DATE DUE

Paolo Giovio

Paolo Giovio

The Historian and the Crisis of Sixteenth-Century Italy

T. C. PRICE ZIMMERMANN

PRINCETON UNIVERSITY PRESS

Copyright © 1995 by Princeton University Press
Published by Princeton University Press, 41 William Street,
Princeton, New Jersey 08540
In the United Kingdom: Princeton University Press, Chichester, West Sussex

Library of Congress Cataloging-in-Publication Data

Zimmermann, T. C. Price, 1934–
Paolo Giovio : the historian and the crisis of
sixteenth-century Italy / T. C. Price Zimmermann.
p.   cm.
Includes bibliographical references and index.
ISBN 0–691–04378–7
1. Giovio, Paolo, 1483–1552. 2. Historians—Italy—Biography.
3. Biographers—Italy—Biography. 4. Bishops—Italy—
Biography. 5. Catholic Church—Italy—Bishops—Biography.
6. Italy—History—1492–1559—Historiography. I. Title.
DG465.7.G56Z56   1995
945′.07′092—dc20
[B]   95–4302

This book has been composed in Galliard

Princeton University Press books are printed on acid-free paper and meet the
guidelines for permanence and durability of the Committee of Production
Guidelines for Book Longevity of the Council on Library Resources

Printed in the United States of America by Princeton Academic Press

10 9 8 7 6 5 4 3 2 1

*To all our friends of Como
and to the memory of
Matteo Gianoncelli and
Dante Visconti*

Contents

Preface

> . . . so steht Giovio vor uns, zum Greifen nahe, im Guten und
> Bösen der echtgeborene Sohn seines Jahrhunderts, und
> trotzdem—ist das nicht wunderbar?—hat es noch niemanden
> gelockt, das Buch "Paolo Giovio und seine Zeit" zu schreiben.
>
> —Emil Schaeffer, *Von Bildern und Menschen der Renaissance*

> . . . so Giovio appears to us, easy to grasp, in his good qualities
> and bad the true son of his century, and yet—is it not
> strange?—it has not occurred to anyone to write the book,
> "Paolo Giovio and His Times."

IN THE EIGHTY YEARS since Schaeffer called for a biography of Paolo
Giovio set in his times, the genre itself has virtually passed into oblivion.[1] Yet there are good reasons for resurrecting it. Seldom has the interplay of life and times reflected more vividly the nature of an era than
with Paolo Giovio. An articulate sounding board for the political, social, and intellectual turmoil of the Cinquecento, he resonated with the
life of a brilliant, yet troubled epoch. His deep frustrations with princes
and politics betrayed the devastation that Italy's political calamity
wrought on the morale of an individual Italian. Not having been a systematic thinker, he mirrored all the more clearly the diffusion of new
ideas among the educated classes. In their frankness and in the range
of their interests his letters reveal an astute mind that encompassed his
age without having the power to transform it.

   Educated first by his elder brother at Como in the traditions of Quattrocento archaeology, philology, and humanism; trained in dialectic,
natural philosophy, and medicine at the universities of Padua and Pavia
in the midst of acrimonious debate over Averroistic philosophy and
Greek philology; reeducated at Rome to fit the prevailing Ciceronianism of the Roman academy; shaped, finally, by the milieu of Leo X into
an adroit ecclesiastical careerist, Giovio spent his life clinging with de-
spondent tenacity to Leonine culture as the armies of Charles V trampled the *libertas Italiae*, the vernacular movement stripped the laurels
from Latin, and the Counter-Reformation attacked the ecclesiastical
pluralism that supported him. Throughout he served as an *arbiter elegantiae* and political analyst for the Roman curia and the principal
courts of Italy. There were few makers of his era he did not know. As a
historian he probed insistently among captains and courtiers to un-
cover "the real truth of events and plans." His much-circulated letters,

his widely read history of his own times, and his biographies of scores of his contemporaries—some of the most characteristic works of the age—painted large areas of the Renaissance's self-portrait. In addition, Giovio offers an unusual portrait of a working historian. Thanks to his correspondence, his immediate reactions to events can be compared with the perspective adopted in his histories and biographies after the benefit of hindsight and fuller information.

While each new age approaches the study of the past with fresh questions stemming from contemporary interests and concerns, biography is perennially rooted in understanding how our predecessors saw themselves and how they came to terms with the demands of their times. It tempers the abstractions of the social sciences and the generalizations of history. Whatever can be learned through abstract methodologies must ultimately be absorbed into a humanistic framework. We do not think of ourselves as abstractions or as statistics in a trend, nor do we act that way in a political or social capacity. A sense of the individual restores humanistic truth to discussions of society in the aggregate.

The struggle to keep afloat on the intellectual and political currents of Italy's crisis involved Giovio in strategies great and small. I have tried to convey a sense of the little pleasures that were a large part of his means for coping. So truly was he "the son of his century" that his personal tragedy recapitulated the peninsula's. As a narrow view of their immediate self-interests kept the Italian states from banding together against the foreigner to preserve their independence, so Giovio's quest for the tangible satisfactions of fresh linens, mature wines, villas, gardens, art, family, friends, and access to great persons eventually compromised his reputation as a historian. Yet despite the patronage he sought so assiduously, he was not the "venal," "partisan," or "shallow" historian he has been accused of being, and at the risk of some revisionism I have tried to document his fundamental honesty and acuity of perception. In recent times his fame and reputation have been largely kept alive by art historians interested in his remarkable museum of portraits at Como, but with the imminent completion of the *edizione nazionale* of his *opera* through the cooperation of the Società Storica Comense and the Istituto Poligrafico dello Stato, we can look for fresh studies of his major works.

A word, finally, in regard to translations and editions. The exertions of Edmund Burke and nineteenth-century English grammarians notwithstanding, Latin syntax has little congruence with English. Indeed, it had little congruence with sixteenth-century Italian, as Giovio himself was well aware. The effect in modern English of a literal translation of Giovio's highly idiomatic Latin is stilted verbosity. I have accordingly rendered his Latin—usually after consulting the sixteenth-century

Italian translations—with a certain amount of stylistic freedom, adopting the expedient of one of his sixteenth-century translators and "following the sense rather than the words."[2] To preserve, on the other hand, the sense of unfettered colloquialism that Giovio's letters convey, I have tried to follow their grammatical structure as closely as possible, while occasionally substituting English equivalents of Italian expressions. Unless otherwise indicated, translations are my own. Whenever feasible I have cited from the *Iovii opera*, but unfortunately some of the volumes appeared too late for me to use. The same was the case with Vincent J. Pitts' important biography of Charles de Bourbon, *The Man Who Sacked Rome*.

THE DEBTS contracted over thirty-five years of study are manifold, and warm memories come with their acknowledgment. The first are to my widely beloved mentor at Harvard, the late Prof. Myron P. Gilmore, and to his wife Sheila. A Fulbright-Hayes Fellowship, an I Tatti Fellowship, an American Council of Learned Societies Fellowship, and sabbatical leaves from Reed College and from Davidson College have made the research and writing possible. For hospitality in Florence I am happily indebted to Consul General and Mrs. Merritt N. Cootes: Αὐτός δ' ἀρίστων τῶνδε τυγχάνω ξένων.

My first introductions in Como came through the hospitality of Dott. Sergio Cerofolini and his distinguished family. At every stage of research and writing I have received priceless assistance from friends and colleagues in the Società Storica Comense, beginning with the late Prof. Dante Visconti and the late Dott. Matteo Gianoncelli, who over many years provided me with moral encouragement, sage advice, dinners on the lake, and an abundance of documentation. In recent years their places have been taken by Prof. Avv. Giorgio Luraschi and his family, and by Prof. Ing. Stefano Della Torre and Prof. Avv. Sergio Lazzarini, who have continued to provide hospitality, documentation, and countless time-consuming assistances. To Prof. Ernesto Travi I owe an inestimable debt for assistance over many years and for freely sharing with me transcripts of Giovian manuscripts and typescripts of his own fundamental studies. I am obliged as well to Msgr. Pietro Gini, the distinguished honorary president of the Società, and to its librarian, Dott. Cinzia Granata. Others who have helped in one way or other are Dott. Alessandro Bortone, Sig. Marzio Botta, Dott. Gian Giuseppe Brenna, Dott. Lanfredo Castelletti, Sig. Giuliano Collina, Dott. Bruno Fasola, the late Maestro Venosto Lucati, Dott. Magda Noseda, Dott. Furio Ricci, Dott. Cesare Sibilia, Dott. Riccardo Terzoli, and Dott. Mariuccia Belloni Zecchinelli.

For help with various problems I am obliged to my former colleagues at Reed College, Prof. Marvin Levich, Prof. Smith Fussner, and the late Dr. Luella Pollock, and to my colleagues at Davidson College, Profs. Peter Ahrensdorf, Robin Barnes, Gary Fagan, Dirk French, Alberto Hernandez-Chiroldes, Stephen Lonsdale, William Mahony, Alfred Mele, Nina Serebrennikov, and Michael Toumazou. To David Shi, now president of Furman University, I am greatly indebted for stylistic suggestions. Dr. John Casey and his colleagues, Marilyn Ainslie, Lydia Lorenzin, Lee Norris, and Marc Overcash, have shepherded me through nerve-wracking crises with the dimly understood computer. The exemplary staff of the E. H. Little Library at Davidson have provided continual and gracious assistance. At various points I have had assistance from historians, art historians, librarians, antiquarian booksellers, archivists, and friends including Prof. Roberto Abbondanza, Dr. David Alan Brown, Mr. Herbert Cahoon, the late Prof. Delio Cantimori, the late Prof. Eric Cochrane, Dott. Gino Corti, Prof. Gaetano Cozzi, the late Dott. Deoclecio Redig De Campos, Mr. Roland Folter, Mr. John Kebabian, Prof. Samuel Kinser, Prof. Linda Klinger, the late Mr. Hans Kraus, Mr. Joshua Lipton, Prof. Edward P. Mahoney, Dott. Fiammetta Olschki-Witt, Prof. Leandro Perini, Contessa Federica Piccolomini Cinelli, the late Marchese Roberto Ridolfi, Dott. Renzo Ristori, Dott. Lucia Rossetti, Prof. Nicolai Rubinstein, the late Mr. Edward Sanchez, Dr. Robert B. Simon, the late John Sparrow, Esq., Msgr. Vincenzo Striano, Dott. Vanni Tesei, Prof. Raymond Waddington, Prof. David Wright, and Prof. Paola Zambelli. Dott. Silvia Castellani generously shared with me her valuable *tesi di laurea* from the University of Florence. Ms. Lia Franks prepared the bibliography. Davidson's Administrative Services cheerfully reproduced many drafts.

For their encouragement, for their penetrating comments after reading various chapters or versions of the manuscript, and for saving me from manifold errors, I am particularly indebted to Professors William J. Bouwsma, Gigliola Fragnito, Riccardo Fubini, Kenneth Gouwens, Werner L. Gundersheimer, Sir John Hale, John M. Headley, Julian Kliemann, Paul O. Kristeller, Thomas F. Mayer, the late Charles B. Schmitt, and Ronald G. Witt. I am uniquely indebted to Dr. Cecil H. Clough, who read the earliest version with patience and incomparable erudition. To Lauren M. Osborne I am grateful for perceptive editorial advice, and to Roy E. Thomas for wizardry in copyediting. It has been a pleasure to work with all the Princeton University Press staff.

My last and irredeemable debt is to the loyal encouragement of my wife, Margaret, and to her gentle insistence that books, even this one, not only could, but should one day be finished.

Abbreviations Used in the
Notes and Bibliography

ASC	Archivio di Stato, Como
ASF	Archivio di Stato, Florence
ASI	*Archivio storico italiano*
ASM	Archivio di Stato, Mantua
ASMo	Archivio di Stato, Modena
ASV	Archivio Segreto Vaticano
Atti	*Atti del convegno Paolo Giovio*
BAV	Biblioteca Apostolica Vaticana
BNF	Biblioteca Nazionale, Florence
BNR	Biblioteca Nazionale, Rome
Brandi	Karl Brandi. *The Emperor Charles V*
CT	*Concilium Tridentinum*
DBI	*Dizionario biografico degli Italiani*
GS	*Giornale storico della letteratura italiana*
ML	Pierpont Morgan Library, New York City
Pastor	Ludwig von Pastor. *The History of the Popes*
IO	*Pauli Iovii opera*
Jedin	Hubert Jedin. *A History of the Council of Trent*
Knecht	R. J. Knecht. *Francis I*
PSSC	*Periodico della Società Storica Comense*
Sanudo	Marin Sanudo. *I diarii*
Setton	Kenneth M. Setton. *The Papacy and the Levant*
SI	Francesco Guicciardini. *Storia d'Italia*
SSC	Società Storica Comense, Como
UCM	Università Cattolica del Sacro Cuore, Milan
WJ	*Journal of the Warburg and Courtauld Institutes*

Paolo Giovio

CHAPTER ONE

Origines (1486–1511)

At ego eum, Patriam historiam et librum de bellis et moribus
Helvetiorum elegantissime conscribentem, honesta commotus
invidia aemulari ex occulto non desinebam.

—Giovio, *Dialogus de viris et foeminis
aetate nostra florentibus,* pt. II

But motivated, as it were, by an honorable kind of envy, I did not
cease secretly wishing to emulate him [my brother], writing most
elegantly the history of our city as well as a work on the wars and
customs of the Swiss.

PAOLO GIOVIO was born shortly before the outbreak of the wars that
form the focus of his *Histories.* The traditional date is 1483, but Giovio's
own statements seem to point to 1486.[1] His family, the Zobii, traced
their origins to the small island in Lake Como, the site of a thriving
community in the earlier Middle Ages and a refuge in time of war. In his
Larius, a description of the lake, Giovio boasted that his ancestors had
founded the hospice and church of St. Mary Magdalen on the nearby
mainland and had maintained the patronage for six hundred years.[2] The
family arms featured—appropriately—a castle on an island, augmented
by the imperial eagle which according to tradition had been conferred by
the emperor Frederick Barbarossa during the Lombard wars. Giovio
himself would later vaunt of having added the crest of yet another emperor. After the destruction of the island by Como in 1169, the Zobii
migrated first to Varenna and eventually to Como, where they intermar-
ried with some of the principal families. Only in 1436, however, when
Giovio's grandfather Giovanni became a *decurione,* or member of the
municipal council, were they formally enrolled in the ranks of the urban
patriciate. From this ancestral tradition Giovio derived an orientation to
history and a strong sense of place.[3] He himself was responsible for the
familiar form of his surname, having Latinized Zobio to Jovius, whence
the more elegant Italian, Giovio.[4]

The biographer of so many Renaissance personalities left no memoir
of his own life. He once made a sketch for an autobiography, but it was
nothing more than a chronological summary of his movements and activities beginning in 1528 and ending abruptly in 1537.[5] He revealed
almost nothing about his parents, Luigi Zobio and Lisabetta Benzi, save

that he attributed his powers of memory to his father, a notary in both the episcopal and municipal jurisdictions, who died sometime about 1500, leaving the future historian a ward of his elder brother Benedetto.[6]

By all accounts, Benedetto Giovio was a remarkable person. Alciato called him the Lombard Varro. A notary by profession, a savant by predilection, he collected classical inscriptions, translated Greek, composed Latin poetry, edited Vitruvius, and corresponded with renowned scholars including Melanchthon and Erasmus. He seems to have known some Hebrew and perhaps even a little Arabic. Paolo admired his gift for languages and his "incredibly vigorous memory for facts and names." In addition to his history of Como, for which he used documentary sources, Benedetto wrote essays on the history and customs of the Swiss and on the nature of human society. His personal qualities won the lasting affection of his compatriots, and various anecdotes attest to his modesty, steady temper, and lack of ambition that his younger brother possessed in such abundance. Even today in Como there is a proverb, "May you have the brilliance of Paolo but the goodness of Benedetto."[7]

One interest of his brother's, the two Plinies, was reflected in Paolo's earliest surviving composition, a Latin letter he wrote in 1504 describing the family's country place at Lissago.[8] Benedetto had engaged in archaeological researches to determine the site of Pliny the Younger's two villas on Larius, as Lake Como was known in Roman times, making it natural enough for Paolo to model his letter on Pliny's descriptions of his villas.[9] Lissago was a hamlet on the southern flank of Monte della Croce just before the main road descended to Como. In a distinctly Plinian idiom, the aspiring Latinist attempted to imbue the modest rural structures and unexceptional family routine with the aura of life in a Roman villa. While candidly admitting that he was awakened each morning and frequently interrupted in his studies by the lowing of cattle, the barking of dogs, the creaking of presses, the coming and going of carts, and the noisy voices of the peasants, he nonetheless transformed his environs into a Roman villa.

The entrance hall became a *cryptoporticus*, the dining room a *coenatio*, the upstairs living room a *triclinium*, the woods *opacissimae sylvae*, and the small brook a *frigidus rivulus*. Led by the nymph, the *genius loci*, he even discovered adjacent to the house an *argenteus fons* which provided the family with sparkling water. The young author seemed quite familiar with the architecture of the Roman villa, owing perhaps to the work of contemporary theorists such as Francesco Maria Grapaldo, whose treatise *De partibus aedium* (1494) he evidently knew. He gave informed attention to architectural subtleties such as the situation of rooms, their relationship to the sun and seasons, and the views framed by windows and doors.[10]

Beyond architecture, Giovio's youthful letter broached many of the familiar themes of Roman villa literature: the cultivation of philosophy and letters in an atmosphere of rural leisure, the celebration of peaceful country delights over wearisome urban turmoil, and the reluctant acknowledgment of the tension between the charms of country retreats and the compelling vitality of urban centers. Retiring to the country, Giovio imagined himself in the company of Cicero in his villa at Tusculum, Aulus Gellius in the villa of Herodes Atticus, Silius Italicus in one of his Neapolitan villas, and Pliny in his retreat at Laurentium; but he also identified himself with Landino in the monastery of Camaldoli and Politian in the Medici villa at Fiesole, suggesting that he credited the Quattrocento humanists with having recaptured the manner of life of the ancients. It was to follow their example, he solemnly reassured his cousin, not to spurn his *patria*, that he had withdrawn from the city and his companions there. Already the future humanist was constructing a life based on the myth of antiquity.[11]

How significant classical values became for Giovio was evident from his later confession that in the dark hours of the sack of Rome he was able to attain more peace of mind from Cicero's *Tusculan Disputations* than from sacred Scripture.[12] Passages in this 1504 letter, moreover, such as his refusal to join in the fashionable urban disparagement of country folk, revealed a fair-mindedness and an openness to diverse human values that would characterize the work of the mature historian.[13] Eventually, his urge to seek out a new life would draw Giovio far from the modest provincial orbit of his birthplace, but he never forsook his early loyalties. At the height of his fame, he returned to found in his *patria*, on a site he believed had been admired by Pliny the Younger, a reconstruction of a Roman villa dedicated to the muses and to the celebration of human personality.

The tenor of his brother's regimen and the formative influence of humanism on Giovio's outlook was evident from his remark that the *De ingenuis moribus* of Pier Paolo Vergerio had remained a popular text with educators during his boyhood.[14] Written at Padua in the first years of the Quattrocento for the young Ubertino da Carrara, Vergerio's little treatise combined the educational philosophy of late Trecento Florentine humanism with perceptive insight, gentle wisdom, and common sense. Vergerio encouraged on the one hand the aristocratic ideal of cultured leisure, and on the other the democratic ideal of merit and the honor inherent in striving for glory. Traces of Vergerio's influence can be found throughout Giovio's life and works—in his insistence that learning should not merely inform but civilize; in his preference for comeliness of manners, morals, and persons; in his Ciceronian conception of history; in his admiration of *virtù*; in his lifelong cult of fame and glory, and his strong sense of the interdependence of heroes and historians; and, finally, in his hard work and somewhat old-fashioned morality, which would preserve him from the worst excesses of life in the capital. Indeed, the letter of Lissago revealed that he was already shrinking from the excesses of his youthful friends, liberated by the wars from their normal restraints and routines.[15]

Another feature of Giovio's youth was his family's fondness, widely shared in that epoch, for medieval chivalric romances. Among the first books the future historian acquired was a fifteenth-century manuscript of the *Cantare di Fierabraccia*. From this love of romances sprang not only Giovio's keen appreciation of Ariosto but also his salient qualities as a narrative historian, particularly his unwearied enthusiasm for describing battles and individual deeds of valor, his admiration for knightly virtues, and his sense for military pageantry and the drama of events.[16] His aversion to gunpowder as the nemesis of knightly valor would later sire a persistent but otherwise unsubstantiated tradition: that Paolo Vitelli and other noble condottieri despised the new, unchivalrous mode of warfare in which a gallant knight fighting for honor and glory with lance and sword could be brought low by a common foot soldier with a gun.[17]

Yet another interest of Giovio's youth was astrology. In his Ischian dialogue he admitted that "from a very young age" he had been "passionately occupied in this art, with an exquisite apparatus of instruments and books."[18] Although by the time the dialogue was written he professed to have developed a complete intellectual and moral revulsion for these "most fallacious of studies," astrology did not entirely vanish from his work. In book 13 of the *Histories*, for example, he speculated that the nearly simultaneous appearance of heresy in both Christian and Muslim lands might have resulted from a malign conjunction of the stars.[19]

Giovio may have continued the studies begun under his brother's tutelage at the *studium* of Como, as a school of grammar and rhetoric flourished there in the late Quattrocento under Teodoro Lucino. The Swiss soldier-ecclesiastic Matthäus Schinner, cardinal of Sion, was an alumnus, as was probably Benedetto, if Giovio's claim was indeed true that his brother had never left Como except to learn the pronunciation of Greek from Demetrius Chalcondylas in Milan.[20] Sometime between the years 1501 and 1506 Giovio himself frequented the Milanese lectures of Chalcondylas as well as those of the Latin rhetorician Giano Parrasio of Cosenza.[21] It was probably at Milan that he formed a friendship important for his future with Ottobuono Fieschi, a scion of the prominent Genoese family, who invited him home "according to the custom of students."[22]

Despite Giovio's preference for literary and humanistic studies, the family's exiguous financial situation led his brother to demand that he prepare himself for a more remunerative occupation, and he elected medicine, although with evident resentment at the slight to his literary gifts.[23] Pavia would have been the logical university to attend, and perhaps he commenced his studies there, but by the autumn of 1506 he was enrolled at Padua, where he witnessed the debates between the eminent philosophers Alessandro Achillini and Pietro Pomponazzi. These only began with Achillini's arrival at Padua that autumn, and by the spring of 1507 Giovio seems to have been back at Pavia.[24]

In the early sixteenth century Padua was the preeminent Italian university. Erasmus, who had spent a couple of months there in 1508 after completing his work with Aldus Manutius, called it "the wealthiest and most celebrated emporium of good learning."[25] Medicine held a central position in the curriculum, and, as today, the liberal arts were a prerequisite for medical study. Giovio would have started with work in logic and natural philosophy; medicine would have come later. He became the pupil of Pomponazzi and followed with keen interest his debates with Achillini, whom he seems to have felt was actually the better philosopher.[26] In fact, in his *elogium* of Achillini, he accused his own master of "insidious ambition" in seeking to depopulate his rival's lecture hall, not so much by his learning as by his mastery of the techniques of soliciting and flattering students.[27]

One of the issues in the debates between Pomponazzi and Achillini was Averroës' interpretation of Aristotle on the nature of the soul. Paduan Averroism was still flourishing. "All agreed to the positions of this author," Giovio's contemporary, Gasparo Contarini, later recalled, "and took them as a kind of oracle. Most celebrated was his position on the unity of the Intellect, and he who thought otherwise was considered worthy neither of the name of peripatetic nor of philosopher."[28] Repercussions of his debate with Achillini found their way into Pomponazzi's lectures, but it is difficult to assess their impact on Giovio. He was clearly well informed on the issues, but he avoided exposing his own views on so delicate a topic. Still, one wonders if an Averroistic skepticism inherited from his university studies did not underlie or at least reinforce the classical outlook he later acquired in the Roman academy.[29]

It is easy to ascertain Giovio's position in the controversies at Padua on the revival of Greek; he consistently asserted that Aristotle and Galen had been reborn from direct acquaintance with the original texts. Greek had been taught at Padua since the establishment of a chair for Chalcondylas in 1463, and Giovio's enthusiastic and warmly personal *elogium* suggests that he attended the lectures of Chalcondylas' pupil, Niccolò Leonico Tomeo, the incumbent of a new chair instituted in 1497 for the teaching of Aristotle in Greek.[30] Slowly the contention of the humanists was winning acceptance that interpretative debate was valueless without sound philology.[31]

Having followed the lectures of Chalcondylas at Milan, Giovio was well prepared to join the ranks of the Greek scholars and seems to have enjoyed his advantage. Indeed, his *elogium* of Leonico Tomeo had an outright polemical tone. Tomeo, according to Giovio, had "hooted out the teachings of the sophists," demonstrating that "to be salubrious, philosophy must be drunk from the purest springs, not from muddy ditches."

> For with their figments of dialectic, dreamt up with barbarian subtlety, the doctors were referring physical questions not to the light of truth but to the inane chattering of disputations, and the poor youth of the university, following the commentaries of the Arabs and barbarians, were led from the straight and secure path onto the rough ground of ignorance.[32]

The inscription, "Pauli Zobii 1506 Nov.," found in a copy of Nicoletto Vernia's edition of Walter Burley's commentary on Aristotle's *Physics*, indicated that Giovio was following courses in natural philosophy as well as in logic.[33]

The hypothesis that Giovio was enrolled at Pavia by the spring of 1507 turns in part on his claim to have been present when the king of France attended a lecture by Giasone del Maino. Arriving victorious in May 1507, after subduing rebellious Genoa, Louis XII had chosen this means of honoring the great jurist, whom his government had persuaded to resume teaching. Not only did Giovio attend the lecture, wherein Maino treated of the Salic Law and the ancillary question of whether a knighthood conferred by the king's own hand was hereditary, he claimed to have been present at the banquet which followed and to have heard Maino's witty response to the king's inquiry as to why he had never taken a wife.[34]

A unique relic of Giovio's university studies at Pavia was a series of academic exercises he completed during the summer vacation of 1508 and titled, "The Como Nights of Paolo Giovio."[35] The allusion to Aulus Gellius' *Attic Nights* was purely ironic. This was no collection of entertaining tales and miscellaneous lore culled from the conversations of languid summer nights in pleasure villas on the banks of the Cephisus. Giovio's "Nights" consisted of exercises in scholastic debate, *quaestiones disputatae*, putting and defending propositions in natural philosophy—for example: "According to the Commentator [Averroës] form is the beginning of individuation"; "The possible intellect is purely potential nor does it understand itself"; "The agent intellect is God"; "All nature is subject to the laws of physics." There was even the bold proposition, which the mature Giovio would have certainly rejected, "Medicine is a lofty science and the human body, subject to it, is curable by human industry." The draft of an academic oration to the doctors and citizens of Como concluded the exercise. While Giovio came to prefer the methods of humanistic discourse, his training in scholastic disputation evidently left its stamp on him. In the Ischian dialogue he described himself as "a sharp dialectician," an epithet later echoed by the secretary of Charles V who had heard that Giovio was "extremely sharp."[36]

Giovio completed his medical studies under the brilliant young Veronese anatomist, Marco Antonio della Torre. Like many on the Paduan faculty, della Torre had fled during the war of the League of Cambrai, and in 1510 he accepted the invitation of the French government to teach at Pavia.[37] An accomplished Greek scholar who preferred to lecture on Galen directly from the original, he brought to Pavia a polemical enthusiasm for Greek texts. To Giovio, whose *elogium* of him was, for once, a true eulogy, he seemed "in the subtlety of his expositions" to surpass the oldest and most authoritative professors of medicine.[38] In language that preserved the partisan flavor of academic debate, Giovio claimed that his mentor had been quick to demonstrate "the many shameful errors destructive of human life into which the botanists and anatomists had fallen through ignorance." He even provided an example of della Torre's cutting humor at the expense of his former colleague at Padua, Gabriele de' Zerbi. Having confidently undertaken to cure a Turkish pasha of dropsy, Zerbi was returning to Padua with his substantial fee when his patient suffered a relapse and died. Overtaken by the pasha's vengeful servants, the physician was assassinated on the spot. It was almost justice, della Torre would say, that a teacher who had injured his pupils by so many inept dissections of dead bodies should himself be cut into while still alive.[39]

Giovio's *elogium* recalled that while lecturing at Pavia, della Torre was engaged in writing a new text intended to supplant not only the fourteenth-century anatomical text of Mondino de' Liuzzi but the more recent text of the unfortunate Zerbi. According to Vasari, della Torre had been collaborating in dissection with Leonardo da Vinci. Since Giovio and della Torre seem to have developed a warm personal friendship, the mentor may have introduced his pupil to Leonardo during the months of their partnership.[40] Unfortunately, della Torre did not live to complete the work in which he was engaged. In the summer of 1511, not long after sponsoring Giovio for the *laurea*, he met a tragically premature death while ministering to victims of the plague at Riva on the shores of Lake Garda.

Among the mourners for della Torre was Giovio's friend, the poet Count Niccolò d'Arco. In later years d'Arco recalled in verse the boisterous side of their student days at Pavia and the "keen witticisms and jests" with which Giovio was wont to season "the bright and sunny days of blessed leisure."[41] D'Arco's lines celebrating the beauties of Pavia have all the freshness of youth and the candid sensuality of young manhood. He also wrote some "salutary elegies" for his witty friend, "moved to pity," Giovio said, by "the cruel flames" of "juvenile passion" which were then devouring him, and which he had been vainly attempting to assuage by writing a piece, now lost, called the *Anterotica*.[42]

This may have been the mysterious love affair to which Giovio alluded in the *Dialogo dell'imprese*, when he related that "being smitten by love as a youth in Pavia, in order not to provoke even worse for myself I was forced to pursue a damaging course to save my life." What the course may have been he did not say, but the episode acquired certain Abelardian tones from the *impresa* (device) he adopted in consequence. "Wishing to demonstrate that it was necessity which forced me to take this course, I assumed as my device that animal called in Latin *fiber ponticus* and in the vernacular beaver, which, as Juvenal relates, when pursued on account of the great medicinal properties of its testicles, cuts them off with its teeth as a last resort and leaves them for the hunters." Above this device Giovio placed the motto ANANKE, "which means in Greek 'necessity' and to which, as Lucian attests, both gods and men obey."[43]

Along with *amore* Giovio was caught up in the other great avocation of university students—politics. For Italy these were troubled years, and Giovio was already demonstrating an intensity of interest foreshadowing the historian of his own times. While a student at Pavia he witnessed the battle of Agnadello, or Ghiaradadda (May 14, 1509), the great debacle in which Venice lost in a day the terra firma empire garnered over the course of a century.[44] Agnadello was less than thirty miles from Pavia, but it would have taken more than casual curiosity to leave books, lectures, and the safety of Pavia's walls to wander in the dangerous lee of hostile armies. Either the future historian craved to see a major battle or he felt that issues were at stake engaging major loyalties of his own—perhaps both. By all indications, Agnadello marked Giovio's emergence not only as a historian but as an Italian patriot.

As a child Giovio would certainly have heard talk of the French conquest of Naples in 1494 and the battle of Fornovo the following year as Charles VIII and his troops fought their way back to France against the allied forces of Italy. In September 1499, Giovio himself witnessed the flight of Ludovico Sforza through Como en route to Germany after the fall of Alessandria to the troops of Louis XII. "With great wonder" he heard the duke speak to the citizens, "displaying admirable constancy, dilating on his plans and on the treachery of many."[45] The first French occupation of Milan ended with Ludovico's triumphal return the following February, again via Como where he was joyfully welcomed, but two months later he was betrayed to an invading French army by his Swiss mercenaries and led away to miserable captivity in France. The wondering boy had not yet reached his judgment as a mature historian that Ludovico il Moro was "a man born for the ruin of Italy," but the French occupation left him with a hearty aversion to all foreign rule and particularly that of the French.[46] His heroes became the Italians who strove to free Italy of "barbarians," and chief among them Bartolomeo d'Alviano, whose boldness had helped defeat the French at the battle of the Garigliano (1503) and the Germans in the war of the Cadore (1508).

The battle of Agnadello was the sequel to the war of the Cadore. In vexation at losing to Venice, the emperor Maximilian turned to Louis XII of France, and subsequently to Ferdinand of Aragon and Pope Julius II, with all of whom he formed the League of Cambrai in December 1508 to despoil the Serenissima of her mainland possessions. The following spring the French army, commanded by the king, was attempting to force an engagement with the equally matched Venetian troops under d'Alviano and Niccolò Orsini, count of Pitigliano. Following orders from Venice, Pitigliano had been fighting a war of attrition, maneuvering to protect the area around Cremona while avoiding a conflict. By crossing the Adda, however, the French succeeded in drawing the Italian rearguard into an engagement which the impetuous d'Alviano allowed to become a full-scale battle. The rearguard was annihilated and d'Alviano himself wounded and captured. In this war Giovio's sympathies lay decidedly with Venice. The league he termed "a cruel conspiracy of foreign nations," nor did the participation of the pope sanctify it in his eyes.[47] Only two years later, when Julius II turned on his former allies, the French, and drove them from Italy, did he win the young patriot's esteem.[48]

Among intellectuals, the wars commencing with the invasion of Charles VIII in 1494 were beginning to generate a new wave of historical reflection that would eventually culminate in the histories of Guicciardini and of Giovio himself.[49] One of the professors of anatomy at Padua, Alessandro Benedetti, was with the Venetian army at Fornovo and let Aldus publish his *Diaria de bello carolino* in 1496.[50] D'Alviano had several humanists and historians in his camp before Agnadello, and he himself, while a prisoner of the French, wrote a commentary on his *res gestae*. His secretary Girolamo Borgia later produced a history endorsing the idea that 1494 had been a turning point in Italian history.[51] After the invasion of the French, the Venetians began to see themselves as the defenders of the *libertas Italiae*, an attitude d'Alviano and his circle fostered. When he started writing his *Histories*, Giovio appealed to the fiery champion for details on the battle of Agnadello and the preceding war of the Cadore, hailing him as a patriot "who has always fought against barbarians for the honor and safety of the Italian name."[52]

In the spring of 1511 della Torre sponsored Giovio for the double *laurea* in liberal arts and medicine.[53] A public examination was required for each degree, but the critical test was the private examination attended only by doctors of the college. After reading and expounding a text, the candidate was obliged to respond to questions, beginning with the most junior doctor and proceeding in order of seniority.[54] When he emerged successful from these ordeals, Giovio felt that he had joined the republic of merit. Following an oration by della Torre "praising my studious vigils," he boasted, he received "the laurel and ring, the ornaments of proven merit."[55]

His university studies completed, Giovio returned to Como, presumably to begin his career as a physician. That was certainly the expectation of his brother, who "lovingly urged that I should repose in those studies in which I had spent my best years and begin redeeming the expenses I had created while pursuing with distinction the more useful arts by proceeding to earn the anticipated emoluments." In other words, he was to practice medicine. But Giovio had other ideas. "Motivated," he later explained, "by an honorable kind of envy, I did not cease secretly wishing to emulate my brother, who was writing most elegantly the history of our city as well as a work on the wars and customs of the Swiss." He had already decided to become a historian. "And so," he continued, "setting out not long afterward for Rome, when Como was afflicted by pestilence, I had no sooner left my brother than that sordid motive of utility was conquered by my liberal genius, which was irresistibly stirred by an innate desire to write history."[56]

No doubt Giovio's decision to leave Como had several components. Plague was clearly a factor. His mentor had just died of it in the summer of 1511, and in 1512 a new outbreak spread throughout Lombardy as a consequence of the French sack of Brescia. Giovio had none of the martyr in him, and the prospect of losing his life ministering to plague victims had little appeal. It was, moreover, a time of warfare in Lombardy, and Giovio was innately a lover of quiet.[57] By 1511, Julius II had turned against the French and was attempting to drive these erstwhile allies from Italy. The army of the Holy League which he organized with Venice, Spain, and England had begun its attack with a siege of Ferrara. Despite a brilliant victory at Ravenna on Easter Day 1512, the French forces in Italy rapidly collapsed owing to the death of their general, Gaston de Foix, and an energetic offensive directed by the cardinal of Sion.[58] By early June the French had lost Pavia, and by the twelfth they had been driven from Como. Shortly thereafter they abandoned Milan, and in December a Sforza government was reestablished under the imperial aegis by Ludovico il Moro's son Maximilian. With the French clinging to

Novara, however, the threat of hostilities lingered. Rome was not only safer but—importantly for an aspiring historian—a cosmopolitan setting. Already Como may have seemed too provincial to the newly minted doctor, whose university studies had carried him far from the retiring youth seeking refuge in the country from the dissolute society of his peers. And so in 1512, with what companions and in what circumstances we do not know, Giovio set out for Rome.[59]

CHAPTER TWO

Humanist Physician (1512–1527)

Medicina igitur est cognitu pulcherrima, et ad salutem corporum
commodissima; verum exercitium habet minime liberale.

—Pier Paolo Vergerio, *De ingenuis moribus*

Medicine is a very fine study and of greatest utility for the health
of the body, but its practice is not at all liberal.

GIOVIO'S FIRST STEPS in Rome are difficult to retrace. There are no letters from these early years, and the historian himself said little, save that
his career had begun with considerably more service to Aesculapius than
to Clio.[1] For the practice of medicine he had no real vocation; to "exit
from the hospital" was his dream from the start.[2] Another motive for
obscuring his early days in Rome was the spectacular disgrace of his first
patron, the Genoese cardinal Bandinello Sauli. How Giovio became physician to Sauli is uncertain, although it may have been through the Fieschi and his Genoese contacts.[3] As one of the younger cardinals who
engineered the election of Leo X, Sauli had received lucrative benefices,
and his palace in Rome was the scene of banquets, festivities, and a life
replete with every luxury. A great Roman household was expected to
include not only a doctor but a humanist or two, and Giovio qualified in
both capacities.[4] He was one of three retainers portrayed in Sebastiano
del Piombo's 1516 group portrait of the cardinal, where he appears engaged in animated conversation with a figure identified as the cardinal's
secretary, Giovanni Maria Cattaneo, a Greek scholar and former pupil of
Chalcondylas and Merula.[5]

In 1514 Giovio received an appointment as lecturer in philosophy at
the Roman university. Cardinals normally procured offices and benefices
for their dependents to ease the burden on their own treasuries. Giovio
appeared on the roll of 1514 as lecturer in moral philosophy with a salary
of 130 gold florins.[6] Much as his father Lorenzo the Magnificent had
restored the University of Pisa, Leo X had determined that Rome should
yield "neither to Padua nor Bologna in the excellence of its doctors and
the throngs of its students."[7] In the first year of his pontificate he reformed the university and began recruiting the most eminent professors
with handsome emoluments. Unfortunately, the financing of his political initiatives eventually undermined his support of learning, and by the
end of his pontificate the Roman *studium* had reverted to its usual medi-
ocrity. For the moment, however, it enjoyed renewed vitality.

In 1515 Giovio transferred to a lectureship in natural philosophy.[8] Although he placed his duties as a courtier above his teaching, leaving a substitute to lecture when he was traveling with the cardinal, he seems to have been a competent philosopher. His distinguished colleague, Agostino Nifo, whose editions of Aristotle he had used as a student at Pavia, paid tribute to Giovio's philosophical acumen with the dedication of his 1542 commentary on Aristotle's *Topics*.[9] Giovio's subsequent *elogium* of Nifo revealed that he continued to keep up with developments in philosophy even after he ceased teaching it, although his distaste for the scholastic tradition was evident in his complaint that Nifo wrote his commentaries on Aristotle "with rude and disordered prolixity, as was then the custom, suitable for crass and unabashedly barbarian ears; for philosophers of his generation eschewed the faculty of writing Latin correctly, as if it were the enemy of good learning, and particularly of philosophy."[10] Once in Rome, Giovio quickly shed the medieval dialectical tradition of the universities for the discursive style of the humanists.

The early years were strenuous, full of "vigils" and "labors."[11] In addition to lecturing at the university and serving as courtier and physician, Giovio was laying the foundations for his work as a historian. In 1515 the first book of his *Histories* to be circulated came to the attention of Leo X. "I am in excellent shape," Giovio exulted to the Venetian historian and diarist Marin Sanudo; "I am following my cardinal, by whom I am rewarded; I am writing the History, nor think of aught but finishing and publishing it. The pope has read a quire of it and commended us greatly, however unmeritedly."[12] In a later recounting, Giovio added that after praising his work, the pope had led him "by the hand" and introduced him to his cousin, Cardinal Giulio de' Medici.[13]

For reasons never clear, Giovio's first patron chose to humor the Sienese cardinal Alfonso Petrucci in his wild plottings against the pope—the so-called conspiracy of cardinals, which surfaced in April 1517. Arrested along with Petrucci, imprisoned in the Castel Sant'Angelo, tried and convicted, Sauli was eventually pardoned but died the following year—of humiliation, perhaps, or of disease contracted in the foul dungeon into which he had been cast during his imprisonment.[14] For Giovio it cannot have been an easy moment; the college of cardinals itself was terror-struck. Giovio's hour of danger may explain the lingering resentment evident in his contemptuous treatment of his former patron in his account of the conspiracy.[15] He not only survived, however, but entered the service of none other than the cardinal de' Medici, whose household expanded considerably in 1517 when he became vice-chancellor at the death of Cardinal Sisto Gara della Rovere.

With his new patron, Giovio moved into the great Riario palace, which Cardinal Riario had been forced to surrender as a result of his implication in the conspiracy, and which was known thereafter as the

Palazzo della Cancelleria.[16] Despite his dream of exiting from the hospital, Giovio was to serve his new master as physician and humanist for the next decade, well into his papacy.[17] In fact, he developed a considerable reputation as a physician. In a letter datable between 1519 and 1521, the Ferrarese humanist Celio Calcagnini referred to him as "primi nominis medicus [a physician of the first rank]," praise Giovio wryly echoed when describing himself as "a physician not only renowned but even successful."[18]

Early in the papacy of his new patron, Giovio's medical reputation was attested by a bizarre episode, out of character with his usual philosophy but well documented. In a letter dated August 4, 1524, the Mantuan agent in Rome described to the marquis Federico an experiment performed by order of the pope with a miraculous antidote for poison compounded by a certain ex-friar. According to the agent, Giovio administered aconite to two condemned criminals, one of whom was subsequently saved by the friar's antidote, the other of whom was allowed to expire. The formula was purchased by the pope and published for the common good in a letter "To all good mortals," dated August 13, 1524, from Pietro Borghese, senator of Rome, Paolo Giovio, papal physician, and Tommaso Biliotti, master of papal spices.[19]

Giovio's more customary practice was illustrated by two works he wrote during the early years of Clement VII's pontificate, the *De romanis piscibus* (Of Roman fish, 1524) and the *De optima victus ratione* (On the best regimen of diet, 1527). The *De romanis piscibus*, a treatise on ichthyology and something of a *regimen sanitatis*, stemmed from Giovio's university training in both medicine and natural history.[20] Chapter by chapter he proceeded through forty different kinds of fish available in the Roman markets, correlating ancient and modern nomenclature, commenting on medical and nutritional properties, and offering suggestions for cooking. For relief from the erudition, he sprinkled in anecdotes about Roman banquets. Pierio Valeriano warmly praised the treatise for having at last resolved the many confusions between ancient and modern names of fish.[21] Giovio carefully distinguished between the properties attributed to fish by the standard medical authors and his own empirical observations, which were generally pragmatic and astute. For example, while citing Athenaios and Pliny on the beneficent properties of cuttlefish, Giovio observed that all soft fish "are digested with the greatest difficulty by the stomachs of scholars and other physically inactive persons," recalling his frequent but unheeded admonitions to Clement VII, "an avid diner on dishes made from these kinds of fish."[22] Giovio's constant invocation of the Hippocratic canon of naturalness to exclude exotic remedies and fanciful lore betrayed the influence of the Greek revival in medicine.

Greek influence was also evident in the *De optima victus ratione*, written during the sack of Rome for Clement VII's datary, Felice Trofino, in hopes of restoring his health.[23] Other than systematizing and commenting on the Greek originals, the chief contribution of the medieval Arab physicians had been their pharmacology, which Giovio energetically repudiated. Prophylaxis, he stressed, was infinitely better than cure: "I do not deny that there may be marvelous properties in foreign and exotic medicines, but that they should be commended with bland labels and through the insidiousness of unskilled physicians brought into domestic use I cannot tolerate; for they are abhorrent to nature and since they are of doubled power they murder men more cruelly than the fevers themselves, as we have seen in the cases of the most noble engraver, Caradosso, and the professor of rhetoric, Matteo da Camerino, who were straightway killed in the flower of health by rash doses of cassia."[24]

For Giovio the foundation of good health lay in a threefold regimen of sensible diet, moderate exercise, and alleviation of mental stress. His treatise for Trofino reinterpreted the Galenic canon with sound common sense. One of the hallmarks of Galen's teaching had been his insistence on the unity of an organism and on understanding its relationship to its environment. Another had been his stress on the effect of psychological factors on physical function. A third had been his emphasis, following Hippocrates, on the recuperative powers of nature, the *vis mediatrix naturae*.[25] Each of these canons was incorporated in Giovio's recommendations, compounded with a dose of Hellenistic philosophy. "The one thing," he said,

> that will most effectively preserve your health is tranquility of mind, wherein the ancient philosophers thought that perfect well-being consisted; for our bodies must endure the continual vexations of our minds, and variable humors are induced by diverse appetites for food. When appetites are balanced in accordance with the sure practice of nature, they produce a temperature that is durable and suitable for maintaining life. Thus philosophy is not only the guide to a good and blessed life, it seems to be the most certain conserver of health as well.[26]

To avoid "perturbations of mind" in times of stress, Giovio suggested reading the ancient philosophers, in particular Cicero's *Tusculan Disputations*.[27] He also prescribed moderate exercise such as riding or playing ball, and dinners with congenial friends. With their "singular and perpetual zeal for exercise," he argued, the ancients conserved their health, and with thermal baths to cleanse the body "they had no need of these pharmacists which the troublesome crowd of sophist physicians and the multitude of quacks force upon us, open-mouthed as we are with credulity."[28]

As its title implied, Giovio's treatise focused on the third component of health, a good diet. With Galen as his authority that most serious illnesses stemmed from digestive malfunctions, Giovio prescribed a regimen for sensible eating. To avoid insomnia dine lightly at night. Foods should be lightly seasoned and cooked as simply as possible. Meats are better and more digestible roasted or boiled than baked in pastries. Heavily seasoned foods may spur the appetite, but they tax the stomach. Avoid especially the doctored and sculptured foods found on the tables of prelates; they are for the eyes rather than the stomach. *Mens sana in corpore sano* and *Ne quid nimis* (nothing to excess) were the maxims most in evidence. In both treatises, in fact, Giovio reinforced Galen with Renaissance Epicureanism—Lorenzo Valla's perhaps and certainly Platina's as set forth in the *De honesta voluptate et valetudine tuenda* (1474?).[29]

In his treatise *The Best Physician Is Also a Philosopher*, Galen argued that the healer must be versed in logic, the science of thinking; in physics, the science of what is; and in ethics, the science of right action. As a mature humanist-physician Giovio reinterpreted the Galenic canon with the same determination he demonstrated in the letter of Lissago to reconstruct in their integrity classical modes of life and thought. Given the nature of many contemporary "cures," a patient would have been fortunate to find a temperate physician like Giovio, whose philosophy was to favor the curative powers of nature.

After becoming a bishop in 1527, Giovio gladly laid aside a profession that had never been more than a means to the end of writing history. He revealed his continuing distaste for the limitations of medical practice in an observation made after learning that the ailing duchess of Florence was about to be submitted to a cure when she suddenly gave birth to a premature fetus of six months which no one knew she had been carrying. "From this," said Giovio, "one sees that medicine is blind and that the physician can be called *invidiae pelagus, erroris oceanus* [a sea of envy, an ocean of error]." And just to show how serious he was, he challenged his correspondent to have the eminent physician Fallopio, then teaching at Pisa, construe the Latin.[30]

Great as its limitations may have been, however, medicine was a way of knowing and, as Vergerio implied, a means of understanding the human condition. Giovio's medical training offered him a systematic guide to observing human nature.[31] The good physician reads closely every sign and symptom, referring them to the framework of an overall diagnosis. So, over the years, Giovio formed his diagnoses of Charles V, Francis I, and Clement VII. His medical interests continually appeared in the *Histories*, whether the diet that gave Turkish soldiers so much vitality and the sanitary arrangements of the camps that protected them from disease, or the temperance by which Paul III preserved his health into extreme old age.[32]

The *Elogia* abounded with medical observations, particularly on diseases and the causes of death. Infirmities Giovio regarded as part of the whole personal ethos he was endeavoring to capture with portrait and character sketch. At times, the subject's use of medicine even provided a window to his underlying psychological state, as when Girolamo Aleandro's self-prescription of drugs revealed his excessive anxieties.[33] As physician, Giovio commended a dictum of Pomponio Leto that successful pursuit of the liberal arts depended upon three faculties characteristic of a well-ordered and healthy body: abundant energy, resilient nerves, and good complexion.[34] Giovio's belief that mental attributes were linked to, if not actually grounded in, physical constitution, underlay his interest in physiognomy and his never-failing surprise when physical appearance belied the mental gifts within.

The relationship of medicine to history in Giovio's scheme of priorities appeared in a medal cast for him in the last year of his life by Francesco da San Gallo. The obverse displayed a splendid portrait bust showing Giovio still full of vitality, wearing a fur-collared gown and prelate's cap. The reverse featured a figure garbed as a physician, holding a large volume under his left arm and raising a naked man from the ground. An inscription read *Nunc denique vives* (Now at last you live). With the book representing the recently published folio edition of Giovio's *Histories*, the physician raising an infirm man to health became the *figura* of the historian, who raises us, not merely to an uncertain and transient state of health, but—as Giovio affirmed in the preface—to the immortality of everlasting fame.[35]

CHAPTER THREE

Leonine Rome (1513–1521)

Dem glänzenden Bilde des leonischen Rom, wie es Paolo Giovio
entwirft, wird man sich nie entziehen können, so gut bezeugt
auch die Schattenseiten sind.

    —Jacob Burckhardt, *Die Kultur der Renaissance in Italien*

We can never tear ourselves away from the brilliant picture of
Leonine Rome as drawn by Paolo Giovio, however well-empha-
sized the darker sides may be.

WHEN GIOVIO ARRIVED in Rome sometime in 1512, the city was beginning to assume the visual and intellectual splendors of the High Renaissance, inspired—or rather, impelled—by Pope Julius II and his vision of
Roman grandeur restored under the aegis of the papacy.[1] Michelangelo
was finishing the Sistine ceiling and Raphael was at work on the Vatican
stanze. Bramante had begun the new St. Peter's and the *cortile* of the
Belvedere. Inspired by the Roman ruins and the recent uncovering of the
Laocoön (1506), Roman classicism was in full spate. To Jacopo Sadoleto, whose poem on the statue had won him instant celebrity, its discovery symbolized the reawakening of Rome to the full *dignitas* of the Augustan era.[2] While Julius II was establishing the political *imperium* of the
papacy, the humanists, led by Paolo Cortesi and Raffaele Maffei, were
fashioning a linguistic *imperium*, restoring the Latin current during the
height of Rome's civilization and power.[3] When Leo X, at his accession
in 1513, took Sadoleto and Pietro Bembo as his secretaries, the triumph
of classicism in letters was assured.

    Giovio quickly fell under the spell of the new *Romanitas*. The *alma
urbs* became to him "the most certain home and free *patria* of all peoples," the source in ancient times of "the legitimate laws and insignia of
empire," and subsequently of "the rites of true religion."[4] The papacy,
not Venice, now appeared as the chief defender of the freedom of Italy
and Julius II as the pope "endowed with singular ferocity of character
and girded with inexhaustible strength, who defended the freedom and
dignity of the Church in realms both sacred and secular."[5] And it was
jointly in the ecclesiastical authority of the papacy and the supremacy of
Latin letters, Giovio came to believe, that Rome's primacy over the nations and "the dignity of the Italian name" were maintained.[6] For the
aspiring historian seeking to make his reputation in Roman literary cir-

cles, the acquisition of a fully classical Latin style was both a practical necessity and a political, almost a moral, imperative.

Looking back a decade and a half later, Giovio bemusedly recalled his reeducation by the "fathers" of the Roman academy. In an extended metaphor that occurred to him amid the gardens of Vittoria Colonna's castle at Ischia, he described being weaned by the senior members of the academy from "silver" Latin models and converted to the prevailing preference for "golden" Latin.

> Nor were there wanting under that sky, as opportune guides to the imbibing and perfecting of eloquence, learned men, versed in antiquity and replete with sound judgment, who took me as a young pilgrim wandering incautiously beyond the Roman walls in the topiaries and luxuriant shady bowers of Quintus Curtius and Tacitus, and who, after admonishing me, led me with singular humanity back to the Sallustian gardens, the famous arches of the Caesarian court and the Livian portico, as if from the dank shadows into the most limpid air and salubrious light of day.[7]

The metaphor of "Sallustian gardens" may well have been a compliment to one of the principal patrons of the Roman academy in these years, Angelo Colocci, a patrician of Iesi and papal secretary whose gardens near the church of Santa Susanna were thought to lie on the site of the ancient gardens of Sallust. Although somewhat less formal in structure than in the days of Pomponio Leto, the Roman academy still met for dinners in the houses and gardens of its members, particularly of Colocci and the Rhinelander Johann Küritz.[8]

Gatherings of the academy during this era had a golden aura. Northern humanists such as Erasmus or Ulrich von Hutten took back to their homelands a lifelong memory of "honeyed conversations." Especially memorable, as Sadoleto recalled, were alfresco banquets on summer evenings in fragrant gardens and vineyards adorned with classical artifacts, where, over simple but delectable food and the celebrated wines of Latium, a learned and mirthful company would grow increasingly spirited as the evening progressed, seasoning the customary declamations and recitations with witticisms, and forging among the members "the sacred bond of friendship."[9]

Occasionally Giovio provided a vignette of the academy's reunions, as when the celebrated improviser Camillo Querno was hailed with the epithet "Archpoet" at a banquet on the island in the Tiber. After an evening of deep drinking and incessant recitation to the lyre, he was crowned with the customary laurel—interwoven, however, with cabbage leaves as a hint to restrain his drinking.[10] Following a tradition begun by Pomponio Leto, newly admitted members often assumed a Latinized epithet or name, which probably accounted for Giovio's adoption of *Jovius*.[11]

Küritz, affectionately identified with the old man in Virgil's *Georgics*, Corycius *senex* (4.127), was an apostolic protonotary and receiver of petitions who became enduringly associated with Renaissance Latin verse. In the same year that Giovio arrived in Rome, Andrea Sansovino finished for Küritz's chapel in the church of Sant'Agostino a much-celebrated statue of St. Anne with the Madonna and Child, a work of refined classicism to which for more than a decade the poets of Rome would affix verses on the feast of St. Anne.[12] Eventually the apostolic secretary Blosio Palladio (Biagio Pallai) gathered the best and published them as the *Coryciana* (1524).[13] Giovio was represented by a rather pedestrian quatrain invoking the commonplace *topos* of nature and art, but while his verses substantiated his claim of being no poet, his interest in Latin poetry was sufficiently perceptive for his fellow physician Francesco Arsilli of Senigallia to dedicate to him a poetical treatise, "On the Poets of Rome [*De poetis urbanis*]," which appeared as an appendix to the *Coryciana*.[14]

The members of the Roman academy often made excursions to the ruins of Rome, following the grand tradition begun by Flavio Biondo and the academicians of the Quattrocento, and, as befitted a historian, Giovio eventually became one of the acknowledged experts on the *relicta Romae*. In his seventh satire, Ariosto spoke of the pure and elevated intellectual pleasure of studying the ruins of Rome in the company of friends such as Bembo, Sadoleto, "the learned Giovio," Blosio Palladio, and the poets Marco Cavalli, Francesco Molza, Girolamo Vida, and Antonio Tebaldeo.[15] With all this Romanizing, Giovio's interest in Greek began to fade, and he sided with the Ciceronians of the Roman academy in condemning Greek studies as an end in themselves rather than as an aid to Latin.[16] He even began to hold with the most ardent that Latin could only be perfected "under the Roman sky," and that native Romans alone could hope to pronounce Latin with a "pure" accent.[17] In short, his acculturation was complete.

"To have been known in Rome," Erasmus observed, "was a great part of felicity."[18] Giovio's felicity began in 1515 when Leo X praised book VIII of his *Histories*. A witty quatrain by Blosio Palladio welcomed him into the circle of papal protégés,

> Esse aliquid volui, quod cum populi aura negasset,
>   Illud, Paule, aliquid coeperat esse nihil.
> Rursus cum incipiant mea dicta placere Leoni,
>   Illud, Paule, nihil incipit esse aliquid.[19]

> I wished to be something, but when popular favor denied it,
>   That something, Paolo, began to be nothing.
> But when my work began to please Pope Leo,
>   That nothing, Paolo, began to be something.

A sense of felicity pervaded the "brilliant picture" Giovio later drew of Leonine Rome in his *Vita Leonis X* (1548), the work that more than any other perpetuated the legend of the Golden Age. As the century progressed and the wars of Italy exacted their crushing toll, the Leonine epoch glowed with distant brightness. "In addition to its uncommonly salubrious air and clement sky," Giovio sighed, "Rome then flourished with outstanding talents and an abundance of everything, which explains why it was that Leo X—a pope of preeminent virtue and amplitude—was said to have founded after many centuries an age of gold."[20]

The ten folio pages devoted to Leo X's character, court, daily life, and amusements became the basis for most subsequent literature on Leonine Rome.[21] Giovio's description of the pope conformed to the portrait by Raphael or the statue by Domenico Aimo in the church of Santa Maria d'Aracoeli. There were the delicate hands, the corpulent body, the legs too small for the bloated torso, the large head, fat cheeks, and protruding eyes. But what the brush and chisel could not convey, Giovio's portrait completed—the animation, the play of intelligence across those features, the suave and courteous manner, the soft and gentle voice, the flow of speech always appropriate to the sentiments, in serious matters grave, in conversation agreeable, in lighter moments spontaneous and urbane.[22] The pope's Latin verses were good, his Tuscan lyrics "delectable." His knowledge of Greek, Giovio observed with evident satisfaction, was "not for ostentation but as an aid to Latin." The historian was delighted that a pope whose acute literary criticism was respected, even feared, by the Roman academy, was also well versed in the history of all epochs and nations.

Although the biography of Leo X had been commissioned by members of the Medici family, Giovio evidently felt obliged to honor Cicero's charge to tell not only the truth but the whole truth, and so he also revealed "the darker sides" of Leo's character and pontificate, the political ruthlessness surprising in so amiable an individual, and the faults of his private life and character. The "outstanding virtues of a liberal and lofty mind," Giovio cautioned, in a particularly Senecan passage, "were often obscured not only by an excessively luxurious style of life but by passions of a nature opposed to those very virtues."[23] Despite his efforts at urbanity, the young man who shunned the licentious behavior of his companions in Como could never quite reconcile himself to the secular levity of Leo X's Vatican, and he noted with disapproval the pope's familiar banter with his chamberlains—handsome young men from noble families—and the advantage he was said to take of them.

So, while he described the less decorous episodes of Leonine Rome, including the mock triumph of Baraballo and the inaugural of Cardinal Bibbiena's licentious comedy, *La Calandria*, Giovio preferred the more

elevated events he witnessed, including the festivities of 1513 to confer
Roman citizenship on Giuliano and Lorenzo de' Medici, which he
thought renewed "the vanished splendor of the ancient city," particularly
Tommaso Inghirami's staging of the *Poenulus* of Plautus, which "recalled
the Roman youth to the dignity of the ancient pronunciation."[24]

Giovio himself benefited from Leo X's celebrated and also much-dis-
puted patronage. According to Benedetto Giovio, his brother's Latin
style prompted the pope to declare that "after Livy he had heard nothing
fuller or more elegant in that genre."[25] To his new Livy, Leo X awarded
half the revenues of a cavalierate, a benefice established for supporting
talent, and subsequently the priorate of Caruco, or Monte Regale, in the
diocese of Mondovì. The bull described Giovio as a cleric of Como and
papal familiar, indicating that he had already taken minor orders.[26]

The Latin style admired by the pope had come with much "huffing
and puffing," Giovio confessed, through imitating ancient authors, the
method advocated by the fathers of the Roman academy.[27] It was also
the method recommended by Lucian in a treatise translated by Cattaneo,
which Giovio thought his colleague intended to dedicate to him, *How to
Write History*. Although Cattaneo evidently changed his mind in respect
to the dedication, Giovio became a disciple of Lucian and began adopting the methods of Greek eyewitness historiography.[28] For Roman historical practice there was the whole tradition of humanist historiography
as a guide, recently codified by the eminent Neapolitan humanist and
historian Giovanni Pontano in his dialogue *Actius* (1507).[29]

Giovio later described the niche he had discerned for himself among
the luminous talents of Leonine Rome:

> For although the ancient writers were a source more of desperation than
> hope of imitation, deterring me from my arduous undertaking, nonetheless I
> was sustained by one certainty, namely that those skilled in eloquence were
> either occupied or unsuited to collecting the materials necessary for relating
> the multitude of events; while those occupied in diplomacy and warfare, who
> were said to have the knowledge of events, did not appear to have even such
> faculties as I could muster for the writing of history. And living in that Roman
> light, in the home of all nations, it was easy to seek the illustrious friendship of
> great commanders as a means of satisfying my urge to know the real truth of
> events and plans.[30]

In other words, the humanists had no interest in history and the diplomats and generals had no interest in writing, leaving him the opening he
wanted.

If the Roman academy shaped Giovio's concepts of style and Greek
historians his methodology, the court of Giulio de' Medici was to provide his education in politics and diplomacy. Following his master in his

vicissitudes from cardinal to pope, Giovio came to know virtually all the great figures of the age. While not usually a participant in diplomacy, he nonetheless perfected the technique of the interview and learned to plot his gleanings from courtiers against his own penetrating judgments of character. And whatever considerations his own imagination failed to supply were readily available from the curial gossip of Rome.

With access to the makers of history came greater insight into its workings. Under the cataclysmic events of sixteenth-century Italian history, Giovio's political outlook deepened and matured. From his early letters, coupled with his retrospective judgments in the biographies and *Histories*, the stages appear by which the young patriot came to envision a political configuration offering Italy some degree of liberty within the confines of de facto foreign hegemony.

What prompted Giovio to undertake universal history? Apart from Flavio Biondo, most humanists had written on more restricted subjects—a city, a dynasty, a war. Benedetto implied that his brother's decision was an early one, as did Giovio himself. "For the last 1400 years," he boasted, "there has been no one of resolute enough temperament to dare to undertake the history of his times, universal throughout the whole world, attaching the fringes of chorography, a necessary mirror for seeing and understanding the *ubi, quomodo, quando* [where, how, when] of events."[31] His affirmation of universal history and the importance of geography were so reminiscent of Polybius as to suggest that the great Greek historian had been an inspiration to him.[32] The apparent slight to Flavio Biondo and his decades *Ab inclinatione Romani imperii* (From the decline of the Roman Empire), which Giovio actually seems to have admired, probably indicated that he did not regard the Quattrocento historian as a model for contemporary history.[33]

The early nature of Giovio's decision to write universal history was underscored by the fact that the first of his *Histories* to circulate in manuscript was book VIII—the present books 13 and 14—the book praised by Leo X in 1515 (Roman numerals will be used to designate Giovio's original manuscript books, Arabic numerals the books of the *Histories* as published).[34] Book VIII commenced in 1514 with the peasant revolt in Hungary and briefly sketched events in Poland, Lithuania, and Russia before addressing its principal theme, a survey of Persian and Turkish history concluding with the defeat of Shah Ishmael of Persia by Selim I at Chaldiran in August 1514.

News of the battle of Chaldiran reached Rome on October 30, 1514, where it had an effect similar to the fall of Constantinople on an earlier generation. After a sleepless night, the pope summoned all the ambassadors in Rome and read them a copy of the sultan's official dispatch announcing his victory.[35] Leo X now joined the long line of popes, humanists, and clerics who had been attempting to arouse Europe to a sense of the danger from the steady Ottoman advance. Giovio's friends in the Roman academy had often heard the pleas of John Lascaris to turn their attention to the growing power of the Turks.[36] A major theme of Raffaele Maffei's *Commentariorum urbanorum octa et triginta libri* (1506) had been the need for Christians to cease fighting each other in order to unite against the Ottomans.[37] Beginning with the inaugural address of Giles of Viterbo, the Fifth Lateran Council had received numerous appeals to heed the Eastern peril. On May 4, 1515, Stefano Taleazzi, titular archbishop of Patras, admonished the tenth session that the Turk "like a ferocious dragon moves swiftly forward to devour us."[38] It was evident that the expansive force displayed at Chaldiran could not be long in turning westward again. To relate the conflicts of East and West in a way that dramatized the debilitating effects of internecine Christian warfare became the grand scheme of Giovio's *Histories.*

But the spirit in which Giovio embraced universal history was broader even than a vision of Christendom's struggle against Islam within the confines of the old *orbis terrarum*. It partook of the Renaissance discovery of the world, of Pius II's *Cosmographia* and of Leo X's delight in accounts of newly discovered countries. It encompassed Russia and the Baltic, the furthest reaches of the Nile, and the New World. The Rome in which Giovio embraced universal history was the Rome in which Giles of Viterbo hailed the discovery of America as the prelude to the last age, the *plenitudo gentium*, the spiritual unity of mankind.[39] Giovio's perennial sense of wonder in discovery and his interest in all peoples reflected the best spirit of his age and informed his sense of universal history with the expectant air of the emperor Charles V's motto, *Plus ultra* ("More Beyond"), displayed over the pillars of Hercules in his crest.[40]

While immersed in the Near East, Giovio was also gathering materials for recent European history. In 1514 he requested from Bartolomeo d'Alviano a commentary on the war of the Cadore (1508) and the battle of Agnadello (1509) similar to one he claimed to have seen for the great commander's more recent campaigns. Tactfully advancing the example of Hannibal to draw any sting from his request for an analysis of Agnadello, Giovio mentioned having had interviews with "almost all the commanders, both Italian and foreign, from whom we have heard the truth and sequence of events . . . in these wars."[41] "I did not want to publish before consulting you," he told d'Alviano, implying that his account of "these wars" had been largely compiled. But which wars did he mean? Did Giovio start his *Histories* with the invasion of Charles VIII, or did he begin with more recent wars only to realize that their thread led back to his boyhood, to 1494? If in 1515 he assigned the number VIII to a book dealing with events of 1514, it would seem he was intending to begin considerably earlier. The year 1494 may well have been his starting point *ab initio*. But this is conjectural. What is certain is that the *Histories* were well under way by the time Giovio accompanied Cardinal Sauli to Bologna to witness his first great diplomatic "summit," the meeting of Leo X with Francis I in 1515.[42]

CHAPTER FOUR

Leo X and the Quest for the *Libertas Italiae* (1513–1521)

E certo é gran fatica volere essere signore temporale et essere
tenuto religioso, perché sono due cose che non hanno con-
venienza alcuna insieme.
—Francesco Vettori, *Sommario della storia d'Italia*

It is certainly difficult to wish to be a temporal lord and to be held
religious, because they are two things that have nothing in
common.

THE BRILLIANT VICTORY of Francis I over the new duke of Milan and his
veteran Swiss troops at Marignano on September 14, 1515, had
thwarted the plans of Leo X for the *libertas Italiae*. A personal embarrassment for Giovio was the fact that Venice had allied itself with France
and that the tide had been turned by his hero, Bartolomeo d'Alviano,
who arrived on the second day of the battle with fresh Venetian forces.[1]
Although a papal army was in the field to protect the newly acquired
territories of the Church in Emilia and Lombardy, the pope was not
eager for a fight and had been glad to agree to a meeting at Bologna.

For the Venetian diarist Marin Sanudo, Giovio drew a lively picture of
the victorious king as he entered Bologna on December 11, riding between two cardinals.

He was wearing a robe of silk and silver brocade and a beret of black velvet
with a small black plume, and holding in his hand a rod; he was mounted on
a dark bay horse decked in black velvet with tassels of gold. His complexion is
very fine, his nose longish, his mouth speaks and laughs, his hands do not
stand out; in short, his appearance is worthy of a ruler. He is of greater than
normal stature and full of force and vigor.

The outcome of the negotiations was as yet unknown, "because it was a
very secret colloquium," but Giovio predicted "the effects" would reveal
it.[2] Pondering the effects of Leo X's diplomacy over the next six years
helped him to devise his own solution to Italy's problems as he watched
the pope maneuver to guard the independence of the papacy and the
libertas Italiae while at the same time advancing the Medici family.

After four hundred years, historians are still reduced, like Giovio, to deducing the terms of the Concordat of Bologna from its effects. It was known that Leo X had conceded the cities won in war by Julius II: Parma and Piacenza to France, and Reggio to France's ally Ferrara, along with Modena if Duke Alfonso d'Este could reimburse him the sum he had recently paid the emperor for it. It also became clear that Francis I had agreed to abandon his other Italian ally, Francesco Maria della Rovere, leaving the pope free to seize the duchy of Urbino for his nephew, Lorenzo de' Medici. Della Rovere, had, indeed, been a disobedient vassal, but in his biography of Leo X, Giovio depicted the war as naked aggression, noting that only after the death of Giuliano de' Medici in March 1516 had the pope felt free to move. Until then, his brother's aversion to harming his hosts in exile had stayed Leo X's hand. Giovio also blamed Lorenzo de' Medici's mother, Alfonsina Orsini, and the "blind ambition" that he increasingly saw as cause of the ruin of Italy.[3] The campaign itself was an easy one, since the duke fled to Modena to spare his people the horrors of war.

In his account of Cardinal Petrucci's conspiracy a year later, Giovio not only underscored Leo X's ruthlessness in putting cardinals to the torture and conducting the trial without the customary cardinal-judges but reported speculation that the pope's real purpose had been to raise money for a renewal of the Urbino war, since in January 1517, just prior to the discovery of the conspiracy, della Rovere had emerged from Mantua and marched with a small expeditionary force to Urbino, where he was welcomed "with incredible rejoicing by all the people."[4] The reconquest by the papal forces under Lorenzo took until September, but its success gave Leo X such pleasure, Giovio reported, that he did not miss the enormous sum of 800,000 ducats which he had spent on it. Then, having described the pope's joy at his triumph over a Christian vassal, Giovio briefly recounted Selim the Grim's triumph over the Caliph of Egypt, concluding with Leo X's barefoot procession on March 14, 1517, to Santa Maria sopra Minerva to commend to the Virgin the safety of Christendom. Such ironic juxtapositions—a characteristic strategy of Thucydides—became one of Giovio's principal means of ethical comment. In his first biography, written in the 1530s, he was already telling his patrons "bitter truths."[5]

Giovio was ahead of most Europeans in his knowledge of the Turks, gained from extensive reading and questioning of travelers and merchants.[6] A historian's detachment let him understand the strengths and weaknesses of the Turkish empire without abating his passionate belief that Christendom should unite to overcome it. There was also a pragmatic element in his crusading zeal, as Muslim pirates were an ever-present threat for Italians near the seacoast. In 1516 a band of corsairs from Tunis had landed at Ostia and almost captured the pope while he was hunting near the mouth of the Tiber. Giovio took such a keen interest in the crusade that Leo X now proposed that twenty-one years later he could still recount the details for Charles V, but the conflicts of the European monarchs undermined the project. Despite the emperor's enthusiastic support, the French were indifferent and the Venetians were pursuing their own policy of coexistence and rapprochement. "Through the fatal negligence of our princes," Giovio lamented, "each of whom envied the glory of the other, those plans so full of piety and honor were ruined."[7]

In April 1518, while negotiations for the crusade were still in progress, the emperor Maximilian I divulged his plans to have his grandson Charles elected king of the Romans, setting off a year of frenetic maneuvering by Leo X to avoid what his medieval predecessors had always fought to prevent, an encirclement of the papal states by the emperor. As king of Spain, Charles was already king of Naples, and as emperor he could be expected to reassert the imperial suzerainty of Milan. Maximilian's death in January 1519 only increased the pope's alarm. Thus the problem of Milan and the empire, so central to Giovio's *Histories*, enveloped the papal curia not long after Giovio himself joined the household of Giulio de' Medici.

Until 1518 the prime mover in papal diplomacy had been Cardinal Bibbiena, but by the end of the election his Francophilia had begun to isolate him in a court that was veering away from France, and Giovio's new patron, a proponent of accommodation with Charles V, gained the ascendancy. After first supporting the elector of Saxony, Leo X overcame his fear of encirclement enough to make his peace with the young Hapsburg, whose election as emperor finally took place on June 28, 1519. Disappointed in his bid to renew the empire of Charlemagne, Francis I was to prove as determined to retain Milan as Charles V to reclaim it, and the stage was set for the epic struggle of twenty-five years. Like his master the cardinal, Giovio inclined toward Charles V or, at any rate, away from Francis I.[8]

When Lorenzo de' Medici fell into a mortal illness during the later stages of the election, the pope sent Cardinal Giulio to Florence, and for the next several years he and his immediate household were there almost continuously. Giovio had a low opinion of Lorenzo, "a spirit neither civil nor temperate," but he was full of praise for the government of his patron, who he felt restored "the state of liberty" and "the happy conditions of earlier times."[9] While in Florence, Giovio was hard at work on his *Histories*. A colophon to the manuscript of book X reads, "Florentiae elucubratus conscriptusque MDXX [composed by lamplight and written at Florence in 1520]."[10] Giovio meant "elucubrated" quite literally. Only after a day attending the cardinal was he able to work on his *Histories*. On November 5, 1520, he reported to his brother that he had recently sent to His Holiness "the tenth and ultimate book of the most marvelous things of the world," and most of the earlier books of the first decade now seem to have taken shape.[11]

While living in Florence, Giovio was admitted into the circle of prominent citizens and men of letters who met regularly in the Rucellai gardens.[12] After Bernardo Rucellai's death in 1514, his place as host had been assumed by his sons Palla and Giovanni, together with his grandson Cosimo. Florentines Giovio would have met among the rare plants and shady walks included the philosophers Francesco da Diacceto and Roberto Acciaiuoli, the poet Luigi Alamanni, the biographer Lorenzo Strozzi, the historians Francesco Vettori, Filippo Nerli, and Francesco Guicciardini, the tragedian Alessandro Pazzi, the mathematician and man of letters Piero Martelli, the ambassador Giovanni Corsi, and perhaps Niccolò Machiavelli, who was working on his *Discourses on the Decade of Livy* and who was commissioned by Cardinal Giulio in 1520 to write his *Florentine Histories*.[13]

"In between witty, lighthearted conversations," Giovio recalled, "we discussed the weightiest matters."[14] All shades of opinion were represented. Roberto Acciaiuoli, Francesco Guicciardini, Giovanni Corsi, and Francesco Vettori were destined to play an important role in the Medicean restoration of 1530. Luigi Alamanni and Francesco da Diacceto's son Iacopo, on the other hand, were implicated in the conspiracy against Cardinal Giulio that surfaced in May 1522. As the elders passed away, Giovio said, their successors began entertaining "the vehement ideas" that ultimately led to the restoration of the republic in 1527. These younger men were equally affable to him, however, and somewhat easier company because of their ready laughter.

Some of the major themes that appeared in the first book of Giovio's *Histories*, as in Guicciardini's, had been developed in Bernardo Rucellai's history (completed in 1509) of Charles VIII's invasion. History was a frequent discussion topic among "the friends of the cool shade," and in his Ischian dialogue Giovio boasted of sitting under the shade of the Ionic portico and the plane tree where the *De bello Italico* had been composed.[15] Many in Florence, Machiavelli among them, endorsed Rucellai's view that thanks to Lorenzo de' Medici's statesmanship, Italy in the late Quattrocento had enjoyed unparalleled peace and prosperity.[16] Another of Rucellai's views, shared with the Neapolitan historian Giovanni Pontano and the Milanese historian Bernardo Corio, was that the dissension and folly of the Italian princes had drawn the foreigner into Italy.[17]

The historiographical tradition originating with Rucellai and his contemporaries that 1494 had been a turning point for Italy constituted the first attempt to define distinct periods within the general notion of a rebirth of civilization after the fall of Rome, and Giovio was the first historian to approach universal history in terms of the new division. His concept of Italy flourishing in peace before being plunged by the invasion of Charles VIII into a war that eventually involved all Europe and even Asia in fifty years of blood and ruin may well have been influenced by conversations in Florence; likewise his belief that the Italian princes themselves had been largely to blame.[18]

It is also possible that Giovio enlarged his knowledge of Greek historiography in Florence, where a continuing interest in Greek historians stemmed from the founder of humanist historiography, the great chancellor Leonardo Bruni. Through his relationships with the philo-Hellenic members of the Rucellai circle, Machiavelli encountered in these same years the theories of the yet untranslated sixth book of Polybius, with its analysis of the mixed constitution of the Romans.[19] Although Giovio did not mention Machiavelli as a frequenter of the Orti, he knew him personally and may even have had a hand in Cardinal Giulio's commission.[20]

Giovio admired Machiavelli's comedies and his Tuscan style. He particularly relished the *Mandragola*, which he implied having seen at one of its performances, either in Florence or in Rome.[21] He felt that Machiavelli had taken Tuscan prose, "which was becoming diffuse in the period that separated it from its founder, Boccaccio, and bound it with new and patently Attic bonds."[22] Indeed, Machiavelli was one of only three vernacular writers whom Giovio included in the *Elogia* (the others being Boccaccio and Corio). His reservations regarding the secretary seem to have arisen later, after reading the completed *Istorie fiorentine*. Even these he found "shrewd and impressive" except where he felt that Machiavelli had "ignored the strife of factions" or had taken liberties with his material to advance his own political views.[23]

Giovio's primary quarrel with Machiavelli and Florentine theorists was over republican liberty. In reflecting on the history of their native city, both Giovio and his brother had concluded that the factionalism of the late medieval republican period had brought Como nothing but misery. While perhaps regrettable from the standpoint of local pride, the city's surrender to Azzone Visconti in 1335 had gained it tranquility and prosperity.[24] The tradition of Lombard humanism had been to support the prince as a bringer of peace, and, as a Lombard, Giovio tended to see in the discussions of the 1520s regarding the best government for Florence a latter-day chapter of a political issue settled in his own region almost two centuries earlier.[25] What the Florentines termed liberty, Giovio thought (not without reason) was illusory for most of the population, and he was most skeptical of the way in which government was habitually used to enrich the party in power and to impoverish its enemies.[26] While harboring no illusions about Italian princes and their failings, he came to feel that only the principate offered the internal stability requisite for prosperity and resistance to foreign powers.[27]

Giovio's acquaintance with the other great Florentine historian, Francesco Guicciardini, seems to have dated from these same years. Although Guicciardini was normally away from the city as governor of Modena and Reggio, he was in Florence periodically for rest and for discussions with Cardinal de' Medici.[28] An interesting echo of Giovio's conversations in the Rucellai gardens which linked him to Guicciardini (as well as to Thucydides) was his analysis of the Florentine character in book 25 of the *Histories*.[29] Themes in Giovio's portrait of the Florentines, such as their restless egalitarianism, also surfaced in Guicciardini's *Dialogo del reggimento di Firenze*, composed largely in 1521.[30]

Giovio's life in Florence seems to have been agreeable enough, and his hopes for the future were high. The cardinal's retinue soon forgot Rome in "the pleasant and salubrious leisure we enjoyed among the amenities and tranquility of a most distinguished city."[31] While Giovio would not have been accepted as a social equal by the great families, his patrician background, affable manners, learning, and friendship with the cardinal brought invitations to parties, weddings, and retreats at country villas. Always a lover of the life of the villa, he left a charming and nostalgic picture of the hills and villas that ringed the city, most of them subsequently destroyed in the siege of 1529–30.[32] Among the Florentine ladies he came to know was his hostess in the Rucellai gardens, Dianora di Pietro Ridolfi, whose marriage to Palla Rucellai was celebrated with dances and comedies "most delightfully written" by members of the Rucellai family.[33] Giovio was even moved to compose a little tractate in praise of Florentine women, later subsumed into the third part of the Ischian dialogue.[34] He found them graceful in dress and movement, quick-spirited and sharp in their opinions, their clothing handsome rather than ostentatious, their household cuisine simple and frugal. They seemed to him very religious, which he thought accounted for their being judged more chaste than other Italian women.[35]

Giovio's letters to his brother reflected the concerns of the aspiring careerist and the pressures exerted by the demands of a numerous and needy family. After reviewing plans for the university educations of Benedetto's sons, for which he had agreed to pay, Giovio's exasperation burst out. "I have told you at other times," he protested, "how I have made up my mind that all I have acquired with sweat and servitude will be for the benefit of your children."[36] Evidently Benedetto had accused him of niggardliness, because much of Giovio's letter was taken up with an explanation of the large expenses he was incurring in his present situation. "Spare me your pettiness," he charged. "It was ever the mark of our family to complain, just as eminent families tend to boast." He was living hand to mouth, he declared, despite what people might report about his style of life—his servitor, his chaplain, or his growing collection of cameos and rings. "I am not trying to accumulate pennies," he protested, "because he who wishes to do that cannot properly serve these lords." A certain style was necessary "for anyone who wishes to look and live like a man." Nonetheless, Giovio was prepared to turn some of his bene-fices over to his nephews for their support, and he urged his brother to keep an eye out for potential vacancies, as "it is necessary that the death of others aid our own lives." Unattractive as they seem, such nepotism and pluralism were a normal pattern for ecclesiastical careerists of the period.[37]

While living in Florence, Giovio continued to acquire portraits of fa-mous men of letters and began adding rulers, statesmen, and generals to form the core of the collection that ultimately inspired his museum.[38] His knowledge of history, astrology, and art were all put to use when the cardinal asked him to coordinate the scheme for the frescoes of the re-cently completed banqueting hall of Lorenzo the Magnificent's villa at Poggio a Caiano. According to Vasari, Lorenzo had wanted the hall painted with scenes from Roman history. It may well have been Giovio's inspiration to select episodes, such as Cicero's return from exile, which could be seen as prefiguring the history of the Medici family. In Pon-tormo's celebrated lunette, the closest in spirit to the Quattrocento frieze on the portico, a complex reworking of Ovid's myth of Pomona and Vertumnus invoked the cycles of nature and perhaps even of cosmic time to celebrate the Laurentian golden age and its return under Pope Leo X.[39]

In these Florentine years, Giovio established fruitful relationships with the courts of Ferrara and Mantua. Supported by the Ferrarese agent, who described him as "a most celebrated writer of histories, in which he has most honorably written and spoken of Your Excellency," Giovio re-quested and received from Duke Alfonso d'Este of Ferrara a portrait of the great physician and Greek scholar Niccolò Leoniceno.[40] With his thanks Giovio sent to Ferrara the draft manuscript of book VIII of the *Histories*, asking that the duke share it with Leoniceno.[41] His friendship with a prince whose relations with the apostolic see were greatly strained—indeed, to the point of Alfonso's imminent excommunica-tion—was characteristic of Giovio's lifelong independence from the poli-tics of his patrons, an independence that served him well as a historian, although it eventually denied him some of the rewards that came from unambiguous loyalty.

Given the rapprochement with the papacy initiated by Isabella d'Este in 1520, Giovio's cordial relations with the Mantuan court were less sur-prising.[42] He kept in touch through Baldassar Castiglione in Rome and through Isabella d'Este's portly, garrulous secretary, Mario Equicola, whom he knew well how to handle. In 1521 Equicola was publishing his history of Mantua, and in thanking the secretary for having praised a book of his own *Histories*, Giovio lifted a phrase from Cicero, avowing himself deeply gratified "to have been lauded by a much-lauded man."[43]

Once the imperial election was over, continuing hostilities between the contestants confronted Leo X with difficult choices. His old fear of encirclement returned, and in September 1519 he concluded a league with Francis I. Disillusion with the sincerity of his confederate quickly set in, however, when far from abandoning the duke of Ferrara as the terms of the league required, the French king began demanding that the pope honor his commitment of 1515 regarding the restoration of Modena and Reggio. In the face of a hostile wind from France, Leo X jibbed and began to sail toward the emperor. This was the course desired by Giovio's patron, Cardinal Giulio, who went so far as to lodge the imperial ambassador, Juan Manuel, in the palace of the Cancelleria when he arrived in Rome in April 1520. For a while the pope actually had alliances with both sovereigns, but by the end of 1520 he had resolved not only to rid himself of his vexatious French allies but to drive them from Italy, a resolve made easier by Bibbiena's death in November 1520.

Leo X's treaty with Charles V, signed on May 8, 1521, contained key elements of the Italian political settlement that Giovio himself came to champion. The French were to be expelled from Milan and Genoa and the two cities ruled by the Sforza and Adorno families as vassals of the empire. The emperor was to transfer Parma and Piacenza to the pope, who was also to retain Modena and Reggio. The emperor promised the pope assistance in dealing with his recalcitrant vassal, the duke of Ferrara, as well as in maintaining the Medici family in Florence. The pope, in turn, promised the emperor the investiture of Naples and assistance in enforcing imperial rights over the terra firma possessions of Venice. Some of these terms merely confirmed historic jurisdictions and boundaries; others represented either enlargements or reassertions of long-unexercised papal or imperial jurisdictions and threatened new contentions. Parma, Piacenza, Modena, and Reggio had always been imperial, not papal fiefs, and imperial jurisdiction over most of northern Italy had been dormant at best. Given the prospect of Italy's domination either by France or the empire, however, the settlement's appeal to Giovio lay in having indigenous Italian families ruling as imperial vassals.

For Leo X, who had been Julius II's legate to the papal armies during the Holy League of 1511–12, the pact of 1521 embodied the *libertas Italiae*. Guicciardini recorded that when the cardinal de' Medici was trying to dissuade him, not from an imperial alliance but from the war it entailed, Leo X had exclaimed that death itself would be welcome if he could regain Parma and Piacenza for the Church.[44] Doubtful, like his master, about a papal military offensive, convinced after the fact by its success and by his own yearning for the *libertas Italiae*, Giovio came to recognize in Leo X's treaty with the emperor the starting point of a whole new series of ruinous conflicts for Italy. By the time he wrote his *Vita Leonis X* in the early 1530s, he had clearly begun to regard 1521 as a second turning point in Italian history, a view that Guicciardini, who was much less favorable to Leo X, subsequently adopted with even greater emphasis. After dilating on the peace and prosperity Leo X had brought to Italy, Giovio observed that "fatal necessity entangled him in the French war."[45] Time only deepened this conviction. In the *Histories* he portrayed the decision of pope and emperor to drive the French from Italy as an extension of the hostilities between Charles V and Francis I, begun in Belgium, continued in Spain, and finally transferred to Italy "by the most dire counsels, since from this point onward Italy lost almost all of its ancient honor and pristine liberty."[46]

Of all the reasons Giovio offered in his life of Leo X, public and private, for the pope's decision to bind himself to Charles V in an offensive alliance against Francis I, the one most resembling "fatal necessity" was the need to combat the "Lutheran poison." Since Giovio's source for Leo X's policies had been the cardinal de' Medici, the pope's chief adviser in this period, his analysis deserves attention. Alarm over the spread of Luther's ideas, Giovio argued, coupled with Charles V's willingness to combat them, as demonstrated at the diet of Worms, predisposed the pope to ally with the emperor "should the war between France and Spain be transferred to Italy." Leo X had not moved against Luther during the election because he had been endorsing the candidacy of the elector of Saxony, but now that he realized the full gravity of the situation, he felt impelled to take all possible measures. To obtain support against Luther, Giovio concluded, as well as to recover Parma and Piacenza, the pope had allowed himself to be drawn into Charles V's war with Francis I and recruited to the plan of reasserting the ancient imperial suzerainty over Milan and Genoa by expelling the French from Italy.[47]

Giovio's own opinion of "brother Martin" was informed and independent. In the *Vita Leonis X* he acknowledged Luther's "eloquence and skill in sacred letters." He condemned the "detestable avarice" of preaching that upon payment for indulgences, the souls of the departed would straightway be snatched from the pains of purgatory. He excoriated the parading of "huge parchment bulls" in the churches as "impudent corruption" and deplored the diversion of the funds raised by these means from the building of St. Peter's to financing the redecoration of the Vatican palace, including the loggias and tapestries of Raphael. He even went so far as to speculate that, had Luther confined himself to contesting papal abuses, he might have earned "unambiguous praise."[48] It was the alteration of rites, the repudiation of his religious vows, his marriage, and his contesting the authority rather than the mores of the Roman pontiff which made Luther an abominable heresiarch.

Luther's actual theology was of little interest to Giovio. By the 1530s, when the final version of the *Vita Leonis X* was drafted, he had learned enough to observe that it revived errors condemned at Constance and Basel, but that sufficed.[49] He reflected the Roman curia's failure to understand the revolutionary nature of Luther's theology and its appeal to people profoundly weary of the shortcomings of the established church. It has been observed that with its emphasis on human dignity and freedom, Roman humanism ill prepared Renaissance clerics such as Giovio to comprehend the stress upon sinfulness, guilt, and atonement which was the mainspring of so much Protestantism.[50]

For the time being the treaty of May 8, 1521, between Charles V and Leo X was kept secret. In early June the curia celebrated news that the Edict of Worms had been promulgated (on May 26). Then, on the 27th came the consistory in which the pope announced his intentions to expel the French from Italy, using their recent (June 23) attempt on Reggio as justification.[51] In the ensuing weeks Prospero Colonna was named supreme allied commander, Federico Gonzaga captain-general of the Church, and Francesco Guicciardini commissary-general of the army. Francisco Fernando d'Avalos, marquis of Pescara, was given command of the imperial infantry, Antonio de Leyva of the imperial cavalry, and Giovanni de' Medici of the papal cavalry.

Hostilities began with an allied siege of Parma. In late August 1521, Giovio apprised his friend Küritz of the initial successes of the imperial arms but expressed the hope that papal diplomacy could yet resolve the differences between the two kings and turn the assembled armies against the Turk.[52] Colonna's leisurely conduct of the siege Giovio attributed to a laudable desire to avoid a storm and sack. Yet a fortnight later the allies raised the siege at the approach of a Franco-Venetian relief force commanded by the French viceroy of Milan, Odet de Foix, viscount of Lautrec, and fell back to the Enza. Later, after arriving at the front himself, Giovio blamed the withdrawal on conflict between Colonna and Pescara.[53] Alarmed by the deteriorating military situation and desperate to avoid defeat and the vengeance of Francis I, Leo X appointed Cardinal Giulio legate *a latere* to the armies, begging him to restore the lost impetus and recover "the victory just snatched from our hands" by dissensions among the captains. Although not very optimistic, Giovio said, Giulio obeyed loyally, departing posthaste for the allied camp "with doubtful hopes but a ready will."[54] So began Giovio's firsthand acquaintance with camps and the conduct of war.

The cardinal's presence and—Giovio noted—the large sum of money he brought had the desired effect. Reinforced by a contingent of Swiss recruited by the energetic cardinal of Sion, Matthäus Schinner, the allied army marched toward Milan, taking advantage of Lautrec's error in not joining up with the Venetian forces. In his *Storia d'Italia* Guicciardini left an unforgettable picture of the two cardinal legates (Sion and Medici) riding with the army, their silver crosses borne before them, surrounded by guns, pikes, cannons, and a vast horde of blasphemers, thieves, and murderers.[55] Giovio's impressions were similar. When a violent quarrel broke out between the Italian and Spanish troops during the march to the Adda, the cardinal de' Medici rushed to the scene, preceded by his cross but in peril of his life, and "with many entreaties" succeeded in avoiding bloodshed. Bad feelings nonetheless persisted up to the moment of crossing the Adda when the generals were finally able to resolve the conflict. Such was the relief of the troops "that first the officers and ensigns and finally the soldiers of all the nations flocked to the legate Giulio and with earnest entreaties sought to have him absolve them by virtue of the pontifical authority of all the sins of their past lives." In cardinal's robes, his cross mounted on a spear shaft, the obliging legate solemnly purified the violent host, "his right hand frequently making the sign of the cross."[56]

Deserted by his Swiss troops and unable to prevent the allies from crossing the Adda, Lautrec fell back to Milan where he expected a respite; but despite the pouring rains and muddy roads, the allied forces pressed on, reaching Milan in the afternoon of November 19. After Pescara stormed the suburb of Porta Romana, the Milanese Ghibellines seized the gates and opened them. The Porta Ticinese was opened to Colonna and the marquis of Mantua while Lautrec and his forces were fleeing by the Porta Comasina in a disordered rout.

The capture of Milan, Giovio felt, had resulted largely from lack of preparation on the part of Lautrec, from the pride which caused him to spurn the better advice of his captains, and from the arrogance and cruelty which had alienated the Milanese. Despite qualities that ranked him with the generals of antiquity, he "was so proud in mind and spirit, whether through a long succession of good fortune, or because of the adulation of his friends—to which the greater part of mankind readily succumbs—that in devising strategy he scorned the opinions of others, apparently preferring to err rather than accept advice."[57]

To illustrate the temper of captains and their dissensions, Giovio related an exchange that took place shortly after the victory. The allied leaders had gathered in the palace of the Crivelli, near the church of San Lorenzo.

> After arriving and saluting the others, Pescara kissed the hand of the cardinal de' Medici, demanding with an engaging smile, "Will you not thank me one day, legate, for the things that I have done today?" These words, by which he seemed to usurp for himself alone all credit for the victory stung Prospero so

profoundly that with a taut neck and savage expression, barely controlling himself, he demanded to know just what it was that Pescara had done all by himself. At this Pescara, blazing with anger, his hand grasping the hilt of his sword and his face full of scorn, responded sarcastically that he had done nothing at all. And without doubt he would have gone on to do something atrocious had not his wrath been momentarily assuaged by reason and had not the legate, interposing his hand as a peacemaker, placated them both with praise for their contributions to the success of the day.[58]

After this incident neither commander had a good word for the other.

The cardinal de' Medici and his entourage were guests in the palace of the Bergonzi, but Giovio did not remain in Milan. Along with some other members of the household he was sent by the cardinal on a mission to Mantua, where he was able to cultivate Isabella d'Este and make friends among the court and members of the Accademia di San Pietro.[59] Then, leaving Mantua on November 26, he returned to the army with one of the cardinal's secretaries, arriving just in time to be a horrified witness to the sack of his *patria*.

After regrouping, Lautrec had left a garrison in Como and gone to reclaim Cremona. Taking advantage of his absence, Pescara marched to Como with his Spanish, German, and some of his Swiss troops. Their first assault was unsuccessful, but Pescara was able to cut off supplies and reinforcements coming by way of the lake, whereupon the French commander, Jean de Chabannes, sire de Vandenesse, surrendered on condition of the garrison's being allowed to depart with baggage and ensigns and no injury being done the townspeople. "Pescara was happy to accept these conditions," Giovio wrote, and upon their acceptance Vandenesse himself came down from the wall in armor and with his own hand delivered to Pescara the keys to the gates of the city. To prevent unauthorized entry of soldiers, the master of the camp, Juan de Urbina, was stationed to guard the breach in the walls made during the assault, and the citizens, "free of fear, came out to the camp to look, and, after swearing obedience to Pescara, were added in the name of the sacraments to the ranks of the allies."

Relieved of "the onerous presence of foreign masters," the citizens rejoiced. But the Spanish troops were muttering ominously that the pact had cheated them of the opportunity of sacking the city and that victories of this nature gave all the honors and rewards to the captains, leaving the soldiers with nothing but fatigue and wounds. Although these seditious grumblings reached Pescara's ear, Giovio said he did not expect the gross insubordination that followed; for virtually under his eyes, on December 3, the soldiers began crossing the moat on a transverse wall so narrow in the middle they had to pass one by one, and when they arrived at the breach, rather than repulsing them, de Urbina and his ensign Vargas extended a hand and helped them cross. "So, with incredible rapidity, first the Spanish and then the German soldiers entered the city."[60]

There followed all the horrors of a sack. The wealthy were tortured and held to greater and greater ransoms, nuns were violated in the convents, the altars of the cathedral were despoiled of sacred vessels—all as if the city had been taken by storm. Such were the troops who just a few weeks earlier had been begging the cardinal legate for absolution. Spanish soldiers tortured Giovio's brother Benedetto by twisting his arm to make him reveal where the family silver was hidden.[61] The outraged Vandenesse protested that he had surrendered not to soldiers but to brigands and challenged Pescara to a duel, but Pescara simply sought to restore their stolen effects to the French garrison.

In his biography of Pescara, Giovio relived his horror and his desperate pleas to the commander. The marquis said he knew his soldiers were bringing infamy upon him and vowed he could die of sorrow but would only promise to punish the leaders. Giovio later heard Prospero Colonna assert that Pescara should have decimated his whole force, or at least the company that had been posted as guards, but Colonna had his own ax to grind, and the reality was as clear to Giovio as to everyone else: Pescara was unwilling to offend the soldiers on whose valor his military reputation depended. "He was often wont to observe," Giovio recalled, "that for those engaged in warfare nothing was more difficult than to adore both Mars and Christ, because in this corrupt business of fighting the customs of war were completely adverse to justice and religion."[62]

For Giovio, the cost of fighting for the *libertas Italiae* was now apparent. If, like Cardinal Giulio, he had been doubtful about the war to begin with, he certainly had no cause to alter his opinion. Subsequent wars only deepened his aversion to the shedding of Christian blood in the quarrels of princes, until by the end of his life he reached a truly Erasmian disgust with all warfare, no matter what the justification. While he believed that personal comment was inappropriate for a historian, he made his point by depicting the horrors of war and its devastating impact on innocent populations, holding up to popes and princes a picture of the suffering imposed by their grandiose policies of aggrandizement. In his correspondence, he never ceased to deplore the afflictions of his beloved Italy, to whose protracted humiliations he was an unwilling but lifelong observer.[63]

Scarcely had the sack of Como subsided than news arrived which suspended the campaign against the French and caused the two cardinals to ride posthaste to Rome. In the midst of his jubilation over the capture of Milan the pope had died.[64] One of the cardinal's secretaries, Paolo da Reggio, had galloped with the news from Milan to Rome, and on finding that His Holiness was hunting at La Magliana, had gone with Gian Matteo Giberti to find him. When they arrived he was saying Lauds, having just reached the verse in the Benedictus, "That being delivered from the hand of our enemies, we may serve Him without fear."[65]

"The news of so great a victory," Giovio wrote, "gave the pope incredible joy, for he had been tormented by anxiety, having just three days previously received tidings of wavering loyalty on the part of the Swiss." During his celebrations that evening, November 24, he had a fit of fever, and a week later, around midnight on the evening of December 1, he expired. "A few hours before his death," Giovio had heard, "humbly clasping his hands and raising them, his eyes piously rolled toward heaven, he thanked God, professing most firmly that he would bear the outcome of even a fatal illness with a calm and tranquil mind, since he had recovered Parma and Piacenza without losses through a brilliant victory over a proud enemy." His death at the early age of forty-six raised suspicions of poison, and Giovio believed that he had, indeed, been poisoned, but that "with notable prudence" the cardinal de' Medici refused to allow examination of the pope's cupbearer, "lest the name of some great prince emerge."[66]

Giovio's final judgment on Leo X's papacy was positive. The first Medici pope had in the end given Italy and the Church strong leadership, and despite the costs of achieving it, Giovio felt that Leo X's settlement for the Italian peninsula as expressed in the treaty with Charles V was superior to any other; for as time went on, a papal-imperial alliance seemed to offer the greatest hope of peace and stability and the greatest degree of freedom for the Italians. The joy of the Milanese at receiving back their duke, even as a vassal of a powerful emperor, was for Giovio the best justification of Leo X's policies.[67]

The *Vita Leonis X* was completed in the latter years of the papacy of Clement VII, when Italy had suffered a series of unprecedented disasters culminating in the sack of Rome. By then the papacy of Leo X truly appeared to have been a golden era.

> For without any doubt he had founded the age of gold, to the benefit of mankind, whereas immediately after the departure of this best prince we have truly experienced the age of iron. Thanks to our own fatal errors the fury of barbarians has brought us murders, tortures, pestilence, famine, devastation, and all other miseries, with the result that literature, above all, and the fine arts, abundance, the public welfare, happiness, and all good things are now as surely mourned as if they had been interred in the same tomb with Leo.[68]

CHAPTER FIVE

Adrian VI (1521–1523)

Ita ut hinc liquido constet pontificatum fato dari, comitiorumque suffragia nequaquam libidine decretoque hominum, sed certa ac incredibili deorum immortalium providentia gubernari.

—Giovio, *Hadriani Sexti vita*

Thus it is crystal clear [through the election of Adrian VI] that the pontificate is awarded by fate, and that the votes of the assemblies are determined not at all by the pleasure and decree of men, but by the certain and incredible providence of the immortal gods.

WITH THE CARDINAL de' Medici having departed posthaste for Rome, there would have been little for his entourage to do but pack and follow. No doubt Giovio gave what comfort he could to his family before setting out on the long journey over muddy winter roads to Rome. The conclave for electing Leo X's successor met on December 27, 1521, and by January 4, 1522, it was totally deadlocked. As Giovio later heard from Giberti, who was acting as the cardinal's *conclavista*, their patron controlled a large number of votes but not enough to secure "that honor to which he aspired with such zeal, wealth, and destined—although not yet mature—felicity."[1] The French party opposed him, as did the older cardinals, especially Cardinal Soderini, and a group of dissident imperialists led by Cardinal Colonna. Time, Giovio thought, was a major factor. Although the allies were holding their own in northern Italy and Guicciardini was successfully defending Parma for the Church—a feat for which Giovio gave him full credit in his *Histories*—Francesco Maria della Rovere had lost no time in returning to Urbino and in helping Matteo Baglioni repossess Perugia. By early January news reached Rome that della Rovere was threatening Siena. Like most observers, Giovio assumed that fears for the Romagna, Tuscany, and Milan prompted his patron to end the deadlock by nominating the emperor's former tutor and current regent in Spain, the aged cardinal of Tortosa, Adriaan Floriszoon of Utrecht.[2]

The choice was not unpremeditated; the Fleming had already been selected as an alternate in case of an impasse, and on January 9, "either despairing of the pontificate," Giovio speculated, "or despising it," Cardinal Giulio nominated him. When Cardinal Cajetan—normally Giulio's opponent—supported the nomination, the other cardinals began to accede, and before they fully comprehended what they were doing, "boldly and as if impelled by the deity," they elected the cardinal of Tortosa, "a foreigner known by hardly anyone, who resided in the most distant parts of the world." Only then did they begin to fathom what they had done. The cardinal de' Medici, on the other hand, "was almost as pleased as if he had been elected himself, having avoided a defeat by his enemies."[3]

Giovio's *Hadriani Sexti vita*, commissioned by the faithful Cardinal Enkevoirt and written between 1529 and 1534, mirrored the hopeless mismatch of pope and curia. Regarded at the time as a masterpiece of irony, it delighted even conscientious reformers exasperated by the Flemish pope's pious but inept leadership.[4] Nowhere was Giovio more "curial" than in the famous opening lines, where—in the sort of Ciceronian terminology Adrian VI most deplored—his election was ironically attributed to the Holy Ghost.

> No one in the history of the sacred assemblies was ever elected to the pontificate from among those famous for learning and virtue with less ambition on his part or with less activity on the part of his friends than was Adrian VI; for, having overcome without any contention on his part so many candidates relying on grace, merit, or wealth, while being known personally to no one at Rome—indeed, scarcely even heard of—from Spain and the furthest shores of Germany he arrived effortlessly at the highest position of all in an event as lucky as it was unlooked-for. Thus it is crystal clear that the pontificate is awarded by fate, and that the votes of the assemblies are determined not at all by the pleasure and decree of men, but by the certain and incredible providence of the immortal gods.[5]

The Roman populace was outraged. Most thought the Sacred College, in a fit of madness, had decided to betray Rome, and a rumor quickly spread that the new pope would remain in Spain or, worse, return to the Low Countries. When a mob of Romans accosted some cardinals returning to their palaces, Cardinal Gonzaga thanked them for hurling insults when stones would have been more appropriate.[6] Giovio thought the worst result of the conclave were the calumnies spread by the candidates to discredit their opponents, but which mainly served to increase the contempt for Rome among the nations whose soldiers were soon to sack it.[7] As for the new pope, Giovio depicted him as far more delighted by the arrival of the jawbone of St. Lambert than by the news of his election to the papacy.

No greater unity prevailed in the Sacred College after the election than during it, and until the new pope arrived it was decided that each month a triumvirate of cardinals should govern the Church. When the first triumvirate turned out to be composed of his opponents, Giulio de'

Medici left Rome, ostensibly to attend to his duties as legate for Tuscany and the Romagna but really to hold together the alliance against the French. Going by sea to Pisa to avoid the army of Francesco Maria della Rovere, he reached Florence on the night of January 22.[8] Giovio's first surviving letter from 1522 was a long commentary on the Italian situation written from Florence for the benefit of Giberti, who had been sent to confer with the emperor in Flanders.[9]

The urgency of Giovio's letter revealed how strongly he had committed himself to the imperial cause. With French troops being massed for an assault on Milan, Charles V had sent Girolamo Adorno to recruit reinforcements at Trent. Scion of a rival Genoese family, Adorno had joined the imperial party in the hopes of recovering the lordship of Genoa from doge Ottaviano Fregosi. At Trent he found several thousand troops already enlisted by the new duke of Milan, Francesco II Sforza, with the help of Georg von Frundsberg, the German captain who was to play such a devastating part in Italian history. Although the principal passes were blocked by the Venetians, Adorno and his reinforcements managed to slip through the mountains north of Bergamo, a feat that filled Giovio with admiration. "We are now very much alive again," he exulted to Giberti, "having been like Lazarus, and Signor Girolamo was our Christ, who merits a eulogy beneath a statue in the alpine snow up to his knees." As if to energize Giberti, Giovio repeatedly stressed the urgency of the emperor's coming to Italy.

> If he does not come he will be deader than King Arthur; if he comes he will be Caesar indeed. . . . For the love of God, make some oration *in genere impulsivo et destativo*, since Chièvres [the late chancellor] is now in the claws of Malebranche [Dante, *Inf.* 21.37], *et perorate*. Otherwise we are done for.

Despite the emperor's persistence in journeying to Spain, events in Lombardy continued their favorable course. After hesitating a long time in Pavia, Sforza was persuaded in early April to risk a dash through French-patrolled areas to Milan. His acute awareness of the miseries of his father's imprisonment in France, Giovio heard, was finally overcome by the tireless Adorno, who convinced him that to delay longer was to risk defeat. Traveling by night over back roads, the duke was able to rendezvous with the forces of Pescara, who had come out seven miles to meet him, and the next morning he entered his city in triumph.[10] The delirious joy of the Milanese at recovering their native dynasty gave Giovio all the justification he needed for the imperial alliance. Meanwhile, Lautrec's Swiss troops, discontented with the results of their desultory campaign to regain Milan, demanded to be led into battle or dismissed. Thus it was that the French general agreed to accost the imperial army where it had ensconced itself in the fortified villa of La Bicocca a few miles from Milan in the direction of Monza.[11]

Prospero Colonna had occupied La Bicocca as a means of keeping his army between the French and the city of Milan after Lautrec had fallen back to Monza following his failure to seize Pavia from the marquis of Mantua. Prospero's cousin, Fabrizio Colonna, was wont to hold that victory depended less on the valor of soldiers than on good earthworks, a dictum borne out on April 27 at La Bicocca. Even more, the battle showed that muskets could overcome the once invincible Swiss pikes.[12] Colonna kept his forces behind the trenches, ready for the Swiss who had insisted "with barbarian pride," as Giovio expressed it, on a direct assault. Pescara had lined his arquebusiers four deep. At his signal the first row fired and knelt to reload, clearing the way for the second to fire, and so on to the fourth, by which time the first row was ready to fire again. Exposed "to an almost perpetual hail of bullets," the Swiss crumpled. "Not only squadrons, but whole companies fell to earth." After successive waves had struggled vainly through the heaps of their fallen comrades, the Swiss abandoned the hopeless contest. The French fell back to Cremona and Lodi, the Venetians to Brescia, the Swiss—no longer the arbiters of Lombardy—to their mountain valleys, and Lautrec to France to explain to his sovereign, as best he could, the loss of Milan.

While the allies were defending Lombardy, Giovio worried as the cardinal de' Medici was "assailed by the arms of his enemies and the plots of his own people."[13] To defend Florence against the condottiere Renzo da Ceri, who was recruiting troops with French funds channeled through Cardinal Soderini, Cardinal Giulio had been forced to come to terms with his former enemies. He gave Malatesta Baglioni's brother, Orazio, a *condotta* and made Francesco Maria della Rovere captain-general of the Florentine Republic for a year. Then, in May 1522, he discovered that some of the younger participants in the Orti Oricellari discussions, notably Iacopo da Diaceto, Zanobi Buondelmonte, Luigi Alamanni, and Battista della Palla, had conspired to murder him during the coming Corpus Christi procession (June 19), apparently because of his reluctance to reintroduce some of the republican magistracies abolished under Leo X. Nerli believed that the conspirators had been more easily recruited by Cardinal Soderini because of their indoctrination by Machiavelli with examples of ancient tyrannicides. The whole affair was kept as quiet as possible, but when it was over Giovio felt that a great cloud had passed. On May 22 he told his brother that he was restored, "now that God and fortune have given the grace to the cardinal my patron to remain alive, great, and vanquisher over his adversaries."[14]

Meanwhile the imperial army under Colonna and Pescara had arranged for the surrender of the French garrison in Cremona, the last in Lombardy, and had marched to Genoa intending to terminate the dogeship of Ottaviano Fregoso and install the Adorno family as imperial vassals. Despite the pleas of Girolamo Adorno to allow time for negotiations, Pescara stormed the city on May 30. Guicciardini believed that Genoa was attacked in the midst of surrendering, and in his biography of Pescara, Giovio admitted as much. His account evoked all the horror and brutality suffered by a gracious city that in better times had so hospitably entertained him. Once again Pescara had obliged his soldiers. Only the belated approach of a French relief force gave the two generals a pretext for recalling the army after four days of sack, laden with the booty of what had been one of the richest cities of Italy. Giovio's biography of Pescara was written solely to please Vittoria Colonna. Understandably, he had little sympathy for his subject, who emerges as a man of appalling ferocity and pride.[15]

With the French driven from Lombardy and Renzo da Ceri no longer a threat, the cardinal de' Medici had gone to Bologna to try to reestablish the authority of the Church in the Romagna. Receiving word from Giberti that Adrian VI had reached Liguria, he hastened to the coast with the other Tuscan members of the Sacred College to meet the man he had helped to the papacy.[16] In the *Hadriani Sexti vita*, Giovio described the pope as they found him on that August day, accepting their congratulations "with a tranquil rather than happy countenance," responding without haughtiness but also without the familiarity that they and those "accustomed to the blandishments of the curia" expected. His demeanor, Giovio said, was immediately taken "as a lack of humanity bordering on contempt," particularly when, after dining by himself, the pope ordered his boat to set sail without alerting the cardinals, who were dining nearby. Giovio painted a vivid scene of the astonished cardinals abandoning their dinner and scurrying down the dock to their boats.[17] The party arrived in Rome on August 29 in suffocating heat, and on the 31st, nearly eight months after his election, Adrian VI was solemnly installed on the throne of the apostles.

If Giovio had accompanied his master and the other cardinals to Rome, he was almost immediately sent northward again on a mission to Genoa, where, "despite westerly winds and the galleys of the enemy," he arrived by September 13 with letters to Girolamo Adorno from the cardinal de' Medici and the marquis of Mantua. Since Federico Gonzaga had been among the group at Livorno welcoming the pope, Giovio's mission must have developed from conversations there. "I would dare to say," he reported to the marquis, "that there was never a triumvirate so well linked in love and true benevolence as Your Excellency, my patron the cardinal, and the said *signore* [Adorno]." By holding fast to their alliance, he suggested, the triumvirate would be able to command "those normally accustomed to commanding"—presumably the new pope.[18]

Other remarks in the letter suggest that Giovio was striving to impress the young marquis with his suitability for the well-known pastimes of the

Mantuan court. He had carried out, he boasted, "un eruditissimo papagallo [an erudite flirtation]," and he had obtained a promise from his old friend Count Ottobuono Fieschi to provide Federico with as many pairs of gloves a year as the marquis had known women "in the manner of the friars." Despite the horrors of the recent sack, Genoese life was apparently beginning to resume some of its famous gaiety. A century earlier Aeneas Silvius had found the city "a paradise of women," and our sixteenth-century humanist was no less enchanted. "We have here," Giovio wrote, "for consolation at not being in Rome with our patron, a squadron of gracious women who are at home and keep open house without a light until the fourth hour of the night with a domesticity that even your ladies would find incredible. Truly," he exclaimed, "they are everywhere beautiful, gallant, pleasing, and learned, and they have no fear of an armed Spaniard or of an Italian."[19]

Delights of the moment did not distract Giovio from the seriousness of the political situation. Belgrade had fallen at the end of August 1521, and the Turks were already blockading Rhodes. Two carracks were being readied at Genoa in hopes of running the blockade and reprovisioning the defenders. Charles V had succeeded in repressing the rebellion of the Comuneros in Spain and was preparing an army to recapture Fuenterrabía from the French. Flattering the heroic image of himself Federico had acquired defending Pavia, Giovio hoped that the emperor might call him to lead a couple of Italian legions in the coming Anglo-imperial campaigns against the French in the Netherlands and Picardy, from which he would return with triumphs rivaling his father's.[20]

Even at this early date, however, Giovio was beginning to perceive that friendships with princes, while enabling him to achieve the "great things" he had promised his brother, might compromise his independence of judgment as a historian. Federico should not expect adulation in the *Histories*, he cautioned, because along with some of the other captains he had helped him acquire "the little house above the garden." Rather he should expect honor for the liberty he has brought to Italians, "a gift more precious than gold."[21]

Giovio did not indicate how long his mission would keep him in Genoa, and he may have left directly from there to join his master in Florence. Things had not gone well with the new pope. Adrian VI had declared that he felt no obligation to any cardinal—indeed, as Giovio reported, he regarded the papacy as a burden, not a gift—and to the astonishment of the curia, the cardinal de' Medici was being treated like any other.[22] Not only this, but in the very first week of his papacy the pope had announced his intention of reforming the Church, beginning with the Sacred College. An outbreak of plague in September afforded many cardinals a pretext for absenting themselves from further unpleasantness, and on October 13 the cardinal de' Medici departed for Florence.[23] There he was to remain not only until the plague abated but for all the following winter, having fallen under a cloud when Cardinal Soderini accused him of having purloined some of the treasures of the Church, a charge not only false, Giovio asserted, but ridiculous, considering how well known it was that Leo X had pledged the treasures of the Church to usurers. Nonetheless, the charges seemed plausible to "a foreigner, suspicious by nature and little experienced in the court of Rome."[24]

In November, Adorno requested Giovio's services on a mission to Ferrara and Venice. The imperial ambassador, the abbot of Najera, had persuaded Charles V to send the indefatigable Genoese to detach Alfonso d'Este and the Venetians from the French. Giovio had evidently made a good impression on Adorno, who was allied with his friends the Fieschi. Perhaps Giovio's good relations with Alfonso d'Este also promised to be useful. Certainly he would have been an enthusiastic proponent of rapprochement, not only with Alfonso but with the Venetians, whose support of the French had been a consistent disappointment to him since 1515. Characteristically, the Venetians had never formally broken off relations with the emperor. Indeed, their ambassador Gasparo Contarini had accompanied Charles V on his journey from the Low Countries to Spain.

Adorno left Genoa on November 13, 1522.[25] On the 19th the Ferrarese agent in Florence, Benedetto Fantini, informed the duke that the cardinal de' Medici was sending "Master Paolo Giovio, his physician, along with Signor Girolamo, who had requested him for a few days." Giovio had been commissioned by the cardinal, the agent said, to convince Adorno "how good it would be for the emperor, the duke of Milan, His Lordship, and Genoa to gain Your Excellency." Giovio would greet the duke on the cardinal's behalf. He had just left today, Fantini concluded, advising the duke that he was someone "to caress well, because he is a person of vigorous speech, and whom he wishes to extol he does so without restraint, and so the converse"—a description suggesting that Giovio was beginning to acquire the sort of reputation for which Aretino became feared and famous.[26]

Curiously, Giovio did not mention this 1522 mission in the life he later wrote of Alfonso d'Este, even though it had laid the foundation for a rapprochement between the duke and the emperor based on the latter's promise of support for the return of Modena and Reggio to the Este.[27] Given the bitter opposition of Giulio de' Medici to surrendering these two cities, one suspects that Giovio had not been made a full participant in the discussions between Adorno and the duke. Giovio, too, opposed the return of the cities and may have felt in retrospect that he had been deceived by his friend. Although unwilling for the present to detach himself from the French, Alfonso did consent to allow free passage of the imperial troops through the territories of Ferrara, a considerable advantage to the allies.

In Ferrara, Giovio had time to meet the great physician Niccolò Leoniceno, renew his friendship with Celio Calcagnini, and admire the "lavish and festive" landscapes of Dosso Dossi before the party went on to Venice, arriving on December 2, 1522, after a brief pause in Padua to allow Adorno to recover from an attack of gout.[28] They had been preceded in Ferrara and Venice by the English ambassador, Richard Pace, who was also working to win over France's remaining allies in Italy.[29] On arriving in Venice, Adorno was still feeling the effects of his gout and needed a couple of days of rest. Not until the morning of December 4 did he make his formal appearance before the doge and senate to present his credentials, attended by the forty members of his own party and a brilliant cortege of ambassadors and Venetian nobles. Walking with difficulty owing to his gout, and assisted by a servant, he made his way forward to salute the doge, the aged and doddering Antonio Grimani, who came down from the tribune to meet him. Business began on the morrow at a session with the doge and Council of Ten, to which Adorno came dressed in black damask, accompanied by the resident imperial ambassador.[30]

The Venetians were in no hurry to respond. Wanting to ally with the victor in the contest for Milan, they were waiting and looking for signs. Charles V's grandfather, the emperor Maximilian, had been an aggressive neighbor, and despite their experience of a strong French presence, they feared even more an expanding imperial power. By Christmastime they were still unable to come to a conclusion, with the result that three commissioners were appointed for negotiations, the English ambassador by common consent acting as mediator.[31]

As talks dragged on through the winter, Giovio found himself with time to revise the first book of his *Histories*. He told Equicola that it featured "the immortal exploits" of Federico's father, the marquis Francesco (commander of the allied Venetian and papal forces at the battle of Fornovo), and that he yearned to see the Serenissima join in a new coalition against the French in which Federico would play an equally brilliant role.[32] The stay in Venice afforded the historian an opportunity of interviewing other protagonists of his *Histories*, the gleanings of which no doubt figured in the revisions he was making. In the *Elogia* he mentioned conversations not only with Doge Grimani but with the soon-to-be doge, Andrea Gritti, regarding the debates in the senate in 1499 as to whether to prefer an alliance with Milan or France.[33]

The desertion of Ludovico Sforza by Venice in 1501 and her alliance with Louis XII in return for Cremona and the Ghiaradadda had been deeply disturbing to Giovio, as it had introduced a major rift in the Italian unity created at Fornovo.[34] With the aid of Grimani he now came to understand Venice's volte-face as the victory of the younger senators, eager for new territories and piqued at Sforza for contesting Pisa with them. The alliance had proved a personal disaster for Grimani, who was sent to command the Venetian forces when the Turks came to Sforza's defense by attacking the republic in the Morea. Lepanto was lost, and an angry senate ordered Grimani arrested and returned in chains to Venice. Giovio told the moving tale of the distinguished patrician being led away by the criminal officers, supported by his four sons, one of whom, a cardinal of the Church, held up his fetters as the old man mounted the steps to the prison. He escaped a death sentence, probably owing to his own eloquence, and was banished to one of the Dalmatian islands. For a time thereafter he lived in Rome. Recalled in 1509 by an overwhelming vote of the senate, he was subsequently elected a procurator of San Marco and in 1521, at the age of eighty-seven, was elected doge—an outstanding example, Giovio said, of a hero swept away by a wave of bad fortune who nonetheless refused to be drowned by it. More than anything, Giovio admired "unconquered spirits" whose stoic fortitude enabled them to triumph over the vicissitudes of Fortune.[35]

During the numerous social occasions of the embassy, Giovio enlarged the circle of his acquaintances in the city.[36] It was not his first visit. In the Ischian dialogue he spoke of having visited Venice in his younger days, probably while he was at Padua, seeking "good letters and, as youth demands, the more erudite pleasures."[37] His friend and correspondent Marin Sanudo had been ill for much of 1522, but during the latter days of the embassy, he seemed to enjoy better health.[38] Sanudo had just finished his history of the expedition of Charles VIII and was no doubt ready to defend his view, if Giovio had not already come to share it, that the invasion of the French was owing to the folly of Ludovico il Moro and that the Venetians had been responsible for the allied victory at Fornovo.[39] The Venetian role had also been celebrated in the *Diaria de bello carolino* of Alessandro Benedetti, published by Aldus in 1496, which Giovio evidently used for book 1 of his *Histories* and which he must have discussed with Sanudo, particularly since the commentaries of Pianella and the history of Equicola both contested Benedetti's viewpoint on the Venetian contribution. Benedetti, a former pupil of Merula's, had been a physician to the Venetian army at Fornovo, and although he himself had died in 1512, his work was still current, even if his boast that the French fury had been vanquished was by now a little outdated.[40]

Another intellectual friend Giovio acquired in Venice was Giovan Battista Ramusio, secretary to the senate and eventually the publisher, in his celebrated series of *Navigationi*, of an Italian version of Giovio's description of Muscovy. Hearing from Ramusio of his presence in Venice, Bembo invited Giovio to spend eight days with him and enjoy the learned circles of Padua. "What he [Giovio] says is true;" Bembo told Ramusio, "I can assure you, he is very much my friend, for the reason that I am very much his."[41] To help pass the time, Adorno was having his portrait painted by Titian, and Giovio no doubt found occasion to meet the renowned painter, whom Adorno had asked to sketch out one of Giovio's ideas for an *impresa* so that he could have it made into a cameo.[42]

As at Genoa, the women of the city attracted Giovio's enthusiastic attention. In the Ischian dialogue he recalled a marriage feast in the Trevisan palace where he admired more than sixty of the most beautiful ladies of Venice. From these, he said, he and Adorno selected ten, whom the ambassador with the senate's permission invited to a banquet. Four of the ten Giovio singled out for particular praise: Lucrezia Venier, Lucia Barbarigo, Benetta Gritti (granddaughter of Doge Andrea), and—most beautiful of all—Isabella Giustiniani, wife of Vettore Grimani (a grandson of the doge), who after dinner danced for the company and our now ecstatic historian.

> She so attracted and inflamed those who beheld her, myself included, seated opposite her among the diners, that she might have been able, if not to scorch me with fire, at least to scald me a bit with steam, were it not that, being not altogether ignorant of the perils of loves suddenly initiated, I had already determined that any such impulses were to be resisted in the line of duty. After the tables were cleared away she danced for us. What graceful posture! How well composed! How flexible and lively her movements! She was wearing a mantle with solid gold fringes reaching to her elbow, the border of which, wider below, was covered with sable. She had hung a necklace of twisted gold, not from her neck as the custom is, but from her left shoulder, letting it circle most fittingly around her back. A garland of exceptional pearls graced her white and swelling breasts. Her hair was gathered in a golden net, but so gently that when it was slightly wafted by the breezes the looseness of the mesh allowed it to spread and shine.[43]

Giovio's praises of Venetian women were enthusiastically seconded by another interlocutor in his Ischian dialogue, the marquis del Vasto, who had joined Adorno's party during the second week in December, along with some of his officers. Giovio took it upon himself to introduce the soldier to the beauties of Venice, both architectural and feminine, including the treasures of San Marco and the famous Venetian nuns, although the latter were now much inhibited by the strict ordinances of doge Loredan. The sins of the nuns Giovio attributed to the greed of the fathers and the excessive size of dowries, which forced young women into religious "vocations" against their wills.[44]

Midway through Giovio's visit came news that dismayed Europe and gravely alarmed his hosts. After a siege of many months, the Knights of Rhodes were finally compelled to surrender their island fortress to the Turks. Suleiman I had continued the expansionist policies of his father, Selim I. In 1521 his forces had succeeded in storming Belgrade, and the following summer he led them in person against Rhodes. The seven hundred knights, assisted by five thousand soldiers, held out against enormous odds, hoping for relief, but none came. Venice was fearful of provoking the Turks, and the monarchs of the European countries were embroiled in their own quarrels. On December 21, 1522, the grand master capitulated. Magnanimous in victory, the sultan allowed the knights generous terms and forbade a sack, an act of nobility which Giovio—mindful of the recent sacks of Como and Genoa by Christians—celebrated in extenso.[45] The Venetian senate first heard of the surrender negotiations on the morning of February 1 when Adorno's secretary brought them news received from the viceroy of Naples, and in the afternoon the surrender was confirmed through their own sources. The senate was greatly moved.[46] Venice began to fear for her colonies in the Dodecanese and her island possessions in the Mediterranean—Cyprus, Crete, Zante, and Corfu.

Giovio blamed the catastrophe on the pope's dilatoriness in arranging for a relief force, as well as on the indifference and quarrels of the Christian princes.[47] The cardinal de' Medici, a knight of Rhodes himself, had in fact suggested that Adrian VI send to Rhodes the fleet which had brought him from Spain, in hopes that so clear a gesture would shame the Venetians into cooperating, but the Spanish had been reluctant to sail to the relief of Rhodes when they were threatened by the French in Lombardy and in the Tyrrhenian Sea. Nor did the pope have the means for raising a fleet, Leo X having spent, as Giovio observed, not only his own revenues, together with the accumulated treasure of his predecessor, but the income of his successor. In anguish over his apparent helplessness, the unfortunate Adrian VI exclaimed that he would much rather be rector of the University of Louvain than pope.[48] It was a telling insight into the misery of a man formed by nature for scholarship and thrust by circumstances into tasks of governance to which he was unequal.

The prospect of having to face increased Turkish pressure on her eastern empire made Venice all the more anxious to be on the winning side in the great contest looming between Charles V and Francis I. In the end the Serenissima opted for Charles V, but before an imperial alliance could be concluded, much had to be resolved regarding territories contested with the empire. By the end of February the only questions remaining were the terms and amount of Venice's contribution.[49] Then in March, just as negotiations on these were nearly over, Adorno fell gravely ill, and on the 20th he died.[50] A state funeral was held in the great Gothic church of San Stefano on Sunday afternoon, March 22. In his diary Sanudo described in detail the long procession from the chapel of San Giovanni in San Marco, where the coffin had lain in state, to San Stefano, proceeding via the bridge and square of San Maurizio. As a close personal friend, Giovio walked directly behind the coffin with the scarlet-clad vice-doge, Andrea Magno.[51] So ended the brilliant career of a friend and patron, "a singular man," as Giovio recalled him, "on account of the quality of his intellect and his experience in the affairs of war."[52]

With Adorno's exequies over and the last duties of friendship rendered, Giovio rejoined his master in Florence. No sooner had he done so, however, than the cardinal was summoned to Rome. Thanks to the vigilance of the imperial party, a courier had been intercepted bearing missives of Cardinal Soderini which suggested that the cardinal was conspiring with the French to stir up a rebellion in Sicily that would necessitate the sending of imperial troops from Milan and open the way for a French invasion. Deeply shaken by the treachery of his trusted confidant, Adrian VI sent for the cardinal de' Medici. Accompanied by a princely retinue of a thousand horsemen, Giulio de' Medici made his entrance into Rome on April 23, 1523. At the ancient Milvian bridge he was met by a throng that included not only cardinals and notables but even one-time enemies such as Orazio Baglioni, Fabio Petrucci (brother of Cardinal Alfonso), and Francesco Maria della Rovere.[53] After appearing in conclave on the 25th and 26th, the cardinal spent the afternoon of the 26th in secret audience with the pope. On the 27th Adrian VI summoned the cardinal of Volterra, confronted him with the evidence, and, despite his pleas, sent him to the Castel Sant'Angelo. With the anger of a man betrayed, Giovio said, the pope pushed forward the trial, which was generally expected to end in Soderini's condemnation and perpetual imprisonment. With his wonted trenchancy Giovio described the proceedings to the marquis of Mantua as "the syrup for giving him the cassia of the cap [cassia is a violent cathartic]." Better still, he thought, would be the Tarpeian Rock.[54]

Despite the return of his patron to a position of influence, Giovio found life in Adrian's Rome annoying and hoped for a speedy return to Tuscany once the trial of Soderini was concluded. "If I had to write the truth about this court," he complained to the marquis Federico, "it would be necessary to write not history but invective and satire, dealing as we are with men of wood."[55] Like most Italians, Giovio saw little positive in the pope. His quarrel was not a personal one; in the reform of the curia he had fared better than many. One unfortunate curial, driven mad by despair when the office in which he had invested his whole patrimony was suppressed, even attempted to assassinate the pope.[56] Giovio's half-cavalierate was taken away when Adrian terminated these sinecures, but he was compensated with a canonry in Como. Apparently, Cardinal Trivulzio had been pressing for a candidate of his own when the pope silenced him by declaring that Giovio was a historian and "not a poet like the rest."[57]

Had Adrian VI merely chased Leo's "simians" from the Vatican he would have enjoyed the plaudits of the whole curia, but his opposition to the classicism of the Leonine age went far deeper. He disliked poets, Giovio explained, because he suspected their sincerity as Christians, and he deplored their celebration of the pagan gods. He would even have ordered the statue of Pasquino (a point for fixing licentious satires) thrown into the Tiber had not the imperial ambassador warned that it would croak from the bottom like a frog.[58] So great was Adrian VI's hostility to classical sculptures that some feared he would make lime of them all. Reverently shown the Laocoön, he retorted that these were the idols of the ancients.[59]

Giovio's portrait of Adrian VI—confirmed by the testimony of most other observers—was of an aged man, crabbed in manner, ungracious even with his loyal supporters, and distrustful of all the rest. In a short time he had alienated almost everyone in Rome, even those who felt reform was mandatory.[60] To its implementation he brought the zeal of a Grand Inquisitor (which he had been for Spain), but through lack of imagination and personal warmth he failed to inspire the loyalty necessary for building a reform party in the curia and so lost all possibility of achieving his goals. He had failed for similar reasons, Giovio suggested, in governing Spain and even in inspiring the youthful Charles V to learn Latin.[61] His closest counselors were the "men of wood," his trusted Flemings, who, "while abundant in loyalty, lacked judgment and skill in matters of state."[62] In ecclesiastical matters the pope's slowness to reach a decision lest he make a mistake was a source of ever-deepening despair to all the curia.[63] His habitual response to recommendations or requests, *videbimus et cogitabimus* (we will see and will think about it), became a byword for Giovio and his friends.[64]

Much of Giovio's impatience with Adrian VI stemmed from the urgency with which the imperial party was promoting an alliance with Charles V. In anticipation of the 1523 campaigning season, Francis I was gathering yet another army for the reconquest of Milan. Although outraged by the treachery of Cardinal Soderini and the French, Adrian VI was still hesitant to make common cause with the emperor. "We are washing bricks and plowing sand," Giovio lamented to the marquis of

Mantua. "God help us!"[65] In his biography of Adrian he recounted the barely suppressed laughter of the cardinals at the expression on the pope's face when Ferdinand of Austria's ambassador, the bishop of Gurk, told him in full consistory that whereas Fabius Maximus by delaying had saved Rome, he by delaying was going to ruin not only Rome but Europe to boot.[66]

Nonetheless the pope did gradually move toward the desired goal. In the spring he instructed his legate, Tommaso Campeggio, bishop of Feltre, to promote the alliance of Venice with the emperor.[67] The resident imperial ambassador, Alonzo Sanchez, had been continuing Adorno's negotiations, but Giovio was fearful that, unless tempered by Charles V, the demands of Ferdinand of Austria would prevent agreement. Adorno's death, he told Equicola, was a sign of the hostility of the gods, yet he hoped they were not so adverse to Italy that they wished to see it destroyed.[68] With the arrival of the apostolic protonotary Marino Caracciolo in June 1523, negotiations resumed in earnest, and by the end of July they were completed.[69]

On July 29 a secret alliance was ratified between the emperor, Austria, England, Milan, and Venice, the terms of which pledged Venice to defend Francesco II Sforza in Milan and to indemnify the emperor for the imperial territories the city had seized over the years. So stung was the pope by the haughty conduct of Francis I, who had gone so far as to threaten him with the fate of Boniface VIII, that five days after the conclusion of this alliance he entered into a purely defensive agreement with the emperor, Austria, England, and Milan, as well as with Florence, Siena, Lucca, and Genoa, which were represented by the cardinal de' Medici. The pope undertook to contribute 15,000 ducats a month toward raising an army and appointed Charles de Lannoy, viceroy of Naples, as commander-in-chief. The triumph of the imperial party was complete.

Giovio was elated. "Now," he exulted, "a way is being found to preserve Italy in perpetuity from the French." His thoughts turned to his departed friend. "O Girolamo Adorno!" he lamented, "Where are you? Why did you die so soon without seeing your wish fulfilled?"[70] In the eyes of those Italians who had worked so long for them, the alignments of the summer of 1523 represented the optimum prospects for the liberty of Italy and the future stability not only of the Italian peninsula but of Europe as well. At the Fifth Lateran Council, Egidio of Viterbo had prophesied that the key to the unity of Europe, necessary for a crusade, would be an alliance between pope and emperor, each with clearly defined roles.[71] As if in fulfillment, the language of the treaty of July 29, 1523, expressed the desire of Caesar "as befitting a good emperor," not only to end the calamities afflicting Italy but to create there a peace which should soon extend to the whole Christian Republic.[72] This was the vision animating Giovio and the imperial party in Rome, and at its core was the perpetuation of Sforza rule in Milan, so infinitely preferable for the Italians to the rule of a French viceroy. As long as the Sforza dynasty lasted, Giovio loyally supported the imperial claim to the suzerainty of Milan.[73]

Guicciardini likewise emphasized the importance to Italians of restoring the Sforza. The speech he attributed to the Venetian procurator Giorgio Cornaro stressed the emperor's returning the fortress of Milan to the duke as a reason for preferring an imperial to a French alliance.[74] The restitution, which so impressed the Italians, had been the triumph of Charles V's Grand Chancellor Mercurino Gattinara, who favored governing Italy through existing Italian powers.[75] The league of 1523 thus represented a broad coalition of statesmen seeking the peace, security, and self-government of Italy.

The defensive treaty was solemnly proclaimed on August 5, after a pontifical mass in the basilica of Santa Maria Maggiore. It was the feast of the miraculous snow, which, according to tradition, had revealed to Pope Liberius the site for the basilica. The heat was intolerable, and Giovio found Vincenzo Pimpinella's long-winded Latin oration no less stifling.[76] As head of the imperial party in Rome, Cardinal Pompeo Colonna gave a solemn banquet for the cardinal de' Medici and the ambassadors of the signatory states at the Villa Antoniana, while the pope, worn out with the heat and fatigued by the ceremonies, sought repose and a simple supper in the neighboring gardens of the Mellini family.[77] So terrified were the French party by "this superb league," Giovio reported to Federico Gonzaga, that "at least two of them here have died of grief—I'm not joking."[78]

As part of the treaty arrangements, Federico was confirmed as captain-general of the Church and appointed captain-general of the Florentines. Giovio's satisfaction with the treaty turned into jubilation when he discovered that his patron had obtained for him the honor of conveying to Mantua the baton of the Florentine Republic and the papal briefs renewing Federico's captain-generalship. He gleefully wrote the marquis that he had been selected not for lack of eager volunteers but for being "Gonzaghissimo."[79] He was preparing "a pompous oration" to declaim at the solemn mass, he said, but he also hoped for a banquet "with ladies of the first rank," promising to reciprocate when the marquis came to Florence. "I can assure you," he confided, "that you will find mounts on those slopes of the Apennines which have as gentle and soft a gait as that dapple gray nag Your Excellency acquired at Milan from the spoils of Lautrec."

On a more serious note, Giovio speculated that to discourage the French "and rid afflicted Lombardy of troops and cavalry," it might be necessary to carry the war into Provence; and on an equally ominous note he recounted a few of "the stupendous things" he had learned of the siege of Rhodes from the grand master, whom he and Giberti had welcomed at Civitavecchia on behalf of the cardinal de' Medici. Federico's reply was suitably cordial, promising both banquets and enjoyable conversations. No messenger, he assured Giovio, could be more pleasing: "For a long time now we have numbered you in the list of our intimates . . . and we count ourselves honored to have such a friend."[80] On August 26 Giovio left Rome for Florence and Mantua bearing the papal commission and, according to his friend Girolamo Negri, high hopes "for a good tip [una buona mancia]."[81]

In Florence, Giovio was welcomed and his business expedited by Francesco del Nero and the magistrates of the Otto di Pratica. On September 2, 1523, he set out from Florence with the Florentine standard, which he described to the marchese as "very handsome."[82] Savoring every moment of his mission, he requested an escort to meet him at Bologna, and so, on the afternoon of September 5, he rode in style into Mantua.[83] Despite urgent calls for Federico's presence in the field, the festivities lasted for over a week, in part because of the marquis' displeasure that the Florentines had not sent the whole of the promised stipend. On the morning of September 9, following a solemn mass in the cathedral sung by the archbishop, the letters of appointment were read and the baton and standard of Florence blessed and consigned to the marquis.[84] Giovio's wish to be numbered among the servitors of the house of Gonzaga was gratified by a grant of Mantuan citizenship, dated September 10, an unusual distinction, or so the charter proclaimed.[85]

But while the palace of Mantua glowed with festivities in Giovio's honor, a large French army under the command of the admiral of France, Guillaume Gouffier, sire de Bonnivet, was occupying Asti, Alessandria, and Novara.[86] A paragon of eagerness now that he had committed himself, the pope had been bombarding Federico with missives urging him to hasten to Milan and join forces with Prospero Colonna. Federico finally departed on September 15, having enlisted Giovio's assistance in obtaining expeditious payment of the balance of his stipend from the Florentines.[87] Since Isabella d'Este was not in Mantua at the time, there would have been no reason for Giovio to tarry, and presumably he left with the marquis. Only on his return journey would he have learned of the death of the pope.

Even as he attempted to rally his armies, Adrian VI himself had been failing. A fever that attacked him the evening following the ceremonies in Santa Maria Maggiore had grown worse. Giovio blamed the "adula-tion" of his physicians for withholding treatment lest they alarm him about his condition. On September 10 the dying pope held his last con-sistory, at which he had to plead with the Sacred College to approve the purple for his datary, the faithful Enkevoirt. Only the support of the car-dinal de' Medici and the imperial ambassador made it possible. He died, Giovio noted, on the same day that Bonnivet had crossed the Ticino, "leaving a great task to his successor."[88]

The wag who pinned to the door of the pope's physician the inscrip-tion "LIBERATORI PATRIAE S. P. Q. R. [The senate and people of Rome to the liberator of our country]" expressed the sentiments of the Romans for their deceased shepherd.[89] Adrian VI's unlovable personality and his draconian measures for reforming abuses *urbe et orbi* had aroused a deep hostility in the city and curia, a hostility amply reflected in the *Hadriani Sexti vita*. Even in narrating the pope's last moments Giovio was unable to repress a touch of malice, suggesting that the old man's death might have been hastened by excessive drafts of his favorite herb beer.

Yet with all its witty sallies and studied ironies, Giovio's biography did at times bridge the gap between the rough-hewn Flemish pope and the urbane world of the Roman curia. For one thing, Giovio's sensitivity as a biographer led him to appreciate the pathos of an earnest and well-meaning man saddled late in life with a dignity he did not desire, slowly and painfully learning the names of the cities over which he now ruled, thwarted by penury and the discords of Christian monarchs from mount-ing the crusade he ardently purposed, at odds with the culture that sur-rounded him, deceived by those he had trusted, and hated by those whose lives he sought to reform. "It is ever the custom of the populace," Giovio observed, "given by nature to dissolute licentiousness, to detest the qualities of the present prince and to praise to the skies the virtues of the last." So it was with Adrian VI, who used to lament the truth of the classical dictum that reputation depended largely on the circumstances in which preeminent virtue found itself.[90]

To Italians accustomed to vivid emotions, Adrian VI's steady piety, so characteristic of the Brethren of the Common Life, seemed cold and hostile, especially when linked with the effects of old age. The pope was laconic to the point of curtness and straightforward to the point of brusqueness. There was nothing about him that could be described as *perblandus, lepidus, urbanus, suavus,* or *elegans,* adjectives that pervade Giovio's biography of Leo X. He lacked that galaxy of virtues summed up by the Italians as "umanità." Giovio himself attempted to understand Adrian VI's personality as a form of stoicism, searching for the appropriate Latin terms, as in the "sedati animi habitu frigidioreque laetitia" with which he received the news of his election to the papacy.[91] And for all his Ciceronianisms and his curial ironies, Giovio rose at the end to a moment of transcendent frankness. "And so," he wrote, "refusing the cure of Christian medicine, we persevered in our corruption to such a point of madness that we aroused the indignation of gods and men, provoking the horrible ruin of the city which even then threatened us, exposing ourselves, body and soul, to every sort of cruelty and ignominy which inhuman barbarians could inflict."[92]

CHAPTER SIX

Clement VII and the Sack of Rome (1523–1527)

> . . . durò una gran fatica per diventare, di grande e riputato cardi-
> nale, piccolo e poco stimato papa.
>
> —Francesco Vettori, *Sommario della storia d'Italia*

> . . . he endured a great labor to become, from a great and re-
> spected cardinal, a small and little-esteemed pope.

THE DEATH OF Adrian VI was a severe setback but, as in 1521, the allies
saved the situation by their resolution. The league had been drawn up to
outlast by a year the death of any one signatory, so while the Roman
populace was venting its joy at the death of its shepherd, Prospero Colonna—now so aged and ailing he had to be carried in a litter—was fall-
ing back to defend Milan. He was even prepared to abandon the city if
attacked, its fortifications and defenders were so weakened, but instead
of launching an assault, Bonnivet settled down to a siege.

Taking advantage of the presence of the French army, Alfonso d'Este
moved swiftly to repossess Reggio and Modena, which not even Adrian
VI had been willing to return to him. With too few troops to defend both
cities, Guicciardini garrisoned the citadel of Reggio, pleaded with the
college of cardinals for Spanish reinforcements, revised his will, and settled down in Modena to wait.[1] On September 28 Alfonso and his troops
appeared before Modena, but at dawn the next day they moved on to
Reggio, which surrendered at once. With these developments as background, the Sacred College assembled in the Sistine Chapel on October
1, 1523, to begin the conclave.

Throughout the previous summer, when Adrian's health was failing,
the duke of Sessa and other agents of Charles V had been working to
have the cardinal de' Medici elected and found it highly propitious that
he was assigned a cell directly beneath Perugino's fresco depicting Peter
receiving the keys. Although he controlled the largest bloc of votes,
Giulio de' Medici was again confronted by unremitting opposition from
the French party and the dissident imperialists surrounding Cardinal
Pompeo Colonna. The senior cardinals, moreover, led by Cardinal Farnese, were jealous of the younger cardinals appointed by Leo X. In his
biography of Pompeo Colonna, Giovio recounted in detail the maneu-
verings of the several parties. This time Giulio had no intention of yield-

ing and stood his ground, knowing that his opponents were held together only by their opposition to him.[2]

As the days and weeks dragged by, the libels in Rome became more licentious, and a schism was rumored. The French were pressing Milan, while the Venetians were temporizing, waiting to learn the outcome of the election before committing their forces. From Milan, according to Giovio, Prospero Colonna pleaded with his nephew for the sake of the imperial cause to accede to the cardinal de' Medici. Eventually, as their elderly supporters begin to sicken in the fetid air of the chapel, the French party proposed Cardinal Franciotto Orsini, a Francophile but also a friend and relative of Cardinal de' Medici's.

Alarmed at the threat of an Orsini pope, Cardinal Colonna rushed to his rival and, as Giovio learned, put the question in its bluntest terms: "Will you be grateful to me if I elevate you to the papacy?" To which Giulio replied, "If you are speaking in earnest I shall indeed treat you surpassingly well, and not only will you be serving your own interests, you will, above all, be rendering the public welfare and the cause of Caesar a distinguished and timely service." Colonna's demands included a free pardon for Cardinal Soderini and several other active opponents. Giulio de' Medici responded by offering his right hand and promising that in token of his sincerity he would take the papal name of Clement.[3] Thus on November 19, 1523, on the second anniversary of his triumphal entry into Milan, Giovio's master became pope.

For Giovio the antagonism of Pompeo Colonna and Giulio de' Medici had been both a personal and a political embarrassment. His ties to Cardinal Colonna predated his service to Cardinal de' Medici, and the effectiveness of the imperial alliance depended upon the cooperation of the two cardinals. In his biography of the marquis of Pescara (although not, understandably, in that of Cardinal Colonna), he went so far as to describe Pompeo Colonna's opposition as "seditious" in view of the grave danger of losing Milan.[4] On the other hand, the secretary to Cardinal Cornaro marveled that Colonna had acceded at all, so bitter had been the rivalry between the two cardinals.[5]

Except for the French party, Rome greeted Cardinal de' Medici's election with expectant rejoicing, amid visions of a return to the golden Leonine age. "Praised be the Lord forever!" exclaimed Vittoria Colonna.[6] Giulio de' Medici had been a great and respected cardinal. It was widely thought that he had been the éminence grise of Leo X's pontificate, responsible for those sterner measures that seemed discordant with the pope's genial nature.[7] Through all the subsequent vicissitudes of fortune he had steered a steady course. Many anticipated, with Bembo, that he would be "the greatest and wisest, as well as the most respected pope whom the Church has seen for centuries."[8] The news gave heart to the imperialists and restored order to the papal states. Alfonso d'Este abandoned the attempt to capture Modena and returned with his army to Ferrara. The Venetians expressed their rapture and ordered their general, the duke of Urbino, to play a more active part in the league, even though the immediate danger to Milan had passed.

Battered first by the rains and mud of autumn, then by early snows and bitter cold, the French had given up the siege on November 14 and gone to winter quarters. In December the viceroy of Naples, Charles de Lannoy, arrived with the marquis of Pescara and the desperately awaited Spanish reinforcements. They were barely in time to assist at the deathbed of Prospero Colonna, who passed from the world on December 30, rejoicing at having saved Milan from the French. The people of Milan mourned him "with incredible lamentation," Giovio recorded, and the more so as they soon found their substance wasted more by their German and Spanish defenders than by their enemies.[9]

For Giovio the "great things" he had been pursuing now seemed at hand. Moving from the palace of the Cancelleria to the Vatican, he was assigned quarters beneath the Sistine Chapel ironically known as "il Paradiso." These had been created by Pope Sixtus IV to house the chapel's clergy by converting a former prison nicknamed "l'Inferno," but to Giovio the original name often seemed more appropriate. "In summer because of the sun," he complained, "in winter because of the colds [the Paradiso] many times seemed to me like the Inferno."[10] Already a papal familiar (*familiaris*), he now became one of the permanent members of the pope's official household, entitled to meals in the papal dining hall (*continui commensales*). As a resident papal physician, moreover, he became a member of the more intimate domestic household, comprised of the courtiers who attended the pope personally, the so-called palatine family (*famiglia palatina*).[11]

How did Giovio fit into the new order? He certainly continued to serve as physician, but since his patron had several of these, his principal role was probably the one attributed to him by the poet Francesco Berni: historian and conversationalist. As secretary to Giberti, Berni was a court "insider," familiar with the routines of the papal household, and his satirical stanzas depicting "Maestro Feradotto" plying his wit to entertain King Gradasso at meals were based on Giovio.[12] Berni's sketch was underscored by an episode in Giambattista Giraldi's collection of moralistic tales, *Gli ecatommiti*, which also featured Giovio entertaining the pope at meals.[13]

Giovio's first years in the Vatican found him enjoying his new prominence and busy assisting his friends. He seemed to have commerce with half of Mantua, he protested to the marquis, and he good-naturedly accused Equicola of trying to bury him with letters.[14] Through Castiglione, Federico sent him a handsome present, evidently something from the spoils of the French camp, because Giovio reported back in great delight that His Holiness spoke of it every day. Best of all, it was a source of chagrin to the French cardinals. His principal thanks, Giovio told the marquis, would come in his *Histories*, when memory brought to mind again the glorious deeds "which make me no less proud that I am, with gilded charter, your servitor, than does living in the Vatican or taking the pulse of Clement VII."[15] To take Clement VII's pulse was one thing, however; to have him keep a promise was another. Federico still had not been paid the sum owed for his *condotta*, and for over a year and a half Giovio kept assuring him that his friends were working on it.[16] Meanwhile, to cure the marquis of his urinary complaints, about which he and the pope spoke "as often as the sea laps at the Tyrrhenian beaches," Giovio recommended the baths of Lucca, whose waters had cured him of urinary stones "as big as barley."[17]

The d'Este archives reveal a constant commerce of information and favors between Giovio and the Ferrarese ambassador Giacomo Alvarotti or the agent Matteo Casella.[18] The duke of Ferrara also sent a present, a big one it would seem, for in thanking him Giovio likewise promised that his gratitude would be evident in the *Histories*, where, beyond celebrating the magnificent deeds of the duke with his "feeble eloquence," he would show himself a true servitor of the house of Este "as it will be commanded and indicated to me."[19] Unfortunately, Giovio's overly eager responses to the sudden fruitfulness of these friendships confirmed his reputation for venality when his correspondence began to be published after his death, even though one looks vainly in the *Histories* for exaggerated praises.

While working for his friends, Giovio was not neglecting his own interests or those of his family. A letter of 1525 shows that the needs of the nephews were endless. Giulio was to be trained in composition so that his uncle could find him a place at the curia. Alessandro, now at the university of Bologna, was behaving like the archetypical student. "God give him grace not to pull any more mad tricks," Giovio warned, "because this is his last chance with me, as I have told him." Giovio was still waiting to hear what his other brother, Giampietro, desired for his son, Giannandrea. Benedetto needed money for building the garden adjoining the family palace, and Giovio asked for plans and a sketch for the project. Most of the letter was taken up with details of the hunt for benefices. Giovio was hoping to exchange his priorate for another canonry in the cathedral of Como. "Keep an eye out," he urged.[20] Just the previous year (1524) he had received *in commendam* the preceptory of Sant'Antonio outside the walls of Como, and the following year (1526) he obtained *in commendam* the church of Santa Vittoria in Piacenza, or else a pension from its revenues.[21]

During the first years of the second Medici pope some of the old gaiety returned to Roman life, commencing with the carnival of 1524. "Now begins the process of dressing up the world," Giovio wrote testily to Federico Gonzaga, "and here they are going about in masks and jesting about the flood of water" (an allusion to the flood and destruction prophesied for 1524 by the astrologer Luca Gaurico).[22] For all his love of banquets and witty conversation, Giovio felt ill-at-ease during the license of carnival. Apparently he was the victim of a courtier's prank devised by no less a person than his friend Giberti, who had been appointed datary at the beginning of the new papacy. When the historian appeared in mask and costume, as Castiglione related to Federico, Giberti attached to his back a sign reading in capital letters, "I AM MASTER PAOLO GIOVIO." This simple trick so upset Giovio, said Castiglione, "that he wished to give himself to the devil," and so, "having compassion on him," the courtiers withheld another trick they had planned.[23]

Papal dinner parties resumed as a focal point of Roman social life. Giovio's *De romanis piscibus* (On Roman fish) was conceived at a banquet the pope gave for François Louis, cardinal of Bourbon. During the meal, the nomenclature of the fish available in Rome had been "subtly disputed," and in response to a suggestion of the cardinal's, Giovio produced his "erudite yet festive" little treatise. Though attractively printed by Francesco Calvo in the summer of 1524, Giovio's first publication came a cropper. In old age he confessed to a friend that the cardinal had rewarded him with "a fictitious benefice situated on the island of Thule, beyond the Orkneys." And so, "repenting of having rummaged through all the rummagable in vain, and being condemned to bear the expense of it, I returned to writing history, a task more in keeping with my talent."[24]

Some of the brilliance and festiveness of old returned to the republic of letters as well. Sadoleto was recalled from his diocese of Carpentras and reappointed papal secretary, along with Giovio's friends from the Roman academy, Colocci and Blosio Palladio. Colocci and Küritz reconciled their differences, and the humanist sodality flourished once more in gardens, vineyards, porticos, and other *loci amoeni*. Sadoleto later remembered Giovio as having been one of the leaders of the academy, the successor to Inghirami and Porzio in Latin eloquence, "in writing history grave and eloquent, and most polished in every field of literature."[25]

Giovio's stature among the academicians is evident from a mock invective composed by Fabio Vigile, a curial humanist and one of the fellowship of the *Coryciana*. The narrator, Jovius, recounts his adventitious discovery of Blosius Palladius devouring "an enormous pheasant" all by himself. To make him atone for this outrage of gluttony, Jovius reveals that he has commanded Blosius to provide an Apician banquet for all the friends who might have been invited to share the pheasant with him. The fun lay in the witty borrowings from the classics used to denounce the miscreant and to threaten him with all sorts of agricultural disasters at his suburban *vigna* had he refused his penance:

> All your projects will go belly up.
> Destructive barrenness will invade your poultry houses,
> And your dovecote shall teem with mice,
> Until their gnawing teeth collapse it. [etc.]

The culminating punishment was to have been eternal infamy in Jovius' *Histories*.[26]

Giovio seemed to move in every circle: the Vatican; the old Roman academy; the brilliant new academy of Giberti at his palace in the Borgo; the court of Cardinal Colonna; perhaps even the "achademia tragica" formed by Giangiorgio Trissino and Giovanni Rucellai while Rucellai was castellan of the Castel Sant'Angelo.[27] Too little is known of Giovio's relations with Roman printers and calligraphers, with his compatriot and publisher, the scholarly Francesco Calvo of Menaggio, or with Ludovico degli Arrighi, the calligrapher of book VII of the *Histories*.[28] Giovio himself had adopted the chancery hand and wrote it reasonably well before his gout, and he insisted on a high quality of calligraphy for all his manuscripts.

While happily joining in the renewal of Roman social life, Giovio was at work on two of his major biographies and the first of his descriptive geographical pieces.[29] The ambassador of Charles V, Luis Fernández de Córdoba, duke of Sessa, had commissioned him to vindicate the reputation of his father-in-law, Gonzalo Fernández de Córdoba, the most brilliant general of the age. After winning the kingdom of Naples from the French, the "great captain" had been forced into retirement in Spain by the jealousy of Ferdinand of Aragon, who suspected him of wanting the crown of Naples for himself, and the duke of Sessa feared that the great soldier's's reputation was being diminished by official annalists and "foolish poets."[30] Giovio was also working on a life of Leo X, which at the suggestion of Felice Trofino he began enlarging with the history of the Medici family going back to Cosimo *pater patriae*, an expansion that must have caused him to take a particular interest in Machiavelli's visit to Rome in late May 1525 to present to the pope his *Istorie fiorentine*.[31]

Another visitor to Rome in 1525, Dimitri Gerasimov, ambassador of the grand duke of Moscow, added interest to a lackluster jubilee and prompted the first of Giovio's "descriptions" of various countries, an outgrowth of his passionate interest in exploration and discovery. With an eye to gaining the imperial title coveted by the grand dukes, Basil III was dangling before the pope the prospect of union with Rome. According to Giovio, Gerasimov's embassy was the indirect result of the intrepid Genoese merchant Paolo Centurione's indefatigable (and to Giovio insane) search for a northern route to India. Unfortunately, the grand duke did not want strangers entering the troubled frontier area (a very modern-sounding response), but he took the occasion of Centurione's visit to renew contacts with Rome.

Gerasimov was received by Clement VII with great splendor in the Vatican and assigned as host and guide the well-traveled bishop of Teramo, Francesco Chieregati of Vicenza, Adrian VI's luckless nuncio to the diet of Nuremberg. Having been educated in Livonia, Gerasimov spoke good Latin, and Giovio said he sought him out almost daily to gather background in Russian history. For the wars of Ivan III against the Tartars in book VIII (13), Giovio had already interviewed one of the Italian architects of the Kremlin, Pietro d'Arezzo, and the military engineer Paolino da Milano. Now at the urging of Giovanni Ruffo Teodoli, archbishop of Cosenza and one of Adrian VI's few confidants among the Italians, Giovio interrupted his other work to write up his interviews with Gerasimov. The *Libellus de legatione Basilii magni Principis Moschoviae* was dedicated to Ruffo, although it was Chieregati who took it and had it published by Calvo.[32]

Giovio's "little book" was a piece of chorography, or political geography, a mélange of geography, natural history, history, social customs, literature, and religion. "Chorography," Giovio contended (echoing Polybius), was "the mirror necessary for whoever wishes to see and clarify the where, how, and when of events."[33] Some of what Gerasimov had told him sent Giovio to the Vatican Library to check and subsequently to correct Pliny, Strabo, and Ptolemy. His description of Muscovy had a charming freshness to it, in part owing to his having retained the simple, unaffected Latin of Gerasimov's replies, in part because his questions themselves embodied the wonder of Europe's enlarging horizons during the Renaissance.[34]

Yet another visitor to Rome in these years, and full of marvelous tales, was the historian (and survivor) of Magellan's heroic voyage, Antonio Pigafetta of Vicenza, who arrived in 1523 to fulfill a vow made on the voyage.[35] In book 34 of the *Histories*, where he recounted the discovery of the New World, Giovio ranked Magellan as the greatest of the generation of explorers who followed Columbus. Somehow Giovio acquired— no one knows how—the portrait of Columbus now considered to have the greatest probability of authenticity.[36] He knew Cortés, and he may also have known Giovanni da Verrazzano, who appears to have named "Jovium promontorium" (Point Judith in present-day Rhode Island) for him.[37]

Giovio now found himself incomparably situated for writing the history of his times: lodged in the Vatican palace, immersed in the mainstream of events, an intimate of the pope, sought out by ambassadors of princes. "Now," he exulted to Federico Gonzaga in 1524, "the time has come when I can work and write without looking behind me."[38] Many contemporaries felt that he had preempted the field of contemporary history, a perception he aggressively encouraged. In 1523 Girolamo Negri reported with much amusement that Giovio had broken with Clement VII's rough-hewn protégé, Pietro Alcionio, "because he has been given to understand that Alcionio is writing history, which he will not yield to anyone." Although Alcionio was only writing an oration in praise of the knights killed in the siege of Rhodes, Giovio had been told otherwise "in order to stir them up against each other."[39]

Yet precisely where they promised to be most authoritative, Giovio's *Histories* abruptly stopped. The entire decade 1517–1527 is missing, from Francesco Maria della Rovere's return to Urbino to the sack of Rome (books 19–24). So are the years 1498–1512 (books 5–10). What accounted for lacunae of such magnitude? At different points in his life Giovio advanced various reasons, all of them contradictory. He presented his "official" version for the lacuna of books 5–10 in the first edition of the *Histories* (1550), following the conclusion of book 4. In anticipation of the sack of Rome, he explained, he had hidden the manuscripts of his *Histories*, along with his silver, in a reinforced chest stowed under the main altar of Santa Maria sopra Minerva, but under torture the sacristans revealed the hiding places of the church's treasures, and Giovio's chest fell into the hands of two Spanish captains, Antonio Gamboa of Navarre and (Hernando Alonzo de) Herrera of Córdoba.

Gamboa was content with the silver and threw away the manuscripts, some of which were written on parchment and bound in red leather, others of which were on paper. Herrera, being somewhat literate, recognized that the manuscripts might have some value and brought the leather-bound parchment volumes to Castel Sant'Angelo seeking a ransom. Moved by Giovio's distraught pleas, the pope conceded the captain a Spanish benefice he wanted for his family, and the vellum manuscripts were redeemed. Those written on paper, however, had been discarded and used by soldiers as toilet paper.

Giovio thought it a grace of God that his manuscripts had fallen into the hands of Spaniards rather than "the barbarian Germans who, in the Campo dei Fiori and in every intersection, burnt an infinite multitude of books." Given the historian's habit of interviewing captains and his presence with the army of the league in 1521, a veteran Spanish captain might well have recognized the significance of the manuscripts. In fact, in the Ischian dialogue Giovio said that they had been recovered "with the aid of certain famous generals who understood their import for their own fame."[40]

While plausible, however, this story was not wholly consistent with the opening of the Ischian dialogue, composed immediately after the sack, where Giovio congratulated himself on having escaped Rome safe and sound together with his *Histories*, "redeemed at a great price." Here he made no mention of books lost.[41] In a letter to Giberti, moreover, written in July 1527, just after his departure from Castel Sant'Angelo, Giovio spoke of his *Histories* as redeemed from Herrera "cum prejudicio argentorum [at a cost of money]" and stored in the castle with Vespasiano Colonna. Giberti was to see to the publication of "at least those eight well-revised books" should their author be drowned en route to Ischia.[42]

If Giovio had begun writing his *Histories* with the events of Leo X's reign, but then, seeking root causes, had gone back to 1494 and worked forward, the "missing" books would have been the last to have been completed. There is thus a possibility that his story about the lost books was merely a convenient fiction introduced years later to cover his failure to complete the history of the pontificates of Alexander VI and Julius II, a hypothesis supported by his mention in the 1527 letter of eight "polished" books. Of the original first decade, the manuscripts of books V–X still survive, and books I–II are at least mentioned by Giovio as being revised at Venice in 1523. That would leave books V–VI, corresponding to the missing books 5–10. In the dedication to *De romanis piscibus* (1524), Giovio announced he was soon to publish the first decade of his *Histories*, suggesting that he had indeed been planning to complete books V–VI, an intention confirmed by his 1514 letter to d'Alviano seeking information for the battle of Agnadello, which would have formed part of the missing book VI (9).[43]

Giovio's explanations for the lacuna stretching from the later years of Leo X to the sack of Rome are also puzzling. This time there was no tale of books lost. He admitted that books 19–24 had never been completely written, but he was evasive, if not flatly contradictory, as to whether or not they had been written in part. In the dedication of volume two of the *Histories*, penned in the last year of his life, he told Cosimo I de' Medici that he could not have written the missing books without giving extreme offense to "certain persons." Unwilling to compromise his integrity as a historian, he had preferred for the sake of his reputation and health to leave them unwritten. The history of these years, he said (echoing a passage in Castiglione), could not "be remembered without sorrow, nor written without floods of tears nor told to posterity without disgrace and shame."[44]

Nonetheless, Giovio concluded his dedication by reminding the duke that the missing history was covered in his biographies and that if God spared him he would do his best to make up the gaps in the *Histories* themselves. In similar vein, he declared to Cosimo I's minister, Lelio Torelli, that out of prudence he was leaving some "windows" in his histories which his nephews could close after his death with materials that he would set in order for them, but no trace of these materials has ever been found.[45]

The most plausible of Giovio's later excuses was probably his reluctance to write the history of the years leading to the sack of Rome, since so many of his patrons shared responsibility for it. To have written truthfully would not only have been disagreeable but would have exposed him to charges of ingratitude.[46] It has even been suggested that Giovio may have been secretly pleased by the parallel with Livy, a number of whose books were either lost or known only through epitomes.[47]

Yet in 1528 Giovio had an entirely different explanation for the gap in his *Histories*: lack of support from the pope. "Indeed," he declared, in the Ischian dialogue,

> you would have read some time ago several books full of great events had this pontificate even minimally fulfilled my moderate, although reasonably conceived, expectations, and if Giberti, who relieved my consternation of spirit out of his own pocket, had been able to assist me in his official capacity [as datary]. But, in truth, thinking I had already acquired sufficient praise for my labors on my *Histories*, I began in my indignation to employ my talent elsewhere, since those very persons who ought to have been eager for honor and immortality—as if stupefied in a deep hibernation of indifference—seemed oblivious to my own studious vigils, as well as those of others.[48]

Obviously Giovio felt that his being given the bishopric of Nocera dei Pagani four years into Clement's pontificate was too little and too late. Perhaps he had been denied a subsidy for publishing the first decade. Years later he repeated the charge with equal warmth: "By Hercules, had not Giberti, inflamed with love of talent and letters and—to the happy fortune of the age—the pope's intimate in the administration of the Church, recalled a denying and hard pope to the grace of beneficence by softening and even deceiving him, some outstanding talents would have perished in grief and sterility."[49]

In his disappointment with Clement VII's patronage, Giovio had considerable company. Those who anticipated the lavish outlays of Leo X were quickly disillusioned. "It is the innate grace of the Medici to favor the muses," Girolamo Negri had observed at Clement VII's election, but four months later he was reporting, "All our curial friends are consuming themselves with hopes, but of this pontificate up to now nothing has been seen but smoke."[50] Some of the officials purged by Adrian VI were restored to their offices, but no cornucopia was uncapped, then or ever.

In its parsimony, in fact, Clement VII's court more resembled his predecessor's than his cousin's, in part owing to the exhaustion of the treasury from Leo X's extravagances, but also to differences in temperament. Like Adrian VI, Clement VII was by nature sparing, parsimonious. Even in prosperous times he had been a discriminating rather than a prolific patron.

Giovio never got over his personal disappointment with the patron who "wanted to send us to bed with cold feet and no supper," but in the public realm he experienced an even deeper disappointment with this master whose personal virtues, while admirable in themselves, proved unequal to the greater tasks that now confronted him. During the papacy of Leo X, Giovio had come to feel that the best hope for Italy's peace and prosperity lay not in attempting to oppose the overwhelming power of Spain but in cooperating with it. From his new vantage point in the Vatican, however, he watched, his anguish heightened by his powerlessness, as his patron deserted the *pax imperii* for a course that he had neither the resources nor the character to sustain, and that precipitated Italy into a pit of ruin.[51]

When the election of Clement VII was proclaimed on November 19, 1523, the triumph of the imperial party and its Italian settlement had seemed complete. "The pope is entirely Your Majesty's creature," wrote the duke of Sessa shortly after the conclave.[52] Giovio himself assured Mario Equicola that "the Pope wants to die a Caesarian and he wants Francesco Sforza in Milan and the French alive in France."[53] With benefit of hindsight, however, Giovio later scaled down his estimate of the pope's loyalty, observing merely that in the first year of his pontificate "Clement judged it expedient not to depart from the league made by Adrian."[54]

Things had begun well enough. Early in 1524 the pope gave the league 20,000 ducats and ordered the Florentines to pay the remaining 30,000 of their obligations.[55] Confident of the new pope, the Venetians ordered the duke of Urbino to take a more active role in the warfare. In mid-February the traitorous duke of Bourbon arrived in Milan, hoping to obtain investiture from the emperor, and at a conference of all the generals it was decided to take the initiative. On March 2, under Pescara's command, the imperial army crossed the Ticino, forcing Bonnivet to fall back to Novara. "Now, O captains," exulted Pescara, "we have the Gauls in a cage!"[56] With an energy unusual in Italian warfare, Pescara pursued the retreating French and fell on them as they were attempting to cross the Sesia. Beaten and ravaged, the French army made its way to Ivrea and thence to France, abandoning in failure Francis I's second attempt to recover Milan.

The policies for which Clement VII had long striven were now triumphant. As pope he was in a position to harvest as their fruits the peace and stability of Italy. Yet to the astonishment of everyone and to the deep chagrin of the imperialists, he now seemed bent on repeating the mistakes of Adrian VI, adopting the neutrality even that moralistic schoolman had found impossible to maintain and which, as cardinal de' Medici, he himself had worked so hard to overcome. How was this possible? Some scholars have reasoned that in order to win the papacy, Clement VII may have secretly bound himself to the French cardinals henceforth to be neutral. Others have argued that once pope he found himself prisoner of the age-old imperative to maintain the independence of the Holy See by balancing other monarchs against the emperor, particularly the sovereigns of France.[57] Still others, noting his habitual indecisiveness, have surmised that personal weakness hampered his good intentions.

From the beginning of Clement VII's pontificate, contemporary observers noted an impediment: the pope was indecisive, even timid. "He is a prudent man and wise," wrote Matteo Foscari, "but long to resolve."[58] "He is very slow to decide," observed Gasparo Contarini, "and not a little timid."[59] While His Holiness debated, suitors were put off with ambiguities. "I have never spoken," declared the former confessor of Charles V, Don Garcia Loaysa, "with one whose sayings were so hard to decipher."[60]

Worse than the pope's slowness was his irresolution. Leo X had been agonizingly long in deliberation, and Charles V's councillors were often reduced to despair by his deliberateness. But once resolved, Leo X was swift in action and Charles V was doggedly steadfast. Clement VII, on the other hand, having decided, would waver, reconsider, draw back. Guicciardini, who was familiar with his decision-making processes, gave a devastating account of them in book sixteen of the *Storia d'Italia*, concluding that, "as a result of his complicated nature and confused way of proceeding, he often permitted himself to be led by his ministers, and seemed directed rather than counselled by them."[61] Since his two chief ministers diverged in their views (Giberti favoring a French policy and Nikolaus von Schönberg an imperial one), it was said that the pope's current mind could be read by observing whichever was spending the most time with him.[62]

Giovio knew his patron as well as anyone and better than most. In his biography of the marquis of Pescara, he went against common opinion by explicitly discounting the notion that Clement VII's ministers were anything other than executors of his wishes. Whatever their own views, he affirmed, they were faithful vehicles of the pope's policies.[63] While agreeing that indecisiveness weakened Clement VII's statecraft, Giovio attributed his inability to hold a firm alliance principally to an ill-conceived desire of making himself the arbiter of Europe by balancing its monarchs one against the other.[64] The trait most responsible for his master's failures, Giovio felt, was not irresolution but avarice. At several critical junctures he saw the pope's unwillingness to commit the necessary resources cripple the implementation of his strategies or cause them to miscarry. While he was aware of Clement VII's constant financial difficulties, Giovio's use of the term *avarice* suggested a deep personality trait, a view shared by his friend the duke of Sessa, imperial ambassador from 1523 to 1526.[65]

Spurning appeals for an offensive league against the French, Clement VII would do no more than discharge his obligations under the existing treaty, meanwhile sending Schönberg to the courts of France, England, and Spain to argue the cause of Christian concord and crusade against the Turk. Peace was quickly made impossible, however, by Charles V's ill-fated invasion of Provence in 1524. Trusting the traitorous duke of Bourbon's promises that the populace would rise to his banner, the emperor sanctioned the invasion, a victim, Giovio charged, of Bourbon's "wicked temerity," "insolent desire," and "vain hopes." Giovio's distress stemmed from his belief that the ill-advised invasion convinced Italians that the young emperor could not be trusted, particularly as he had been slow to invest Sforza formally with Milan, and that "with immoderate desire he aspired to the empire of all Europe."[66] Giberti's self-justification confirmed Giovio's analysis.[67] Although intended to frighten Francis I from further attempts on Milan, the Provence campaign had exactly the reverse effect. The counteroffensive of 1524, led by the king himself, not only drove the imperial armies out of France but pursued them across the Alps and swept the French back into Milan.

Instead of entering the capital in person, Francis I turned south to besiege Pavia, whereupon many Italian adherents of the league began to waver, reasoning, Giovio explained, that if "the fatal misery" of foreign masters had to be endured, the French at least regarded Milan as their own country, whereas the Spaniards had "oppressed and robbed it with every example of cruelty and avarice like a foreign country that they would one day abandon."[68] Despite his own frustration, Giovio clung to his belief that the restoration of the Sforza under the imperial aegis was the best Italy could hope for, but to his evident anguish, a contrary view began to prevail in Venice and in Rome.

At the end of October 1524 the pope dispatched Giberti to the French and imperial camps with proposals for a truce, each side to retain what it had so far acquired or held. The pope's object, Giovio maintained, was to enhance his own position as mediator, but under the present circumstances the proposals meant the abandonment of Francesco II Sforza, who had fled from Milan before the French. In his biography of Pescara, Giovio exposed the perverse chain of reasoning whereby doubt about the emperor's intentions to invest Sforza with Milan became the reason for abandoning him.[69] On January 5, 1525, Clement VII announced an agreement with Francis I, which he justified by the sudden danger to the papal states. In return for a guarantee of Parma and Piacenza to the Church and Florence to the Medici, the pope would consent to Francis I's acquisition of Milan and assure French troops the right of passage through papal territory. The real motive, Giovio asserted, was fear that Francis I would succeed in taking Pavia and the "blind" suspicion that Charles V's slowness to invest Sforza with Milan indicated a wish to retain it for himself as a stepping stone to the mastery of all Italy. While not unreasonable by the standards of the time, Giovio said, the suspicion was not an accurate assessment of the emperor's character and intentions.[70]

Suspecting some sort of negotiations, the imperial ambassador had warned the pope that Caesar would regard as enemies those who refused to support him in his present need. When the treaty of January 5 was revealed, Charles V was outraged. To the Florentine ambassador he protested his incredulity that the man who as cardinal had led him into a long and difficult war for the liberty and well-being of Italy, and whom he had supported during two conclaves, should now desert him.[71] To Sessa he complained of having poured out for the cardinal de' Medici "streams of gold." To his confidants, tradition held, he exclaimed, "I shall go into Italy and revenge myself on those who have injured me, especially on that poltroon, the pope."[72]

Meanwhile in Italy the situation of the imperial commanders was becoming every day more difficult. Cut off from their Milanese subsidies, deserted by the pope, Florentines, and Venetians, the generals were unable to pay their troops, whose morale was rapidly ebbing. Still, Charles V would not hear of truce, and the commanders were forced to devise expedient after expedient to maintain the soldiers' loyalty. Morale was briefly raised by the appearance of Bourbon, who crossed the Alps in midwinter with reinforcements, including the twenty companies of Georg von Frundsberg. Francis I obtained Swiss reinforcements, however, and the stalemate continued.[73]

The pope had conceived the worry that in the present circumstances a clear military victory would annihilate the loser, leaving Italy at the mercy of the victor. Some of his advisers suggested sending a papal army to Piacenza, combining forces with the Venetians, and forcing the belligerents to accept a truce; but destiny, Giovio lamented, prevented the pope from taking a part "full of security and honor" through fear of the expense. "By nature sparing and never liberal with money," he charged, Clement VII "delighted in temporizing and delay, being accustomed to measure his own counsels in accordance with the success or failure of the undertakings of others."

> This habit, while suitable for a holy and moderate pontiff who, like the ancient popes, confined himself to sacred matters, was inopportune and disastrous for one who wished to guard the safety of all with strong and generous counsels in order that Italy, ravaged by the obstinate arms of great nations, might conserve herself free and safe from the ruin which was fast coming upon her.[74]

As of Christmas the imperialists were completely without resources. Pescara negotiated an agreement with the troops to serve one more month without pay, and in late January he moved the army out of winter quarters in Lodi to encamp within a mile of the French, hoping to find some way of provoking an engagement. Francis I's troops had taken up a highly defensible position north and east of Pavia in the park of Mirabello and in the environs of the abbey of San Paolo, which the king had made his headquarters. Here the representatives of the pope urged him not to submit himself to the risks of battle against an army about to disintegrate from lack of pay.[75] For three weeks the armies engaged in skirmishes, until in the night of February 23–24, 1525, on the very eve of the expiration of his agreement with the troops, Pescara succeeded in breaking through the northeast wall of the park. The French ran to the defense, and the fateful battle was joined.

The large number of conflicting and often self-serving contemporary accounts makes the battle of Pavia difficult to reconstruct in congruent detail.[76] Beginning in the half-light of dawn after a foggy winter night, it was fought with extreme confusion and was over almost before anyone realized what had happened. Guicciardini was unable to reconcile eyewitness memoirs to his own satisfaction and left his account unfinished. Giovio personally interviewed many of the surviving participants, including Francis I, but achieved vividness and clarity by holding for the most part to Pescara's contemporary account of the battle to Charles V.[77]

Difficult as the battle may have been to reconstruct, its outcome left no uncertainties. Francis I was a prisoner and the imperialists were again triumphant. The third French attempt to retake Milan had fared even worse than its predecessors. Charles V received the news of his awesome victory with no sign of exultation. Forbidding the usual cannonades and displays of fireworks, he ordered instead processions and services of thanksgiving in the churches, while he himself sought release for his emotions in prayer. Clement VII was deeply shaken. In the sedate Latin of his *Histories* Giovio described the pope as *perturbatus*.[78] With more immediacy a contemporary reported that he "was like a dead man."[79] The indomitable Pescara had succeeded in forcing the issue, and all Clement VII's hopes disappeared in Francis I's catastrophe. The Colonna, who had never deserted the imperial star, gave themselves over to wild rejoicings and then fell on the French and Orsini troops returning in early March from an unsuccessful expedition against Naples. Disdaining the pope's threats, they carried the fighting right to the Orsini houses on Monte Giordano, an affront, Giovio noted, that "sank deeply into Clement's heart."[80]

The pope was now torn between the advice of the imperial party to re-create the league and the urgings of the French party to raise an army and rescue the king, a plan Giovio dismissed as the product of "immoderate and impudent minds."[81] Defeated in what Giovio saw as his "dangerous and undistinguished course" of neutrality, Clement VII concluded a new league, offensive and defensive, with the viceroy of Naples, Charles de Lannoy. In return for a large papal and Florentine subsidy, the viceroy promised recognition of Francesco Sforza as duke of Milan and restoration of Reggio to the Church. Lannoy's agreement to such favorable terms for the pope was owing to his overwhelming need for money to pay the troops.

On May 1, in the Colonna church of Santi Apostoli, the league was formally announced with a solemn mass celebrated by Cardinal Colonna, followed by a lavish banquet.[82] The scorn of the imperial commanders for the pope was transparent. Far from enforcing the provisions of the new league regarding Reggio, Lannoy accepted a bribe from Alfonso d'Este and put the pope off with various pretexts. Not only did Clement VII find himself "wondrously deceived," Giovio related, but in addition he had to listen to the pleas of the wretched citizens of Parma and Piacenza, whose territories—also in violation of the treaty—were suffering continual depredations from the insolent imperial troops.[83] Was, then, the settlement so near in 1523 still possible in 1525: the duke of Milan ruling as imperial vassal in Lombardy; the states of the Church augmented by Parma, Piacenza, and Reggio; Italy pacified and crusades launched against the Lutherans and the Turks?

Along with Schönberg and Castiglione, Giovio still believed that the emperor could be counted upon to make a just, even a magnanimous settlement of Italian affairs, but unfortunately for those who had faith in his good intentions, the imperial ministers in Italy often had their own agendas. Bourbon, in particular, wanted Milan for himself. Moreover, when Francis I was spirited away to Spain to negotiate with Charles V directly, Giovio saw the pope and Venetians fill with new dread lest from Francis' desperation and Charles' strength came "new and perilous designs" and a "conspiracy for the ruin of Italy."[84] In concert with Lodovico Canossa, bishop of Bayeux and ambassador of France to Venice, Giberti now began promoting an alliance between the pope, the Venetians, the Swiss, the Milanese, and the regent of France, Louise of Savoy, mother of Francis I. Giovio did not approve, but he could see the pope's reasons. "Deprived of his hopes, defrauded of his money, and goaded by his many injuries," he wrote, Clement VII began contemplating a league with the Venetians and the French.[85]

At this point the Milanese chancellor, Girolamo Morone, also despairing of the emperor's intentions, made a bold—and in the outcome disastrous—gamble. Knowing that Pescara was still smarting from his failure to receive a substantial reward for his crucial role in the victory of Pavia and that he was enraged at Lannoy for having removed Francis I to Spain without consulting either himself or Bourbon, Morone approached the commander with the proposition that he lead the armies of Italy in a war to rid Italy of foreign domination, with the crown of Naples as his reward. To Morone's joy Pescara seemed interested, desiring only evidence of the pope's sincerity and the opinion of jurists both as to the pope's title to the kingdom and as to how he and the other barons could be discharged from their oath of loyalty to the emperor.

Although the d'Avalos were in origin a Spanish family, Pescara himself had been born in Italy, and his title was a Neapolitan one. Giovio depicted Giberti as suspicious until convinced by his own envoy's report. Then he threw himself into the scheme. "I see the world transformed," he wrote, "and Italy arising from the depths of misery to the summit of prosperity."[86] But when he had the incriminating evidence he needed, Pescara sent it all to the emperor. On October 14, 1525, he arrested Morone at Novara, occupied Milan with his troops, encircled the citadel, charged Francesco Sforza (who had been ill all this time) with treason, and deprived him of the government of Milan.

Giovio's account of the "conspiracy of Morone" evinced all the ambiguities of his own position as Italian patriot, imperialist, and biographer, and the stirring speech he placed in Morone's mouth urging Pescara to "become the glorious bearer of Italian liberty rather than the ignoble and hated minister of foreigners" was no doubt expressive of his own deepest emotions.[87] Did Giovio think Pescara was tempted? His analysis was comprehensive and shrewd, combining the intuition of the biographer with the instinct of the historian. He was, moreover, extraordinarily well-informed. Although he had been unable to interview Pescara before his death, by the time the *Histories* were published he had had occasion to question not only Giberti, Sforza, Morone, and Morone's courier, Domenico Sauli, but Pescara's widow, his cousin and protégé del Vasto, and his trusted Neapolitan captain, Giambattista Castaldo, who carried the evidence of the conspiracy to Spain.

In his account of Pescara's first reaction to Morone's proposal, Giovio followed the general's own words to Charles V, "I hesitated for one moment."[88] But whereas Pescara went on to tell his master that his hesitation was whether to arrest Morone there and then or to draw him out, Giovio has him weigh his injuries against the dangers and infamy of treason. A spirit "born for great enterprises," Giovio surmised, was tempted by an opportunity to vindicate itself against ingratitude and to gain a kingdom, "for which," he observed (in a possible allusion to Machiavelli's *Prince*), "some people believe that divine and human laws can be violated."[89] Giovio even explored the theory—although in the end rejecting it—that Pescara had only told the emperor after conceiving the fear that Marguerite of Navarre would reveal the plot as a gesture of goodwill.[90] Giovio also had good reason to believe that Pescara had hesitated long enough to write of Morone's offer to Vittoria Colonna, who told the historian that she had adamantly protested her preference for remaining the wife of an honored captain rather than becoming a queen under such circumstances, no royal rank being so exalted that it was not excelled by "the loftiness of perfect virtue."[91]

Giovio's narration of the conspiracy makes clear his belief that it had been a mistake to mistrust Charles V's intentions and that Pescara had behaved correctly in not breaking faith with his master. On the other hand, his own deepest emotions clearly lay with "the princes of Italy, who bitterly lamented that they had been malignly tricked and deceived by an Italian who had not hesitated to reveal plans entrusted to him in good faith to an emperor who aspired to the *imperium* of all Italy, an Italian who had not scrupled to sow the seeds of a great war in order to acquire, through injuring others, the reputation among foreign nations of an incorrupt and constant loyalty."[92]

Without any doubt Pescara had greatly exacerbated the situation and, according to Giovio, he now joined those ministers of Charles who were urging the emperor to repossess Parma and Piacenza "from our Holy Mother the Church," arguing that the riches of Italy were easily acquired because of the incredible madness of factions.[93] Pescara did not live long enough to enjoy the fruits of his loyalty and the general's baton sent him from Spain. He died the night of December 2–3, 1525, from an illness probably resulting from wounds suffered at Pavia. He had summoned Vittoria Colonna to attend him in his last moments, but she had barely set out before the news of his death reached her.[94] His command was assumed by Antonio de Leyva, and the siege of the citadel of Milan continued.

Meanwhile in Spain the emperor was attempting to decide how to deal with the king of France. Giovio's account of the debate at the imperial court, as given in his biography of Pescara, shows that he was exception-

ally well-informed. Not only did he understand what appear to have been
the positions of Lannoy, Pescara, and others, he was well-apprised of the
arguments of the imperial chancellor, Mercurino da Gattinara. In fact,
Giovio's summary of Gattinara's advice to Charles V to strengthen his
empire by winning the confidence of the Italians seems to have been the
basis for Guicciardini's account of the debates at the imperial court.[95]

To Gattinara, Giovio attributed an emotional appeal for the liberty of
Italy, embodying the fervent belief shared by Castiglione (Clement VII's
nuncio in Spain), by Cardinal Salviati (his legate), as well as by
Schönberg, Cardinal Colonna, and the rest of the imperial party in Italy,
that despite recent events, an honorable settlement was still possible.
Were the emperor to take the "pacific and humane" part of freeing the
people of Italy from their "blind fear" of servitude, a people "born to
liberty," Gattinara urged, he would ride to his coronation in Rome
through jubilant throngs, and "his armies would pass through streets
covered with carpets and flowers, shaded with hangings, and sprinkled
by fountains."[96]

To appreciate the reasonableness of Giovio's continued support of the
imperial party, it is important to understand the strength of the Italian
party at the imperial court and the qualities in Charles V on which its
hopes were based. Subsequent research has confirmed Giovio's understanding of Gattinara's objectives, including the establishment of Francesco Sforza in Milan as the cornerstone of imperial policy for Italy despite Bourbon's claims.[97] His faith in the continued possibility of a just
imperial settlement for Italy was shared by some of the most authoritative and patriotic Italians of his day. Like Giovio, Castiglione was a devotee of the *libertas Italiae*, but he, too, after confronting as a political
realist the "fatal" disunity of the Italian states and the overwhelming
power of Spain, felt that the best choice consisted in conciliation and cooperation between pope and emperor. Castiglione was close to Gattinara
and shared his confidence that ultimately Charles V could be counted
upon to make a just and magnanimous Italian settlement.[98] Giberti, on
the other hand, was convinced of the "malissimo animo" of Caesar.[99]

In the outcome, Castiglione and Giovio were right. Three years after
this debate, with his power even greater than it had been after the victory
of Pavia (although admittedly after the death of Bourbon), Charles V
consented to the pardon and restoration of Sforza to Milan, vindicating
the perspicacity of Castiglione and Giovio in regard to the emperor's
character.[100] Giovio's refusal to write the history of Clement VII's pontificate betrayed the anguish of a patriotic Italian who had correctly interpreted the political realities of his day but who had been forced to suffer
himself and to witness even worse sufferings while a lesson in realities was
meted out to his friends and patrons in blood and iron.

After the death of Pescara, events moved rapidly toward formation of the League of Cognac, the instrument, in Giovio's view, of Italy's undoing. Despairing of the emperor and exasperated by the treatment of Sforza, Clement VII had decided once again to desert a league with Charles V, convinced by Giberti and Lodovico Canossa that "Caesar's greatness was perforce his own servitude."[101] In early February, Guicciardini arrived in Rome to help with the diplomacy. By late February 1526 the terms of the treaty of Madrid were known in Rome, by which Francis I was to be freed in exchange for the ancient territories of Burgundy. In mid-March the king was released, his sons taking his place as hostages, and by the end of the month the papal emissary had arrived at the French court to negotiate a Franco-papal alliance. On May 22 the League of Cognac was formally ratified by the pope, Francis I, Sforza, and the Venetians, and shortly thereafter Guicciardini was appointed lieutenant-general of the papal forces. The army of the league was to be commanded by the former foe of the Medici and now general of the Venetian forces, Francesco Maria della Rovere, duke of Urbino.

Within a few short months of the conclusion of the League of Cognac, all the hopes that inspired it were dashed to pieces. Without the promised aid from France, the duke of Urbino hesitated to relieve Milan, and Sforza was compelled to surrender the castle. While the army of the league maneuvered ineffectually in Lombardy, the forces of the Colonna, allies of the emperor, suddenly marched on Rome and sacked the Vatican. By the end of autumn, not only was the viceroy of Naples advancing on Rome from the south but, unchecked by the army of the league, an unruly imperial army full of angry German troops had crossed the Po and was massing for a southward march.[102] On the last day of 1526, Filippo Strozzi, now a hostage for the pope in the citadel of Naples, warned his friend Francesco Vettori that the bark of St. Peter was sinking. "If you believe that it cannot perish," he said, "I will soon enlighten you to the contrary."[103]

No letter of Giovio's survives from 1526, so his reactions must be deduced from the dialogue he wrote immediately afterward on Ischia, or from the abbreviated account in his biography of Pompeo Colonna. He clearly blamed the pope for assuring the success of the Colonna raid by discharging his troops, trusting in a truce made after the Colonna seized Anagni in August 1526. Just before the seizure, Giovio had had an opportunity of assaying the family's intentions when the pope sent him to their stronghold of Marino to attend the ailing duke of Sessa. Giberti was echoing his own sentiments, Giovio suggested, when he strongly advised the pope against reducing the defenses of Rome.[104]

When the Colonna marched into the city on September 20, the Romans watched as if attending a parade. Thanks to the cruelty and greed of Clement VII's officials, Giovio said, the populace hated the papal government. Nor could the pope long hold out in the castle of St. Angelo, he added, since, owing to the greed of the same officials, it had not been adequately provisioned. It was even rumored that only the truce arranged by the ex-viceroy of Sicily, Don Hugo de Moncada, had prevented Cardinal Colonna—to his great disgust—from removing Clement VII and substituting himself as pope.[105] For Giovio, the Colonna raid was a personal disaster. The "paradiso" was sacked, and his losses were only limited by his having acted on his intuition and hidden his valuables with the sacristans of Santa Maria sopra Minerva.[106]

In the *Pompeii Columnae vita* Giovio's narrative of the war against the Colonna and the events leading to the sack of Rome was telescoped but, at the time, the events and frustrations they engendered seemed interminable—the fluctuations of the pope's fortunes, the vacillations, the reversals, the alternation between fits of aggressiveness and moods of passive despair as now the imperial, now the papal and French expeditionary forces, gained the upper hand. In his desire to revenge himself on the Colonna, Clement VII raised troops and sacked their territories south of Rome. A consistory deprived Pompeo of the cardinalate, but when cited to appear he appealed, like Luther, to a general council of the Church.

In the *Storia d'Italia* Guicciardini broke his normal pattern by introducing 1527 as "a year full of atrocities and events unheard of for many centuries"[107] As it began, the imperial troops were still congregating near Piacenza for a march on Rome. The main hope of the papal forces, the captain Giovanni de' Medici, had been fatally injured in November 1526 while attempting to block Frundsberg from crossing the Po near Mantua. The terrified Florentines were appealing to the pope to come to terms. To the south of Rome, Lannoy had begun a siege of the papal town of Frosinone. Destitute of funds, Clement VII was in the process of accepting the terms of Charles V's latest ambassador, Cesare Fieramosca, who arrived on January 25 bringing what Giovio described as "the most humane" letters from the emperor offering terms for a three-year peace. Hardly had the pope accepted these terms on a provisional basis, however, than the arrival of the Angevin pretender to Naples, René de Vaudemont, with 30,000 ducats revived his spirits, and on the 29th Giberti ordered the papal forces to take the initiative. By February 4 Lannoy was defeated and Frosinone liberated. When Francis I's admiral, Andrea Doria, arrived in Rome on February 7 to command the papal fleet, it was decided to carry the counterattack to Naples itself.

On February 14, 1527, Giovio wrote to a friend in Venice who passed his letter on to Marin Sanudo. "In order not to write envenomed satires about the paradoxical conduct of this miserable war," Giovio began, "I have refrained from boring you with my letters." The only thing that gave him comfort was the comportment of the Italian troops trained by Giovanni delle Bande Nere. "In effect, our troops have improved so much," he boasted, "they will no longer fear another nation." At a review of the victorious troops in Rome, many had wept for joy.

> O what faces! What beards! What helmets! What arquebuses! What expressions! What gait! The captain, Lucantonio Gazizza, was in the dress of Patroclos, with a powder horn of gold and gilt arquebus, and a countenance to make Venus jump out of the bath and Vulcan rush in alarm from his forge.

Despite this martial show, Giovio's realism forbade optimism. Lannoy, he felt, would fight to the very end. There were several impediments to a vigorous allied advance on Naples, and with the young princes still hostages in Spain there was no telling when Francis might come to an agreement with Charles, "leaving the world *in bordello.*" Finally, there were the Landsknechts gathering ominously on the Po. If the defenses of Emilia, the Romagna, and Tuscany were as poor as reported, assaulting Naples had been a grave mistake. "True it is," Giovio concluded, "that the picks of madmen often smash the plans made by the pens of wise courtiers."[108]

Events soon proved Giovio right. Clement VII's unpaid, unprovisioned troops began deserting, the Neapolitan campaign fell apart, and in early March the pope was forced to summon Fieramosca back to Rome to negotiate a truce. Despite a last-minute effort by Giberti to forestall it, the truce took effect on March 15. Clement VII was now so fearful for Florence that nothing could dissuade him from ratifying the treaty, which even Giovio the imperialist would term "the beginning of the greatest misfortunes for Rome and Italy."[109] To renewed pleas the pope would only respond with the words of Pilate, "Quod scripsi scripsi," and he began in good faith to recall and discharge his forces.[110]

Clement VII now pleaded with Lannoy to stop Bourbon, presuming as viceroy he had the authority. But the imperial soldiers were completely out of control. For eight months they had endured every kind of hardship and received no pay, only promises. On hearing that negotiations for a truce were under way they stormed the commander's tent, forcing Bourbon to hide for fear of being murdered then and there. In his fury at the insubordination of his Landsknechts, Frundsberg himself suffered a stroke of apoplexy—a condign punishment, Giovio thought, for his impious boasts that he was going to hang the pope with a gilt noose he often displayed.[111] When Cesare Fieramosca arrived at the camp with the treaty and a mere 30,000 ducats, the anger of the soldiers was so terrifying he fled for his life to Ferrara. "They were like raging lions," he explained to the emperor.[112] A virtual prisoner of the mob of desperate, unpaid soldiery, Bourbon now announced that he was unable to abide by the terms of the truce and began crossing the Apennines.

From Bologna, on the same day on which he learned of Bourbon's intentions, a chastened Guicciardini wrote Giberti that three courses remained open to the pope: to make a new treaty, to fight to the death, or to flee. All had their costs, he warned, but none would avail if it were not chosen immediately and resolutely. "May God illumine you," he prayed.[113] Unfortunately, resolution was the last of the pope's qualities. Trusting to the new peace, he had already recalled his troops from Naples, and in the belief that Lannoy had arranged to ransom Florence from Bourbon's forces he dismissed his remaining Swiss, along with the last of Giovanni de' Medici's Black Bands. This he did, Giovio said, despite the strenuous pleas of everyone. The court was in despair. Totally bewildered, Federico Gonzaga could only conclude that "God's will has so ordered this, that the Church and its leaders may be destroyed."[114] Whether ignorant of or indifferent to the pope's financial plight, Giovio concluded that a single flaw undermined Clement VII's natural prudence and experience in the affairs of the world, his "fatal streak of avarice, which so affected his judgment that he had no fear whatever for things that worried everyone, while placing the greatest confidence in things that no one else, neither leaders nor people, thought worthy of any confidence at all."[115]

Only when Bourbon, by then encamped north of Borgo San Sepolcro, began to escalate his demands for ransom while simultaneously moving his army toward Florence did Clement VII see that he had been tricked by Fieramosca's truce. Luckily for Florence, the Venetians ordered the duke of Urbino to move to its defense. Thwarted in its expectations of a sack of Florence, Bourbon's army set out on a rapid march for Rome. When Clement VII realized the gravity of his situation, he asked to rejoin the League of Cognac and began making frantic preparations for the defense of Rome. In his consternation, Giovio said, the pope could not make up his mind whether to fight or flee—now demanding, now begging aid from the cardinals and Romans, now debating whether to escape on the galleys or to destroy the bridges and take refuge behind the walls of the city, hoping in the latter event either to buy off Bourbon with a huge ransom or to be rescued by his allies.

The defense of Rome was entrusted to Renzo da Ceri, "a captain," Giovio lamented, "calamitous to his country." Having reenrolled whatever soldiers he could find, and having armed the totally unpracticed Roman militia, Ceri proceeded to boast that he could hold the Leonine city and all Rome for two days—long enough, thought the pope, for the duke of Urbino to reach Rome and relieve a siege. Along the summit of the Vatican hill, Ceri erected puny earthwork defenses which, Giovio recalled, were a joke to the enemy, "but which we beheld with grief and tears."[116]

On May 5, having outstripped the army of the league, Bourbon arrived with his famished troops on the heights of Monte Mario. From there he showed them the city of Rome—a vision of wealth surpassing even their avid expectations. He suggested an assault the following morning where the defenses appeared to be weakest; and so, toward dawn on May 6, 1527, they attacked the walls of Rome near the Porta Torrione (now Cavalleggeri) of the Leonine city. The Swiss guard, Giovio wrote, valiantly resisted the first assault. Bourbon himself was hit in the thigh by a ball from an arquebus (a hit later claimed by Benvenuto Cellini), but a thick fog was rising from the marshes, making it impossible for the defenders to train their artillery, and even as the duke lay dying his troops were pouring over the walls. Once inside they tore to pieces the Roman militia gathered inside the Porta Torrione, and all resistance collapsed. Those who fled were nowhere safe, Giovio lamented, not even at the altars respected by Goths and Vandals.

At the moment of crisis, Giovio was with the pope, who had been "vainly wearying an adverse God with his prayers." Only when he heard the clamor in the Vatican palace did he start to flee down the fortified corridor to the Castel Sant'Angelo, "groaning and lamenting his betrayal by everybody." While he fled he could see through the fenestrations "the miserable rout of the Romans, with the spears and halberds of raging barbarians at their backs." As they hurried along, Giovio had been holding up his master's robes to assist his flight. When they came to the open wooden bridge into the castle, he hastily threw his own violet cap and cloak over the pope's head and shoulders, lest he be recognized by his white vestments and shot at by a soldier.[117]

From the ramparts of the castle the view was of universal sack and pillage. No one was spared. Even the ambassadors of kings were treated like the Romans. After their initial fury, Giovio said, the Germans were content with relatively light ransoms, taking what they found, carousing and visiting their Lutheran sensibilities on the churches. The Spaniards, however, "with more astute and implacable cruelty" devised tortures to force their victims to reveal the hiding places of their treasures. The Italians, Giovio lamented, "having learned the vices of their allies, although none of their virtues," equaled them in crimes, with all the more ignominy for showing neither pity nor love for their common *patria*.[118]

To emphasize the ruthlessness of the siege of the castle, Giovio told of an old woman strangled with a halter for trying to take some lettuce to the pope and strung up for the citadel to see, and of boys shot while trying to attach vegetables to ropes to be hauled up by the besieged. From the ramparts, the pope could see the smoke rising from the villa that Raphael had designed for him on Monte Mario and understood that Pompeo Colonna was retaliating for the destruction of the Colonna villas in Latium.[119]

On May 22, not two days as Clement VII had hoped, but two weeks after Bourbon's arrival, the duke of Urbino and the forces of the league reached the outskirts of Rome. From Monte Mario they surveyed the city and decided against any attempt to relieve the castle. "What, indeed," Giovio observed with feeble irony, "could seem more foolish to a practiced and prudent general than to descend to a disadvantageous location and battle an unconquered enemy, one without doubt superior in forces, position, and spirit and emboldened by their recent victory, unfurling his banners and fighting with no hope of victory for the safety and liberty of Italy?"[120] Provisions were scarce and plague was beginning to break out among his soldiers, so without striking a blow the duke retreated to Urbino.

Meanwhile in the castle, where over a thousand people were crowded together, conditions were becoming intolerable. The inadequate store of comestibles was fast running out, and cardinals, Giovio recalled, "were eating the flesh of asses as avidly as if they had been guests at solemn banquets." Negotiations with the army were going badly, as Clement VII had neither the sums demanded as ransom nor the credit to raise them. Declaring to his advisers that he could only be cured by the lance of Achilles, he begged Pompeo Colonna to come to an audience. And so, as the allied army was beginning its withdrawal and the last hope of relief had vanished, the two bitter rivals came face to face.[121]

Giovio had been commissioned to write the biography of Pompeo Colonna by the cardinal's nephew Francesco Colonna, archbishop of Rosano. This, combined with his own personal ties to his subject, placed him in a delicate position, but in the dedication he confronted his problem forthrightly. He told the archbishop that he wished that Pompeo had never become a prelate, but rather a great condottiere in the tradition of the Colonna family, so that his admirable loyalty to the empire need never have compromised the loyalty which as a cardinal he owed to the Church. Despite his sympathies for the imperial party and his exasperation with the pope's inadequacies, Giovio made no effort to conceal the part that Pompeo's fierce and intractable pride had played in provoking the catastrophe. He even pointed out that the Colonna were marching on Rome at about the same time that the Turks were annihilating the Hungarians at Mohács.[122]

Giovio only began the cardinal's rehabilitation when he came to narrate his arrival in Rome. Colonna had reached the city rejoicing in the humiliation of his adversary, Giovio said, but when he "saw it full of corpses and mourning and heard the wailing of women and children, the screams of leading citizens being tortured, both clerical and lay, vainly beseeching help, and the houses in all the quarters full of groaning, he was unable to restrain his tears, and his sorrow was made the more piercing by the reflection that his native city lay ruined, while to the exact contrary of his intentions the pope had escaped safe and unharmed and the calamity and suffering had fallen instead upon the innocent."[123]

When Colonna arrived at the castle, the pope's appreciation of the perils of his position removed any thought of pretense, Giovio related, and he received with unfeigned relief the one person who could now help him.[124] In tears the bitter rivals deplored "the calamities of Rome, the erosion of the dignity of the priesthood, and the universal insanity of the times, in which—far longer than had befitted priests—they had themselves participated, to the ruin of things human and divine." Inevitably, despite Pompeo's help, the terms to which Clement VII was forced to submit were harsh. He was to surrender the fortresses around Rome as well as those of Piacenza, Parma, and Modena. He was to pay 400,000 ducats—100,000 of these at once, 50,000 in twenty days, and the remainder in subsequent installments. Until payment was complete he was to remain a prisoner, along with thirteen cardinals, and he was to furnish seven hostages, including Giberti. The Colonna were to be restored to all their possessions and all censures were to be removed from the imperialists. On June 7 four companies of Spanish and German soldiers took possession of the castle. Charles V was again the victor.[125]

CHAPTER SEVEN

Ischia (1527–1528)

... arce eiectus in Aenariam veni ad Victoriam Columnam.
    —Dialogus de viris et foeminis aetate nostra florentibus

... ejected from Castel Sant'Angelo, I came to Ischia, to Vittoria
Colonna.

WHILE THE HOLOCAUST raged in stricken Rome, Giovio remained with
the pope in Castel Sant'Angelo. Clement VII was a virtual prisoner.
Spanish troops guarded his chamber. His days were spent in desperate
negotiations over his ransom. To help meet the soldiers' exorbitant demands, Benvenuto Cellini was set to melting down gold and silver artifacts in an improvised furnace on the ramparts. Provisions were short and
conditions grim. As the implacable heat of summer came on, plague
broke out, and the stench of rotting corpses made it impossible to remain
on the battlements when the wind blew from the city.[1] To combat de-
pression and while away the anxious hours, Giovio composed his little
treatise, *De optima victus ratione* (On the best regimen of diet), a somewhat optimistic undertaking when the flesh of asses was passing for a
great delicacy. Implying in the preamble that he had not yet been able to
attain "the fruit of Christian constancy," he said that had found Cicero's
Tusculan Disputations "an overflowing help" in liberating himself "from
fear and anguish." He did not elaborate, but Cicero's eclectic stoicism
seems to have spoken to his distress.[2]

On July 6, 1527, came the reward for a decade of service when Clement VII conferred on Giovio the bishopric of Nocera dei Pagani near
Salerno, just vacated by the death of Cardinal Jacobacci.[3] Not long after
his promotion, Giovio was forced to leave the pope's side, as the soldiers
demanded more reductions in the number of retainers to avert the
spread of plague within the fortress. He departed with mixed emotions,
he recalled, his pleasure in being free diminished by the continued suffering of his master and colleagues.[4] He first took refuge in the house of his
banker, Francesco Formento, near the church of Santa Lucia, but although he seems to have enjoyed the protection of the master of the
imperial camp, Juan de Urbina (who was perhaps hoping to atone for the
sack of Como), Giovio decided to join Vittoria Colonna and the small
company seeking refuge from war and plague on the island of Ischia,

preferring "the uncertainties of Neptune and the risk of tertian fever," he told Giberti, to "dying here to no purpose." At Ischia he felt he would be able to write "quietly" and "freely" of "this singular catastrophe of Rome." A safe-conduct requiring papal officials to provide him escort if necessary was issued on July 17.[5]

Vittoria Colonna had retired to Ischia late in 1526 to wait out the hostilities between the Colonna and the pope. Having experienced the shipwreck of the times, Giovio said, she took pleasure in aiding others, especially men of letters, and received him "with such charity and liberality that the rest of her household thought I was not merely a friend or client but a longed-for relative." In the 1520s she had developed a close rapport with the pope's counselors, particularly Giberti, and Giovio's description of her management of the Colonna household suggests that he had already been her guest in Marino or in Rome.[6]

The castle of Ischia belonged to Vittoria's husband's family, the d'Avalos. For splendor of situation it had few rivals. Giovio admired its sweeping view of the bay of Naples framed by nearby Procida and distant Vesuvius.[7] The castle had been a retreat for the Aragonese kings of Naples and often guarded their prisoners and treasure. Even now it held some of the pope's ransom, stowed by the marquis del Vasto, and in its dungeons had recently died the vanquished doge of Genoa, Ottaviano Fregoso, a prisoner of the marquis of Pescara.[8]

Vittoria Colonna was still in deep mourning for her husband. Her marriage had not been particularly happy, but despite Pescara's long absences and many infidelities she had devoted herself to celebrating his deeds during his lifetime and now sought to perpetuate his glory after death. The daughter and granddaughter of soldiers, she had seemingly accepted the customs as well as the demands of the profession. Dressed in widow's weeds, she kept largely to her own apartments, avoiding festivities in order to pursue an ascetic regime of prayer, self-discipline, and religious study. Her extended mourning notwithstanding, she was a solicitous hostess, Giovio said, and the center of the literary salon.[9]

Giovio found himself among remarkable women. The castle's *châtelaine*, Costanza d'Avalos, duchess of Francavilla, had been Vittoria's guardian during her adolescence. In 1503, when Vittoria was just thirteen, the duchess had displayed her fortitude by defending Ischia against a French fleet while Iñigo d'Avalos, her brother, was on the mainland with the Spanish army, an act of valor for which Ferdinand the Catholic made her *châtelaine* in her own right after Iñigo's death later that year. At Ischia she raised Iñigo's orphaned children, Costanza and Alfonso, the future marquis del Vasto, as well as their elder cousin and Vittoria's fiancé, Francisco Fernando, marquis of Pescara. Fluent in Latin and a poet of some merit in Italian, the duchess saw to it that all her wards were educated in letters as well as in the arms traditional with males of the family.[10]

When war first threatened the southern mainland, Costanza the younger, now duchess of Amalfi, had sought the safety of the island, as had the two princesses of the house of Aragon, Maria and Joanna. Maria was married to the marquis del Vasto, Joanna to Vittoria's brother, Ascanio Colonna, constable of Naples and commander of the imperial cavalry. Raphael immortalized Joanna's beauty in a famous portrait now in the Louvre; Giovio celebrated her gift for music, her intriguing mixture of gravity and grace, and the charms that consigned the beholder to "perpetual torment," especially when she was "carelessly dressed, forearms bare, hair loose," and nature triumphant over art.[11] With Maria and her husband Giovio was to form a deep and lasting friendship, but for the moment he was enchanted by her "small black eyes," her "rosy cheeks," and "lively countenance."[12]

Still other refugees arrived during the winter of 1527–28, including the young and beautiful princess of Salerno, Isabella Villamarina, a brilliant pupil of Pomponio Gaurico, and the renowned Lucrezia Scaglione, whose vivacity and charm had so captivated the viceroy Lannoy. While tending her during a bout of quartan fever, Giovio heard the story of one luckless admirer who, transported by desire, had been attempting to lower himself to her chamber by a rope when he slipped to his death from the parapets of her villa, thus furnishing "noble material" to the poets of Naples. Giovio found her well-formed and graceful, with "a luminous countenance" and a winning personality.[13]

Throughout Giovio's stay the marquis del Vasto returned frequently to the castle. Having served his apprenticeship under his formidable elder cousin and risen to be commander of the Spanish infantry, he was now advanced to the command of the entire imperial infantry. After the sack he had played a significant part in the negotiations between the pope and the army, not the least of which was convincing Clement VII to restrain from further enraging his captors by excommunicating them.[14] In the autumn of 1527, when the French army sent to recover Milan was ordered to march on Naples instead, he was alternating between Rome and Naples, attempting to persuade the soldiers to leave Rome and struggling to organize the defense of the Regno. In 1527 he was just twenty-six years old, already an accomplished soldier and commander, well-educated, something of a poet, handsome, and energetic.[15]

A frequent guest at the citadel was the Neapolitan lawyer and agent of Charles V, Giovanni Antonio Muscettola, a member of the viceroy's council who was closely involved in all del Vasto's negotiations.[16] For several years he had been a good friend of Vittoria's and had evidently known Giovio in Rome before the sack.[17] Although versed in humanistic studies and a member of the circle of Pomponio Gaurico, Muscettola was a forceful and eloquent champion of the new vernacular literature. Another wartime refugee to the island, whom Giovio introduced to Vittoria Colonna's salon, was the young Latin poet Antonio Sebastiani of Traetto, called "il Minturno" from the Roman name of his city.[18]

On Ischia and at Naples, Giovio encountered a number of the members of the old Pontanian academy. Pietro Gravina he already knew from Rome, but now he met Jacopo Sannazaro, with whom he had long conversations on history and literature. The academy's critiques of society following the invasion of Charles VIII and its debates as to whether rational control of human destiny was possible—questions embodied in Pontano's dialogues *De prudentia* and *De Fortuna*—were influential on Giovio's own searching discussions of Italian politics and society after the sack.[19]

At Vittoria's urging, Giovio distilled his conversations into a *Dialogue Concerning Men and Women Flourishing in Our Times*, ostensibly as a diversion for Giberti, who was one of the hostages seized by the soldiers toward the end of September 1527 and marched off in chains when they became impatient at continued delays in paying the pope's ransom.[20] The dialogue's setting is thus Ischia between the end of September and the dramatic escape of the hostages engineered by Cardinal Colonna on the night of November 29–30, 1527.[21]

The dialogue is a key to Giovio's state of mind and a mirror of a cataclysmic moment in the crisis of the sixteenth century. The sack of Rome seemed to embody all the discontinuities that had been developing with disorienting rapidity not only in the political configuration of Italy and the Mediterranean world, but in warfare, social values, religion, and even in humanistic studies and the arts. Especially for Roman humanists, it seemed to signal the end of an era.[22] How to reorient one's life, how to hold to cherished traditions and pursuits in the wake of universal upheaval, how to find the continuity necessary for mental equilibrium—these suddenly became overriding demands for Giovio and his friends, shaping the dialogue as they had shaped the conversations that engendered it and the lives it reflected. So perfectly, in fact, did the dialogue embody its moment in time that when occasions of publication presented themselves in 1530 and again in 1535, Giovio began revisions only to conclude that it could not be made to fit changed political circumstances.[23]

The *Dialogus de viris ac foeminis aetata nostra florentibus* differs significantly from the models of humanist dialogue developed in the Quattrocento. Historical more than rhetorical in nature, it aims to record the achievements of the early Cinquecento, its genesis evidently being debate as to whether the leaders of the present could compare with their predecessors of the Quattrocento. The defense of the present in confrontation with an idealized past is also a theme of *Il cortegiano*, especially in the preface to book two, but whereas Castiglione adhered to the rhetorical format in developing an ideal type through argument, Giovio offers a more conversational survey of outstanding captains, writers, and noblewomen of the day. Although ideal types emerge, they are a by-product of the discussion of actual individuals. Giovio's rhetorical strategy lies rather in energizing his presentation by means of tensions between the interlocutors—all friends, but each representing a diverse social type and viewpoint—as the discussion of notable individuals provokes argument on the changes remaking politics, society, and literature. While the Quattrocento dialogue usually involved a considerable degree of fiction, Giovio's seems to be closely based on actual conversations and personalities.[24]

Del Vasto is very much the soldier. While asking intelligent questions about literature, he generally leaves judgments to the others. His experience and authority as a commander would make the reader forget his youth, were it not for his complete detachment from Quattrocento warfare, which he knows only through history and tradition. Muscettola, who is Giovio's age, is very much the lawyer, constantly introducing considerations of law, equity, and due procedure. As a literary amateur and member of a learned profession, Muscettola advances his critical judgments with much greater confidence than del Vasto, particularly with regard to vernacular literature. Giovio is the principal resource for the conversations, speaking with authority on matters of history, tradition, and Latin literature. On the great issues of the times, however, he claims no particular wisdom, although his passionate involvement often forces the issue conversationally. As del Vasto attempts to understand the present through its warfare and Muscettola through its diplomacy, Giovio turns to history, ancient and modern, in an attempt to find patterns of meaning which will illumine current perplexities.

In deference, perhaps, to Sannazaro's *Arcadia*, the dialogue's mise-enscène contrasts the natural beauty and serenity of the island with the dark shadow cast upon it by the turmoil of the world beyond. A hunt for waterfowl, organized by del Vasto to distract the ladies from worry, is in progress around the island's small lake when a galley is sighted, which lands on the beach nearby.[25] It turns out to be bringing Senator Muscettola, coming on behalf of the viceroy to induce the marquis to return as soon as possible to the mainland. Del Vasto is reluctant to heed the call, and the two men walk for some time in the fields about the lake in tense discussion. Uneasy about leaving the women when a Venetian fleet has entered the Gulf of Pozzuoli, del Vasto is also doubtful if the army is

ready to submit to leadership. Having been passed over for the supreme
command in favor of his slightly younger contemporary, the prince of
Orange, he is unenthusiastic about pulling someone else's chestnuts out
of the fire.[26] Unable to agree, the two men call Giovio to join them for
a respite in their contentions. Muscettola warmly congratulates Giovio
on his escape from Rome, to which Giovio responds that he might better
congratulate him on the salvation of his *Histories* and tells the story of the
loss and recovery of the manuscripts.[27]

The stage is thus set for a discussion of the tragedy of the sack, its
causes, and the broader question of the servitude of Italy. Giovio's treatment of these great issues is impassioned, rich in complexity, fearless in
candor, and startling in acuity. In the dedication he warns Giberti that
the dialogue will display "that same trust and freedom of speech we used
among ourselves—Muscettola, d'Avalos, and I—as we sat at leisure in
familar conversation in a pleasant bower among the myrtles near the
lake."[28] Again and again the searing question recurs: Why did Italy lose
its independence and what can be done? To read Giovio's pages is to
comprehend the depth and strength of Italian identity among sixteenth-
century intellectuals.[29]

Although he allows d'Avalos to speak convincingly of his horror on
beholding the scenes of slaughter and torment that greeted him in Rome,
Giovio cannot wholly acquit him of complicity in the sack, despite his
deliberate absence, and on several occasions turns to him with a sharp
rebuke. Muscettola, too, was involved in the aftermath, pressing the pope
for hostages and ransom and driving him to tears of humiliation and despair.[30] Imperial partisan though he was and disgusted as he may have
been with Clement VII's misguided course, Giovio cannot suppress his
fury at the sack of Rome, "the sacrosanct home of all nations." Charles V
and his ministers have reduced themselves to Goths and Vandals. Even
the Turks respected the altars of Jerusalem, Rhodes, and Buda, Muscettola is made to confess, whereas at Rome, "we see not only everything
sacred stripped and profaned, but in St. Peter's, the most venerable tem-
ple in Christendom, the high altar flowing with blood and heaped with
the bodies of those who vainly sought refuge with the Deity."[31]

Giovio uses del Vasto's suggestion that the stars may be responsible
for Italy's collapse as an occasion for advertising his recent renunciation
of astrology. Just when he might have been most tempted to resort to the
traditional explanations of astrology or Fortune, Giovio shows the greatest independence from them. The stars, he holds, may influence events
but cannot determine them.[32] Muscettola's broaching the popular notion that the sack may have been God's punishment for Italy's moral
degeneracy allows Giovio to expound his own views.[33] Not surprisingly,
these reflect his studies in classical moral philosophy, his many conversa-

tions on politics in Florence, Venice, Rome, and Naples, and the humanist historian's predisposition to seek human causes for historical outcomes. Our natural instincts are sociable and docile, he explains, but
good customs require good laws and good examples. If princes are corrupt, the populace will soon degenerate. Corruption has caused the disasters of Italy—not God, Fortune, or the stars. The insane ambition of
our princes first called the foreigner into Italy, unleashing the war and
turmoil that have brutalized the innate Italian humanity and destroyed
the honorable customs of the Quattrocento. Immersed in banquets and
wine we have lost the old values, the modesty of our women and even,
through neglect of letters, the intellects of our children. Now in our
blindness we curse Fortune and scrutinize the stars.[34] Giovio's adapta-
tion of Aristotelian and Platonic political and ethical theory to understanding Italy's problems somewhat resembles corresponding passages
of Castiglione's *Courtier*, which Vittoria Colonna possessed in manuscript. Indeed, at times it seems as if the shade of Ottaviano Fregoso has
risen from the dungeons of the castle to channel through Giovio the
views he has presented in book four of *Il cortegiano*.[35]

Giovio's analysis of Italy's decline also reflects some of the characteristic ideas of Machiavelli. It even begins with the metaphor of a flood as
found in chapter twenty-five of *The Prince*, although after Luca Gaurico's
1524 prophecy, flood and destruction were probably in the back of everyone's mind. But as floods in nature are followed by renewed fertility,
so Giovio hopes that the flood of invasion may ultimately have a reinvig-
orating effect on the institutions and society of Italy.[36] While endorsing
the commonplace humanist view that the barbarian invasions destroyed
the arts, letters, and sciences until their revival in the Trecento, Giovio
adds a Machiavellian twist by coupling the revival with Giangaleazzo Visconti's renewal of the military arts, ending Italy's subservience to foreign
mercenaries.[37] Still more recognizably Machiavellian is d'Avalos' assertion that martial *virtù* is but the reflection of civic *virtù* and that military
discipline is perfected under either good kings or free republics. He argues that a good general requires the support of a good government, and
that it is Italy's princes who have stripped the Italian soldier of his ancient
glory by their malign or reckless policies and by their neglect of military
discipline.[38]

Giovio's culprits for the invasion of Charles VIII—the commence-
ment of Italy's miseries—begin with Ludovico il Moro, followed by
Alfonso II of Naples, the Venetian senate, and Pope Alexander VI. Evidently he had not been persuaded by his conversations with the Venetians in 1522–23 and continued, like many Italians, Machiavelli included, to blame them for "immoderate ambition." His condemnation
of Alexander VI, who in the end opposed the French invasion, suggests

that Giovio may have become familiar with the pope's part in the League of San Marco of April 22, 1493, although it is not mentioned in book 1 of the *Histories*. Giovio expresses his satisfaction in the eventual punishment of each of the responsible parties—Sforza dying under strict confinement in France, Alfonso II driven from his kingdom to die in exile, the Venetians totally humiliated at Agnadello, and Alexander VI stricken by his own poison.[39]

Machiavellian echoes resonate as the interlocutors compare the military practices of the Quattrocento and Cinquecento. Although the Quattrocento has been lauded for its flourishing culture, stable politics, and humane warfare, when it comes to comparing the captains of the present day with their fifteenth-century predecessors, Giovio and d'Avalos deride Quattrocento warfare. Their exaggerations about bloodless battles and wars less strenuous than tournaments seem almost to derive from Machiavelli's *Florentine Histories*. Especially in comparing generals of the two eras, Giovio and del Vasto vigorously champion present commanders, who have to cope with far deadlier combat in far more difficult circumstances.[40]

Another Machiavellian echo is Giovio's disparagement of mercenaries, whose disadvantages are all detailed, including lack of a sense of responsibility to their employers. Del Vasto, however, makes an important distinction—seemingly a counterargument to Machiavelli's—between cadres of trained and disciplined professional soldiers and the undisciplined, thieving, murdering rabble that now afflicts the Italian peninsula. A continuously maintained and adequately paid professional army has no reason not to be loyal, he argues, and Giovio agrees that the custom of raising troops at need and then discharging them to save money—the habit of popes—has forestalled the development of a well-trained, loyal, and formidable Italian soldiery.[41] A recurrent theme in Giovio's works is the destruction and misery spread in Italy by the license of soldiers, just now so frightfully demonstrated in the sack. D'Avalos himself concedes that Milan is being destroyed by the exactions of the troops posted there for defense against the French.[42]

Entirely Machiavellian, finally, is the urgency to find a solution to the present predicament. Can Italy be saved? Can liberty be regained? Hatred of servitude and frustration with Italy's paralysis pervade the entire dialogue, yet no obvious solution emerges. Instead, the problem baffles every attempt at resolution, owing to the conflict on so many levels between patriotism and the *particolare*. At times Giovio's longing for the *libertas Italiae* is no more than a resigned hope. At other times, like Machiavelli, he dreams of a military savior, a hero of extraordinary spirit and immense resources who can persuade the Italians to unite behind him. Yet even enumerating the necessary qualities induces a sense of hopelessness. Giovio thinks of his friend Count Sinibaldo Fieschi of Genoa—able, resourceful, enormously wealthy—who refuses to stir, protesting that whatever he did would eventually redound to the advantage of some foreign king and the further misery of Italy. Giovio's pessimism contrasts revealingly with the optimism of Quattrocento moralists regarding the opportunities wealth afforded for leadership and public service.[43]

Despair turns to exasperation with the ineffectual leaders of the present, most notably with the pope. Giovio's pent-up frustration surfaces when del Vasto asks how a man as experienced and prudent as Clement VII could have been moved to trust men he had never before trusted and to have employed servants (viz. the duke of Urbino) who had been enemies of his house. Giovio's only recourse is to fall back on explanations he has already rejected—Fortune and Fate, a transparent evasion of blaming his master for failed leadership.[44] Ostensibly, he places the blame on the avarice, pusillanimity, and greed of the pope's advisers, the public posture taken by Charles V, yet among Clement VII's many virtues—his intelligence, subtlety, prudence, dignity, piety, and fortitude—the interlocutors find one missing, the virtue "by which pope Leo ascended to the heavens." Giovio clearly means magnanimity—a mind equal to great enterprises—the same quality Cesare Gonzaga demands of a great prince in *The Courtier* (4.36). For Giovio magnanimity is not the self-imposed patience of Clement VII but the vigorous resolution of Andrea Gritti, who had impressed him so deeply in 1522 as one who by despising fortune and suffering with equanimity every disaster, even chains and prison, in the end saw the greatness of Venice restored and himself elected doge.[45]

Discussion of the duke of Urbino raises fundamental questions about the war of the League of Cognac. Despite objections by Giovio, d'Avalos tenaciously defends della Rovere's conduct. It would have been folly, he argues, expounding the classic military theory of the Quattrocento, for the duke to have thrown his less well-trained troops against the battle-hardened and now desperate Spanish and German regulars of Bourbon and Frundsberg, either in Emilia or in Latium. In one battle the last remaining military power of Italy would have been annihilated and the whole peninsula would have been prostrate at Caesar's feet. Rather than blaming the duke, del Vasto suggests exploring the delicate question of whether, given the paucity of resources available to the league, the war ought to have been commenced at all.[46]

D'Avalos' eventual rejoinder to Fieschi's despair is to declare that his own motive for serving the emperor has been his expectation that the coming victory of Caesar will secure for Italy a lasting peace. In the religion, temperance, equity, and justice of Charles V—successor to the Augusti of old—del Vasto sees the best and most realistic chance for peace and prosperity, if not the ancient liberty of which all dream. Once Caesar comes to Italy and hears for himself the groans of its people, del Vasto is certain he will take the necessary measures. For Giovio, of course, the hegemony of Charles V had all along been the preferable alternative to French rule. Although as a curial humanist he probably considered the Church, not the emperor, the true successor of the Caesars, he nonetheless accepted the Holy Roman Emperor in his historic role as suzerain of northern Italy.[47] He again endorses the imperial settlement, although, in his present mood, without enthusiasm.

Muscettola's advice for Italians is henceforth to live like discreet servants, unbroken in spirit but prudently dissimulating, serving with cheerful faces while patiently awaiting the day of freedom. Giovio agrees that stoic discipline is necessary to endure the irresistible floods of the times, but he suggests that Italians at least decline to row with too versatile an oar. How much can we stand? he wonders. Will the day ever come when we can rebuild our states, our thoughts, our plans, our hopes themselves? Clearly everything depends on the moderation (*clementia*) and justice of Caesar. Our best hope is that these will soon be exhibited.[48] Significantly, del Vasto has already expressed the conviction that, despite all opposition, the natural magnanimity of Charles V will restore Milan to Sforza, the cardinal point of Giovio's vision of the reconstructed Italian state system.[49]

All these themes have been woven into a discussion of eminent contemporary commanders. The remainder of the first day is given over to delineating the qualities of the ideal general, a challenge posed in book seven of Machiavelli's *Art of War*. Giovio's search for the model general forms a modest analogue to Castiglione's quest for the model courtier, so pleasing to Vittoria Colonna. Not, perhaps, surprisingly, but not altogether unmeritedly, the paragon of generals turns out to have been Vittoria's husband, and the discussion concludes with a eulogy of the marquis of Pescara as a commander and Giovio's promise to write his biography. As dusk approaches the friends gather the rest of the party and return to the castle to present the day's bag to Vittoria Colonna.

Since the beginning and end of the second day are missing from the manuscript, the setting is not apparent. The text begins as Giovio is describing the tearful reconciliation of Cardinal Colonna with Clement VII—a touch Vittoria would have appreciated—and the cardinal's subsequent efforts to rehabilitate the pope. The day's theme is a comprehensive survey of contemporary authors in both Latin and Italian. Coming just on the eve of the eclipse of Latin by the vernacular, it is a unique document for the literary history of Italy in the Cinquecento. Giovio was an astute, if not a profound, critic and abreast of the chief controversies of the day, including the polemic between Latin and the vernacular; the debates on imitation as a means of developing talent; and the arguments regarding the respective roles of talent and training, "nature" and "art," in the formation of writers and poets. In Florence and Rome he had come to know the best of the new vernacular literature.[50] While Ciceronian in form, recalling the evaluation of orators in the *Brutus*, the dialogue seems to owe even more to Quintilian, particularly the survey of authors in book ten and the precepts for the acquisition of stylistic facility through imitation.[51] A more recent prototype would have been Paolo Cortesi's dialogue *De hominibus doctis* (composed ca. 1490), a review of Latin authors of the Quattrocento which circulated in Rome in manuscript, but Giovio's survey avoids Cortesi's polemics. An oblique reference may indicate that Giovio had seen an early manuscript of Lilio Gregorio Giraldi's dialogue, *De poetis nostrorum temporum*, begun in 1514. Obviously he knew the Latin poem dedicated to him by Francesco Arsilli, *De poetis urbanis*, a commentary on the best of the contemporary Roman poets.[52]

Not surprisingly, Giovio casts himself as a staunch partisan of Latin, although not inflexible, while Muscettola is made into a resourceful defender of the vernacular.[53] In its revised form the dialogue undoubtedly reflects the linguistic "summit" at Bologna during the coronation of Charles V. Giovio readily concedes the coming triumph of Italian and has Muscettola liken Dante, Petrarch, and Boccaccio, the founders of Tuscan literature, to Ennius, Cato, and Varro, who prepared Latin to be a literary language. He agrees that for most writers the mother language with its immediacy and spontaneity will be preferable to a language that can only be acquired with perseverance and sacrifice.

Moreover, having been enriched and regularized, Muscettola argues, Italian is now capable of many, although not all, of the effects of Latin, and Giovio is forced to acknowledge that Latinists from Pontano to Bembo have been increasingly tempted by it. Muscettola supports him, however, in cautioning that none of these eminent bilingual poets believed that any and every effect could be "impudently" borrowed from Latin.[54] Like his friends Trissino, Valeriano, Equicola, and Castiglione, Giovio favored the common Italian of the courts rather than the "pure" Tuscan advocated by Bembo. The interlocutors of the dialogue seem to agree that the vernacular is preferable for love poetry, but Giovio can scarcely share Muscettola's belief that with further polishing Italian may come to be regarded as a nobler language than Latin, and he never misses the opportunity to link its origins to the conquest of Rome by barbarians.[55]

Nonetheless, Giovio's defense of Latin is heavy with pessimism. Latin may already be in decline, he acknowledges, since no contemporary can excel Ermolao Barbaro, Merula, or Politian.[56] Oratory is clearly in decline. Rewards are no longer given for humanistic funeral orations, as executors now prefer the less expensive friars.[57] Law courts are even beginning to use the vernacular. The great Roman plays are no longer performed at festivals, and histories—Giovio confesses with a sigh—are being translated into Italian to render them accessible "to the uneducated." The pessimism inherent in the Roman academy's doctrine of imitation surfaces in Giovio's acknowledgment that even after expending the enormous amount of time and energy necessary to acquire an Augustan Latin style, one still cannot hope to equal, let alone exceed, the great writers for whom Latin was a native language.[58] Unlike Vasari, Giovio never speaks of surpassing the ancients but rather of the hopelessness of doing so.[59] What, then, justifies the effort to maintain Latin? Giovio's answer comes late in the day.

Although Giovio toes the line for Bembo and the Roman academy, stressing the "purer eloquence which has resulted from a subtler imitation of the ancients," the moderate nature of his Ciceronianism appears in his respect for Politian, Barbaro, Merula, and other greats of the previous century who wrote—and defended—a more eclectic Latin. In fact, in actual practice, Giovio himself never came completely into the Ciceronian camp.[60] The pinnacle of achievement, he maintains, echoing the profounder aspects of Bembo's position, is a style that is fully classical, yet individualized by that natural force of the writer which alone can impart vigor and organic unity.[61] The transcendence of natural talent in Giovio's view appears in his admiration for Machiavelli, whom he considers a demonstration of the triumph of natural gifts over the lack of formal training.[62]

Discussion of talent leads, *mirabile dictu*, to the author of the dialogue. Although he allows himself to be larded with compliments for his productivity, his memory, and his feats of Latinization, Giovio modestly attributes his own success to hard work.[63] He denies having a secret memory aid, contending that memory schemes such as Cicero's are suitable only to oratory. With Plato as his authority that the use of notes weakens memory, he claims merely to have strengthened by practice "a certain natural vigor" of memory inherited from his father.[64] Thanks to his access to captains and generals, Giovio predicts that his *Histories* will be imperishable, even if lacking in eloquence, since future ages will want facts rather than style.[65] Giovio's work ethic was strong and he felt that his productivity had earned him the right to full-time support.[66] Had the pope been swifter in rewarding, he says, several books would already have been published. But now he has been recalled to the writing of history by the "benign liberality" of Vittoria Colonna and by his own desire of relating to posterity "the criminal magnitude" of the sack of Rome.[67]

The diminution of patronage owing to the Italian wars has been a continuous note in the discussion, and Giovio's dismay is heightened by the threat from the northern countries to Italy's one remaining hegemony—Latin. Too cosmopolitan to close his eyes to the merits of northern humanism, Giovio still hopes in the midst of Italy's political ruin to perpetuate her supremacy in Latin literature—the last relic of Rome's ancient sovereignty.[68] His cult of Latin is rooted in his Italian patriotism. He is beginning to comply with Muscettola's request to know more about the talents of foreign Latinists, however, when the manuscript of the second day breaks off.

As the third part of the dialogue opens, the three friends have embarked by boat one afternoon to explore "the queen's rocks," a rocky point and adjacent islets where the Aragonese queens of Naples and their ladies-in-waiting created a series of small gardens connected by wooden *ponticelli* (bridgelets). Rumination on a vanished way of life raises the question of whether such women will ever be seen again. Giovio vigorously demurs. The ladies gathered in the castle are proof, he says, that the women of today not only equal but surpass their counterparts of the past.

Giovio's assertion is the keynote for comparing the excellences of the women of the different regions of Italy, their physical and mental endowments, charms, proclivities, manners, and pastimes. It clearly draws upon some of Giovio's fondest memories, with glimpses into privileged worlds of elegance, beauty, and refinement. But on a deeper level the discussion, suspended as it is between past and future, betrays a remarkable desire to transcend stereotypes to reach a new concept of the sexes, their roles and relationships.[69]

Giovio's precedents are evident. There are numerous echoes of Giuliano de' Medici's adumbration of the female courtier in book three of Castiglione, including his defense of the equality of women, although with the exclusively male company of Giovio's dialogue the descriptions of women are more overtly sensuous.[70] Giovio pays yet another compliment to Vittoria Colonna by orienting the conversation along the lines of the treatise, "In Defense of Women," which her cousin, Cardinal Pompeo, had recently dedicated to her. The cardinal's *Apologia mulierum* was a vigorous denial of the purported inferiority of women, beginning with Aristotle, continuing with numerous *exempla*, ancient and modern, and concluding with a lavish encomium of Vittoria herself as the embodiment of all virtues, masculine and feminine.[71] Giovio follows suit, commencing his preamble with Aristotle, although in a historical rather than a biological context, asserting the capabilities of women and citing Socrates in *The Republic*, whose belief in feminine equality, he argues, is vindicated by some barbarian nations today, particularly the Persians. Several Persian women fell fighting against the Turks at Chaldiran, he claims, and were buried with honor by Selim.

Muscettola is quick to agree. It was indeed illiberal of the Greeks and Romans, he declares, to shut women up in the home with the drudgery of raising children, denying them participation in public affairs. With the training of the lawyer, he expounds the shameful legal handicaps of women in Roman law, dwelling on the ease with which a Roman could put aside his wife or even, as Cato the Younger, lend her to a friend. The sex that seems so soft and foolish, he proposes, is equally capable of the virtues we call virile and is lacking not in nature but in opportunity; the loss is ours if men force women to serve in a lowly condition.

Muscettola argues that the differences between men and women are owing not to nature but to custom. It cannot be, he says, that women are incapable of the behaviors we call masculine. We are conceived in their wombs, nourished by their milk. We share the same affections of the mind and senses, the same vulnerability to illness, the same love of life, the same span of years, the same nerves, fiber, mind, and soul. Of necessity women must be capable of everything that pertains to reason. They should be trained from infancy not in working fabrics and in needlepoint but in the expectation of earning distinction in all the arts and virtues. Our ancestors did not, nor do we, nor will our descendants lack women of prudent and virile disposition, of acute and perspicacious spirit, capable of discharging arduous responsibilities in all theaters of action. As Giuliano and Pompeo, Muscettola recites examples of resolute women who led great armies to memorable victories, founded temples and cities, wrote great poetry, or ruled peoples. Right at hand he points to Vittoria Colonna, esteemed not only for her achievements in literature but respected for her highly successful governance of seditious Benevento following her husband's death.[72]

At this point, d'Avalos the soldier brings the discussion back to reality, declaring that in the tumult of the present we will be fortunate if we can preserve laws and customs, let alone reform them. The wars of Italy, Giovio thus intimates, have been a barrier to social progress. Three qualities, according to d'Avalos, render a woman of good disposition praiseworthy: distinction of family, beauty of form, and manners equal to all occasions. Literary studies make her admirable and equal to men, and chastity makes her divine. With del Vasto's traditional aristocratic standards as a guide, the dialogue now unfolds in more predictable directions, dwelling on the physical attributes of women in winsome detail. Although Muscettola and Giovio continue to stress intellectual culture and, indeed, imply a serious incompleteness when it is lacking, there is no further attempt to confront the issue of equality. Even the blatant inequality inherent in del Vasto's repeated insistence on feminine (as opposed to masculine) chastity remains unexplored, presumably out of deference to Vittoria's own exaltation of feminine chastity.[73]

Giovio uses d'Avalos' disquisition on the present decline in chastity as an opportunity to deprecate the occupation of Milan and its effect on Lombard morals, drawing a brutal picture of foreign occupation—the city surging with violent, impulsive soldiery, and captains not above using their troops to force their suits on reluctant wives or to punish uncooperative husbands. With the occupation have come laxity and luxury: sumptuous clothing, lavish banquets, and costly wines.[74] A kiss may be nothing among the French, del Vasto contends, but one kiss and Italians think a woman is half-corrupted. Worst of all, taxes and the depredations of the soldiery are clearly ruining the city's wealth. Giovio blurts out that he can scarcely restrain his tears when he thinks of Como being ruined by the continual robberies of del Vasto's guards. Yet again, the times have intruded, and the three must agree anew to limit themselves to pleasant topics.

After praise for all the ladies of the castle, the dialogue culminates in tribute to Vittoria Colonna. Its themes have reflected her interests in the heroic ideal, in vernacular poetry, and in the role of women in society. The sympathy repeatedly expressed for the plight of the women of Italy, deprived of husbands, relatives, and homes by the struggle for the mastery of Italy, has spoken directly to her widowhood. As the first day has ended with an extended tribute to her husband, the third day now concludes with a protracted paean to Vittoria herself—six quarto pages of it. From her radiant black eyes and ivory skin to her graceful figure and aristocratic bearing, from her undulating breasts—swelling and subsiding with her breathing like a pair of nesting doves—to the adornments of her mind and the loftiness of her morals, she is the embodiment of every human perfection. She vanquishes all other women as Rome conquered the world. Compared to her, as Giberti is wont to say, other women are like mosaics, admirable only at a distance. She has no flaw. A goddess in similitude, she warms to human friendship. Her aristocratic dignity is without stiffness or haughtiness. Her chastity is without prudishness, her religion without severity, her wit without malice. She combines the masculine virtues of magnificence (*splendor*), fortitude, and justice with the feminine virtues of modesty, chastity, and charity. She is a philosopher among philosophers, a poet among poets. Like the fires lit for festivals on the tops of the pyramids, her letters illumine all her other virtues.[75]

A century ago Carlo Volpati drew a heavily shaded contrast between Giovio, the epicurean, servile courtier, and Vittoria Colonna, the loftily idealistic, profoundly religious aristocrat, but the truth is more complex.[76] The Vittoria Colonna of 1527–28 was not yet the disciple of Ochino, Pole, and other religious reformers. Although loosened from her worldly moorings by the death of her husband, she was still drawn to the cosmopolitan culture of Castiglione, much as Giberti himself at this time combined refined conoisseurship with spiritual fervor.[77] Although Giovio observed that she was already debilitating her joints with kneeling and her body with discipline, Vittoria's overriding preoccupation in these years was to secure immortal glory for her bellicose husband, and who better to aid her than the bishop-elect of Nocera?[78] Who, indeed, had a comparable command of both history and the Latin style requisite for true immortality? It is no wonder that Giovio felt welcomed to Ischia not as a client but as "a longed-for relative." Vittoria's sonnet, "Di quella cara tua serbata fronde," breathed her unfeigned gratitude for the life that Giovio's histories would give her husband.

> Di quella cara tua serbata fronde
> ch'a' rari antichi, Apollo, ampia corona
> donasti, alor ch'a l'alma tua Elicona
> gustar l'acque più chiare, e più profonde,
>
>   or che 'l gran Iovio ne l'estreme sponde
> del pario Oceano a l'Indico risona,
> con sì lucido onor che si ragiona
> le prime glorie altrui girli seconde,
>
>   orna di propria man la fronte altera,
> ché la sua dotta musa oggi è sol quella
> che rende il secol nostro adorno e chiaro.
>
>   Questo al Sol vivo mio sua luce intera
> serberà sempre, e quel subietto raro
> farà sì degna istoria eterna e bella.[79]

> With that prized, reserved branch, Apollo,
> Which you gave, an ample crown, to those
> Rare ancients who tasted the clearest,
> Deepest waters of your spring at Helicon;
>   Now that the great Giovio resounds
> From the Parian to the Indian ocean,
> With such blazing honor, that the glories he bestows
> Reduce earlier ones to second place;
>   Deck by your own hand his lofty forehead,

Since his learned muse is now the only one
Which renders our century adorned and famous.
   He will preserve for my living Sun his entire light,
Forever, and that rare subject will make
So worthy a history eternal and splendid.

To Vittoria's desire to celebrate the memory of her husband "not with vain tears, but with eternal honors," Giovio's response was a deep and gallant sympathy. Nothing was more praiseworthy, he assured her, than the quest for "true glory" and its perpetuation through letters to "eternal praise."[80]

In the spring of 1528, war tightened its grip on the inhabitants of the castle, and the gloomy forebodings of d'Avalos were fulfilled in ways that not even he could have foreseen. In early February the French army under Lautrec had entered the kingdom of Naples, moving south from the Romagna along the Adriatic coast. At roughly the same time, after lengthy negotiations conducted by Orange and del Vasto, the rebellious imperial troops had finally been induced to leave Rome and had begun marching to defend the Regno. Luckily for the imperialists, Lautrec lost time reducing towns in Apulia, so that some defenses were in place on April 30 when he rode into the environs of Naples and pitched his tent on the estate of the duke of Montalto, the father of Joanna and Maria d'Aragona.[81]

Despite the grace of time, the defenders of Naples were in a precarious situation. Antagonisms between the Landsknechts and the Spanish soldiers smoldered beneath the surface, while dissensions between del Vasto and Orange plagued the command. To make matters worse, a French-Genoese fleet under Filippino Doria, a young cousin of the admiral Andrea Doria, had blockaded the imperial fleet in the bay of Naples. On April 28, without waiting for Venetian reinforcements, the imperial fleet attempted to break the blockade, attacking Doria off Capo d'Orso, between Salerno and Amalfi. From Ischia the reverberations of the cannon had been audible over the water, and afterward rumors of an imperial defeat had drifted in but no certain tidings. Desperately anxious for their husbands and relatives, the ladies implored Giovio to visit the fleet, since, as a friend of the Doria family, he could be certain of a welcome no matter which side had won. And so, gathering together what medicaments he could, Giovio set out from Ischia on his mission of mercy, as he called it, in a small sailing craft manned by stout oarsmen.[82]

At Capo d'Orso, Giovio found that the imperial fleet had been completely destroyed. The battle had lasted four hours and had cost the lives of fifteen hundred men. Pompeo Colonna later called it "the cruelest and most bloody sea battle of our times."[83] In the heat of battle

Doria had taken the unusual expedient of freeing and arming his Moorish galley slaves, who fell on the hated Spaniards with the ferocity of unchained lions. Hugo de Moncada, the viceroy (successor to Lannoy), and Cesare Fieramosca, the famous Neapolitan captain, were both dead, while del Vasto, together with Ascanio and Camillo Colonna, had been taken prisoner.

After a cordial reception, Doria gave Giovio permission to visit the prisoners, who were being held on board another galley. At seeing his friends so reduced he was scarcely able to restrain his tears. The marquis del Vasto had been wounded in the neck, Ascanio Colonna in the right hand and in a foot. Having tended their wounds and heard their story of the battle, Giovio returned over a sea strewn with floating corpses to hear Doria's account. As a special favor the young captain granted him the gilded armor of del Vasto, which the marquis had feared to see set up as a trophy in a church in Genoa.

Giovio stayed to assist in negotiations over ransoms, and thanks to Doria's "humanity" he was able to secure some mitigation in terms for his friends. Then, on the first of May, after interviewing not only captains but common soldiers, he sat down on the victor's galley to describe the battle to the pope.[84] While he had been deeply moved by the plight of his friends, his sentiments were less tender for the remainder of the Spanish and German prisoners. It was a great satisfaction, he confessed, to see the harsh treatment meted out to the troops responsible for "the ruin of the world," many of whom had already been put in chains at the oars as replacements for the liberated Moors.

Particularly sobering was the end of Hugo de Moncada. Just a few days earlier he had been feted at a splendid open air banquet at Capri amid splashing fountains and flourishes of trumpets. Now, after having lain naked for a couple of days between two barrels, exposed to the taunts of the Moors, his legless body was being interred at Amalfi. "I write this," Giovio explained, turning moralist, "to tell of human pride, and to what misery it is reduced in a single hour." Still unforgiving, years later, Giovio concluded book 25 of his *Histories* with an account of Clement VII's satisfaction in the deaths of Hugo de Moncada and Cesare Fieramosca, the former because he had led the sack of the sacristy of St. Peter's, the latter because of his deceptions while the emperor's ambassador, both deaths being signs to the pope "that God immortal would be no tardy avenger of that whole impious and perfidious crime."[85]

With del Vasto and Colonna destined to be conveyed as prisoners to Andrea Doria, Giovio returned to Ischia to offer what comfort he could to their wives. Vittoria Colonna plunged into a campaign of letter-writing, begging the pope to intercede with Doria for honorable treatment of the captives. When Muscettola left on an embassy to Clement VII on behalf of the prince of Orange, he bore her personal plea. The pope was at Viterbo, where he had recently taken up residence after leaving Orvieto, his first refuge after gaining his freedom in December.[86] On June 3 the apostolic protonotary Giovanni Battista Sanga, Giovio's fishing companion in quieter times, wrote to Vittoria to say that Muscettola had arrived in Viterbo and that His Holiness had not only written Doria but had received a reassuring response. Sanga also said he had been commanded to request a safe-conduct from Filippino Doria for Monsignor Giovio, whose presence, "pleasing to His Holiness at any time, would be particularly pleasing in these trying times." However, Sanga assured Vittoria that the pope did not want to deprive her of Giovio's company as long as his presence on Ischia suited them both.[87]

The defenders of Naples were now in even worse straits, but as Giovio observed in book 26 of the *Histories*, Fortune continued to lavish her unpredictable favors upon the emperor.[88] Plague broke out in the French camp in July, and Andrea Doria switched his allegiance to the imperial side. For over a year he had been receiving overtures. In June 1527 no less a person than Gattinara had made a trip to Genoa to court him. Offended, Giovio said, by peremptory demands that he hand over his prisoners of Capo d'Orso, disgusted by failures to honor the terms of his contract, and angry at French plans to enlarge the rival port of Savona, Doria began to ponder del Vasto's invitations to enter the service of Charles V. As a result of negotiations conducted through his prisoner, the admiral returned to Francis I the collar of the order of St. Michael when the term of his contract expired and on August 10 became the emperor's servant. It would have been better to give up six Savonas, Cardinal Wolsey remarked, than to discontent Doria.[89]

The French position now rapidly disintegrated. On August 16 Lautrec succumbed to the plague, and on the 28th his subordinates began the withdrawal that their commander had been too headstrong to accept.[90] Just the day before, Doria had landed del Vasto and Colonna at Ischia for a brief, joyful reunion with their wives, after which they hastened to Naples to organize pursuit.[91] Decimated during the retreat, the French were surrounded in Capua and forced to surrender. Giovio closed his account of the war in the south with words of heartfelt pity for these "half-dead shadows of men" herded into the royal stables, where they were fed by the charity of the Neapolitans. This was the army whose presence had forced the imperial troops to relinquish Rome, and out of many, few returned.[92]

From among the French officers, del Vasto liberated Count Guido Rangoni, despite Spanish opposition, and sent him to Ischia where he provided Giovio with details of the French command.[93] On the day Doria disembarked del Vasto and Colonna, Giovio narrowly missed finding himself in the thick of a naval battle. He had gone down to the harbor to pay his respects, and while he was aboard Doria's galley, it was sighted by a French and Venetian fleet emerging from the straits of Procida. When the enemy began firing, the admiral ordered his men to battle stations and sent a fast galley out to reconnoiter. For a moment it seemed as if he were going to engage, but on finding that he was badly outnumbered he decided to remain under the protecting guns of the castle, and to his evident relief Giovio lost the opportunity of gaining firsthand experience of the terrors of battle.[94]

After the Venetian contingent had departed for the straits of Messina, Doria tarried to harass the French, then sailed off on his famous mission to liberate Genoa.[95] Giovio himself lingered a while longer, but on October 6 the pope reentered Rome and on the 14th he summoned all the absent cardinals. The time for return had come. On the 28th the historian took his regretful leave of "the blessed isle," and by November 8 he was once more in Rome.[96]

CHAPTER EIGHT

Papal Courtier (1528–1534)

Aliqui enim, ut in libera urbe impune accidit, eum sapientis-
simum appellabant quod neptem suam maximi regis nurum et in
domo sua Augusti Caesaris filiam rara foelicitate conspiceret; et
contra alii criminose admodum id factum vituperarent quasi, de-
posita sacrosancti Pontificis persona, privatis familiae commodis
quam publicae quieti consulere maluisset.

—Sui temporis historiarum liber XXXII

Some, as happens without rebuke in a free city, called him most
wise, since, with rare felicity, he saw his niece become the daugh-
ter-in-law of a great king and the daughter of Augustus Caesar
become a member of his own house; while others called it a crime
that having, as it were, divested himself of the sacrosanct persona
of the pope, he had placed the private interests of his family above
the public welfare.

GIOVIO RETURNED to a city in misery and a master in travail. Destruction, desolation, and poverty lay all about. There was a deep sense that
the world had changed, perhaps forever. The pope's white beard, seen in
Sebastiano del Piombo's portrait (now in Parma), told of his personal
sufferings.[1] Even the artist complained, "I do not seem to be that Sebastian I was before the sack. . . . I cannot return to the same mind."[2] Giovio's own mood was scarcely expansive. Everything he had saved was
lost. To increase his sense of universal catastrophe, his family was still
struggling to rebuild after the sack of Como and vainly looking to him
for help, but his offices were not rendering "so much as a chestnut."
Nocera had been sacked, he explained, and expediting the bulls for his
appointment as bishop had taken everything he could scrape together; it
was only thanks to the marquis del Vasto and the marchioness of Pescara
that he was alive at all.[3] The sack of Rome seemed to signal the end of any
dependable order in the public sphere. Giovio's motto, *Fato prudentia
minor* (Prudence unequal to fate), reversing an epigram from Virgil's
Georgics (1.416), expressed his anomie. Increasingly he devoted himself
to creating a private order that would enable him to live securely amidst
the turmoil of his times.[4]

Exhausted by hardship and uncertain where to plot his course, Clement VII fell so ill in January 1529 that recovery seemed doubtful. In book
25 of the *Histories* Giovio recounted being at the pope's bedside to hear

him express what everyone expected would be his last exhortation to the Florentines.[5] Of all his burdens, the revolt of Florence had been the heaviest. Seizing the moment of his captivity, the citizens had expelled the two young Medici bastards, Alessandro and Ippolito, and restored the republic. Careggi was burned and the Medici arms were everywhere defaced.[6]

To everyone's surprise, however, Clement VII recovered from his illness—miraculously liberated, Berni said, from the attentions of his eight physicians—and as health returned so did the determination to regain Florence.[7] "What use is it to me, O Giovio," he demanded,

> to have retained the papacy and reacquired health and life, if I am driven by ungrateful citizens from my native city to lament in perpetual exile the grandeur of my ancestors, the reputation of my family, and the fortune of the principate? I shall certainly be called slothful for losing them unless I and the exiled youths recover them with the same vigor by which they were acquired and so long preserved, and unless you write in your histories that Fortune did not always mock my just desires.[8]

In the interests of his family, Clement VII abruptly made peace with his erstwhile captor. The treaty of Barcelona, signed on June 29, 1529, was a triumph for Gattinara's Italian policy. The pope consented to abandon Francesco II Sforza, should he be proven guilty of treason, and the emperor agreed to abandon Alfonso d'Este and allow the pope to deprive him of Ferrara as punishment for his aid to Bourbon in 1527. The emperor confirmed the possession of Modena and Reggio by the Church, and the pope lifted the ancient ban against imperial possession of the kingdom of Naples (a papal fief). Most importantly for the pope, the emperor assured him his assistance in recovering Florence. A separate agreement provided for the marriage of Alessandro de' Medici—called the natural son of Lorenzo de' Medici but widely presumed to be the pope's own son—to Margaret, the emperor's natural daughter.[9] The subsequent treaty of Cambrai (August 3) between Charles V and Francis I—called the *Paix des dames* because it was negotiated by the mother of Francis I, Louise of Savoy, and the aunt of Charles V, Margaret of Austria—gave the emperor a free hand in Italy. Francis I surrendered his claim to Milan and abandoned his Italian allies, including Alfonso d'Este, with whom he had recently concluded an alliance cemented by the hand of Renée of France.

Having destined Alessandro de' Medici to rule Florence, Clement VII had prepared Ippolito for a career in the Church, and when death had appeared imminent, he had won the consent of the Sacred College to making his teenage cousin a cardinal. Giovio attached himself to the new prelate, very likely by request, since the pope wanted him surrounded with mature advisers. In August 1529, Ippolito was appointed one of the legates to welcome the emperor to Italy, and so Giovio found himself bound for Genoa in the train of his new patron.

The emperor disembarked at Genoa on August 12 with great pomp and ceremony.[10] Caesar's youthful appearance, courtesy, and modest demeanor had quickly dispelled the hostility of the Genoese, and Giovio felt the same effect.[11] He came furnished with a letter of introduction from the imperial ambassador at Rome, the irascible *Micer* Miguel Mai, who said that, "beyond serving the pope," he was "writing with much care and diligence the history of what occurs," in which, "as in all other things, he shows himself and is the servitor of Your Majesty."[12]

On August 30 Charles V departed for Piacenza. In book 27 of his *Histories* Giovio described the administration of the ancient oath by which the emperor-elect swore, somewhat belatedly, never to use force against the liberty of the Church. Having so sworn, however, he declared that he had not thereby renounced any of his own prerogatives, an indication of his dissatisfaction with the retention of Parma, Piacenza, Modena, and Reggio by the Church.[13] Nevertheless, after receiving the keys to Piacenza in the *duomo*, he returned them to the papal governor.[14] While the pope prepared himself for the journey to Bologna, having agreed—for obvious reasons—to a coronation there rather than in Rome, the emperor spent a couple of months in Piacenza and Parma. News that Suleiman the Magnificent had raised the siege of Vienna lent a joyous note to the coming festivities. On October 24 the pope made his solemn entry into Bologna, and on November 5 the emperor was received with magnificent display and "incredible rejoicing."[15]

Giovio's description of Charles V's entry into Bologna is one of the most vivid passages in the *Histories*. With the eye for color and texture of a Veronese, he captured the brilliance of the scene and all its human drama, particularly the moment when the emperor mounted the platform before San Petronio where the pope awaited him and all eyes turned to watch the expressions on their faces as the two heads of Christendom, after all their past antagonisms, laid eyes upon each other for the first time. "Caesar's countenance was grave and martial but suffused with a certain gentleness and modesty." The pope had been expecting another Ariovistus, but when he beheld the young emperor his face "showed a sudden exhilaration, as if rejoicing to find him much more august and humane than he had anticipated."

Charles V, then twenty-nine years old, was in the flower of his age and fortune. Thanks to his temperance and immersion in affairs of state, Giovio thought, he exuded both the splendor of youth and the gravity of old age, with blue eyes that were gentle rather than severe or frightening, a curly yellow beard that compensated for "a chin a little too prominent," a slightly aquiline nose that suggested "the magnanimity of the ancient kings of Persia," and golden hair cut like a Roman emperor's.[16] In his renewed enthusiasm for the young sovereign, Giovio only hinted at the famous features noted by other Italians, the lantern jaw and mouth which could not close.[17]

With personal rapport established, diplomacy followed more smoothly. Pope and emperor were lodged in adjoining suites in the Palazzo Pubblico (the present Palazzo Communale). For Giovio the agreements made before the coronation redeemed the emperor's reputation and atoned for the crime of the sack. He sensed that Charles V was eager to settle Italian affairs in order to deal with Germany and the Turks, hence "what he had refused to allow to be taken from him with armies he now conceded with lofty magnanimity."[18] The absolution of Francesco II Sforza and his confirmation as duke resolved all the anguished uncertainty surrounding Milan and justified the faith of the imperial party. In his *Histories* Giovio pulled out all the stops, declaring that this one act displayed "to the stupefaction of all, how much greater and loftier Caesar was than all his fortune."[19] In his exultation Giovio even managed a tribute to Clement VII's diplomacy, allowing himself only the slightest irony in noting the general praise for the pope's "industry, judgment, and unwonted felicity."[20] Much to Giovio's satisfaction, Charles V was freed by the agreements of Bologna to deal with the Lutherans and Turks, the Venetians were reconciled to the emperor and made part of a universal peace for Italy, and the "insane," ungrateful Florentines would bend their necks again to the "easy" Medicean yoke.[21]

The radicalism of the restored Florentine republic, displayed in the banishments of optimates, the destruction of Medicean villas, and confiscations of property, had confirmed Giovio's belief that this government was a demagogy and a threat to the political stability of Italy. Even the old Florentine republic had seemed to him no more than a vehicle for the enrichment of whatever party was in power, and the "liberty" defended by this republic he termed in the *Histories* "crueler not merely than the gentle principate of the Medici, but the harshest tyranny you can name."[22] As a result of the treaty of Barcelona, an imperial army under the command of the prince of Orange had invested Florence in October 1529, and in late December the besiegers were augmented by another force under the command of the marquis del Vasto, which made its way south with great hardship through the wintry Apennines.

While negotiations were in progress at Bologna, Giovio profited from one of the most brilliant assemblages of the Renaissance to enlarge his acquaintance with the protagonists of his *Histories*. Princes, prelates, ambassadors, grandees, humanists, artists, and musicians were converging from all over Europe to participate, and Bembo looked forward to the memorial of the festivities "which our Msgr. Giovio will draw with his learned and graceful style in his histories."[23] With his new rank of domestic prelate enhancing his status as historian and papal intimate, Giovio found ready access to the endless round of social events. The Ferrarese envoys saw him assisting the pope at the knighting of a young nobleman of Parma; on another occasion they ran into him as they were leaving the palace of the legate.[24] Giovio's new patron, Cardinal Ippolito, entertained lavishly, as did his friend the marquis del Vasto until he departed for the siege of Florence.

At a dinner where Giovio was the guest of the ambassador Don Diego de Mendoza and the general Antonio de Leyva, conversation turned naturally enough to the biography Giovio was writing of Gonzalo de Córdoba. Both men had been his officers, and the historian learned that the "great captain" had gone to his grave with three regrets, two of which involved having broken his word—even though at the command of his king: once to the young prince Ferrando, the last of the Aragonese dynasty of Naples, whose surrender he accepted at Taranto; and once to Cesare Borgia, whom he received after the death of Alexander VI. To both he had given safe-conducts, and both he sent as prisoners to Spain. The third regret Gonzalo would never reveal, but Mendoza and de Leyva believed it was allowing Ferdinand to lure him back to Spain where he was conveniently retired.[25]

Giovio paid court to Isabella d'Este, who was giving lively parties in the palazzo Manzoli.[26] Literary luminaries were flocking to the palazzo Marsili in via San Mamolo where the flamboyant poet Veronica Gambara was entertaining rank and virtue of every sort.[27] The coronation festivities were the occasion of an informal "summit" designed to reach agreement on rules for the vernacular following controversy provoked by Bembo's *Prose della volgar lingua* (1525). The great dream of Bologna was a vernacular humanism made possible by linguistic reform, a dream described in Sperone Speroni's *Dialogo delle lingue* (1542), which was set at the time of the coronation.

The projected summit was somewhat overshadowed, however, by the confrontation with Latin promoted by Romolo Amaseo, once the pupil of Musurus at Padua and now a star in the intellectual firmament of Bologna. In two spectacularly rhetorical lectures delivered at the opening of the academic year, not long after the arrival of pope and emperor, Amaseo marshaled all the arguments for the supremacy of Latin. Dismissing the vernacular as the fruit of the barbarian invasions and a testimony to servitude, he urged Latin, the language of universal empire, as the true Italian birthright. "Can you allow the glory of that language of your forefathers," he demanded of the youth of Italy, "to flee into exile into the bosoms of foreign nations, driven out by the iniquity of this age and the perversity of certain enemies?"[28]

With Amaseo unfurling the banner of Latin, Giovio began to think of publishing his dialogue. Through Giangiacomo Calandra he asked Isabella d'Este for enough "fine white paper for the luxurious Dialogue, in which that famous house [of Gonzaga] has a distinguished part." The marchioness obliged with seventy reams of Mantuan paper, but although he enlarged the portions dealing with the Gonzaga family and readied the dialogue for the typesetter, Giovio drew back. After an initial rush of enthusiasm, he probably realized how little he stood to gain by opening old wounds now that pope and emperor had composed their quarrels and a new day was dawning.[29]

Late in life, when taxed with being hostile to the French, Giovio rehearsed the many times the imperialists had accused him of being a Francophile, beginning at Bologna when "I had to justify myself and clear things up with the emperor himself."[30] It may have been that he had actually circulated the dialogue, only to find it sounded a discordant note, reminding people of things they would rather have forgotten. Dependent as he was on patronage to achieve the security he coveted, Giovio was always vulnerable to the sensibilities of the great, a circumstance that caused him constant difficulties and that made him retard the appearance of his *Histories* until the end of his life.

Fortunately, Giovio succeeded in appeasing the emperor, if this was the occasion in Bologna to which he was referring, for as part of the coronation bounty he received a patent of nobility for himself and his family, creating them counts palatine of the Holy Roman Empire and augmenting their arms with Charles V's personal crest, the pillars of Hercules and the motto *Plus ultra*. The charter, which cited Giovio's devotion to the emperor, read as if the imperial agents had found his help significant, and it would be interesting to know who had been his principal advocate at court.[31]

Charles V had elected to be crowned on his birthday, February 24, 1530, which was also the fifth anniversary of the battle of Pavia. As Bembo had hoped, Giovio's description of the ceremonies was both graceful and full, commencing in early January with Amaseo's moving oration on the peace long yearned-for by the afflicted people of Italy and now at last achieved.[32] Had Giovio himself resolved to serve "with smiling face"? Warmly as he welcomed the imperial peace for Italy, with the restoration of Sforza, he also emphasized in his *Histories* the darker side to the arrangements of Bologna, the preponderance of power they gave the emperor.

Notwithstanding Clement VII's strong representations, Charles V had refused to live up to all the terms of the treaty of Barcelona, having been won over by the wily Alfonso d'Este during a stay in Modena.[33] Contrary to his expectations, the pope was forced to pardon his disloyal vassal and confirm him in possession of Ferrara, despite Alfonso's having furnished his assistance to Bourbon in 1526–27. And not only this; the continued resistance of Florence made Clement VII so dependent on Charles V's goodwill that after the coronation he was compelled to allow the duke of Ferrara to come in person to Bologna and to consent to the immediate transfer of Modena and Reggio to the empire pending a final adjudication of rights by the emperor alone. As a client of Alfonso's, Giovio could perhaps forget this distasteful setback to the Church in the happy outcome for Milan, but even while forced to pardon his own disloyal vassal, the pope was compelled to acquiesce in the punishment of the emperor's vassal, the papal loyalist Alberto Pio, an assiduous antagonist of Erasmus and Luther. For joining the League of Cognac, Pio was deprived of Carpi, an imperial fief, which was then granted to Alfonso d'Este, adding to Clement VII's humiliation. The signal favor, moreover, that the emperor showed the duke of Urbino must have been a bitter sight for all the sufferers of 1527. Not surprisingly, Clement VII returned quietly to Rome, without formal ceremonies of welcome.[34]

Charles V, on the other hand, went on a triumphal progress to Germany, where grave matters awaited his attention. Cardinal Ippolito and the other legates having been instructed to accompany him as far as Mantua, Giovio had the opportunity to enjoy still more festivities and the renewal of old friendships on the Mincio. Federico Gonzaga's problems were less complex than those of Alfonso d'Este, but he, too, had conflicting obligations. Although Mantua was an imperial fief, there had been no problem in his having been captain-general of the Church in 1520–21, but after being rebuffed in his bid for a renewal of the captain-generalship during the war of the League of Cognac, he had kept a low profile, aiding neither emperor nor pope. He was fortunate in avoiding the customary fate of neutrals when Gattinara and Charles V decided to win his loyalty by elevating Mantua into a duchy. Although he had not attended the coronation out of pique at losing a contest over precedence with the marquis of Monferrat, he was prepared to spend lavishly on the emperor's reception in order to promote his aspirations for an advantageous marriage.[35]

Federico and Charles V were exactly the same age and quickly developed a rapport which helps explain the unusual concessions the emperor was willing to make for his vassal of Mantua. For nearly a month he lingered in the city to enjoy the spectacular entertainments, some of them held in the partially completed palazzo del Te, the *capolavoro* of Giovio's old friend, Giulio Romano.[36] On one occasion, Giovio and Ariosto, friends from the latter's Roman visit, amused themselves and onlookers in the square by comparing living heroes to characters from *Orlando Furioso*—del Vasto to Ruggiero, the count of Sarno to Sacripante, Cardinal Medici to Mandricardo, the duke of Urbino to Zerbino, Luigi Gonzaga to Rodomonte, and the count of Caiazzo to Gradasso.[37]

Eventually a marriage contract was struck between Federico and Giulia of Aragon, the emperor's aunt, after which the marquis was elevated to duke in an imposing ceremony; but by then the legates and Giovio were already in San Benedetto del Po, and by the beginning of May they were back in Rome.[38]

After returning, Giovio recalled, he "mainly passed the time" with the cardinal de' Medici.[39] In the *Elogia* he painted a dazzling picture of the luxury of Ippolito's court, which so distressed the pope—the theatrical performances, the jousts and tournaments, the great hunts with infinite numbers of blooded dogs and horses, the banquet tables set in woods by tinkling springs for all the court and noble youth of Rome.[40] It was no secret that Ippolito, like Pompeo Colonna, despised the clerical life and would have preferred to govern Florence. A young man in the flower of his age, as Giovio described him, he had the irresistible personal charm, the love of life, and the gift for music and poetry of his grandfather, Lorenzo the Magnificent. He translated Virgil and Hippocrates into Tuscan. When he took up music, Giovio marveled, he learned to play all the instruments—lute, viol, recorder, cornet, drum, and even the military trumpet and kettledrums. The fruit of an affair between Giuliano de' Medici, the brother of Leo X, and a lady of Urbino, he was brought to Rome at the age of three and raised in the Vatican by his uncle, who found him a particular delight and let him play at his feet during audiences. When he was old enough to learn letters, Pierio Valeriano was assigned him as a tutor, and he was groomed for the ecclesiastical career he so resented. He was just eighteen when made a cardinal.[41]

In March 1531 Giovio described for the duke of Milan the tournaments and sea battles in flooded arenas which Ippolito staged for his idol, Giulia Gonzaga Colonna, the widowed young duchess of Traietto.[42] The historian's efforts to keep up with his young master and his high-spirited retinue ended in misfortune one day on a hunt in the Tiburtine marshes near Tivoli. As Giovanni Morone, bishop of Modena and son of the former chancellor, explained to the duke of Milan, "I have not been able to undertake the embassy to Giovio because he is absent owing to a disgrace he suffered, which I dare not describe to Your Excellency, although it is ridiculous enough. He will soon be back, and meanwhile the calumnies will cease."[43] Morone's reference was probably to an incident described with ample curial malice by a pasquinade in the Corsini collection. Apparently while crossing a marsh Giovio had failed to spot a ditch and fell into it with his horse, muddying all his fine vestments.

> Vescovus est quidam galantior omnibus unus
> Historicus, prorsus imberbis, fronte ita latus,
> Ut merito dici frontator possit ab omni.
> Hic cupiens magno in coetu se ostendere pulchris

Vestibus indutum scarlattibus atque velutis
Heroem quemdam est per campos forte secutus
Ad cacciam, sed dum buffonum maximus esse
Et dici studet, umquam cessante cicada,
Ecce tibi est foveam pantani lapsus in amplam
Purpureis illis cum vestibus atque caballo
Quem, ceu cuncta solet, emit Frontone magistro.

There is a certain bishop, more gallant than all the rest, a historian this one, quite beardless, with a forehead so wide that truly he can be called an affronter by all. Desiring to show himself in a large company decked out in beautiful vestments of scarlet and velvet, this one followed a certain hero through the fields to the hunt. But since he is the greatest of buffoons and eager for the title, this never-ceasing cicada, lo! he falls into a big ditch in the swamp with those purple vestments and his horse, which, as is his wont, he bought with Fronto as his master.

According to the "poet," Giovio crawled up out of the ditch, all covered with mud, remounted, dug in his spurs and vented his mortification on the poor horse:

Ni te ultus fuero paucis scelerate diebus
Expensis vivam propriis, tangarque pudore,
Non episcopalis eris sonipes, sed portovaligia.[44]

If I do not avenge myself on you in a few days at my own expense, you wicked beast, as I live, I shall be ashamed of myself. You will no longer be the steed of a bishop but a beast of burden.

The sneers, the stifled laughter of the courtiers, and Giovio's chagrin are all lovingly depicted.

This pasquinade was not the only barb Giovio suffered in these years. In May 1532 the Ferrarese agent Antonio Romei reported to Cardinal Ippolito d'Este, "I also wanted to say that one day recently there was found attached to Pasquino one of these dishonest animals that go fluttering all night with outspread wings into the sweet nests of the women of Ferrara and Rome, and which are painted on walls of the taverns with feet and wings, and underneath there was this distich:

Si tale genus volucrum scinderet aera pennis
Venator Jovius sollicitus fieret."[45]

If such a flying creature cleaves the air with its wings
Giovio the hunter becomes aroused.

Other, undated pasquinades accused Giovio of sodomy; one called him "a bishop worn out by indulgence." Still others accused him of venality.[46]
Giovio himself lamented that Rome was a city in which "ill is said of

everyone," and it is easy enough to see how the historian laid himself open to charges of partiality.[47] Accusations of sodomy were so common among clerics and humanists as almost to form a literary genre. By all admissions, his own and others', Giovio had a sharp tongue, and many pasquinades attacking him read like attempts to settle a score with any convenient weapon. Other than inference or innuendo, there is little reliable evidence for Giovio's sexuality. His letters to Federico Gonzaga boasted of heterosexual liaisons, and he appears to have had an illegitimate son.[48] A famous distich attributed to Aretino called him a hermaphrodite, a state of which Aretino could certainly write with authority.[49] Giovio was a gossip and perhaps this trait was coupled with manifestations of effeminacy, but despite his best intentions he could never quite overcome his old-fashioned provincial morality, which may have kept him from the worst excesses of curial Rome. He clearly had a gift for friendship and formed a number of sentimental friendships during his lifetime, as with Annibale Raimondi or Giorgio Vasari. Although a victim of pasquinades, he collected them himself, as evident from his commonplace books.[50]

In addition to his bons vivants, knights, musicians, and other virtuosi, Ippolito enjoyed the company of men of letters, having a poetic spirit himself, Giovio said, "of marvelous vigor."[51] Among the many virtuosi he drew to his court was Giorgio Vasari, whom he met in Arezzo after his abortive attempt to seize the government of Florence in April 1531. Arriving in Rome the following winter, Vasari found as protectors Giovio and the cardinal's two secretaries, Claudio Tolomei and Gabriele Cesano, all three of whom, he wrote, "favor me, love me, and guide me like a son."[52] Later that spring, Vasari told his Florentine patron, Ottaviano de' Medici, that he had gotten lantern oil in his eyes and would have gone blind "but for the diligence and medicine of Monsignor Giovio."[53]

The cardinal's entourage became for Giovio a substitute for the old Roman academy, which never quite recovered from the sack, even though Colocci, who had lost his library and collections and twice had to ransom himself, did his best to resume his customary role of host and patron.[54] Küritz had died in Verona, fleeing the stricken city. Eventually, Blosio Palladio was able to build a handsome villa on Monte Ciocci, a spur of Monte Mario behind the Vatican, where he entertained his friends amid the parterres and ponds of his enchanting gardens, prompting Valeriano's epigram,

> Extinctas siquidem Blosius nunc suscitat aras,
> Instauratque tuos docta Minerva choros.[55]

> Blosio now indeed restores your ruined altars,
> learned Minerva, and resuscitates your choruses.

Giovio himself suggested that reunions of the Roman academy were relatively rare, however, by the wording of his invitation to Mario Maffei, on a visit to Rome in 1534, to dine with Vigile, Colocci, and Blosio Palladio "so that the joyous sodality of the old academy can be renewed."[56]

As the man of letters began to replace the humanist in the 1530s and 1540s, literary gatherings were more likely to take place in the palaces of great prelates or in academies organized for specific subjects, such as architecture or Italian poetry. While hardly an enthusiast for the vernacular, Giovio seems to have been an occasional participant in these new academies, particularly when formed by his friends. About 1530 Uberto Strozzi, from a Mantuan branch of the great Florentine family, organized the Vignaiuoli, whose members all took names connected with viticulture or husbandry (wild grape, must, pale, willow, fig, quince, and so on). Several of Giovio's friends from Ippolito's circle, including Francesco Maria Molza, Berni, Giovanni della Casa, and Gianfrancesco Bini, were among its members, and he himself is sometimes said to have been one, although this may be through confusion with Giuseppe Giovi of Lucca.[57]

The jovial tenor of gatherings, as Rome recovered from the sack, was evident from the description of a dinner for poets given in 1531 by Giovio's friend Giovanni Antonio Muscettola, a frequent visitor during the latter years of Clement VII's pontificate. "On the evening of Santa Lucia," as Giovanni Mauro d'Arcano, secretary to Cardinal Cesarini, related to Gandolfo Porrino, secretary to Giulia Gonzaga,

> Signor Muscettola gave a dinner for the poets, to which I also as a poet was invited, and no other wine was drunk than that of the vineyard of Pontano, brought by the posts from Naples. This is of such poetic vigor that all were warmed, not only in beholding but in tasting and in drinking it, more than seven or eight drafts for each, and some there were who arrived at the number of the muses. . . . At the end of the dinner our messer Marco da Lodi sang to the sound of the lyre, which was played by Messer Pietro Polo [Paolo?], and he sang:
> Per me si va nella città dolente [Dante, Inf. 3.1].
> If peradventure you would like to know the names of the banqueters I will list them for you from head to foot. And first came signor Muscettola, then bishop Gambara [Uberto Gambara, bishop of Tortona], Pietro Paolo [Vergerio?], Blosio, Sanga, the secretary dall'Occhio, the bishop of Cava [Giovanni Tommaso Sanfelice], M. Marco da Lodi, Molza, Bini, Fondulio [Girolamo Fondoli of Cremona], il Bardo, Maestro Ferrante [Balami] the Sicilian. I cannot recall any others, except for myself. Giovio and Messer Claudio Tolomei were missing, taken from us by the cardinal de' Medici, and you were missing.[58]

Giovio's attendance on the cardinal de' Medici did not preclude his customary service to the pope. In late November 1531, when the ambassador and agents of Ferrara went to the Holy Father to announce the firstborn of Ercole d'Este and Renée of France, they found Giovio in the audience chamber, along with Cardinal Ridolfi, the Florentine ambassador, and Lorenzo Cibo.[59] Clement VII's fortunes had improved somewhat with the capitulation of Florence in the summer of 1530. On August 12, after withstanding a siege of nine months, the republican government was finally forced to surrender by the total defeat of its army at Gavinana nine days earlier. For Charles V it was a cheerless victory, since it cost him the prince of Orange, and Giovio later heard from the Neapolitan captain, Fabrizio Maramaldo, that he had murdered the captured Florentine commander, Francesco Ferrucci, because he could not bear to have him live when Orange had been slain.[60]

The heroic resistance of the Florentines won the grudging admiration of many who disapproved of their cause, Giovio among them. His letter to Marco Contarini after the battle of Gavinana showed how carefully he had been gathering the particulars of what he eventually termed in his *Histories* "the most stupendous thing to be read in any author," excelling any resistance chronicled in Greek or Roman history.[61] At the time, however, he was not quite so charitable, callously punning that "the *arrabiati* will bend the neck to the soft yoke of the most clement balls [the Medici symbol]; otherwise they will feel what pain of the testicles is, because the army . . . is ready to indemnify itself for the privations of a whole year with a lucrative sack; for truly, there has never been a siege of this length."[62] In Giovio's mind the last barrier to the peace of Italy had fallen. "Now we can hope for quiet and prosperity in poor Italy," he exclaimed to Federico Gonzaga, "and Your Excellency can triumph over Turkish rather than Christian blood, if, as the good Caesar wishes and Clement desires extremely, you turn your victorious eagles to the East."[63] This was no idle turn of phrase. The Turks were increasingly dominating Giovio's political thought, not only because of the campaigns of Charles V and Ferdinand of Austria to check them in Hungary but because of the incessant danger they posed to the coasts of Italy.

During 1530 Giovio's correspondence showed him grafting new friendships onto old ones and using his access to the pope to advance the interests of his friends. By acting as a literary intermediary between Vittoria Colonna and Pietro Bembo, he stood godfather to one of the great friendships of the Renaissance. At Bologna, Giovio had shown Bembo some of Vittoria's verses celebrating the glory of her husband, and now the marchioness used him to forward additional verses. The two poets had undoubtedly met during the papacy of Leo X, when Vittoria was living in Rome, but in 1530 she was coming increasingly under the spell of Bembo's verses and turned to Giovio as a mutual friend to pour out her admiration.[64] "The more one reads his poems," she wrote in June 1530, "and the more one ponders them, the more admiration they evoke . . . so that I have concluded that I am totally enamored of him, nor do I seek to have you involved in this love which is beyond any sensual appetite."[65] Courteous at first, rather than genuinely interested, Bembo was soon won by the perspicacity of Vittoria's criticism, and the marchioness no longer needed an intermediary.[66] Giovio feared no rivalry, he confided to Bembo, since he was certain that Vittoria's love for him was, as Giovio's for her, "celeste, santo e platonicissimo [heavenly, holy, and most platonic]."[67]

On a somewhat less Platonic note, Giovio helped hold Clement VII to a promise made to free Bembo's benefices from the tithe.[68] Eventually, the great poet's thanks for these and other favors over the years were expressed in his graceful tribute of 1538 linking Giovio forever with Vittoria Colonna:

> Giovio, che i tempi e l'opre raccogliete
> > del faticoso e duro secol nostro
> > in così puro e sì lodato inchiostro
> > che chiaro eternamente viverete,
> Perché lo stile homai non rivolgete
> > a questa, novo in terra et dolce mostro,
> > donna gentile, che non di perle et d'ostro
> > ma sol d'honor, e di virtute ha sete? etc.[69]

Giovio, you who gather events and the times of our harsh and wearisome century in ink so pure and praiseworthy that clearly you will live forever, why do you not turn your style to celebrating this new and sweet marvel on earth, a gentle lady who thirsts not for pearls and purple robes, but only for honor and virtue? etc.

In the autumn of 1531 a pastoral visit to his see gave Giovio an opportunity to revisit Ischia. According to his autobiographical fragment, he left Rome for Nocera on September 28. Almost nothing is known of his administration of his see, which, as Cardinal Jacobacci before him, he governed through vicars. The only document at Nocera reflecting his episcopacy is a late sixteenth-century charter citing his sanction for the formation of the Congregation of the Body of Christ on April 6, 1548.[70] He endured the sort of administrative vexations complained of by the bishops at the time of the Council of Trent, particularly the activities of exempt orders. For example, his appeal to Cardinal Campeggio, cardinal-protector of the Dominicans, having failed to stop the friars of La Cava from interfering in the administration of the city and diocese, he was forced to obtain a letter from the pope.[71] For managing the financial affairs relating to his see, he relied on the services of Vittoria Colonna's agent, the Florentine businessman Tommaso Cambi.[72]

From Nocera, Giovio went to Naples and then Ischia, returning by sea to Ostia in mid- to late November.[73] While at Naples he seems to have called on Pompeo Colonna, whom he found chatting amiably with other callers as he planted exotic species in his gardens near the lake of Avernus and ancient Cumae. The cardinal's affable and courtly side did not, however, blind Giovio to the extreme rigor with which he was exercising the office of viceroy, a rigor long remembered by the Neapolitans.[74] Renewed contacts with southern humanists resulted in Giovio's brief, largely anecdotal life of his old friend from Roman academy days, the Neapolitan poet and critic Pietro Gravina, a dignified and genial epicure whose verses had celebrated the exploits of Gonzalo de Córdoba. Dedicated to Giovanni Francesco di Capua, count of Palena, the life was included in the 1532 edition of Gravina's poems collected by his friend Scipione Capece. Giovio's desire to give an authentic picture of Gravina, including his penchant for facile praise, his laziness, and his misogyny, aroused the ire of another Neapolitan humanist, Girolamo Scannapeco, whose criticism spurred him to formulate his theory of biography. Although the biographer, unlike the historian, has traditionally been licensed to omit unflattering materials, Giovio argued, everyone has faults, and not to speak of them, albeit gently, is to forfeit credibility. Adulation brings only contempt.[75]

A decade had now passed since Giovio had seen his family, and his brother was urging him to return home. Another reason for visiting Lombardy was to cement relations with Francesco II Sforza. Giovio's cultivation of the duke stemmed partly from his eagerness to bolster the native Milanese dynasty, but he had private reasons as well. A rival family was seeking to dispossess his nephew of the office of *referendario* in Como and he needed the duke's support. Before the struggle was over he had to make two strong protests to save the office for Francesco.[76] He also made it clear that he would like a little help in refurbishing the adjacent house he had bought to enlarge the family dwelling, or else in buying "a most beautiful spot" about a mile from Como. He had already sent his chaplain to Como with two wagons full of "gentilities," he told the duke, to "live a life worthy of the philosophy of body and soul"—a characteristically breezy Giovian quietus to debates in the *Tusculan Disputations* and in Quattrocento moral dialogues as to whether a measure of wealth was necessary to the perfection of virtue.[77]

Giovio had planned to visit in 1531 to help celebrate the withdrawal of the Spanish garrison from Como, but the "war of Musso" intervened.[78] Benedetto's letter renewing his invitation the following year related the upturn in the family's prosperity thanks to Paolo's support. Refurbishing of the house and an addition was nearly complete, and Giovio's suite was ready for him to the right of the atrium, comprising living room, bedroom, museum, and garden room.[79] The lower garden opening onto the atrium had been put in good order, as well as the upper garden on the ramparts of the city wall. The silver service Giovio had provided to replace the one lost in the sack was safely stored for use on great occasions, tin and maiolica being sufficient for everyday use. Under the impetus of Paolo's growing prosperity, Benedetto was now dreaming of acquiring the house on the other side of the family dwelling, as well as a garden on the lake that would only cost sixteen hundred gold *scudi*, he urged, and in better times would "easily be worth two thousand."[80] Giovio's own thoughts also turned to lakeside property when the pope hinted that he might make him a present of the Fonte Pliniana, the famous intermittent spring described by Pliny on the east side of the lake. "In the name of God," Giovio urged his nephew Giulio, "find out whose it is, how much it would cost, and let me know, so I can make a test of the pope's liberality."[81]

Thanks to Giovio's intervention with the duke of Milan, the eldest nephew, Francesco, was exercising the office of *referendario* in Como. His youth outgrown, he was now at an appropriate age for marriage. Alessandro had completed his studies at Bologna and was practicing medicine. Apparently he had not exhausted his uncle's patience with any more "mad tricks." Celio was installed in the canonry of the cathedral of Como granted Giovio by Pope Adrian VI and was studying music. Giulio was studying law at Pavia, supported by the commenda of Sant'Antonio which Giovio had obtained from Clement VII in 1524. Scarcely had Giovio been designated bishop-elect of Nocera, in fact, than he had begun proceedings to resign his earlier benefices to these two nephews.[82] Cesare, the youngest nephew, was still an adolescent and, according to his father, showing more propensity for Mars than Minerva. Rosa, the only daughter, was now thirteen, attractive, prudent, and would soon be nubile (needing, of course, a dowry from uncle).

His brother's letter also indicated that Giovio was again thinking of publishing his *Histories*. Benedetto had learned of Paolo's intentions from their mutual friend, the publisher Francesco Calvo, and, like the cautious scholar and older brother he was, he suggested that Giovio bring the books to Como for editorial criticism before rushing them into print. But before Giovio could revise and publish the completed portions of the *Histories*, he was swept up in great events that moved him to resume his narration.

One of the subjects of earnest discussion between pope and emperor at Bologna had been the defense of Christendom and the recovery of

Hungary from the Turks. Clement VII had been so shaken by news of the annihilation of King Louis and the Hungarians at Mohács in 1526 that he had even debated going in person to Spain to speed agreement between Charles V and Francis I and promote a European crusade against the Turks.[83] Alone among Christian princes, Giovio asserted, the pope had sent Louis aid for the defense of his kingdom.[84] The siege of Vienna, raised just three weeks before the emperor's entry into Bologna, had lent new urgency to the Turkish threat, and Giovio was only expressing the common opinion when he suggested to the emperor that the siege had been a timely warning from God.[85]

Charles V had left Bologna in 1530 with the intention of pacifying Germany and uniting it in a great crusade. At the diet of Augsburg he vainly struggled to reach agreement with the nascent Protestant party, hoping to find some formula for religious peace that would allow him to respond to the urgent pleas of his brother Ferdinand for aid in Hungary. In Rome, Clement VII was likewise promoting a crusade. Despite news of the formation of the League of Schmalkalden and the demands of Charles V for a general council of the Church, the only topic of conversation at the curia during the winter of 1530–31, said a Florentine envoy, was the Turks.[86] Not only was it certain that Suleiman would return to Hungary, his fleets were a constant menace to Mediterranean travel and to the coasts of Italy.

As a contribution to the coming crusade, Giovio composed his treatise on the origins and nature of Turkish power, the *Commentario de le cose de' Turchi*, which he dedicated to Charles V on January 22, 1531. He had probably begun it as soon as he returned to Rome from Bologna, but the great flood of the Tiber in October 1530 would have disrupted his work. The *Commentary* was printed by Antonio Blado, at least by August 1532 when the Ferrarese agent at Rome sent a copy "newly printed" to the cardinal d'Este. Several subsequent Italian printings (1533, 1535, 1538, 1540, 1541, 1560) indicated its popularity, as did a Latin translation by Francesco Negri, which was published in Wittemberg (1537), Antwerp (1538), and Paris (1538, 1539) and translated into German by Justus Jonas (1537), with a preface by Melanchthon.

Of the various treatises written for Charles V on the Turkish menace, Giovio's was probably the most realistic, the least moralizing, and the most informative. Recalling the emperor's difficulties with Latin, he made his offering in simple Italian. The text was economical. As the Ferrarese envoy remarked, by reading it, "Your Excellency will learn in a short time what he would not perhaps learn even in a very long time without the book."[87] Despite his love for the paladins of romance, Giovio regarded this crusade as a practical matter. He understood the Ottoman expansionist drive better than most, and he had a new appreciation of the impact of oriental events on Western history.[88] His objectivity as a historian and his openness to divergent human values enabled him to discern the real strengths of the Turkish state and to present them in full relief. He even took a kind of ironic satisfaction in holding up instances of honorable behavior on the part of "barbarians" as a reproach to Christian commanders and princes. An enemy who was steady, honorable, magnanimous, disciplined, and valiant was much more to be feared than the degenerate barbarians of popular imagination. So unprejudiced was Giovio in assessing the strengths of the Turks that he often had to defend himself against the accusations of contemporaries such as Jiminez de Quesada that he was "aficionado a la nación turquesca."[89]

Beginning with Othman, Giovio traced the growth of Turkish power, sultan by sultan, creating a vivid tableau of the internal struggles that ensured the succession of the most ruthless sons to the throne and highlighting the pressures on each succeeding sultan to imitate the conquests of his forebears. Clearly, from enemies such as these Christianity could expect neither peace nor quarter. Moreover, the present sultan, Suleiman the Magnificent, was a ruler whose many virtues had strengthened the Turkish state by cementing the loyalty of subjects and soldiers.

> Your Majesty should know that he is resolute and minutely informed on the affairs of Christianity and that he keeps his mind and forces in instant readiness for more wars. He has marvelous intuition. Not only is he adorned with many virtues, he lacks the salient vices of cruelty, avarice, and treachery which marred his predecessors, Selim, Bajazet, and Muhammad. Above all, he is religious and liberal, and with these two qualities one flies to heaven. For religion produces temperance and justice while liberality wins the spirit of the soldiers and sows the hope of certain reward in men of all conditions who seek through talent to rise to better fortune.[90]

Although Giovio believed that in military discipline Turkish armies surpassed the ancient Roman, let alone contemporary Christian armies, he nonetheless believed that German pikes could break the charges of the Janissaries, the nerve of the Turkish forces. Like the soldiers of Mark Antony advancing against the Parthians, the emperor's cavalry and infantry should be provided with shields to protect them from Turkish archers. Above all, Giovio urged the emperor to seek a decisive engagement and avoid a drawn-out tactical campaign. A vigorous offensive in Hungary, he argued, was the best defense for western Europe. Rhodes, Belgrade, and Buda should have banished thoughts of awaiting the Turks in Austria or Italy, a feasible strategy if peace among the Christian states permitted a swift, united response, but not as things stood currently.[91]

In the late winter and spring of 1532, Rome was again full of rumors of an impending Turkish offensive. In March the imperial court confirmed Venetian reports that a large fleet was being readied for attacks on Sicily and Apulia and a large army for invading Hungary. Implored by his brother Ferdinand, Charles V began preparing in earnest to defend Hungary, while the pope began fortifying the Marche and fitting out a fleet for Andrea Doria. The danger to Rome seemed real enough to cause Giovio to plan on spending the summer inland in Como.[92] When summer came, however, he found himself not in Como but in Germany with the armies of Charles V. To assist the emperor's crusade the pope had raised 50,000 ducats by means of a tax on the Italian clergy of half their yearly revenues, cardinals included, and Ippolito was designated as legate to take the treasure to Germany. On July 8 he left Rome with a numerous suite of prelates, secretaries, and curial officials, and a guard composed of 40 captains, 130 arquebusiers, and up to 200 cavalrymen.[93]

For the initial stages of the journey, Giovio seems to have been following a couple of days behind the cardinal. During a night with Guicciardini, now governor of Bologna, conversation naturally enough centered on the Turks. Two days later Guicciardini confessed to his friend Bartolomeo Lanfredini that Giovio had succeeded in frightening him with everything he had to say "regarding the power, the preparations, the quality of justice, and the temperance of the Turk and of Pasha Ibrahim [the grand vizier]." As usual, Giovio's open-mindedness was taken amiss, and some of the party had facetiously suggested that his propaganda might almost win Europe for the Turk.[94] For Guicciardini, talking of Turkish matters had been partly a personal convenience. On the eve of Giovio's arrival the formidable Tuscan had confessed to Landfredini that he feared Giovio's importunities, perhaps anticipating probing questions on his role in the events of 1526–27 or the situation in Florence with the deadly antagonism between Alessandro and Ippolito.[95]

In Mantua, Giovio caught up with the cardinal. From there the party headed for the Brenner Pass, Ippolito dressed not as a cleric but as a soldier, with sword and dagger, a red hat with a white plume, and a cut cloak.[96] At Verona, Giovio had a brief reunion with Giberti, and at Riva on Lake Garda he spent a night with Count Niccolò d'Arco, who hailed him with an ode recalling their joyous times together at Pavia.[97]

During the legate's solemn entry into Regensburg on August 13, the Venetian ambassador noted Giovio among the prelates in the cortege.[98] By the end of July the emperor had succeeded in bringing about the semblance of a religious peace in Germany and preparations for the crusade were in full swing. Ippolito busied himself in raising eight thousand Hungarian cavalry with the advice of King Ferdinand and the treasure he had brought from Rome.[99] On August 27, just before his departure from

Regensburg, Giovio wrote to his brother describing the preparations and his own emotions. The entire army, he calculated, including the Hungarian and Croatian soldiers recruited by the legate, would number 100,000 foot and 25,000 horse, with another 75,000 followers. The Turk had 150,000 fighting men, he had heard, in a total host of 500,000. "We will drink from the chalice to escape fear," he confided, "and we will hope for a [decisive] victory if battle is joined, because in a long war we will not do well." He reassured his family that he would remain "in a secure place to be able to write of the outcome" but left instructions for the disposal of his possessions should he not return.[100]

In book 30 of his *Histories* Giovio observed that not since Roman times had the Danube seen so many boats and soldiers as embarked from Regensburg on September 3, and he painted a vivid picture of the noisy scene, with the trumpet flourishes, the drum rolls, and the soldiers all shouting to their friends as the boats full of troops moved down the river. Even as they embarked, however, the chance for the decisive engagement Giovio hoped for had been lost. Once again, the divisions within Christendom had prevented timely action. On August 7 the sultan had arrived in western Hungary with his huge army and laid siege to the small fortress town of Köszeg (Güns) near the Austrian frontier, about sixty miles south of Vienna. Miraculously, it held out for three full weeks while Charles V was still making preparations in Regensburg, until on August 28 Suleiman finally raised the siege. It was the heroism of the defenders of Köszeg, not the imperial armies, that saved Hungary. In his *Histories* Giovio explained that the resistance was possible because Suleiman lacked heavy artillery. The sultan had brought only light artillery, expecting not sieges but an engagement with the emperor "in battle for the empire of the world." The historian had seen the haughty challenge to Charles V, written on serrated paper with Arabic letters of blue and gold and seals of gold.[101]

Charles V arrived at Vienna on September 23, too late for fighting but in time to receive some Turkish standards captured in skirmishes and to enjoy a magnificent review of his forces that took two days. Although the onlookers "wept with joy," Giovio said, "at the hope of a certain victory over the barbarians should the proud enemy be audacious enough to present himself," Suleiman had already turned southward and the emperor was in no position to pursue.[102] The soldiers had already refused Ferdinand's pleas to follow the retreating army and unseat the Turks' client-king, John Zápolya. As usual their pay was in arrears, and the deep divisions in religious and political loyalty were making themselves felt. The mighty host was mainly facade. On learning that Suleiman had crossed the Drave and marched to Belgrade with 30,000 captives, the emperor turned his thoughts "somewhat sooner than expected" to Italy. Despite Ferdinand's pleas to use this great army for the reconquest of Hungary, Charles V would only consent to leave the Italian troops while he himself took his Spanish veterans and some of the German regulars back to Italy, where he wished to have a colloquy with the pope before embarking for Spain.

Giovio's narrative of the great crusade filled the thirtieth book of his *Histories*. It was imbued with the immediacy of eyewitness history and his optimistic view of Charles V engendered by the coronation settlement. It opened magniloquently, promising to narrate a greater assemblage of arms than had ever been described by any historian. Yet even as Giovio extolled the magnificence of the army being marshaled, he rent the veil of splendor with observations betraying the underlying social, political, and economic problems that had already sapped the vitality of this crusade. In Germany, for example, he made clear that religious conflict had only been set aside, not resolved. He took note of the efforts at subversion on the part of Francis I and his ambassador to the Sublime Porte, although he argued (not unrealistically) that Ottoman expansionism was a sufficient reason for Suleiman's invasion and that French encouragement was not a material factor. He was realistic, as well, about the complex political situation in Hungary itself and the treacherous rivalries among the Christians there. The only significant negative factor he ignored was Venice's abstention from the emperor's crusade because of its own truce with the Turks.

Giovio depicted the pope as eager to impress the Protestants with his concern for the welfare of Germany, but having spent a million gold florins for the subjugation of Florence, the Holy Father had nothing left to give. He had accordingly taxed the Italian clergy half a year's income, the bulk of which had been extracted with incredible rapacity from those least able to pay, the lower clergy, hospitals, and convents of nuns. And while priests fled from their churches to escape the tax gatherers and altars were denuded of their furnishings, the cardinals managed to evade the tax, "as if for the preservation of the dignity of the Roman curia it were permissible for cardinals to abate nothing of the customary splendor of their style of living even when the mass of the needy were being stripped of the last sustenance for their lives."[103] Moreover, the money forcibly gathered from the rank and file of the Church—Giovio's Latin here (*coacta pecunia*) was deliberately phrased—was entrusted to the legate, Ippolito de' Medici, whose "insane expenses" had only begun to be matched by augmented revenues from the benefices of the recently deceased Pompeo Colonna.[104] In describing the Church's response to the Turkish menace, Giovio thus managed to point out the sort of abuses—pluralism and clerical luxury—that were fueling the Lutheran movement and dividing Christendom. This was certainly telling his patrons "bitter truths."

In Vienna, Giovio had been able to interview the castellan of Köszeg, Nicholas Jurišić, who became for him that rare individual in sixteenth-century warfare, a valid hero in a valid cause.[105] But beyond celebrating the small garrison's determined resistance, Giovio used it to expose the lack of mission in the rest of the Christian forces, moving directly from the siege to an ugly incident in Vienna where the competition for quarters among the emperor's soldiers threatened to become a war of its own, a dismal contrast not only to the heroism of the defenders of Köseg but to the admirable discipline of the Turkish foe.[106]

In narrating the march of del Vasto's troops from Italy to Germany, Giovio had sarcastically described the aversion of rich Spanish captains to the fatigues and hardships of fighting the Turks as opposed to plundering the people of Italy.[107] Yet another display of indifference to the welfare of Christendom occurred when the emperor's Italian units learned they were to be left behind to endure campaigns in the Hungarian winter while their Spanish compeers returned to the delights of Italy. At first they began to grumble and demand triple pay. Then, in October, about eight thousand of them, led by Tito Marconio of Volterra, mutinied and headed back to Italy, crossing the Drave at Villach and marching to the Tagliamento where they disbanded.[108] Hence, despite some creditable fighting that occurred in skirmishes, the shortcomings of the crusade all stood revealed: leaders preoccupied with European politics, Protestants more concerned with confessional advantage than the defense of Christendom, and mercenary soldiers preferring to prey on civilians rather than fight against the enemies of their faith. In sum, all Giovio had to say about the great endeavor was that the emperor led a mighty host to Vienna and that this was more than had hitherto been done. The denouement came in the partition of Hungary the following year.[109]

Giovio's account of the return march further demonstrated his capacity as a historian to recount both good and bad of his patrons. Traversing the mountain passes in an unusually cold autumn was not a comfortable experience; in his autobiographical sketch he described it as *per ignem et aquam in refrigerium* (through fire and water into deep cold).[110] For the youthful legate, "of an age and vigor of spirit more disposed to bearing arms than performing sacred rites," the crusade had been a great adventure, almost the military command he coveted, and because of this he chafed all the more at the position the emperor assigned him at the rear of the march with the "gowns"—the ambassadors, prelates, and secretaries.[111] To the plaudits of his "adulators" but to the dismay of his "mature advisers," he had shed his wearisome cardinal's biretta and robes during most of the crusade and donned secular garb, with a fur cap. To Giovio, who wanted nothing more than to put on a cardinal's cap, it must have seemed a great waste.

Volatile by nature, impatient, and, "as with those in great fortune, accustomed to obey no one," Ippolito broke the appointed order. Giovio was not specific as to when, but reports to the Venetian senate indicated that the legate had already left Vienna ahead of time on October 6. Between October 8 and 10 he and his escort of cavalry officers succeeded in slipping by the emperor and riding ahead with the officers and troops sent to keep watch on the column of rebel Italians.[112]

To those who knew the twenty-one-year-old cardinal, Giovio contended, it seemed a harmless enough escapade, but Charles V was disturbed by the fact that Ippolito not only had a good deal of money in his possession but numbered among his companions Pietro Maria de' Rossi, count of San Secondo, in whose company the Italian mutiny was thought to have begun, and who was suspected of scheming to free his native Arezzo from Florentine domination. When Ippolito refused to obey his summons to return, Charles V began to fear he was hoping to enlist the rebel Italian soldiers and make another attempt to seize Florence from his cousin Alessandro. At St. Veit in Carinthia, therefore, the emperor had Ippolito taken into custody, along with Rossi, and held five days.[113]

Shortly after this drastic step, the emperor summoned Giovio to his side. As they rode, Charles V explained that he had acted much against his will but in the interests of the peace of Italy and the good of the Medici family, and he asked Giovio, as the confidant of everyone involved, to write to the pope. Although Giovio thought the measure "a little harsh," he could not but sympathize with the emperor's concerns and did as he was bidden. The pope, he said, took things in good part. Actually Clement VII protested the measure to the envoys of Charles and Ferdinand with tears in his eyes, but Giovio was right in that he quickly swallowed his feelings so as not to mar the meeting with the emperor then being arranged.[114]

Ippolito, once freed, rushed with a small guard to Venice, where he was reluctantly and quietly received, sans ceremony, and where he consoled himself with the company of Aretino and the charms of Aretino's friend, the renowned courtesan "La Zaffetta."[115] He also sat for Titian's famous portrait of him in Hungarian dress, which Giovio later had copied for his collection. The legate held a mace and the scimitar he was given by his Hungarian captains, and (as if in mockery of a cardinal's biretta) he wore a purplish-red cap with peacock feathers. A thin, black beard and eyebrows accentuated his finely molded features—the mouth set, the gaze dark and defiant.[116]

After Ippolito's release, Giovio continued on in the emperor's train to Mantua, where Ippolito quietly rejoined the party. The emperor's reception was again sumptuous. Giovio doubtless avoided the hunts, but there were lavish banquets and performances of comedies directed by Calandra with scenery by Giulio Romano.[117] At a ceremony which took place on the feast of St. Andrew, the emperor bestowed the Order of the Golden Fleece on the marquis del Vasto.[118] Once again there were visits to the palazzo del Te to admire the progress of Giulio Romano's frescoes. Since the emperor's last visit, Giovio had supplied portraits of King Matthias Corvinus of Hungary and Gonzalo de Córdoba to help the sculptor Alfonso Cittadella, "il Lombardo," complete the statues of famous condottieri for the loggia of David.[119] As usual, the festivities provided Giovio with occasions for interviewing captains and soliciting details of campaigns. He was present in the palace of Cardinal Ercole Gonzaga, where Ippolito was lodging, when a discussion arose between the duke of Urbino, Antonio de Leyva, and the marquis del Vasto over charges made by the French that Count Guido Rangoni had lost them the battle of Landriano.[120]

While at Mantua, Charles V learned that Clement VII was willing to meet him again at Bologna. When the emperor made his entry on December 13, 1532, he was awaited by a pope who, as Giovio emphasized, had been deeply alienated by the decision, published in April of the previous year, to award Modena and Reggio to Alfonso d'Este. Indeed, the emperor's adjudication had been so hard for the pope to swallow that Giovio doubted he would ever be able to digest it. Nor had it helped that news of it had reached Rome on the fourth anniversary of the sack.[121] In his biography of Alfonso d'Este, Giovio described the scene he was later called to witness when Alfonso's ambassadors arrived with the 100,000 ducats stipulated as payment for Modena and Reggio, and the pope refused to accept them. When the ambassadors had left with the money, Clement VII

> descended from the lofty throne which had been set up for the morning's conclave and, turning to me, whom he had summoned to witness his refusal, said with a beaming face, "Will you describe me in your *Histories*, Giovio, as avaricious and eager for money when I have just voluntarily repudiated this great heap of gold? Or will you perhaps think me inept and out of my mind to put the dignity and reputation of the papacy above lucre and the convenience of the moment?[122]

Giovio saw a clear link between the emperor's decision on Modena and Reggio and the pope's subsequent rapprochement with Francis I. Shortly after learning of Charles V's decision, Clement VII had consented to a marriage between Catherine de' Medici and Francis I's second son, Henry, duke of Orléans, a match that so disturbed Charles V, who had wanted Catherine for Francesco II Sforza, that many feared Clement VII had thrown away the peace of Italy; but the emperor needed the pope's support for the council demanded by the diet of Regensburg, and Clement VII was disposed, Giovio said, "by artifice and temperament [*magno sibi artificio et temperamento*]" to placate both sovereigns. The friendship of just one king, he said, meant servitude for the pope.[123] Despite the widening rift between them, therefore, pope and emperor greeted each other in Bologna with every outward sign of cordiality and were lodged as before in communicating suites.

Giovio wrote book 31 of the *Histories* during the high tide of his admiration for Charles V, but despite optimism over the cooperation of pope and emperor resulting in Andrea Doria's capture of Koron and Patras during the autumn of 1532, he was unenthusiastic about their second colloquy.[124] He could forgive the decision on Modena and Reggio and acquiesce in the pope's explanation that the imperial judges had been corrupted by bribes, but he had discerned the inner workings of Charles V's mind and realized he would never give up a fief of the empire.[125] Had Giovio known that Clement VII had been prepared to grant Catherine not only Modena and Reggio but Parma and Piacenza as dowry for a French match, he might have been even more sarcastic than he was about the pope's digestion.[126] He said almost nothing about the council demanded by the emperor, perhaps knowing that the pope's promise to pursue it was empty, if not actually deceitful, because of the resolute opposition of Francis I, and he deplored the pope's capitulation to the emperor on the question of Catherine of Aragon. The admonition—issued in Bologna to Henry VIII to set aside Anne Boleyn within thirty days or be excommunicated—Giovio thought an "empty threat, untimely in its severity," which helped force the English king onto the path of schism.[127]

One outcome of the second colloquy of Bologna filled Giovio with unfeigned gratitude, however, and that was the league for the defense of Italy which pope and emperor drew up with Austria, Milan, Mantua, Ferrara, Genoa, Siena, and Lucca, and the tacit compliance of Venice. Milan would be garrisoned by de Leyva as captain-general, but the rest of the hated Spanish troops would be dispersed—some to Koron, some to garrison the cities of Sicily, some to guard Otranto, and some to return to Spain. This was the most praiseworthy achievement of Clement VII's entire life, Giovio declared. Rejoicing to be free of "the cruelest and most rapacious soldiery," the people of Lombardy could "begin to anticipate for the first time having life, liberty, and property."[128]

One event during the colloquy marked another milestone in the expansion of Europe's horizons. In 1521 Manuel I of Portugal had informed Pope Leo X that a Portuguese mission had fulfilled an age-old European dream of establishing contact with the Christian king of Ethiopia, popularly known as "Prester John." The mission returned to Portugal in 1527, but Manuel's successor, João III, was less enthusiastic, and only in 1532 did he allow the chaplain, Francisco Alvares, to bring the pope two letters proffering the obedience of David III (Lebnä-Dengel) to the Roman See. Alvares was received as the king's ambassador in a public consistory held on January 29, 1533, in which he presented a small golden cross together with the letters. These the Portuguese ambassador asked Giovio to translate from Portuguese into Latin, along with two letters from the *negus* to the king of Portugal, all of which were immediately published by the Flemish printer, Jacob Keymolen of Alost, with a description of the ceremonies.[129]

In his introduction, Keymolen mentioned a description of the geography, history, religion, and customs of Ethiopia compiled by Alvares, which he said Giovio had also been asked to translate, but none ever appeared. In book 18 of the *Histories* Giovio gave a remarkably accurate history and description of Ethiopia (even if he could not refrain from inserting a few elements of European legend, such as the unicorn) based probably on Alvares' information, supplemented by interviews with an Abyssinian monk, Täsfa-Seyon, who came to Rome about 1535 and lived there until his death. Growing reservations in Lisbon and Rome about the Judaizing tendencies of the Ethiopian church impeded further efforts at union and perhaps kept Giovio from proceeding with a translation of Alvares' commentary, but he had at least helped in reclaiming "Prester John" from legend.[130]

Charles V departed from Bologna on February 28, the day after the new league was ratified. In a final show of goodwill he had requested Ippolito as legate to Spain, but the cardinal adamantly refused. Enough was enough.[131] At Pavia the emperor stopped for a tour of the battlefield with the marquis del Vasto, then enjoyed the hunting around Vigevano until he heard from Andrea Doria that the galleys were ready and the weather propitious; and so, after another triumphal welcome in Genoa, he departed for Spain.[132] Giovio left Bologna on March 10 with Clement VII, who again avoided Florence by traveling through the papal states. For Giovio it was a chance to follow the ancient Via Flaminia down the coast to Ancona and to see the shrine of Loreto before crossing the mountains via San Severino and Camerino. By April 3, 1533, he was back in Rome. On the 16th he received his episcopal consecration from the papal sacristan, the venerable archbishop of Durazzo, Gabriele Mascioli Foschi, who was assisted by Rodolfo Pio, bishop of Faenza. In the Ischian dialogue Giovio had anticipated an earlier consecration, and the long delay was probably owing to the times, his travels, and the necessary preparation for priestly orders. Two other bishops consecrated with him were likewise appointees of 1528, one of whom, Bernardo de' Medici, had also been with Cardinal Ippolito in Germany.[133]

Scarcely had he recovered from a half year of constant travel than Giovio set out again for Marseilles, where Clement VII was to meet with Francis I to celebrate the marriage of Catherine de' Medici with Prince Henry. The pope had overcome opposition in the Sacred College to his two-faced diplomacy and had "subtly" persuaded the French to acquiesce in his league with the emperor by pointing out that it had resulted in the dispersion of imperial troops from Milan.[134] The papal party left Rome on September 9, 1533, following the Via Cassia to Siena. At San Miniato al Tedesco, where the old Via Francigena joined the road from Florence to the coast, the pope stopped to meet with Michelangelo to negotiate a contract for a *Last Judgment* in the Sistine Chapel.[135]

At Livorno the papal party embarked on October 5 on the galleys of the duke of Albany, who had already landed Catherine at Nice for her overland journey to Marseilles. The pope's galley was splendidly hung with gold brocade. Leaving port, Giovio recalled, they were overtaken by Andrea Doria and the fleet returning victorious from Koron—a stirring sight—standards flying and cannons roaring a salute to His Holiness.[136] Despite this propitious beginning, an attack of quartan fever turned the voyage into a trial for Giovio.[137] After a stop in Villa Franca (present-day Villefranche), the convoy arrived in Marseilles on October 11, where a reception had been prepared for the following day by the constable of France, Anne de Montmorency, "with incredible apparatus and expense." On the 13th, King Francis, Queen Eleanor, and the three princes made their entry and obeisances to the pope, attended by "all the nobility of France." Fortunately, Giovio had recovered enough to enjoy the "splendid" Latin oration by Jean du Bellay, bishop of Paris, which concluded the ceremonies.[138]

Following the precedent of Bologna, pope and king were lodged in apartments communicating by an inner door, and it was clear from the *Histories* that Giovio's enjoyment of the festivities had been marred by fears of the mischief their conversations might bode for Italy. In contrast to Guicciardini, who stressed the personal nature of the talks and the fact that no formal agreements resulted, Giovio emphasized the length of the private conversations during the four weeks of the visit and the suspicions they aroused in the mind of the emperor. In Giovio's weighted prose the communicating door between the apartments became "a secret door." Mere discretion was made to seem ominous: "So great was the silence surrounding their plans that not even a servant with a candle was admitted to their nocturnal colloquies."[139]

Both king and pope had suffered the miseries of imprisonment at the emperor's hands—a certain bond between them, Giovio suggested—and he dwelt again on Clement VII's anger at Charles V's decision to return Modena and Reggio to Alfonso d'Este. Indeed, he drew an even more vivid picture of the pope, "lamenting to everyone the injury done him and, contrary to custom, freely expressing his emotions, stroking his beard the while, first with one hand then with the other."[140] Hinting at possible outcomes of the meeting, Giovio recounted a witticism of Filippo Strozzi's, who affected to soothe the disappointment of the French treasurers at the small size of Catherine's dowry by predicting that three inestimable jewels were yet to come—Genoa, Milan, and Naples.[141] Giovio did not even mention the council sought by the emperor, probably because it was so obvious that neither Clement VII nor Francis I wanted it, each for his own reasons.

Despite his distaste for French rule and his fears of losing the peace so recently acquired, Giovio admired Francis I, and in book 31 he unstintingly praised his magnificence and generosity. The men of letters in the papal cortege, he said, were "received most familiarly by the king, an arbiter of all elegance and an acute judge of all the fine arts." Giovio himself was granted an audience in which he was able to question the king about the battle of Pavia and other events relating to the *Histories*. No one, he said, ever answered his questions more freely or at greater length, a graciousness reflected in Giovio's moving narration of the chivalrous king's capture at Pavia.[142] Besides an interview, Francis I granted Giovio a pension, as he did a number of other papal courtiers.[143]

After Guicciardini, on behalf of the pope, had concluded the final negotiations over the marriage contract, Catherine and Henry were wed by Clement VII in a solemn ceremony on October 28. She was fourteen years old, he fifteen and none too happy with this alliance.[144] After creating four French cardinals on November 7, the pope departed on the 12th aboard the galleys of the duke of Albany. At Savona he dismissed the French fleet and sailed on the ships of Andrea Doria to Civitavecchia. For Giovio the return voyage was an ordeal that nearly ended his life. He had been ill much of the time at Marseilles, and a recurrence of quartan fever on the voyage was so severe he made a new will.[145] Heavy autumn storms tossed the vessels, exacerbating the miseries of fever. The Mantuan envoy reported at one point that a galley with Giovio aboard had been driven off course in heavy seas and was not yet accounted for.[146] "I touched the hand of Charon in the thieving port of Agay," Giovio recounted to Cardinal Ippolito, "and I saw him again at the island of Gallinara."[147] At Albenga he found some old friends and decided to remain there to regain some strength. Finally, as autumn turned toward winter, he made his way overland to Como with further hardships crossing "the frozen Apennines." Not until December 9, 1533, could he rest at home.

Giovio's homecoming after more than a decade was an event for his family and the city. Although living "by the scales of medicine" and subject to bad days when the fever left him hot and stupefied, he was gradually improving thanks to a strict regimen and the warmth of the German-style stove he had ordered for his room. He predicted that he would be cured when the sun reached Aries. Meanwhile the visits of physicians, doctors, and grammarians gave him great amusement. His sixty-two-year-old brother he found "without a single white hair and as energetic in all literature as Aleandro is in councils." Vitruvius, he said, "would have laughed at my remodeled house on account of the foolishness of plastering over old designs with modern ones, but he would not have been angry because of the commodiousness of some cheerful, largish rooms and the air of amenity afforded by the two gardens and the square courtyard."[148]

When the sun did come around to Aries, Giovio found himself only two-thirds cured, despite his prediction. Writing to Molza he confessed his "marvelous desire" to make up a third with him and Valeriano "in those sweet dialogues that I know you are holding for the entertainment of our common Maecenas and patron," and at cherry time he hoped to be able to entertain his friends in Rome with the opinions of the *litterati* of Como, "full of words, points, and secrets, up to the fringe."

> They are learned but bizarre; and among others there is one most obstinate who adores the style of Erasmus, and another knows by heart all of the *Polyantha* [a grammatical repertory used in schools] and another recites page by page the *Margarita poetarum* [an anthology by Albrecht von Eyb]. My brother functions as a sort of Palamon and sustains these controversies without giving judgment, and this is my amusement. Here I have found all that the son of Cicero and Apicius could have desired.

For the son of Apicius there were "wines to make one fling the wine of Rome on the floor, . . . everything [to eat] that flies or runs," and "the confections manufactured in devotion to San Biagio" that "would make every Neapolitan dine in the morning."[149]

All in all, Giovio's stay in Como was a satisfying one. Benedetto, who had just completed his own estimable history of Como, had presumably read and critiqued the *Histories* as he had offered to do.[150] Giovio himself had had a chance to pay court to Francesco II Sforza and had recovered the cost of the addition to the family house as a souvenir of the duke's friendship.[151] Observing Lombardy firsthand, he had been able to render a good account of Sforza's government and the progress being made in rebuilding after the long Spanish occupation. Giovio's continual laments about the misery caused by the Spanish troops emphasized the destructiveness of the wars to the economy and people of Italy.

Between the loss of Parma and Piacenza to the Church, the dislocation of the rural economy, the flight of peasants from the fields, the disruption of commerce, and the confiscation of working capital through taxation, the ordinary revenues of the duchy of Milan had, in fact, fallen from 600,000 ducats to 170,000. To stimulate the economy Sforza had done his best to reduce taxation, but the contributions he was obligated to pay the emperor forced him to levy extraordinary imposts which ruined many families.[152] Little wonder Giovio found that the pope's journey to Marseilles had alarmed the Lombards with the prospect of renewed warfare.[153]

So anxious was Giovio about his place in Ippolito's retinue and potential mischief from the "thorn sowers" always found in courts, that he did not wait for Sforza's thirteen-year-old bride, Christina of Denmark, to make her long-anticipated entry into Milan but set out with the coming of good weather on the long journey to Rome. He arrived on May 12, shortly before the onset of the pope's last illness, a recurrence of his stomach disorders.[154] All during the summer, as Clement VII hovered between life and death, the problems that had beset his reign erupted anew. Relations deteriorated between Francis I and Charles V. Ippolito and Alessandro quarreled. The Moslem pirates resumed their dreaded attacks, carrying off not only treasure but their customary human booty: men for the oar, women for the harems, and boys for the sultan's armies. First they struck at Sicily, then Procida; then, on August 18, they raided Fondi in a brazen attempt to capture the beautiful duchess of Trajetto for the sultan's harem. Through all of this the pope's condition steadily worsened, until finally, in the afternoon of September 25, 1534, his sufferings ceased.

With sublime understatement, Lorenzo Grana, whose proficiency as an orator Giovio had always admired, asked the cardinals assembled at Clement VII's funeral to elect a new pope equal in virtue "but somewhat luckier."[155] There were those who went so far as to thank the papal physician, Matteo Corti, whose treatments were presumed responsible for the death of a man who was only fifty-seven years old and of generally robust constitution. Giovio himself had little positive to say for the patron in whose service he had achieved prominence and wealth. By the time he finished book 32 of his *Histories*, it was all too obvious that in "wishing to provide for the private good of his family rather than for the public peace," Clement VII had sown at Marseilles the seeds of a new war for Milan and a harvest of misery for Lombardy.[156] His one great service, Giovio noted, had been to allow himself to be led by the emperor into the pacification of Italy and its liberation from mercenary soldiers; yet with his fatal propensity for balancing one force against another to enhance his own position and aggrandize his family, he had immediately begun to undo his own best work, just as by switching allegiance from side to side he had earlier brought on the sack of Rome.

Although similar to Guicciardini's memorable sketch of Clement VII's character in the *Storia d'Italia*, Giovio's final assessment was tinged with personal bitterness, particularly in regard to the pope's parsimony with men of letters. "To these," he complained, "he gave the blandishments of words to hold them in the appearance of grace, but in secret he hated them like his creditors."[157] Those whom he loved "for some secret reason," or whom he was forced by circumstances to cultivate, he shamelessly promoted to the greatest honors, while overlooking those who served him loyally. Of the thirty-one cardinals he created, Giovio charged, the pope had really admired only one or two.

Giovio did not dissent from the common interpretation of Clement VII as basically a good, if weak, man, but he implied that in positions of leadership, goodness without strength is no better than vice. He readily conceded the natural dignity, exemplary patience and self-control that were matched by humanity and discriminating judgment, but he felt that Clement VII's mind and spirit were unequal to the papacy. He was more of a nature to follow detailed account books and to master the secrets of artisans. "And certainly he was one whom no one ever deceived in small matters, although by the same token it should not be cause for marvel if in great matters that touched the welfare of the world he was very often deceived."[158] The strength of his judgment was vitiated by the weakness of his resolve, and while agonizing over expenditures he lost the moment for action.

"A fatal parsimony" ruined Clement VII's statecraft, and weakness engendered the ambiguity that became in its way a dishonesty just as real as the deliberate dishonesty of less high-minded popes. Giovio repeatedly expressed his belief that Clement VII's vain attempts to appear strong and to enhance his own position by balancing contending monarchs against each other were responsible for two of the greatest disasters to the Renaissance papacy—the loss of England and the sack of Rome. To Cardinal Alessandro Farnese, he later explained why, among so many biographies, he was unwilling to write the life of Giulio de' Medici: "Because I could never write the truth without prejudice to my honor, having been his servitor, nor could I write falsehood without charge to my conscience, wishing to be withal a just and honest writer."[159]

CHAPTER NINE

Transitions (1535–1538)

A far questo non si può l'uomo allambicar il cervello *impensis propriis.*

—Giovio to Rodolfo Pio of Carpi, 1535

A man cannot be expected to rack his brains at his own expense.

WITH THE DEATH of Clement VII, Giovio entered a new phase of his career. No longer would he rely on one patron. Although he eventually attached himself to the new pope's grandson, Cardinal Alessandro Farnese, he began using his reputation as a historian to develop a galaxy of patrons who collectively did much better by him than the single patron of times past. The field of force that held this galaxy in place was his correspondence. To maintain relations with his patrons Giovio developed into one of the great letter writers of the age, the creator of a new genre of lively political commentary.

To the duke of Milan, Giovio confessed that he did not have the same familiarity with Paul III's secretaries as with Clement VII's and that henceforth his news would have to come from Campo dei Fiori—that is, from the gossip of Rome.[1] Yet far more of his letters were preserved from this new period than from his years as a papal intimate. In Ferrero's edition, only 25 letters date from the reign of Clement VII, while 384 are from subsequent years—230 of them from the last seven years alone. Some letters may have been lost in the sack of Rome, but two factors were chiefly responsible for the imbalance: first, the new importance of the letter in Italian literary life and the growing inclination to preserve, circulate, and publish good examples of the genre; second, the growing virtuosity of Giovio's letters themselves. Deprived of privileged information, he was compelled to become a commentator on events and to develop the "journalistic" qualities that made his letters so sought-after. To compete with the detailed reports flowing to the courts of his patrons from merchants, ambassadors, and other agents, he had to offer something more than mere information, and so he started incorporating the perspective he had gained from his vast knowledge of fifteenth- and sixteenth-century history. Giovio's commentaries on events, Cosimo I de' Medici once declared, said "all that can, in my opinion, be said," and, what was more, said it pungently and vivaciously.[2]

Too eclectic and undisciplined for the crafters of literary Italian, Giovio's style appealed immensely to the audience he most desired—captains, prelates, and princes. The correspondence of the Roman curia was sprinkled with his linguistic coinages and bons mots.[3] His effects were carefully calculated. In one of his letters to Francesco II Sforza, for example, he apologized for exceeding "philosophical gravity, episcopal dignity, and historical continence . . . in order to give some entertainment to Your Excellency when, for the sake of sanity, he needs to shake off the heavy cares of state." It was an eminently successful approach. The "sweetness" of Giovio's letters was such, the duke declared, "that the more they are read by us the more they arouse the desire to reread them."[4]

Giovio aimed at the spontaneity of everyday speech. His grammar was basically Tuscan, but compounded with intentional grammatical infractions and extraneous linguistic elements that made for a free-flowing, indeed, effervescent, medium. Wary, like Bembo, of the Latinizations of the Quattrocento—"falsi Latini in volgare"—but, unlike Bembo, contemptuous of "pure" Tuscan, Giovio appropriated the "parlare alla cortigiana," the common Italian of the courts.[5] Linguistically speaking, his epistolary prose had five major strains: the Latin expressions and Latinisms natural to a humanist and cleric; Italian dialect expressions, particularly Lombard and Venetian; Spanish expressions and occasional Gallicisms; the old *lingua zerga*, or *gergo furbesco*, a kind of humorous slang (e.g., the use of the term *agresta* [verjuice] for money); and his own idiosyncratic coinages.[6]

Medical metaphors were the vehicle for some of Giovio's most trenchant irony, as, for example, his terming a blunder by a would-be cardinal "the cassia of the cap [cassia is a violent purgative]." Proverbs and proverbial locutions added earthiness to his style and reinforced its deliberate anticlassicism. Another element, Giovio's *burlevole cifra* or "humorous cipher," was not strictly speaking linguistic but a kind of code frequently found in diplomatic dispatches and based on humorous epithets of the court, as, for example, his pseudonym for Cardinal Farnese, "Efestione," stemming from the perception that Alessandro was as dear to his grandfather as Hephaestion had been to Alexander the Great.[7] Much of Giovio's *burlevole cifra* probably derived from the epithets, pseudonyms, and conceits of the Vignaiuoli and other academies, his use of it being in fact most frequent in the years in which he was a participant in their reunions. With his plurilingualism, his deliberate lexical deformations, and his frequent metaphorical dilations—as often as not ironic—Giovio created out of "the tongue common to all Italy" a highly expressionistic language that brought him to the threshold of literary mannerism. He has been called "in all probability the most experimental writer of the century."[8]

It has been more than once observed that Giovio wrote his own autobiography in his letters, and indeed his letters flowed with the currents of his life.[9] Unpremeditatedly conversational, they mixed the loftiest sentiments with the most trivial personal concerns. In one and the same sentence Giovio could praise Venice as the standard-bearer of Italian liberty and lament the fact that the doge had forgotten his promise to send glass for the windows of the museum.[10] Few autobiographers have revealed themselves as unstintingly. He shared the hopes that sustained him, the defeats that depressed him, and the realities he accommodated with a pungent sense of irony. He alternately displayed the impassioned Italian patriot, the broad-visioned European commentator, the shrewd analyst of human propensities, the gossiping, flattering courtier, and the ambitious careerist. As two sides of one coin he showed the critic of clerical excesses and the self-serving pluralist. He demonstrated his love of all the good things of life: of fine food and delicate wines, literate conversation, the society of accomplished women, of villas, gardens, and the fine arts. He revealed his self-serving tenacity in financial matters as well as his admirable stoicism with the fevers that beset him and the attacks of gout that crippled him. The only elements lacking for a true autobiography would have been a theoretical structure, a unified vision, and a consistent sense of the self over time (although the lack of these elements may well qualify Giovio as a "postmodern" autobiographer).

Giovio's letters revealed, finally, a political and moral vision of surprising acuity and disinterestedness—although hopelessly mixed with personal concerns that often ran counter to it. He was willing to confront the issues of his day with rare directness and to talk of matters normally passed over or treated by periphrasis, such as the ills of the Church or the failings of individual princes. Frequently he used humor as a means of making strong points palatable. In 1543, for example, when the Venetian agent at Milan passed on to the Council of Ten a letter from Giovio, he cautioned, "It is best to make it clear that Giovio's letters are sometimes self-serving, that he has a licentious and satirical manner of writing, and that the letters are always in this same style; however, one can pay attention to what he intends to say on the subject by ignoring the superficial meaning of his words."[11] Using humor to mask propositions of great seriousness was Giovio's way of dealing with his deep frustration at the realities of Italian political life. Francesco Campana, Cosimo I's chancellor, found Giovio's letters "not only entertaining but impassioned."[12]

In his autobiographical fragment, Giovio recorded that after Clement VII's death he went on living in the Vatican palace. Since Paul III had been elected in October 1534, with the active support of Cardinal Ippolito, Giovio probably felt reasonably secure for the time being, although with the ever-deteriorating relationship between Ippolito and his cousin

Alessandro, he was forced to "tread warily."[13] In February 1535 he told his friend Rodolfo Pio of Carpi, nuncio in France, that he was still spending his mornings with Ippolito, and that as one who would die a loyal servitor of the Medici he hoped each cousin would follow his predetermined career and cooperate with the other. If not, he prophesied, "the pheasant and the peacock will each lose his tail."[14] As usual, Giovio was clairvoyant. Far from cooperating with his cousin, Ippolito was entertaining the Florentine exiles, those of 1530, augmented by refugees from Alessandro's increasingly sinister rule, and Giovio learned of the bizarre conspiracy masterminded by Giovanbattista Cibo, archbishop of Marseilles, to hoist the duke with gunpowder when he came to sit in the bedroom of a Florentine lady he was frequenting.[15]

To complicate the situation for Giovio, Ippolito's relations with the pope unexpectedly soured after Paul III deprived him of the legation of Ancona. When the pope detained one of Ippolito's chief henchmen, Count Ottaviano della Genga, the cardinal suspected collusion with Alessandro and fled to his castle near Tivoli. Not long afterward, in the summer of 1535, he set out with a brilliant retinue, including Filippo Strozzi and some of the leading Florentine exiles, to join the emperor in his campaign against the pirates of Tunis. His ultimate intentions were impossible to ascertain. Charles V had agreed to hear the complaints of the Florentine exiles when he came to Naples after the conclusion of the Tunis campaign, and many thought Ippolito intended to press their case before he reached Italy. Giovio, on the other hand, believed he had repented of his quarrel with his cousin and had resolved to seek the emperor's mediation, a view partially endorsed by Varchi.[16] No doubt the excitement of another crusade was a factor. While his agents were attempting to obtain ships, Ippolito and his court tarried at Itri to enjoy the company of Giulia Gonzaga at nearby Fondi. There he developed a fever that on August 10, 1535, turned mortal.

The cardinal's death in the flower of young manhood, coupled with the suddenness of the onset of fever, naturally aroused suspicions of poison, particularly given Alessandro's sinister reputation and the attitude of the pope. Even before Ippolito died, his cook was apprehended by the exiles and put to the *strappado*. Although he confessed under torture to having poisoned his master, his retractions immediately afterward coupled with pleas not to administer remedies for poison to the cardinal left a lingering uncertainty. In relaying the news to Pio, Giovio mentioned the suspicion of poison and the continuing interrogation of the cook at Rome.[17] Not only in the *Histories*, however, but in his *elogium* of Ippolito, written long after he would have had anything to gain from protecting Alessandro, Giovio dismissed the idea of poison, as did the papal judges at the time.[18] In his letter to Pio, he noted that death was "less harsh" to the cardinal "because of the presence of the lady Giulia, who attended him with virtuous courtesies." In the *Elogia* Giovio gave a vivid description of the funeral: the cardinal borne to his last rest on the shoulders of his weeping Ethiopian and African guards, followed by his singular household of Moors, Tartars, Indians, and Turks all demonstrating their grief according to the custom of their nation, "some beating their breasts, others tearing their cheeks with their nails, all with the same grief but with different expressions and a babble of voices." So disappeared Giovio's impetuous patron, like the comet of his *impresa*, "fatis et pravis hominibus ita impellentibus me protestante et deprecante [the fates and crooked men so impelling, I protesting and deprecating]."[19]

It was probably the uncertainty felt by Giovio after the death of Ippolito that caused him to invest so much energy in his efforts to secure payment of the pension awarded him by Francis I at Marseilles. Whatever advantages Francis I hoped to gain by marrying his second son to the niece of the pope had vanished with the death of Clement VII and likewise any inclination to maintain promises to the dead pope's courtiers. For two years Giovio kept badgering Pio to induce the king, the constable Montmorency, and the cardinal of Lorraine to have the pension paid. The correspondence reveals Giovio's preoccupation with living well and the delicate relationship this had to his work as a historian. Part of him was willing to use the *Histories* as a threat to extract the pension, part of him wanted to remain independent in the service of truth. Even though the cardinal of Lorraine had forgotten the honor of his ancestor, the crusader Godfrey of Bouillon, Giovio preached to Pio, "it is contrary to faith pledged that he does not cause to be paid to me at Lyon, in care of Neri Capponi, the barely tasted and publicly awarded royal pension; and to the living and the dead, from Cathay to Tenochtitlan, I say this in order that one day, when [His Majesty] is admiring the admirable [memory] theater of the learned Giulio Camillo, you may remind him that with sleeves rolled up and nightcap on my head I am all ready and in order to do him a fine piece of work according to my weak but expedited talent, according to what will please His Majesty." But then, as if suddenly recalling his integrity as a historian, Giovio added,

> I say this except for the universal history, because in writing that I do not want to have any obligations; it is enough that I will have ambergris and musk on my pen when the glorious name of His Majesty passes under my lined paper. . . . Please explain to him my candid mind, because His Majesty has need of deeds, not words.

How Pio succeeded in explaining such a divided mind is not known. He was asked to do the same with the constable Montmorency as well, whom Giovio jokingly threatened to hide under a haystack in the *Histories* if the pension were not paid.[20]

Giovio felt the historian ought to be respected and rewarded because of the singular power he held over the living and the dead; yet he recognized that if the historian was sincere in his calling, he did not use his power arbitrarily. How then to claim reward if one will tell the truth in any event? Gratitude, Giovio suggested, was owing to the historian for undertaking the labors in default of which great deeds are forgotten, and on this basis he felt he merited substantial support from the beneficiaries of his toil. In fact, owing to disappointment at his failure to gain support, he had once again ceased working on the *Histories*. "You know that at present I am at leisure and not working," he reminded Pio, "quia nemo nos conduxit, idest imperavit quidquam Minervae vostrae [because no one has led us, that is, has requisitioned anything from your Minerva]." In addition to the *Histories* he had begun "to describe the empires of the known world," utilizing his knowledge of modern history, "with chorography on the crupper," and he had even thought of treatises on politics, religion, medicine, and natural history, "but I never found a pale to support my vines."[21]

Support was necessary, Giovio explained,

> because you well know I do not wish to study if not in the fur of marten or lynx, because fox and beaver give off too much smell; and I do not want mules squeezed in a hat press or dry pasta at table; and I do not want servants with broken heels on their shoes and no soles on their stockings; and I want to eat two times a day, and with *minestra*; and I want a fire from St. Francis [October 4] to St. Gregory [March 12]; and I do not want debt to saffron me in the chancery. A man cannot be expected to rack his brains at his own expense.[22]

In his dilemma between the patronage he solicited and the integrity he sought to maintain, Giovio dramatized the lack of provision for a historical profession. With no vocation for the cloister or, for that matter, the practice of medicine, he rejected two possible sources of relative independence. Had he been content to live modestly and retire to his diocese, he might have found, even amidst the cares of ecclesiastical administration, the time and energy to write his *Histories* and the independence to keep them above suspicion. But the real undoing of his reputation as a historian was his thoroughly Renaissance love of magnificence. It was not eating twice a day with *minestra* that betrayed him so much as his aspirations to maintain a rich lifestyle, acquire land, build a Roman villa on Lake Como, convert the ancestral house into a palazzo, and provide for a numerous family of nieces and nephews. These secular ambitions drove him to seek the gifts and pensions that compromised, if only through appearances, his independence and reputation as a historian.

With all its evident ambiguities, Giovio's letter of 1535 to Pio did his reputation incalculable harm when it was published by Domenichi in his

Lettere volgari di Monsignor Giovio (Venice, 1560), where it could be interpreted literally by unfriendly critics. When badgering Pio about the pension, Giovio would have done well to recall the admonition he had received a decade earlier from Benedetto Tagliacarne, an Italian humanist at the French court. After recounting compliments paid Giovio in the king's presence, Tagliacarne cautioned, "I beg you, my Giovio, see that whatever you write for posterity agrees completely with the truth itself, whose persona the historian puts on, and that nothing transmitted by you to posterity be perceived to have been influenced by love or hate; for outstanding fecundity of style can never add as much as even the least suspicion of mendacity can detract."[23] Had Giovio heeded those words, he might have lived less splendidly but his reputation as a historian would have been more secure.

Mornings during the winter of 1535 Giovio spent with Cardinal Ippolito, afternoons he passed attending the new pope.[24] In his youth Paul III had been a pupil of Pomponio Leto and had been active enough in the gatherings of the Roman academy to have been considered a member. Indeed, he was one of the interlocutors in Paolo Cortesi's influential dialogue *De hominibus doctis* (On learned men). Giovio had not known Farnese well enough to have formed any expectations about his papacy, however, and his admiration grew rapidly during these first months. "Every day," he declared to Francesco II Sforza, ". . . I find him more humane, more courteous, more learned, more lofty of concept, more Christian, and more just; and this is the truth, for I see that for the good and like a good ecclesiastic he is swift and resolute, and in worldly affairs he knows when he needs to put on the ears of a Genoese merchant, or speak in ambiguities like a Florentine merchant, or keep his back to the wall like a Bergamasc farmer." Giovio was particularly relieved to see that the new pope gave no sign of willingness to abet the designs of Francis I on Milan, despite his own evident designs on the duchy of Camerino.

Giovio quickly divined that Paul III's worst problem was finding the money to take care of his beloved family. Describing the pope at leisure with his grandchildren, Giovio allowed himself the faintest touch of irony: ". . . and Your Excellency knows how much grandchildren please grandfathers." The fifteen-year-old Alessandro had been created a cardinal the previous December, and Giovio described his future patron as a youth "of good cheer, with the Orsini lip of the count of Pitigliano his grandfather." But then irony yielded to one of Giovio's startlingly candid analyses:

> So, My Lord, everyone has things to do in his own house, and the opulence of the ancient papacy has been annihilated through having attended more to the temporal than the spiritual; and so, bit by bit, losing the reputation and

authority of religion, the shop no longer prospers, and we are led to where we are, to the necessity of a great council from which no good can be hoped unless God lend us his right hand.[25]

Aside from his efforts to obtain payment of the French pension and give good counsel to Ippolito—both unavailing—Giovio's attention throughout the winter, spring, and summer of 1535 was increasingly absorbed by the emperor's forthcoming crusade against the pirates of Tunis. For several years the formidable corsair Kair-ed-din, nicknamed Barbarossa, had been terrorizing the coasts of Italy and Spain. After driving out the indigenous ruler Muley Hassan, he had made Tunis his base, a short sail from Sicily. Suleiman the Magnificent had given him the titles of pasha and admiral, along with the governorship of Algiers. In June of 1535, after months of diplomatic preparations during which he shamed most of Europe into a state of truce, Charles V launched his *cruzada* from Cagliari. Andrea Doria commanded the fleet, the marquis del Vasto the infantry.

Giovio had followed preparations with mounting interest. Throughout the winter of 1535 he had collected descriptions of Barbarossa's defenses from travelers and was proud to have been able to furnish d'Avalos with a topographic sketch of the fortifications of Tunis. By July 14 he had seen the emperor's letters to the pope giving details of the preliminary skirmishes, and by late July or early August he himself had a letter from del Vasto announcing the expedition's complete success. The fortress guarding the port, "La Goletta," was taken after an arduous siege and the Moslem army routed in a pitched battle. When the emperor's army reached the walls of the city, the Christian slaves revolted and seized the citadel. Barbarossa fled and Charles V was master of Tunis. Proud of his own part in the fighting, the emperor reinstalled Muley Hassan as his vassal and set sail for Sicily on August 17, disembarking at Trapani on the 22nd and arriving at Naples on November 25 after a triumphal progress through Sicily and Calabria.[26]

Sometime in November, Giovio left Rome to pay a pastoral visit to Nocera and then go on to Naples, intending, as Girolamo Negri expressed it, "to confront his marquis del Vasto and the emperor with his histories."[27] From Naples the historian reported with evident gratification that he had been warmly received by Caesar both on arriving and departing. When he went to take leave on December 10 in order to be in Rome for Christmas, "His Majesty recounted, and partly at my interrogation, many fine things about Goletta that were relevant to the history," he boasted, "and I have persuaded myself that the history will please him, which I have already shown to Granvelle [Nicolas Perrenot de Granvelle, imperial councillor] and other savants."[28] Giovio's admiration for the crusader-emperor was at its height, and so, too, were his expectations: "His Majesty is even more gallant than one can imagine. I expect for myself a lame mule [Giovio's jargon for a gift], but even without it I wish to be his servitor in my heart and with my pen in hand, *gratis*."[29] This was proof, indeed, of admiration, and perhaps a passing impulse, for in a subsequent letter the old Giovio reappeared: "It seems to me he would like the flesh of the lark, but if he wants it on parchment I will first need to ride a lame mule; otherwise I will leave the job to a friar newly minted as *cronista* of his Majesty [Guevara?], who writes in Spanish and refectory Latin."[30]

Throughout his stay in Naples, Giovio was busy interviewing participants in the crusade. Along with the emperor, the marquis del Vasto, Andrea Doria, and other captains, he was pleased to be able to question a Genoese who had been one of Barbarossa's slaves and could give him an eyewitness account of the revolt inside the citadel. As usual, he relished the festivities, including a *ballo in maschera* to which Caesar came masked. The emperor had seen the fabled Lucrezia Scaglione, whom Giovio found more beautiful than ever. There had been a little row with the youthful duke of Alba when, with "libera bocca," she had remarked on his resemblance to a none-too-handsome Neapolitan.[31] On a more elevated plane, there was a reunion with Vittoria Colonna, and once again Giovio considered publishing the dialogue, to which he made a few final revisions.[32] He was invited to dine with the emperor's secretary, Francisco de los Cobos, in company that included Alfonso d'Avalos, Pedro de Córdoba, and Lope Hurtado de Mendoza, all of whom would have had particulars of the expedition for the *Histories*. Perhaps this was the occasion upon which Cobos presented Giovio with an Aztec chronicle bound in leopard skin that had probably been given him by Cortés.[33]

The marquis del Vasto, who was now signing his letters "fratello e servitore," gave Giovio "incomparable treasures" from the booty of Tunis, including a Koran and a theological text; a mullah's ceremonial robe and a jacket of Barbarossa's made of deep blue velvet ornamented with gold flowers; a basin used as a birdbath by the pirate's tame magpies; a large porcelain serving bowl; a brass bowl inlaid with gold and silver, Damascus style, in which the king of Tunis once washed his feet; the scepter of Muley Hassan; the scimitar of the castellan of Tunis, which had formerly belonged to the king; a sapphire of Barbarossa's; a silk carpet that had belonged to Barbarossa's eunuch; various musical instruments; a turban; shoes; and two keys to the treasure chest of Tunis, finely wrought in gold and silver, which the nuncio, Francesco Chieregati, had borne in the triumphal entry into Naples.[34]

Giovio's admiration for Charles V and his exploits at Tunis by no means blinded him to the sober realities of the political and military situation. The rest of the Barbary coast was still in Turkish hands and Barbarossa himself had escaped to Algiers. The prospect of continued raids on Italy was a real one, and there was already talk of an expedition to Algiers.[35] Money was a major problem. This one expedition had cost a million and a half gold *scudi*, much of which Charles V was now trying to recoup from Italy. The emperor had everything "except the soul of the Florentine," Giovio quipped, "that is, cash."[36] Some good news for Giovio came in a letter of Guicciardini's reporting that Alessandro de' Medici had prevailed over the exiles. When the duke had gone to kiss the emperor's hand, Charles V had suggested, "Better go kiss your bride," indicating that he had rendered judgment in Alessandro's favor and that he was confirming the marriage negotiated at Marseilles to his daughter Margaret. And so, Giovio concluded, "Marzocco's tail has been amputated."[37]

The death of Francesco II Sforza on November 1, 1535, had been a major blow to Giovio and his hopes for the future of Italy. "Cursed be that evil enema," he would often exclaim, "given on that night to Francesco Sforza, and cursed be that pestiferous hand of Lorenzo delle Teste [his physician]."[38] Never in good health, the chief hope of the Italian imperialists and last of the dukes of Milan expired at the age of forty without leaving an heir. Giovio's friendship with him had ripened to the point where the duke had been addressing him "tanquam fratri honorando [like an honored brother]."[39] Even as recently as June, Giovio's disappointment at failing to obtain the provostship of the Umiliati in Borgo Vico outside Como had led him to contemplate forsaking Rome and accepting Sforza's invitation to join his court in Milan.[40] Now the fate of Milan rested once more in the hands of Charles V.

The new pope agreed with the emperor on the necessity of a council to settle the Lutheran question, but the requisite peace between Francis I and Charles V remained elusive. If peace depended on Charles V's giving Milan to Francis I, Giovio opined in his jargon, that was "tart sugar." He knew that Granvelle was suggesting that Milan be given to Francis I's youngest son, the duke of Angoulême, along with the hand of Charles V's niece, Christina of Denmark, widow of the duke of Milan, and he thought it was "the only solution," but he doubted that the emperor would consent.[41] What Giovio most anticipated and feared was heavy pressure on the pope to join a league against France. Later, he became convinced that the real peril of Naples had been a secret agreement reached there between the emperor and the Venetians giving Charles V a free hand with Milan provided he did not make an Austrian Hapsburg its duke.[42]

As the emperor tarried in Naples during the unusually mild winter of 1536, preparations went forward for his reception in Rome. Giovio described for his brother the dismantling of medieval churches to restore the Roman temples incorporated into their fabrics and the tearing down of "an infinity of houses" to create broad, straight streets (including the present via San Gregorio). Because of the temporary nature of the decorations on wood, cloth, and buffalo hide, the Romans were already deriding the entry as "Testaccia," or "Festival of Potsherds," an allusion to Monte Testaccio and the traditional carnival festival of Testaccio. Nor were they very happy about the taxes imposed to finance it.[43] On April 4 Charles V reached the outskirts of Rome, lodging at San Paolo outside the walls, and the next day he made his solemn entry into Rome, the first imperial entry in sixty-five years.[44]

Book 35 of Giovio's *Histories* opens with an abbreviated but darkly dramatic account of the entry as the joyless Romans recognized among the Spanish soldiery the faces of their tormentors of 1527. The emperor entered by the Porta San Sebastiano and followed the ancient *Via triumphalis* through the arches of Constantine, Titus, and Septimius Severus to a fourth arch constructed by Antonio da San Gallo in the piazza San Marco. From there his procession followed the *Via papalis* to the Ponte Sant'Angelo and St. Peter's, where the pope awaited. All the decorations had been contrived to represent to the emperor his heritage and responsibilities. Giovio had conceived the expectation that he might be the one to show him around the ruins of Rome, but that honor went to the director of the vast program of tearing down and rebuilding, the pope's superintendent of monuments, Latino Giovenale Manetti. As it turned out, Giovio would not have been able to discharge the office in any event, as a mild but persistent attack of gout toward the end of March had made it very difficult for him to negotiate stairs.[45]

After briefly mentioning the emperor's ascent of the dome of the Pantheon, book 35 of the *Histories* moves at once to the principal event of his stay, his indignant denunciation of Francis I on Easter Monday, April 17, in the Sala dei Paramenti of the Vatican. Although he had anticipated pressure on the pope to create an anti-French alliance, Giovio had no way of foreseeing the startling events that prompted Charles V's speech. Moving in late winter to gain control of the passes into Italy, Francis I had launched an attack on the imperial fief of Savoy, seizing Bourg-en-Bresse in February 1536, the fortress of Montmeliano in March and, on April 3, Turin itself. Speaking in Spanish, which he thought most of the Italians could understand, Charles V vehemently denounced the French king, rehearsing the long history of broken treaties that had ended in the recent assault and offering, as a way of sparing further bloodshed, to meet him in single combat. Not surprisingly to Giovio, Charles unequivocally refused to relinquish Milan to any of Francis' sons, and after quitting Rome he hastened north with his forces to strike a counterblow in

Provence. Whether he had hobbled up to the Sala dei Paramenti to hear the emperor in person Giovio did not say, but he reported the speech at length. While recognizing that Charles V would never cede Milan, Giovio did not at this time share the suspicions of many in the curia that he was aiming at "monarchy," that is, the empire of all Italy.[46]

Despite his gout, Giovio did climb the stairs to wait on the cardinal of Lorraine, in Rome because of the emperor. Lorraine confirmed what he had already told Rodolfo Pio the previous summer, namely that the pension would be paid beginning with the two earliest unpaid terms, a prospect so heartening to Giovio he gave His Most Reverend Lordship a medallion from Syracuse that had come from Alfonsina de' Medici, promising to follow it with portraits of Barbarossa and the king of Tunis. To the cardinal's secretary, the abbé d'Onecourt, he gave a medallion and a ring with a fine cornelian found in Pompei.[47] It was not only the French pension, however, that was in arrears. In May, Giovio wrote to Guicciardini, now Alessandro de' Medici's chief minister, explaining that Ippolito had rewarded him for the biography of Leo X with a pension on the provostship of Sabbioneta, which the cardinal had subsequently renounced to Bernardo de' Medici, bishop of Forlì. Since the return from Marseilles, however, Forlì had ceased to pay and in fact had assigned the provostship to his creditors, leaving Giovio owed 250 *scudi* which he hoped the duke would help him collect.[48] Pensions were one of the worst features of the ecclesiastical patronage system, and many a bishop was impoverished by them. Giovio's constant struggles to collect his pensions were symptomatic of their evil.[49]

This same month of May 1536, Giovio succumbed to an illness that brought him, he said, within sight of the Stygian marsh and made his hand tremble as he wrote of it. He cured himself by leaving Rome in September, still "half dead" but bit by bit regaining appetite and color as he traveled through the Farnese territories to Tuscany.[50] There was an evident note of self-satisfaction in his description of this novel cure, a journey in the sixteenth century being more often a way of losing one's health than regaining it. While in Florence, Giovio received an invitation from Alessandro de' Medici to join him in Pisa. Despite his apprehensions, Giovio had been successful in preserving good relationships with both cousins; indeed, just after Ippolito's death, Duke Alessandro had turned to him for help in securing the cardinal's effects and had expressed his regard for the historian as for "an honored father."[51] From Pisa, Giovio accompanied Alessandro to Genoa to meet the emperor, who arrived there on September 23 after the collapse of the Provence campaign. Despite Giovio's presence among the ambassadors, Charles V, "being out of sorts with himself," did not grant him another personal interview. "His Majesty did not care to narrate these Provençal and Picard escapades like the African victories this past year," Giovio related sarcastically, "and so the duke remounted a galley and I a horse and came here to Como ."[52] While Giovio was at Genoa, the duke of Alba fulfilled a promise made at Rome by giving him a white horse, but unfortunately this was not the horse he chose to ride to Como, and despite the careful arrangements made for its conveyance he was never to see it again.[53]

A couple of days before he left Genoa, Giovio was forced to write in some alarm to Cardinal Farnese. His servant at Rome had gotten word to him that he had been asked to vacate his rooms in the Vatican. A proto-notary of the Sacred College, "like some God the Father," he wailed, "wants to chase me from Paradise like a brother of Lucifer." Before leaving Rome, Giovio reminded Alessandro, he had secured his protection "in universum" for his honor, his goods, and his person. A canny move. At Ippolito de' Medici's death, Paul III had conferred on his grandson the immensely lucrative vice-chancellorship, together with all of the late cardinal's benefices that lay in the papal gift, and with the instincts of the consummate courtier Giovio had begun to pay court to the new vice-chancellor. A cordial rapport soon developed between the sixteen-year-old cardinal and the fifty-year-old bishop, similar to the rapport between Ippolito and Giovio at a similar stage. Nonetheless, Giovio had been deeply offended at being rebuffed in his first request of the Farnese, the convent of the Umiliati in Borgo Vico, and he may have left Rome in 1536 with a view to exploring new possibilities.[54] In fact, contrary to his announced intentions, he was to remain in Lombardy for almost two years. He was not ready to cut any ties, however, and his new patron was evidently able to conserve his quarters, the "paradiso," for him.

Arriving in Como sometime in November 1536, after a wintry journey through the Apennines, Giovio began to work on the *Histories*, roused from a decade of inactivity by his renewed optimism and the excitement of recent events. Not only was he stirred with admiration for the emperor, he was heartened by Paul III's decisive leadership and the end to policies that "disgrace the Italian name."[55] Ten books (the first decade?), he told Pio, were being readied for the printer; the rest were not "safe" enough for present publication.[56] A year and a half after his return to Como, he told Cardinal del Monte that he had been working steadily and would bring to Rome five books treating of recent events. These are most likely to have been the present books 30–34 (1532–1535), comprising Charles V's crusade in Hungary and the expedition to Tunis.[57] In all probability Giovio resumed composition of his *Histories* with book 30, leaving a gap of eleven books and fifteen years (books 19–29, 1517–1531). Despite his renewed incentives, however, he threatened to Pio that if the French pension were not soon forthcoming he would forsake history for satires in the manner of Aretino, who, he had just learned, had obtained a handsome pension from the emperor on the revenues of Milan.[58]

In December 1536, to Giovio's relief and pleasure, Alfonso d'Avalos became military governor of Milan, and he went to celebrate the Christmas holidays with him. The arrival of Maria d'Avalos during the carnival season of 1537 was the occasion for more festivities, and Giovio spent much of that spring in Milan. The marquis was hard-pressed in defending Lombardy against the French ensconced in Piedmont, as well as in defending Tuscany against the Florentine exiles; for in January had come the shocking news of the assassination of Alessandro de' Medici (January 5, 1537). Giovio's first reaction was that "the comedy of the Medici has finished in a tragedy; and I say, *in parvis quies et paucos novit secura quies* [the quiet life consists in having little, and security comes to few]."[59] Thanks, however, to the decisive action of Guicciardini, Vettori, and the *Palleschi*, the eighteen-year-old son of Giovanni delle Bande Nere and Maria Salviati was quickly named head of the Florentine Republic. Nonetheless, Strozzi and the exiles were planning an attack, aided openly by France and covertly by Pier Luigi Farnese.

In February it was thought that Francis I was going to the Flemish front with a large army, while sending the count of St. Pol to Italy with reinforcements for Turin and the other French-held towns. Count Guido Rangoni would aid the Florentine exiles. Meanwhile it was learned that Suleiman, now formally the ally of France, was preparing to attack the Hapsburg domains by land and sea.[60] In the hopes of a successful opening of the council in Mantua on May 23 as scheduled, Paul III was clinging to his neutrality and apprehensively watching "these two great princes insanely rage together." Unless he lacked all sense, Giovio thought, the pope would proceed during the winter to Bologna to give evidence of his intent to be present in Mantua in the spring. That being the case, Giovio saw no point in riding to Rome "just to come hurrying back, breaking my bottom, and being condemned to bear the expense of it."[61]

In late February or early March 1537, Giovio made a sortie from Milan to pay his respects to Giberti and his traveling companion, the newly created cardinal Reginald Pole. The reform commission on which both were serving had ended its work with the *Consilium de emendanda ecclesia* (Plan for reforming the Church), and the two were en route to the Low Countries where Pole intended to launch a mission to win back Henry VIII. Giovio's interest in Pole's mission, strong enough to lure him onto the dreaded winter roads, probably stemmed from his desire to see the errors of Clement VII annulled and England brought back into the fold, a desire evident in the latter parts of his *Descriptio Britanniae, Scotiae, Hyberniae, et Orchadum* (Description of Britain, Scotland, Ireland, and the Orkneys).

The *Descriptio*'s idealized portrait of Pole and his mission suggests a propagandistic intent unusual for Giovio and may have been his way of seeking to undo the harm done by Clement VII. It may also be evidence of a deeper connection between Giovio and reforming circles than might otherwise be thought.[62] His numerous friendships with reformers and Giberti's esteem for him are difficult to explain absent any sympathy on his part for reform. Giovio may have been more secular in outlook than some, but the leading reformers were scarcely plaster saints. Rigid stereotypes do little to explain complex historical movements.[63]

Having seen the cardinals, Giovio went to Piacenza at the invitation of the vice-legate Filiberto Ferreri, bishop of Ivrea and soon to be named nuncio to France. He had "certain business" there—perhaps his pension on Santa Vittoria, perhaps laying the foundation for further efforts to collect the French pension, which, despite his fine gifts to the cardinal of Lorraine, had still not been paid.[64] As of March 10 Giovio thought the pope would spend April in Bologna, but by early May he had learned of the postponement of the council to the first of November and decided to summer in Como and Milan, where he could devote "the good part of the day" to work on the *Histories* and the rest to the society of friends such as Cardinal Marino Caracciolo, civil governor of Milan, the marchioness del Vasto, and "the flower of the fat and loyal people of St. Ambrose."[65] Giovio had quickly come to enjoy the confidence of Caracciolo, who appointed him to a special commission to investigate the violent controversy between a canon of the cathedral of Como, Pier Martire Maggi, and his colleagues.[66]

Giovio's visibility in Milanese life was attested by his presence at two special sessions of the deputies for the construction of the cathedral, together with a number of senators, officials, and the painter Gaudenzio Ferrari, to consider the plans of the architect Cristoforo Lombardo for a new portal.[67] It was during this Milanese sojourn that Giovio had his patent of nobility ratified by the senate of Milan. Why he had waited seven years was something of a mystery. The act of ratification, dated March 26, 1537, noted the delay.[68] Given his friendship with the late duke, it cannot have been the political situation that restrained him from presenting the charter. Perhaps it was the cost of ratification. Still more likely was that in 1530 he did not feel he had accumulated sufficient wealth to enable his family to maintain the style of counts, whereas now, with the family house enlarged to the size of a small palazzo and suitably furnished, the time was opportune. Another little family matter Giovio took care of during this Lombard residence of 1537 was the adoption of his natural son, Feliciano, by his brother Giampietro.[69]

As the spring progressed, Giovio feared for Cosimo's hold on Florence, particularly if the emperor would not grant him the hand of Alessandro's widow, Margaret, but this did not keep him from pestering the young head of the Florentine state about the arrears of the pension owed by the bishop of Forlì.[70] He even enlisted the aid of the marquis del Vasto, who wrote Cosimo somewhat wearily, "I pray that you satisfy him, for if he does not receive what he justly desires, he will complain more of Your Lordship and myself than of his principal debtor."[71] The defeat and capture of the exiles at Montemurlo on the first of August removed one source of worry for Giovio, although Cosimo still had far to go in winning the *bene placet* of Charles V.

With summer had come the resumption of hostilities in Piedmont. Initially, del Vasto succeeded in retaking a number of towns seized by the French the previous year and in setting siege to Turin. Francis I was not minded to relinquish his gains in Piedmont, however, and in October a French army under the dauphin and the constable Montmorency crossed the Alps via the Mt. Cenis pass, forcing the marquis to abandon the siege and driving him back to Carmagnola. In early November, after the conclusion of his campaign in Picardy, the king himself joined the army. Siege and countersiege made slow warfare, however, and by mid-November Francis I was just as glad to negotiate a truce. Finalized at Monzón in Spain on November 16, the truce was subsequently prolonged until the following June. "We are so happy at this holy truce," Giovio exclaimed after learning of it, "that we cannot eat for joy."[72]

Autumn brought mixed tidings from the Ottoman front. True to predictions, Suleiman had attacked by land and sea. In early October the Turks inflicted a crushing defeat on the forces of Ferdinand of Austria at Osijek, leading to a truce with the Turks' client-king John Zápolya and the continuing partition of Hungary. Barbarossa had sacked the Apulian town of Castro, with a large fleet and the French envoy present. Suleiman himself had attacked Corfu, and although he withdrew at the approach of a relief fleet under Andrea Doria, his attack ended the long Venetian neutrality and brought about an alliance with the papacy against the Turks. "Viva Papa Paolo e messer San Marco!" Giovio exulted when he heard the news.[73] In late October he learned of the second postponement of the council, this time to May 1, 1538, at Vicenza, so again there was no point in returning to Rome.

Much of the autumn of 1537 Giovio seems to have spent in Milan. Andrea Doria was in the city during the second week in December after the cessation of hostilities, and besides enjoying his company, Giovio enlisted his aid in pressing Cosimo de' Medici to round up the duke of Alba's gift horse, which was apparently grazing in Tuscany, having been given away by the captain to whom Giovio entrusted it. The horse was no small matter for Giovio, who professed his readiness to "mutiny against Paradise to avenge myself for this trick."[74] His friendship with the great admiral continued to grow, and it was sometime during this decade 1530–1540 that Giovio obtained for his collection one of the great portraits of the Renaissance, Bronzino's *Andrea Doria in the Guise of Neptune*, now in the Brera.[75] At Christmastime, Giovio left Milan to be with his family in Como. "I shall go say mass at Como and eat *pan giallo*," he told Angleria; then he would return to Milan for the birth of Maria del Vasto's child in January.[76]

During these months, Giovio was again experiencing the hardships inflicted on Lombardy by the hostilities of Francis I and Charles V. As in the previous decade, Charles V was seeking to finance his wars from Italy. "In the end they want to flay us," Giovio lamented to his friend Girolamo Angleria, "since the gold is so slow in coming from Peru." Recounting the miseries of the previous summer, he declared,

> I tell you, we stood in such fear that we did not know which side to take. The Spanish troops mutinous, the Landsknechts lazy, ready to return and mutinous; the Italians few and money extremely scarce; the French, big and victorious, menaced us with extreme ruin; but we feared even more our own, who had already prepared a bridge over the Ticino in order to hide by billeting themselves in the villages, leaving the countryside to the French to sack.[77]

In August Giovio had added his own prayers to those of the ambassadors of "our poor and afflicted city of Como," pleading with Caracciolo for "some mercy" in the new impositions necessitated by the warfare.[78] Explaining to Cosimo de' Medici why del Vasto could not send funds to pay the mutinous troops of Tuscany, even though Battista Ricasoli had "orated like a great Guicciardini," Giovio said flatly that there was no money even to pay the mutinous troops of Lombardy and "rid this country of these locusts."[79]

Giovio's *Histories* recapitulated his contemporary protests. In book 37 he related that the monthly tax on every person ordered by the emperor to support the troops was exacted with such harshness that the marquis del Vasto himself was moved to tears of frustration, "believing that the emperor would maintain a firmer hold on his dominions if he would seek to hold them with benevolence rather than coercing them with insolent and rapacious governments."[80] Books 36 and 37, composed probably in the early 1540s, not long after the events they describe, reflected Giovio's growing exasperation with the antagonism of the two sovereigns who seemed so oblivious to the human suffering their ambitions entailed. Under the pressure of renewed warfare in Lombardy, Giovio's admiration for Charles V the crusader was beginning to erode. Book 36 opened with a stinging denunciation of the ambitions of the warring Christian monarchs. The year 1537 would be marked by continuing struggles in diverse parts of the world, Giovio declared, rather than by signal victories, and yet this in itself would serve to display the minds of great princes, "who prefer to extend their power, breeding wars from wars, rather than enjoying the fruits of peace, and who, in attempting to enlarge their domains, seek for themselves, with prideful contention and anxious labors, a dubious honor subject to all the tricks of Fortune."[81]

After this preamble on the ambitions of princes, book 36 took up the warfare with the Ottomans during the summer and autumn of 1537, beginning with Suleiman's attack on Corfu and concluding with Ferdinand's ill-fated campaign against Zápolya and the Turks and his defeat at Osijek (Eszék) in October. Giovio detested Francis I's Turkish alliance and highlighted the role of the French ambassador Jean de la Forêt in promoting a Turkish attack on southern Italy in concert with the French descent on Piedmont. Likewise, he stressed the presence of the French agent Troilo Pignatelli in Barbarossa's fleet. Book 37 both opens and closes with a reminder that the warfare it narrates between Charles V and Francis I in Piedmont was occurring simultaneously with the fateful campaign in Hungary and the Turkish attacks on Castro and Corfu. By such "Thucydidean" juxtapositions of Western and Eastern events, Giovio made clear that Francis I's ambitions were being paid for by the innocent people of Italy and the Christians of Hungary.

Throughout the winter of 1538 Giovio watched the negotiations of Charles V and Francis I with a wary eye. He continued to be encouraged by Paul III's efforts for peace, so much more efficacious than Clement VII's.[82] March found him at Vigevano, where the marquis and marchioness del Vasto were holding court in the former summer residence of the Sforza dukes. Despite the pope's departure from Rome on the 23rd, Giovio still did not believe his projected meeting with king and emperor at Nice would actually take place, and he was making no plans to attend. Despite his long preference for the imperial settlement, his war-weariness had reached the point where he was even willing to see the French in Milan again—whatever would bring peace and restore the health of "St. Ambrose, who will become jaundiced and consumptive if the bloodlettings . . . continue on top of the deep wounds of the past."[83] As for the "concilietto di Vicenza," scheduled now for the first of May, Giovio did not expect to see more than "three luxurious sessions."[84]

In the spring of 1538 Giovio accompanied the d'Avalos on a tour of the marquisate of Novara, which the emperor had just conceded as a fief to Pier Luigi Farnese. Returning just before Easter, they found the pope already at Piacenza. Giovio had previously decided to accompany the marquis to Piacenza, beseeching Cardinal del Monte to find him lodging, "be it even in a house of friars," and now he decided to continue on "to enjoy the marvelous view of Nice and to chronicle it in letters of gold to the eternal glory of the most fortunate Pope Paul."[85] Giovio had begun to feel real admiration for this pope who had just turned seventy and who seemed to be winning out over the skeptics, himself included.

At Piacenza the weeks following Easter were cheered by increasingly favorable developments. On April 28 the legates Pio and Jacobacci returned from France with the promise of Francis I's presence at Nice, and by the first of May it was learned that the duke of Savoy would lend the pope the citadel. Journeying overland by way of Alessandria, symbol of Guelf power in the Middle Ages, Paul III sailed from Savona on May 15 in a fleet provided by the emperor. He reached Nice two days later but, despite the duke's promise, the townspeople and garrison refused to hand over the citadel to Pier Luigi Farnese, and so even the pope was forced to take up residence "in a house of friars" outside the city. The heat and discomfort were great. On May 19 the pope received his first visit from the emperor, who found it cooler on his galley in the harbor at Villa Franca (Villefranche).[86]

In the complex series of comings and goings that constituted the colloquies at Nice, Giovio had a small ceremonial part to play. Believing that the negotiations might actually result in Milan's being given to the duke of Orléans, del Vasto had arranged to introduce a group of Milanese noblemen to the king of France. The marquis was ill on the appointed day, however, and asked Giovio to conduct the group to Villeneuve and make the introductions. Francis I received Giovio and the Milanese with his customary courtesy and every sign of goodwill. Giovio took the occasion of securing details on the Provence campaign of 1536, asking in particular why His Majesty had not harassed Charles V's rearguard as he retreated. Among his reasons the king cited the old maxim of Quattrocento warfare, "Build golden bridges for a retreating enemy," but he said he was especially reluctant to have his Swiss attack the emperor's Germans, their historic enemies, for fear of provoking them to extremes.[87]

Giovio may have deftly raised the Turkish problem, for he claimed to have heard Francis I avow his intent to live up to his title "Most Christian."[88] The embassy itself proved pointless. In book 37 of the *Histories* Giovio commented that del Vasto had been "wondrously deceived" in his expectation that Milan might go through marriage to a son of Francis I. "Those skilled in affairs and familiar with the intimate natures of each prince believed that in the end Charles would never cede Milan nor Francis cease his attempts to win it"—for Giovio and Italy a recipe for despair.[89]

This time Charles V was willing to grant Giovio an audience, and the historian presented him with a little treatise he had written at the instigation of d'Avalos on the best way of making war against the infidel. Believing another crusade was possible if the colloquies at Nice proved successful, the marquis thought it would be helpful to review the strategies planned under Leo X in 1516–1518. Giovio's *Discorso dell'impresa contro al Turco* was cast in the form of a letter to del Vasto, taking up where the *Commentario de le cose de' Turchi* had left off.[90] It began in the guarded optimism that the twin offspring of "this holy peace" of Nice would be a universal council and a crusade. While the Turks were strong, Giovio argued, they were far from invincible and had been weakened not only by their recent wars with the Persians, but by internal rivalries, by their failures at Vienna in 1529 and in Hungary in 1532, and by "certain prophecies."

Some of the treatise reflected the thinking of Leo X's time, some was entirely Giovio's. His analysis of the respective strengths and weaknesses of the Ottoman and Christian armies drew on his own observations of 1532, as well as on his historical researches. The treatise concluded with some practical advice on provisioning and diet as well as the quite wonderful suggestion that monks and friars be released from their vows to serve as oarsmen and supply officers to the army. All should share appropriately in the burdens of taxation to support the crusade, Giovio emphasized, cardinals included.

The colloquy of Nice was probably the occasion on which Charles V granted Giovio a pension of 300 ducats from the revenues of the see of Pamplona, and the presentation of his treatise with the support of the marquis del Vasto may have provided the pretext.[91] The pension to Aretino suggested that the emperor was becoming somewhat more solicitous of his fame and reputation among men of letters. However, he seems to have been anxious to avoid the appearance of patronage. Juan de Sepúlveda, a Spanish humanist, formerly a protégé of Clement VII and, since 1536, *cronista* of Castile, asserted in his *De rebus gestis Caroli V* that Giovio had sought a pension from the emperor at Bologna, supported by Alessandro de' Medici, and had been refused. According to Sepúlveda, when Giovio subsequently complained to his friends at Rome, "Will Charles Caesar ever be induced to give me a lame mule as a gift," word reached the emperor who retorted, "If Giovio thinks that because he writes history he will receive a tribute from me he is greatly deceived. It is precisely because he writes history that he ought not to expect a gift from me."[92]

Although there were several improbabilities in this story as related, there were nonetheless elements of truth.[93] According to Sepúlveda, when Charles did eventually concede Giovio a "pensionette" he made it appear as if he had yielded to the earnest entreaties of his son-in-law, not to the merits of the historian or any expectation of partiality. If a suitable pretext other than historiography was what Charles V wanted, the Turkish treatise and the support of del Vasto would have provided a plausible justification for a pension that did not ostensibly recognize Giovio's writing of history. Certainly at this point the project of a great *cruzada* was very much in the emperor's mind and heart.[94]

In the very last hours of the arduous meetings at Nice, Paul III was able to arrange a ten years' armistice on the basis of the status quo—a major achievement given the refusal of the sovereigns to meet personally. After this diplomatic victory he set sail for Genoa on June 20, followed by the emperor, with whom he entered the city in state on the 22nd. The pope was lodged in the Fieschi palace high up in Violà, the emperor in the palazzo Doria, whose magnificent gardens, built above the dungeons of the galley slaves, would have been sweetly redolent in the warmth of early summer.[95] Here in Genoa agreement was reached regarding the marriage of Margaret to Ottavio Farnese and the postponement of the council to Easter 1539. On arriving at Genoa, Giovio suffered "a little fever and a little gout," which kept him in bed for a week. The gout had broken an eighteen-month truce, he explained, employing the diplomatic language of the hour.[96] An invitation from Cardinal Farnese to rejoin him in Rome struck Giovio as so gracious that he was determined to be there by the feast of St. Luke (October 18), bringing in "a well-ruled quire, the flower and fruit of this most holy glory of His Holiness."[97]

Even though it was probably written in the early 1540s when Giovio was still relatively enthusiastic about the Farnese papacy, the account of the colloquy of Nice in book 37 of the *Histories* was by no means the promised paean to Paul III. A counterpoint to Giovio's praise for the pope's peacemaking was his growing sense of disillusionment with the extent of Farnese nepotism. Thus, while one sentence told the reader that in undertaking the arduous journey to Nice the pope was demonstrating a greater concern for Christianity than for his own health, the next sentence suggested that one of the reasons for the unwillingness of the two monarchs to meet together personally under the pope's aegis was suspicion of his private motives for arranging the meeting, namely Margaret's hand for Ottavio Farnese and the duke of Vendôme for Pier Luigi's daughter Vittoria. If Giovio appeared to share the skepticism of the sovereigns regarding the pope's motives, however, he also appeared to share the pope's skepticism regarding the long and ostensibly friendly conversations that Charles V and Francis I subsequently held at Aigues Mortes, arranged by Montmorency as part of his assiduous diplomacy of reconciliation.[98]

In addition to venting his skepticism about the true motives at Nice, Giovio's account ended on a particularly bitter note. Learning of the truce while negotiations were still in progress, the imperial soldiers in Lombardy had begun to demand their back pay, and not finding it immediately forthcoming had ravaged the countryside, sacking, wasting, and seizing the harvests. As he was about to embark from Nice, a delegation of Milanese citizens had reached the emperor to demand relief from "the cruelty of these shameless brigands." Giovio's handling of the interview revealed his own bitter feelings. When a sullen emperor refused to respond and had Granvelle rebuke the delegation for their outspokenness, Giovio described the leader, Battista Archinto as "foaming at the mouth [spumanti ore]" and challenging Granvelle: "If not a thoroughly cruel man, Granvelle, as president of the council how can you suffer a city second to none in faith and affection to the emperor to be ruined by the incessant depredations of a nefarious soldiery, when for many years that city has not only enriched all of you with stipends but has borne the cost of the emperor's whole court?"[99] Not only did the delegation return to Lombardy with no promise of relief; yet another levy was imposed to satisfy the rebel troops.

At this point Giovio described the Milanese as ready to accept any new lord who offered promise of milder treatment. Charles V now seemed indistinguishable to them from the German emperors of the Middle Ages, who looked on Italy as a source of booty for their soldiers. And not only did Giovio tell sovereigns "bitter truths," he was prepared to do the same to his friend and patron, Alfonso d'Avalos, author of the new levy, who was compelled by his mutinous troops to leave his son as a hostage while he went to Milan to raise the money. This spineless response Giovio contrasted with the severity of Ferrante Gonzaga, who punished an outbreak of insubordination among the Spanish troops in Sicily by decimation. When it was learned that the emperor had rewarded Gonzaga and docked del Vasto's salary, Giovio noted that the Lombards at least felt vindicated. Unfortunately, Giovio's Maecenas, while a competent general, was proving an incompetent, if not actually corrupt, governor.[100]

In this same somber mood Giovio's narrative in book 37 moved from Italy to Greece, where the Christians lost their superiority at sea. The Venetian-papal league against the Turks, which had given Giovio such satisfaction in the autumn of 1537, had been joined by the emperor, and final arrangements had been made at Nice and Genoa for the viceroy of Sicily, Ferrante Gonzaga, to command a united offensive to seek out and destroy the Turkish navy. The fleets finally met on September 27, 1538, off Préveza, a town lying at the entrance to the Gulf of Ambracia, opposite the ancient promontory of Actium. Giovio's vivid account was based on descriptions he obtained from Andrea Doria and the Venetian commander, Vincenzo Capello. It evoked all the intensity of debate among the commanders over strategy and painted a particularly memorable picture of the hostile fleets in full battle panoply floating silently on the calm waters of the Ionian sea—a test of nerves—each waiting for the other to make the first move.[101]

The wily Barbarossa, considerably outnumbered, had executed a flying eagle formation with great precision to place himself in readiness but had every reason not to attack. To the disgust of the Venetian and papal commanders, impatient all summer for battle, Doria would not take the initiative, and after spending the day in vain attempts to provoke the Moslems, the Christians finally retreated in great disorder during a sudden squall at sundown. Doria never explained his strategy to Giovio's satisfaction, and it was clear to the historian that the admiral had forfeited much of his reputation.[102] Indeed, Giovio was among the first to see that at Préveza, where Mark Antony had lost the empire of Rome, the Christians had surrendered their maritime superiority to the Turks.[103] His only explanation was the common opinion that Doria distrusted the Venetians. From princes to captains, the Christian powers could not trust one another or cooperate among themselves. The Holy League broke up in quarrels as to who had been at fault, and Venice soon made a separate peace with the Turks.[104]

From Genoa, Giovio returned to spend the summer of 1538 alternating between Milan and Como. At Como there were festivities for the wedding of his nephew Francesco, the *referendario*.[105] At Milan he found a complimentary letter from Aretino. The marquis, who, after forgiving a few wounds, had become Aretino's newest patron, insisted on reading the letter aloud so that Giovio could savor the grandiloquent praise for the *Histories* which "the scourge of princes" now found it convenient to substitute for "apostolic parasite" and other, less aureate, epithets of the past.[106]

Summer for Giovio always meant Lake Como. Throughout his life it was a source of pride and, in a way, moral strength. His roots were there. Its beauty moved him deeply. Above all, it offered him through the two Plinies a direct and personal link to the classical past. Other than the founding of his museum on its shores, nothing better demonstrated his deep attachment to the lake than the little description he had written the previous autumn (1537) for one of his new Milanese friends, the senator Francesco Sfondrato.[107] Sfondrato had been Charles V's ambassador to Savoy, and as a reward for retaining the duke's loyalty during the Provence campaign of 1536, he had been invested on October 23, 1537, with feudal rights over a number of territories on the eastern shore of the lake.[108] He wanted to know something about these new possessions, and

Giovio decided on the spur of the moment to visit them. Good weather must have lingered that autumn, because he expanded his mission into a tour of the whole lake, making a complete circuit by boat in six days.[109]

The little treatise that resulted from the tour, *De chorographia Larii Lacus*, was more and less than Sfondrato had desired—more because it was a description of the whole lake and less because it did not describe his fief in much detail. Instead of a practical help in administration, the senator received a humanistic travelogue from lakeshore to lakeshore. Giovio hinted at the discrepancy when he suggested that Sfondrato, who was something of a Latin poet, might want to use his treatise as the basis for a poetic description of the lake in imitation of Bembo's *Benacus* (a verse description of Lake Garda published at Rome by Calvo in 1524).

After surveying the geography and history of the lake from Roman times, Giovio took the reader into his *battèll* (the distinctive boat of Lake Como, now called "Lucia"), and set out. His affection and pride were everywhere evident: in his portrayal of the Roman past; the mildness of the climate; the unwearied beauty of the vast and limpid lake; the steep and sheltering mountains; the churches, villas, gardens, orchards, and vineyards on their lower slopes; the deep forests, icy springs, and frothing torrents above; the abundant fish and game; the sweeping panoramas; the enchanting small vistas. No wonder that Caesar founded a colony here, or that Pliny and Cassiodorus praised a spot created for the delight of human kind.[110]

Giovio dilated on the Isola Comacina and its history; on the presumed villas of Pliny at Lenno and Bellagio;[111] on the ruined fortress of Musso, seat of the pirate empire of Giangiacomo de' Medici;[112] on the Fiumelatte, a milk-white seasonal torrent studied by Leonardo da Vinci;[113] on the lake of Pusiano southwest of Lecco; on the Fonte Pliniana, the intermittent spring that fascinated Pliny the Elder;[114] and on the particular virtues of the wines made along the eastern shore of the Como branch.[115] His little treatise was copied in a fair hand and sent to Nicola Boldoni, professor of medicine at Pavia, his companion on the expedition to the Fiumelatte who wanted to add a letter of his own with further details. The manuscript remained in the library of the Sfondrati for twenty years until Dionisio Somenzi found it so evocative of his own trip to the lake that he obtained the permission of Francesco's son to publish it, and so was born the long and delightful tradition of descriptions of Lake Como.[116]

Giovio's idea of founding a portrait museum on the lake was his most original contribution to European civilization. While *Wunderkammern* and princely collections were not new, the idea of filling a villa with portraits of famous people on canvas or on bronze medallions, calling it a museum, and opening it *ad publicam hilaritatem* (for public enjoyment) was a new departure. Giovio had begun collecting portraits of illustrious men of letters sometime before 1521, and by 1522 he was also collecting portraits of rulers, statesmen, and generals. The inspiration had come to him, he said, of adorning his room, "Mercury and Pallas," with the "true images of illustrious men of letters, so that through emulation of their example good mortals might be inflamed to seek glory."[117] Thereafter his correspondence shows him constantly badgering all manner of persons for portraits. As he once confessed to Giberti, "Your Lordship knows that I sin in these portraits."[118]

No idea is born in a vacuum, and there were various precedents for Giovio's inspiration to form a portrait collection, but none was quite what Giovio had in mind.[119] Although intended as *figurae* of glory and incentives to emulation, most collections or cycles featured idealized or imaginary representations, whereas from the very start Giovio demanded an exact likeness, preferably done from life but otherwise from sound evidence such as coins, medallions, portrait busts, or earlier authentic portraits. His insistence on realism partook of the more scholarly approach to archaeology developing at Rome and the spirit in which Raphael had copied the features of Socrates for the *School of Athens* from an ancient cameo or statue.[120]

From the beginning, Giovio's collecting had a public and didactic purpose, and he often called his museum a *templum virtutis*, suggesting something of a cult.[121] No doubt his didactic purpose justified his boldness in soliciting portraits, for bold he certainly was. Few notables of the day escaped his solicitations for their own portrait or one of a famous compatriot. As with his *Histories*, Giovio's vision in collecting was universal. Local portrait collections already existed, such as Isabella d'Este's or Gianfrancesco Zaninello's at Ferrara, but Giovio conceived of a worldwide archive of portraiture, an idea whose novelty and utility must have struck donors as well, since, even allowing for his notable persistence, he enjoyed a remarkably high rate of compliance with his not inexpensive requests. When he had the inspiration of enlarging the identifying inscriptions to *elogia*, or capsule biographies, his innovative scheme was complete. For each worthy there would ultimately be a nexus of features, moral character, and deeds, a scheme that constituted the fullest expression of individuality reached during the Renaissance.

By 1535 the collection had grown so large that Giovio was thinking of sending it to adorn the renovated palazzo in Como but feared for the special levies the duke of Milan was being forced to exact. "He who sits low in the saddle," he explained to Rodolfo Pio, "keeps from getting his neck broken."[122] Thanks to Benedetto's continued vigilance, however, he eventually acquired the ideal site for his project in Borgo Vico, just

outside the city, between the lake and the road to Cernobbio, and building began shortly before autumn 1537.[123] In his last will Giovio declared
that the museum was constructed "with the perpetual liberality of the
marquis del Vasto." A gift from the marquis in 1537 probably enabled
him to begin construction, and with his old friend as military governor
he must have felt reasonably safe from the teeth of the tax gatherer.[124]

In the *Larius* Giovio declared that his museum was being built close
to the site of an ancient plane tree admired by Pliny the Younger. Pliny's
tree did not stand on the grounds of his own villa, but on those of a villa
belonging to his friend Caninius Rufus, the remains of which Benedetto
thought he had located in Borgo Vico.[125] Giovio certainly knew that the
Roman villa of Borgo Vico had not belonged to Pliny. Correcting an
early draft of a description of the museum, Benedetto had reminded his
brother that the villa had belonged to the poet Caninius Rufus, not to
Calpurnius Rufus, as Giovio had apparently stated.[126] Yet in the final
version of the description, prefaced to the 1546 edition of the *Elogia*
when Benedetto was in his grave and no longer able to correct him, Caninius Rufus disappeared and Giovio spoke with considerable hyperbole
of his museum's being situated "in the very ruins of a Plinian villa."[127]
Perhaps "Plinian" was to be understood as meaning "with Plinian associations." Whatever the case, Giovio's legerdemain demonstrated his
yearning for a palpable link with the classical past.

Classical precedent was also apparent in the name *musaeum*, although
Giovio gave the term its modern meaning.[128] He and his brother were
using it as early as 1532, when Benedetto referred to one of the rooms
prepared for him in the refurbished family palazzo, probably a place to
house some of his collection, as a *museum*.[129] It may be that Giovio had
in mind something analogous to the museum founded by the Ptolemies
at Alexandria, a splendidly housed academy with a great library and tradition of lectures and symposia in which the Hellenistic rulers of Egypt
themselves took part; but if so he was not explicit. In the *Larius* he
merely declared that his museum was being constructed in memory of
Pliny and in honor of Apollo and the Muses.[130] In his own description of
the museum, Benedetto similarly remarked that the part most appropriately called a museum was the great hall giving onto the lake, on whose
walls were depicted "the nine Muses and Apollo, with musical instruments and other insignia attributed to them by the ancient poets."[131]

The work begun in 1537 continued during the whole of Giovio's second sojourn in Lombardy and was not completed until his fourth sojourn, in 1543. All through the intervening years, "the mad caprice of
building" was to prove a constant drain on his income and capital,
prompting numerous appeals to his patrons for assistance and ceaseless

efforts to collect his pensions. Already in 1538, on his way back from Nice, he was suggesting to Cardinal Farnese that his forthcoming account of the colloquies "might merit a loggia on my Museum on the shore of Larius out of the liberality *in solidum* of Father, Son, and Holy Ghost."[132] In addition to the marquis del Vasto, Giovio identified Francis I and Henry II as contributors to the museum, and among "other minor dukes and princes," the duke of Florence, the duke of Alba, the viceroy of Naples, and Cardinal Francisco Mendoza.[133]

As the summer of 1538 drew to a close, Giovio began preparing for the journey back to Rome. From the few months originally projected, his sojourn in Como and Milan had been protracted to almost two years, and it was clear that further absence would imperil his standing in the curia. If he had left Rome with the idea of exploring new modes of existence, it is clear that for the present he had decided not to adopt them. Although he had told Cosimo de' Medici the previous January that he was ready to renounce "the papal favors of taffeta of our lord Pope Paul" and spend the rest of his life in Cosimo's service, the taffeta favors apparently still beckoned.[134] And so, at the beginning of September 1538, armed with his letter from Cardinal del Monte requiring monasteries along the Via Emilia and Via Cassia to offer him hospitality, he set off with his retinue.[135]

An important stop en route was to be Florence, where Giovio wanted to cement relationships with the newest head of the Medici family and where he hoped to recover the arrears of the pension owed him by the bishop of Forlì, not to mention the duke of Alba's horse.[136] As it turned out, the visit was protracted owing to an accident near Barberino in the Apennines when Giovio's horse fell beneath him. But, as he explained to Pio, "such was its prudence and discretion that it fell in a manner so as not to break my leg; and so with a foot half-crippled, *ad felicem convalescentiam* I have been here with my leg in bed twelve days, staying with Duke Cosimo, who has paid me more reverence than a lord." After the festivities for the Medici patrons, Saints Cosmas and Damian, Giovio was preparing to put his welcome to the proof by bringing up the matter of the pension.[137] Then he hoped to be in Rome by the feast of the coronation of Mary (November 8), having been invited to enjoy the hospitality of the cardinal del Monte as long as the pope remained in the palace of San Marco (the present palazzo Venezia). Thereafter he would resume life in the *paradiso*. He was coming *allegro*, he declared, because his hopes were no longer great ones. From Cardinal Farnese he hoped for "some little choir stall," a pension of a hundred *scudi* somewhere north of the Alps, and furnishings for a room at the museum; from Pio himself perhaps a tessellated chimney. He would finish his *Histories*. He was resolved "to work up this fine end of the wars and beginning of holy peace to the honor of Pope Paul; and a cancer to that bungler [Clement VII] who wished me to have to stay in bed while my stockings were being repaired for lack of another pair." The signals were mixed but the import was clear: "Spes mea in Farnesii gratia."[138] For the next decade Giovio pursued his fleeting hopes down the corridors of the Vatican and through the thronging piazza of Campo dei Fiori.

CHAPTER TEN

Courtier of the Farnese (1539–1544)

"Spes mea in Farnesii gratia"
—To Cardinal Rodolfo Pio of Carpi, 1538

"My hope is in the grace of the Farnese"

NO CROWD ASSEMBLED in the piazza del Popolo for Giovio's return to Rome, but after an absence of nearly two years he was heartened to find himself welcomed and "caressed" by the pope and Cardinal Farnese.[1] Because of the increasing eminence of his new patron, now first secretary as well as vice-chancellor, he found himself the historian and oracle to an emerging statesman, a role he could scarcely expect with the pope, and the young cardinal soon developed a genuine fondness for the jovial, if ceaselessly importunate, historian.

Giovio's conflicting loyalties involved him almost immediately in tensions between Rome and Florence over a succession of issues—the fate of Filippo Strozzi, the inheritance of Margaret of Austria, the patronage of the *badia* of Altopascio, and the friars of San Marco. Through all these disputes, Cosimo's agents used Giovio as a source of counsel and support. Francesco Babbi assured the duke that Giovio knew all the subtleties of negotiating at the curia.[2] Giovanni Fabrini advised the duke's majordomo, Pierfrancesco Riccio, to cultivate Giovio "and become as intimate as possible, because he is a person whose services are to be used often; for beyond his other qualities he is so intimate with the pope and Cardinal Farnese that he speaks as freely as he wishes, and when he acts for a friend away from Rome he performs whatever is requested and is, moreover, a mouthpiece not only of this court but of all the others and a source for all the people that matter in Rome."[3] So efficient was Giovio's network that when Agnolo Niccolini wanted a letter of Ugolino Grifoni's to be widely read it occurred to him that "there was no better trumpet than Giovio's."[4]

As the winter of 1539 wore on, Giovio grew pessimistic about an offensive against the Turks. The amity of Charles V and Francis I at Aigues Mortes seemed tenuous at best: Caesar would never give up Milan, Giovio concluded, nor Francis I cease to desire it.[5] As for "Messer Concilio," called now for Easter, he would remain suspended at Vicenza like an executed criminal, "hung by one foot and blowing in the wind."[6] When the news came in March of Cosimo's engagement to Eleanora de Toledo, daughter of the viceroy of Sicily, Don Pedro Alvarez de Toledo,

Giovio decided to attend the festivities and then go on to Como. The suspension sine die of the council, announced in May, confirmed his plans. Despite Cosimo's disappointment in losing Margaret of Austria to Ottavio Farnese, the marriage to Eleanora would prosper. The couple would quickly become inseparable, and the duchess would produce so many male offspring that worries about the Medici line would vanish; but meanwhile the engagement plunged papal-Florentine relations to a new low, as Paul III had been hoping to see his granddaughter Vittoria become duchess of Florence.

Giovio left Rome on June 21, 1539, in time to be present for Eleanora's triumphal entry on the 29th, the banquet and pageant on July 6, and the performance of Antonio Landi's *Il comodo* on the 9th.[7] The festivities over, he made his way to Como where he discovered that the marquis and marchioness del Vasto had paid a couple of visits to the museum and found it so delightful they were talking of underwriting an addition. Between visits to Pavia and Milan, Giovio settled amid his portraits, working on the *Histories* and enjoying "the most delicate wines, marvelous fish, divine figs, and gracious air."[8]

The historian's labors during the summer months of 1539 probably included books 36 and 37 of the *Histories* (1537–1539), and the lives of the twelve Visconti dukes of Milan, commissioned at Nice by Francis I's third son, Charles, then duke of Angoulême, who with the prospect of becoming prince of Lombardy was taking a more lively interest in his Visconti ancestors.[9] In addition, Giovio was probably putting the finishing touches on the life of Muzio Attendolo, founder of the Sforza dynasty.

Commissioned by Cardinal Guido Ascanio Sforza, a grandson of Paul III, and published in Rome at the end of 1539 by Antonio Blado of Asolo, the *Vita Sfortiae clarissimi ducis* was not one of Giovio's best biographies.[10] For one thing, he did not know the period well. Muzio had been dead seventy years before the Italian wars began. Nor could Giovio employ his customary method of eyewitness interrogation. Despite efforts to interview old soldiers of the house of Sforza and ascertain the oral tradition at Naples, he was almost totally dependent on written sources. Perhaps for this reason he did something quite unusual in early historiography. He appended to his biography, as a critical apparatus, a list of the sources he had used. The list reveals that beyond consulting the standard humanist authors, such as Crivelli, Simonetta, and Merula, Giovio had rummaged in the chronicles and annals of several cities, especially Naples, and had even gone to the Vatican archives for clarification of events during the papacy of Martin V.

Despite his critical preparation, however, Giovio's biography differed little from previous historiography. Unable to make intuitive contact with his subject, he fell back on many of the least valuable props of the humanist tradition, including astrological portents. He did strive to separate legend from fact, even while exaggerating the virtues of his subject in the manner of an *exemplum* rather than a biography, and there was evident sincerity in his admiration for Sforza's rugged strength, his stoicism, and, above all, his part in ending the dominance of foreign mercenary captains. The condottiere's death crossing the river Aterno near l'Aquila was movingly narrated. "Impelled by his fatal destiny," Sforza rode into the swelling flood to encourage his troops, extended a hand to rescue a drowning page, and was drowned himself when the gallant gesture threw his horse off balance. Gallantry was perhaps the touchstone of the biography, which included a vigorous condemnation of gunpowder—an invention, Giovio charged, "for the destruction of humanity and the corruption of true soldiering," since "now the reputation of outstanding valor no longer pertains to a strong and admirable right hand in hard battle, nor to unconquered vigor of spirit and body, but to the fortuitous trajectory of flying projectiles, blind chance, and often a lucky temerity."[11]

While writing and supervising construction at the museum, Giovio continued to worry about the European situation. The recapture of Castelnuovo (Hercegnovi) by the Turks on August 7, 1539, heightened his fears. Taken by the Christians after Préveza on October 27, 1538—the one bright spot in that disastrous campaign—the town was recaptured by the Turks after a siege begun in the spring and concluded with a bloody assault.[12] The marquis del Vasto mourned the death or enslavement of many of his veteran Spanish troops, but the Milanese, said Giovio, flocked to the altars of St. Donatus, on whose feast the Turkish victory had occurred, to give thanks that the rapacious Spanish troops had been so swiftly and condignly punished for their outrages on the population of Lombardy.[13] Still, a Turkish victory was no cause in itself for rejoicing, and in letters from Vienna Giovio always heard the sound of hoofbeats. Even more he feared new attacks on the Italian coast by Barbarossa, predictably emboldened by Préveza.[14]

Although he had promised to return to Rome in October with "perfumed papers" demonstrating his loyal service to the Farnese, Giovio became so persuaded that emperor and pope would meet in northern Italy he thought he would remain in Lombardy for the winter of 1539–40.[15] Instead of going himself, however, Paul III sent Cardinals Farnese and Cervini on a special mission to both Charles V and Francis I, seeking peace and support for a council. The mission was conceived shortly after Don Luis d'Avila arrived in Rome on November 20, 1539, to announce that the emperor intended to accept the invitation of Francis I to make his forthcoming journey to Flanders through France. D'Avila's arrival prompted Nicolas Raynce, secretary of the French ambassador, to ask

Giovio what he thought of these new developments. The response was well-informed, shrewdly perceptive, historically based, accurate, and expressive. Although full of characteristically trenchant Giovian metaphors, it used almost no *lingua zerga*. It was, rather, a *cri du coeur* over the seeming hopelessness of establishing the unity necessary to confront the relentless Turkish advance.

Too long, too narrowly political, and too dated to find its way into anthologies, the letter remained unpublished until 1956. Had it been known earlier, it might have confuted the nineteenth-century critics' image of Giovio as a shallow journalist and "reporter."[16] Despite his opinion of what Charles V ought to have done, and despite the ostensible signs during 1538–39 of a rapprochement with Francis I, Giovio's anticipation of what Charles V actually would do proved entirely correct. The colloquy of Aigues Mortes, the declaration of Toledo of February 1539, implying that Milan might go to a French prince, and the friendly demonstrations as the emperor passed through France in December and January 1539–40 were followed by a breakdown in negotiations and renewed warfare. Moreover, just as Giovio predicted, the Venetians reached an accord with the Turk. The death of Andrea Gritti at the very end of 1538 had opened the way, and the new doge Pietro Lando initiated the exchanges that led to the treaty of October 2, 1540, by which Venice gave up its last outposts in the Morea in return for peace. As for the council, negotiations dragged on quite as Giovio had anticipated until the diet of Regensburg (1541) convinced just about everyone on the Catholic side of the futility of further discussions with the Protestants.[17]

Most remarkably, Giovio's letter to Raynce embodied a dramatic reversal in his thinking on Milan. Even allowing for the fact that Raynce was secretary of the French ambassador, it is clear that Giovio had abandoned the former linchpin of his political vision for Italy. Milan had always made him an imperialist, but with the Sforza line extinct and Lombardy ravaged by taxes and troops, his priority shifted from the maintenance of Milanese independence to peace at any price, even by a return of the French. Exasperation with incessant fighting, so evident in his letters, brought him to accept a settlement based not on an independent duchy of Milan but on a balance of power in Europe between France and Spain.[18] His new disposition was all the more striking given the financial support he was receiving from the imperial governor of Milan and the difficulty he was experiencing in securing payment of his French pension.[19] It demonstrated his capacity to rise above his own *utile* to a European vision of events, a vision carried over into the books of the *Histories* written in these and subsequent years. Giovio's narration of the last phase of the Hapsburg-Valois wars, in both Italy and the north, had a darker tone than any preceding part of the *Histories* and the greatest number of *obiter dicta* on the vanity of princes and the suffering their ambitions visited on their people.

Not long after writing his letter to Raynce, Giovio had an opportunity to assay the mood of Venice for himself. Knowing of the republic's exhaustion and her negotiations for a truce with the Turks, Charles V had maneuvered Francis I into sending a joint mission in hopes of dissuading the Serenissima from making a separate peace. The proposal had been the first item on his agenda when he descended the Pyrenees into France in December 1539. As his emissary, Francis I selected the marshal of France, Claude d'Annebault. Charles V appointed the marquis del Vasto, who invited Giovio to join his suite.

Once admired by Giovio as a defender of Italian liberty, Venice now stood very low in his esteem. Frequent dark allusions in his correspondence indicated that he blamed the city for encouraging Charles V to retain Milan after the death of Francesco II Sforza and to reject the suggestion, made not only by Paul III but even by Granvelle, that he grant it as a fief to the third son of Francis I, the then-duke of Angoulême (Orléans after 1536). For Giovio the attraction of this particular route to peace was the likelihood that the duke would have become an Italian prince. Just why he blamed the Venetians for obstructing the proposal is unclear, especially since it was unacceptable not only to Charles V but to Francis I as well, who wanted Milan for his second son, Henry, but blame them he did. "Peace was in the snare," he charged in his letter to Raynce, "and they cut the cord."[20] Now, he noted with grim satisfaction, "St. Mark has a wolf by the tail," a haughty pagan enemy demanding tribute and two Christian princes ready to form a new League of Cambrai should Venice appease him too much.[21]

The embassy was given a splendid reception. The doge, Pietro Lando, came out to meet the ambassadors in the Bucentoro, accompanied by a fleet of gilded galleys. D'Annebault and del Vasto spoke to a crowded senate chamber, but the Venetians were justly suspicious of the monarchs' good faith, and the mission bore no fruit. Giovio's letters from Venice reported that del Vasto had offered himself as commander for a joint effort to seize control of the sea from Barbarossa, and in the *Histories* the marquis has a fine speech concluding with a stirring plea to let one great victory cancel all the reverses to date; but after the performance of Andrea Doria at Préveza, his offer was given little credence.[22] Giovio's investigations led him to believe that while many thinkers wanted Milan given to the duke of Orléans, the imperial party was strong in the senate, where votes were counted, not weighed. Nonetheless, it was difficult for an outsider to gauge the real state of things, he confessed, even though likening the once tight-lipped senate to the slave in Terence's *The Eunuch*, "who, full of cracks, was leaking here and there."[23]

Whatever the outcome of the talks, there was always good entertainment to be had in Venice, and Giovio savored the "dolcissima compagnia" of the literary circles.[24] With del Vasto he visited Aretino, through whom he began negotiating with Francesco de' Rossi, "il Salviati," for some work at the museum.[25] Apparently doge Lando had declined the opportunity to contribute to its construction, but another patron was willing to supply glass for the windows. To his new friend Donato Rullo, a Calabrian living in Venice, Giovio confessed that he had "a wondrous desire to spend a year away from the sound of drums," and were the Turks to come to Italy, Venice would be his "refuge and secure paradise."[26] Still, as he and the marquis were ferried across the lagoon to terra firma and the towers of that "paradise" receded in the maritime haze, it was clear to Giovio that he had seen greatness beginning to slip into decline.

On the outward journey, Giovio and del Vasto had gone by way of Verona and Vicenza. They had glimpsed Giberti, most likely at Verona, and at Vicenza they had seen Gian Giorgio Trissino—one would like to think in the midst of his Accademia Trissiniana at Cricoli, where he had just completed a splendid villa based on the theories of Vitruvius. After perusing some of the books of the *Histories*, which Giovio habitually carried with him, Trissino composed a graceful sonnet in his honor.[27] On the return from Venice, Giovio and d'Avalos came through Mantua, where they stopped to observe the feasts of Christmas, St. Stephen, and St. John (December 25, 26, and 27). During the festivities they undertook at Aretino's behest to reconcile him with Duke Federico, with whom he had been in disgrace since 1531.[28] "In raising that little bit of mist which had gathered above the serene forehead of the lord duke of Mantua," Giovio crowed to Aretino,

> "there was so little work that you need be obliged to us for a scruple only, and this goes for the lord marquis as well as for messer Titian and myself, fortunate and skillful ruffians in these sorts of matters. It is enough to say that the organ sounded well, the keys were well-touched, and the bellows gently inflated with astrolabe in hand. All you have to do is write a gracious letter to the lord duke without the ceremony of crystal liquids and without purple childishnesses— that is, in your own divine manner—and the duchy will be as fruitful as the former marquisate; you read me, I know."[29]

Resuming their journey, Giovio and d'Avalos reached Milan in time to observe New Year's Eve. Then, on the first day of 1540, while the marquis and court moved to Vigevano, Giovio went to keep Epiphany at Como, where he planned to work on his manuscripts. As long as Cardinal Farnese was away on his peacemaking embassy to the emperor, he was in no hurry to return to Rome, and he remained in Lombardy throughout the winter of 1540 to write and to supervise construction of the museum. Pier Luigi Farnese had aided him in buying additional land and in laying out "a fine piazza" in front of the entrance, "in the style of a fifth-rate cardinal."[30]

While Giovio was celebrating carnival with the d'Avalos at Vigevano, he learned that the emperor had completed his journey through France and was now in the Netherlands conferring with his sister Mary on the punishment of Ghent for its revolt, but there was no word on the outcome of the conversations with Francis I. Skeptical as ever, Giovio attributed the apparent friendliness of the two monarchs to financial exhaustion and predicted that their dilatoriness in reaching a solid agreement was hastening the "circumcision" of Venice, as he called its peace with the Turk. The del Vasto–d'Annebault mission had merely enabled the senate to gain time to follow the course "that necessity showed to be the less ill." The republic's emissary to the Porte, Alvise Badoer, might already have reached Constantinople, he speculated, and del Vasto had heard that Barbarossa was plotting new attacks on Brindisi. Those who discounted these rumors, Giovio said, were optimists who believed that Charles V and Francis I had in their pockets a ten-year truce with the Turk negotiated by Francis I's emissary to the Porte, Antonio Rincón.[31]

Giovio's skepticism was fully justified. Although Francis I had suspended his subsidies to the Protestants during the talks as a sign of goodwill, the emperor's ultimate terms for peace, proposed in March, 1540, after the suppression of Ghent, were as unacceptable to Francis I as the latter's own counterproposals were to the emperor. Charles V would not give up Milan, and Francis I would not accept anything else. By June the talks had collapsed and Montmorency, the architect of rapprochement, had fallen. On October 11, Charles V proceeded to invest his heir Philip with Milan. Giovio was also right as to the rumored truce with the Turk. Suleiman had long before refused the ostensibly joint overtures of Francis I and Charles V, conveyed through Rincón in the winter of 1538–39, and had let it be known that he was prepared to make peace only with Venice. Unbeknownst to Giovio, it was actually this rebuff which had prompted the emperor to propose the d'Annebault–del Vasto embassy.[32]

Despite promises to return to Rome in the spring, Giovio remained in Lombardy. The intention of the d'Avalos to pay an extended visit to the museum was reason enough, but thoughts of Barbarossa in Civitavecchia may have played a part.[33] The international situation continued to look worrisome. Giovio now expected Venice to have concluded a treaty with the Turk by mid-September, relinquishing the Morea, and the emperor would have lost forever the occasion of launching a crusade.[34] France had played away all its friends at the gaming table. The pope had been unmasked before everyone in "this laughable council" and was now afflicted by the rebellion of Perugia (February 1540). The Turk alone seemed capable of prudent diplomacy. Indeed, by the expected treaty with Venice, Suleiman had effectively removed the possibility of a Christian offensive. "Now, *signor mio*," Giovio lamented to Rullo, "this would be material for a satire, except that I am not a poet, so I shall reserve the occasion to do it in prose in the books of life when I find myself in a secure time and place."[35]

True to his word, Giovio incorporated his reproaches in the *Histories*. Composed in all probability within a year of these events, book 39 commenced with the emperor's trip through France in December and January 1539–40. The introductory sentences were steeped in irony: not only the French, who by their nature believe the things they hope for, but even persons knowledgeable in the ways of the world thought that by accepting Francis I's splendid hospitality, Charles V could not long defer the concessions that would lead to the longed-for peace between the two monarchs.[36] In narrating the joint embassy to Venice, Giovio made clear the extent to which he blamed the wars of Charles V and Francis I for the Republic's alarming condition, the result of staggering losses in hostilities with the Turks—defeats by land and sea, territories lost, peoples enslaved, trade destroyed, merchants imprisoned, goods confiscated—all stemming from the unwise alliance with the emperor that had led to the disaster at Préveza in 1538, a disaster that Giovio had already made clear in book 37 was not of Venice's making.

The immediate context in which Giovio set the arrival of the d'Annebault–del Vasto mission was a famine that Venice was unable to alleviate with Sicilian grain, despite her pleas, because of an imperial export tax equal to the price of the grain itself, making her best hope Macedonian grain imported with the permission of the sultan. In these circumstances the embassy was doomed to failure, particularly since the ambassadors could not offer a single concrete detail of the supposed peace impending between the two monarchs. Thanks to the leaks Giovio had mentioned in his contemporary letters from Venice—a sign to him that "the madness of factions" was disrupting the once-serene Republic—he had been able to learn that the emperor's opponents in the senate believed that Charles V had inherited the ambitions of his grandfather Maximilian and was aiming to add Venice to his Italian dominions. The deterioration of Venetian morale culminated in Giovio's account with the treason of the brothers Cavazza and their betrayal of state secrets that Francis I had not scrupled to reveal to Suleiman.[37]

The context in which Giovio put the collapse of peace negotiations between Charles V and Francis I was the emperor's punishment of Ghent, an act he described as a calculated piece of severity designed to stifle any thought of rebellion in the emperor's other domains, all of them burdened with his oppressive taxation. From the grim fortress constructed to make Ghent feel the yoke of its servitude, Giovio moved directly to Charles V's final break with Francis I, incorporating details provided by Cardinal Farnese of his humiliating treatment. The emperor had kept him uninformed not only about negotiations with France but even about the proposed colloquy at Hagenau and plans for conciliating the Protestants, until the astute young diplomat finally learned them from the women of the court and, after bitterly reproaching Granvelle, departed in disgust.

It was obvious to Giovio, as to later historians, that Charles V's ultimate offer to Francis I, a marriage between the duke of Orléans and Charles V's daughter Mary, with Flanders as dowry, was ungenerous, even arrogant. The emperor had reneged on the declaration of Toledo (1539), proclaiming instead that Milan was the head of his Italian dominions and inseparable from them. In his growing disillusion, Giovio's terms for the emperor, once celebrated as another Charlemagne, turned dark. Charles V was "harsher than necessary." His public utterances in favor of concord, consensus, and crusade were merely veils for "a secret plan to increase his greatness." Under the appearance of seeking peace he was scheming to become lord of all Italy.[38] Once again, Giovio put the failure of negotiations in the context of the Ottoman peril. On hearing the news, the Venetian envoy to Constantinople, Alvise Badoer, moved swiftly to conclude peace. The great crusade was dead.

Giovio concluded this section of book 39 with a prophetic excursus:

> I know that I have been somewhat more prolix than appropriate for someone writing the history of nearly the whole world in this explication of the councils of princes, by which we are doubtless to perish; but my good readers will certainly forgive me if I have dwelt too long on the causes of public sorrow and the mourning soon to come when they understand how the insane raging of the greatest kings lost an exceptional occasion not only of repulsing but of destroying the enemy in a mighty victory; an enemy who holds a bloody sword to our throat insolently and successfully while our kings, ruling with no piety but with abundant ignominy, fight with nefarious arms among themselves and lose the world; for it is evident that after exhausting their mutual strength they will abandon not only the empire of the East but everything else to the unopposed barbarian faith.[39]

As Giovio proceeded to explain in the remainder of book 39, the "exceptional occasion not only of repulsing but of destroying" the Turks was the death, in July 1540, of John Zápolya, the Turks' client-king of Hungary.

Giovio was no clerical zealot sanctimoniously promoting a crusade. He condemned the warfare of Christian kings as a political realist who saw the prosperity of Christendom crumbling as barbarian fleets attacked her shores and crippled her trade while her kings drained off immense wealth through confiscatory taxation to support, not a rational plan of defense and counterattack, but their own dynastic pretensions. No democrat, Giovio nonetheless spoke for the common humanity of the age.

Sometime about June 22, 1540, the marquis and marchioness del Vasto arrived in Como for their promised visit. Their large entourage was lodged partially in the museum, partially in the family palace in the city, and Giovio boasted that all were enjoying "salubriousness, views, freshness, delightful architecture, cool waters, suave fruits, and perfect fish." On the 23rd a great company, numbering some three hundred, went to dine at the Fonte Pliniana across the lake, requiring a "pygmy armada, like Barbarossa's."[40] Giovio had at last achieved the ambition of every *homo novus* to cut a great figure in his *patria*. He asked Carlo Gualteruzzi to tell Vittoria Colonna that the marchioness was occupying her room, "della Vittoria," in which her portrait testified to her bounty and liberality.[41] While the d'Avalos were staying at the museum, word came of the death of Duke Federico Gonzaga on June 28, creating a moment of sadness for all. Giovio had lost one of his earliest patrons, and del Vasto had wept, Giovio told Cardinal Ercole Gonzaga, as if he had lost his alter ego.[42]

On July 14 the d'Avalos departed, compelled by affairs of state to return to the stifling heat of Milan, and Giovio began to think more seriously about his return to Rome. Before consenting to go he had sounded out both the pope and cardinal-nephew, not only indirectly but directly.[43] Aside from exemptions from the tithe, there had been no "datarial graces" so far, only a disappointment over the Umiliati of Borgo Vico, and Giovio emphasized to the cardinal that his willingness to return was owing entirely to assurances that "the recent dryness of Rome in my regard will be benignly irrigated by the fresh and living waters of the perennial font of your liberality toward the likes of me."[44] To Giovanni Poggio, nuncio to Spain, Giovio explained that he was returning to "the customary service" at the express invitation of the Farnese, even though he had been tempted to continue enjoying the leisure and literary quiet "at my jocund and salubrious museum on the lake of Como, without thinking of enriching myself further, or of meriting the red hat, which belongs to the sons of good Fortune."[45]

As usual Giovio was transparent. In his heart he still wanted the hat. The astrologer Luca Gaurico had predicted it for him, and even if he himself put little trust in Gaurico's predictions, there was always the reflection that Paul III put a great deal of trust in them.[46] One of the panels in the *sala d'onore* of the museum depicting events of Giovio's career had been left conspicuously blank.[47] Despite his protests to Pio that he was not accustomed, like Ariosto or Chieregati, to envisioning himself once a week in consistory or to dream of seeing himself in the mirror with a red biretta, he had clearly been disappointed at not being among the twelve cardinals of Paul III's sixth promotion on December 19, 1539. The pope had now created the very large number of thirty-nine cardinals, among them several men of letters including Sadoleto, Aleander (*in pectore* December 22, 1536), Bembo (*in pectore* December 20, 1538), and, in this last promotion, the protonotary Uberto Gambara, bishop of Tortona, whom Giovio had often derided for his ill-concealed ambitions.[48]

Were Giovio's hopes realistic? Paul III's criteria for promotion were normally service to the Church or to the Farnese family and, as always, the advocacy of princes. The Church had not benefited conspicuously from Giovio's service, nor had the Farnese family. Giovio was not a dexterous and serviceable diplomat like Marcello Cervini, the cardinal's secretary just elevated; and while he had too many extraneous ties to be considered a Farnese loyalist, none of Giovio's princely patrons were urging him for the purple. Promotion would have had to have come, as with Bembo, for his writings, and while Paul III evidently appreciated the lively commentary that made Giovio's letters universally welcome, it was ominous that, for whatever reason, he did not accept the historian's offer to write his biography.[49] Giovio's model, Bembo, had been a long-time friend of the pope, and Giovio himself was well aware of the objections Cardinal Carafa had raised to the promotion. "Not only for the likes of me," he confessed to Pio, "but even for distinguished men, the rigorous and fierce pseudodisciples of Daun Cato will have snatched from the girdle of the good pope the key of the chest of the red hats and thrown it in the well of San Patrizio [at Orvieto]." Still, he hoped "one fine autumn" someone might retrieve it with a fishhook.[50]

Most prejudicial of all to his hopes, perhaps, was Giovio's attitude toward the campaign being initiated as he negotiated his return to Rome. Early in 1540, Paul III had finally begun implementing the recommendations of the reform commission appointed in 1536, whose report, *De emendanda ecclesia*, had been issued just before Giovio met with Giberti and Pole on their northward journey in 1537. In the consistory of April 21, 1540, the pope authorized Cardinals Carafa and Contarini to begin reforming the Apostolic Penitentiary, despite the vigorous opposition of the grand penitentiary, Cardinal Pucci. Giovio's alarm was evident in the letter he wrote Cardinal Farnese on July 16 to announce his imminent return. Praising the elevation of Cervini allowed him to contrast the virtues of spirituals with the defects of Theatines, "who with strange appetites want tart sugar and who want to bind the elements of this ancient machine, and put them in a sack and reduce them to make them more beautiful and do not see that the wish to reduce them down to the primary materials would be to bring the machine itself to destruction."

Giovio urged moderation, employing—significantly—a classical apothegm. "*Vitia erunt donec homines* [As long as there are men there will be vices: Tacitus, *Hist.* 4.74]," he warned, "nor can one use extreme severity to reform the customs and manner of the Roman court; one would do better with sweet dexterity to lessen abuses, castigate avarice, repress luxury, revise the composition of the tribunals, abbreviate suits, correct monopolies, and then let whoever wants to wear pleated shirts and cloaks without hoods, and let bishops attach fringes to the trappings of their mules in the manner of cardinals, the attempted reform of which, by edict, threw Chieregati into such a fury against the reforming Cardinal Sanseverini."[51] Giovio had taken the measure of Carafa and it alarmed him. His advice to attack fundamentals rather than superficialities and to proceed moderately was sensible and, indeed, reflected the pope's own cautions of March 1535, based on the failure of Adrian VI's clumsy attempts at reform.[52] Yet despite Giovio's personal ties to the spiritual party and his intellectual recognition of the need for reform, his instinctive alarm at its imminence linked him to the obstructionists and made him seem increasingly anachronistic.[53] Nonetheless, if Aretino could dream of the hat, so at least could Giovio.[54]

In August 1540, as he prepared for the journey back to Rome, reports reached Giovio of the failure of the conference of Hagenau. Although called by Charles V in the hopes of reaching accord with the Lutherans on doctrine, the colloquy had mainly revealed the deep divisions among Catholics, let alone between Catholics and Protestants. It had not been in progress more than a month when Giovio called it "a diet of goats." Despite the united front of the Protestants, who clung steadfastly to the Confession of Augsburg, Giovio perceived the fissures among them as well: "In effect the Lutherans, divided into forty-eight sects, laugh at Christ and do not believe in God and want to enjoy the goods of the churches, sleep with nuns and eat meat on Friday, avoid the fatigue of going to mass, do away with the cost of exequies for the dead, and not ruin their stomachs with Lent."[55]

Giovio's skepticism about Hagenau reflected the curia's aversion to doctrinal discussions with heretics, particularly under circumstances not controlled by Rome. His cynicism about Lutherans kept him from understanding the force of the Protestant movement, a characteristic failing of the *politique*. For Giovio, religion consisted in conventional piety coupled with correct observance of traditional forms, and he easily equated revolt against those forms with moral license and atheism.[56] He could sympathize with Luther's initial protests because he could understand the alienation caused by venality and corruption, but he had no sympathy with alterations of doctrine or ritual. The Lutheran princes he saw as mere political opportunists. Not withstanding this, his contemporary letters revealed an astute sense of the political situation in Germany and the probable outcomes of the emperor's various initiatives.

Word of the death of John Zápolya in July 1540 made Ferdinand of Austria hasten from the colloquy of Hagenau to press his claim to all of Hungary, as befell him by the treaty of Grosswardein, but Giovio foresaw that to prevail against both the Turks and the shifty barons of Hungary, he would need more support from the emperor than he was likely to get. The Protestant princes would ultimately fight against the Turk, Giovio prophesied, "but not in a time or place opportune for the king of the Romans." He was correct on both counts.[57]

"Booted and spurred," as August 1540 drew to a close, Giovio was waiting for the first rains to end the worst of the heat and drought before setting out for Rome. The young Marco Gallio, older brother of the future cardinal Tolomeo Gallio, entered Giovio's service as secretary and amanuensis about this time and may have accompanied him on the journey.[58] The first stop was to be Vigevano, where del Vasto had asked Giovio to join the court for the inauguration of the September hunting season. While there he expected to learn how the marquis planned to defend his gains in Piedmont against a French attack timed to coincide with the anticipated Turkish offensive in Hungary. A visit had been promised Count Giulio Landi in Piacenza, and in Florence there would be the festivities for Saints Cosmas and Damian (September 27).[59] With so many diversions en route, Giovio did not reach Rome until the evening of October 6, 1540, but his purpose seems to have been firm. He had arrived, the secretary Bernardino Maffei informed Cardinal Farnese, "of a mind to finish the rest of his life in the service of Your Most Reverend Lordship."[60]

The Rome to which Giovio returned after the absence of a year and a half was both old and new. While court life continued in forms traditional to the papal "monarchy," with banquets and fireworks on the anniversary of the pope's election, new and unaccustomed currents were flowing.[61] The day Giovio was celebrating the feast of Cosmas and Damian in Florence, the pope had published the bull *Regimini militantis ecclesiae*, the first great success of the reform movement and a gauge of his determination to forestall conciliar action by an internal reform of the Church.[62] Then, on December 13, almost before Giovio had settled himself in the "paradiso," the pope summoned the more than eighty bishops and archbishops resident in Rome to an audience and represented to them the necessity of returning to their sees to guide their flocks. "If other acts correspond with this beginning," Gregorio Cortese exulted to Contarini, "I behold already, in the spirit, the Holy Church renewed in beauty and comeliness."[63]

Although the circumstances of Alessandro Farnese's election to the Sacred College and his early life as a cardinal belonged to the Rome of Alexander VI, from the moment of his ordination to the priesthood at the age of fifty-one, he had not only lived a blameless life but had taken a serious interest in the administration of his diocese. It was characteristic, therefore, that in beginning a reform of the Church he should have turned to the episcopacy. Because the signature sheet has been lost, it is uncertain if Giovio signed the bishops' response protesting that the nearly total usurpation of episcopal authority by exempt orders, legates, nuncios, curial familiars, and even secular authorities, made residence futile.[64] Although the pope resolutely maintained his stance throughout the winter 1540–41, the bull converting his exhortation to an imperative was never promulgated, and whatever shock Giovio experienced at the prospect of forced residence in Nocera was at least mitigated when the waters of Farnese grace finally irrigated the parched terrain of his needs. Shortly after the historian's return, Cardinal Farnese wrote to the nuncio of Venice to confirm an exemption from the tithe, past, present, and future on Giovio's pension of 100 *scudi* on the bishopric of Verona, and similar letters may have been written for his other benefices as well.[65] Then, on December 16, he received *in commendam* the church of San Giuliano at Como.[66] Still more graces were to follow during the next two years including a half-cavalierate, two archpresbyteries on Lake Como, and a pension of 100 *scudi* on the see of Lavello.[67]

The carnival of 1541 was particularly brilliant, despite the incipient revolt of Ascanio Colonna, which created for Giovio the specter of 1527 should the emperor decide to support him.[68] One of the season's highlights was a party given by Cardinal Farnese for the resident ambassadors and papal *familia* featuring a performance of Machiavelli's *Clizia* directed by Molza with costumes by Giulio Clovio and a few alterations in the text in obeisance to the new reform currents.[69] Although she had tried to talk sense to her brother, Vittoria Colonna was so distressed by the ruthless spring campaign in which Paul III crushed once and for all the independent power of her family that she went into retirement, first at the convent of San Paolo in Orvieto and then at the convent of Santa Caterina in Viterbo. Perhaps in deference to her, Giovio omitted this unhappy episode from the *Histories* altogether.

Diplomatic events of 1541 moved forward at a rapid pace, culminating in the meeting of pope and emperor at Lucca in September. Giovio had heard much talk of another meeting but was skeptical about its usefulness.[70] The chief incentives for the meeting were the situation in Germany and, above all, the council. Although increasingly suspicious of the compromises Contarini was attempting to work out with the Protestants in the "Book of Regensburg" (April–July 1541), Rome heeded his eloquent warning of "the great fire now spreading from Denmark and Sweden all over the north and overleaping Alps and rivers even to the regions of Italy," particularly when it was reinforced by a report from the marquis del Vasto on the spread of heresy in Lombardy. Truly alarmed, a consistory voted on July 8, 1541, to resume the council called earlier for Vicenza, and with the council at least partially resuscitated, Paul III was more determined than ever to seek a meeting with Charles V.[71]

The emperor himself was about to embark on a new project. Financially unable to mount a great crusade in Hungary, he had resolved to attack the Turks in Algiers, a more feasible project and more popular in Spain, to which he was returning after his failure to effect a settlement in Germany. He was also calculating that Francis I would not risk public opprobrium by attacking him in Piedmont while he was on a crusade, a consideration of some urgency, since the likelihood of war—continually present after the break-off of negotiations in 1540—was never greater than in the summer of 1541 after the murder of Antonio Rincón.

One of the most brilliant and intriguing diplomats of the sixteenth century, Rincón was a refugee from the Spanish Comuneros uprising of 1521. Entering French service, he continued the struggle against Hapsburg power by mastering the unknown byways of what had been a no-man's-land of diplomacy. The success of the French alliance with the Turks rested in no small measure on his resourcefulness and skill. He was on his way back to Constantinople, traveling incognito with Cesare Fregoso, a Genoese in French service, when the two were stopped along the Po by troops of the marquis del Vasto on July 4, 1541, recognized and murdered. After Castelnuovo, Rincón would have been especially unpopular with the Spanish veterans. Del Vasto disclaimed all responsibility and the emperor opened an inquiry, but the harm had been done. When he learned of it, Giovio thought it was only a matter of time before the French took up arms.

Disregarding the remonstrances of his physicians and the protests of the Francophiles in the curia, Paul III left Rome on August 27 for Lucca, where Charles V had agreed to meet him. After an arduous journey up the Via Cassia in the heat of summer, the pope made his solemn entry on September 8. Cardinal Farnese had gone ahead with a small escort to greet the emperor at Viareggio, leaving most of his familiars, Giovio included, to join him at Lucca. Four days after the pope's entry, the emperor arrived from Genoa with Cardinal Farnese and the dukes of Ferrara, Florence, and Camerino (Ottavio Farnese).[72]

Paul III and Charles V had held six conversations in Lucca with one yet to come when Giovio expressed the universal astonishment that "despite Doria, del Vasto, Neptune, and Aeolus," the emperor was persevering in his plan to attack Algiers in October, a month of frequent storms. As the pope was descending the stairs of the bishop's palace for one of his calls on the emperor, he had caught sight of Giovio and asked him what he thought of this "paradox." Baffled himself, Giovio could only invoke the common opinion that it was fate and the emperor's inner nature. "We will hear bizarre tales and discourses of vessels dispersed throughout the Mediterranean," he prophesied, "and we will see plenty of ex-voto paintings in Santa Maria del Popolo." Despite his skepticism, however, he had begun collecting material for his narrative and had already acquired a plan of Algiers.[73]

There is no indication that Giovio had an audience at Lucca with the emperor, for whom his *linga zerga* epithet had subtly changed from "cima d'arrosto (top of the roast)" to "cima d'arrosto freddo (the top of a cold roast)," but he had heard some of the rival accusations in the inquest the pope had agreed to open on the Rincón affair, and from the many captains and soldiers present he had been assimilating details of Suleiman's reconquest of Buda earlier in the summer.[74] He was shocked at the sultan's uncharacteristic cruelty in ordering the mass execution of the Germans captured in their precipitate flight until "the many mountains of heads" appalled even the Turkish troops. The immediacy of eye-witness detail, the grim nature of the warfare, and Giovio's own dark sense of the tragedy of it all made his narrative of the fall of Buda one of the more gripping parts of his *Histories*. Much of the old kingdom of Hungary now vanished for several centuries into the Ottoman empire.[75]

Charles V left Lucca on September 18, 1541, and Paul III departed on the 20th, intending to return to Rome by way of Bologna and Perugia. This time Giovio did not go on to Como but stayed with the papal party.[76] Shortly after their return, on All Hallows' Eve, 1541, Michelangelo's *Last Judgment* was unveiled, following which the pope celebrated High Mass in the Sistine Chapel. Giovio admired the Sistine ceiling but left no opinion of the *Last Judgment*. Although enthusiastic about Michelangelo's work, he disapproved of the "incredible squalors" of the artist's private life and does not seem to have been on friendly terms with him (few, of course, were).[77]

In 1541 Giovio ceased to serve on the College of Deputies for St. Peter's. He had been named to the college when Paul III resumed construction early in his pontificate, and he functioned regularly until 1539 and sporadically until 1541 because of his absence in Como.[78] In a letter from there of January 1540, he thanked the deputies for some honor he felt they had done him.[79] Why he should drop from the college just as he returned to residence in Rome is puzzling. From 1536 to 1540 he would have been closely associated with Antonio da San Gallo and Baldassare

Peruzzi during the construction of San Gallo's great model and the evolution of the plans that, although accepted by Paul III in 1540, subsequently drew such vigorous expressions of Michelangelo's scorn when he was appointed architect following San Gallo's death in 1546.[80]

In a letter of early November 1541, Giovio claimed he was living with his customary modest expectations and "jocundity of mind" amid the fortunes and misfortunes of the Roman courtiers, transmitting to posterity "the disasters of our times."[81] Foremost among those disasters was the emperor's Algerian crusade. All Giovio's predictions came true. The emperor and troops had disembarked on October 23 and invested the city, but the following night a gale tore the fleet to pieces before the bulk of the artillery and provisions could be unloaded. Attempts to reprovision from the remaining ships were foiled by renewed storms, while the army was soaked by the rains and savaged by the Moorish defenders. Eventually, the emperor and survivors saved themselves by reaching Bougie, west of Algiers, where they were able to embark on the remaining ships. Even then, Cortés (who had come out of retirement for this crusade) thought Algiers could still be won, but the emperor and Andrea Doria saw the storm as a sign from God and sailed back to Spain.

By early December, Giovio had examined "an infinity of letters," including the emperor's widely circulated report to his brother Ferdinand and another by Andrea Doria, from which he had pieced together his own reconstruction of the disaster. He calculated that the emperor had lost 12,000 men, 1,800 horses, 183 transport ships, 17 galleys, and untold pieces of artillery.[82] His account of this hapless crusade—one of the great set pieces of the *Histories*—was probably composed in the winter and spring of 1542. That June, Giovio commented to Giovanni Poggio, nuncio in Spain, that Charles V could expect more praise from him for Algiers than for Tunis, since at Algiers he had shown the kings of the world "the value of constancy in an intrepid spirit," the very note on which book 40 concluded.[83]

In the wake of the Rincón affair and the disaster at Algiers, winter and spring of 1542 were marked by growing tension and uncertainty. The imperialists in Lombardy were braced for a French attack, and an attempt to poison the marquis del Vasto was traced to Piero Strozzi. The impasse in Germany continued. "The diet of Speyer has expired," Giovio quipped to Stefano Colonna, "with nothing done for the faith of Christ," at least not on the religious issue. The diet did promise Ferdinand 40,000 foot and 8,000 horse for the reconquest of Buda, and Giovio hoped for a great battle, since, regardless of who won—German or Turk—Italy would lose a host of enemies. The pope, who was engaged in raising a contingent of 3,000 foot and 500 horse, remarked to Giovio that he wished to devote the rest of his reign to saving Europe from the

Turks. Unity being the prerequisite, he would strive to bring the two "obstinate and enraged" monarchs together for another colloquy. Giovio remained skeptical. It was a good design, but it would not be colored in, he predicted, "because God wants to castigate us more thoroughly." By May he knew that the work of Morone at Speyer had borne fruit in at least one respect: the German estates had accepted Trent as the site for the council, and on April 26, 1542, consistory followed suit, with the opening date set for the first of November.[84]

In retrospect, the agreement on Trent was a turning point, but at the time it seemed merely another step in a never-ending saga of proclamation and prorogation. In fact, Giovio was more interested in the effect of the announcement on the creation of cardinals. One consequence was the elevation of the nuncio who had labored so effectively at Speyer, Giovanni Morone. Another was the promotion *in pectore* of the bishop of Trent, Cristoforo Madruzzo, to whom Giovio quickly penned a graceful note of congratulation, affirming that in his case fortune had indeed been the companion of virtue.[85] It would only be a few days, Giovio predicted, before the actual elevation, but in fact the bishop was destined to wait four years before it was certain that the long-expected council would assemble in his episcopal city and he could swath himself in scarlet. The bull convoking the council, *Initio nostri huius pontificatus*, dated May 22, 1542, was composed by Sadoleto and stressed the Turkish dangers so prominent in the pope's mind, and in Giovio's as well.[86]

While following Ferdinand's preparations for the recovery of Buda, Giovio was watching apprehensively as war clouds gathered again over Piedmont and Lombardy.[87] By late July he had heard of the French declaration of war and hoped Francis I would not be completely outwitted by Charles V—the evident likelihood, since he did not match his rival's attention to detail—but he feared the French-Ottoman connection, knowing that Suleiman was ready "to pick up the legs and feet of Italy in his beak" if Caesar held onto the head.[88]

Enveloped all summer by the fog of rumors, Giovio begged Cardinal Farnese for news. The city had become a sepulcher of false tidings, he complained, and he was constantly being sought out by ambassadors, cardinals, and courtiers for reliable news.[89] By mid-December, Alessandro Vitelli and the other captains had returned from Hungary, and Giovio was in possession of the outcomes of the various campaigns of the summer and autumn. It was a dismal enough harvest. The county of Roussillon in the Pyrenees had been ravaged to no effect and destruction spread in the Netherlands with similar results. In Piedmont the French had retaken Bicocca, thanks to the arrival of Marshal d'Annebault after the Roussillon campaign, and were besieging Chieri. Owing to impositions to pay for the war, Giovio lamented, "the poor Milanese state is going to its final ruin." With inadequate leadership and poor morale, the crusade in Hungary had utterly floundered. After an ineffectual assault on Pest, in which only the papal troops had distinguished themselves, the army had dispersed.[90] So ended the hope of regaining Buda.

These events of the summer and autumn of 1542 formed the material of books 41 and 42. Since Giovio was composing the more recent books within a year or two of events, the two books must have closely mirrored his mood of 1542, particularly his anger and despair at the breakup of the Christian force before Pest. After describing the emotions of the retreating troops as they watched the slaughter of their wounded comrades, abandoned on the further bank, Giovio inserted into his narrative yet another bitter condemnation of the Christian princes: "Now in truth our generals, having to their heavy shame experienced for the third unhappy time the force and skill of the Turks, deplored with sad musings their lost military reputation; for it was now admitted that all hope of regaining Hungary had to be forgotten and counsel taken rather for saving Germany, since the greatest monarchs, oblivious to true honor and piety while pursuing private quarrels, have undertaken, with wicked obstinacy of spirit, to sap and destroy the Christian commonwealth for the benefit of barbarians."[91] By 1540 Giovio was even less concerned by the rights and wrongs of the Hapsburg-Valois quarrels. "A plague on both your houses" was the new attitude of the old imperialist.

The year 1542 brought Giovio personal as well as political sorrows. In August he reported to the cardinal on a visit to poor Molza, painfully disfigured by advanced syphilis. Trying to cheer him with a little Giovian humor, he had asked him, when he passed to the other life, to see if the recently deceased Contarini's opinions on free will had landed him in purgatory and to report back in a vision. "Ah, humorist!" cried Molza, laughing in spite of himself, "my first concern will be to seek out the cauldron being readied for you and to report on that."[92]

Not long after Giovio's visit to Molza, a letter arrived from Benedetto announcing the death of their brother. In an exchange that indicates how intrinsic Ciceronian philosophy was to their inmost thoughts, each advised the other to seek consolation in the immortality of letters, promising to do the same himself. Benedetto, in particular, pleaded with Paolo not to let his death rob their family of the glory of his *Histories* but to speed them to publication. Paolo assured him that in the spring he would bring to Como at least a dozen of "the less dangerous" books to revise for publication with his help, using a phrase which suggests that his condemnations of the wars of Charles V and Francis I were part of the contemporary composition of the *Histories* and not interpolations of his old age.[93]

The year 1543 was to bring new hopes and new disappointments. Since mid-December 1542 Giovio had known of the pope's intention to travel north with the swallows in pursuit of three objectives: drawing the king of France to an interview at Turin, intercepting the emperor at Alessandria on his way from Spain to Germany, and reinforcing by his own proximity the prospects for a council at Trent. Cervini had been pressing the Italian bishops to ready themselves for the journey to Trent but, as Paul III and Giovio both understood, without peace there could be no council. Thus, despite the solemn entry of the three legates into Trent on November 21, 1542, Giovio saw little hope. Francis I was still refusing to accept the city as a venue, and in his anger at the pope's steadfast refusal to declare himself against France, Charles V had dismissed the legate bearing the invitations to the Spanish bishops. A surprise appearance at Trent by Granvelle, however, on January 7, 1543, accompanied by his son Antoine Perrenot, bishop of Arras, and by Don Diego Hurtado de Mendoza, the Spanish ambassador to Venice, made the pope decide to anticipate the swallows, and Giovio was preparing himself for the rigors of winter travel even as he condemned Arras' harangue to the legates on clerical abuses as "excessive."[94]

Ignoring the pleas of his family, Roman officials, and the Sacred College, Paul III set out on February 26 through the papal states, hoping to be in Bologna by Palm Sunday (March 18).[95] Although he thought the pope was going so fast he would find the "most lame" council in the ditch by the roadside, Giovio asked Cardinal Farnese to revalidate his old charter granting him the hospitality of monasteries and then set out on the direct route through Tuscany, making a little detour through the mystical landscape south of Siena to see Cardinal Cervini's new villa under construction in the Maremma. By dint of riding every day and never spending a second night in the same place, he managed to reach Bologna on March 13, four days ahead of the pope, who made his formal entry on the 17th.[96]

While attending the pope at Bologna, Giovio was being entertained by Giovanni Campeggio, bishop of Parenzo, a nephew of Cardinal Campeggio, and had managed to finish a chapter of his *Histories*. Sending it to Cardinal Farnese, he hoped that "some foggy or rainy day" the pope "might even deign to read part of it, prudently noting any badly stitched point so that it can be emended." He would have liked to have had Romolo Amaseo give it a final stylistic polish, he said, but Amaseo had become too much the courtier to occupy himself with such matters. The letter sounded the same cautionary note Giovio had used with other patrons. The Farnese should expect of him "sincere service," he cautioned, not "courtly adulation." He also promised Farnese that while the pope was traveling he would work on what he called "your book, *De imperiis*," using a metaphor which suggested he had been discussing it with Fra Leandro Alberti, who was then at work in Bologna on his *Descrittione di tutta Italia* (1550).[97]

Delayed in settling the affairs of Spain, the emperor finally landed at Savona on May 24 and went immediately to Genoa, where Pier Luigi Farnese was waiting to invite him to a colloquy with the pope. The emperor's purposes in coming were still unclear, but Giovio believed they were connected with Germany rather than Italy. Conversations in Bologna with Sfondrato had deepened his grasp of the emperor's situation, especially his need for papal money. Caesar's problems were, indeed, many. His rebel vassal, the duke of Cleves, was on the march in Gelderland, nourished by French money, and the diets of Nuremberg had achieved no reconciliation for Germany. Suleiman was preparing another offensive by land, Barbarossa by sea. The nonopened council Giovio expected to be closed about the first of June with a bull *ad perpetuam rei memoriam* protesting the discords which had thwarted it.[98]

On June 7, when Giovio wrote from Bologna to his friends Raynce and Angleria, the pope and curia were awaiting the return of Cardinal Farnese, who had been dispatched in alarm after the emperor had refused Pier Luigi's invitation. By the time he composed book 43, Giovio had concluded that because of his secret alliance of February 11, 1543, with Henry VIII, Charles V had felt obliged to give the impression of being forced into an unavoidable meeting with the pope. On the positive side, Giovio could report that Ottavio Farnese, who was returning with the emperor from Spain, had at last been admitted by Margaret to the conjugal bed, where he had performed creditably, after which he had come to Bologna to salute his grandfather. Giovio had been cultivating "Madama" since her arrival in Rome following Alessandro's death and was genuinely glad that things were improving.[99] There was still talk of Charles V's ceding Milan to Margaret and Ottavio in return for a half million ducats, which Giovio foresaw the poor Milanese (and Comaschi) would have to pay, and he cursed again the physician and fatal enema which he blamed for the death of Francesco II Sforza.

The day after Giovio's letter, Cardinal Farnese returned to Bologna bearing the emperor's counteroffer of a meeting at Parma or Mantua. With the reluctant consent of the cardinals, the pope left Bologna on June 11, and when Giovio wrote again to Raynce and Angleria on the 15th, the papal court had just reached Parma, the pope having made his formal entry that morning with twenty-two cardinals and a like number of bishops. Giovio had heard that the emperor was now at Cremona with a strong force of cavalry and 2,500 foot, vastly outnumbering the papal guard. He had also learned of Cosimo de' Medici's trip to Genoa and successful negotiations for the return of the fortresses of Florence and Liguria upon payment of 150,000 *scudi*. He was delighted for Italy and pleased that the emperor was "not so engorged with Monarchy as people have been saying." Milan, he hoped, might still go to Margaret and Ottavio, which would be pleasing to everyone provided the money were used for war against the Turks and not against France.[100] By now it was clear that the armaments Charles V had been raising all fall and winter were destined to be used against the duke of Cleves in "pitiful Flanders" and the French in Champagne. "There is no more talk of the Turk," Giovio sighed, despite a tearful embassy from Ferdinand led by the bishop of Vienna. Suleiman was on the march, building bridges over the Danube, and Barbarossa was at the Gulf of Lepanto.

Owing to the fears raised in the papal court by the size of the emperor's force, it was finally agreed to meet, not at Parma, to which the emperor had an ancient claim, but rather at the small town of Busseto, between Cremona and Fidenza, where he had once been the guest of the Pallavicini family. The pope and cardinals arrived on June 21 and Caesar on the following day, all the papal court going to meet him. From then until the evening of June 25, the two heads of Christendom had numerous interviews to discuss their respective views and disagreements. The venue was not to Giovio's liking. The town was "a fetid hole where sleep was banned," and he vowed upon returning home to stay in bed for a week amidst cool linens.[101] Nor were the meetings a success. Charles V was still distrustful of the pope and angry with him for not disowning Francis I because of his alliance with Suleiman. Paul III, on the other hand, feared another schism if he did. As a peace measure, Giovio heard, the pope had suggested settling Milan on Margaret and Ottavio, an initiative that only convinced Charles V that family aggrandizement dominated papal diplomacy. The emperor's intentions with regard to the duke of Cleves had become abundantly clear. When Giovio went to wait on him, he chided, "You had better hurry up and write what I have already done, Giovio, because this war is going to give you a new and great labor."[102]

On the evening of June 25 the emperor departed for Germany, and the pope returned to Parma. Giovio made his way to Como, where "Fortune, which always amuses itself with my little plans," made good his vow to stay in bed a week by sending him a fever and catarrh.[103] While the pope was celebrating the feast of St. Peter (June 29) at Bologna, Barbarossa's flotilla appeared at the mouth of the Tiber, striking consternation into Rome until the city was reassured by the French envoy, "Captain Polin [Antoine des Escalins, baron de la Garde]," that he was conducting the fleet to southern France as a base for attacking the cities of Spain. The Rincón affair, as Giovio explained in the *Histories*, had thrown Francis I and Suleiman back into a working partnership negotiated by Polin. While the sultan led an army into Hungary during the campaigning season of 1543, Barbarossa was to attack the Spanish coasts. All eagerness for this congenial task, he had anticipated his work in Spain by sacking Reggio Calabria and enslaving the city's imperial guard just about the time the emperor was sailing for Italy.[104]

Book 43 of the *Histories*, on which Giovio began work almost immediately, placed the colloquy of Busseto squarely in the context of the Turkish peril. An exordium related the fears of all Europeans that their sovereigns would do nothing to defend them against the Turk. Giovio depicted the emperor as wholly engrossed in the effort to punish his rebellious vassal, the duke of Cleves, and the pope as unable to overcome the emperor's long-standing hatred of his French opponent, who, Charles insisted, "with so many broken treaties had forfeited credibility," and yet, "with immoderate appetite for the lands of others, would never accept peace or lay down his oft-vanquished arms."[105] For emphasis, Giovio quoted at length the appeal of Cardinal Grimani, dean of the Sacred College, but the perils of Hungary, Ferdinand's plight, and the suffering of the peoples of his own lands—ravaged by fighting, brutal soldiers, and constant imposts—failed to move the emperor, who responded to Grimani's pleas with a recitation of Francis I's unceasing attempts to undermine him in Italy, Germany, and Flanders by means of arms, Protestants, and now the very infidels that he, the emperor, alone had attempted to combat.

Recent historians have stressed Paul III's dynastic ambitions as the stumbling block of Busseto.[106] While Giovio had already condemned Farnese nepotism in letters and in the *Histories*, at the time of Busseto he felt it might actually work for peace, in that giving Milan as a fief to Ottavio and Margaret might placate Francis I. He certainly knew of the intrigues of the Venetians and his friend, del Vasto, that led the emperor to insist on retaining the citadel, the proximate cause for the failure of the proposal; but the ultimate blame for the failure of Busseto he laid to the emperor's anger at the pope for refusing to abandon his neutrality and enter into an alliance against France.[107] Significantly, Paul III now had Giovio's full support. Twenty years earlier, the historian had vigorously condemned a similar neutrality on the part of Clement VII. Now he accepted the traditional view of the popes that a preponderance of the emperor was the greater evil, no matter how culpable the behavior of the French king. After England, moreover, Giovio feared the loss of France to the Church should the pope side openly with the emperor. In Charles V's paramount determination to punish the duke of Cleves, Giovio perceived the character of a ruler whose guiding principle was *mon droit*. The duke's Protestantism, he thought, weighed far less in the emperor's mind than his lèse-majesté. Perhaps Charles V was, indeed, aspiring to "monarchy."[108] Under the circumstances the pope's July 6th suspension of the council would have come as no surprise.

Once recovered from his fever, Giovio began enjoying the breezes at the museum. With his brother as critic he was revising the earlier books of the *Histories*, expunging the "delicta iuventutis meae [the sins of my youth]," as he put it, in hopes of an edition by Priscianese "in that type more luxurious than Messalina [Nero's third wife]."[109] On visits to Milan he admired the refurbished citadel and corrected the treatments of the marchioness' physicians for "mal della verula."[110] Consoling her in July for the death of her father, he again revealed his reliance on Cicero's *Tusculan Disputations* and his admiration for stoic fortitude.[111] In mid-August he was summoned by the marquis, who, in a moment of disgust with his deteriorating position at the imperial court, "unbuttoned his chest" and asked Giovio to explore the possibility of service with the pope.[112] Despite the French declaration of war, the only invasion of Lombardy so far had been of grasshoppers, which the peasants were attempting to scare off with pealing of bells, fusillades of arquebuses, and "unheard-of clangors."[113]

Work on the museum was almost complete. On arriving, Giovio had found the gallery of Virtù and the portico of Parnassus already finished and their inscriptions in place testifying to the liberality of the Farnese. Since then he had extended the garden and embellished one of the piazzas. From Cosimo I de' Medici he had obtained the promise of a subsidy for the *stanza d'onore*, which was dedicated to the duke and which displayed his *impresa*.[114] Not only this, but for the bargain sum of 900 gold *scudi* he had been able to buy the "magnificent" house used by the governors of Como, which stood just north of the family palace and communicated with it via the rear gardens. Now prompt payment of the French and Spanish pensions was more necessary than ever.[115]

A visitor during this summer of 1543 paid an enthusiastic tribute to Giovio's accomplishment. The renegade friar and man of letters Anton Francesco Doni had settled in Piacenza the previous winter. In April he sought Giovio's assistance in finding a suitable position, and in July he paid the historian a visit. To Tintoretto he sent a short, facetious account of the museum, and to his new patron in Piacenza, Giovio's friend Count Agostino Landi, he sent a fuller description centering on the *imprese* and inscriptions. The ensemble made a vivid impression. "I have seen an infinity of palaces in my day, My Lord," Doni's letter to Landi began, "but this one I am going to sketch for you pleases me far more than all the others."[116] Doni's interest in the inscriptions and *imprese* preserved many that were lost when the museum was destroyed in the seventeenth century, including the dedication Giovio had placed on the principal facade during this residence of 1543, proclaiming his public and didactic purposes: "Paolo Giovio bishop of Nocera, who on account of the fecundity of his erudite talent merited the favor and liberality of the greatest kings and popes, while he was composing during his lifetime in his native city of Como the history of his own times, dedicated this museum with its perennial fount and pleasant porticoes on Larius [Lake Como] to public enjoyment. 1543." Here in his *patria*, Giovio was affecting, as far as his means permitted, the Aristotelian virtue of magnificence cultivated by his patrons at Rome.[117]

A slightly earlier description of the museum came from Benedetto's Latin muse in a letter written in late 1542 or early 1543 in anticipation of his brother's arrival.[118] It might well have been penned by Pliny the Younger, so uncannily Plinian is its style, but like Pliny's letters it was also vague regarding the actual plan. For this, Giovio's own description was somewhat better, even though he focused more on the setting and life than on the construction and decoration. He composed it during this summer of 1543 at the request of the young soldier, Ottavio Farnese, with whom he had been discussing his portraits, museum, and *Histories* at Busseto, and three years later he incorporated it into the preface to the *Elogia* (1546).[119]

As Pliny with his villa "Comedy," Giovio delighted in his museum's proximity to the water—so close, he boasted, he could fish from the balcony of the great hall.[120] In the depths of the water below lay the ruins of the Roman villa, invisible today, which he somewhat freely linked to Pliny, the "square blocks of marble, great shafts of columns, and sunken pyramids which once adorned the entrance of the crescent-shaped mole forming the harbor." The strong sense of place evident in Giovio's youthful letter of Lissago reemerged in his evocation of the museum's rapport with the lake and in his whimsical chronicle of his efforts to lead the reluctant oread of a mountain spring through clay pipes to rise in the fountain of the principal courtyard.

This fountain was the one feature for which Giovio claimed "perfection of elegance," a quality he thought was lacking in the villa as a whole owing to its piecemeal construction. Located in a doric portico with an eastern exposure that made it ideal for summer lunching or dining, the fountain was complemented by a mural depicting a *gradus ad Parnassum* according to Ovid's *Metamorphoses* (5.250–68), a theme often encountered in Roman gardens of the Cinquecento. From the summit of Parnassus a winged Pegasus struck water from a rock, which cascaded to the fountain—a statue representing the goddess Nature—around which "a multitude of poets" were crowning each other with wreaths of laurel. Ascending the *gradus* to the summit, Doni recognized a number of contemporary literati, including Antonio Tebaldeo of Ferrara, Veronica

Gambara and Vittoria Colonna (one in a carriage, the other on horse-back), Ariosto, Molza, Luigi Alamanni, Navagero, Michele Marullo, Pontano, Sannazaro, the marquis del Vasto (armed and on horseback), Benedetto Giovio, Sadoleto and Bembo (in cardinals' robes, on mules), Vida, Fracastoro, and Giovio himself.[121]

Giovio's efforts to recreate the classical life, visible everywhere in mottoes and inscriptions, predominated in the portico of the masks, where gilded comic masks—an apparent allusion to Pliny's villa "Comoedia"—seemed "to be uttering with Laconic brevity precepts for a life of elegance."[122] The architecture likewise strove to re-create a classical milieu. To his patron Cardinal Farnese, Giovio declared that the museum had "a Vitruvian aspect, air and quality," and while the exact proportions of the plan cannot be reconstructed, deliberately Vitruvian elements of design were nonetheless discernible, especially in the courtyards and in the disposition of the rooms according to the seasons. The portico of the masks led to "the spacious and brilliant hall" dedicated to the Muses, from which the villa as a whole derived its name, a grand summer room cooled by breezes from the lake.[123] A portico on the north side of the central courtyard collected the sun for enjoyment in winter. Various other galleries and rooms housed Giovio's collections of books, coins, gems, tapestries, portrait medallions, and historical curiosities, including the spoils of Tunis, artifacts from the New World, classical inscriptions, and sculptures. The portraits, with the *elogia* appended on parchment, were eventually dispersed throughout.[124] On the upper story were bedrooms and winter rooms—all having windows of glass, Giovio boasted. Another feature in which he took pride was the location of the kitchens, stables, and servants' apartments outside the villa proper, making it "a blessed abode of golden peace, a calm and refreshing haven of that liberty we hope for rather than possess." No more awakening to the creaking of oxcarts and the noisy shouting of peasants!

Although the conclusion of the *Musaei Ioviani descriptio* suggested that Giovio was looking forward to a life of dignified retirement *in villa*, his present intention had been to return to Rome in the fall, accompanying Maria del Vasto for most of her journey to visit her family in Naples. During the last days of August, however, he was struck by a crippling attack of gout and, despite his impatience to be off, healing came too slowly for travel that autumn. In compensation for his continued absence from Rome, he promised Cardinal Farnese to make good use of the long nights to work on the *Histories*, lantern in hand. Meanwhile, he required his patron's assistance in securing payment of his pensions and in retaining his exemption from the tithe, his desire to see Europe defended from the Turks not apparently extending to a personal contribution for the maintenance of papal troops in Hungary.[125]

Autumn brought news from the various campaigns of the summer and the eyewitness reports Giovio relied on. Francesco Franchini of Cosenza, once tutor and now secretary to Ottavio Farnese, sent him an account of the storming of Düren and the overthrow of William of Cleves (August 24). Four Spanish and Majorcan soldiers, fugitives from the sultan's army, provided details of the taking of Esztergom (Strigonia) in Hungary. He was particularly pleased that all confirmed his portrait of Suleiman, sent him by the duke of Urbino, as "the spitting image." All likewise confirmed the sultan's rumored ambitions of "seeing" Rome. By marching through the Friuli, they said, the Turks estimated they could be in Milan in twenty days, greatly reinforcing Giovio's fears of an inland attack. "Tell the cardinals to believe in the Turk, My Lord," he hastened to warn Farnese, "because they will soon touch him with their hands."[126] By mid-November Giovio had learned of the cardinal's latest peace mission to Germany, and while he thought it a waste of time, it made him less uneasy about his own absence from Rome.[127] In December he went to Vigevano to obtain firsthand details from del Vasto of the French-Turkish siege of Nice.[128] All this gave him materials for what he said would be another tragic book to be written during the winter.

The "tragic book" turned out to be book 43 and much of book 44, both written by the autumn of 1544.[129] After narrating the failed colloquy at Busseto and the scenes of panic in Rome upon the dramatic appearance of Barbarossa at Ostia, book 43 moves to Hungary and the triumphant progress of Suleiman through Esztergom (Strigonia), Tatabanya, and finally Székesfehérvár (Alba Regia), where the Hungarian kings were traditionally crowned. It is an unrelieved chronicle of Christian shame, of loss of nerve by defenders and failure by kings to mobilize for the defense of Christendom. The book ends bleakly with the hope that disasters of such magnitude may finally raise Europe's rulers from their folly.

As book 43 closes with the victories of the sultan, book 44 opens with the victory of the emperor over a rebellious vassal, contrasting by this juxtaposition the unified Turkish advance with the internecine quarrels of Christians. Once again, Giovio's portrait of Charles V is remorseless and dark. Speaking to his troops in full armor, the emperor promises them booty and glory. Despite the recollection of Düren's defenders that Caesar's legions had been torn to pieces nearby, the modern Caesar is victorious. After a relentless artillery barrage the city is taken, sacked, and put to the torch (August 24), an "atrocious spectacle" intended as a lesson to others. Even the cathedral with its beautiful tower is destroyed. Jülich and Roermond immediately open their gates, and the emperor marches to besiege Landrecies. With no help coming from Francis I, occupied in besieging Luxembourg, the duke of Cleves has no option but to throw himself on the emperor's mercy.

If Giovio darkened his portrait of the emperor, he did the same with the French king's by emphasizing his alliance with the Turks. While Suleiman was taking Esztergom and the emperor Düren, Captain Polin and the count of Enghien (François de Bourbon) were assisting Francis I's new ally, Barbarossa, in his assault on Nice. Giovio also included a puzzling episode from the siege: inexplicably, Barbarossa wasted an opportunity of annihilating Andrea Doria's disordered fleet when it was crippled by a sudden storm as it landed del Vasto's troops at Nice. "To the wonder and then the amusement of his officers," Giovio wrote, although to the exasperation of Polin, the old pirate made haste so slowly that the chance was lost. Contemporaries, including Giovio, began suspecting the two admirals of collusion, surmising that Barbarossa was repaying the favor done him by Doria after Tunis, when he delegated the pursuit of the disordered Turkish fleet to an incompetent commander. The admirals seemed to be playing games with each other at their masters' expense. With each passing year, as Giovio perceived, the Turkish conflict was losing more of its religious dimension and evolving into a purely political, economic, and military rivalry.[130]

During the winter of 1543–44 Giovio was often with del Vasto at Vigevano, his presence at one point being enough to frighten Giulio Camillo Delminio from making a visit to interest the marquis in subsidizing his projected memory theater.[131] In the frequent discussions of the political situation, what weighed most heavily in Giovio's thoughts was the presence of Barbarossa's fleet at Toulon. Forced after the campaign against Nice to provide the Turks with winter quarters, Francis I took the remarkable step of handing them the seaport town of Toulon, which the unlucky inhabitants were compelled by royal edict to vacate. This unholy outrage, in Giovio's view, was a consequence of the contest for Milan, and in a letter written the last day of January to the Venetian resident there, Vincenzo Fedeli, he yet again cursed the physician and the enema that sent Francesco Sforza to his death.[132]

Like Paul III, Giovio was also disturbed by the emperor's new alliance with Henry VIII. It was apparent, he told Fedeli, striving to comprehend the Charles V of Ghent, Busseto, and Düren, that something had alienated Caesar from his normal good and pious nature, so evident to one who had watched him wash the feet of the poor in Rome in 1536. Giovio's hope in writing Fedeli was to induce the Venetian senate to join with the pope to save Italy from the Turks. It was a deeply felt plea. "Because of the infinite madness of our factions," he lamented, "men today are so extraneous to their own natures that there are few good Italians to be found; everyone attends without heed to his own passions, so that at Rome good Italians are wanted, that is, true servitors of Holy Church and of the great Evangelist [St. Mark], standard of the liberty of Italy."[133]

Fedeli forwarded the letter to his masters, so Giovio had his chance to be heard on the Rialto. Despite its failings, Venice was still his best hope, if not for a crusade then for preserving the *libertas Italiae*. But what of the need for good Italians at Rome? Was this a veiled criticism of Farnese nepotism and Cardinal Farnese's current mission to Francis I and Charles V? As early as February, Giovio had learned of the inhospitable reception which the emperor had accorded the embassy and his rejection of what Giovio termed "honest efforts made for peace."[134]

Interpretations of the real purpose of Alessandro Farnese's mission of November 1543–January 1544 varied widely at the time and still differ. Some accepted it as sincere, and others saw it as a stratagem of Farnese nepotism for promoting a marriage between Vittoria Farnese and the duke of Orléans. Charles V saw it this way and preferred not to receive the cardinal. When finally obliged to, he delivered an even more indignant repetition of his speech at Busseto. Cardinal Ercole Gonzaga, who shared the emperor's opinion, speculated that Cardinal Farnese had returned to Rome bringing "the union of Vittoria with the duke of Orléans in his sleeve."[135] Although aware of the skeptical view of the cardinal's mission, Giovio had his own reason for approving the pope's policy of conciliating Francis I, and that was the fear of yet another break from Rome. If nepotism made the pope take the right course, Giovio was prepared for the moment to overlook it. Denouncing Protestants and the "abominable exhalations that expire from the mephitis of Speyer," he declared to Fedeli that he would mount his white horse and form Cardinal Farnese's rearguard on his return to Rome.[136]

As it turned out, Francis I's price for a marriage alliance was higher than the pope was prepared to pay. Paul III was reserving Parma not as dower for Vittoria but as a great dukedom for Pier Luigi. Nor did Cardinal Farnese stop at the museum on his return from Speyer, as Giovio had hoped, but urged the historian to join him in Rome. As soon as the sun was in Aries (March 18), Giovio promised to put on his winged sandals and come bringing the two and a half books written during his sojourn at Como, but his departure was delayed when the marquis del Vasto announced his intention of spending part of Holy Week at the museum (April 6–13). As nearly every room of the museum bore witness, Giovio was deeply obliged to "the pious and generous Italian," his patron, and he willingly postponed his departure. Besides, he had hopes that d'Avalos, like Neptune, might strike the earth with his trident a couple of times "to produce a good pair of horses" for the journey.[137]

If the marquis del Vasto did spend part of Holy Week at the museum, he went from there to the numbing defeat in which he lost his army and his reputation. Since January, the French under the count of Enghien had been besieging Carignano, a town on the Po southeast of Turin.

Both sides were in a belligerent mood. Blaise de Monluc had made a quick trip to France to obtain the king's permission to engage the forces del Vasto was massing for the relief of the town. Giovio thought his friend's original plan was well conceived: to break the siege by fording the Po and cutting off the French provisions from the other side. In unremitting heavy rain, however, his army became bogged in muddy roads, spread out, and weakened from inadequate victuals. At this point, despite the bad conditions and the advice of his civilian counselors, del Vasto determined to provoke a direct engagement. Money was running out, provisioning was breaking down, and in the terrible weather disease was bound to set in. He found the French army awaiting him to the southeast of Carignano near the hamlet of Ceresole d'Alba, where he attacked it the day after Easter, April 14, 1544. For a while the imperialists had the better of the fighting, as the veteran Spanish and Germans under Ramón de Cardona broke the French left, but in the center del Vasto's newly recruited Landsknechts could not stand the joint onslaught of the Gascons and Swiss. Their ranks broken, they were set upon by their mortal enemies, the Swiss, with terrible slaughter. Twelve thousand soldiers were slain, mostly German. Del Vasto himself was wounded by an arquebus and had to fight his way out of the battle with his sword. After collecting the remnants of his fleeing troops he arrived at Asti toward sunset, stunned by grief and the peril of his situation. Fortunately, Enghien elected not to follow up his victory by pressing on to Milan.

Giovio had never looked upon del Vasto as a Giovanni de' Medici but, despite his ineffective discipline, he respected the marquis as a commander. As he listened to his old friend recounting the battle and his failed strategies, one wonders if Giovio thought back to their conversations on Ischia about the reluctance of old-school generals, such as Francesco Maria della Rovere, to give battle. He had clearly retained them in mind, for on the wall of the armory of the museum he had placed the inscription, MELIOR EST CERTA PAX QVAM SPERATA VICTORIA (Better certain peace than hoped-for victory).[138] He also knew on whom the weight of the governor's disaster would fall, and that the Milanese state would have to "fill up his coats and socks [with money]."[139]

Giovio's account of the battle of Ceresole was even-handed and did nothing to absolve the marquis of responsibility, beyond allowing him to explain his reasons for giving battle and analyze the causes of his defeat. The duke of Alba thought that Ceresole illustrated the deadly impasse reached in sixteenth-century warfare owing to the addition of the arquebus to the pike, making any old-style battle between equally matched forces an indecisive bloodbath.[140] And indeed, despite the enormous cost, Ceresole entailed no lasting harm to the imperial side or gain to the

French. As if seeking consolation somewhere, Giovio concluded his account with the reflection that the battle displayed the unpredictable judgment of God, His chastisement of the proud and His punishment of "the wicked impiety" of the German Lutherans, who formed the bulk of the slaughtered troops.[141]

Sometime in May, despite all the springtime beauty of the lake and the freedom of his museum, Giovio set out with his household for Rome, bent on resuming "the customary service." Before leaving Lombardy he stopped to obtain an account of the disaster at Ceresole from the marquis.[142] It was to be their last reunion. Giovio did not return to Lombardy for another five years, and Alfonso d'Avalos died in April 1546.

By June 7 Giovio was in Rome, and before the month was out fearful tidings came from Naples. The Turkish fleet had destroyed the castle of Procida, burned the town of Forio on Ischia, captured thousands of inhabitants for galley slaves, and ravaged the Neapolitan coast around Pozzuoli. This was the force that had wintered in Toulon and was now on its way back to Constantinople, looting and burning the coastal towns of Italy as it went. "And so the miserable kingdom of Naples is simultaneously lashed by sea and land," Giovio lamented, by the Turks and by the Spanish troops sent to defend it.[143] After recounting these raids in the final book of his *Histories*, he concluded with one of the most powerful indictments of the Hapsburg-Valois wars to be found anywhere, an indictment placed, appropriately enough, in the mouths of the miserable captives chained in the fetid holds of the Turkish galleys. Tortured by hunger and thirst, they spend the long voyage to Constantinople and slavery "cursing the cruelty of the king of France and the emperor, whose obsession with their old quarrels makes them oblivious to the suffering of their innocent subjects, and whose unbridled and obstinate selfishness, in despising mutual concord, invites these calamities— to their great infamy."[144]

During the winter of 1543–44, while Giovio was composing his account of the war of Cleves, Charles V was maturing his plans for a decisive blow against France. On December 31, 1543, he reached a new agreement with Henry VIII for a joint invasion to take place by June 20, 1544. Charles V was to invade Champagne, Henry VIII Picardy; both would then converge on Paris.[145] With the plans of the two kings nearing completion, Francis sent Cardinal Ippolito d'Este the Younger to Rome in a last-ditch effort to seek a Franco-papal alliance. As Giovio predicted, the pope would not abandon his neutrality, but as a goodwill gesture he gave the cardinal a precious stone found in the recently uncovered tomb of Maria (d. 404), daughter of Stilicho and first wife of the emperor Honorius, which Giovio identified as an *ammochrysus*.[146]

During the wearying months at Speyer, Charles V had worked to conciliate the German Protestants so as to win support for the humiliation of France. Their price was the imperial proclamation embodied in the recess decree (June 10) guaranteeing the religious status quo and the rights of the Protestants to worship as they chose until the meeting of "a general, free Christian council of the German nation." These were the "abominable exhalations" from Speyer which Giovio had denounced in the winter and spring.[147] By the end of June he learned that the forces of the emperor, commanded by Ferrante Gonzaga, had taken Luxembourg and Commercy and were marching on Ligny in Lorraine.[148] From Metz, where Charles V lingered until July 6, letters had come indicating that his intentions were to strike at Paris. To Giovio it seemed as if a decisive moment might be approaching in the endless Hapsburg-Valois wars. "Were I dead," he exclaimed to Cosimo de' Medici, "I would want to be resuscitated to see and write that Gallican tragedy, which I would like to become a comedy with the customary peace and marriages and good cheer; but everything stands in the hand of God."[149]

Having crossed the Meuse at Commercy in order to take Ligny, the imperial army advanced to the Marne, besieging Saint-Dizier and storming Vitry. Here the emperor joined it with the rest of his forces. Despite the failure of the French army to come to its relief, however, Saint-Dizier held out for forty-one days, until August 17. Giovio had heard of its fall and of the emperor's subsequent march toward Chalons-sur-Marne when he responded to Cardinal Farnese's request for an analysis of the situation. As these momentous events unfolded in rapid succession, the cardinal and his staff often turned to Giovio for interpretation. Few, even in Rome, could match his knowledge of history, geography, strategy, and tactics, or his insight into the characters of the two monarchs gained from observing them for nearly three decades. From the papal states, where the cardinal was attending to affairs, secretaries forwarded copies of the latest dispatches and eagerly awaited Giovio's responses. On the sixth of September, Maffei had pleaded, "you know how much your letters are desired by us. Therefore my lord, if you will, purge yourself of contumacy and write us a long letter full of discourses on these last reports which show the two armies are already within three leagues of each other."[150]

Giovio's detailed analysis of September 11 concluded that the emperor would be forced to abandon the march on Paris, a prediction borne out on the very day he made it.[151] Charles V confirmed Giovio's assessment of his military acumen and that of his commanders by not besieging Châlons but moving northwest along the Marne starting on September 2, bypassing Francis I's army and capturing Epernay, Château-Thierry, and Soissons. His light cavalry even reconnoitered as far as Meaux, spreading terror in Paris. But the emperor's purpose in the march was political rather than military. He knew his provisions would not last beyond late September, and that Henry VIII, who had duly landed in July, was much more interested in besieging Boulogne than in aiding a march on Paris. Francis I had already put out feelers in mid-July, and by the end of August Charles V was ready to talk in earnest. Saint-Dizier had saved Paris.

In early September 1544 the terms of two treaties were worked out, one public and one secret. The fall of Boulogne on September 13 only increased Francis I's eagerness to reach agreement, and the public treaty was signed at Crépy on the 18th. By its terms Francis would assist in the war against the Turks with 10,000 foot and 600 heavy cavalry; the territorial status quo of the time of Nice was to be restored and recent conquests on each side forfeited; the duke of Orléans was to marry either Charles' daughter Mary or Ferdinand's daughter Anne (if Mary, he was to receive the Netherlands and Franche-Comté as dowry; if Anne, Milan—the decision would rest with Charles; the groom would receive the duchies of Bourbon, Châtellerault, and Angoulême); Francis renounced his claims to Savoy and Piedmont, Charles his claim to Burgundy. In the secret treaty, a draft of which only came to light in the twentieth century, Francis promised to aid the emperor in the promotion of a council, in the reformation of the Church, and in the recovery of the German Protestants for the Church, including the furnishing of an equivalent number of troops if it had to be done by force.[152]

Giovio's anxieties during the month of September, while tidings were trickling in, showed the interplay of his deepest political feelings with his instincts as a historian. When the first rumors of the treaty reached him, he was skeptical. On September 18, the actual date of the public treaty, he told Cardinal Farnese that not even if his Swiss troops had the plague, his Germans had mutinied, the dauphin was mortally wounded, the duke of Orléans a prisoner, all the superintendents of finance bankrupted, Brittany in revolt, and Boulogne taken by the English should Francis I accept the rumored terms he had just heard from the bishop of Cortona. He laughed, he said, at the thought of Francis' surrendering Savoy and Piedmont, his gateway to Italy. Nor, he insisted, would Charles ever give away Milan. Peace would not come through a truce such as this but through the proposals outlined by the pope at Busseto. Growing exasperation pervaded the letter. With their money exhausted fighting each other, the princes will have no resources for opposing the Turk when he returns next year. They have "neither clemency nor pity for their miserable people and will never cease to torment them." Giovio's advice to the cardinal and pope was to plan a council on their own, hold it in Italy, and let all good Christian bishops who want come to it. Then let God punish the authors of "this venomous dissension."[153]

By September 23 Giovio still had no satisfactory news, only conflicting rumors. He was rapidly concluding that Caesar's march toward Paris was more bravura than substance, and when he learned that the bishop of Arras had gone to Henry VIII's camp he suspected the making of secret plans. All Rome was on tenterhooks, he said, the partisans of each side suspended "with sweating temples in the balance between hope and fear."[154] By September 27 reliable news of the peace had reached Rome, although not the terms, but the relief was such that "no one is doing anything," Carlo Gualteruzzi reported to Giovanni della Casa, "but embracing one another and thanking the Lord God that by His goodness he has vouchsafed this to us."[155] By October the terms of the public treaty of Crépy were definitely known and Giovio hoped it would at least prove "a holy cooling off period [refrigerio] for the afflicted people of every nation and a remedy against the audacity of the Turk."[156] Writing to congratulate the cardinal of Tournon on his role in the negotiations, he anticipated concluding his *Histories* with this peace, which would be a fitting close to an era of warfare opened exactly fifty years earlier.[157]

Despite the certainty of the terms, Giovio still could not repress his skepticism. He thought Francis I's position had been too strong for him to concede so much; in attacking Paris, Charles V would have fared about as well as Charles the Bold. All the ambivalence surfaced between the historian and the Italian patriot. Much as he yearned for peace, he was irritated with Francis I for accepting it in a fashion so unlike his gallant self. He was incredulous that after fighting twenty-three years for Milan, the French king would acquiesce in the alternate marriage and that Orléans would be content "to fish herrings" in the Low Countries, never coming to Italy except "with pilgrim staff and a shell on his cap." The only trick remaining for Charles V to play on the French, Giovio lamented to his friends in Rome, was to seduce their mistresses.[158] To an unknown French correspondent he went so far as to describe himself as in despair at not having Orléans for his lord in Milan. Some of this sudden peevishness and Francophilia may have stemmed from the realization that now Charles V was, indeed, the arbiter of Italy.[159] Giovio at last became a believer in Caesar's march toward "monarchy."[160]

In the first euphoria after Crépy, Giovio was the object of merriment in the cardinal's *familia* owing to his offer, if the rumors of peace proved true, to become a friar in the convent of San Salvatore in Lauro.[161] At the first certain news of the peace, the cardinal wrote to remind Giovio of his vow, comforting him with the reflection that the life of the convent would afford him the necessary leisure to write of the great crusade against Suleiman that would surely follow.[162] Redefining his vow, Giovio reaffirmed his readiness to go in earnest the day Caesar actually gave up Milan. The picture of Giovio the connoisseur, enophile, and gourmet among observant friars continued to divert the courtiers, and on the first of November Giovanni Bianchetti reported to Giovanni della Casa that the prospective novice was rumored to have bought the cloth for his habit.[163]

In the end, Giovio's skepticism regarding the terms of the "lean" peace of Crépy, as he began to call it, was entirely justified. Beyond returning the fortified town of Stenay in Lorraine to Charles V, Francis I did little to implement its terms. Nor did Charles V press him, being ambivalent about his own concessions. The tragic death of the duke of Orléans the following year relieved him of making a difficult decision and even more difficult renunciations. Francis I had no intention of joining in a holy war against his firmest ally, the Turk, and despite the initial anger of the sultan, who threatened to impale the resident French ambassador. Polin and Monluc were soon received again at the Sublime Porte, where they attempted to act as intermediaries (lukewarm ones, it must be admitted) in Charles V's efforts to secure a truce.

Ironically, while its actual terms were soon a dead letter, Crépy proved the start of a de facto peace. France was financially exhausted, and the English still held Calais and Boulogne, for which Francis I was to struggle unsuccessfully for the remaining three years of his reign. Charles V was likewise at the end of the resources he had assembled for this effort and now wanted more than anything to deal with the German Protestants. The best-kept terms of Crépy were those of the secret treaty, which Giovio had no way of knowing, although he suspected the existence of one. Ultimately, the discontinuation of French aid to the Protestants made possible—or at least easier—the emperor's great victory at Mühlberg. In response to the visits of papal legates dispatched to congratulate the two monarchs, each duly called for a council to assemble at Trent. Losing no time in circumstances suddenly turned favorable, Paul III hastily drafted and published on November 30 the bull *Laetare Jersualem*, calling for the convocation of a general council at Trent on March 15, 1545. A new era was at hand.

Giovio's *Histories* closed with the peace of Crépy. A brief summary, probably added at the time of publication, carried them to the deaths of Henry VIII and Francis I in 1547 and redeemed a promise made to Charles V by briefly mentioning the battle of Mühlberg; but for all intents and purposes the narrative ceased at Crépy on September 18, 1544. Within a short time it was obvious that the wars of Francis I and Charles V had come to an end, and as Giovio had remarked to the cardinal of Tournon, there was a roundness in closing upon a half century of conflict. The historian's interest turned to filling in the unwritten portions of the *Histories* and to completing and publishing his biographies and *elogia*.

Following his recent pattern, Giovio probably began the concluding book of the *Histories* (45) soon after the events it related. As the Italian captains returned from Flanders, he gleaned most of the particulars needed for his narrative. Any remaining questions regarding the emperor's strategy could have been settled by Ferrante Gonzaga before the final version was drafted. As in all the later books, the narrative was keenly sensitive to the sufferings of the civilian population. Between the destruction of crops as a defensive maneuver by the French army on the one hand, and the aggressive ravaging by the imperial army on the other, Champagne presented an "aspect of horrible ruin truly worthy of compassion, because the inhabitants of that exceedingly fertile country found on neither side any remedy for their misery."[164]

In this last book Giovio darkened his portrait of Charles V still further. In his growing apprehension that the emperor was, indeed, aiming at "monarchy," by which he meant "the empire of all Italy"—the historic core of the world-empire dreamt of by the medieval emperors—Giovio accused Charles V of duplicity in negotiating the terms of Crépy, suggesting that he had been "astutely" seeking to gain time by making promises with respect to Milan that he had no intention of keeping, and he charged him with using the council as a stratagem to prevent the pope from guarding the *libertas Italiae*. By placing on Paul III "the heavy chains of the Council of Trent," he wrote, the emperor restrained him from acting "as defender of the public liberty."[165] These twin fears—the emperor and the council—were to become major preoccupations of Giovio's declining years.

CHAPTER ELEVEN

The Elusive Prize (1545–1549)

Vi vo in parte volentieri, per visitar gli amici e signori miei, e anco per veder se potessi presso Sua Santità beccarmi qualche aiuto di costo.

—To Alfonso d'Avalos, March 25, 1544

I am going there [to Rome] of my own accord, in part to visit my friends and patrons and also to see if I can cadge some worthwhile subsidy from His Holiness.

GIOVIO'S HABITUAL CANDOR explained why he was still willing, at the age of fifty-eight, to forsake the freedom of his delicious villa for "the customary service" in Rome. It was the hope of "some worthwhile subsidy."[1] Although he never entirely gave up hope of the hat, there were other prizes that would complete the empty panel in the museum, such as a major bishopric. He started taking a keen interest in the health of the aging bishop of Como, Cesare Trivulzio.[2] He had always felt that Nocera dei Pagani was below his deserts, both in income and in prestige. Clement VII had given him a thin spouse, he lamented to Cardinal Farnese, with unfulfilled promises of a rich dowry.[3] For a minor bishop without other subsidies life could, indeed, prove a financial misery, his rank requiring a style that his income could not sustain. In his second satire, Ariosto consoled himself for not having received preferment from Leo X by dilating on the many woes of a minor bishop, laden with obligations and debts.[4] Fortunately, Giovio had his pensions, and provided these were paid—admittedly a somewhat uncertain proposition—he confessed to Cardinal Farnese that he could live in *summa opulentia*.[5] His 1520 rebuke to Benedetto comes to mind: "It is not penny antes we are seeking, but great things."[6]

Giovio's key asset in his quest for preferment was his increasingly close relationship with Cardinal Farnese. Their correspondence makes plain what a privileged relationship the historian had come to enjoy with the influential cardinal-nephew. Few courtiers or dependents would have dared the familiarity evident in Giovio's letters. Not only was the tone intimate—within, of course, the conventions of sixteenth-century address—the content was often no less personal than the style. Giovio felt quite free to make spicy, even scurrilous, comments about a whole range of persons great and small; he offered advice on the cardinal's conduct of affairs, his health, and even his confessor; he chided him for actions he disapproved of; and in an age where elaborate humility was the convention, he pressed his incessant demands for favors with astonishing directness.[7] Yet the cardinal's responses indicated that he accepted Giovio's familiarity and that he held him in particular esteem. In February 1545 the historian could say that he felt "well-regarded by the pope and well-treated by my Cardinal."[8]

The young diplomat found Giovio a source of historical knowledge and political comment on the affairs into which he had suddenly been thrust as a major protagonist. Giovio's familiarity with the Roman court and its ways was so extensive that even seasoned prelates valued his judgment.[9] In cultural matters, too, he enjoyed Farnese's ear, as shown by the commissions he obtained for Vasari and the deference he received from other courtiers, even when they cordially disliked him. Time alters all relationships, however, and by the peace of Crépy, Alessandro Farnese was becoming the intelligent and self-confident young cardinal depicted by Titian two years later in his portrait of Paul III and his grandsons. Moreover, the times themselves were changing, and for the great issues of the Counter-Reformation, Giovio had little interest. Thus, even as his ambitions were soaring, his value as an adviser was waning. Still, there remained the Giovian wit and the gift for friendship which had won and continued to win him the patronage and esteem of an impressive series of younger men of rank and power, such as Alfonso d'Avalos, Federico Gonzaga, Girolamo Adorno, Francesco II Sforza, and Ippolito and Cosimo de' Medici.

Toward the end of 1544, Giovio received a pleasant compliment from his friend Nicolas Raynce, who dedicated to the "father of history" an Italian translation of the first six books of the memoirs of Commynes. To the captain Stefano Colonna, Giovio explained that having seen the work in the hands of the emperor, King Francis, and Pope Clement, he had begged Raynce to undertake the translation into Italian "to afford delight with utility to my lords."[10] Why Giovio did not have Raynce translate the last two books dealing with the wars of Italy is something of a mystery, especially as they were available by then in print.

Giovio's frequent and protracted absences from Rome during the years 1536–1544 had caused him to lose touch with some of the Roman literary movements. Although he had associations with many of their members and shared their interest in Vitruvius, he seems to have played little part in the influential academies formed in the 1530s by Claudio Tolomei, such as the lively Accademia della Virtù, first patronized by Cardinal Ippolito (ca. 1535), or the Accademia della Poesia Nuova (ca. 1539). When Dionigi Atanagi sent him Tolomei's *Versi et regole della nuova poesia toscana* (1539), containing poems by some of his friends among the *padri virtuosi*, Giovio responded from Como with an appreciative letter saying that he had discussed the new poetry with the marquis del Vasto but frankly admitting that the experiments with quantitative meter and "queste longole di versi [these drawn-out verses—i.e., hendecasyllables]" did not inspire him with much enthusiasm.[11] The poets Giovio encouraged and patronized were mainly the minor Latin poets whose celebratory verses were published in the *Elogia*. In a letter of July 12, 1546, to Cardinal Farnese, Giovio mentioned being frequented by several of his poetic protégés, including Onorato Fascitello, Giovanni Battista Possevini, Antonio Vacca, Giano Vitale, and Girolamo Britonio. Other poets he encouraged were Marcantonio Casanova, Pietro Mirteo, Anton Francesco Raineri, Gabriele Faerno, Agosto Coceiano, and Angelo Costantini.[12]

Giovio continued to maintain touch with Vittoria Colonna, immersed ever deeper in discussions of theology and reform with Carnesecchi, Flaminio, Pole, and the *ecclesia viterbensis*. He seems to have seen her at Viterbo on his trip north in 1543; at least he told a friend that with her endorsement one could lodge in the guest house of the convent of Santa Caterina and be sent a good meal. Having heard reports at Vigevano of an illness and return to Rome in December 1543, he wrote to a mutual friend for more definite news.[13] She returned to Rome to stay shortly after Giovio himself did, and he must have continued to see her in these last years, because the *impresa* he designed for her alluded to the troubles her friendships with Contarini and Ochino were causing her with theological reactionaries. Giovio had no sympathy with either heresy or Ochino, whom he wanted to see returned from Geneva to Rome in chains (probably because of the troubles his flight was causing his friends); but one of his most congenial qualities was his detestation of zealots, and it angered him to see a friend of devout Christian discipline disturbed in "her lofty concepts" by "invidious and malign persons." Her consolation, he said, was that by their attacks such persons harmed themselves more than her, and to express this idea his thoughts must have returned to Ischia, because he devised the image of cliffs battered by waves, surmounted by Vittoria's long-standing motto, CONANTIA FRANGERE FRANGVNT (They break those trying to break them).[14]

During these years Giovio was in frequent contact with Carlo Gualteruzzi, Pietro Bembo, Giovanni della Casa, Marcello Cervini, and other reformers. Other good friends of the mid-1540s included Nicolas Raynce, with whom he often dined, and his old "compare" Girolamo Angleria.[15] His correspondence shows him in congenial relations with many of the Farnese courtiers and servitors, including Bernardino Maffei; the Aristotelian philosopher Antonio Bernardi of Mirandola; Claudio Tolomei; Angelo Perozzi of Camerino; Romolo Amaseo; Cardinal Farnese's steward Curzio Frangipane; and the bishop and nuncio Girolamo

Dandino, with whom he developed a close intellectual rapport based on a shared longing for peace in Europe and exasperation with its two principal sovereigns.[16]

Following the peace of Crépy, the issues dominating European diplomacy were the Council of Trent, the Protestants, and reforming the Church. Unworkable as it seemed to Giovio at the time, the peace of Crépy proved a real turning point in European events. The deaths three years later of Francis I and Henry VIII altered substantially the nature of the Hapsburg-Valois struggle, and the preoccupation of Suleiman the Magnificent with his Persian frontiers brought to a standstill the incursions of the Turks. None of this, however, could have been immediately apparent during the early months of 1545 when Giovio waited, with all of Europe, to see which of the two alternatives stipulated at Crépy the emperor would choose, giving up Milan or the Netherlands.[17] Although Giovio had begun to suspect that Charles V was aiming at "monarchy," even now he hoped he was wrong.[18] He was widely quoted in sixteenth-century diplomatic correspondence, and by one channel or another his confident prediction that Charles V would never give up Milan, neither in the eight months given him by the treaty of Crépy, nor in his lifetime, made its way to the ear of the emperor himself. "I would like to know the reason that moves Giovio to say this," demanded Caesar, to which Philibert de la Baulme, seigneur de Montfalconnet, replied, "Because he is a Francophile." To Giovio this merely demonstrated the truth of the dictum, *Veritas odium parit* (Truth generates hatred).[19]

The untimely death of the duke of Orléans on September 9, 1545, convinced Giovio that fate was as determined as ever to advance Charles V, and he recalled his own motto, *Fato prudentia minor*.[20] Still, he thought the emperor was practical enough to see the impossibility of ruling the whole world, and he continued to explore ways in which giving Milan to Margaret and Ottavio Farnese, to be combined at Pier Luigi's death with Parma and Piacenza, might work to everyone's benefit. In another startling reversal of his earlier thinking, Giovio accommodated himself to Pier Luigi's creation as duke of Parma by reasoning that henceforth popes would no longer be "gnawed by the red ant of recovering Parma and Piacenza" for the Church. The emperor, he surmised, well understood the need for containing the "engorged" apostolic state, and a dukedom of Parma would be a buffer state. In fact, it had really been a perception of the territorial and political logic of Italy, he reflected, not the bribes of Alfonso d'Este which had caused Charles V to take "stomach and life" from Clement VII in 1531 by awarding Modena and Reggio to Ferrara.[21]

Giovio's yearning for peace thus led him to acquiesce in the boldest schemes of Farnese nepotism and to repudiate the expansionist policies of Julius II and the Medici popes. He even went so far as to suggest that, by renouncing territorial ambitions, future popes might be content with the peace and security of Italy, "at which the spiritual obedience will flourish ever more—the certain and true patrimony of Holy Church."[22] Unfortunately, Giovio's genial visions of Margaret and Ottavio visiting "the fresh and jocund museum" from their capital at Milan were not to materialize. Once relieved of the obligations of Crépy, Charles V gave up all thoughts of subinfeudating the duchy, and as this became clearer, Giovio began to think the emperor really was aiming at "monarchy." The ensuing complications with the pope over Parma and Piacenza only confirmed his suspicions.

While waiting in the early months of 1545 to see what the emperor would decide about Milan, Giovio was also watching with disquiet the progress toward the Council of Trent. After the elation in November 1544 over the promulgation of the bull *Laetare Jerusalem*, convoking the council for March 15, 1545, Rome had relapsed into apathy borne of second thoughts and mistrust of the emperor's intentions. In mid-March Giovio was reporting to Cosimo de' Medici that the curia suspected the emperor of having a secret understanding with the Protestants.[23] Nonetheless, the appointment of the cardinal legates on February 6 convinced him that the council would go forward. In mid-April 1545 he learned along with everyone else that Cardinal Farnese was being dispatched as legate to the emperor at the diet of Worms.[24] The mission was a response to hints that the emperor was contemplating a major offensive against the Protestants, but this was kept as secret as possible.[25] In the dark for once, Giovio speculated that the mission was for concerting action against the Turk.[26] Despite pleas to the cardinal and his secretaries for information, and despite some leaks at Trent from the cardinal and his suite on the return to Rome, Giovio gave no indication of having learned the true reason for Farnese's journey. Every effort was being made to conceal the emperor's plans from the Protestants, and Giovio's "journalistic" propensities were well known.

Another development of 1545 that Giovio watched closely was Charles V's negotiation of a Turkish truce, duly assisted by France under the terms of Crépy. Without a truce, Giovio foresaw, the emperor would be forced to continue making concessions to the Protestants in return for aid, and the council would languish. Ironically, a truce was conceded by Suleiman on October 5, 1545, the day before news reached Istanbul of the death of the duke of Orléans, which virtually invalidated the treaty of Crépy.[27] On October 10 Giovio ventured to suggest to Cardinal Cervini that while it was being said in Rome that the council would not open, he himself felt that favorable tidings from Istanbul would rescue it. Cervini was impressed enough with Giovio's analysis, even though humorously couched, to send the letter on to Madruzzo, and by November

21, 1545, the legates at Trent could write joyfully to Farnese that they had just learned from Giovanni della Casa in Venice of the Turkish truce.[28]

During September and October 1545, the pope had been vainly attempting to persuade the emperor to allow him to move the council to a city other than Trent, but in the end he yielded to the pleas of the legates to honor the commitment already made. On November 7 the prelates in Rome were informed that the opening of the council had been set for the third Sunday in Advent, December 13, and that attendance was mandatory. Indeed, Cardinal Farnese apparently indicated that the bishops could choose between Trent and Castel Sant'Angelo (the papal prison).[29] Giovio's only surviving letter from the last months of 1545 was a gloomy one written five days after the formal opening of the council but did not mention it. His gloom came from the fact that the disintegration of relations between Charles V and Francis I following the death of Orléans had removed all prospects of war against either the Turk or the Lutherans. The only thing that seemed to prosper was Paul III's nepotism, the pope having just the previous day conferred the hat upon his fifteen-year-old grandson, Ranuccio Farnese, along with the emperor's candidate Pedro Pacheco, George d'Amboise, and Henry of Portugal.

Giovio was beginning to see a pattern, the pope accommodating the emperor on one issue—in this case the hat for Pacheco—in order to cover yet another act of nepotism. By now he had learned of the projected campaign against the Protestants and its postponement until the summer of 1546, which the pope had accepted with surprising good grace in order to secure Caesar's grudging acquiescence in Pier Luigi's investiture with Parma and Piacenza (August 1545). From this point onward, sarcastic little allusions in Giovio's correspondence indicated his disenchantment with the scale of the pope's nepotism and his uncertainty in any situation as to which interest would dominate, Church or family.[30] Little wonder Giovio's own nepotism gave him no qualms, as he increasingly sought in his old age to ensure the future of his family.

Giovio had, in fact, become head of his family. Benedetto died on August 3, 1545—a sad surprise, for he had been active as a notary through the end of May. He was buried in the cathedral, an honor accorded few laymen, borne to his last resting place on the shoulders of noble youths with tolling of the great bell and a vast throng of fellow-citizens.[31] His death deprived the historian of his best critic and the anticipated companion of his old age, whose approach he was increasingly feeling. All resentment on the part of the younger sibling vanished as he penned an *elogium* in tribute to his "brother by nature and by love, an excellent father in the utmost solicitude which affection inspired, a temperate educator and diligent master in letters who performed for me, bereft of a father before adolescence, every duty imposed by perfect virtue."[32]

During 1545 Giovio composed the *Elogia* of men of letters, which were published by Michele Tramezzino in Venice toward the end of 1546.[33] With his museum virtually finished, he had thrown himself more energetically than ever into collecting portraits. Shaping his approach to the personality and the purse of the intended donor, he alternately begged, pleaded, flattered, bribed, or extorted additions to his collection. Even so, he was forced to pay for many himself.[34] In the later stages he had the idea of composing biographical inscriptions on parchment to hang beneath the portraits, "lives written with laconic brevity," to which he gave the name *elogia*.[35]

The Latin term *elogium* denoted a maxim or inscription, as on a tombstone or on one of the busts of ancestors which adorned Roman homes. It was not the equivalent of the Greek word *eulogia*, meaning praise. In fact, in Roman legal usage *elogium* signified what would now be termed a criminal record. Giovio's *elogia* obviously derived from the inscriptions on ancestral busts, although compounded with something of the criminal record in that they were intended as capsule biographies after the humanist tradition of *exempla*, examples of good traits and bad furnished for moral reflection. Character was paramount.[36]

The *elogia* were rhetorical in form: brief, vivid, and memorable. Ferdinand Gregorovius, in a happy metaphor, called them "a species of historical fresco-painting."[37] Burckhardt found them as readable as he found the *Histories* tedious and mined them for some of the striking portraits in the *Civilization of the Renaissance in Italy*.[38] Giovio himself described his *Elogia* as "more pleasantly written, with a certain license, for the delight of the gentler spirit."[39] They reflected Quintilian's guidelines for *laudationes*, as well as Giovio's familiarity with classical prototypes, particularly the biographies by Suetonius.[40] A recent precedent may have been Bartolomeo Facio's *De viris illustribus*, modeled on Pius II's *De viris aetate sua claris*, although broadened in scope with the inclusion of lives of artists, sculptors, and men of letters who did not subsequently become important cardinals or popes.[41] Unlike Facio's laudatory sketches, however, Giovio's *elogia* abounded in biting judgments on personal, professional, and moral shortcomings, reflecting the authentic spirit of the classical tradition.

The "certain license" Giovio allowed himself in the *elogia* has been the bane of scholars seeking to verify details which appear nowhere else, such as Egidio of Viterbo's giving his face an ascetic pallor by eating cumin and inhaling fumes from burning damp straw. Giovio composed the *elogia* rapidly, sometimes without verifying details, and at times he may have contented himself with gossip or legend when he felt it dramatized a character trait he wished to illustrate. The technique had classical precedent and a theoretical defender in Quintilian.[42] Just as in his portraits Giovio wanted the actual physiognomy, not an idealized *figura*, so he wanted a rounded picture of the actual human character, not an idealized *exemplum*. "By a most unkind decree of Nature," he explained in the *elogium* of Egidio, "no bright shape of perfect virtue can shine forth, but all show some ugly spot of vice to mock their felicity," and sometimes it was gossip that brought this spot to light. Thus, even if Giovio had no proof that the cardinal inhaled fumes of smoldering straw, the tale would have illustrated the streak of hypocrisy in his overly severe bearing.[43] Moreover, lack of corroboration from other sources does not necessarily mean that Giovio used hearsay; he may well have incorporated evidence of character traits normally disregarded in biography. Indeed, he sometimes found himself in trouble for not glossing over defects of character.[44]

The great originality of Giovio's museum lay in combining written lives with portraits so as to give historical authenticity to likeness.[45] For this endeavor there were few precedents. Varro's *Imagines*, a great collection of seven hundred Greek and Roman notables, were, of course, lost. The most important recent antecedent was the *Illustrium imagines* of Andrea Fulvio, published in 1517, a book of woodcuts of worthies copied from coins with brief, rather lifeless biographies by Sadoleto.[46]

Despite the flowering of individualism in the Renaissance, the concept of human personality—of a totality of the self, the sum of its interior and exterior relationships—was still in its infancy. Apart from the notion of character inherited from ancient historians and biographers (grounded principally in ethical judgment), a little Aristotelian psychology, the theory of the four complexions and humors derived from medicine, a typology of sinfulness inherited from the Middle Ages, and a few necessarily vague notions about physiognomy, the Renaissance had scant theoretical basis for its cultivation of individuality. On a practical level, at least, Giovio's museum remedied the deficiency by coupling a traditional analysis of character, as revealed in deeds, with an authentic likeness from which the beholder could draw intuitively the same global inferences about personality that one draws in life. Giovio's scheme expressed the same analytical spirit as Guicciardini's *Storia d'Italia*, the same urge to understand human actions by exploring inner recesses and probing for the wellsprings of conduct. His museum supplanted humanist *figurae* and *exempla* with concrete, historical persons. Founded after a century and a half of experiment in portraiture by Renaissance artists, it was an early attempt to bring system to the study of the individual.[47]

Giovio divided his portraits into four categories: deceased men of letters; living men of letters; makers of great works of art and renowned wits; and popes, kings, and generals.[48] Eventually, he hoped to publish the *elogia* in each category with woodcuts of the portraits, somewhat in the manner of Varro, but he lacked the resources.[49] To promote his collection he resolved to take advantage of the recent interest of Ottavio Farnese, who apparently offered him a subsidy for paper and ink, to publish immediately, without woodcuts, the *elogia* of deceased men of letters.[50] On October 10 he told Cervini that the "most jocund book" of the *elogia* of the deceased was finished, from Albertus Magnus to Albertus Pighius (105 in all) and that he was thinking of making a second book of the living.[51] Preparation of the manuscript and printing by Tramezzino took most of 1546. During the process Giovio decided to add an *elogium* of his recently deceased brother and the briefer *elogia* of deceased scholars for whom he did not have portraits, some forty of them. By early December 1546 he had obtained privileges from Francis I, Paul III, Charles V, the Venetian senate, and the dukes of Florence and Mantua, and by late January 1547 he was sending out copies. The title, *Elogia veris clarorum virorum imaginibus apposita quae in Musaeo Joviano Comi spectantur*, was probably a generic title intended to serve for later editions that would include the remaining categories.[52]

The year 1546 began poorly for Giovio. In January he complained to Cardinal Farnese that he was suffering from asthma and a cough, forcing him to lead a "vita teatina, primitivae ecclesiae [a Theatine life, of the early Church]."[53] He told Cosimo de' Medici he was planning to go to Trent.[54] When Cardinal Madruzzo made him the incredibly generous offer of a room in the episcopal palace—on the ground floor, even, to accommodate his gout—he accepted.[55] Still, he did not go. He dreaded the long-winded theological debates, and he was haunted by the fear, widespread at Rome, that Trent would repeat the councils of Constance and Basel, at best limiting the powers of the papacy and at worst provoking a schism in the Church. Like most Italian prelates, he expected the translation of the council to an Italian city and kept exhorting his patron to accomplish it.[56]

As Paul III grew older and weaker, Giovio harped on the danger of the pope's dying while the council was sitting in an imperial city, creating a situation that would give the emperor undue leverage in the choice of a successor. Paul III's own strenuous efforts in the summer of 1546 to persuade the emperor to agree to a translation suggested how fully he shared Giovio's concern. Despite the emperor's obduracy, Giovio went on hoping that before the medlars had ripened the pope would find a way not only to transfer the council but to suspend it, "because this point contains the health of the apostolic see." The council had served its purpose merely in being opened "to close the mouths of slanderers," Giovio warned Cardinal Ascanio Sforza, and papal authority could achieve a moderate reform of the Church.[57] He had become so mistrustful of the council that he told the cardinal he was beginning to think the failure of the peace of Crépy might have been for the best, since the two monarchs, being at peace with each other, would have "become severe auditors of the saddles, spurs, and cruppers of the Apostolic See."[58]

To risk the unity of the Church and the authority of the papacy for the chimera of reconciliation with the Protestants, Giovio thought was a reckless course. Along with his detestation of reforming zealots and his impatience with theological "double talk" about justification, the patriot in him feared that a papacy shorn of power, patronage, and revenue would be unable to defend the *libertas Italiae*, and the humanist in him dreaded its losing the means to patronize letters and the arts.[59] He derided the conciliatory party as "lords traffickers in justification," and he made a hero of the bishop who had loudly exclaimed in the midst of a debate—inspired, Giovio was certain, by the Holy Ghost—"We are deluded indeed!"[60] Like Cervini, Giovio was a traditionalist, a moderate reformer but neither a "spiritual" nor an "intransigent."[61]

To Giovio, the proper doctrinal work of the Council of Trent was not the conciliation but the refutation of Protestantism. When he thought the September draft of the decree on justification was ready for adoption (the version desired by Rome), he commented approvingly to Farnese, "the winnowed justification is ready to become a decree and the pronouncement will come before St. Luke [October 18], in defiance of Melanchthon and Bucer." His alarm therefore reached a peak in late December 1546, when he learned that Charles V had refused to ratify the compromise over justification, translation, and papal control worked out by Cardinal Farnese and Don Diego de Mendoza, and he began to fear even more intensely that the emperor was aiming at making his own pope at the council.[62] To his friend Pietro Bertano, bishop of Fano, Giovio recommended studying the fifth session of Constance (in which the decree *Sacrosancta* was passed, establishing the superiority of a council over the pope). "Believe, My Lord, in Giovio," he demanded, "who was always an enemy to opening the council, as a thing not necessary *in tanta desperatione pacis solidae* [in such great desperation of solid peace]."[63]

The other great movement of 1546 was the emperor's campaign against the League of Schmalkalden, postponed from 1545 and launched with substantial papal assistance in July after the futile diet of Regensburg. The council called for in the recess decree of Speyer (1544) had met, and the Protestants had refused to attend. Coercion was now the order of the day. At a solemn ceremony on July 4 in Santa Maria in

Aracoeli on the Capitoline, Ottavio Farnese received the marshal's staff and standard as commander-in-chief of the papal forces, and Alessandro the legatine cross.[64] For once Giovio was surprised; he had thought the emperor would not move against the Protestants without a guarantee of peace from France. He followed the campaign with the keenest interest, constantly begging his patron for letters. As soon as one arrived, he said, the "paradiso" was full of courtiers copying it; they were knocking on his door up to midnight, even "the greatest cardinals."[65] At one point the cardinal sought the precedents for having his legatine cross borne before him in the army.[66] Along with the gossip of Rome and medical advice for a stomach problem, Giovio kept plying his patron with arguments for making translation acceptable to the emperor. Now that conciliation had yielded to coercion, there was no reason for the council's remaining in Trent. As for relocating in an Italian city, the cardinal should remind the emperor that he was already master of Italy, commanding "head, shoulders, arms, breast, belly, legs, and heels."[67] If Farnese could persuade the emperor to recover Hungary, he would have shown him the way to win the hearts and minds of the Italians, the path to empire in ancient times.[68]

Giovio offered military advice as well. Having correctly determined that the emperor was less well-prepared than the League of Schmalkalden, he urged Farnese to press on Caesar the wisdom of switching from the aggressive tactics of Marcellus to the defensive strategies of Fabius Maximus.[69] Despite his high opinion of the landgrave of Hesse as a soldier, he was quick to see his error in not moving to block the papal militia at Innsbruck or to dislodge the emperor from Regensburg, later termed a serious mistake by Charles V in his memoirs.[70] Giovio predicted that the landgrave would at some point make a surprise attack but that the emperor would not allow himself to be drawn into a decisive encounter, and on learning that the imperial army had withstood the league's assaults at Ingolstadt on August 31 and September 2, he burst into Latin, adapting Livy and Virgil to congratulate his patron: "Facere fortia et pati Romanum esse, magne Romane, memento: hac enim via in coelum onusti gloria proceres iere Romani [Remember, Roman, to be brave and suffer is Roman: by this road the Roman nobles have gone to heaven laden with glory]."[71] The emperor's tenaciousness gave him good reason to hope for a "total victory," as did the continuing mistakes of the league. He said he would not "forgive" the landgrave in his *Histories* for failing to prevent Maximilian of Buren's army from joining the emperor after Ingolstadt, although he credited the landgrave with "unheard-of bravery" for his attack of August 31.[72] After a last futile attempt to provoke a major engagement on October 14, Hesse withdrew and Cardinal Farnese took his departure.

On greeting Giovio, who had gone out to meet him under Monte Mario, the cardinal teased, "You are enthroned throughout the imperial camp as a landgravian, but don't be discontent at having made such a good judgment of him, because he is, in truth, a good soldier."[73] Giovio again reflected, *veritas odium parit,* but he wrote to Ottavio Farnese with words intended for the emperor's ear, praising him for having avoided the bloody battle fearfully anticipated in Rome and for imitating Julius Caesar's virtually bloodless victory over Pompey's forces at Ilerda. After attempting to win father and grandfather with a vignette of the children babbling happily and playing with his cane on his recent visit to Margaret, Giovio urged that it was time for the emperor to demonstrate his clemency and magnanimity by seeking not to destroy the Protestants but to unite with them against the Turk, having first made an enduring peace with France and ending the miseries of his war-torn subjects. In view of the pope's extreme age, he urged the young soldier to represent to his father-in-law the danger of a schism should he not allow the Council of Trent to be suspended. The death of Paul III during a sitting council would pose the risk of "two popes at once," Giovio warned, one created by the council, another by the conclave.[74]

Giovio's letter embodied his own and the curia's alarm at Charles V's rapid progress toward "monarchy." Some of his arguments came directly from the pope. Just two days earlier, he said, His Holiness had stressed to him the need for peace with France as the basis for continuing the council and remounting a crusade. Paul III's anger at discovering that Charles V had concluded separate truces with the Protestants without abrogating the freedom of religion granted at Speyer soon led him to believe that he was merely helping to finance the emperor's greatness in Germany, and he began to meditate withdrawing his troops. Toward the end of 1546 Giovio dilated further to Pier Luigi Farnese on the emperor's progress to "monarchy," listing the events where Fortune had remedied his lack of prudence, as in undertaking a war against the Protestants before he had made a real peace with Francis I, or before his own forces had been fully assembled. Now Charles V was seeking to prevent promulgation of the decree on justification, so necessary to the papal position, while at the same time, with a pope at an age reached by "two in a million," forbidding the suspension or translation of the council. Who knew, Giovio speculated, but what the emperor was planning to make his own pope at Trent. "The generous Pope Paul" who opened the council "for his own and the public honor" had been tricked.[75] To Dandino, Giovio expressed the fear that by opening the council to achieve the unity of Christendom the pope might have created a new Barbarossa or Frederick II. "This blessed 1546" had, indeed, proved "a year of paradoxes."[76]

During the time Cardinal Farnese was in Germany, Giovio was supervising the painting of Vasari's famous frescoes of the life and pontificate
of Paul III. He had introduced his protégé to the cardinal in 1543 and by
unflagging efforts had procured him the commission to decorate the audience hall in the palace of the Cancelleria.[77] As Vasari himself related,
to gain the commission Giovio had him do "molti disegni di varie invenzioni [many designs of various inventions]" until the cardinal was satisfied. Like an *impresa*, the cycle was to be a synthesis of word and image
depending for decipherment on the learning and acuity of the observer.
For the principal panels Giovio employed the same scheme he had used
for Tommaso Cambi's house at Naples, where he had chosen four episodes in Charles V's career to illustrate "the virtues of His Majesty in all
the rest of his actions."[78] To avoid the "adulation" that Giovio detested,
the Cancelleria inscriptions were generalized and nowhere included the
Farnese name, so that by means of his historically demonstrated virtues,
Paul III became the *figura* or *exemplum* of a virtuous pope. With a delightfully Giovian twist, the chief nexus between Farnese and *figura*
(aside from the coats of arms) became the individual features of Paul III.

The principal panels depicted Paul III receiving the homage of the
nations, promoting universal peace (Nice), rewarding merit, and building St. Peter's. Each panel was to be read in concert with the surrounding inscriptions, with the personifications of virtues in flanking niches,
and with the *exempla* from classical history in the frieze above. In the
Cancelleria, Giovio amplified the scheme he had used at Poggio a Caiano
into one of double prefigurement. As a *figura* of papal virtues, Paul III
prefigured popes to come, just as he himself had been prefigured by great
rulers of the past, most notably Alexander the Great.[79] *Synkrisis*, the
comparison of the subject with heroes of the past, was a figure of the
rhetoric of encomium, and in fact the hall can be read as an attempt to
transform the rules of encomium into a decorative system.[80] Each principal scene represented a well-developed topos in the rhetoric of the ideal
pope, and the general arrangement bore a striking resemblance to the
rhetorical memory system of the pseudo-Ciceronian *Rhetorica ad Heren-
nium*, by which points of a speech were to be imagined as located in a
building with niches, angles, and columns.[81] To the knowledgeable and
responsive observer, the whole room would function as a speech. Giovio's familiarity with ancient memory systems, his previous *invenzioni*,
and his practice designing decorative schemes for his own museum, had
all prepared him for creating an *invenzione* of astonishing sophistication
and complexity.

But if the Cancelleria cycle demonstrated Giovio's command of
rhetoric, it also expressed his predominant political, social, and moral

convictions of the 1540s. Each topos emphasized a major Giovian preoccupation. The "Tribute," embodied his view of the papacy as the true
successor of Rome and his passion for the *libertas Italiae*; "Paul III Promoting Peace" expressed his deepest yearning for Europe—peace between Charles V and Francis I and prosperity for their subjects; "Building St. Peter's" symbolized his belief in papal leadership in patronage of
the arts; and "Rewarding Merit" epitomized his philosophy of ecclesiastical service and his fondest hopes. To Giovio the careerist, high office in
the Church was not so much the opportunity for broader service as it was
a reward for merit. A neglect of *iustitia distributiva* was one of his principal complaints against Clement VII. Doubtless not by accident, Vasari
chose to depict Giovio in this particular panel, gripping his cane as he
watched the distribution of cardinals' hats, his eyes fixed on Bembo, the
prototype of his hopes.[82]

The commission for the cycle was awarded to Vasari on March 29,
1546, and painting began on July 16, after the cardinal's departure for
Germany. Giovio's "management style" during the realization of the
frescoes was characteristic. He constantly meddled in the work while at
the same time promoting it in glowing terms to the absent patron. To
avoid the sort of scandal that had attended Michelangelo's *Last Judgment*, he told the cardinal, he had made Vasari cover up the masculinity
of the personification of the Vatican (after objections by the steward,
Curzio Frangipane).[83] On August 25 he reported that Vasari was at work
on the fourth panel and that the cardinal would salivate when he saw how
much he had gotten for the price. "It is a wonderful thing," he exclaimed, "to see in a glance a population of three hundred figures done
from life."[84] With Giovio's interest in portraiture, it is not surprising that
many of the figures were actual portraits, and that he was exacting in his
standards.[85]

In the end, even Giovio's abilities as a promoter could not conceal the
defects of the work. Because of the speed at which it was done, anticipating some event the cardinal had wished to hold upon his return from
Germany (probably in connection with the projected marriage of Vittoria Farnese), the room became known as the "Hall of One Hundred
Days," prompting a famous witticism of Michelangelo's.[86] As soon as he
finished, on October 23, Vasari left Rome, and it was not until December
18 that Giovio could inform him that the cardinal had seen the frescoes
and was satisfied. It was not a rave review. "He liked very much the best
portraits," Giovio reported, "and overall the work came out better than
he had anticipated, particularly considering the short time allotted you.
It is enough that you have been praised by seven-eighths of the gentle
spirits."[87] The comfort this gave Vasari can be imagined. The painter

regretted having accommodated the cardinal's schedule, he later confessed, and resolved never again to lose control of a project by employing too many assistants.[88]

Fortunately for posterity and for art, Vasari and Giovio were linked in the genesis of a far more successful project than the *Sala dei Cento Giorni*: Vasari's *Lives of the Artists*. "During this time," Vasari related in the memoir of his own works, "the day's work being over, I often went to see the most illustrious Cardinal Farnese dine, where there were always present to entertain him with fine and noble discussions Molza, Annibal Caro, Messer Gandolfo [Porrino], Messer Claudio Tolomei, Messer Romolo Amaseo, Monsignor Giovio, and many other literati and gallants of whom the court of that lord is always full."

One evening, Vasari said, the topic had turned to Giovio's museum and the *Elogia*, then in the process of publication, and Giovio was dilating on his intent to follow them with "a treatise discussing the men illustrious in the art of design from Cimabue to our own times."[89] When he had finished, the cardinal turned to the painter to ask, "What do you say, Giorgio. Will not this be a fine piece of work?" "Fine," responded Vasari, "if Monsignor Giovio will be aided by someone from the arts to put things in their proper place and say how they truly stand; I say this because while this discourse of his was marvelous, he has confused many things." To the reader, Vasari explained that Giovio "certainly demonstrated great knowledge and judgment in matters of our arts," but had been inaccurate in details, being chiefly interested in "the larger picture." Urged by the cardinal and company, Vasari agreed to put together a chronological outline of artists and their works to serve as a basis for Giovio's project; but when he brought the historian his "notes and writings," which he had been making since youth, "as a pastime and because of my affection for the memory of our artists," Giovio recognized their merit and insisted that Vasari undertake the project himself. "Not knowing the styles and the many particulars which you would know," Giovio said, "if I were to do it, I would do at best a little treatise similar to Pliny's." To overcome Vasari's diffidence, Giovio insisted that he show his work to Caro, Molza, Tolomei, and others for confirming opinions.

Vasari's vignette betrays some evidence of literary reconstruction, although not as much as sometimes supposed. The context in which he set the conversation was undisputably his work on the Cancelleria frescoes, and most indicators point to an actual occasion in the spring of 1546, after the commission had been awarded and before Cardinal Farnese had departed for Germany.[90] Giovio continued to lend encouragement. "Attend to your book," he urged Vasari after his return to Tuscany. "I hereby offer myself as reviser, and I can tell you it will be immortal."[91] Just over a year later, in December 1547, the eagerly awaited manuscript arrived in Rome, and Giovio wrote to express his delight: "I devoured your book just as soon as I had it, and I am impressed to the point that it seems impossible you could be so good with the brush, when you advance yourself so with the pen."[92] At Giovio's suggestion the work had already been shown to Varchi in Florence, and Giovio himself now circulated it to Caro and others in the cardinal's circle. At the end of January 1548 he returned the manuscript with the suggestion it be entitled *Le vite de gli eccellenti artefici*, recalling Nepos.[93] After further revisions in Florence by Vincenzio Borghini, Vasari's masterpiece went to press in 1549, appearing the following year.

Recent scholarship has stressed Vasari's intellectual debt to the humanistic milieu of Rome and the friendships begun in 1532 among the courtiers of Ippolito de' Medici. Giovio's prominence in this milieu, his interest in the theory of history and biography, his recent composition of the *Elogia*, his wide knowledge of the arts, and his strong affection for Vasari all suggest a major impact on Vasari's ideas of history and biography and probably on his criticism as well.[94] Although Vasari would occasionally complain of "this chatterbox of a Giovio" and chafe under Giovio's insistent demands for portraits, he continued for many years to maintain a friendship that had been important to his thought and career.[95]

While helping Vasari with the Cancelleria frescoes and readying the first series of *elogia* for the press, Giovio was composing a sequel of *elogia* of the living and revising "the sacred History."[96] At the end of December 1546 he announced to Pier Luigi Farnese that he was ready to publish fourteen books. "The book of life" now stretched, he said, from the invasion of Charles VIII to the "lean" peace of Crépy. His wording was somewhat confusing, but Giovio's intention seems to have been to "fenestrate" some books and withhold others for posthumous publication, "because I do not want the travail of justifying things that are undoubted." The cavils of the imperial court must have been wearing on him. In addition to the present books 1–4 (the remains of the original books I-V) and books 11–18, he had probably written at least major sections of books 30–34, 36–37, 39–45, and parts of others. Evidently the bulk of the *Histories* had been composed by 1546.[97]

Another work to which Giovio gave the finishing touches in 1546 was the *Descriptio Britanniae, Scotiae, Hyberniae, et Orchadum*, a piece of chorography intended to form part of the series conceived in 1535, the *De imperiis et gentibus cogniti orbis*. In the dedication to Cardinal Farnese he remarked somewhat bitterly that it had provided him a respite from chronicling "the fortunes of this calamitous century," and a temporary "oblivion" from the miseries of Italy, "burning in continual warfare, bereft of its ancient dignity, stripped of its liberty and wealth."[98] But even the *Descriptio* could not avoid the contagion of a calamitous century, finishing as it did with the "raging" of "the bloody and cruel tyrant," Henry VIII. By an unknown agency, George Lily's eulogies of the principal English humanists—two of them martyred by Henry VIII— came to be added to the volume as published by Tramezzino in Venice by June 1548. Giovio had high praise for Lily in the text, and it was probably through Lily's patron Cardinal Pole, whom Giovio hailed as the chief hope for Henry VIII's repentance and return to Rome. The *Descriptio Britanniae* may, in fact, have stemmed from Giovio's mysterious encounter with Pole and Giberti at Voghera in 1537, as his own contribution toward winning England back to the fold.[99]

The year 1546 brought a heavy and unexpected sorrow in the death of Giovio's close friend and munificent patron, the marquis del Vasto. At the time of his death, Alfonso d'Avalos was only forty-four, but he had never enjoyed a happy day after his crushing defeat at Ceresole d'Alba. His position in Milan had steadily deteriorated as his enemies at court began to press for his replacement. A trip to Spain early in 1546 had not succeeded in annulling charges of maladministration, and his health had worsened under the stress. His widow penned the sad news to Giovio the very morning of his death, March 31, 1546. Giovio responded with the type of consolation the humanists had perfected through the aid of classical philosophy, frankly acknowledging the pain of bereavement and accepting earthly grief as natural and legitimate. "The teachings of the faith of Christ and the precepts of philosophy have been so insufficient to console me," he confessed, "that I have no remedy for this incurable sorrow, either to offer Your Excellency or to use for myself." He could only comfort Maria, truthfully enough, that her husband had escaped "the intricate miseries of the corrupt world," that he was without doubt in Paradise, and that his glory was immortal. It had always been "the fatal destiny of the house of d'Avalos" to die young, Giovio reminded her, leaving progeny who decked themselves with splendor. This he augured for Don Alonso and Don Iñigo, promising them and her the most reassuring thing he could, the sympathetic support of the pope and Cardinal Farnese requested by his dying friend. Other than that, he concluded, abruptly taking a pragmatic view of the circumstances, a Christian stoicism would best serve her interests and theirs, both for enduring this life and for gaining the world to come.[100]

The year 1547 proved a fit sequel to 1546 in its harvest of dramatic and paradoxical events. It opened well, in Giovio's eyes, when the Council of Trent adopted on January 13 the decree on justification as approved by Rome, the decree that remains to this day the foundation of the Roman Church's teaching on the respective roles of faith, grace, and works in salvation. "We have cleared the post," Giovio exulted to

Dandino, "in despite of Martin Luther and in confirmation of the apostolic authority." In its next descent he hoped the Holy Spirit would inspire the closing of the council so that Paul III could go to heaven without the stain of a schism or a coup by "him who aims *plus ultra* ["more beyond," Charles V's motto]."[101] Instead, less welcome debates followed on the reform of the episcopate, culminating in the decrees adopted on March 3 obligating bishops to reside in their sees.

Meanwhile, with south Germany pacified, Charles V was extending his campaign against the Protestants into electoral Saxony—this despite his fury over the withdrawal of the papal troops shortly after promulgation of the decree on justification. On April 24, 1547, the emperor decisively routed the elector at Mühlberg, and on June 19 the landgrave of Hesse capitulated. Charles V opened the diet of Augsburg on the first of September as emperor in fact as well as name, and Giovio was genuinely elated. When the news of Mühlberg reached Rome, he sent to his friend, the Neapolitan general Giambattista Castaldo, a letter obviously intended for the emperor's eyes. Such a victory, he declared, made it evident that His Majesty was "a consummate and perfect captain, worthy not only of the reputation of Fabius Maximus for strategic delay but of Caesar for the swift and sudden fury of war." If Charlemagne, after laboring thirty years to subdue Saxony, merited the cognomen *magnus*, Giovio continued, betraying no fear of hyperbole, Charles V, after subduing it in only thirty weeks, merited the cognomen *maximus* "on the triumphal arches and in the sacred *Histories*, a memorial of triumph more durable than marble sculptures." The duke of Alba would also receive "an immortal tunic of shining virtue," Giovio guaranteed, and Castaldo himself could count on "fringes of gold" and "perfumed ink."[102]

Charles V's triumph was rendered even more dazzling by the recent death (March 31, 1547) of his great antagonist, Francis I.[103] Building on the new prospects for peace with France under Henry II, Giovio concluded his letter by attempting to reinforce what he professed to know were the emperor's own inclinations to confront "this deluded beast of a Suleiman," and promising him the moral and financial support of the pope. In responding, Castaldo related that he was unable to finish reading the letter because the duke of Alba took it and handed it to the emperor, "who read and reread it, noting with great satisfaction those passages which dealt with his valor, and likewise the duke with those dealing with his, so that it was concluded that the letter had no peer, except the one written to the emperor by the pope, and this was also the opinion of Don Luis d'Avila." The part about the crusade, Castaldo affirmed, pleased the emperor most of all.[104]

In August Giovio also wrote in courteous terms to the two defeated commanders, still captives of the emperor, seeking the reasons for what he surmised were their principal tactical errors.[105] Requesting Alba and Castaldo to encourage the two Protestant leaders to respond, Giovio again emphasized his reliance on eyewitness testimony. "The true light of history," he affirmed to Alba, "consists in clarifying events and in explicating the counsels of those who have conducted wars" (a thoroughly classical view). "And well I know," he went on, "that history cannot attain perfect dignity, if the truth of matters is not extracted from the breasts of great men." As if to reassure the duke that no harm would come from his soliciting the perspective of the defeated parties, he added, "And I know how to weigh and measure the circumstances of both sides."[106] Charles V and Francis I had both submitted to his questions, Giovio concluded, and if the landgrave and elector refused to do so, they would have no cause to complain of him subsequently.

Ironically enough, just as he was triumphing over the Protestants on the battlefield, the emperor was losing control of the council that had once been his hope for the religious peace of Germany. Not only was the January decree on justification a complete victory for Rome, the curial party was able to take advantage of an outbreak of typhus in March to secure the long-desired translation to an Italian city. Cardinal Cervini, chief author of the translation to Bologna, took Giovio's view that the council had to be removed from imperial influence.[107] Congratulating the legate on securing the translation of "this badly opened and well-transferred council," Giovio confided that even Cardinal Farnese, who had generally been more pliant than his grandfather, was beginning to see the emperor's insincerity, an insight that elicited from Cervini an appreciative reply. What was necessary now, Giovio concluded, was a temperate and dexterous reform that would stop the mouths of the blasphemers in Germany without despoiling the Holy See of its prerogatives.[108] To the bishop of Nagyvárad (Grosswardein), Giorgio Martinuzzi, Giovio rejoiced that the danger of schism was now past.[109] While the translation relieved him of one set of worries, however, it created another, namely the fear that he might be forced to attend. His first reaction was that he would attend "a session or two," then "decree" himself a trip to his museum, with a week in Florence en route.[110]

On April 21, 1547, the date specified in the final session at Trent, the council duly reconvened at Bologna but postponed further meetings until the second of June. When it met again then, it prorogued itself until September 15. Sometime in August, Giovio's attendance must have been seriously suggested, for on the 21st he wrote an urgent letter to Cardinal Farnese asking to be excused.[111] His reasons were large and small. He was neither a theologian, he protested, nor a canonist, nor even a student of Church history. Only in his métier of history was he worth anything, and for that he needed the quiet of Rome. In the foggy

Bolognese winter he feared another attack of gout, such as the three months' attack he had suffered there in 1532. Moreover, he had lost a molar at Bologna and had too few left to risk another. In point of fact, given his decision to terminate his *Histories* in 1544, Giovio had little to gain as a historian by attending the council, and the prospect of lengthy discussions on uncongenial issues horrified him. With advancing age, he needed the time for completing and publishing the *Histories*, biographies, *elogia*, and other works.

While other prelates were leaving for Bologna, Giovio remained in Rome, still expecting to be excused because of age and gout.[112] Ironically, he might have spared himself the necessity of even pleading. Although unwilling to have the council return to Trent, the pope decided early in September to conciliate the emperor by postponing the September session to await the outcome of the diet of Augsburg, called to settle the affairs of Germany after the emperor's victory over the Protestants. Then, on September 10, Pier Luigi Farnese was assassinated in the castle of Piacenza. It soon became apparent that the conspirators had acted under the influence of Charles V's new governor of Milan, Ferrante Gonzaga, who swiftly took possession of Piacenza for the emperor and who would have seized Parma had it not been for the resolution of its commandant. The council was at a standstill.

Even before the conspiracy, relations between pope and emperor had been tense. In his heart Charles V had never really consented to the investiture of Pier Luigi as duke of Parma and Piacenza; he had simply refrained from objecting. Now Gonzaga's zeal had forced his hand. Paul III was mortally offended and, as Giovio observed, the deed being done, the emperor was more likely to seize Parma than to give up Piacenza.[113] As usual, Giovio had been enjoying profitable relationships with both sides. He had been corresponding with Pier Luigi all summer, sharing his reservations about the emperor's increasing power, but he had been honored by Ferrante Gonzaga's visit to the museum in July and gratified by the governor's promise to be no less generous a patron than Francesco II Sforza or the marquis del Vasto.[114]

In May Giovio had cited a dictum of pope Martin V: "With how little sense the world is governed!"[115] Now he poured out his apprehension and concern to his old Tuscan friend and patron, Cardinal Niccolò de' Gaddi. "One must live from day to day," he lamented, and, above all, avoid making "vain judgments about the future," like Paul III's astrologer, Luca Gaurico, who had just predicted prosperity and long life for Pier Luigi. Favored by Fortune, Charles V goes toward monarchy "with sails and oars"; Henry II is in difficulties with England; only the Venetians can now oppose the emperor; Caesar's condolences to the pope on the death of Pier Luigi and those of the Most Christian King are nothing but "dust in the old man's eyes."[116] Once again Giovio was flowing with the stream of papal thought. Paul III was, in fact, at that moment negotiating with the Venetians and the French for an alliance against the emperor.

To Giovio, however, nothing seemed to block the emperor's road to "monarchy." Even "the Turkish dog" which the king of France once held over him had been restrained, at least temporarily, by the five-year Turkish-Hapsburg truce concluded in July 1547. Although many were surprised, Giovio was not, knowing of Suleiman's desire to profit from internecine disputes in the Persian royal house and his fears of a coup by Mustafa should he be away in Hungary.[117] Even the tumult in Naples over the introduction of the Inquisition would strengthen the emperor's position there, Giovio thought, through the repressive measures it would enable him to take.[118] And while Giovio could report to Giovanni Poggio, nuncio in Spain, that "the generous Pope Paul stands solid as a pyramid of Egypt against the harsh blow of thieving Fortune," he also surmised that His Holiness was debating whether to be ruled by the spirit and keep the council in Bologna, or by the flesh and accept some possible quid pro quo from the emperor (such as the return of Piacenza) for the return of the council to Trent.[119] Thus 1547 drew to a close amid fresh uncertainties.

In the personal realm, 1547 had brought Giovio a gain and a setback. The gain was that thanks to the efforts of Dandino and the cardinal d'Este, Henry II ordered the bishop of Toul to pay Giovio his pension.[120] The setback was Giovio's failure to secure for his nephew, Alessandro, the coadjutorship of Nocera with right of succession. Apparently, he had earned his doctorate in medicine and settled down.[121] Perhaps with the Council of Trent still in session, Cardinal Farnese did not wish to press the pope for this particular grace, despite the precedents Giovio cited of Sadoleto and Biagio Martinelli of Cesena. The reforms of Trent had limited coadjutorships to the pope's *motu proprio*. At the end of the year there was at least good news when Ferrante Gonzaga confirmed the office of *referendario* at Como to the Giovian family.[122]

The year 1548 began badly for Giovio, with a prolonged attack of gout that came on right after Christmas and lasted thirty-four days. By the end of January he was barely able to move from his bed to a couch by the fire.[123] Throughout the winter the political situation remained tense, as the emperor pressed the pope to return the council to Trent. On January 23, Don Diego Hurtado de Mendoza appeared in consistory, attended by all the other ambassadors, "to intimate sword, plague, and fire if the council did not return to Trent." The pope's response had not yet been given when Giovio reported to Cardinal Ippolito d'Este that "all Rome stood in gravest suspense, wondering whether some stimulus to the flesh would not suffocate the spirit," that is, whether the pope would not consent to the return of the council to Trent in exchange for the return of Piacenza to the Farnese.[124] When Paul III's response, given in consistory on the first of February, proved negative, Mendoza left Rome and Charles V determined to proceed on his own. In March the famous interim decree was drawn up allowing Protestants clerical marriage and communion in both kinds. Despite the opposition of the nuncio, Giovio's friend Sfondrato, the decree was presented to the diet of Augsburg in May and published as part of the recess of June 30; imperial-papal relations had reached their nadir. In Rome, some feared another 1527.

The emperor's decrees put Giovio in a belligerent mood. Now was the time, he told the nuncio Dandino, for "the old man to pull off the biretta, spit in his hands, and jump into the trenches." He had recommended to Cardinal Farnese that the pope enlist four thousand Swiss to guard the passes to Rome. Still, he was uncertain which in the end would weigh the most with him, the spirit or the flesh.[125] Unbeknownst to Giovio, His Holiness was participating in a counterconspiracy against Ferrante Gonzaga. At the beginning of August, Henry II of France had even descended to Piedmont to await its outcome. To Giovio, "the pious and generous and most powerful King Henry" now seemed, at least potentially, the savior of the papacy.[126] Gonzaga discovered the conspiracy in time, however, and Henry II returned to France, disappointed that Paul III was unwilling to accept his terms for assistance, which were the transfer of Parma from Ottavio Farnese to Henry's son-in-law Orazio Farnese.[127]

The year 1548 saw the publication in one volume of three of Giovio's major biographies, all of them fundamental contributions to sixteenth-century historiography: the lives of Leo X, Adrian VI, and Cardinal Pompeo Colonna.[128] Each represented a type of biography perfected by Bruni and the humanists of the Quattrocento—historical biography. Giovio claimed to have written his lives "in imitation of Plutarch—a philosopher of the greatest gravity—although with a somewhat freer style," but his biographies differed from ancient biography in their basic approach.[129] Whereas Plutarch and the ancients had used history as a vehicle for the exposition of character, Giovio and the humanists left character to be deduced from history, an inversion that made history predominant. Only in the *Elogia* did Giovio adopt the Plutarchan or Suetonian approach. The "Plutarchan" component of Giovio's major biographies was rather his willingness to include his subjects' bad deeds as well as good so that they might furnish material for the moral inferences which made history, according to humanist theory, "philosophy teaching by example." Although Renaissance theory accorded biographers the convenience of glossing over bad qualities, Giovio's lives were rigorously historical. Everyone had bad traits as well as good, he maintained, and "adulation" only invited ridicule.[130]

The *Vita Leonis X* was Giovio's masterpiece. It defined the first Medici pope by his role in history and fixed in print the tradition of the Leonine Golden Age. Its melancholy final lines epitomized the nostalgia of the humanists for the vanished life of Rome before the sack, a life which, indeed, glowed with aureate splendor when recollected in "an age of iron." As historiography, Giovio's work was immensely influential, not only for the tradition it perpetuated but for the interpretive structure it gave to Leo X's reign. Historians have returned to it again and again, from Guicciardini, who used it in manuscript for his *Storia d'Italia*, to Burckhardt, who remarked that he could never quite tear himself away from Giovio's picture of Leonine Rome, however much it emphasized the darker aspects. Giovio himself professed to have written it "with integrity, without malignity, and without the boot-greasing of pseudo-praises," and in its forthright portrayal of the pope's virtues and flaws, it was, indeed, "Plutarchan." It remained the standard life of Leo X until the appearance of Fabroni's in 1797 and Roscoe's shortly thereafter, in 1805.[131]

Like many of Giovio's works, the *Vita Leonis* was a long time in preparation. A first version, suggested by Felice Trofino, may have been composed before the sack of Rome. The actual version was commissioned by Cardinal Ippolito as he and Giovio journeyed to meet the emperor at Genoa in August of 1529. Later, Pope Clement VII requested the addition of a book on Cosimo *pater patriae*, beginning in 1433, for which he furnished a second pension, as well as information and critiques. On his own initiative Giovio interposed "with strict and amiable brevity" the intervening material on Piero di Cosimo and Lorenzo the Magnificent. The finished manuscript, calligraphed and bound in five volumes, "luxurious *utroque modo*," was given to the cardinal sometime before his death, probably in 1533.[132] Owing to the difficult period in Medici fortunes following the death of Clement VII, however, it lay unpublished, despite a second dedication to Duke Alessandro, until Giovio began pressing Duke Cosimo to have it printed. He sent the manuscript to Florence in January 1546, and in February he suggested that the recently revised life of Adrian VI be printed along with it—"on the crupper," as he put it. Because of delays in Florence, however, the actual *editio princeps* of the *Hadriani Sexti vita* became the version published at Venice as an appendix to the *Elogia*.[133]

The life of Adrian VI was commissioned by the dutiful Enkevoirt and was probably completed soon after the unfortunate pontiff's death, but in any event before Enkevoirt's death in 1534. It was held by contemporaries to be a masterpiece of irony. The author himself told Cosimo I it would be a foil to the life of Leo X, fulfilling the motto of Giuliano de' Medici, GLOVIS, which reads in reverse, SI VOLG (It turns).[134] In no other work did Giovio translate so many ecclesiastical terms into classical Latin, furnishing an example of the Ciceronianizing scathingly attacked by Erasmus and detested by Adrian VI. Giovio was seemingly participating in the curia's revenge on the pontiff who had expropriated the livings of so many of the humanist tribe. Although he himself had actually fared better than most, Giovio found it impossible to forgive the old man for failing to provide competent leadership, just as he was subsequently unable to forgive Clement VII. That his views were shared, even by earnest reformers, was evident from Cardinal Seripando's confession that the lives of Leo X, Adrian VI, and Pompeo Colonna had afforded him "infinite pleasure" owing to their "divine passages, particularly in the life of Adrian."[135]

Last "on the crupper" came the life of Pompeo Colonna, composed sometime between 1534 and 1544 and dedicated to the cardinal's nephew, Archbishop Francesco Colonna, who had probably commissioned it. In this, more than in any other biography, Giovio experienced a tension between his personal esteem for his subject and his adverse judgment as a historian. With an almost twentieth-century concern for possible subjectivity, he used the preface to warn the reader of his personal conflict, and his narrative, although objectively formulated, stressed the grave damage done the papacy by the Colonna raid of 1526.

Despite his evident impatience, Giovio was forced to wait two years to see his biographies in print. While Cosimo and his courtiers were anxious to establish a press for printing the output of the Florentine Academy and for publishing the treasures of the Laurentian Library, their experiment with Doni's press was not working out, and not until 1548 was Torrentino's press ready for what the court intended to be a major publishing event. The handsome folio edition, which appeared in May 1548, carried a preface by Piero Vettori hailing Cosimo for the establishment of the press and announcing its mission. For Giovio, its inauguration turned out to be an event of lasting import, as henceforth all the first editions of his works were printed and published in Florence.[136]

Laurens Leenaertsz van der Beke—Lorenzo Torrentino as he was known in Italy—was lured to Florence from Bologna in 1547 with substantial incentives.[137] Contemporaries praised his typefonts, which came from Frankfurt-am-Main, as handsome and eminently readable.[138] His press gave new life to the Florentine Academy and spawned an academy of translators. The life of Leo X immediately found two, Cosimo Bartoli of the Florentine Academy, and Lodovico Domenichi of Piacenza, who was commissioned by the press itself.[139] A proofreader and corrector, Domenichi had come to Florence from Venice with a recommendation from Aretino, working first for Doni and subsequently for Torrentino. His translation of the *Vita Leonis X* marked the beginning of a collaboration which resulted in his translating the greater part of Giovio's works during the ensuing four years. Throughout the process of printing and translation, Giovio's principal link with the court and press was Cosimo's trusted minister, Lelio Torelli of Fano, whom, together with the duke, Giovio appointed judge and censor of his work, *in spiritualibus et temporalibus*—an office that Torelli discharged with intelligence and tact.[140]

The *Vita Leonis X* was followed in 1549 by the *Illustrium virorum vitae*, consisting of the lives of the twelve Visconti dukes of Milan, with the dedication to Henry II of France while still dauphin; the life of Muzio Attendolo Sforza, with its dedication to Cardinal Ascanio Sforza; the life of Gonzalo Hernandez de Córdoba, with a dedication to the duke of Sessa; and the life of the marquis of Pescara, with the dedication to Vittoria Colonna. As with its predecessor, the entire volume was dedicated to Cosimo, this time by Giovio himself with a letter dated from Rome, April 21, 1548. Final arrangements for printing were made during the spring of 1549, and during the autumn Giovio was occupied with reading proofs passed on to him by the ducal agents at Rome.[141]

As Giovio desired, the *Vitae duodecim Vicecomitum* was published simultaneously in Paris by Robert Estienne.[142] The work itself, as he explained in the preface, had been commissioned by Charles, duke of Orléans, at the colloquy of Nice when it seemed he might be given the duchy by the emperor as a means of cementing peace with Francis I. By the time it was finished, however, its raison d'être had vanished in the renewal of warfare. After Crépy, Giovio had probably been waiting for the emperor's decision on whether to give the duke Flanders or Milan and so lost his opportunity of presenting the volume when the young man unexpectedly died. Thereupon he dedicated it to the dauphin Henry. The epilogue, explaining the genealogical basis for the French claim to Milan, was only completed in January 1547, probably in an effort to give the work added utility but also reflecting Giovio's current political thinking on the Milanese question. Because it was a "research job" and not based on eyewitness testimony, the *Vitae duodecim Vicecomitum* has not had any recognizable life in subsequent historiography, although the Paris edition is sought after for its fine woodcuts. It was quite otherwise with the biographies of Gonzalo Hernández de Córdoba, the great captain, and Francisco Fernando d'Avalos, marquis of Pescara.

The life of the great captain was originally commissioned by his son-in-law, Luis de Córdoba, duke of Sessa, while he was serving as ambassador to Clement VII. Giovio had almost finished the life, when the Colonna raid (in good part the work of the duke of Sessa) interrupted his work, and subsequently much of it disappeared in the sack of Rome. The original composition can thus be assigned with fair certainty to the period 1525–26.[143] At the instigation of Cardinal Francisco de Mendoza, Giovio rewrote the life, rededicating it in 1547 to Gonzalo's grandson, the then duke of Sessa, hoping, as he confessed to Giovanni Poggio, to get a subsidy from him as well.[144] Owing to the range and authority of Giovio's eyewitness sources the life of the great captain has been of lasting historiographical significance, and no historian of the wars of the period can ignore it.[145] Giovio himself termed it "copiously" written.[146] Historians have been troubled by minor confusions and inaccuracies, in part owing to Giovio's extreme distaste for chronicle, which led him to use too few dates, in part because of his probable—and certainly understandable—memory lapses in rewriting the work twenty years later. Another shortcoming was Giovio's tendency to make Gonzalo into one of his beloved paladins. Nonetheless it was a solid, coherent, and mature work—"a major contribution," to use the current jargon of reviewers.[147]

In July 1548 Giovio reported to Cosimo de' Medici that he was revising the life of the marquis of Pescara in order to have it printed following the life of the great captain.[148] Commissioned by Vittoria Colonna in 1528, the work was evidently completed before the death of the marquis del Vasto in 1546, since the dedication mentions him as living.[149] A second dedication to Giambattista Castaldo, Pescara's chief lieutenant, may indicate an additional subsidy after Vittoria's death in 1547. Like the life of Gonzalo, the life of Pescara was the basis of much subsequent historiography. Both contained extensive materials that would have formed part of the missing books of the *Histories*. Because of Giovio's close association with many of Pescara's lieutenants, including the marquis del Vasto, his companion on most of his campaigns, the life was particularly well-based on accounts of eyewitnesses, among them, of course, the author himself.[150]

During the early months of 1548, Giovio had been working on the *elogia* of heroes and a life of Alfonso d'Este commissioned by Cardinal Ippolito d'Este, from whom he was trying to obtain necessary information.[151] The arrival in September of a prospectus from Doni for a book on antique medals renewed his hope that the *elogia* of heroes might also be illustrated with woodcuts, as Doni was planning for his volume.[152] Giovio was also beginning to collect materials for a life of Giovanni delle Bande Nere promised to Cosimo de' Medici.[153] In July he had even contemplated a trip to Florence to deliver his *Histories* in person, indicating that the decision to publish them there had already been made. Eventually the visit was postponed until the following summer, but to reveal the importance Florence was assuming for him, Giovio hinted that he was thinking of dedicating the *Histories* to the duke, a resolve soon reinforced by events.[154]

In August 1548 Giovio's long career of expectation reached its crisis. With the death of Cesare Trivulzio, the see of Como, long a preserve of the Trivulzio family, at last fell vacant. Giovio's candidacy was obvious to all, to some his elevation a foregone conclusion. During an illness of Trivulzio's in 1543, Giovio had observed to Cardinal Farnese's secretary, Bernardino Maffei, that "everyone augurs me the episcopacy of Como," modestly adding, however, that he himself thought the see was "a morsel for messer Bernardino Maffei and for me a little pension."[155] As soon as news of the vacancy was out, Giovio rushed to the palace of San Marco, which Paul III habitually used as a summer residence. "In San Marco I threw myself at the feet of our lord," he later told Cardinal Farnese, "and I said, 'Holy Father, if with your generous courtesy you wish to honor me, your immortal slave, with the miter of my native city, I will voluntarily relinquish my present bishopric [certainly an understatement] and I will accept the payment of pensions up to 1,000 *scudi*, since it is worth 2,000; and if Your Holiness has in mind a person more suitable than me, I beg him to reserve me an honest pension so as not to discredit me completely with my fellow citizens, and so that I appear a person of some consideration in your house.'" For the gouty old man, to throw himself at the pope's feet must have been a supreme effort. The pope responded, "In this we cannot fail you and so we shall effect it," an ambiguous answer, which could have been interpreted as meaning either that it would be done, or that the bishopric was out of the question but that the pension was a certainty.[156]

A month or so later, on September 19, the see was awarded to another of Paul III's secretaries, Bernardino della Croce. On the preceding day, Cosimo de' Medici's chargé d'affaires in Rome, Benedetto Buonanni, had written the duke informing him that there would be a consistory at which Como would be awarded and that Giovio wanted to see if he could get "a good little pension" from it "in order to come with more gaiety to kiss the hands of Your Excellency." From what the secretary could discern, "There is a great wish to make him a cardinal, but the many who importune will generate some difficulty, and perhaps some other factors as well."[157] Four days later the secretary wrote a chastened postscript. "Giovio will do well to get a pension of 150 *scudi* on Como, and that is how scantily the outcome has supported the prescience of the rumor I reported to Your Excellency."[158] At the time, Giovio himself had been slightly more optimistic. Five hundred ducats had been reserved for pensions, "which," he later recounted, "made me certain that

I had to be one of those persons." Assignment of the pensions was reserved until della Croce could take possession of the see, and, owing to the hostility of Ferrante Gonzaga, that might be some time.

As Buonanni had ascertained, the autumn of 1548 saw a large number of aspirants to the cardinal's hat. A great flight of "pendocanti," as Giovio termed them in his jargon, awaited "the time of Santa Lucia [December 13] to hood themselves like peregrine falcons."[159] With his own hopes fast fading, satire was now Giovio's refuge. Come December, nomination of new cardinals was deferred until April 1549 when, despite pressures from princely families, only four were created, all intimates of the pope and all selected to resist any influence from Ferrante Gonzaga in the choice of his successor: Girolamo Verallo, Gian Angelo de' Medici, Filiberto Ferreri, and Bernardino Maffei.[160]

While waiting for his pension, Giovio continued working on the *elogia* of heroes and the life of Alfonso d'Este, seeking accurate information from informants such as the Ferrarese chronicler, Gaspare Sardi.[161] With his customary interest he followed the campaigns of Suleiman in Persia and the aggressive campaigns of the sultan of Morocco in North Africa. On the eve of Don Diego Mendoza's arrival in Rome in March 1549 to negotiate the matter of Piacenza, Giovio was, as usual, dubious. "We are like sparrows on a swing," he said, "picking at bits that are thrown to us." The emperor, he knew, was resolute. The pope, he also knew, was torn by "the duel of the flesh with the spirit," and he could not foresee which would prevail.[162]

By August Giovio could wait no longer. Three-hundred *scudi* had been given to Latino Giovenale Manetti, and despite Cardinal Farnese's many assurances, Giovio had reason to doubt that the pope intended to award him the 200 *scudi* remaining. It was more than age could bear. Protesting that with his gout he could not remain on his feet for an audience, he penned an ultimatum to the cardinal. "To me it appears strange," he declared, "that Pope Paul, who thirty-two years ago read and praised my histories to messer Bartolomeo Saliceto, should esteem me so little, given that I was so esteemed, even though *in minoribus* in respect of style, by Pope Leo, Pope Adrian, King Francis, and Charles V." Thanks to the past benefactions of Clement VII, Giberti, and Ippolito de' Medici, he said, it was not so much the money he needed as "that the pope and Your Most Reverend Lordship take care not to dishonor me in my *patria*, in which I still amount to something." He felt his services to the Farnese with his pen should certainly have obliged them at least to this extent. "What I wish to say in my language is that with fifty fine strokes in honor of His Holiness and all your house in the universal history, which I shall presently bring to the press in Florence, I should merit a good bit more than this remnant." The letter ended as peremptorily as it began. "Let Your Most Reverend Lordship deign to undertake whatever offices seem best to him with His Holiness; I do not intend to annoy him any longer."[163]

Giovio's timing was not of the best. Cardinal Farnese was deeply involved in the crisis developing within his family over Piacenza and Parma. Far from surrendering Piacenza, Charles V was now insisting on having Parma as well—just as Giovio had predicted—and Henry II was obdurate about supplanting Ottavio with Orazio in Parma as the price of his support, a prospect Ottavio was determined to prevent. No doubt the cardinal would have liked to oblige Giovio, but his influence with his grandfather had its limits. Indulgent as he was to his family, Paul III retained his strong grip to the end. He was not at their beck and call, and it was evident that he had no particular affection for Giovio. But above all, it was clear that Giovio's inability to furnish the exclusively loyal service demanded by the Farnese had at length caught up with him. Paul III was well aware of the historian's ties to the imperial establishment in Italy and probably knew of his credit with Ferrante Gonzaga, who was preventing della Croce from taking possession of his see. As long as the Farnese loyalist della Croce was barred from Como, there would be no "little pension" for Paolo Giovio.[164]

As nothing came of Giovio's ultimatum, even after a final interview with the pope on the loggia of Castel Sant'Angelo, the long-planned trip to Florence to publish the *Histories* took on an air of finality. Forsaking Rome after thirty-six years, Giovio declared, he would henceforth live only to commend himself to posterity through his works.[165] His emotions can be readily gathered from his subsequent letter to Cardinal Pio. "I swear to Your Most Reverend Lordship, by this remainder of my life, which is very dear to me as it will be the means for living after death, that I did not dare to come to kiss your hand, fearing to lose the gravity of the philosopher, because I would have been forced to bathe my eyes and cheeks with tender tears as old men are wont to do for both joy and sorrow, taking leave of a patron of such affection and benevolence toward me, and especially considering that the occasion of seeing him again will be difficult."[166] On September 3, 1549, amid the final packing, Giovio dispatched a note to Cosimo's majordomo, Pierfrancesco Riccio, giving instructions for the care of a trunk containing "his true soul," the *Histories*, which would arrive ahead of him in Florence.[167] On the morrow he had his last glimpses of Rome, before his equipage clattered across the Ponte Milvio and headed north along the Via Cassia toward Ronciglione and Viterbo.

CHAPTER TWELVE

De Senectute (1549–1552)

SENECTVS IN LIBERTATEM ASSERVIT

"Old age liberates" (the final motto in a series in the frieze of the *sala d'onore* of the museum describing the major episodes of Giovio's career)

IF GIOVIO'S DEPARTURE from Rome was a defeat, his journey to Como was a triumph. Thanks to good mules and the luxury of wagons, he survived the rigors of the road so well he thought he might even live another seven years.[1] Host after host showered him with flattering hospitality. On the second day Captain Bartolomeo of Mirandola entertained him at lunch, probably at Viterbo, and accompanied him to Bagnaia, where Cardinal Ridolfi received him "like a Lucullus." The cardinal had just added a pair of loggias to the governor's castle, affording a view of the countryside around Monte Cimino, and in the adjacent hunting park he had begun what would become one of the greatest gardens of the Renaissance. Giovio found it all "an enchantment."[2]

On reaching Florence the historian was warmly greeted by Duke Cosimo's majordomo, Pier Francesco Riccio, and "pompously" lodged in the palazzo della Signoria, although he expected to be moved to the palazzo Medici for greater convenience in conferring with Torelli on the publication of the *Histories*.[3] The duchess Eleanora ordered a litter to expedite his coming to Poggio a Caiano, but heavy rains detained him in the city for several more days.[4] By September 16 he had joined their excellencies, and the secretary Jacopo Guidi reported that there was almost no one "who has not passed the hour of meals in listening to the eloquent Giovio."[5] After four days Giovio returned to Florence with the duke to assist as physician at the deathbed of the cardinal of Ravenna, Benedetto Accolti. Announcing the demise of this antagonist to Cardinal Farnese provided Giovio the perfect opportunity to let his patron know he had not forgotten his obligations to the Farnese—or theirs to him.[6]

On September 28 Giovio was back at Poggio a Caiano "with another book" of the *Histories*, reported Giovanni Conti, "and every evening goes on reading a portion, to the great satisfaction and pleasure of His Excellency." Caught up in the general admiration, the secretary confessed staying up to the fourth hour of the night (about 11:00 P.M.) reading "the history of the wondrous colossus Giovio."[7] By now the courtiers knew that Giovio intended to dedicate his magnum opus to the duke.[8] In part the dedication expressed his appreciation for Cosimo's patronage, in part his pique with the Farnese over the pension, but most of all it embodied the admiration of an "ancient servitor" for this latest head of the Medici house.[9]

Giovio had been watching Cosimo gather strength and independence. To his amazement, he had seen him defy the redoubtable Paul III and hold his own. He had observed the good effects of his rule in Florence.[10] Now he could truly celebrate the young duke for sparing the Florentines the servitude of an imperial governorship. As Giovio's reservations about Charles V increased, so did his support for anyone who preserved a measure of independence from the imperial "monarchy." He made his point obliquely and with characteristic Giovian impertinence in the dedication of the second book of the *Elogia virorum bellica virtute illustrium*, where he likened the benefits of Cosimo's rule to those of the fourteenth century *signore*, King Robert of Naples. Called to defend the Florentines against "threatening tyrants," King Robert had brought the city not "the empty title of liberty," but "true liberty with tranquility and wealth." Now, Giovio reminded the Florentines, these benefits were being received not from "an external king" but from "a humane citizen and sanctified prince."[11] The duke and his courtiers were equally genuine in their admiration of Giovio and in their appreciation of his great compliment. Torelli had told Riccio he thought the dedication of the *Histories* would have been "no small honor" for the emperor or the king of France.[12]

By the time Giovio reached Florence, the *Illustrium virorum vitae* was either in the final stages of printing or off the press. Domenichi's translation of the life of Muzio Attendolo Sforza was being printed by the Giunti. Domenichi had also finished translating the lives of the twelve Visconti (Venice: Gioliti, 1549) and was working on those of the Gran Capitano (Florence: Torrentino, 1550) and the marquis of Pescara (Florence: Torrentino, 1551).[13] Giovio had already sent the duke a list of the heroes he intended to celebrate in the *Elogia* of captains and rulers, and there was even talk of printing them with copper plate engravings made from the portraits at Como.[14] Most importantly, the order for the printing of the *Histories* had been established and, pending the arrival of "a magnificent paper" on which to print them, they were being read by Cosimo and Torelli, the duke and his minister having been made by Giovio "judges and censors of all my affairs, *in spiritualibus et temporalibus*, to correct, suppress, or enlarge."[15]

With everything so satisfactorily arranged, Giovio began to think of continuing on to Como before the roads became difficult and returning "with the storks" in the spring. Excited by the prospect of seeing his life's work in print, delighted with the kind treatment he had received during the three weeks of his stay, and overcome with Cosimo's insistence on paying for the seven tapestries he had ordered, he wrote to Pio extolling the duke as "a king of courtesy." Then, on October 3, he resumed his progress in style, accompanied through the passes of the Apennines by a ducal steward who sent a courier ahead each day to prepare the evening's reception "among those alps and rocks."[16]

As recounted to Angleria, Giovio's stages from Bologna to Milan read like a triumphal progress, with legates and governors vying with each other in lavish hospitality. The highlight of the journey was Giovio's meeting at Lodi with Ferrante Gonzaga, who reassured him that he would prove no less generous a patron than the marquis del Vasto had been. At Melegnano (Marignano) the marquis Gian Giacomo de' Medici insisted that Giovio dine and spend the night, the historian having earned the gratitude of the reformed pirate-king a dozen years earlier by securing him and his brother better treatment during their imprisonment by del Vasto when they were suspected of conspiring against the emperor.[17]

At Milan, where he had agreed to visit Gonzaga's sick children, Giovio was met at the Porta Romana and escorted to the governor's secretary, Giovanni Maona, who was ready with "a good fire, white linens, and perfumed rooms." The children's maladies turned out not to be serious, and the next day Giovio lunched at Gonzaga's "fantastic" villa, "La Gualtera," built at the end of the Quattrocento by Ludovico il Moro's chancellor, Gualtiero Bascapè, and now being refurbished by the architect Domenico Giunti of Prato.[18] So, with far more danger to his gout from repasts than roughness of the roads, Giovio at last reached Como and "sweet repose."[19]

Once arrived, the historian quickly settled into a productive routine. Mornings were spent readying the *Histories* for publication, afternoons in boating and fishing or visiting properties he had acquired and improved.[20] Evenings brought more work on the manuscripts. Gabriele Faerno had drafted an inscription for Giovio's dining room commemorating his prandial customs in old age:

> Convivas frugi ac faciles tres accipit arctam
> Ad mensam prandens Iovius: sed vespere solus
> Quam leviter coenat, quo vividiore senecta
> Scribat facta virorum saeclis memoranda futuris.[21]

Dining, Giovio entertains three affable and temperate companions at his modest table, but in the evening, alone, how lightly he sups, so that in his lively old age he may record the deeds of men for future ages.

In November 1549 came news of the death of the pope. Alessandro Farnese's last days had not been happy ones. Unable to break the deadlock with the emperor over Parma and Piacenza, he had concluded by reclaiming both for the Church and sending Camillo Orsini to take possession of Parma in the name of the Holy See. Refusing to brook the loss of his state, Ottavio rushed to Parma and, on being refused admission by Orsini, appealed to none other than the mortal enemy of his house, Ferrante Gonzaga—an act of the most flagrant disobedience. Aflame with indignation, the pope contracted a violent fever in the November chill and within five days, on November 10, he was dead. Giovio received the tidings from Gonzaga, who summoned him in haste to Milan for briefings on the state of the curia and the prospects for the conclave.[22]

Giovio's analysis, based on the known "humors" of the curia, was astonishingly prescient. Before the dramatic and protracted conclave that saw Cardinal Pole fail of the papacy by one vote and Cardinal del Monte emerge as Julius III, Giovio predicted that the memory of Adrian VI would make the Italians resist a foreigner. If the struggle between concilarists, Farnese partisans, imperialists, and Francophiles reached an impasse, he thought the cardinal Verulano (Ennio Filonardi) was old enough for an interim choice and that Pio and del Monte were upright enough to satisfy the reformers and serve as compromise candidates.[23]

Had it not been for the loss to Cardinal Farnese, Giovio confessed, he would have been pleased by the death of Pope Paul, "who, ingeniously tricking everyone, in the end tricked himself."[24] When the news of del Monte's election reached him, he was delighted. Not only was the new pope a friend of many years, he was on good terms with Farnese and had already made Giovio's old friend Cardinal Pio one of his chief advisers.[25] Not surprisingly, Giovio immediately renewed—if it had ever lapsed—the campaign for the pension. Even though its revenues had all been assigned to others, he hoped that these people could be compensated with other income and the pensions on Como assigned to him in order to "save his honor with his fellow citizens."[26] He promised to pay his homage to the new pope in person when good weather came and a mild attack of gout had subsided, although he had been vexed to learn that the paradiso had been taken from him.[27] When summer came he talked about a return to Rome in the fall when the medlars had ripened. Meanwhile he was working hard on the *Histories*. He had done more in the last months, he said, than in the previous two years.[28]

The first four books of the *Histories* had been left with Torelli in Florence. After about a month in Como, Giovio sent down books 11 and 12, and during the succeeding winter and spring he sent six more, which, together with the summaries of the six supposedly lost in the sack of

Rome, were to make up the first volume of eighteen books.[29] He urged that printing begin as promised before Christmas, "because I do not want to be surprised by death, like Pope Paul."[30] Printing did begin, and by mid-January 1550 the proofs were being forwarded to Como for correction.[31] Torelli attempted to parry Giovio's complaints of lack of care in proofreading by commending the diligence of the proofreader, "Messer Arnold of Haarlem," and blaming the "bestiality" of the typesetters and their incorrigibility when drunk.[32]

Despite a mild attack of seasonal gout, Giovio was hard at work during the winter of 1550 with proofreading and preparing material for the second volume. His thoroughness can be seen in the fact that, despite its having been praised some years before by Bembo, he sent the latter half of book 18, dealing with the Venetian campaigns of 1516 against the emperor Maximilian, to a friend in Venice, hoping for a final scrutiny by some knowledgeable patrician or even the doge.[33] He sent the parts of book 25 covering the aftermath of the battle of Capo d'Orso to the Genoese jurist Marcantonio Sauli.[34] Needing some detail on the capture of Castelnuovo, he turned to Don Juan de Luna, now castellan of Milan, in the hopes that he might have among his soldiers a veteran of the campaign. He did, and he sent the man to Como for the historian to interview himself.[35]

Sometime in May, Torrentino evidently suggested postponing publication until both volumes were complete, precipitating Giovio into a state of intense agitation. "If this happens," he raged to Torelli, "I would throw myself out the window in desperation, because I want it to be published now, with the proem in front and the epistle of Alciato, according to the order established with Your Lordship." If the volume was thinner than Torrentino wished, Giovio fumed, that was his fault for leaving such small margins, compressing the lines, and not leaving space between the end of one book and the beginning of another.[36] In responding, Torelli was at pains to soothe the historian's agitation, explaining, with the slightest touch of irony, that to keep him from throwing himself out the window he and the duke had decided to have the first volume finished and published immediately—this very week, if possible. As if to justify Torrentino's idea of waiting until both volumes were ready, Torelli adduced the example of Guicciardini's heirs, who were still delaying the appearance of the *Storia d'Italia*.[37]

In thanking the minister, Giovio explained his anxiety with the Browningesque example of that cautious jurist of Parma whose tomb bore the inscription, *Nolens stare discretioni haeredum suorum hoc sepulchrum in vita sibi fieri iussit* (Not wishing to leave things to the discretion of his heirs he ordered this sepulcher for himself while still alive).[38]

Torelli's allusion to Guicciardini set Giovio on a course of reflection about the perils of publication during one's lifetime. He was not looking for quarrels, he said, "in this, my old age, which seeks tranquility." Nothing would be more inept and foolish than to elicit hatred where one expected favor. He well knew why Guicciardini's heirs were retarding publication of the *Storia d'Italia*, having seen how "it bites too freely those who merit it for truth alone, always odious to those who wish to be flattered with false adulation." He had experienced similar pressure himself, he said, when asked to drop from his *Histories* his praises of Marco Foscari.[39] His solution to the problem of publishing in his lifetime would be to leave certain "windows" in the text which his nephews could then close after his death with materials he would have prepared. Just where these "windows" were left is unclear, and the materials he mentioned have never been found.[40] Meanwhile, publication proceeded as Giovio had so emphatically desired. Printing was completed on August 2, 1550, and by mid-month he had in hand the pledge of the immortality he hoped for from his life's work.[41]

As August turned to September, Giovio gathered up the materials for volume two and took leave—for the last time, it turned out—of Como and everything he had created there, intent solely on completing the *Histories*.[42] Beyond the logistics of publication, he needed ready access to Cosimo de' Medici and Florentine sources to finish the books dealing with Florentine history from the sack of Rome to the establishment of Cosimo's principate.[43] With his lingering gout, he found the journey more difficult this time, and he arrived at Bologna "rather worn out."[44] After he had rested four days, however, the governor, Girolamo Sauli, provided him with a litter for crossing the Apennines, and by September 11 he was again enjoying the customary welcome on the Arno.[45]

Almost immediately, Giovio began sending volume one to various crowned heads, being anxious, as he had told Granvelle, "to enjoy some sweetness" from it during his lifetime.[46] His original intention had been to sojourn a bit in Florence and then go on to Rome, although "as a Polish pilgrim," he reassured Torelli, visiting but not staying.[47] A crescendo of summonses from his friends had culminated in Cardinal Farnese's declaration that, "in short, this absence of yours from the court can no longer be tolerated."[48] Although old, gout-ridden, and, as he claimed, proof against worldly vanity, Giovio was not insensible to these appeals, but having left Rome for his honor, he was not willing to return without some tangible satisfaction. He was no longer disposed to be a speculator, he said.[49] Yet even as he wrote, the first waves of the storm were breaking which was to confine him to the security of Cosimo's court. The repercussions from the publication of the *Histories* had begun.

The first wave was created by the letter of Andrea Alciato inserted in the first edition (it was removed in subsequent editions). Its inclusion had been largely a matter of chance. In June of 1549, Torelli had suggested adding something after the dedication to Cosimo in order to fill up the first gathering, which otherwise would have contained two blank pages.[50] By April 1550 Giovio had determined to use a letter the great jurist had written him the previous fall in response to his complaints about the pension. A fellow Lombard, Alciato had been a longtime friend of both Giovio brothers.[51] The decision must have been made not long after Alciato's death on January 12, 1550.[52]

Although an immediate campaign was begun by Alciato's heir to discredit the letter as a fabrication, recent scholarship has accepted it as genuine, while allowing for retouching here and there.[53] The taste involved in printing it was another matter. To deck the appearance of his magnum opus with the tale of his disappointed hopes for the bishopric of Como was certainly a major lapse of judgment on Giovio's part. "You write," the letter began, "shaken by a grave injury and soon to forsake Rome (which I should never have thought possible), unwilling any longer to bear indecorous witness to the contumely dealt you in that court where for many years you have been as clearly fortunate in a prosperity consonant with the golden mean as you have been famous for the authority of your studies." It was indeed strange, Alciato declared, that Pope Paul would have preferred anyone over Giovio for the bishopric of Como. And yet whom has he chosen? "Someone who was not born in Como, who has never been seen there, and who, as I understand, has suddenly been produced from the sordid recesses of the cubicle."[54] Giovio's deception by the inveterate cunning of the old pope has confirmed his wisdom, Alciato asserted, in rejecting offers to teach at Rome and dismissing "a vain and uncertain hope of the purple."

From consolations and exhortations to enjoy the literary *otium* of the museum, Alciato turned to praising Cosimo, "a cosmos among the princes of his age," a "grave emulator of the glory of his ancestors," by far "the best of patrons." Indeed, Alciato continued, he himself had come close to accepting the duke's offer of a chair at Pisa.[55] After praising Giovio's biographical style as rivaling Plutarch's, Alciato repeated cautions he claimed to have expressed to Giovio during a discussion of history with Francesco Sfondrato and Gualtiero Corbetta at the dining table of Carlo Borromeo. In particular the historian should avoid speeches inappropriate to the speaker, such as the one put in the mouth of Tullio Marconio, leader of the 1532 mutiny of Italian troops in Austria, an oration so accomplished as to make it seem that instead of being called to the ensign from the fields of Volterra, he had been "snatched from the schools of Cicero and Hermogenes."[56]

The letter contained some interesting comment on Giovio's style. In the *Histories*, Alciato found, Giovio had adopted neither the Livian "milky fullness [*lacteam ubertatem*]" nor the Sallustian "sobriety [*sobrietatem*]," but to his own "solid, and recognizably individual style" had added "a few flowers culled with a discerning hand," not from the Tacitean "briar thicket," but from the "meadows" of Quintus Curtius. The letter concluded with prospects of the pleasing conversations the two friends would have—both of them now lame with gout—on boating excursions on Lake Como, once Alciato had retired from Pavia to his villa at Buccinigo, a mere three hours from the museum.

If Giovio's judgment was warped by the temptation of clothing himself in the praises of one of the greatest intellects of the age, so was Cosimo's, whose assent was necessary for the letter's publication. In Rome, however, where the cardinals had just demonstrated their admiration for the late pope by setting aside an unusual sum of money for a monument, Alciato's letter provoked an outrage. Giovio's friends were deeply embarrassed. "Believe me, please," begged Pio, "it would be best if that letter of Alciato's could be annulled, and if you restrained yourself a bit from the lengths to which the memory of that cursed pension drives you."[57]

Giovio reacted querulously. "Can nature be such that my friends have no compassion for the wrongs done me," he wrote testily to Angleria, "that they do not even wish other, illustrious friends to console me with their condolences, as Alciato did so justly and opportunely in this instance?" Even slaves are allowed to weep when they are mistreated. "Alack, what woe is mine! that having labored forty years to honor the living and the dead and afford a useful exercise to posterity, I find no one who thanks me for it, or who gives me even one dry kiss, but all assail me ferociously in the flanks with pikes and furious spears." The letter was only printed by chance, Giovio protested, "and if Alciato, who expected the red hat in a box, was semimutinous and wanted to tell it as he saw it, the fault is not mine." He was not such a fool that he did not see Alciato's drift in the letter, but was he therefore to forgo the gratification of "being lauded by a lauded man?"[58]

With regard to Pope Paul, Giovio assured Angleria that in writing the *Histories* he never allowed himself to be swayed by personal feelings. "When I write history I dismiss from my mind everything that might alter the purity of historical truth."[59] He did indeed have angers, but they were transitory. He had even forgiven the marquis of Pescara for the sacking of his *patria* and house and for not securing restitution of his silver from the two soldiers who had extorted it from his brother by torture. Besides, he declared, the greater part of his gifts had come from the cardinal, not the pope. His return to Rome would depend on fulfill-ment of an unspecified datarial grace, probably the appointment of his nephew as coadjutor for Nocera. The letter's blend of what might be called, in Giovian jargon, "the spirit" and "the flesh" was characteristic of the era, although the truculence was entirely Giovian.

Giovio's initial impulse was to maintain the identical posture with Cardinal Farnese, although somewhat less truculently. On August 30, while vacationing at the family's country retreat at Gradoli near the lake of Bolsena, the cardinal had had Annibale Caro draft a gracious letter urging Giovio's return. "We shall have, now in one spot, now in another, our little dinners, ordered by you yourself with the company you choose, and you can imagine that the garden in Trastevere [the Villa Farnesina] is your Museum and that the river is the lake."[60] And if, indeed, Giovio had experienced some "stormy weather" in the matter of the pension, it was not such that his ship could not be brought to port, especially since they would not have "to overcome the parsimony of our old man," but had instead a pope "who will not fail us in some honest favor we seek." Having been sent to Como, however, the letter did not reach Giovio until the end of September, after the eruption of the affair of the Alciato letter. In thanking his old Maecenas, Giovio remained noncommittal, averring that he had sufficient income for his worldly needs and was only thinking of assuring himself life after death by finishing the *Histories*. Because of his gout, travel to Rome now would be risking death, and he was thinking rather of returning to Como and tranquilly awaiting the end of his days at the museum. As far as the second volume of the *Histo-ries* was concerned, Farnese need have no fears, knowing the obligations Giovio had to the cardinal himself and to the dignity of the deceased pope, "even though he could have taken more account of me than he did."[61] Indeed, Giovio had recently reflected that he had always been Astolfo in the house of Cardinal Farnese, franker than Orlando, more diligent than Rinaldo, and now he felt the time had come to lay down the role.[62]

After he had penned this response, however, disquieting news from Rome prompted Giovio to inquire discreetly of Pio just how he really stood with the cardinal. He was sending a personal emissary, he said, to broach a matter too confidential to write. It seems that he had received an anonymous letter advising him not to go to Rome lest he be poisoned for having written things dishonoring the late pope and for "showing disdain" by printing the letter of Alciato.[63] Eventually things reached the point where Cosimo himself thought he should intervene. "To Giovio it seems very strange," the duke informed his ambassador at Rome, Ave-rardo Serristori, "that after producing so many fine works he has to suffer the contrary of what he anticipated, having celebrated so many learned and valorous men of this century." Serristori was bidden to raise the matter with Cardinal Farnese and the pope, "who with a blessing could take care of everything."

> And we, who are most desirous of enjoying this good old man with his jovial disposition, neither brusque nor bitter, are very fond of him, for even if slow of leg he is swift of wit and so fresh of memory that he continues to write things which we read with great pleasure as soon as they are written. And since he appears to us worthy of affection and unaltered by these winds of hate and evil-speaking, so we hold him—a relic of the ancient servitors of our House.[64]

Meanwhile, apart from the letter of Alciato, repercussions were being created by the *Histories* themselves. From Tivoli, where he had just made his formal entry as governor, the amiable Cardinal Ippolito d'Este the Younger, a competent Latinist, had written an encouraging letter declaring that he was reading the first part of the *Histories* "with the utmost pleasure," but from Rome came news that the new ambassador of France, Claude d'Urfé, had taken vigorous exception to Giovio's use of the phrase "barbarian savagery [*barbara feritate*]" to describe the killing of women and of children in their cradles by the French during the sack of Mordano di Romagna in 1494.[65] To Angleria, the recipient of many complaints in these days, Giovio protested that he had never called the French *Gallos barbaros* "except when they used inhumanity and cruelty in war, which at that time was not in use among soldiers." Angleria was bidden to remind the ambassador of the many things Giovio had written to the honor of the French nation and to "tell Orpheus and Euridice that I shall not fail to show the world in this history that I have held neither art nor part." It was ridiculous, he mused, to think one could satisfy everyone.[66]

With his letter to Angleria, however, Giovio included another letter for Cardinal Ippolito asking him to mollify the ambassador. Since August, Giovio had been seeking to have the cardinal of Guise force the bishop of Toul to resume payment of his French pension, which was once again in arrears, and were he now to gain the reputation of a Francophobe it might needlessly imperil the negotiations. Luckily, Guise himself seems to have had no adverse reactions to the *Histories*.[67]

Unfortunately, a budding reputation of being anti-French did not save Giovio from the charge of being anti-imperial. One of the last things he had done before leaving Como was to send the emperor's court a draft copy of book 34, narrating Charles V's Tunis crusade, urging that it be read and, where necessary, emended. In a covering letter to the younger Granvelle, Antoine Perrenot, bishop of Arras, Giovio explained that he was submitting the book at the urging of Giambattista Castaldo, from whom he had learned that the emperor was attending personally to conveying his achievements to posterity.[68] In addition to subsidizing the work of Guevara and Sepúlveda, Charles V had, in fact, begun dictating his memoirs that very summer to his personal secretary Guillaume van Male, utilizing in part Don Luis d'Avila's account of the German wars.[69] This desire for immortal fame elicited Giovio's ready sympathy. It was "a great consolation to foresee life after death," he remarked to Arras, "when deeds are read of by those who were their authors; for this, as Cicero says, is to be among posterity and to know what history will say of oneself six hundred years from now." A short letter to the emperor emphasized the sincerity of Giovio's desire for comment and correction.[70] He had, in fact, circulated many other books in the same fashion, most recently book 18.

Upon receiving book 34, Arras had responded courteously enough, excusing himself with the pressures of work from personally translating and editing the manuscript but informing Giovio that he had entrusted the task to d'Avila, a veteran of the expedition, who was already at work annotating various passages "to inform Your Lordship of what really happened in this war."[71] In mid-November the official reply arrived in the packet of the Florentine ambassador to the imperial court, Bernardo de' Medici, bishop of Forlì. Drafted by d'Avila, the commentary had been put into Latin by van Male, but the emperor's involvement was confirmed by Cosimo's ambassador, who informed the duke that d'Avila and Arras were "secretly commissioned by His Majesty, who is so covetous of glory that he has regarded this history with an extremely jaundiced eye; for it seems to him that Giovio has detracted from his figure and from the truth."[72]

This was not the first time that Giovio had been obliged to defend himself against the emperor's touchiness or the charge of Francophilia. Years before he had been forced to do it in person at Bologna, and more recently Castaldo had done it for him in Germany.[73] In the volume of the *Histories* just published, Cosimo's ambassador elaborated, the emperor felt that he had been slighted by Giovio in order to please the French, "perhaps owing to natural affection which inclines him to the other side." The emperor especially wished to prevent this from happening in the second volume. Having been constantly pestered by Giovio over his pension, Forlì seemed only too happy to oblige the emperor. From "well-informed sources," he said, he knew that "His Majesty confides in the care of Your Excellency to have Giovio correct the errors or else to prevent the printing and cease patronizing him."[74]

Cosimo's reply to this broadside was ambiguous. "We have afforded Giovio the convenience of printing his histories here in Florence," he declared, "to give this universal boon to the living and to posterity, and we lay no charge upon him unless it be to write without passion or partisanship, and we are confident that in so doing he cannot fail to satisfy His Majesty, whose actions have ever been beneficent and just." In cipher, however, the duke appeared to bow to political necessity. "And if in what he has written of Tunis he has not satisfied His Majesty, advise me where there is particular need of correction and I shall not fail to do as His Majesty desires, and I shall also inform him of all the remaining parts before they are printed." Evidently the matter was subsequently discussed with Giovio, who had come down to Livorno to be with the court, because at the end of the letter there was a somewhat relieved postscript in the duke's own hand: "Giovio has told us that he will revise the book on Tunis in an accommodating fashion and that it was for this very reason that he sent it to His Majesty."[75] When this reply of Cosimo's was brought to Charles V, according to d'Avila, the emperor repeated three times, "The duke of Florence will keep an eye on the writings of Giovio, eh? You think he really will?"[76] So much for the tale of Sepúlveda.[77]

Two days after returning to Pisa, where he had taken up winter quarters (probably in the Medici palace), Giovio wrote to Arras thanking him with elaborate irony for his suggestions, which he knew "came from perfect judgment accompanied by the light of truth, faith, and charity." He would take such account of them as was appropriate, and he had no doubt that the revised product would satisfy the world, "which already knows in great part that I proceed sincerely without art or part, neither bought by favors nor driven by hate, which in this lowness [*bassezza*] of mine has never happened." His intentions were to celebrate appropriately in his *Histories* "the glory and the name of the most unconquered emperor Charles V." As for his being a Francophile, Giovio retorted that the French already considered him an imperialist. "I have to laugh at this," he declared, "because truth stays in its place and time will clarify it." He was too old and gouty to spend his time drafting apologies, he grumbled, although he would no doubt speak with less freedom in the second part, since hatred was his reward rather than benevolence.[78]

For d'Avila, Giovio reserved his sharpest irony. After thanking him for the "marvelous" service to their old friendship represented by his "most delightful [leggiadrissimo]" commentary, he promised, "I am going to correct all these things according to their order, and so much the more willingly as the authority of your name excels the good faith of all the captains and soldiers that have recounted these things to me."[79] Giovio's account of the Tunis crusade had indeed been gathered from a wide range of eyewitness testimony. While it reflected his admiration for the crusader-emperor, it was intended as history, not *laudatio*. D'Avila's own commentary on Charles V's German wars was so excessively laudatory that it had actually provoked resentment among the German princes. Giovio had always seen the futility of adulation and appears to have believed in good faith that the emperor did not really want it. He had recommended to Tommaso Cambi that in designing a fresco cycle commemorating the achievements of Charles V he avoid "adulation of Caesar, which when done inappropriately by people who think to praise him, brings instead shame to His Majesty because of the laughter it provokes from gallants, as on the triumphal arches at Naples, Rome, Siena, Florence, Bologna, Milan, and Genoa."[80] D'Avila's commentary revealed that the quarrel of the court lay not in matters of substance, but rather in Giovio's failure to inflate the image of the emperor sufficiently.

Thus Giovio's hopes of enjoying "some sweetness in this life" from his historical labors were rapidly fading.[81] In biography, he had always maintained, it was permissible to be laudatory. History followed a stricter canon. In fact, Giovio's biographies were by no means uncritical, while his *Histories* aimed at a high standard of impartiality. As he had prophetically written to Ottavio Farnese, explaining why he would not entrust them to the mail carriers, "No writer of history, even the most impartial, has ever been able to satisfy victors and vanquished alike and to avoid making himself unacceptable or even actually hateful to both parties, since one may readily be subject to partisan and insolent criticism, who, in his desire to do a service to posterity, speaks frankly of the living and writes of the sport of fortune with envy always watching him."[82]

Now that his forecast had come true, how did Giovio react? Although he declared to Arras that henceforth he would allow himself less liberty in writing, having received odium in place of thanks, he evidently did nothing to abridge the second volume's ironic prefaces on the ambitions of princes, its Thucydidean juxtapositions, and its trenchant condemnations of war, which, far more than in the previous volume, raised the *Sui temporis historiarum libri* to the plane of humanist moral commentary. In his old age Giovio seemingly recognized the folly of trying to please everyone and resolved not to "flatter the world between the bed and the grave."[83] And despite continuing dispatches from Forlì describing the urgency of the emperor's desire to censor the rest of his work, the duke strongly encouraged his resolution.

At Pisa, Giovio worked hard on the remaining books. He had chosen the milder maritime climate for his winter quarters, even though he had once discouraged his nephew Alessandro from studying there because "the Pisan air, which is very depressing, makes me fearful."[84] The winter of 1550–51 proved unusually severe, even near the coast. "Eolus blew so much" that the Arno was full of ice and the mountains were covered with snow. His eyes watered with smoke from keeping close to the fire, Giovio complained, and his body was roasted. The nerves of his knees continued to torture him. Still, he kept on working. The first of the unwritten books to be taken up was book 38, comprising the murder of duke Alessandro, together with Cosimo's succession and the consolidation of his power. Begun after extensive interviews with the duke, it was finished by mid-April, save for the attempts of the exiles to seize Borgo San Sepolchro and Sestino and for their final rout at Montemurlo. Seeking eyewitness testimony as always, Giovio turned to Benedetto Varchi, who had been with the exiles on the rainy march to Sestino, gently reminding him, lest he prove in any way recalcitrant, that the duke had by no means forgotten his presence there. Varchi obliged and by May 20 the book was done.[85]

A vivid piece of narration, book 38 bore the imprint of Giovio's ever-increasing disillusion with political life. Although it did little to endear him to Florentines of his own and subsequent generations, it was a balanced and informed piece of historiography, even if written from an antirepublican viewpoint. The historian himself was pleased with it.[86] He produced a gripping account of the grisly murder of Alessandro by his cousin Lorenzino and, for all his affection for the Medici and friendship with Alessandro, he indulged in no whitewashing of the former duke or his behavior. His narrative of Cosimo's creation as "head" of the Florentine republic, based on conversations not only with the duke but with Guicciardini in previous years, was unrelentingly realistic about the deceptiveness on both sides. Giovio frankly termed Cosimo's modest comportment a piece of dissimulation, although he apparently indulged old antagonisms a little by casting a thin veil of irony over his prose when he came to depicting the maneuvers of Guicciardini and the optimate leaders, who, caught between their dislike of a prince and their fear of a mob, sought to protect themselves with a principate while salvaging the republic by eliminating the authority and title of duke. The effort to limit Cosimo's stipend to two-thirds of Alessandro's, Giovio sarcastically termed "Tuscan frugality," and he mercilessly depicted the pale and trembling councillors hearing the shouts of Vitelli's impatient soldiery in the piazza outside, calling for a duke. The stark military power of the empire was about to overwhelm the last daydreams of the Florentine optimates.[87]

As might be expected, Giovio drew a flattering portrait of Cosimo, replete with "folkloristic" details, but he had been in earnest when he repeated to Torelli his understanding that the duke did not expect "boot greasing," and despite a personal conviction that a strong Florentine principate was to Italy's best interest, he made no effort to conceal the harshness of the measures used to sustain it, particularly Cosimo's treatment of the prisoners of Montemurlo including Filippo Strozzi, whose desperate tale is told in sympathetic fashion. Giovio duly recorded Cosimo's hypocritical regrets at Strozzi's suicide and his protestations of intended pardon, but in a manner creating more sympathy for Strozzi, not less.[88]

In addition to working on book 38, Giovio also took time during the winter of 1550–51 to ready the *Elogia virorum bellica virtute illustrium* for printing. When he requested the return of the partially completed manuscript, left with the duke early in the winter, he drew a thoughtful reply. While declaring himself pleased by the prospect of publication of these *Elogia*, Cosimo nonetheless suggested that Giovio ought rather to be perfecting the *Histories* and bridging "the vast gap" of the six missing books. "Moreover," he argued, "truth being the nerve of history, which Your Reverend Lordship, having professed to serve in the previous books is also expected to serve in the remaining six, it will be difficult to maintain credit should Your Lordship turn himself wholly to the *elogia*, in which it is permitted in a certain manner to pass over and to shade the truth." If suspicion were to be cast on the *Histories*, he suggested, all Giovio's labor would have been in vain. Cosimo concluded his clairvoyant observations with a strong appeal to Giovio to set aside his reservations about completing the missing books,

> nor fear on account of anyone to say the truth, which no historian should have to fear, and Your Lordship so much the less as he is already at an age where nothing ought to give concern. And I shall receive from this that contentment which can be imagined on the part of one most desirous of the immortality of Your Lordship's name.[89]

This dignified and perspicacious letter makes it difficult to believe that Cosimo intended to honor his promise to Charles V to censor the remaining books of the *Histories*.

Despite the admonition, Giovio persevered in finishing the *Elogia*, an indication of the importance to him of his collection and museum. The fifth book was composed immediately after book 38 of the *Histories*, evidently with great speed, since the whole edition in seven books, each dedicated individually to Cosimo, was off the press by the end of July.[90] While not particularly valuable as a historical source, the *Elogia* of heroes, as Giovio sometimes called them, merit reading.[91] The list, although including only one woman, Isabella of Aragon, is otherwise a catholic one, ranging from Roman emperors to Moorish sultans, and comprising such diverse "heroes" as Attila and Piero Soderini. In the humanist tradition of history as moral philosophy, the *Elogia* furnished examples not only of good conduct but of bad, notable examples of the latter being Ezzelino da Romano "with his fearful pallor and viper's eyes," Cardinal Alidosi, "an example to posterity of a wicked life," and Cesare Borgia "who in his bloody character and pitiless cruelty can be likened to the ancient tyrants."

No doubt Giovio intended to repay some personal debts with the *Elogia* and settle a few scores, as when he excoriated Ludovico Sforza for his ruinous schemes and Georg Frundsberg for his crimes, or when he attempted to rehabilitate the maligned Piero Soderini as a decent moderate.[92] The *Elogia* also enabled Giovio to celebrate patrons who, because of the missing books, did not figure prominently in the *Histories*. The portraits bristle with vigor: the impetuous Bartolomeo d'Alviano, short in stature but with piercing eyes; the indomitable Antonio de Leyva, crippled with gout yet briskly commanding his troops from a litter; the versatile Pompeo Colonna, with helmet in the camp and surplice at the altar; the enigmatic Alfonso d'Este, severe and taciturn except when discussing literature; the "stout" Cortés, burning with desire for Mexican gold.

The *Elogia* reveal many of Giovio's basic values: his fervent Italian patriotism and belief in the destiny of Rome; his stoic philosophy, evident in his admiration for a spirit unconquered by adversity and for that most difficult of all attainments—self-control; his devotion to the cult of glory and to the partnership between men of action and men of letters in serving it; his belief in the power of Fortune as greater than all human prudence; his moral code centering on honor as the font of virtue, the antithesis of all immorality; his admiration for *virtù*; his aversion to duplicity and treachery; his detestation of baseness, whether personal or political; and his ambiguous feelings about war, the theater of great deeds but a tragic waster of kingdoms and peoples. The *Elogia* of heroes give the impression of a Weltanschauung formed by grafting onto ancient stoicism not a little of the spirit of knightly romance.

In February 1551 Giovio had begun soliciting Cardinal Ippolito for the return of the manuscript of the life of Alfonso d'Este, completed at Como the previous spring, so that it could be readied for printing. To spur the cardinal he even concocted a dream vision of the late duke appearing to him at the museum, speedily released from Purgatory thanks to the indulgences of Pope Paul and eager to be clothed in the rich vestments of Giovio's biography before assuming his place beside other great commanders in Paradise.[93] The cardinal returned the manuscript and the life appeared in the fall, along with the second edition of the *Elogia* of men of letters.

Despite its composition during Giovio's maturity as a writer, the *Liber de vita et rebus gestis Alphonsi Atestini* was one of the least convincing of the major lives. Alfonso was a difficult subject, and there were signs of hasty composition.[94] As befitted a biographer, Giovio did his best to take a sympathetic view of the duke's self-serving politics—even his aid to Bourbon in 1527—by accepting the paramount law of self-preservation, but he did not conceal the frequent conflict between Alfonso's *utile* and

Italy's *libertas*, as when he explained Alfonso's participation in the League of Cambrai as a means of recovering the Polesine from Venice, yet depicted the league itself as a vehicle for delivering Italy into the hands of barbarians.[95] Ferrara was a paradigm of Italy's self-destruction. The biography was almost exclusively political, and the duke's involvement in the vicissitudes of the Italian wars afforded Giovio an opportunity for summarizing much of the history that would have gone into the missing books of the *Histories.*

Despite the Alciato letter, appeals to return continued to arrive from Giovio's friends in Rome. Cardinal Pio even cited Berni's poem, "Ser Cecco:" "Come! for Rome has need of you and you of Rome, nor can the court do without Ser Cecco."[96] Such literate summonses notwithstanding, Giovio elected to remain in Tuscany to oversee publication of the *Elogia* and finish the second volume of the *Histories.* He was already at work collecting materials for book 35, dealing with the emperor's ill-fated Provence campaign of 1536.[97] In Tuscany, moreover, he and his household were being fed and lodged by the duke, no small matter. "The expense of Giovio is multiplying daily," one of Riccio's subordinates at Pisa had complained.[98] Both his nephew Giulio and great-nephew Paolo the young were with him now, in addition to Marco Gallio and several servitors.[99]

In fact, Florence was becoming an eminently suitable surrogate for Rome. Cosimo's diplomatic network kept the historian abreast of developments in the larger world. He frequently dined with the duke and often called on the duchess.[100] Since Cosimo has been described as taciturn and Giovio as loquacious, they no doubt made an excellent combination.[101] In addition to geography, history, and politics, the two shared a keen interest in portraiture and in portrait medallions. In 1552 the duke sent Cristofano degli Altissimi to Como to begin copying the portraits in the museum, and he enjoyed learning of Giovio's more important pieces, such as his Pisanello medallions.[102] In Cosimo's own large collection of medallions, now in the Bargello, there was a copy of the fine portrait head of Giovio by Francesco da San Gallo, made in 1552, which traced the striking profile of the old bishop and caught his extraordinary vigor.[103] In August 1551 the duke sent Giovio a medal just cast of the duchess with a request to suggest a design and inscription for the reverse.[104]

Although he did not become active in the Florentine Academy, reorganized in 1547 under ducal patronage and devoted to vernacular literature, Giovio did preside over one stormy session in 1550 when Nicolò Franco, attending in disguise while a guest of Varchi's, was recognized by Domenichi and "courteously assaulted" by partisans of Aretino.[105] Giovio himself preferred not to take part in literary disputes but to maintain good relations with all parties. On an individual basis, he saw Varchi, Piero Vettori, Bernardo Segni, Giambattista Gelli, and Cosimo Bartoli. Gelli translated Giovio's life of Alfonso d'Este, and Bartoli the life of Leo X. After Giovio's death, Gelli spoke eloquently of his regret at losing "the sweet and pleasurable conversation of such a rare old man."[106] Yet another learned visitor was Torrentino's scholarly editor and proof-reader, Arnold of Haarlem.[107]

Varchi and Giovio had maintained a guarded friendship for some time, and now they saw each other frequently.[108] At Cosimo's order, Varchi composed the long verse epistle appended to volume one of the *Histories*, praising Cosimo and Giovio, and the sestet appended to volume two. After reading the first chapter of his nascent *Storia fiorentina*, Varchi later revealed, Giovio gave him the "fraternal" advice, obviously stemming from recent experience, not to tell the truth quite so bluntly, "because today one cannot do so, acquiring only hate from those offended and the esteem of no one."[109] At the duke's suggestion, Nerli submitted part of his *Commentaries* for Giovio's criticism.[110] Except possibly for Busini, none of the Florentine historians seems to have delighted in Giovio's company, but his standing with the duke made him too powerful to offend. All were angered by his account of the Florentine republic and took literary revenge after his death.

Giovio's friendship with his translator, Lodovico Domenichi of Piacenza, deepened in the course of time. Before being called to Florence by Doni, Domenichi had worked for Gioliti in Venice. A former member of the academy of the Ortolani at Piacenza and translator of Xenophon, he had much to offer in the way of learned company. Like Giovio, he came from the urban patriciate, his father having been a notary of Piacenza. Like Giovio, as well, he seems to have had a gift for friendship and to have enjoyed amiable relations with most of the difficult tribe of literati. Giovio thought his translations united fidelity to the original Latin with purity of language and felicity of style. It was gratifying to see his works translated into Italian during his lifetime, Giovio once told Domenichi, although his pleasure was tinged with envy when he reflected that, in Italy, Domenichi's translations would be more sought-after than his own Latin originals, "which will await praises from other more remote and foreign nations."[111]

As always, Giovio delighted in the society of artists. Vasari, to whom he had a strong sentimental attachment, was alternating between Arezzo and Florence. In addition, Giovio had formed friendly relations with a number of other Tuscan artists then resident in Florence, including Bronzino, Pontormo, and the aging Bugiardini.[112]

With the advent of spring 1551, Giovio returned from Pisa to Florence, where he was housed in the old Medici palace in rooms he recognized as having been used by Cardinal Giulio during his Florentine sojourns of the 1520s.[113] In late May, his old friend and patron Cardinal Gaddi arrived in his native Florence and, through a quirk of fate, in July arrived none other than Efestione himself (Cardinal Farnese), exiled from Rome because of the rebellion of his brother Ottavio against Julius III.[114] With profuse expressions of gratitude contrasting notably with the loftier tone of earlier days, the vice-chancellor accepted asylum from the old antagonist of his house. He was lodged along with Giovio in the Medici palace and given use of the villa at Careggi.[115] Although recent events inevitably cast their cloud on all concerned, evenings were passed reminiscent of old times in Rome, with the "dolcissima" Giovian conversation that Gaddi and Farnese had longed to enjoy.

The prospect of hostilities between the pope and Ottavio Farnese, who had secured Parma during the interregnum, was enough to deter Giovio from a summer trip to the museum.[116] Ottavio had refused to abandon his alliance with Henry II of France, to which he had been driven by Charles V, who not only continued to hold Piacenza but insisted on the return of Parma as a fief of the empire. As Giovio had observed, the emperor had not really wanted to surrender the city to the Church in 1529, and now he was obdurate. Declared a rebel on May 22, 1551, Ottavio took the military initiative and on June 12 began ravaging papal territory north of Bologna. Although he was driven back to Parma by a combined papal-imperial force, the appearance of a French army in the Piedmont threatened to revive the horrors of the Hapsburg-Valois wars. For Giovio, with his close ties to both sides, it was a dismal prospect, and he buried himself in work.

By June 23 Giovio was reviewing the last of Varchi's verses for inclusion in the *Elogia* of heroes.[117] He himself was striving to finish the six remaining books of the *Histories,* but the summer of 1551 was proving as hot as the previous winter had been cold and come August he laid aside his more serious work and for respite composed the *Dialogo dell'imprese*.[118] By mid-September the "pleasing and jocund little treatise," conceived during his conversations with Domenichi, was adorned with illustrations and ready for presentation to the duke.[119]

As Alciato's celebrated *Emblemata* of 1531 had become the fundamental text for emblems, so Giovio's *Imprese* became the basic text for devices. Its popularity and influence was attested by six contemporary editions in the original Italian, two in French, and one each in Spanish and English.[120] Although written for enjoyment, the treatise had a more serious dimension, evident even in Giovio's disclaimers. The very nomenclature he adopted, "body" for the symbol and "soul" for the motto, betrayed the Neoplatonic and hermetic background of Renaissance emblemmaking. As so often, Giovio stood at the intersection of the learned world, where his training and education placed him, and the courtly world, where he preferred to move.

The dialogue's intended audience was the society represented by the courtiers, Giuliano de' Medici among them, who are found composing emblems in the first book of Castiglione's *Courtier*. Yet there were numerous links to that continuing universe of hermetic discussion in which many of Giovio's old friends and intellectual acquaintances participated: his brother Benedetto, Alciato, Calcagnini, Valeriano, Bocchi, Delminio, and Doni. On taking up residence in Florence in 1550, Giovio came in contact with a circle of intellectuals who were carrying the traditions of Pico and Ficino into a new generation, among whom Domenichi, a former pupil of Alciato's, was a leading spirit. It was in this same period that Domenichi was preparing his edition of the works of Delminio.[121] Giambattista Gelli had a strong interest in hermeticism, as did Cosimo Bartoli.[122] So did Giovio's new friend the learned canon of Pescia, Antonio Buonagrazia, the translator of Pico's *Heptaplus*.[123] At one time Buonagrazia had been the envoy to France of Galeotto Pico, count of Mirandola, and Giovio sought him out for information on the French portions of the *Histories*.[124] Through Buonagrazia, he came to know his maternal uncle, the abbot Turino Turini of Pescia, translator of Gianfrancesco Pico's dialogue *The Witch*.[125]

In contrast to Alciato, whose *Emblemata* was the product of an interest in symbol as language; or to Valeriano, who invented a symbolic language which he thought was based on the same principles as Egyptian hieroglyphics, mistakenly believing they were ideographs; or to Achille Bocchi, who dedicated to him (somewhat ambiguously) the eighty-sixth symbol of book III of his *Symbolicarum Quaestionum libri quinque* (Bologna, 1555), Giovio was primarily interested in symbol, not as the basis for a systematic and arcane language which might participate on a more immediate level in the realm of divine ideas, but as a restricted form of *explicatio*, the presentation of an individual's life and philosophy to an audience of the educated and courtly. Rather than avenues back to an arcane world of meaning, Giovio's devices were vehicles of disclosure in which the mystery of the symbol served primarily to limit the revelation to the educated and to conceal it from the vulgar. The device was an outward display of the bearer's inner truth. While the image, or body, of the device linked the bearer to a transcendental world of mystical meaning, Giovio's more evident delight was in "conceit," in ingenious artifice, in contradiction, and in the ambiguity of polyvalent allusion. Not surprisingly, he used the *impresa* as an aid to memory, a visual symbol about which to group perceptions of the life, works, and character of an important historical personage. The explicative character of a device thus operated over time in the sphere of history. Like the portrait or the *res gestae*, the *impresa* became another element in the cult of individual personality and of personal immortality through history.[126]

After outlining the use of emblems on shields and helmets, first by ancient heroes, subsequently by his beloved paladins and Arthurian knights, and then by the German knights of Barbarossa's time (as seen in the frescoes of Santa Maria Novella in Florence), Giovio came quickly to the popularization of the custom among the Italians. The initial stimulus, he said, came from the French captains of Charles VIII and Louis XII, although the Italians soon displayed their flair for *invenzione, capriccio,* and *fantasia*.[127] To qualify as a true *impresa* a device had to satisfy five conditions (not always observed, however, even by Giovio). It required an image, or "body," and a motto, or "soul." It had to be neither so obscure it would take a sibyl to interpret it nor so clear it could be comprehended by the vulgar. It had to be visually striking. It could not employ the human form. And for the purpose of veiling its meaning from the vulgar, the motto had to be in another language than the bearer's. A classic example of a device was the one adopted by Aldus, consisting of a dolphin, the symbol of agility and speed, entwined about an anchor, the symbol of stability, with the motto *Festina lente* (Make haste slowly). In discussing well over a hundred *imprese* borne by distinguished personages, Giovio opened a fascinating window into his times. Curiously, although the creator of many successful devices for others, he himself never succeeded in finding a "body" for his own motto, *Fato prudentia minor* (Prudence unequal to destiny).

When the *Dialogo dell'imprese* was finished and the hot summer melted into autumn, Giovio's thoughts reverted to the *Histories.* Of the six books remaining to be written, 25 to 29 dealt principally with the last Florentine republic, and 35 with the warfare of Charles V and Francis I in 1536. While still in Florence, Giovio was preparing materials, writing to Rome, for example, to secure eyewitness testimony for the siege of Peronne (book 35).[128] Unusually heavy autumnal rains prevented his departure for Pisa until mid-November with the result that book 25 was completed in Florence and book 26 begun there.[129]

The same rains that detained Giovio in Florence were also miring the Parma war.[130] Well-informed, as usual, Giovio stressed the pope's lack of money to prosecute the war, and displayed a decided sympathy for Ottavio. With French encouragement, Turkish corsairs were sweeping through the Mediterranean, prompting his reproach, "the good pope has lit a great fire that will not be put out all that quickly."[131] Giovio's sense of déjà vu was increased by the pope's agreement to reopen the council at Trent to please the emperor and, as in the past, he did not see how anything worthwhile could come from a council with war in progress.[132]

On November 15 the historian was finally able to set out on a leisurely progress to Pisa, where he began working on book 26.[133] As a university city, Pisa was proving a quite satisfactory locale. Its Latin academy rivaled the vernacular academy of Florence, Giovio told Varchi.[134] He formed a close friendship with the Neapolitan philosopher Simone Porzio, who had been brought by Cosimo at a high salary to add distinction to the Pisan faculty.[135] When Giovio came to know him at Pisa, Porzio was in the process of composing and publishing his treatise *De humana mente disputatio* (1551), almost certainly translated by Gelli but not published because of the row created by another work of Porzio's which Gelli had translated with the title *Se l'huomo diventa buono o cattivo volontariamente* (Whether man becomes good or bad voluntarily).[136]

Certainly no coward, Porzio had carried Pomponazzi's conclusions about knowledge of the soul to even greater lengths, and Giovio was one of the first to warn him of the scandal his new work was creating among certain "reformed" clerics.[137] Porzio's son Camillo, who was living with his father while studying for a doctorate in law, later attributed the inspiration for his history of the revolt of the Neapolitan barons to conversations at Pisa in which Giovio declared that he wished he had carried the thread of his *Histories* back to the revolt, since it was the exiled rebel prince of Salerno who, in concert with Lodovico Sforza and Giuliano della Rovere, had been so effective in persuading Charles VIII to claim his Angevin inheritance.[138] Other Pisan company included Gabriele Fallopio, the famous physician who held the chair of anatomy; Guido Guidi, formerly physician to Francis I and now professor of medicine; Chirico Strozzi, professor of Greek; Bartolomeo Strada, professor of philosophy; and Piero Angeli of Barga, professor of Latin literature.[139]

At Christmas 1551 arrived the good news that the formalities had been completed for appointing Giovio's nephew Giulio coadjutor for Nocera with right of succession. The "magra sposa," as Giovio called his see, was to have a new bridegroom from the Giovian *gens*. Giovio's exploratory moves, renewed with the accession of Julius III, to have Alessandro succeed him do not seem to have prospered, and in the spring of 1551 he again broached the matter, this time with Giulio as his candidate.[140] With the advocacy of cardinals Medici and Pio the pope gave his assent, and by Christmas the appointment was completed with the additional grace Giovio requested of reduced fees.[141] Conscious, doubtless, that in this new day such graces were less easily obtained, Giovio wrote spontaneously of his gratitude to his old friend Pio, declaring that this favor meant as much to him as the red hat and absolving him from the obligation of continuing to press for the pension.[142] Thanking the pope, however, he could not restrain from a little irony. On November 20 his friends Pietro Bertano and Girolamo Dandino had both received the hat.

Turning theologian, he averred that the grace of the coadjutorship had filled up his little vessel just as surely as the recent promotions to cardinal had filled up the greater vessels deemed worthy of that honor. Old and lame as he was, the pension still rankled and the purple still glistened.[143] And if Pio was absolved of the obligation to press for the pension, it was quite otherwise for Farnese, whom Giovio persisted in reminding of his grandfather's promise.[144]

His other advocate for the coadjutorship, Gianangelo de' Medici, Giovio had thanked in person when he came through Tuscany on his return from Emilia, where he had been serving as legate to the papal army commanded by his brother the marquis. On January 18, 1552, Giovio reported to Angleria that three cardinals had left Pisa the previous morning—Farnese for Florence, Medici for Rome, and Gaddi for the Elysian Fields. "An old and lovable friend," he added sadly, "*in minore et in maiore fortuna.*"[145] Angleria's letter, which Giovio had read "collegially" with Farnese and Medici, had contained the shocking news of the murder of Cardinal Martinuzzi, archbishop of Nagyvárad (Grosswardein) and "a munificent patron" of Giovio's (he had given him at least one horse). In Rome the news had caused an enormous stir, and it left the group at Pisa "quasi astratti [almost stupefied]."[146]

Starting as a simple Paulite friar, Fra Giorgio, as he was usually known, had risen to be the major force in Christian Hungary. On being struck, he had cried, "Why this to me, Lord?" and Giovio wondered the same. Perhaps, he speculated, it was God's punishment for the friar's excessive devotion to John Zápolya's widow and infant son. He had gone to such lengths to defend them against Ferdinand's attempts to enforce the treaty of Nagyvárad (Grosswardein) that he had given Buda to the Turks, opening the way for the eventual fall of Esztergom, Székesfehérvar (Alba Regia), Zoclos, and Valpo.[147] Indeed, the prevalent opinion, which Giovio did not share, was that Ferdinand had taken more account of old scores than of recent services. Recently, Ferdinand had been so pleased by Fra Giorgio's success in bringing Zápolya's widow, Isabella, to honor the previously neglected treaty of Nagyvárad (which provided for the reversion of Christian Hungary to Ferdinand upon Zápolya's death) that he had asked Julius III to make the friar a cardinal.

In September 1551 Giovio had written to congratulate Giambattista Castaldo, who had acted for Ferdinand in the negotiations, and who had been cooperating with Fra Giorgio in the siege of Lipova. In his congratulations, Giovio had lauded the new cardinal as the person who had saved what was left of Christian Hungary from the Turks, and in early October he had again expressed his satisfaction with the general accord.[148] On learning of the murder, the historian's instinct was to fear that Ferdinand and Castaldo might have suspected him of double-dealing with the Turks in hopes of becoming the ruler of Christian Hungary. That such might have been the case Giovio thought hard to believe, even allowing for the excessive ambition that seemed to characterize "friars exited from the refectory" (an allusion, no doubt, to Luther), but it might have appeared otherwise to a simple soldier. "Time always stays buried a while," Giovio cautioned, "before it clarifies itself to men." Meanwhile, in Martinuzzi's murder he saw the tyranny of Fortune, raising men from the abyss only to cast them down as a warning to pride.

Giovio's guess regarding the motives for the murder turned out to be correct. In response to the historian's discreet inquiry and "the letter I seem to see in your mind," Castaldo attempted to explain and justify the deed, which had been committed by his subordinates. Apparently he had indeed come to feel that Martinuzzi was double-dealing with the Turks, planning a "Sicilian Vespers" to gain control of the kingdom for himself. Castaldo's letter had the ring of sincerity. A military man and newcomer to the complexities of life in Hungary, the war-weary old soldier found it difficult to understand the elaborate mechanisms the friar was obliged to use in keeping the Turks at bay without actually enraging them, and Fra Giorgio's release of the Turkish commander from the besieged fort of Lipova apparently confirmed Castaldo in all his worst thoughts.[149] His letter to Giovio ended dramatically with a description of his small, unpaid force surrounded at Sebeş and the enemy's trumpets and drums sounding in his ears. But despite the pope's refusal to exonerate him, he would go to battle, he said, not as Aeneas—*Dii me terrent, et Iuppiter hostis*—but determined to make his enemy's victory, if victory it must be, as costly as possible. So closed another stark chapter in the dismal history of sixteenth-century Hungary. Despite Castaldo's desperate defenses of Nagyvárad, Székesfehérvar (Alba Regia), and Temesvár, Transylvania was completely lost to the Turks. Once again Giovio's analysis had reflected the astuteness of his instincts, as well as his superior grasp of the complex situation on Europe's frontiers.

A second shock of the winter of 1552 was the condemnation of Lodovico Domenichi by the Inquisition for secretly publishing a heretical book. Thanks to the atmosphere of comparative intellectual freedom that Cosimo's chief ministers had encouraged him to allow, religious discussion among some Florentine citizens and visiting intellectuals entered dangerous areas of heterodoxy. Although supportive of Pietro Carnesecchi in his 1546 trial for heresy, Cosimo had permitted the appointment in 1551 of three commissioners by the Roman Inquisition as a gesture of reconciliation with Julius III. The first fruits of their visitation was the auto-da-fé of December 1551, in the piazza della Signoria, consisting of the public humiliation and repentance of twenty-two citizens, chief among them the former Florentine ambassador to France and sometime secretary of the Florentine Academy, Bartolomeo Panciatichi.[150]

Domenichi was found to have translated and anonymously published Calvin's letter to the Nicodemites, *Excuse de Jean Calvin à Messieurs les Nicodémites* (1544), rebuking timid Protestants for their dissimulation and urging them to declare themselves openly.[151] He was probably "fingered" by Doni, who had denounced him to the Inquisition after a quarrel in 1548.[152] Condemned on February 26 to ten years' imprisonment, he was led on March 15 to the fortress of Pisa and immured in the keep.[153] Almost immediately, friends began pressing for alleviation of the sentence. Renée of France, duchess of Ferrara and a Calvinist sympathizer, wrote to Cosimo as early as March 20 to urge his release.[154] Other appeals probably came from the milieu of Torrentino because of Domenichi's importance in translating Giovio's works. On May 19 the duke ordered his transfer from Pisa to a cell in the Florentine prison, Le Stinche, with light so that he could write. In August his sentence was commuted to seclusion for a year in the convent of Santa Maria Novella, but with freedom during the day to leave the convent to work on the translations. In January 1553 he was even granted permission to be absent at night to expedite publication of the vernacular edition of the *Histories.*[155]

Was Giovio among those who interceded with the duke? We do not know. He disliked heretics, but he detested inquisitors and may have intervened while in Como to protect some canons of the cathedral from the inquisitor.[156] Certainly he would have had no sympathy with Domenichi's interest in Calvin. Despite the fact that many of his friends and associates had entertained ideas later declared heretical, no evidence indicates that Giovio himself did so.[157] Quite simply, he lacked the interest in theology to ponder ideas such as predestination or justification by faith beyond what he needed to follow the debates at Trent. As a careerist, his loyalty was to the institution of the Church. Just in November 1551, he had expressed to Angleria his unqualified approval of proceeding against heretics, not only with the pain of perpetual imprisonment but with the stake for those who had come to disbelieve in Purgatory or the afterlife—of which, he said, there were many among the "great and very great, if one may judge by their works."[158]

In January 1552 Giovio interrupted his labor on the books dealing with Florentine history to take in hand the revision of book 34, containing the Tunis crusade.[159] To supplement and perhaps to balance the commentary of d'Avila, he resorted to the unusual expedient of having Moorish galley slaves, veterans of the fighting, brought to him for interrogation. "You can tell Cardinal Mendoza," he told Angleria, "that I often find my room full of Moors from the galleys here—giants of men—for better information."[160] Having heard from Angleria that the first volume of the *Histories* had pleased the cardinal, Giovio sent him the revised book 34, describing it as "very accurately composed," with "singular praise of the emperor and the Spanish name."[161]

Francisco de Mendoza y Bobadilla, cardinal bishop of Coria, was cousin to the imperial ambassador to Rome, the scholarly Diego Hurtado de Mendoza. It was partly at his urging that Giovio had resurrected the biography of Gonzalo de Córdoba after its loss in the sack of Rome. So far as can be determined, he was the only person who received a copy of the revised book. Despite Cosimo's promises to the emperor, searches of the archives of Florence and Simancas have uncovered no evidence of a copy's having been sent to the imperial court. There is no reason to believe that Mendoza was deputed by the imperial court to act as censor, nor is there any trace in the correspondence with Rome of his having reported his apparently favorable opinion. In all probability Giovio was covering himself by submitting his manuscript to a friendly Spanish authority. He certainly gave the cardinal no time to forward the manuscript to the court. Less than a month after sending it, he was soliciting its return.[162]

Did Giovio incorporate the changes demanded by the imperial court? Although the original version of book 34 no longer exists, a comparison of the book as published with the commentary of d'Avila suggests that Giovio changed some details here and there but stuck to his earlier version in important matters. He magnified Caesar's role somewhat, but without whitewashing, and he left as they were some of the details to which the imperial court had taken strenuous exception. Given his admiration for Charles V's Tunis crusade, even his original version must have been highly laudatory. He genuinely believed that he had done well by the emperor, but he was adamant that liberal studies, as the name implied, were free and far removed from "servile and vituperous adulation," and that precisely because of this fact they alone had the power "to give to noble virtue a brilliant and eternal splendor."[163] Avila's commentary justified Giovio's lament that "in these tempestuous times, to have praised sparingly is tantamount to having spoken ill."[164] Fortified, however, by Cosimo's advice that at his age he should fear no one but write for posterity, the historian pressed forward to complete the *Histories* and to gain the lauds he still hoped for from his own and distant ages.

In February Giovio took up the siege of Florence, expecting to complete his account by the end of March. In the interest of speed he ceased receiving visitors, with the result that, despite a touch of catarrh which brought on a little gout, he found he had done two months' work in a fortnight.[165] The intensity of his labors can be gauged from the fact that the siege absorbed a good part of book 28 and almost all of book 29. Work on the *Histories* was not so preemptive, however, as to preclude attention to pressing concerns such as his French and Spanish pensions and the still-hoped-for pension on Como. Another preoccupation, now more timely than ever, was the renewal of papal permission to make a will.[166]

Letters from Angleria in Rome brought news of events in the greater theater of Europe and the recrudescent Hapsburg-Valois conflict. As Giovio had foreseen, the appearance of Protestant delegates at the re-opened Council of Trent during the fall of 1551 and winter of 1552 made no contribution to the reunification of Christendom.[167] In mid-March 1552 he learned from Angleria of the league of Protestant princes with France secretly put together by the treacherous Maurice of Saxony. He was not at all surprised at Henry II's renewed belligerence, and his main concern was that it was bound to provoke more visitations by the Turk.[168] When the forces of the new league seized Augsburg on April 4, the pope decided the time had come to suspend the sessions at Trent. Under these new circumstances Julius III could expect little support from the emperor for the Parma war, and during the same consistory at which it was decided to suspend the council it was also resolved to come to terms with Ottavio Farnese and his ally, Henry II.

As "a good ecclesiastic and Italian" Giovio was gratified by the prospect of peace and an end to what he had seen as a "horrible peril for the bark of Peter," loss of face in Italy if the pope did not discipline his rebellious vassal but the threat of a French schism if he did.[169] No clone of Julius II, Julius III had entered the Parma war mainly under pressure from Charles V and in doing so had become an unwitting pawn between the two monarchs. He lacked a strong personality to match his imposing presence. Giovio feared for the future of the Roman court, "sustainer of so many excellent talents," and for "poor Italy," for which the papacy "conserved the honor of the ancient empire."[170] An armistice between Ottavio and the pope was signed on April 29, and Giovio hoped the emperor would acquiesce.[171] Urged by Ferrante Gonzaga, Charles V did give his reluctant assent on May 10.

The emperor's own position with respect to the army of the French and Protestant league had continued to worsen. He had fallen back to the region of Innsbruck, and when Maurice marched south and seized the city on May 23, the victor of Mühlberg was forced to flee over the Brenner Pass all the way to Villach, a city through which Giovio had seen him pass in triumph some twenty years earlier on the return from the crusade of 1532. The ensuing convention of Passau guaranteed freedom of worship to the adherents of the Augsburg confession until the next diet. Held in Augsburg in 1555, the diet accepted the fact of the Reformation in Germany. Charles V's German policy lay in ruins.

By the end of March, as he announced to the duke, Giovio had finished his narration of the war of Florence (books 28 and 29). He had left out "no particular that seemed honorable and worthy of memory," justifying his somewhat extended treatment with precedents from ancient historians, including Polybius. He went on to say that his account could have been briefer and less fatiguing to write had he not gone to such pains to obtain "true information from public writings and from so many reports of living persons."[172] Taken in context, the phrase "public writings [scritture publiche]" would seem to indicate official documents, suggesting that Cosimo's officials had made available some of the archives of the republic, perhaps the correspondence or deliberations of the Signory, or the records of the Dieci di Balìa, who conducted the war. In any event, Giovio's use of documents was probably limited, for in seeking information from Segni he said he was so well-informed he needed clarification only on certain particulars. He thought his eyewitness account so authoritative it would serve as a basis for anyone subsequently writing of the siege in Tuscan—a prediction fulfilled—and he also felt it would satisfy both victors and vanquished—an expectation sadly disappointed.[173]

Giovio had good material to work with. By any standard the resistance of Florence to the army of Charles V was a magnificent effort. From the initial destruction of the suburbs to the final march of Francesco Ferrucci, it was a tale of heroic will against invincible odds, and so it appeared to Giovio—"the most stupendous thing that was ever read in any author," exceeding anything in Greek or Roman history.[174] "Marzocco [the lion-emblem of the Florentine republic] ought to be very content with me," he declared, "because it is evident that I have not had a glimmer of rancor [amarezza], but a ready propensity for praising them for those virtues that merited it."[175] His account of the siege, Giovio ventured to predict, would be "ever-glorious to the Tuscan name" and please both the living and posterity.[176]

The outcome was otherwise. From start to finish Giovio's account infuriated partisans of the libertas Florentiae, in his own and later ages. Rancor he certainly did not show, but his unbounded admiration for the republic's valor was insufficient to win from him the least sympathy for its cause. If, indeed, the siege was "the most stupendous thing ever read in any author," he made clear that was because of "the constancy and pertinacity of those who under the pretext of liberty wished to defend their state, such as it was, and the perseverance of those who opposed them."[177] His earlier attitude toward the opponents of the Medici did mollify somewhat; he was far more hostile to Francesco Ferrucci in his

1530 letter describing the siege than in the *Histories*. But as in 1530, so even more in 1552, Giovio felt that Florentine "liberty" was deleterious both to the city itself and to Italy at large.

From the opening of book 25, which depicted the Florentines as rejoicing in the calamity of Rome, Giovio betrayed his hostile perspective. His interesting digression on the nature of the Florentines suggests that he might have had in mind the description of the Athenians by the Corinthians in book one of Thucydides (1.70), as well as some of his conversations in the Rucellai gardens. The nature of the Florentines was such, he explained, that their loyalty could not be won by any benefit, no matter how great, and their jealousy was such that they could not suffer the preeminence of any other citizen in dignity, goods, or fortune, but being full of ambition, pride, and envy, all wanted to hold power and advance their own interests. Driven by insatiable cupidity, they found their honor and reputation in gain, even dishonest gain, and yet—to the marvel of everyone—there was no sumptuousness to their lifestyle, but all lived simply after the manner of the ancient Greeks, whose descendants they were. The one exception to the simplicity of their lifestyle was their building, which they did magnificently. Because of their vices they had been torn by the most grievous civil discords for three hundred years, often resulting in the death and exile of some of the noblest citizens and the destruction of some of the finest palaces. In desperation they had turned at times to accepting the yoke of a vile artisan or foreign tyrant. To this race the Medici had for a hundred years brought peace, order, and prosperity. Forgetting all rancor, Pope Leo X and after him Pope Clement VII had opened to them the riches of the Church and the lucrative government of cities and provinces, so that to the rest of Italy it seemed as if the patrimony of Peter had been skimmed by the Florentines. And yet, absent any capacity for gratitude, the minute the pope was overwhelmed with a tragedy that drew tears of pity even from foreigners, the Florentines took the occasion of revealing the full extent of their perfidy and malignity.[178]

For Giovio the last republic was a constant drift toward the left, with "wise citizens" and "good men" overwhelmed by the crowd of "low citizens," people "born to disturb the peace and repose of the republic." As in the times of Soderini, this rabble, "less foolish than bestial," thought the only good citizen was an enemy of the Medici. Carducci, coming from a family that was "old rather than noble," a hater of the pope whose "inquiet and precipitous nature" prompted him to attempt revolution by stirring up the young, exclaimed "like a rabid madman" that Florence would never be at peace until she was rid of Medici sympathizers and the house of the Medici ruined to its very foundations.

The first *gonfaloniere*, Niccolò Capponi, Giovio portrayed as a good and moderate man with the true interests of the city at heart, a statesman who fell victim to the forces of ignorance and malice represented by Carducci and his party. Capponi's speech after his fall, in which he defended himself for having treated privately with the pope, was reported in full by Giovio from eyewitness accounts as a classic plea for moderation. Public concord made a city invincible, Capponi argued, not arms or money. After his disappearance, Giovio commented, practically appropriating the words of Thucydides on Corcyra, the republic lost any semblance of humanity, reason, or justice, their place taken by insolence, cruel pride, and force—all now deemed virtues by the plebs, "maddened by a blind fury, and especially the seditious young."[179]

How Giovio could think that such an account, however accurate its particulars, would "satisfy Marzocco" is difficult to comprehend. His respect for the valor and determination of the republic seemingly never led him to reflect that these qualities, tested in the extreme by a long siege, might have had deeper roots than a mere love of sedition. Understandably, as a Medici partisan, he saw the darker side of the last Florentine republic and its excesses. During the nineteenth century, when the latter had been forgotten and the resistance of Florence had become a symbol of indigenous Italian nationalism, Giovio's account brought him into even worse odor. Ironically, he was, if anything, a stronger Italian nationalist than the Florentine republicans, with a vision less parochial than theirs. Still more ironically, he was discredited as a historian because of his outlook on the republic, while Guicciardini, who made a fortune in the service of the Medici and subsequently helped destroy the last remnants of the republic, was accounted an authentic Italian.[180]

Although hostile, Giovio's account serves as a corrective to a historiographical tradition which erred in the opposite direction by eulogizing the republic and its leaders as martyrs of nationalism and liberty. Giovio's pages remind us that the republican leaders of 1527–1530 were, in reality, more like sixteenth-century Jacobins. In almost no time they had irremediably alienated the optimates, who had initially been sympathetic and whose wisdom and political connections were sorely needed if the republic were to have any staying power, convincing them instead that their only common ground lay with the Medici. As contemporary scholarship continues to redress the romanticism of nineteenth and early twentieth-century Florentine historiography, Giovio's viewpoint becomes more comprehensible than it was to earlier generations.[181]

Giovio's dedication of volume two of the *Histories* to Cosimo bore the date, Pisa, May 1, 1552. Eager as he was to see printing of the remaining parts begin, he had nonetheless tarried in Pisa while the duke was visiting.[182] His journey to Florence was a slow one because of his litter and included a stop at Pescia to acquire some information through Antonio

Buonagrazia and his French contacts, which he needed to finish book 35, the only one still awaiting completion.[183] On returning to Florence on the 11th, Giovio found that instead of rooms in the Medici palace, the duke had reserved him a house near the palazzo della Signoria, in the via de' Cimatori.[184] Printing started on or about May 30 and, in a race with time, Giovio kept pressing Buonagrazia to provide the requisite details on the siege of Peronne and other episodes of the Provence campaign.[185] By September 10 the printing of volume two was complete, and by the end of the month he was sending copies to his patrons.[186]

Once the *Histories* were off the press, Giovio had planned to betake himself to Como.[187] His nephew and now coadjutor, Giulio, had left Pisa for Como in January, and he was looking forward to joining him there to further various projects for his properties and the museum.[188] He also had plans to renounce a canonry in favor of his natural great nephew, Marzio. For all of Benedetto's five sons he had found positions, four in the Church and one in the Milanese administration. Now there were six great-nephews needing advancement, including the son of his other brother, Giampietro. Not only this, but his great-niece Isabella, his nephew Ottavio's second illegitimate child, was getting married and needed a dowry.[189] On August 4 he made his final will, distributing his riches among his nephews, great-nephews and nieces, and leaving Giulio as trustee of the museum, which was established as a perpetual trust.[190]

Come autumn, however, the duke persuaded Giovio not to risk his health in the "snowy" Como winter but to spend another winter at Pisa and return to Como in the spring.[191] Cardinal Farnese, his exile ended in June after the papal armistice with Ottavio, had been urging a return to Rome, but this was quite out of the question. "You should see my legs," Giovio said.[192] Instead, he sent the cardinal a copy of volume two of the *Histories* for reading on his forthcoming trip to France, along with a plea to work for payment of the pension on Toul, still in arrears.

The Italian peninsula was continuing to feel the disruptive influence of hostilities between Henry II and Charles V. Hardly had the Parma war been ended than Siena revolted, evicting the imperial garrison on July 27 and placing itself under the protection of Henry II. On September 30 an embassy to France led by Claudio Tolomei passed through Florence and called en bloc on Giovio.[193] Giovio was not a close friend of the energetic and restless Tolomei, but they had been colleagues since the days of Ippolito de' Medici. It may have been through his association with Tolomei that Giovio had been made an honorary member of the Sienese academy of the Intronati, although he could have been inducted during any one of many visits to the city.[194] If the embassy was seeking his support for Siena's new allegiance, Giovio maintained a discreet silence. Earlier in the month he had observed that the establishment of an imperial enclave at Orbetello in the Maremma, which the Sienese, "like mad-men," had not prevented, would keep southern Tuscany "in the shad-ows." One of the last bastions of Italian communal liberty was about to fall.[195]

All through late September and October, Giovio was busy sending out copies of volume two to various patrons. One he even sent to Capan Bey, grand dragoman of Suleiman the Magnificent, in the hopes of having it translated for the sultan. "Glory being the true food of great lords," he said, he had understood that the sultan took delight "in knowing that his honorable victories and deeds were celebrated throughout the world."[196] Then he sat back to await the responses. In particular he hoped that the pope would "pay the debt for the living and the dead celebrated by me."[197] When forwarding a copy of Domenichi's transla-tion of book 38 to Cosimo, he also ventured the hope that the duke would intervene with the executors of the recently deceased bishop of Forlì to have him paid the arrears of the constantly delayed pension.[198]

Urged by Cosimo, Giovio contemplated filling in the missing portions of the first two volumes and even writing a third. In his last letter to Pio, written on December 3, he congratulated himself on having had the wis-dom to flee Rome in time to complete the second volume, citing the famous line from the *Aeneid* which had sounded to Savonarola like a trumpet, rousing him to seek holy orders, and which, in a more practical vein, had induced Luigi Guicciardini to flee Florence in 1529: *Heu fuge crudeles terras, fuge litus avarum*. Now, Giovio said, he was looking for-ward to a third volume, "for which I have an infinite tickling in the pen."[199] First, however, he wanted to await the outcome of the current war, as he knew that the emperor was marching on Metz, which Henry II had seized in May along with Toul and Verdun. The siege was unsuc-cessful, but Giovio was not destined to learn the outcome.

With the onset of November's chill, the historian's health deterio-rated. On the 12th he wrote to Luca Contile, asking him to beg from his former lady, Isabella of Capua, wife of Ferrante Gonzaga, a box of the candied quince and peaches she received from Naples, whose "celestial vapors" he thought would be better for his weakened head than the fresh eggs, chicken *al pesto*, and broths on which he was currently subsisting. He feared the increasing weakness that was returning him to infancy.[200] To his old friend Annibale Raimondi he confessed sensing the end was near. "May it please God that we see each other again in this world, because to tell the truth, my dear Messer Annibale, I am feeling very battered and for some months now I have not been able to cheer myself, beyond which I sleep very heavily at night and I almost always dream some very strange dreams which frighten me, not only when I am asleep but even when I am awake." The duchess had been "an angel of Paradise" and had tried along with her "most divine consort" to cheer him, telling him it was just a fit of melancholic humor, but there was no concealing that he had at his "backside a flock of 'ties' that sing all night," and that, in fact, it was necessary "to resolve to make this voyage in good spirits, since one cannot avoid making it." He took satisfaction in having arranged all his affairs, with Giulio as coadjutor, and he wished only for ten months or a year in order to finish the missing books, a good part of which he had composed not because he really wanted to but because he felt he could not fail "this my great patron who has strictly commanded it." Then he would gladly sing *Nunc dimittis servum tuum, Domine.*[201]

One thing greatly troubled Giovio in his last days, and he had written Raimondi in an effort to rectify it. He had found that in narrating the siege of Chieri in book 38 he had maligned a Romagnol knight named Azzale, a captain in the service of France, through basing himself on the testimony of two foot soldiers who, he had recently ascertained, bore the captain a grudge that they had artfully managed to conceal when furnishing him details of the siege. He had promised to make amends in the next volume of the *Histories* and meanwhile he begged Raimondi to circulate his letter, thus removing "the great spot this has made on me, body and soul."[202] Giovio's mortification over this mistake and his attempts to correct it even as his life was ebbing were perhaps the most convincing testimony to the sincerity of his efforts to write accurate history. "The sacrosanct history," as he often termed it, was indeed a sacred trust.[203]

The final letters from Giovio's pen were dated December 3. Eight days later, on the night of December 11–12, he had a brief attack of colic, and before the night was out he had breathed his last. His nephew and successor, Giulio, was in Como, but his great-nephew, Paolo the Young, "the Archpriest," was with him at the end.[204] When the news was brought, Cosimo ordered Riccio to prepare the exequies in a manner suitable for a bishop and "persona molto grata" to himself, humanely directing the steward to comfort the archpriest and other members of the household "to bear in peace God's pleasure and not to worry about anything, indeed to trust completely that we will take them under our protection and will demonstrate on every occasion our gratitude with those favors that will be necessary."[205] On the following day, December 13, the funeral was celebrated in San Lorenzo with "rich exequies" attended by Riccio, Torelli, the court, and "a great throng of people."[206]

Staging the funeral ceremonies in San Lorenzo was a mark of special favor, but Cosimo also directed that Giovio should be buried there, in the church normally reserved for the Medici family. The duke may have been contemplating the creation of a pantheon analogous to the Malatesta Tempietto at Rimini. In 1546 he had sought from Rome the body of Bembo, but if such had been his intent, he ceased to pursue it, and the gesture to Giovio remained a rare tribute to a "rare man."[207] Although he expected to die in Como, Giovio had directed that he be interred wherever he succumbed, in a marble tomb for which he had imitated the lawyer of Parma to the extent of providing an epitaph and a design, but these could not be found at the time owing to the sealing of his house by the papal commissary.[208] His body lay in a provisional sepulcher until 1574, when the existing monument was completed and installed in a niche in the cloister near the stairs leading to the Laurentian Library.[209]

The statue commissioned by Giovio's heirs from Francesco da San Gallo resembles the splendid portrait medallion of 1552 but lacks its vital energy.[210] The bearded face wears a pained expression matched by the tumbled confusion of the episcopal robes. One of the huge hands, enlarged perhaps by gout, rests on a volume of the *Histories*, but the historian seems unlikely to stir himself to read a passage or sustain a point. His weariness is unrelieved by satisfaction in achievement or by hope of repose. There is none of the historian's confident expectation of life among future ages. It is not a fitting monument.

For sixty years or so the museum stood on Lake Como as a memorial to its creator, but despite the perpetual trust established by Giovio's will it was eventually sold by his great-great nephews, passing thereafter in a semiruinous state to a nephew of his sometime secretaries, Marco and Tolomeo Gallio, who tore it down to build the present villa Gallia.[211] Henceforth, Giovio's memorial would be his works, which he had always predicted would outlast monuments of bronze or marble.

Ad Sempiternam Vitam

Quando in hac vita, quam natura incertis brevis aevi angustiis
humano generi praescripsit, nihil beatius esse potest quam nominis famam, immortalibus invicti animi monumentis, ad non in-
certam spem sempiternae laudis extendisse.

—Giovio, preface to the Histories

For in this life, which nature has set for humans within the uncertain confines of a brief span, nothing can be more blessed than to
have extended the fame of one's name, through the immortal
monuments of an unconquered spirit, to encompass the certain
hope of eternal praise.

. . . und wenn Paolo Giovio mit all seiner Flüchtigkeit und ele-
ganten Willkür sich dennoch die Unsterblichkeit versprach, so ist
er dabei nicht ganz fehlgegangen.

—Jacob Burckhardt

. . . and if Paolo Giovio with all his superficiality and graceful
caprice promised himself immortality, his expectation has not
been altogether disappointed.

FROM THE MOMENT of publication, Giovio's *Histories* were in great demand. Four editions of the Latin text appeared in Italy and seven in
northern Europe, along with twelve editions of Domenichi's Italian
translation, four of a French translation, and one each of German and
Spanish versions.[1] A complete census has not been made of reprintings
and translations of the biographies and minor works, but there were no
fewer than thirty-two editions of the *Elogia*.[2] The best-known of the
biographies, the life of Leo X, served as the standard biography for two
and a half centuries. Even Giovio's harshest critics exploited his works,
and his explanatory structure became the general property of the age.

Unfortunately for Giovio's reputation, however, a persistent strain of
detraction, lasting well into this century, marred the reception of his
work and often obscured its real merits. The contemporary Florentine
historians were vitriolic. Giambattista Busini denounced Giovio as "a
scribbler, more lying than the French."[3] Donato Giannotti dismissed the
Histories "as something written for buffoonery," and Filippo Nerli found
them "distant from the truth."[4] Benedetto Varchi, who had composed

so many laudatory verses while Giovio was alive, compiled a list of "one hundred errors of Paolo Giovio," a repetitive and querulous catalogue of minor inaccuracies, particularly in regard to Florentine institutions.[5] In a pamphlet published at Lyons, Federico di Scipione degli Alberti castigated Giovio, not so much for errors of fact as for his Medicean sympathies, reworking the proem to Giovan Michele Bruto's *Florentine Histories* (1562) into a defense of the last Florentine republic based on ancient precedents.[6]

As Giovio had remarked, the historian of contemporary events writes "of the sport of fortune with envy always watching."[7] Although he considered publication during his lifetime and the lifetimes of his protagonists a sign of impartiality and good faith, the French continued to believe he was imperial in his sympathies, the imperialists French.[8] Gonzalo Jiminez de Quesada, a veteran of the battle of Ceresole d'Alba, was so offended by Giovio's presumed slights to Spanish honor that he spent the final years of his life countering every one of them in the fifty-five chapters of the *Antijovio*. The iconoclastic physician, Girolamo Cardano, cited a tradition that after reading Giovio's account of the battle of Pavia and its sympathetic treatment of Francis I, Charles V had complained, "Giovio has not described my victory but that of the king of France." Cardano himself thought that Giovio had equaled the historians of antiquity in vice and accused him of obscuring the career of Antonio de Leyva because he had not been bribed—this despite the fact that de Leyva appears in the *Histories* on over fifty occasions and is celebrated as one of the outstanding generals of the age.[9]

Notwithstanding the efforts of Giovio's numerous advocates, including Camillo Porzio, Giambattista Gelli, Francesco Franchi, Aonio Paleario, Carlo Passi, Tommaso Porcacchi, Vincenzo Cartari, Dionigi Atanagi, and Girolamo Ruscelli, hostile criticism persisted. Doubtless inadvertently, Domenichi damaged Giovio's credibility by including in his 1560 edition of the historian's correspondence several letters containing phrases that could be taken as evidence of venality, and others were produced from archives.[10] Bodin concluded that Giovio had been venal and roundly condemned the *Histories* in his *Methodus*: "Not that many things written by him were not truly and elegantly written, but he earned the reward of mendacity, so that even when he wrote true things he was regarded as suspect." What seemed to haunt the Frenchman most was the suspicion that Giovio had reaped a greater reward for telling lies than others for telling the truth.[11] Venality aside, Bodin preferred the archival scholarship of Guicciardini to the eyewitness methods of Giovio, and his aversion formed the basis for the overwhelmingly negative entry on Giovio in Bayle's *Dictionary*.[12]

Bayle also reported the judgments of Pierre de Brantôme, who called Giovio "a venomous pen," and Jacques-Auguste de Thou, Giovio's professed continuer, who nonetheless styled him "a venal inkwell." Both had been deeply offended, inter alia, by Giovio's treatment of Anne de Montmorency—admittedly a complex issue. Despite his admiration for Montmorency as a soldier and his own yearnings for peace between Francis I and Charles V, Giovio felt at the time that his minister was forcing Francis I to cede too much, and in the *Histories* he gave an account of Montmorency's fall which read as if he had obtained it straight from the constable's enemy, Madame d'Étampes. When Domenichi's edition of Giovio's correspondence appeared, critics lost no time in linking the offending passages in the *Histories* to the letter of 1535 in which the historian had facetiously threatened to denigrate Montmorency if his French pension were not paid.[13]

Along with the condemnations of Bodin, Brantôme, and de Thou, the *Dictionary* cited the influential judgments of Joseph Scaliger, G. J. Vossius, and Justus Lipsius. Scaliger, who also seemed to have been offended by the treatment of Montmorency, regarded Giovio as "extremely mendacious and inferior to Guicciardini." Vossius dismissed him as "venal," and Lipsius—agreeing for once with Scaliger—justified his pronouncement, "judicio ac fide ambiguus [untrustworthy in judgment and fidelity]," with Giovio's closeness to the Medici and del Vasto.[14] These and other critiques were diligently copied by Pope Blount into his *Censura celebrorum auctorum*, whose several editions in England and on the Continent further prejudiced Giovio's reputation.

The sneers of the seventeenth century were followed by the sermons of the late eighteenth and nineteenth centuries. Girolamo Tiraboschi thought Giovio capable of capricious inventions, and William Roscoe, after exploiting the *Vita Leonis X* for his own biography of Leo X, pompously excoriated Giovio for venality and moral obtuseness.[15] Francesco De Sanctis accepted the tradition of Giovio's venality, and Cesare Cantù went so far as to exclaim that the *Histories* not only lacked morality but perverted it.[16] Somewhat more gently, John Addington Symonds characterized Giovio as "a sort of sixteenth-century Horace Walpole."[17]

Despite the emergence in the nineteenth century of strong countervailing judgments from Ranke, Burckhardt, and Pastor, echoes of the negative tradition persisted into the twentieth. Eduard Fueter, offended by Giovio's boasting of his "golden pen," dismissed him as "a revolver journalist," and even Benedetto Croce, who prided himself on having "definitively removed every serious support for the legend of the venality of Giovio," hardly commended the *Histories* to serious historians by describing them as "a great collection of historical anecdotes."[18] Roberto Ridolfi revived the Florentine tradition with his epithet "the shameless Giovio," and, cruelest of all, in Giovio's own *patria*, where Counter-Reformation standards were retroactively applied, Felice Scolari challenged the wisdom in naming the Liceo Scientifico Paolo Giovio.[19]

The rehabilitation of Giovio's reputation began in the nineteenth century with Leopold von Ranke, who used him extensively in conjunction with archival sources and who found him well-informed and independent in judgment.[20] Ludwig von Pastor agreed that Giovio had told his patrons "bitter truths."[21] In researching the battle of Gavinana, Edoardo Alvisi found Giovio "much more reliable than others believe."[22] Federico Chabod, who used Giovio extensively for his history of Milan in the epoch of Charles V, found him informed and accurate as well as a source for period style and values.[23] Michele Lupo-Gentile, continuing investigations begun by Giuseppe Sanesi, discovered that, even while reviling Giovio, the Florentine historians had mined his *Histories* for their coverage of peninsular events.[24] Going one step further, Carlo Dionisotti has reaffirmed the basic accuracy of Giovio's whole account of the events of 1527–1530.[25]

In concert with Chabod and Dionisotti, Beatrice Reynolds stressed the exaggeration of Giovio's faults by his Florentine and French critics.[26] Others have ascertained that he stoutly resisted political pressures to change his narrative from what he believed was the truth. Franca Bevilacqua Caldari has demonstrated that Giovio refused to yield to pressure from du Bellay and the cardinal of Lorraine to alter his account of the fall of Montmorency and, in another context, I have sought to show that in revising his account of the Tunis crusade he declined to accommodate Charles V.[27] While adhering to Croce's view that Giovio lacked political depth, Emanuella Scarano Lugnani has followed Croce and Chabod in stressing his narrative gifts, the universal nature of his data gathering, and his provision of a "whole series of episodes and information not to be found in other contemporary historians."[28]

Most recently, Eric Cochrane provided a balanced assessment of Giovio's strengths and weaknesses as a historian, emphasizing his reliance on the testimony of eyewitnesses, the vast draught of his net of causal relationships, and his uniqueness among his contemporaries in undertaking to write universal history. The greatest obstacle to a favorable reception of Giovio's work, Cochrane suggested, lay "in the confusion inherent in humanist historiography between the historian's role as recorder of facts and his role as the bestower of fame," a confusion that Giovio admittedly did little to allay.[29]

In short, as Traiano Boccalini affirmed in the early seventeenth and Carlo Dionisotti in the late twentieth century, the tradition of Giovio the mendacious was more often the product of hearsay than of familiarity with the substance of his work.[30] Giovio had an almost religious respect for his calling as a historian, and he detested "adulation."[31] More than many humanist historians, he honored the Ciceronian injunction to tell not only the truth but the whole truth.[32] Despite the difficulties of writing contemporary history while seeking support from its chief protagonists, he produced a balanced, objective, and penetrating history of his age.

Reputation apart, Giovio's real nemesis has been Guicciardini. The incomparable brilliance of the *Storia d'Italia* has eclipsed the *Sui temporis historiarum libri*. Yet it was Giovio who first renewed in the sixteenth century the Greek tradition of contemporary history and the systematic use of eyewitness sources. If Bruni, the founder of humanist historiography, had revived the critical methods of Greek historians, particularly Polybius, Giovio applied them broadly and systematically to contemporary history. "For more than twenty years," he wrote in 1535, "I have been sweating to write history as cautiously, as clearly, and as faithfully as my weak talent allowed, and to fulfill with diligence the precepts of Lucian."[33]

Lucian, who urged Thucydides as the model for historians, identified the prerequisites for writing history as "political understanding and power of expression," qualities Giovio translated, when speaking in the Ischian dialogue of the historian's preparation, as "judgment and eloquence." For "judgment" he employed the Latin term *prudentia*, which to contemporaries connoted practical wisdom in conducting affairs— "political understanding"—as well as discrimination in weighing evidence.[34] Giovio's apparent debt to Thucydides was most evident in the structure of his narrative, particularly his juxtapositions, and in his use of eyewitness sources. He interviewed as many participants as he could, including common soldiers, and systematically compared accounts to discover "the real truth of events and plans."[35] While he used archival documents when necessary, he preferred the oral interview, which allowed him to probe one witness with information extracted from another. Even the redoubtable Guicciardini feared his technique.[36]

In the preface to his *Histories* Giovio also seemed to be advertising his compliance with the precepts of Polybius, the theorist as well as the exemplar of universal history, who advised the historian to compare and study the sources, scrutinize the topography, and gain the experience of participation in political life. "Having earned friendship and familiarity with the greatest kings and popes and the most distinguished generals," Giovio declared, perhaps thinking of Polybius in the field with Scipio Aemilianus,

we have learned from their mouths the things that we have transmitted in the faithful memorial of letters, distracted by neither fear nor favor. It has also aided marvelously to have followed my lords princes to war in the provinces, where I have seen camps, battle lines, battles, stormings of cities, fields of victory strewn with dead bodies, and stunning examples of each kind of military fortune.[37]

The one Polybian prerequisite that Giovio could not meet was political experience, a dimension lacking in his work, and he strayed from Greek methodology in emphasizing narrative over pragmatic analysis of causes, motives, and consequences—the element that Polybius and Thucydides thought distinguished history from mere entertainment.[38] While he helped advance the humanist tradition in method and scope, Giovio in fact succumbed to some of its most crippling limitations.

As the Ciceronian canon of historiography was interpreted by Pontano, Campano, Cortesi, Facio, and other humanists whose theories dominated the Roman academy when Giovio joined it, rhetoric was paramount, and a classical style had become the overriding imperative.[39] Roman tradition dictated content, making war the principal focus.[40] Speeches were considered a means of adding "texture," and topographical descriptions "variety." "Dignity" and "brevity" were basic canons, not to introduce ignoble or petty matters or weary the reader with burdensome considerations.[41] *Verba* had triumphed over *res*, a triumph secured by the imposition of Augustan models. The nascent historicism of Valla and Politian had been suppressed by the polemics of Facio and Cortesi and, to judge from Leo's X's aestheticism, Valla's affirmation of language as the key to historical truth had been weakened to a preoccupation with style as an end in itself.[42] For the humanist in court service, moreover, it had become all too easy to construe negative facts as *infra dignitatem* and produce history that evaded Cicero's challenge to tell not only the truth but all the truth.[43]

Giovio had come to Rome with an excellent model of a historian in his brother, a good critic who sought out documentary sources. From Vergerio the aspiring historian had learned the importance of methodical doubt, and in conversation with his colleague Cattaneo he evidently strengthened his grasp of Greek methodology. Yet when forced by the "fathers" of the Roman academy to follow Augustan models, Giovio circumscribed his methodological advances in eyewitness history and abridged his presentation of "the real truth of events and plans."[44] He forsook Tacitus, a historian of psychology and motive, and adopted Livy and Sallust, historians of epic conflict. He made military history his principal focus, not politics and diplomacy, and even though he declared on occasion that the literary aspect of history was less important than its substance, he nonetheless sacrificed the detailed analyses of motive so common in his letters to Augustan demands for "dignity," "brevity," and "a smooth and even-flowing style."[45]

Occasionally Giovio introduced, with apologies for contravening the laws of dignity and brevity, precisely the extended causal considerations favored by Thucydides, Polybius, and the modern reader. Normally, however, after finding "the real truth of events and plans" through collating eyewitness interviews, he conformed to the humanist tradition by dismantling his scaffold and excising the elements which account for the strength and fascination of Guicciardini's *Storia d'Italia* but also for its shuffling pace.[46] It is ironic that while Giovio's "huffing and puffing" to acquire an Augustan style gained him his reputation with his contemporaries at Rome, it cost him the interest of the future ages to which he looked with such longing hopes. A modern reader is unlikely to prize the reduction of sixteenth-century events to the language and mindset of Augustan Rome, nor can Domenichi's Italian translation supply a contemporaneity of expression lacking in the original.[47]

No thrall to the cult of antiquity, Guicciardini was far more autonomous than Giovio in accepting or rejecting components of the humanist tradition.[48] It was not so much in method that Guicciardini differed from the humanists as in objective. Bruni had practiced the critical comparison of sources sometimes cited as the dividing line between Guicciardini and humanist historiography, and Giovio had developed the eyewitness approach; but whereas Giovio was a historian of consequences, Guicciardini was a historian of motives and processes.[49] With his empirical reconstruction of intentions and aims from the moves and countermoves of diplomacy, Guicciardini not only restored the pragmatic Greek approach but carried it to new levels. It was not the need to know outcomes that drove him to archival documents, but the desire to reconstruct diplomacy and to unravel the twisted thread of motive through all the changes wrought by outcomes, expected and unexpected, until he reached protagonists' original intentions. For Guicciardini, history was a dynamic process in which individuals were altered by the very events they initiated.[50]

Giovio, on the other hand, by deferring to the Roman and humanist traditions, limited himself largely to outcomes and to the explanatory power of narrative. To some degree this stemmed from his plan for his work. His intention had always been to publish in his lifetime, to present his age with its own portrait, and in the sixteenth century a history so conceived required restraint in analyzing individuals and their motives. The affair of the Alciato letter was proof enough. With no impulse to publish, Guicciardini could write to suit himself. But in confining himself to narrative, Giovio was also following personal preference. Although an exceedingly astute and sought-after interpreter of the contemporary political scene, he lacked Machiavelli's speculative interest in political structure and Guicciardini's patient interest in the moves and countermoves of diplomacy. He was not by nature a theorist, and not having been a diplomat, he never had to construct a "working hypothesis" as to the intentions of his antagonist and revise it hour by hour and day by day. Giovio's chief weakness as a historian lay in his impatience with reflection and control.[51] The nuances of the Florentine constitution were of less interest to him than the temper of the individuals who worked it, the trammels of diplomacy less significant than their consequences.

Not that Giovio obscured motive, diplomacy, or cause: within the confines of the Roman tradition, he included as much explanation as he evidently felt "the dignity of history" would allow. His aperçus of character and reflections on human conduct indicate that, like Guicciardini, he was developing a systematic model of human nature against which to test his analyses of motive.[52] With his dramatic sense for the interplay of reason, rhetoric, and circumstance, he was especially apt to reconstruct the clash of personalities in council prior to battle and the fateful choice that swept the participants onto the field of destiny.[53] For the battles themselves he remains a major authority.[54] In military matters Giovio and Guicciardini should always be read in tandem. Guicciardini tended to reduce warfare to its political and tactical dimensions; Giovio afforded more concrete detail, along with the dramatic power of the Livian *descriptio*.

Nor should it be overlooked that Giovio was the first to reduce the manifold and complex events of his time to a meaningful narrative structure, a feat easily forgotten once it is achieved and absorbed.[55] Giovio's *Histories* began to exert their influence in the manuscript form in which they circulated in Rome and elsewhere for over thirty-five years. Guicciardini himself paid their author the compliment of transcribing extensive passages from manuscripts of the *Histories* and biographies. He made copies from book seven of a manuscript of Giovio's life of Pescara, which he followed closely in the *Storia d'Italia* when narrating the imprisonment of Francis I and the debate at the Spanish court in anticipation of the treaty of Madrid.[56] He followed a manuscript of Giovio's on the captivity and escape of the pope in 1527.[57] He made eighteen folio pages of summary from a manuscript of Giovio's life of Leo X which served him not only for particulars but for organizational sequence and narrative structure, especially in book thirteen.[58]

Risorgimento-era critics commonly excluded Giovio from the ranks of "engaged" historians, and yet he wrote history that was deeply engaged—morally in the humanist tradition, and politically in the crisis of Italian liberty. He cared no less than Guicciardini for "the safety and glory of Italy," and through long experience of disaster he, too, reached a deep understanding of the historical process and a tragic vision of liberty lost. Watching helplessly as the peninsula succumbed to servitude, he sought consolation and a meaning in the power of narrative that eluded him as an observer, although his more evident achievement was a deepening of the moral dimension of traditional humanist historiography and a despair that linked him to his more aloof colleague. In Giovio's *Sui temporis historiarum libri*, humanist historiography reached its most broadly political vision, offering a universal framework and a comprehensive theory of human agency for the wars of Italy.[59] Nonetheless, the problems of a new era were already pushing against the constraints of an obsolete historiographical tradition. With his intellectual power and his independence from Latin models, it was Guicciardini who transformed the old tradition into a new historiography.

Quintilian—the Roman rhetorician who had so deeply influenced the program of Quattrocento humanism—remarked that history was written "not for immediate effect or the instant necessities of forensic strife, but to record events for the benefit of posterity and to win glory for its author."[60] No historian took up the pen with more ardent hopes of everlasting glory than Paolo Giovio, and if at the end of his life he laid it down somewhat less sanguinely than he had taken it up, still he continued to hope for "some sweetness" in his present life and immortality in times to come.[61] In this, as in so many things, he reflected the values of the Quattrocento in which he had been educated and to which he clung despite the changing preoccupations of the Cinquecento. Indeed, by mid-century, the exordium to his *Histories*—a classic tribute to the cult of fame—must have seemed a bit old-fashioned.

If longing for fame and recognition was Giovio's mainspring, the concept of "true glory" was his pendulum. As historian and biographer he shared the traditional humanist presumption (deriving ultimately from the arguments of Cicero in his oration *Pro Archia*) of a close partnership between men of action and men of letters in the quest for fame and glory; and, like humanists from Petrarch to Castiglione, he assiduously promoted the notion that true glory consisted in virtuous deeds and their faithful relation to posterity in the memorials of good prose. It was not by "ambitious and vain titles," he reminded Vittoria Colonna, that her husband's glory had been gained, but by "illustrious deeds"; and it was not by marble sepulchers and equestrian bronzes that it would be preserved—memorials that had also been raised to "vile and timid men"—but by "the monuments of good and veracious letters."[62]

Nowhere did Giovio assert more clearly the value of fame as a stimulus to upright conduct than when castigating "the severe and yet pertinacious sect" of Stoics for their denial of pleasure (*laetitia*) in fame.[63] By "Stoics" he meant not only the sect of ancient philosophers but ascetic Christian theologians and reformers. He took up the anti-Augustinian battle of the Quattrocento humanists and converted their defense of *amor laudis* into a kind of guerrilla war against the encroachments of the Counter-Reformation. Like Machiavelli, he thought the desire for reputation induced socially useful conduct, and, like Petrarch and his Quattrocento followers, he believed the innate desire of human nature for fame and glory was the seed of nobility. Dispraise of glory meant the removal of a primary incentive to virtuous behavior. Over and over Giovio lauded glory as the wellspring of action, "the true food of great lords."[64]

From Vergerio, Giovio early absorbed the humanist conviction that education directed the impulse for fame along the path to "true" as opposed to "specious" glory, and that the most powerful educator was the example of great individuals. Rhetorically minded humanists like Vergerio were fond of spouting the hoary dictum of the first-century B.C.E. rhetorician and historian, Dionysius of Halicarnassus, that history was "philosophy teaching by example."[65] As the aspiring writer learned good style by imitating the great writers of the past, so the aspiring soldier and statesman learned right conduct by "salubrious emulation" of the great figures of history. To Giovio, the historian was both educator and partner of the soldier and statesman, charged on the one hand with furnishing examples of what to emulate and what to avoid in the quest for true glory, and on the other hand with validating the achievement of it. No wonder the role was a difficult one. The ambiguities were many, and never more so than when the historian was tempted to offer patrons the opportunity of "being among posterity," as Cicero had expressed it, by reading now what would be said of them "six hundred years hence."[66]

Giovio's response to the dilemma was to reinforce in his patrons, as best he could, the desire for "true" glory. Thus to Cosimo I he declared that the *Elogia* of statesmen and generals would comprise examples of "detestable lives," since he knew "with what grave and constant judgment, by zealously favoring letters and the fine arts, and by practicing exemplary piety and justice, you are striving toward the true honor, not of simulated but of illustrious fame, and by what principles of an incorrupt mind you are wont to detest and punish wickedness."[67] In his *Histories* and biographies, Giovio held fast to the distinction between fame or glory in the sense of notoriety, and "true glory." Thus he described the duke of Bourbon as eager for "new glory, even if gained by a turpid crime."[68] In all his brilliant achievements Giangaleazzo Visconti had seemingly acquired true glory. Yet his fame would always suffer from his murder of his uncle—except, Giovio ironically suggested, among those who regarded Caligula as a paradigm.[69]

But if history was a form of moral philosophy, what were Giovio's ethical standards? He had been, after all, a professor of moral philosophy. What did he think assured "true" rather than "specious" glory? Were the moral-rhetorical norms he inherited from the Quattrocento altered by the exigencies of the Cinquecento? Did the old educational formulae withstand the test of new times?

The code by which Giovio judged the protagonists of his *Histories*, biographies, and *Elogia* seems to have consisted in a loose mélange of Christian habits of mind compounded in part with medieval chivalric ideals such as nobility, courtliness, piety, liberality, loyalty, and valor, in part with the classical virtues of wisdom, justice, magnanimity (comprising fortitude), and temperance (the backbone of Cicero's moral philosophy as expounded in the *De officiis*, the basis of much Quattrocento moralizing).[70] Like Cicero and most Renaissance moral theorists, Giovio was strongly influenced by Aristotle's *Nicomachean Ethics*, which he enjoyed thanks to the "incomparable benefit" of Bruni's translation.[71] From Bruni, reinforced, probably, by Pontano, Giovio also derived his orientation to Aristotle, an orientation stripped of the theological superstructures of the generation of Salutati, let alone those of medieval commentators.[72] Giovio's approach to ethics was essentially rhetorical and secular. Among his manuscript notes, he left a sketch for a project illustrating the virtues and vices according to Aristotle by means of examples drawn from history, ancient and modern.[73] For humanists stressing the authority of individual experience, the Aristotelian mean and the person of practical wisdom were an eminently suitable basis for morality.[74]

Once at Rome, Giovio resumed the humanist mode of his early education and dismissed—like Petrarch—the Aristotelian dialectical tradition of his university education. To denote the scholastics, he adopted the recurrent humanist term "Sophists." He seems to have had little interest in Plato. Like Cicero, he accepted some Stoic teachings but rejected most, finding them, as did the generality of Renaissance humanists, rigid and uncongenial.[75] He shared the widespread aversion to the misunderstood school of Epicurus; he made no mention of Sextus Empiricus or Cicero's *Academica* although, like many sixteenth-century thinkers, he may have been closer to academic skepticism than he thought.[76] He was a syncretist to the extent that he found it convenient to assume a general compatibility between Christianity and pagan moral philosophy, but unlike the Quattrocento humanists, he had no wish to engage in polemics on the subject. For speculative moral-theological questions such as the freedom of the will, which reemerged in his own era in a new context, he had no concern whatever. He was not a systematic thinker. He interests the historian of ideas principally as he reveals the diffusion of various ideas among an educated elite.

To the historian of rhetoric, on the other hand, Giovio is of much greater interest, owing to the highly rhetorical nature of the *Elogia* and to the manner in which, in new contexts, he continued to affirm the values of the humanist rhetorical tradition. As a kind of sixteenth-century *Wehrmacht* descended on Italy, followed by religious reaction, Giovio's response was not to adapt to either, but to urge a congerie of ethical and cultural standards which he identified with the "rebirth of good letters" and the past preeminence of Italy.[77] Despite the evident failure of humanism as an educational program to mitigate the folly, greed, and "insane ambition" of princes, Giovio went on seeking to temper the extremisms of his own age with the equilibrated classical humanism of the Quattrocento, to the point of coming

> Between the pass and fell-incensed points
> Of mighty opposites.

In the *Histories*, as in the *Elogia*, Giovio was swift to expose unchivalrous conduct such as disloyalty, treachery, cowardice, faithlessness, or brutality, while eager to praise bravery and nobility, and solicitous to honor the memory of valorous soldiers whose careers were cut short before they could acquire the fame of great deeds. A helpless civilian caught in the calamity of Italy, he made a rhetorical weapon of his pen and tried to hold the military to basic standards by detracting from their glory when they failed in bravery or in honor, or when they turned to preying on the people it was their duty to defend. He vehemently denounced cowardice and cruelty, and he took particular satisfaction in rebuking captains and soldiers with examples of bravery and nobility in their Turkish foes—to the point that he acquired the reputation of being a Turkish sympathizer. He praised the temperance and justice of Suleiman the Magnificent, and with ironic satisfaction he recorded Ludovico Sforza's lament that the only person who had kept faith with him was Sultan Bajazet.[78] Giovio's open-mindedness did not extend to compromising the safety of Christendom, however, and alliances with the Turk were always repugnant to him on practical, as well as on chivalric and religious grounds. To Giovio the devotee of romance, the pinnacle of knightly glory was a crusade against the infidel, when "the arms foully and impiously used against us" would be turned on the Turk.[79] Setting out for Tunis, Hungary, or Algiers, rather than Flanders or France, Charles V is praised as seeking the "true glory" of the crusader.[80]

Giovio's notions of vice, derived from the norms of chivalry and humanism, displayed the unself-consciously secular nature of his outlook. Evil had little scope in his thinking. Vices were either behaviors opposed to the virtues of the feudal code, or excesses and deficiencies according to Aristotle's scheme. Louis XII of France Giovio found deficient in liberality and in the accustomed piety of the French kings, that is, in knightly virtues.[81] Others he reproached for failure to behave in the straightforward fashion of a knight.[82] In an Aristotelian mode, he chastised Ludovico Sforza and Louis XII, not for ambition—a form of the desire for glory and hence good—but for "immoderate ambition."[83] When he lamented that pride and contentiousness were the common defect of captains, Giovio was not thinking of the Seven Deadly Sins but signifying that an excess of the aggressiveness needed in a good captain became a vice.[84]

Like the life of ascetic renunciation, the abject humility prescribed by the Benedictine rule was not for Giovio a virtue, but a form of inhuman extremism. He quietly continued the anti-Augustinian polemics of Petrarch and Quattrocento humanists such as Bruni, Poggio, and Valla.[85] Pride, for Giovio, was not the Christian vice, the root of sin, but a superfluity of the Aristotelian sense of self-worth that characterized the noble man.[86] In analyzing the character of the French general Lautrec, Giovio observed that excessive pride undermined his success as a commander because he would never listen to advice.[87] Many brave officers, the historian lamented, went to their deaths in battles foolishly initiated because their pride would not allow them to risk the appearance of cowardice by opposing rash (as opposed to courageous) plans in council.[88]

What substituted for humility in Giovio's humanistic and aristocratic ethic was the Renaissance virtue of "humaneness," a virtue displayed by the great in behaving civilly to those beneath them, as when Francis I received the marquis of Pescara *humaniter*.[89] The popular Italian term *umanità* designated the gracious demeanor to those of lesser social station which Aristotle ascribed to the magnanimous man, although in the Renaissance it became celebrated as a major attribute and the center of a galaxy of related virtues.[90] Cardinal Pompeo Colonna, Giovio noted, thought it shameful to be outdone in humanity, displaying himself as gracious to those who approached him pleasantly and modestly but as scornful to those who attempted to overawe him with arrogance. The Aristotelian virtue of "great-spiritedness," interpreted by Cicero as *magnanimitas*, evoked Giovio's highest admiration. For Giovio, as for Castiglione, it was the essence of the prince, the virtue by which Leo X "flew to the heavens."[91] For having restored Milan to Francesco II Sforza, Giovio praised Charles V as exhibiting "greatness of mind" and as aspiring "not to a shadowy but to a true and lively glory," one that came "not through the assistance of Fortune but from the very font of his own virtue."[92]

Endorsing, like Cicero, selected aspects of Stoic teaching, Giovio lauded Stoic fortitude and a "virile spirit" in adversity, such as displayed by Andrea Gritti, Antonio Grimani, and Maria Pacheco.[93] By maintaining his "ever unconquered spirit" after his overwhelming defeat at Algiers, Charles V showed himself superior to Fortune.[94] Too good a historian to underestimate the power of chance in human affairs, Giovio insisted on the Stoic view (traditional throughout the Middle Ages, as well as in Quattrocento humanism) that virtue should triumph over both kinds of Fortune.[95]

Two characteristically Renaissance virtues completed Giovio's pantheon: *virtù* and magnificence. Giovio used the Latin term *virtus*, as Machiavelli the Italian *virtù*, in a sense closer to its root meaning of "manliness," and hence "strength," "vigor," "courage," or "excellence," rather than to the secondary Latin or primary modern meaning of "virtue" or "virtuousness"; thus the term is better rendered by the Renaissance Italian *virtù*, or the Chaucerian *vertu*. Giovio's primary sense of the word seems to have been force of intellect, character, or talent. The most poignant expression of admiration for *virtù* in his works was perhaps Francis I's exclamation after Pavia to the marquis of Pescara that he found himself compelled to love and respect the *virtù* even of his conqueror, "such is the force of outstanding virtue [*praestantissimae virtutis*], glowing with its own admirable radiance."[96] Significantly, with the restricted opportunities for political participation in Giovio's world, the principal spheres for the exhibition of *virtù* became not politics but arms, letters, and the arts.

For Giovio, *virtù* was an amalgam of celestial force and individual spirit, an individualizing factor in literature and life, the principle of excellence, achieved through a combination of talent and training. Although as a humanist he accepted imitation as a pedagogic strategy, like Machiavelli, he felt that mere imitation was the refuge of the mediocre.[97] Giovio's ideal world was an aristocracy of applied talent refined by manners. In *virtù* the man of letters could find common ground with the warrior, the humbly-born with the nobly-born. Here again, Giovio displayed his Quattrocento orientation, reflecting—despite the harsher realities of the Cinquecento—the theme of many a dialogue on the true nature of nobility. He clearly sympathized with seasoned captains when less experienced officers of higher social rank were promoted over them, as with the marquis del Vasto and the prince of Orange. He had no respect for those who failed to live up to high birth, or for those who were too lazy to employ their talents ("eunuchs," as he called them).[98] One of his most amiable qualities was his open-mindedness, which showed itself in his admiration for *virtù* wherever found, even in the Saracen enemy. His admiration enabled him to write laudatory biographies of enemies of Italian liberty such as Gonzalo de Córdoba. Under the inspiration of Vittoria Colonna he came to recognize the *virtù* of women and their potential for "virile" contributions to society, and in the Ischian dialogue he became an outspoken critic of restricting their access to education, social intercourse, and even politics.[99]

Magnificence, the other characteristic Renaissance virtue, was particularly important to the humanist, as it covered the patronage of arts and letters. For Aristotle, magnificence was part of magnanimity, but when combined with the legacy of medieval chivalry it evolved into a particularly Renaissance virtue, embodying the sense of style, expenditure, and

display necessary for great personages.[100] Its corresponding vice of deficiency was parsimony, as exhibited in Giovio's eyes by Clement VII and
Louis XII; its corresponding vice of excess was ostentation, as exempli-
fied by Cardinal Wolsey, "whose pomp and circumstance easily exceeded
that of the Persian kings."[101]

If Giovio's morality, with its chivalric component, tended to be patrician, so did his mores. Like Giberti and Castiglione, he disliked bad manners.[102] His sense of wholeness demanded that *virtù* be accompanied by
morum elegantia (refinement of manners/good breeding), the goal of
Vergerio and the Quattrocento educators. The *Elogia* of men of letters
often rebuked fellow humanists whose talents had enabled them to rise
in the world, but whose coarse manners remained to denote their hum-
ble origins. Giovio's cosmopolitan urbanity abhorred the rough and
tumble *burle* and *beffe* (practical jokes) of a less polished era.[103] His gaze
was upward. He moved in a closely interconnected, cosmopolitan society of the talented and powerful, the real locus of the Renaissance. Like
most elites, Giovio's society was highly competitive internally, and he
was discontent not to have reached the topmost circle. If he took little
satisfaction in his miter it was because he was less interested in his relationships to those below than to those above him. The cure of ordinary
souls meant no more than the practice of medicine. It has been aptly said
that humanism saved only distinguished souls.[104]

What place, if any, in Giovio's moral framework had the three theological virtues, the virtues embodied in the Sermon on the Mount? The
answer is complex. Renaissance society was still a Christian society whose
ethical norms were perceived as based on Christ's teachings, and Giovio
would have been outraged by any suggestion that he was not a conscientious Christian.[105] Yet in addition to tempering the extremes of Christian
teaching with the Aristotelian mean, he tended to subsume religious virtues in the medieval chivalric virtue of "piety," a characteristic of the
good knight, bound to honor religion but as much from "good breeding" as from deep conviction. As a humanist, moreover, Giovio could
associate piety not only with his beloved paladins but with Roman *pietas*,
the virtue of Rome's founder, the dutiful Aeneas. Locating piety in the
context of Roman virtues would have required no exceptional dexterity
on Giovio's part. In *The Courtier*, Ottaviano Fregoso argues that piety
springs from justice, rather than vice-versa.[106]

Conventional piety is a dutiful reverence for God and the forms of
religious life. It is habitual, ritualistic, and essentially social in nature,
integrating us into the common culture. It characterizes a good king, a
good knight, and a good citizen. It is reassuring to others. It is reassuring
to the individual, creating rapport with human society and the ruling
powers of the universe, yet requiring no deep interior commitment, no

restructuring of values or significant alteration of behavior. It is the antithesis of Augustinianism, but it is the most common form of religion.

For Giovio, conventional piety made possible the easy coexistence of a basically secular humanism with Christianity. Significantly, in writing a letter of consolation to Benedetto upon the death of their other brother, Giovio found classical Latin the most appropriate vehicle for his thoughts on life and immortality. Nothing, he assured Benedetto, "will be able to snatch from either you or me that hope sweeter than any other, immortal life, whether we affect to seek heaven with the ingrained piety of our family, or by means of the monuments of our literary talents we seek a distant fame among posterity."[107] For the Christian a becoming piety and the traditional hope of heaven, for the humanist eternal life in letters; in the ambiguity of the Latin construction the second hope might well be a hedge for the first. Indeed, Giovio publicly asserted to Giambattista Castaldo that if Vittoria Colonna with her Christian piety seemed to have been despising fame, one could presume that she was dissimulating rather than spurning it.[108]

One of Giovio's most revealing comments was made at the time of the sack of Rome when he endorsed, in language close to that of the *Tusculan Disputations* themselves, the Ciceronian view of philosophy as the physician of souls, the cure for fear and stress. It was the basic theme of the *Tusculans* and a view endemic to the humanist tradition from Petrarch onward, one fundamental to a youthful model of Giovio's, Cristoforo Landino, who lectured at Florence on the *Tusculans* and composed his own *Camaldolese Disputations*.[109] Giovio likewise betrayed his deepest values when praising his friend Filippo Sauli, bishop of Sestri, the equal of Gian Pietro Carafa in piety and doctrine, he said, but with "a mild and humane character, far from the gloomy severity of the more religious life, nor abhorring the sweetness of those elegant studies, in which, in the course of human affairs, noble men, their minds made tranquil, take delight with praise and honest pleasure."[110] Giovio's resolute defense of Latin stemmed from a preoccupation, not so much to suppress the vernacular as to preserve the independent value structure inherent in the classical and humanist traditions.

For Giovio and the upper-class society in which he moved, religion was largely external, as evident, for example, in his enumeration of the qualities that commended Pompeo Colonna to Leo X as a churchman: his mastery of sacred ceremonial and his knowledge of the salutations due various orders, his gravity and eloquence in expressing his opinion in consistory, his dignity in celebration of the sacred rites, the order and company of his household, the splendor of his table, and the selection of worthy men as his attendants. Nothing was said of interior spirituality, perhaps because God alone can truly judge it, perhaps because it did not matter.[111]

Giovio's models as prelate and careerist were his patrons the great secular cardinals who lived magnificently, built lavishly, and wove the values of classical humanism into a pliant ecclesiastical framework. Even as a bishop, Giovio felt no need of contriving justifications for combining humanistic culture with an ecclesiastical career, no special reading of history or intellectually cumbersome refashioning of the pope into the head of a new, classically based culture.[112] By a process of compartmentalization, natural to the human mind, the humanists had long been re-creating classical culture while pursuing careers in the Church, and Giovio made the same accommodation. He belonged to the age of Leo X. It was not that the conflict evident in Jerome, Petrarch, and Salutati between classical and Christian values had been resolved; it had simply ceased to be vexatious. In the Rome of the High Renaissance, serving the Church and "living like a man" were eminently compatible goals.[113]

With the advent of the Counter-Reformation, secular and sacred were less easily combined. Giovio knew that Bembo's openness regarding his past had nearly tripped him on the way to the cardinalate. The "spiritual" party Giovio found personally compatible as well as admirable, perhaps because they, too, were observers of the mean, but he dreaded the intransigent zealots, as evident in his remark that the philosopher Galeotto Marzio "also wrote works on sacred and moral philosophy—to his sorrow, for when they read in them that the eternal joys of heaven were in store for all peoples who lived upright and pure lives in accordance with the just law of nature, the monks accused and condemned him."[114]

Giovio was not a polemicist, however, let alone a martyr, hence the actual dimensions of his humanistic culture were normally concealed, perhaps even from himself, beneath conventional phrases such as "the more elegant" or "the more learned studies." Carafa he carefully characterized in the Ischian dialogue as "one who would have excelled all in the more learned studies had not his incomparable piety and unfeigned religion removed him, a despiser of glory, far from human praises."[115] When writing to trusted friends, however, even when they were prominent churchmen, Giovio seldom concealed his contempt for "Stoics" and "Theatines," as in the hope expressed to Cardinal Farnese that God would protect His Excellency "from the Theatines, *ante partum, in partu et post partum.*"[116]

It would doubtless have alarmed Giovio to have known that in the last years of his life he himself had been denounced to the Roman Inquisition. Girolamo Muzio, his antagonist at the court of the marquis del Vasto and the promoter of Giulio Camillo Delminio, had attempted to compensate for a licentious past by embracing the Counter-Reformation with a convert's zeal. Religious dogmatism has always brought out the worst features of human nature, and many of Muzio's stamp found in the new organ of the Holy Office a convenient means for striking at old enemies, just as Doni had denounced Domenichi. Muzio's letter to the commissary general of the Inquisition at Rome, dated November 11, 1550, charged that "in the writings of Bishop Giovio are found things more appropriate to an infidel than to a Christian," specifically auguries and references to "the gods." Moreover, Muzio went on, if someone cited Scripture to Giovio he was accustomed to respond, "What? The Bible to Giovio?"

> "It grieves me," Muzio oozed, "that such things are borne so pleasantly. I understand in Rome, with the domesticity he has with the principal heads of Christianity, that in speaking of God he allows things to come from his lips which if they were uttered by an ordinary person would give rise to a call for the stake, but with him the brigade simply laughs and says that he is a gallant (as he desires to be called)."[117]

The cardinal inquisitors included several of Giovio's friends, who presumably would not have been impressed with Muzio's malice, but whether a file was made will not be known until the archives of the Holy Office are opened. Certainly files were begun on a number of Giovio's acquaintances.[118] Apart from charges that could have been leveled at any Ciceronian humanist, the drift of Muzio's accusation seems to have been not so much infidelity as irreverence or flippancy: "To me it does not seem suitable for one who wishes to make profession of being an honorable writer to play the buffoon; nor does it seem permissible for someone who wishes to be a bishop to speak like an infidel." Giovio's witticisms touched on just about every subject, and no doubt they also touched on religion. While there is no suggestion in Muzio's charges of systematic atheism, they do substantiate the unabashed classicism in Giovio's outlook.

If Giovio's religion consisted of ritual piety complementing a classical Weltanschauung, if he turned first in times of crisis not to the Bible but to Cicero's *Tusculan Disputations*, there were nonetheless mental habits of the medieval Christian worldview imposed on his humanism. He could not accept the Stoic notion of disinterested virtue. His morality was still basically eschatological, the sanctions of heaven and hell being replaced by the secular rewards and punishments of "true glory" or everlasting infamy in history. Beyond the influence of Cicero, his rejection of the doctrines of late Stoicism betrayed an Augustinian hostility to the idea of self-sufficient virtue, that is, a socially based virtue independent of future rewards and punishments, the final hallmark of a secular outlook.[119]

Giovio's universe was still a moral one. His triumphant descriptions of the deaths of each of the principals in the sack of Rome—all ascribed to God's speedy punishment of wickedness—revealed his assumption of a basic morality undergirding human existence. He did not love his world so much that he pardoned all, as Burckhardt implied of the Italian of the age. Giovio was, in fact, at some pains to demonstrate that the victory of evil was neither brilliant nor lasting.[120] He refused to accept a Machiavellian distinction between private and public morality, and after a long flirtation with astrology he disallowed either Fortune or the stars as the final arbiters of human fate. In his very last years he insisted that in his motto, *Fato prudentia minor*, "Fate" was to be construed as "Providence."[121] Perhaps it was because of his acceptance of the universe as fundamentally moral that he never explored the contradiction broached on Ischia between the notion of history as a human creation and the helplessness of the individual caught in the flow of events, the ground of his motto, "ANAGKE [Necessity]."[122]

As an ecclesiastical careerist, Giovio's loyalty was not so much to religion as to the institution of the Church. His accommodation of humanism was undoubtedly made easier by his view that the Church was the contemporary embodiment of the greatness of ancient Rome, an idea he and the Roman humanists derived from Biondo's *Roma triumphans*.[123] For Giovio, the Holy Roman Empire was medieval and German. The papacy had become the true heir of Rome and the guardian of the *libertas Italiae*.[124] In his *elogium* of Romulus, Giovio celebrated the city of Rome as the source of the authority of the Caesars and subsequently of the institutional power of the papacy.[125] With the Roman empire vanished and liberty lost, all that remained to Italy were the papacy and leadership in Latin eloquence. At the root of Giovio's anticonciliarism was the fear that a weakened papacy would result in diminished patronage and the loss of Italy's primacy in Latin. "For we still hold," he wrote at the conclusion of the *Elogia* of 1546, "(if those who have been stripped of almost every vestige of liberty may make even modest boasts) the fortified citadel of true and unfailing eloquence, where (by the grace of the pure Muses) our native Roman honor and integrity is kept impregnable and defended against foreign foes."[126] Giovio's championship of Latin and the papal monarchy was rooted in his humanistic culture and Italian patriotism.

With his cult of fame and the individual, his classicism, his love of magnificence, his connoisseurship of the arts, and his fascination with remote peoples and places, Giovio seems to epitomize the Burckhardtian Renaissance man, and, indeed, his writings were one of Burckhardt's major sources. *The Civilization of the Renaissance in Italy* abounds with references drawn from Giovio's works, particularly the *Elogia*. Yet, while Giovio illustrates the four principal topoi of Burckhardt's model, he himself fell short of the revolutionary creativity central to it. His importance—great as it was—was as an arbiter and popularizer, not as an innovator and epoch-maker.

Giovio certainly regarded history as a human, not a divine creation, but he did not go on to accept the moral autonomy of politics; for him the state was not entirely a work of art in Burckhardt's sense. There remained that lingering need shared by most human societies for reassurance from a cosmic order. Furthermore, Giovio illustrated a change in attitude toward politics between the Quattrocento and the Cinquecento which Burckhardt's essentially static model did little to explore. By the third decade of the sixteenth century, the wars of Italy had produced a deep sense of pessimism, eroding the fifteenth-century confidence in human statecraft and the creative potential of politics and diplomacy. While history remained a human creation, it was now apparent to Giovio, as to Pontano or Guicciardini, that it was dominated by irrational forces no individual human could master or control—*Fato prudentia minor.* The "occult force of destiny" could drive even the wise to madness.[127] The optimistic promise of civic humanism, the heroic aspirations of the era of Julius II and Leo X had yielded to intense longings for peace; order had supplanted initiative and participation as a political goal. Rulers such as Cosimo I de' Medici in Florence were attuned to the new mood, and Giovio to them.[128]

The sense of helplessness, moreover, amid the conflict of greater powers; the feeling of vulnerability to invasion and attack, whether by Saracens or Christians; the realization that neither politics nor diplomacy, no matter how astute, nor rhetoric, no matter how eloquent, could counteract human folly enough to assure stability in the public world—these all magnified the urge to seek the quiet life, to create private worlds of order centered on villas and gardens laid out for literary leisure and the company of chosen friends. If, as De Sanctis argued, humanism in the Cinquecento lost its political dimension and took a purely literary bent, Giovio demonstrated that it did so in response to conditions which had pushed spirits to the breaking point. The tension between public and private life was, of course, a good Roman topos, and it was testimony to the pervasiveness of humanism that, when they succumbed to despair, the elite of Italy fled not to the monastery but to the villa.[129]

Giovio contributed as much as anyone to the cult of individual personality, and in this he exemplifies Burckhardt's concept of the development of the individual. Yet, curiously, he made no serious attempt at the innovative form of autobiography, as did his fellow physician Girolamo Cardano. His biographies and *Elogia* did not significantly advance the delineation of character and personal traits beyond ancient concepts and techniques, although his museum systematically matched character sketches with physiognomy, presumably to facilitate intuitive judgments of a global sort that approximated modern notions of personality.[130]

Giovio's revival of antiquity and its values was certainly Burckhardtian in its sophistication and in its innately Italian character. Some of that

Italian character, Burckhardt stressed, had been formed by the legacy of medieval chivalry, and the *chansons de geste* had, indeed, influenced Giovio's moral code. Yet for Giovio, antiquity was a limiting as well as a liberating concept. Unlike his protégé Vasari, he had not grasped the possibilities for surpassing the ancients; unlike Bembo he did not develop his considerable potential as a vernacular writer. While Giovio adroitly sidestepped the marginalization of the humanists in the sixteenth century—what Burckhardt termed "the fall of the humanists"—the Ischian dialogue showed how keenly he sensed it. The legacy of antiquity remained and collecting continued, but the cult of antiquity was dethroned. The wisdom of the ancients had not availed and the greatness of Italy had not been reborn.[131]

In the discovery of the world and of man, Giovio the biographer and chorographer comes closest to fulfilling the Burckhardtian topos at the level of creativity, although even here his enthusiasm and facility tended to mask a lack of reflection and depth. There was some justification to Gregorovius' murkily Hegelian judgment: "His works, which lack artistic ability as well as depth of thought, are more or less descriptions of persons or events, which, although revealing not the smallest perception of the hidden current of the age, are nevertheless characteristically illumined by it."[132] If not a maker, Giovio was certainly a "true-born son of his century."[133]

Giovio exemplifies almost to perfection the mentality described in Burckhardt's concluding chapters on morality and religion. All his works reveal the state of mind where a belief in fame and historical greatness has supplanted rather than destroyed traditional belief in the afterlife, and where honor, rather than religion, dictates personal conduct. Giovio's ambivalent attitude toward astrology, denouncing but not entirely dismissing it, was exactly as Burckhardt described. Only in one respect did Burckhardt draw the wrong conclusions from Giovio, and that was through a misreading of passages where the historian seemed to be condoning misconduct with antique examples when he was, in fact, using the examples as a means of tactful censure.[134] Giovio cannot be enlisted to show that immorality had been accepted in the Renaissance as the ineluctable consequence of a Promethean re-creation of the individual.

What most reveals Giovio's stature is reading what Burckhardt found tedious, the *Histories*.[135] Even when leisure is lacking to read them in the Latin which appeared to Bembo both graceful and learned, Giovio emerges as an exponent of earnest moral values, an open-minded analyst of events on a Mediterranean scale, and a judicious practitioner of eyewitness historiography.[136] Still, as he himself recognized, for all his energy, versatility, and acuity, he lacked the *virtù* of genius. If, in an era of optimism regarding human potential, the greatest minds were ultimately discouraged by "a sense of the ineffable, indeterminate, and indeterminable in existence, by the reality that evades man's grasp and power," so even more keenly Giovio felt the limitations of his talents and achievements.[137] "Not that I am at all enamored of myself as a historian," he once remarked, "it is enough for me that if the Barbary steeds don't race, the emaciated nag wins the *palio* trotting."[138] Even if he recognized the thoroughbred in Guicciardini's *Storia d'Italia*, which he saw in manuscript, he had already perceived by the 1540s that Latin was doomed to lose the battle with Italian and that his efforts in mastering Augustan prose would mainly be appreciated, if at all, by foreigners and by distant ages.[139] His failure to win the cardinal's hat he took as a judgment on his talents and a sign that he had not reached the plateau with Sadoleto and Bembo. Even his "jocund museum" was not "absolute art," he lamented, because of a lack of overall harmony in the design, the result of his having had to proceed piecemeal as funds were available.[140] We strain at the limits all our lives only to confront in the end the mocking face of Terminus.

So we take leave of Paolo Giovio, historian of his times and creature of his age, full of faults and virtues—loquacious and addicted to gossip, sharp-tongued, a social climber, a little too eager to please the influential, a little too lacking in gravity, an epicure, more than slightly avaricious, tiresome in his tenacity, self-serving, a careerist rather than a churchman, "someone who makes the greatest fuss over nothing," a complainer; yet in his own way a stoic, a victim of severe gout in his later years but unfailingly jovial, a brilliant conversationalist, amusing, warmly personal, a good Lombard, a good uncle, a solicitous and loyal friend, a companion too spontaneous to dissimulate, a correspondent who in his candor left himself to us "warts and all," a conscientious and perceptive historian, a sympathetic biographer who urged, "Let us write of virtues and vices, but with tempered humanity, not angry invective, so that readers can take the virtues like ports at sea and flee the shoals to avoid shipwreck."[141] In writing the biographer's biography, how could we not comply?

Giovio's Ecclesiastical Benefices

Papacy of Leo X:

Half cavalierate. *IO* 2:167; *IO* 6:136.

Priorate of Carrù Monregalese (Mondovì). March 15, 1518. ASV, Reg. Vat. 1142, fols. 22v–25r; *IO* 1:112; *IO* 2:167.

Papacy of Adrian VI:

Canonry in cathedral of Como to replace the half cavalierate taken away (*IO* 6:136). Bulls presented to the chapter (ASC, Notarile 201, Volpi, January 17–18, 1523). Renounced to nephew Cecilio as per letter of Benedetto (*PSSC* 8 [1891]: 245).

Papacy of Clement VII:

Preceptory of S. Antonio fuori le mura, Como. June 13, 1524 (ASV, Reg. Vat. 1252, fols. 139v–142r). Renounced to Giulio (*PSSC* 8 [1891], 245; ASC, Notarile 203, September 1, 1528).

Pension of 25 ducats on canonry in cathedral of Novara. Letter of July 1, 1525 (*IO* 1:112); Litta, "Giovio."

Reversion of San Colombano and 17-ducat pension. 1524–25 (*IO* 1:112).

Pension of 50 scudi on S. Vittoria, Piacenza (1526). C. Poggiali, *Memorie storiche di Piacenza*, vol. 8 (Piacenza, 1760): 342–43; *IO* 1:203, 246.

Canonry in cathedral of Laon. Letter of July 17, 1527, *IO* 11 (forthcoming). Willing to resign it at request of pope.

S. Salvatore fuori le mura, Ascoli. Bulls not yet expedited. Wishes to resign it to Cecilio. Letter of July 17, 1527.

Bishopric of Nocera dei Pagani (Salerno). January 13, 1528. Van Gulik and Eubel, *Hierarchia catholica* 3:230; ASV, Reg. Vat. 1438, fols. 122r–126r.

Pension of 100 scudi on bishopric of Verona (a grace of Giberti?). Card. Farnese to nuncio at Venice, October 15, 1540. Archivio di Stato, Parma, Racc. MSS 114, ins. 2, fol. 19.

Pension of 100 scudi on bishopric of Caserta for life of Leo X, ca. 1533 (*IO* 1:85; 2:225, 235); Cardinal Farnese orders Giovio paid (Archivio di Stato, Parma, Racc. MSS 114, ins. 2, fol. 52).

Pension of 100 scudi on provostship of Sabbioneta by Ippolito de' Medici for life of Leo X, ca. 1533. *IO* 1:185, 325.

Pension of 1,000 francs on priorate in Rouen. Awarded 1533 by Francis I. BNR, MS Autog. 153.1; *IO* 1:251; *IO* 2:60, 169.

Papacy of Paul III:

Pension of 300 ducats on bishopric of Pamplona awarded by Charles V, 1538. ASV, Reg. Lat., 1688, fol. 67v–68r; *IO* 1:236, 253, 320; *IO* 2:239; ML, MA 3313, Giovio to Poggio, February 15, 1542.

S. Giuliano, Como. December 16, 1540 (ASV, Reg. Vat. 1546, fols. 45v–47r). Bulls presented to chapter, January 15, 1541 (ASC, Notarile 207 [Volpi]; *IO* 2:175). Renounced to Alessandro, 1541 (Litta, "Giovio," *IO* 2:110).

Archpresbytery of S. Stephen, Menaggio. February 16, 1542 (ASV, Reg. Vat. 1581, fols. 169r–170r; *IO* 1:307).

Half-cavalierate. By 1543. *IO* 1:307.

Pension of 100 scudi on bishopric of Lavello (Bari). By 1543. *IO* 1:307.

"Benefice of Angri [Nocera]." 1544. *IO* 1:348.

Papacy of Julius III:

Giulio Giovio coadjutor with right of succession and without fee. August 21, 1551. Van Gulik and Eubel, *Hierarchia catholica* 3:230; *IO* 2:215.

Exemptions from the Tithe:

Nocera. October 22, 1537 (ASV, Min. Brev. Paul III [1537], Arm. 41, no. 8, fol. 312r). See also *IO* 1:213, 329). Requests for reconfirmation (*IO* 1:222, 263, 318; 2:165, 234).

Pension on Verona. Archivio di Stato, Parma, Racc. MSS 114, ins. 2, fol. 19, Farnese to nuncio to Venice.

Sequence of Composition of the *Histories*

Old	New	Years	Written	Source
VIII	13, 14	1514–15	By 1515	*IO* 1:85
X	17, 18	1515–18	By 1520	Colophon to X (ML, MA3230); Letter of 1520 (SSC, Archivio Aliati, 28, 5, fol. 159r)
IX	15, 16	1515	By 1522	*IO* 1:96, 98
XI	ep. 21	1521–22	1522	*IO* 1:100 (Asks information)
I	1	1494	1521	*IO* 1:89 (Asks information)
			1523	*IO* 1:101 (Revising)
II	2	1495		
III	3	1495–96	?	Binding ca. 1520–1525
IV	4	1496–97	?	
V—	5—	1498—	Missing	*IO* 1:83 (Asks information on events of 1508–1509)
VI	10	1513		
VII	11, 12	1513–14	By 1523	Arrighi's calligraphy
I–X	1–18	1498–1517	By 1524	*IO* 9:11
	19–24	1518–27	Unwritten	
	34	1535	Draft	*IO* 1:169
	30–34	1532–1535	1533–1538	*IO* 1:204
	36–37	1537–1539	By 1540	*IO* 1:261
	39–40	1540–41	by 1543	*IO* 1:306, 327
	41	1542	By 1544	*IO* 1:337
XXX	42	1542	By 1544	*IO* 1:337
	43–44	1543–44	1544	*IO* 1:349
	45	1544	By 1546	*IO* 2:62
	38	1536–37	1550–51	*IO* 2:194, 196
	25–26	1527–29	1551	*IO* 2:210
	27–29	1529–1531	1552	*IO* 2:224, 226–27
	35	1536	1552	*IO* 2:235–37

First Editions of Giovio's Works (in order of publication)

De Romanis piscibus libellus. Rome: Calvo, 1524.

(coauthor) *De virtute olei contra pestem.* Rome, 1524.

Libellus de legatione Basilii Magni Principis Moschoviae. Rome: Calvo, 1525.

Li veri particulari de la felice vittoria del illustre Signor Conte Philippino Doria contra larmata cesarea sopra Salerno historialmente mandati alla S. di N. S. PP. Clemente VII dal R. et Eccellentissimo M. Paulo Jovio. Rome(?), 1528.

Vita Petri Gravinae a P. Iovio ad Iohannem Franciscum Campaneum. In *Petri Gravinae poemata.* Edited by Scipione Capece. Naples: Sulzbach, 1532.

Comentario de le cose de' Turchi. Rome: Blado, 1532.

Vita Sfortiae clarissimi ducis. Rome: Blado, 1539.

Elogia veris clarorum virorum imaginibus apposita . . . Addita . . . Adriani Pont. vita. Venice: Tramezzino, 1546.

De vita Leonis Decimi Pont. Max. libri IIII. His ordine temporum accesserunt Hadriani Sexti Pont. Max. et Pompeii Columnae Cardinalis vitae. Florence: Torrentino, 1548.

Descriptio Britanniae, Scotiae, Hyberniae et Orchadum. Venice: Tramezzino, 1548.

Vitae duodecim Vicecomitum Mediolani principum. Paris: Estienne, 1549.

Illustrium virorum vitae: De vita et rebus gestis XII Vicecomitum Mediolani principum; Vita Sfortiae; De vita et rebus gestis Consalvi Ferdinandi Cordubae cognomento Magni; De vita et rebus gestis Ferdinandi Davali cognomento Piscarii. Florence: Torrentino, 1549.

Historiarum sui temporis tomus primus. Florence: Torrentino, 1550.

Liber de vita et rebus gestis Alphonsi Atestini. Florence: Torrentino, 1550.

Elogia virorum bellica virtute illustrium. Florence: Torrentino, 1551.

Historiarum sui temporis tomus secundus. Florence: Torrentino, 1552.

Dialogo dell'imprese militari et amorose. Rome: A. Barre, 1555.

Larius. Venice: Ziletti, 1559.

Lettere volgari di Mons. Paolo Giovio. Edited by Lodovico Domenichi. Venice: Sessa, 1560.

Consiglio di Monsignor Giovio raccolto dalle consulte di Papa Leone Decimo per far l'impresa contra infideli. Venice: Bonelli, 1560. Appendix to the *Istorie.*

Fragmentum trium dialogorum: Dialogus de viris litteris illustribus, cui in calce sunt additae Vincii, Michaelis Angeli, Raphaelis Urbinatis vitae. Modena, 1781, in G. Tiraboschi, *Storia della letteratura italiana,* appendix to vol. 9.

De humano victu epistola ad Felicem Trophinum. Edited by Giambattista Giovio. Como: Ostinelli, 1808.

Dialogus de viris et foeminis aetate nostra florentibus. In *Iovii opera* 9. Edited by Ernesto Travi. Rome: Istituto Poligrafico dello Stato, 1984.

Paulus Iovius P. Iano Raschae. Edited by Stefano Della Torre. In *Atti del convegno Paolo Giovio.* Como: Società Storica Comense, 1985 (*Raccolta Storica,* 17), 296–301.

Notes

PREFACE

1. Emil Schaeffer, *Von Bildern und Menschen der Renaissance* (Berlin: Julius Bard, 1914), 180.

2. "seguitando più tosto i sensi che le parole." Giambattista Gelli, preface to his translation of Giovio's *La vita di Alfonso da Este* (Florence: [Torrentino], 1553), 5.

CHAPTER ONE

1. E.g., in 1550 he spoke of his sixty-four years. *Pauli Iovii opera* (henceforth, *IO*), 2:178. See T. C. P. Zimmermann, "La presunta data di nascita di P.G.," *Periodico della Società Storica Comense* (henceforth, *PSSC*) 52 (1986–87): 189–92.

2. *IO* 9:339–40. An inscription, still visible, commemorates the restoration of the hospice during Giovio's youth by the prefect of the foundation, his first cousin, Gabriele Zobio, but there is no documentary evidence before the thirteenth century. See the note of Dante Visconti in his edition of Giovio's *Larius* in Gianfranco Miglio and Pietro Gini, eds., *Larius* 1:95 n. 64. On the history of the island see Matteo Gianoncelli, "Note storiche su l'Isola Comacina," *PSSC* 42 (1968): 37–48.

3. For an introduction to the genealogical literature on the Giovio family see the articles by Luigi Rovelli, Luigi Trombetta Panigada, and Venosto Lucati in *Como*, nos. 1, 3, and 4 (1958); and "Giovio di Como" in Pompeo Litta, *Famiglie celebri d'Italia*.

4. Benedetto Giovio to Francesco Sfondrato, in Santo Monti, ed., "Lettere di Benedetto Giovio," *PSSC* 8 (1891): 128. Paolo was using Jovius at least by 1514 and probably adopted it on being admitted to the Roman academy, whose members customarily Latinized their names. *IO* 1:83.

5. Biblioteca Nazionale, Rome (henceforth, BNR), MSS Autografi, A. 153.1. A single sheet, canceled with diagonal ink lines.

6. *IO* 9:255. Luigi's *rogiti*, running from 1462 to September 26, 1500, are found in the Archivio di Stato, Como (henceforth, ASC), Fondo Notarile, cartelle 70–75. For this reference I am much obliged to Dott. Cesare Sibilia.

7. *IO* 9:255 and 8:126–27. For Benedetto Giovio (1471–1545) see Matteo Gianoncelli in *Larius* 1:101–106 and the introduction of Francesco Fossati to his edition of *Opere scelte di Benedetto Giovio* (Como, 1887), vii–xxvi, both reprinted in Benedetto Giovio, *Historiae patriae libri duo* (1982). See also Paul O. Kristeller, *Iter Italicum* 1:46–48, 2:70, and 5:529a–532b. For the Como proverb I am indebted to Dott. Gian Giuseppe Brenna.

8. For a discussion of the letter and a transcription see Stefano Della Torre, "L'inedita opera prima di Paolo Giovio ed il museo: L'interesse di un umanista per il tema della villa," in *Atti del convegno Paolo Giovio: Il Rinascimento e la memoria* (henceforth, *Atti*), 283–301. The letter is dated the Ides of July, 1504.

9. One of the books from Giovio's library I was able to examine through the courtesy of the late Hans Kraus of New York was a copy of the Aldine edition of Pliny the Younger's letters (*Epistolae*, 1508) with Giovio's inscription and marginalia. For Benedetto's comments on the sites of the Plinian villas see his *Historia patriae* (1982), 232–33. For his archaeological studies see Roberto Weiss, *The Renaissance Discovery of Classical Antiquity*, 117, 129–30, 153; Giorgio Luraschi, "L'età antica di Como," in *Atti dei convegni celebrativi del centenario 1878–1978* (Como: Società

Storica Comense, 1979), 87–105; *IO* 8:67; and Stefano Della Torre, "Un ritratto pliniano tratto dagli affreschi del museo di Paolo Giovio," *PSSC* 46 (1978–79): 169–76.

10. Della Torre, *Atti*, 284; *IO* 8:88.

11. Ernesto Travi, "Paolo Giovio nel suo tempo," in *Atti*, 314–15. In view of Giovio's own later collections it is interesting that in describing Silius Italicus' villa, Pliny the Younger (*Ep.* 3.7) stressed the collections of books, statues, and portraits.

12. *IO* 9:138.

13. Travi, *Atti*, 314.

14. *IO* 8:129. Pier Paolo Vergerio, *De ingenuis moribus*, trans. Eugenio Garin, in Garin, ed., *L'educazione humanistica in Italia*, 49–104.

15. Travi, *Atti*, 314.

16. E. Travi, "Casa Giovio e la tradizione delle leggende cavalleresche," *PSSC* 49 (1982): 9–32.

17. John R. Hale, "Gunpowder and the Renaissance," *Renaissance War Studies*, 400–401.

18. *IO* 9:180. See E. Travi, "La sosta a Napoli di Paolo Giovio," *Quaderni* 4 (1987): 115.

19. *IO* 3:267. In the *Hadriani Sexti vita* (Florence, 1551; hereafter, *Hadriani vita*), p. 132, Giovio noted that the future pope had also studied astrology avidly in his youth and that his horoscope predicted greatness for him.

20. *IO* 8:405, 127.

21. Travi, *Atti*, 315.

22. *IO* 9:290. On the dating I follow Silvia Castellani, "Contributo alla biografia di Paolo Giovio," 38.

23. Giovio described his family as "vetustate quam fortunis clarior" (*IO* 8:126). In the second part of the Ischian dialogues he suggested that he would have much preferred to prepare for writing history but that Benedetto did not think he had the aptitude to make a career of it. *IO* 9:255.

24. Severe prohibitions, often renewed, restricted Milanese subjects to the University of Pavia. See Luigi Franchi, *Statuti e ordinamenti della Università di Pavia* (Pavia: Tipografia Cooperativa, 1925), 147–52. In 1506, however, Pavia was suffering from an outbreak of plague. On Giovio at Padua see Bruno Nardi, *Saggi sull'aristotelismo padovano* (Florence: Sansoni, 1958), 171. I am grateful to Dott. Lucia Rossetti for confirming the absence of any reference to him in the archive of Padua. He is not mentioned in the *Acta graduum academicorum* (1501–1525), ed. Elda M. Forin, 3 vols. (Padua: Antenore, 1969).

25. Desiderius Erasmus, *Opus epistolarum* (ed. Allen) 6:190.

26. *IO* 8:96.

27. *IO* 8:84. For confirmation of Giovio's portrait of Achillini see Herbert S. Matsen, "Giovanni Garzoni to Alessandro Achillini: An Unpublished Letter and Defence," in Edward P. Mahoney, ed., *Philosophy and Humanism: Renaissance Essays in Honor of P. O. Kristeller* (New York: Columbia University Press, 1976), 527.

28. Cited by J. H. Randall, Jr., *The School of Padua and the Emergence of Modern Science* (Padua: Antenore, 1961), 82–83. On Contarini at Padua see Gigliola Fragnito, *Gasparo Contarini: Un magistrato veneziano al servizio della Christianità* (Florence: Olschki, 1988), 4–5. On Averroism see E. P. Mahoney, "Nicoletto Vernia on the Soul and Immortality," in Mahoney, ed., *Philosophy and Humanism*, 144–63.

29. On repercussions of Pomponazzi's debate with Achillini making their way into his lectures see Charles B. Schmitt, "Thomas Linacre in Italy," in F. Maddison, M. Pelling, and C. Webster, eds., *Linacre Studies* (Oxford: Oxford University Press, 1977), 51. In his *elogium* of Pomponazzi, Giovio showed no hostility to Averroism, contenting himself with the observation that the *De animae immortalitate* aroused the violent hostility of the monks—not usually a very serious matter for Giovio—and rather slyly (and correctly) noting that with regard to the mortality of the soul Pomponazzi's interpretation of Aristotle had the support of "the most holy and learned cardinal Cajetan." On the other hand, Giovio attacked the commentaries of Alexander of Aphrodisias, which Pomponazzi utilized in

evolving his own arguments, as being the most pestilent possible means "for corrupting the youth and dissolving the discipline of the Christian life" (*IO* 8:96). In the *elogium* of Contarini, moreover, Giovio attacked Pomponazzi's interpretation of Aristotle and praised Contarini's defense (*IO* 8:121–22). By 1546, when Giovio published the *Elogia*, the Council of Trent was already in session and he may have felt that this was a prudent episcopal sentiment. On Averroism and Alexandrism see P. O. Kristeller, "Paduan Averroism and Alexandrism in the Light of Recent Studies," *Atti del XII Congresso Internazionale di Filosofia* (1958), vol. 9 (Florence, 1960): 147–55; reprinted in P. O. Kristeller, *Renaissance Thought and the Arts* (Princeton: Princeton University Press, 1980), 111–18. On Contarini and Pomponazzi see Elisabeth G. Gleason *Gasparo Contarini* (Berkeley: University of California Press, 1994), 78–82.

30. *IO* 8:114.

31. For a good overview of the debate see Charles B. Schmitt, "Philosophy and Science in 16th–Century Italian Universities," in *The Renaissance: Essays in Interpretation to Eugenio Garin* (London: Methuen, 1982), 297–336.

32. *IO* 8:114. Giovio's language was very reminiscent of phrases used by Chalcondylas at his inaugural discourse at Padua in 1463, and by Erasmus. See Deno J. Geanakoplos, "The Discourse of Demetrius Chalcondyles on the Inauguration of Greek Studies at the University of Padua in 1463," *Studies in the Renaissance* 21 (1974): 133.

33. Walter Burley, *Expositio in octo libros Aristotelis physica*, ed. Nicoletto Vernia (Venice: Bonetus Locatellus for Octavianus Scotus, 1491). See Christie's sale catalogue, *Early Printed Books, Manuscripts, and Autograph Letters*, London, November 17, 1976, p. 74. I was subsequently able to examine this volume in New York through the courtesy of Mr. Hans Kraus. Other volumes offered at the same sale that bore Giovio's inscription or annotations and probably dated from his student days included the commentaries of Aegidius Romanus on Aristotle's *Elenchi* (1500) and *Posterior*

Analytics (1495), and Agostino Nifo's edition of other Aristotelian works (*Opera nonnulla*) with the commentary of Averroës (1496).

34. "So that when you recommend me for a red hat, Pope Julius will know there is no impediment" (*IO* 8:92). For the dating of the event see Ferdinando Gabotto, *Giasone del Maino* (Turin, 1888), 236–39. Two other pieces of evidence support Giovio's presence at Pavia by 1507. The first is his letter of June 1525 to Federico Gonzaga recommending a certain Luigi Mancasolla, whom he attests he knew eighteen years previously at the *studium* of Pavia, i.e. in 1507 (*IO* 1:111). The second is the statutes of the college of arts and medicine of Pavia, which required four years' residence before proceeding to the laurea (Franchi, *Statuti*, 124–29). Castellani, on the other hand ("Contributo alla biografia," p. 40), follows Travi in suggesting that Giovio may have remained at Padua until the interruption of studies there in 1509 by the war of the League of Cambrai and migrated to Pavia in 1510 with his major professor, Marco Antonio della Torre. Ernesto Travi, "Paolo Giovio a Pavia accanto a Marco Antonio della Torre e Leonardo," *Communitas*, 121–25.

35. There is an inscription, "Noctes Pa: Iovii Actae Comi 1508 25 Ivlii Hora I5.a ascendens II mp [Concluded at Como, July 25, 1508, 15th hour, 2nd ascendant, in his own hand]." The rediscovery of this document and its significance was announced by Prof. Ernesto Travi in *Atti*, 316. I am much obliged to him for a copy of the MS, found in the Biblioteca Nazionale of Rome, Fondo Vittorio Emanuele, 1303, and to Prof. Avv. Sergio Lazzarini for a copy of the transcription, which will be published in vol. 11 of the *Iovii opera*.

In the eighteenth century, Count Giambattista Giovio mentioned the MS as being in his possession but mistook it for a *tesi di laurea*, giving rise to the tradition that Giovio received the doctorate in 1508 (G. Giovio, "Elogio di Msgr. Paolo Giovio," in Andrea Rubbi, ed., *Elogi italiani* 8:72). A notarial document dated November 15, 1508, found by Matteo Gianoncelli mentions Giovio as "artium et medicinae scholaris Domini Pauli" (ASC, Notarile 212, fol. 80). For most of the materials from ASC I am indebted to Dott. Gianoncelli. In a letter regarding the education of his nephew Marco Antonio, Giovio recommended lodging at Pavia in the house of a professor as he himself had done (Società Storica Comense [henceforth, SSC], Archivio Aliati, 28, 5, fol. 154). For the SSC archives see Magda Noseda and Cesare Sibilia, "Fondi archivistici gioviani." The dating of the *Noctes* by the ascendant obviously indicates Giovio's astrological interests.

36. "Acer dyalecticus" (*IO* 9:248). For Guillaume van Male's characterization of Giovio's nature as "dicacissima," see *Lettres su la vie intérieure de l'empereur Charles-Quint ecrites par Guillaume van Male, gentilhomme de sa chambre, et publiées, pour la première fois*, ed. Frederick A. F. T. de Reiffenberg (Brussels, 1843), 58. On scholastic dispute in medical education see Brian Law, *The Rise and Decline of the Scholastic "Quaestio Disputata"* (Leiden: Brill, 1993). On medical education see Nancy G. Siraisi, *Avicenna in Renaissance Italy: The Canon and Medical Teaching in Italian Universities after 1500* (Princeton: Princeton University Press, 1987).

37. G. B. de Toni, "Intorno a Marco Antonio dalla Torre," *Atti del R. Istituto Veneto di Scienze, Lettere, ed Arti* 54, ser. 7, vol. 7 (1895–96): 190–203.

38. *IO* 8:85–86. On the importance of Greek philology to the medical advances at Padua see Marie Boas, *The Scientific Renaissance* (New York: Harper and Row, 1962), 25–26. Many of the Latin terms in use had been drawn from Arabic translations of Greek ones.

39. *IO* 8:86. On Zerbi, who held the chair of theoretical medicine at Padua from 1494 to his death in 1505, see L. R. Lind, *Pre-Vesalian Anatomy* (Philadelphia: American Philosophical Society, 1975), 141–56. There are several versions of the story recounted by Giovio, including a particularly grisly one related by Pierio Valeriano in *De litteratorum infelicitate libri duo* (1620), 1:39.

40. Similarity of language suggests that

Giovio was Vasari's source for the collaboration. Giovio's life of Leonardo mentions his going to dissect bodies of criminals "in the very schools of the physicians" (*IO* 8:229). Bernard Schultz points out that careful reading of Vasari's words does not support the oft-encountered notion that Leonardo was going to supply illustrations for della Torre's text. Bernard Schultz, *Art and Anatomy in Renaissance Italy* (Ann Arbor: University Microfilms International, 1985), 96–100. See also Travi, "Paolo Giovio a Pavia," 121–25.

41. D'Arco, *Nicolai Archii Comitis numerorum libri IV*, 71. On d'Arco see the article by Gerhard Rill (although the birth date he gives is improbable) in *Dizionario biografico degli Italiani* (henceforth, *DBI*) 3:393–94.

42. *IO* 9:233. No known manuscript of the *Anterotica* exists. See Travi, *Atti*, 315.

43. *IO* 9:419. On the beaver and his testicles see Juvenal, *Saturae*, 12:34–36.

44. *IO* 9:376.

45. *IO* 8:375.

46. "vir . . . ad exitium Italiae natus." *Histories*, bk. 1 (*IO* 3:14).

47. *IO* 8:63. Giovio also denounced Venice's cooperation with France against Milan, and its "blind lust for expanding its empire" (*IO* 8:374).

48. *IO* 8:381.

49. See Eric Cochrane, *Historians and Historiography in the Italian Renaissance*, bks. 3 and 5.

50. Alessandro Benedetti, *Diaria de bello carolino*, ed. Dorothy M. Schullian (New York: Ungar, 1967).

51. Giovio had seen d'Alviano's commentary (*IO* 8:389). On Borgia see Felix Gilbert, *Machiavelli and Guicciardini*, 264–69. Other friends of d'Alviano's who were with him at Agnadello included the physician and historical theorist Girolamo Fracastoro (like Giovio, a pupil and friend of della Torre's); the poet and geographer Giovanni Cotta; and the Venetian diplomat Andrea Navagero, an orator, poet, and classicist later commissioned as the first official historiographer of the republic. According to Giovio, Cotta actually asked to accompany d'Alviano to prison (*IO* 8:82–83). On

Fracastoro's presence at Agnadello see Antonio Favaro, *L'università di Padova* (Venice: Ferrari, 1922), 20. On Navagero see Gaetano Cozzi, "Cultura, politica e religione nella 'Pubblica Storiografia' Veneziana del Cinquecento," *Bollettino dell'Istituto di Storia della Società e dello Stato Veneziano* 5–6 (1963–64): 215–94.

52. *IO* 1:83. On the growth of Italian nationalism in the sixteenth century see Vincent Ilardi, "'Italianità' among Some Italian Intellectuals in the Early Sixteenth Century," *Traditio* 12 (1956): 339–67, reprinted in Ilardi, *Studies in Italian Renaissance Diplomatic History.*

53. See Travi, "Paolo Giovio a Pavia," 121–25.

54. Franchi, *Statuti*, 124–29.

55. *IO* 8:86.

56. *IO* 9:255. In the preface to his *Histories* Giovio described himself as drawn to history "ab ipsa statim adolescentia," echoing the words of Flavio Biondo, who had felt himself spurred to writing history "ab ipsa adolescentia" by the example of Bruni (*IO* 3:5); R. Fubini, "Flavio Biondo," *DBI* 10:542.

57. Travi, *Atti*, 317–18.

58. In the *elogium* of Gaston de Foix, Giovio asserted that he had seen the French general many times, another indication of his presence in Lombardy in 1511, the year de Foix became viceroy. Castellani, "Contributo alla biografi," 269.

59. On the date of Giovio's departure see Travi in *Atti*, 318. Twice in 1549 Giovio spoke of having been in Rome for thirty-seven years, which would indicate arrival in 1512 (*IO* 2:138, 153). In 1532 Benedetto complained of his brother's not having resided in Como for any length of time in twenty years, thus confirming his departure in 1512 (*PSSC* 8 [1891]: 243). For other evidence see chap. 12, n. 208, below.

CHAPTER TWO

1. *IO* 3:5.

2. *IO* 1:86.

3. In 1515 Giovio referred to "Monsignor nostro de Sauli" (*IO* 1:85). In 1520 he remarked to his brother that "se la disgrazia

della buona memoria del Cardinale de Sauli non fosse intervenuta, forse che non arebbe a stentar più" (*IO* 1:86).

4. Francesco Priscianese, *Del governo della corte d'un signore in Roma* (Città di Castello, 1883), 4–5, 70. See also John F. D'Amico, *Renaissance Humanism in Papal Rome*, 45–60.

5. Michael Hirst, *Sebastiano del Piombo*, 99–100; Charles Davis, "Un appunto per Sebastiano del Piombo ritrattista," *Mitteilungen des Kunsthistorischen Institutes in Florenz* 26 (1982): 383–88. For calling the latter article to my attention I would like to thank Dr. David A. Brown. On Cattaneo see the article by Gianni Ballistreri, *DBI* 22:468–71.

6. *Lettera dell'Abate Gaetano Marini . . . nella quale s'illustra il ruolo de' professori dell'Archiginnasio Romano per l'anno MDXIV* (Rome, 1797), 14, 43. For comparison, Nifo's was 300 florins (the highest salary), Camillo Porzio's 150, Parrasio's 200. In this period it was quite normal for posts in philosophy to be held by physicians. Most of the leading philosophers, including Nifo, held degrees in medicine. A perusal of the *Name List* from *A Medical Register of the Italian Renaissance, 1350–1550*, compiled by Juliana Hill Cotton (Oxford: Privately printed, 1976), in fact reveals how many humanists and men of letters had been trained as physicians.

7. Giovio, *Vita Leonis Decimi* (1551), bk. 3, 67.

8. *IO* 1:85.

9. *Commentaria in octo libros Topicorum Aristotelis* (Paris: Wechel, 1542), verso of title. For calling my attention to this dedication, found only in the rare first edition, I am much obliged to Prof. Edward P. Mahoney. The dedication is also noted by Carlo Dionisotti in his *Machiavellerie*, 424 n. 25.

10. *IO* 8:115.

11. *IO* 9:241.

12. December 15, 1515 (*IO* 1:85). Roman numerals will denote books of the *Histories* in Giovio's original manuscript numeration, Arabic numerals books of the *Histories* as published in Torrentino's edition of 1550–52. For a discussion and rec-

onciliation of the two series see my "Nota storico-critica" in *IO* 5:239–48.

13. *IO* 9:256.

14. Giovio described the dungeons in which Sauli and Petrucci were kept as "subterraneos carceres tenebris ac odore tetro maxime horribiles" (*Vita Leonis* [1551], 90). These infamous *gemellae*, as they were called, have been filled in and no longer exist.

15. *Vita Leonis* (1551), 89. The particulars of the examination of the familiars of Cardinal Petrucci are known, but some of the files for the trial have been lost, including those relating to Cardinal Sauli. See Alessandro Ferrajoli, "La congiura contro Leone X," *Miscellanea della R. Società Romana di Storia Patria* 7 (1920): 153–209.

16. In the Ischian dialogue, set in 1527, Giovio spoke of having served Giulio de' Medici for ten years. *IO* 9:256.

17. In 1522 Giovio instructed his brother to address letters to "Mastro Pauolo Iovio fisico del Rev.mo et Ill.mo de' Medici" (*IO* 1:97). A dispatch of the Ferrarese envoy to Florence dated February 17, 1521, called Giovio "medico de Mons. Ill.mo et R.mo Vicecancelliere et celeberrimo scriptore de historie." Archvio di Stato, Modena (henceforth, ASMo), Cancelleria Estense, Dispacci da Firenze, 12.

An entry in the Salviati account books for 1524 identified Giovio as "medicho di Nostro Signore [i.e., the pope]." Pisa, Salviati Archive, III, 11 (Quaderno di cassa A. di Iacopo di Giovanni Salviati, 1522–29), fol. 88. For this reference (and for much else) I am indebted to Dr. Gino Corti. See also Pietro Capparoni, *Paolo Giovio Archiatra di Papa Clemente VII.*

18. Celio Calcagnini, *Opera aliquot* (Basel, 1544), 101; *IO* 9:248. On Calcagnini and his visit to Rome in 1519–20 see the entry by Valerio Marchetti, A. De Ferrari, and Claudio Mutini in *DBI* 16:492–98. In chap. 3 of his treatise *De pueris recte instituendis*, Jacopo Sadoleto praised Giovio's mastery of "the physician's lore, in which he is distinguished both for his knowledge and his art and for the service and benefit which he brings from it to his friends." *Sadoleto on Education*, ed.

E. T. Campagnac and K. Forbes (London: Oxford University Press, 1916), 72. (For this reference I am obliged to Dr. Cecil H. Clough.)

19. On November 5 the Mantuan ambassador, Francesco Gonzaga, wrote the marquis to say that he had not been able to find a copy of the publication in the bookstores in Rome but that Giovio had promised to let him have at least two copies (Alessandro Luzio, *Lettere inedite di Paolo Giovio tratte dall'Archivio Gonzaga*, appendix, 47–48). Cicogna found a copy in the Biblioteca Marciana (Emmanuele Cicogna, *Delle iscrizioni Veneziane*, 6 vols. [Venice, 1824–53], 3:334–35). On the Biliotti family see Alessandro Ferrajoli, *Il Ruolo della Corte di Leone X*, ed. Vincenzo De Caprio, 210–15.

20. *Pauli Iovii Novocomensis Medici De Romanis Piscibus libellus ad Luduvicum Borbonium Cardinalem amplissimum* (Rome: Calvo, 1524). See Travi's introduction in *IO* 9:3–9 as well as the detailed analysis by Franco Minonzio, "Appunti sul *De romanis piscibus* di Paolo Giovio," *PSSC* 53 (1988–89): 87–128. For linguistic aspects see G. Folena, "Per la storia della ittionomia volgare: Tra cucina e scienza naturale," *Bollettino dell'Atlante Linguistico Mediterraneo* 5–6 (1963–64): 81–82.

21. Valeriano, *Hieroglyphica* (Cologne, 1631), bk. 31, 356.

22. *IO* 9:57.

23. Trofino, appointed datary in 1527, succeeding Giberti, was forced by bad health to resign the office at the end of September and died before the year was out.

24. *IO* 9:140. The Pavian goldsmith, Ambrogio Caradosso, called "il Foppa," died in 1526.

25. See the introduction to Galen's *On the Natural Faculties* by Arthur John Brock, M.D., in the Loeb Classics ed. (London and New York: Heinemann, 1916).

26. *IO* 9:137–38.

27. Cicero's *Tusculan Disputations* was "possibly the single most comprehensive and influential source for Renaissance psychological theory," and "a systematic philosophical guide to psychological health." George W. McClure, *Sorrow and Consola-*

tion in Italian Humanism, 7. For "perturbationes," Cicero's translation of the Greek "páthe," see *Tusc.* 4.5.

28. *IO* 9:138.

29. For a more extensive discussion of Giovio's two treatises see my article, "Renaissance Symposia," in Sergio Bertelli and Gloria Ramakus, eds., *Essays Presented to M. P. Gilmore* 1:363–74. On Giovio's debt to Platina (Bartolomeo dei Sacchi), see Vittorio Cian, "Gioviana," *Giornale storico della letteratura italiana* (henceforth, *GS*) 17 (1891): 284. For Platina's *De honesta voluptate* and a bibliography see the edition by Emilio Faccioli (Turin: Einaudi, 1985).

30. To Simone Porzio, May 20, 1551. *IO* 2:196.

31. Mario Santoro places Giovio among those Renaissance writers who were interested in a more integral comprehension of man through employment of all fields of knowledge in what he calls "humanistic encyclopedism." Mario Santoro, *Fortuna, ragione e prudenza nella civiltà letteraria del Cinquecento,* 20. Prof. John M. Headley has suggested a parallel between Giovio and Thucydides, who on account of his habit of systematic observation has sometimes been thought to have been a physician.

32. *Histories,* bk. 40 (*IO* 5:50, 65–66).

33. *IO* 9:254; 8:120.

34. *IO* 9:250. Complexion is intended in the Renaissance sense of a compounding of basic elements or humors.

35. *IO* 3:5. Needless to say, the physician can also be seen as an analog to Christ raising Lazarus. Copies of the medal exist in the British Museum, London; the Biblioteca Ambrosiana, Milan; and the Museo Nazionale del Bargello, Florence. It is reproduced by L. Forrer, *Biographical Dictionary of the Medalists* (London, 1904–1930), 5:326, and by Ludwig Goldscheider, *Unknown Portraits of the Renaissance* (London: Phaidon, 1952), pl. 19. For the copy in the Bargello see J. Graham Pollard, *Medaglie italiane nel Museo Nazionale del Bargello,* 3 vols. (Florence: Amici del Bargello, 1985), 2:633–34, pl. 309. See also G. Pollard, *Medals from the S. H. Kress Collection* (London: Phaidon, 1963), 64 n. 342. For other medals and portraits of Gio-

vio see Julian Kliemann in Charles Davis, ed., *Giorgio Vasari,* Catalogue of the Exhibition, Arezzo, 1981 (Florence: Edam, 1981), 120.

CHAPTER THREE

1. Charles L. Stinger, *The Renaissance in Rome*, 11–12, 91, and chap. 5.

2. Richard M. Douglas, *Jacopo Sadoleto* (Cambridge: Harvard University Press, 1959), 9.

3. Stinger, *The Renaissance in Rome,* 290–92; Paolo Cortesi, *De hominibus doctis,* ed. Giacomo Ferraù. On Roman humanism see Carlo Dionisotti, *Gli umanisti ed il volgare fra Quattrocento e Cinquecento,* and Riccardo Fubini, *Umanesimo e secolarizzazione.*

4. *Elogium* of Romulus (*IO* 8:237). The font of such Romanizing was Biondo, whose *Roma triumphans* advanced the idea that imperial Rome prefigured papal power. See Fubini, "Flavio Biondo," *DBI* 10:536–59.

5. *La vita del marchese di Pescara,* ed. Panigada (1931), 225. See also *IO* 3:182.

6. *IO* 8:144–45. See also Ernesto Travi, "Dignitas Italici nominis," *Lingua e vita nel primo Cinquecento,* 63–75.

7. *IO* 9:256. Michele Cataudella cautions that Giovio's supposed return to Augustan Latin was "incerto e contraddittorio." See his discussion of Giovio's Latin in *IO* 6:xiv–xvii.

8. For Giovio's affectionate portrait of Colocci see the *elogium* of Eligio Calenzio, *IO* 8:75. On Colocci and his garden see David R. Coffin, *Gardens and Gardening in Papal Rome,* and Vittorio Fanelli, *Ricerche su Angelo Colocci e sulla Roma cinquecentesca* (Vatican City: Biblioteca Apostolica Vaticana, 1979). On the Roman academy see D'Amico, *Renaissance Humanism,* 89–112, and Vincenzo De Caprio, "L'area umanistica romana 1513–1527," *Studi romani* 29 (1981): 321–35.

9. Sadoleto to Colocci, 1529 (*Iacobi Sadoleti Epistolae* [Cologne: Birckmann, 1554], 225–26). For Sadoleto's *vigna* see Coffin, *Gardens and Gardening,* 235. For Erasmus' memories see his letter to Robert

Guibé, February 8, 1512 (*Opus episto-larum*, ed. Allen, 1:499–500).

10. *IO* 8:105–106. "Archpoet" was the title of the chief of the Goliards. Cabbage, according to Pliny the Elder (*Nat. hist.* 20.84), was a cure for drinking.

11. *Elogium* of Sabellicus (Marc'Antonio Cocci), *IO* 8:78.

12. The group was later moved to the pillar of the nave where Raphael had painted for Küritz an Isaiah. See Virginia Anne Bonito, "The St. Anne Altar in Sant'Agostino, Rome: Restoration and Interpretation," *Burlington Magazine* 124 (1982): 268–76. In his *elogium* of Michelangelo, Giovio mentioned the sumptuous banquet given by Küritz to celebrate the dedication of the statue and the many poems written on that occasion (*IO* 8:230). For Giovio's relations with Küritz see *IO* 1:90–91. On Küritz's garden see Coffin, *Gardens and Gardening*, 233.

13. *Coryciana*, with the *De poetis urbanis, ad Paulum Iovium libellus* of Francesco Arsilli, ed. Blosio Palladio (1524). I have not been able to see the article by Msgr. José Ruysschaert, "Les péripéties inconnues de l'edition des 'Coryciana' de 1524" in *Atti del convegno di studi su A. Colocci* (Jesi: Amministrazione communale, 1972), 52 ff. See also Phyllis Pray Bober, "The 'Coryciana' and the Nymph Corycia," *Journal of the Warburg and Courtauld Institutes* (henceforth, *WJ*) 40 (1977): 223–39. Benedetto Varchi copied from Giovio's papers a list of the seventy-eight most prominent members of the Corycian academy, published by Vittorio Fanelli in his edition of Federico Ubaldini, *Vita di Monsignor Angelo Colocci*, 114–15.

14.

An vivunt Coryti Pario sub marmore Divi?
Naturae an potius hoc rear artis opus?
Artis opus, veras natura expromere formas
Si bene vult, posthac discat ab arte opus est.   —*Coryciana* (1524), Kiir.

For Giovio's disclaimer at being a poet see the Ischian dialogue, *IO* 9:243. On his rela-tions with poets see Cian, "Gioviana," *GS* 17 (1891): 277–357. The best edition of *De poetis urbanis* is in *Poesie latine di Francesco Arsilli*, ed. R. Francolini (Senigallia, 1837). On Arsilli see the article by Msgr. José Ruysschaert in *DBI* 4:342–43, and Giovio's *elogium* of him, *IO* 8:124–25.

15. Seventh satire, lines 127–29.

16. *IO* 9:238–39. On the academy's attitudes toward Greek see Ferraù and Delio Cantimori, "Questioncine sulle opere progettate da Paolo Cortesi," in *Studi di bibliografia e di storia in onore di Tammaro de Marinis*, 4 vols. (Verona: Valdonegal, 1964), 1:273–80.

17. *IO* 8:92; 9:234, 259.

18. "Magna felicitatis pars est Romae innotuisse." To Jodocus Gaverius, March 1, 1523 (*Opus epistolarum*, ed. Allen, 5:246). I am told that Erasmus was paraphrasing Seneca, which would have suited the context.

19. Gianfrancesco Lancellotti, *Poesie italiane e latine di Monsignor Angelo Colocci* (Jesi: Bonelli, 1772), 99. The poem is found in the Biblioteca Apostolica Vaticana (henceforth, BAV), MS. Vat. Lat. 3388, 270r.

20. *Vita Leonis* (1551), 68. Francesco Vettori confirmed Giovio's portrait of Leonine Rome with his ironic comment: "Nel suo pontificato, in Roma, non fu peste, non penuria di vivere, non guerra, fiorivano le lettere e le buone arti e vi erano ancora in culmine e' vizi" (*Sommario della storia d'Italia*, in Vettori, *Scritti storici e politici*, ed. Enrico Niccolini, 197). On Medicean traditions of a golden age see Cecil H. Clough, "Chivalry and Magnificence in the Golden Age of the Renaissance," in *Chivalry in the Renaissance*, ed. Sydney Anglo, 25–47. For a bibliography and the concept of the *aurea aetas* see Vincenzo De Caprio, *La tradizione e il trauma*, 9; Stinger, *The Renaissance in Rome*, 298–99.

21. *Vita Leonis* (1551), 95–102, 109–11. Pastor called them "brilliant historical descriptions." Ludwig von Pastor, *The History of the Popes from the Close of the Middle Ages* (henceforth, Pastor), 8:141.

22. *Vita Leonis* (1551), 109.

23. *Vita Leonis* (1551), 96–99.

24. *IO* 3:215, 8:123, 9:251. For the festivities of Giuliano's citizenship see Bonner Mitchell, *Rome in the High Renaissance*, 61–74, and Anthony M. Cummings, *The Politicized Muse* (Princeton: Princeton University Press, 1992), chap. 4.

25. ". . . se nihil post Titum Livium in eo genere volumine illo elegantius et uberius vidisse." Benedetto Giovio, *Historia patriae* (1982), bk. 2, 258. For a negative assessment of Leo X's patronage see Domenico Gnoli's essay, "Secolo di Leone X?" in *La Roma di Leone X*, 341–84. Gnoli suggested that Leo mainly enjoyed letting his ear float on the cadences of the Latin. Giovio's biography makes clear that Leo diluted the good effects of his patronage by subsidizing the mediocre alongside the talented.

26. For the half-cavalierate see *IO* 6:136 and 2:167. The bull of March 3, 1518, is found in Archivio Segreto Vaticano (henceforth, ASV), Reg. Vat. 1142, fols. 22v–25r. For other references to this benefice see *IO* 1:112 and 2:167. The bishop of Mondovì at this time was a member of the Fieschi family, Giovio's friends, and in securing the appointment he may well have had help from them. A wide variety of clerics were entitled to call themselves papal familiars. For a description of the papal bureaucracy, mainly during the Quattrocento, see Peter Partner, *The Pope's Men*.

27. Giovio's expression is *anhelens* (literally, "panting"), *IO* 9:248. See "Il concetto di imitazione nel Rinascimento," in Riccardo Scrivano, *Cultura e letteratura nel Cinquecento*, 315–30.

28. *Elogium* of Cattaneo (*IO* 8:103). As published, Cattaneo's translation contained no dedication to Giovio but rather one to Cardinal Sangiorgio dated 1506. *Aphtonii progymnasmata idest praeexercitationes rhetorum: Luciani opusculum de componenda Historia nuper a Ioanne Maria Cataneo latinitate donata* (Venice: Gregorio de' Gregori, 1522). The recent study of Lucian by Emilio Mattioli, *Lucian e l'umanesimo* (Naples: Istituto Italiano per gli Studi Storici, 1980), does not mention the Cattaneo translation. In a letter to Girolamo Scannapeco, Giovio declared that he had always followed "the precepts of Lucian." *IO* 1:174.

29. *Actius de numeris poeticis et lege Historiae* (Naples: Mayr, 1507). See the modern edition in Giovanni Pontano, *Dialoghi*, ed. Carmelito Previtera, 123–239.

30. *IO* 9:255–56. In Giovio's notebooks there is an entry listing as a "speculum doloris, admirandi sine spe imitationis," Caesar, Livy, Sallust, Tacitus, Velleius Paterculus, and Suetonius. As a "speculum optimae spei, aequandi, si non omnino superandi," Giovio listed Pontano, Callimaco (Filippo Buonaccorsi), Sabellico, Paolo Emili, Bracelli, Campano, Valla, and Simonetta. As "speculum laetitiae, contemnendi extra historiae notitiam" he listed Ammianus Marcellinus, Spartianus, Vopiscus, Eutropius, Trebellius Pollio, and Paulus Diaconus. SSC, Archivio Aliati, 28, fasc. 5, fol. 44r. Incompletely transcribed by Giambattista Giovio, "Elogio," 74–75.

31. Benedetto Giovio, *Historia patriae* (1982), bk. 2, 257–58; Giovio to Lelio Torelli, June (my dating) 1550 (*IO* 2:166).

32. Giovio was probably thinking of Tacitus as the last universal historian, scarcely fair to Biondo or to Ammianus Marcellinus, of whom he seemed to have had a low opinion (*IO* 3:6), probably because Ammianus was not a native Latin speaker. On Giovio and universal history see Cochrane, *Historians*, chap. 13. For Polybius' statements on the importance of universal history see esp. bks. 1.4, and 3.32, both of which were accessible in Niccolò Perotti's Latin translation (Rome, 1473, and Venice, 1498, 1518, 1520, 1521). Giovio's language, in fact, was remarkably similar to the Latin of Perotti's translation of 1.4: "Hoc autem vel in primis nos animavit ad scribendam historiam: simul, quam temporibus nostris nemo adhuc fuit: qui in universum res gestas scribere voluerit etc." (*Polibii historiarum libri quinque* [Venice: Aldus, 1521], 75v). The suggestion that Giovio may have modeled his whole historical work on Polybius was made by Beatrice R. Reynolds, "Latin Historiography: A Sur-

vey: 1400–1600," *Studies in the Renaissance* 2 (1955): 56, and more extensively by Thomas F. Mayer, "Reginald Pole in Paolo Giovio's *Descriptio*: A Strategy for Reconversion," *Sixteenth Century Journal* 16 (1985): 439 n. 35.

33. The *Decades* are praised by name in Giovio's *elogium* of Biondo and either the *Roma instaurata* or *Roma triumphans* is praised by content, it is not clear which (*IO* 8:49). Biondo also stressed universal history over particular, but his style was not admired in the sixteenth century, and his inability to bring explanatory order to the complexities of his own times may have disqualified him in Giovio's eyes as a model. See Fubini's entry in *DBI* 10:536–59; Denys Hay, "Flavio Biondo and the Middle Ages," *Proceedings of the British Academy* 45 (1959): 97–125; and Donald R. Kelley, "Humanism and History," in Albert Rabil, Jr., ed., *Renaissance Humanism* 3:243.

34. In the letter to Sanudo of 1515 the book read by the pope is not specified, but in the Ischian dialogue Giovio reveals that it was book VIII, of which a MS is preserved in the Vatican Library (*IO* 9:256). See my analysis of the composition of the *Histories* in *IO* 5:239–48.

35. Kenneth M. Setton, *The Papacy and the Levant* (hereafter, Setton), 3:153. For the effect of the fall of Constantinople see Agostino Pertusi, *La caduta di Costantinople: Le testimonianze dei contemporanei: L'eco nel mondo*, 2 vols. (Milan: Mondadori, 1976).

36. See Ubaldini, *Vita di Msgr. Angelo Colocci*, ed. Fanelli, 78–83. Giovio recorded Lascaris' epitaph, composed by himself, which laments the slavery of Greece (*IO* 8:64). The Turkish menace was a common theme in Roman oratory of the Quattrocento and Cinquecento. See John M. McManamon, "The Ideal Renaissance Pope: Funeral Oratory from the Papal Court," *Archivum historiae pontificiae* 14 (1976): 45–46.

37. D'Amico, *Renaissance Humanism*, 82–83. Giovio gave a critique of the work in the *Elogia* (*IO* 8:131). See also Cochrane, *Historians*, 49–50.

38. Setton 3:147–48, 151, 154; Stinger,

The Renaissance in Rome, 108–109.

39. Giles thought that Leo X would be the first pontiff of the new era. John W. O'Malley, *Giles of Viterbo on Church and Reform* (Leiden: Brill, 1968), 110–15. O'Malley does, however, caution that Rome "does not seem to have sustained a high level of excitement over the prospect of the New World and the new peoples offered to its pastoral care." There is not a single mention of the New World in the acts and orations of the Fifth Lateran Council. O'Malley, "The Discovery of America and Reform Thought at the Papal Court in the Early Cinquecento," in *First Images of America: The Impact of the New World on the Old*, ed. Fredi Chiappelli (Berkeley: University of California Press, 1976), 187. On possible Joachimite ideas in Sauli's household during Giovio's service see the intriguing article by Josephine Jungić, "Prophecies of the Angelic Pastor in Sebastiano del Piombo's Portrait of Cardinal Bandinello Sauli and Three Companions," in *Prophetic Rome in the High Renaissance*, ed. Marjorie Reeves, 345–70.

40. For Charles V's device see Giovio's *Dialogo dell'imprese* (*IO* 9:379–80). For Giovio's sense of marvel at sixteenth-century inventions and discoveries see *IO* 9:184.

41. *IO* 1:83. In his *elogium* of d'Alviano, Giovio mentioned seeing his commentaries (now lost), written during his imprisonment by the French (1508–13); *IO* 8:389. Giovio's account of the League of Cambrai either was not completed or was lost in the sack of Rome.

42. The argument for Giovio's having begun with current events and followed the thread backward is strengthened by his remark in old age to Camillo Porzio that he wished he had followed the thread of events back to the revolt of the Neapolitan barons. Camillo Porzio, *La congiura de' baroni del regno di Napoli contra il re Ferdinando I*, dedication, in Porzio, *Opere*, ed. C. Monzani (Florence: Le Monnier, 1855), 3. Giovio's wish to go back even earlier may well have come after discussing Pontano's *De bello neapolitano* with Jacopo Sannazaro in 1527–28 (*IO* 1:177). For a discussion of

the currently known evidence bearing on the timing and sequence of composition of Giovio's *Histories* see my "Nota storico-critica" (*IO* 5:239–48).

CHAPTER FOUR

1. *Histories*, bk. 3 (*IO* 3:354).
2. To Marin Sanudo, December 15, 1515 (*IO* 1:84–85).
3. *Vita Leonis* (1551), 81.
4. *Vita Leonis* (1551), 85.
5. The phrase is Pastor's, 8:240.
6. One of his relatives, in fact, was in trade at Constantinople. *IO* 1:149.
7. *Vita Leonis* (1551), 93.
8. Università Cattolica del Sacro Cuore, Milan (henceforth, UCM), Fondo Negri da Oleggio, to Benedetto Giovio, September 1519. The papers are not yet catalogued. See Tino Toffano, "La biblioteca Negri da Oleggio: Una preziosa raccolta di storia lombarda," *Aevum* 48 (1974): 570–75. I owe all citations from this *fondo* to the kindness of Prof. Travi.
9. *Vita Leonis* (1551), 95.
10. Pierpont Morgan Library, New York City (henceforth, ML), MA 3230.
11. UCM, Fondo Negri da Oleggio. For a fuller discussion of the evidence for the sequence of composition and the existing MSS see my "Nota storico-critica" in *IO* 5:239–48, and Cecil H. Clough, "A MS of Paolo Giovio's *Historiae sui temporis, liber VII*: More Light on the Career of Ludovico degli Arrighi," *PSSC* 53 (1988–89): 53–83.
12. Ernesto Travi, "Giovio, gli Orti Oricellari e Machiavelli," *Testo* 5 (1983): 52–61.
13. On the later phase of the gardens see Rudolf von Albertini, *Das florentinische Staatsbewusstsein im Übergang von der Republik um Prinzipat* (Bern: Francke, 1955), 74–90. Giovio specifically mentioned only Roberto Acciaiuoli, Francesco da Diacceto, Piero Martelli, and Giovanni Corsi (*IO* 9:292). He did not mention Machiavelli's participation, which, despite his remarks in *The Art of War*, is problematic. See Roberto Ridolfi, *Vita di Niccolò Machiavelli*, 297–98, but also Carlo Dionisotti, *Machiavellerie*, 138–53.

14. *IO* 9:292–93.
15. *IO* 9:292. Actually, the *De bello italico* was largely composed during Rucellai's self-imposed exile from Florence beginning in 1506 (Bernardo Rucellai, *De bello italico commentarius* [London: Bowyer, 1733]). It is clear that Giovio used it, since in bk. 1 of his *Histories* he incorporated a detail found only in Rucellai's history, namely Piero de' Medici's positioning the French ambassador behind an arras while he held a conference with the Milanese ambassador. *IO* 3:29–30.
16. See the last sentence of Machiavelli's *Florentine Histories.*
17. While Florentine ambassador to Naples in 1495, Rucellai consulted with Pontano, who was one of the first to emphasize the folly of the Italian princes. Some of Pontano's views subsequently emerged in print in his dialogue, *De prudentia* (Florence, 1508). See Santoro, *Fortuna, ragione e prudenza*, chaps. 2 and 5. For the views of Corio (whose history was first published in 1503) on the culpability of Ludovico see Bernardo Corio, *Storia di Milano*, ed. Anna Morisi Guerra, 2 vols. (Turin: UTET, 1978), 2:1479–81.
18. For further discussion of the theme and the historians involved see Cochrane, *Historians*, chap. 7; Giovanni Pillinini, *Il sistema degli stati italiani, 1454–1494*, chap. 1; Anne Denis, *Charles VIII et les Italiens: Histoire et mythe*, 22–23 and passim; and Gigliola Soldi Rondinini, "Ludovico il Moro nella storiografia contemporanea," *Saggi di storia e storiografia visconteo-sforzesche* (Bologna: Cappelli, 1984), 159–204. Felix Gilbert attempted, somewhat ambitiously, to order the contributions to this tradition sequentially but neglected Giovio's part (*Machiavelli and Guicciardini*, 255–70).

Unlike Machiavelli and Guicciardini, Giovio did not specifically celebrate Lorenzo as the architect of peace, which suggests caution in making any definite attributions of intellectual indebtedness to the Orti tradition. With regard to the idea of a turning point, however. it is significant that Pietro Alcionio, who was then lecturing in the *studium* of Florence, praised the first de-

---

cade of Giovio's *Histories* for embracing the history of the world "post quam Carolus VIII Rex Galliae cum maximis copiis transgressus Alpeis tranquillum Italiae statum perturbavit, et prima funestissimorum in Italia bellorum iecit semina" (*Medices legatus de exsilio*, bk. 2, fol. fiiir). In the *Vita Leonis X*, the first-written of his biographies, Giovio was already speaking of Charles VIII as having been "exitiabili dissidio singularique dementia nostrorum principum evocatus" (*IO* 6:21).

19. See Dionisotti, *Machiavellerie*, 139–40. Dionisotti is able to give convincing proof for the hypothesis advanced by J. H. Whitfield that it was through the philo-Hellenic circles of Florence that Machiavelli came to know the sixth book of Polybius and not through a visit of Lascaris as supposed by J. H. Hexter. A similar viewpoint is taken by Eugenio Garin, "Polibio e Machiavelli," *Quaderni di storia* 16 (1990): 5–22.

20. Dionisotti, *Machiavellerie*, 414, 417. See also Travi, "Orti."

21. See Ezio Raimondi, "Machiavelli, Giovio ed Aristofane," in Sergio Antonelli, ed., *Saggi di letteratura italiana in onore di Gaetano Trombatore*, 389–400.

22. *IO* 8:112.

23. *IO* 8:111. Dionisotti notes that in the Ischian dialogue Giovio mentions Machiavelli as *annalium vernaculus scriptor*, suggesting that he had already read the *Istorie fiorentine* in manuscript (*Machiavellerie*, 421). As we now know, Giovio revised the dialogue in 1535, allowing him ample time to have read the published version of 1532. When he came to write the *Elogia* twenty years later, Giovio apparently felt that the Florentine situation was such that his earlier praises of Machiavelli needed modification. Dionisotti points out, however, that it would have been easier to drop Machiavelli from the *Elogia* altogether, and that his inclusion is another demonstration of Giovio's independence and critical sincerity.

24. *IO* 9:338. For Benedetto's outlook see his *Historia patriae* (1982), 72.

25. See Quentin Skinner, *The Foundations of Modern Political Thought*, 2 vols.

(Cambridge: Cambridge University Press, 1978), 1:25–26; or Gary Ianziti, *Humanist Historiography under the Sforzas*.

26. *Histories*, bk. 25 (*IO* 4:24–26). For a similar opinion on Florentine "liberty" see the *Commentaries* of Pius II, bk. 2.

27. The context of Giovio's later views on Machiavelli is really the anti-Machiavellian discussions regarding the need for fortresses which began with the restoration of the principate in 1513. The same context also explains Giovio's comment in the life of Ottone Visconti that "in conserving the principate nothing is more empty or fickle than popular support" (Dionisotti, *Machiavellerie*, 438). Giovio's conclusions regarding the principate were at least in accord with the last chapter of Machiavelli's *Prince*.

28. He was there from July 24 to October 2, 1519, for rest and conversations with the cardinal, and again in late July and August 1520 (R. Ridolfi, *Vita di Francesco Guicciardini*, 134–37). For a discussion of the differences in outlook between Giovio and Guicciardini see Dionisotti, *Machiavellerie*, 418–19, 438–43.

29. *IO* 4:24–25.

30. See the analysis by N. Rubinstein, "Guicciardini politico," in *Francesco Guicciardini, 1483–1983: Nel V centenario della nascita* (Florence: Leo S. Olschki for Istituto Nazionale di Studi sul Rinascimento, 1984), 181–82. The *Dialogo* was written on the campaign of 1521, when Giovio was also present with the army.

31. *IO* 9:292.

32. *IO* 9:293. In bk. 27 of the *Histories* Giovio called the destruction of all these villas in 1529 proof of Francesco Carducci's inexorability. *IO* 4:103.

33. *IO* 9:292.

34. See Travi, "Orti," 58–59.

35. *IO* 9:293–95.

36. To Benedetto, July 3, 1520 (*IO* 1:86–87).

37. On Giovio as representative of a low period in the history of the Church see Msgr. Pietro Gini, "Paolo Giovio e la vita religiosa del Cinquecento," in *Atti*, 31–50. On careerism in the Church see Carlo Dionisotti, "Chierici e laici nella letteratura

italiana nel primo '500," in *Geografia e storia della letteratura italiana*, 47–73. On pluralism among Renaissance prelates see Barbara McClung Hallman, *Italian Cardinals, Reform, and the Church as Property, 1492–1563*. For the practice of alienating benefices to relatives see esp. chap. 3. By 1527 Bembo had twenty-eight different benefices.

38. *IO* 1:92, 100.

39. Vasari, in the life of Franciabigio. For Giovio's scheme see Julian Kliemann, "Il pensiero di Paolo Giovio nelle pitture eseguite sulle sue 'invenzioni,'" in *Atti*, 197–223, and by the same author, *Andrea del Sarto: Il Tributo a Cesare* (Poggio a Caiano, 1986). See also the interesting if controversial reading of Janet Cox-Rearick, *Dynasty and Destiny in Medici Art* (Princeton: Princeton University Press, 1984).

40. Pietro Antonio Torelli, dispatch of February 17, 1521. ASMo, Cancelleria Ducale, Dispacci da Firenze, 12.

41. *IO* 1:88–89.

42. Alessandro Luzio, "Isabella d'Este e Leone X," *Archivio storico italiano* (henceforth, *ASI*), 5th ser., 44 (1909): 118; 45 (1910): 258.

43. June 25, 1521 (*IO* 1:89). Giovio's phrase echoed Cicero's expression in his letter to Lucceius, "qui non tantum laudari se laetatur, sed addit etiam, a laudato viro" (*Ad familiares* 5.12.7). On Giovio's relations with Castiglione see Vittorio Cian, *Un illustre nunzio pontificio del Rinascimento: Baldassar Castiglione*, 164. On Equicola see Stephen Kolsky, *Mario Equicola: The Real Courtier* (Geneva: Droz, 1991).

44. Guicciardini, *Storia d'Italia* (henceforth, *SI*), 14.10.

45. *Vita Leonis* (1551), 102. For Guicciardini's views see *SI* 14.1. In 1521, however, his outlook was quite different. He may, in fact, have been influenced by Giovio (see below, "Conclusion," n. 58).

46. Epitome of bk. 20, probably written in 1551 (*IO* 4:7). In the life of Alfonso d'Este, Giovio stressed Leo X's desire to recover Parma and Piacenza and to avenge himself on the viceroy of Milan, Odet de Foix, viscount of Lautrec, whom he suspected of having aided Francesco Maria della Rovere to return to Urbino in January 1517. Giovio, *De vita et rebus gestis Alphonsi Atestini* (1550), 42.

47. *Vita Leonis* (1551), 103–104. In the summary of book 20 of the *Histories* Giovio also set the alliance of pope and emperor in the context of their cooperation against the spread of Lutheranism in Germany. Guicciardini, while accepting Giovio's reasons, also stressed Leo X's intrigues as a cause of hostility between Francis I and Charles V. *SI* 14.1.

48. *Vita Leonis* (1551), 99. See also Giovio's *Hadriani vita* (1551), 139.

49. *Vita Leonis* (1551), 103. In the *Elogia* Giovio somewhat sarcastically described Aleandro as sent to Germany by Leo X to put an end to the incipient Lutheran heresy "by disputation." *IO* 8:120.

50. Stinger, *The Renaissance in Rome*, 329.

51. By the time he wrote the life of Alfonso d'Este in 1550, Giovio knew the attack on Reggio was only used by the pope as a pretext for revealing long-made plans and said as much. On the basis of Alfonso's personal word, Giovio also discounted the contention (which he said was spread by Guicciardini and Guido Rangoni) that Alfonso had fostered the French attempt on Reggio (*Vita Alfonsi* [1550], 43). Guicciardini did not make this charge in the *Storia d'Italia*.

52. *IO* 1:91.

53. The withdrawal had also been owing, at least in part, to Colonna's not altogether groundless suspicion that with Parma and Piacenza regained the pope would drop out of the league (Pastor 8:52). While noting the rivalry, Guicciardini attributed the withdrawal more to unexpected difficulties in the siege compounded not only by the arrival of Lautrec but by new fears regarding the intentions of Alfonso and the need to protect Modena and Reggio. *SI* 14.5.

54. *Vita Leonis* (1551), 105.

55. *SI* 14.8.

56. Giovio, *De vita et rebus gestis Ferdinandi Davali cognomento Piscarii* (Florence, 1551), 305. Gonzalo Jimenez de

Quesada, the future marshal, who may have been with the Spanish troops as early as 1521, held that the fight broke out because the Italians had been pilfering the Spaniards' baggage. *El antijovio*, ed. Rafael Torres Quintero, 60–61.

57. *Vita Piscarii* (1551), 311. Like Giovio, Guicciardini believed that the successes of the allied armies were almost entirely due to the mistakes of the French (*SI* 14.9).

58. *Vita Piscarii* (1551), 310.

59. Luzio cited a letter of Isabella's to Federico of November 26, 1521, mentioning the departure that day from Mantua of some of the agents and servitors of Cardinal Giulio who had been visiting, including "lo ex.te M.ro Paolo Giovio medico del p.to R.mo et Ill.mo" ("Isabella d'Este e Leone X," p. 259). For the Mantuan personages Giovio encountered on this visit of 1521, including the chronicler Jacopo d'Atri, count of Pianella, see *IO* 1:96, 98, 101, 102, 104, 105, 111. The Accademia di San Pietro took its name from the main square outside the palazzo.

Giovio's praises of Isabella in the Ischian dialogue, while warm, were so generic as to suggest that he may not, in fact, have formed a particularly close relationship with the exacting marchioness. In the *Dialogo dell'imprese* Giovio claimed to have devised the motto *SVFFICIT VNVM IN TENEBRIS* (In shadows one is sufficient), for Isabella's famous *impresa* showing a candelabrum with just one candle lit, but there are doubts. See Mauda Bregogli-Russo, *L'impresa come ritratto del Rinascimento* (Naples: Loffredo, 1990), 172 ff.

60. *Vita Piscarii* (1551), 313. Juan de Urbina (Giovanni d'Urbino, Giovanni Dorbino, Gian d'Urbina, etc.), who later participated in the sack of Rome, subsequently became master of the camp to Giovio's friend, the marquis del Vasto. He is highly praised by del Vasto in the Ischian dialogue (*IO* 9:219) and by Giovio in the life of Pescara (*Vita Piscarii* [1551], 333). See Judith Hook, *The Sack of Rome*, 126. He is identified by Valori and Roth as the prince of Orange's lieutenant general in the siege of Florence, mortally wounded while reconnoitering the walls. Aldo Valori, *La*

difesa della Repubblica Fiorentina (Florence: Vallecchi, 1929), 162; Cecil Roth, *The Last Florentine Republic* (London: Methuen, 1925), 160, 164, 180. Jiminez de Quesada calls him Juan de Hurbina (*Antijovio*, 61). His biographer in the *Enciclopedia Universal Illustrada*, vol. 65 (Madrid, 1929), 1392, says he was born in Alava.

61. In a letter of September 19, 1550, Giovio gave the names of the soldiers who tortured his brother as a certain Gallindo and the ensign Juan de Vargas (*IO* 2:175). An eyewitness account of the sack is also given by Benedetto Giovio in his *Historia Patriae* (1982), 143–45.

62. *Vita Piscarii* (1551), 313–14. Guicciardini recorded that the sack of Como took place "con infamia grande del marchese" (*SI* 14.9).

63. On Giovio's reactions to the crisis of Italy see Ettore Rota, "Paolo Giovio," in *Letteratura italiana: I minori* 2:945–46.

64. *Vita Piscarii* (1551), 315; *Pompeii Columnae vita* (Florence: Torrentino, 1551), 172. In a letter to Isabella d'Este dated December 5, Federico Gonzaga said the two legates had just left Milan. Archivio di Stato, Mantua (hereafter, ASM), Archivio Gonzaga, Corrispondenza estera, 2125.

65. Pastor 8:59, from the account by Bartolomeo Angilelli in Marin Sanudo, *I diarii* (hereafter, Sanudo), ed. Rinaldo Fulin et al., 32:239–40.

66. *Vita Leonis* (1551), 107–108. To the imperial ambassador Leo had declared on returning to Rome that the victory at Milan had given him greater joy than his election to the papacy (Pastor 8:60). In the life of Pompeo Colonna, Giovio also allowed the possibility of a fever contracted in the pestilent air about La Magliana (*Pompeii vita* [1551], 172). Guicciardini also noted the suspicion of poison (*SI* 14.10), and did not hesitate to name the "great prince" as Francis I. November not being a malarial season, Pieraccini suggested instead bronchial pneumonia. Gaetano Pieraccini, *La stirpe de' Medici di Cafaggiolo* 1:227.

67. *Vita Piscarii* (1551), bk. 2, 318. On the importance of the Sforza restoration to

the Milanese see Gino Franceschini in the *Storia di Milano,* 17 vols. (Milan: Fondazione Treccani degli Alfieri, 1953–66), 8:233.

68. As noted, Guicciardini felt that the troubles that continued to afflict Italy after Leo's death were owing to his league of 1521 with the emperor. This, however, was only his final judgment in the *Storia d'Italia,* after he himself had tried his hand at driving the foreigner from Italy. Vettori, who was bitterly opposed to the imperial alliance, commented that fortune's last grace conferred on Leo was to carry him off before he saw the consequences of what he had done. *Sommario,* 168, 190, 196–97.

CHAPTER FIVE

1. *Hadriani vita* (1551), 128. For Giberti as source see *IO* 1:92–93.

2. Giovio's account of the conclave is generally consonant with Guicciardini's (see Pastor 9:15–26). K. J. P. Lowe has come to somewhat different conclusions regarding Colonna's role. *Church and Politics in Renaissance Italy: The Life and Career of Cardinal Francesco Soderini,* 121–24.

3. *Hadriani vita* (1551), 130.

4. Girolamo Seripando to Agostino Cocciano, June 9, 1548, ". . . et vi troverete tratti divini massime nella vita di Hadriano" (*Concilium Tridentinum,* ed. Görres-Gesellschaft [henceforth, *CT*], 2:436). Giovio did not mention the *Hadriani vita* in the Ischian dialogue along with the other works in progress in 1527, so it may be confidently placed between his return to Rome in late 1528 and the death of Cardinal Enkevoirt in 1534. *IO* 9:257.

5. *Hadriani vita* (1551), 115; *IO* 6:109. In addition to the other classical, as opposed to ecclesiastical, Latin usages (e.g., *dii immortales*), Giovio even adopted the term for the ancient Roman electoral assemblies, *comitia,* to describe the conclaves. For an alternate perspective on curial Ciceronianism see D'Amico, *Renaissance Humanism,* 156–58.

6. Pecchiai, *Roma nel Cinquecento,* 7.

7. *Hadriani vita* (1551), 127. For the large number of pasquinades dating from the conclave and election see Valerio Marucci, Antonio Marzo, and Angelo Romano, eds., *Pasquinate romane del Cinquecento* 1:139 ff.

8. Vettori, *Sommario,* 200; Guicciardini, *SI* 14.12.

9. *IO* 1:92–94.

10. Giovio, *Vita Piscarii* (1551), 318; *Vita del Pescara,* ed. Panigada (1931), 282. Burigozzo gave the date of entry as April 4. Gianmarco Burigozzo, "Cronaca milanese, 1500–1544," *ASI* 3 (1842): 437.

11. Guicciardini mentioned arrears of pay as a factor in the Swiss demands (*SI* 14.14). Recent scholarship, however, has shown that Lautrec was not short of money, confirming the accuracy of Giovio's version. See R. J. Knecht, *Francis I,* 115–16.

12. Giovio erroneously gave the date as April 29; *Vita Piscarii* (1551), 321–25; *Vita del Pescara* (1931), 287–94. For a contemporary account see Sanudo 23:213–14. See also the discussion of Piero Pieri, *Il Rinascimento e la crisi militare italiana,* 541–46.

13. *Vita del Pescara* (1931), 281; *Vita Piscarii* (1551), 318.

14. *IO* 1:96–97. Giovio's letter is dated May 12 but is known only through a copy. Its content would suggest May 22 as a more probable date. For the conspiracy see Rosemary Devonshire Jones, *Francesco Vettori,* 157; J. N. Stephens, *Fall of the Florentine Republic,* 120–22; and Lowe, *Soderini,* chap. 11.

15. For Giovio's lack of basic sympathy see particularly the dedication of the *Vita Piscarii.*

16. Letter of Girolamo Negri, August 14, 1522. *Lettere di principi* 1:81r–v (misnumbered as 78). Since vol. 1 was reprinted at least twice, to avoid confusion notes will henceforth carry the year.

17. *Hadriani vita* (1551), 136. The encounter took place on August 23.

18. *IO* 1:99–100.

19. For Giovio at Genoa see also *IO* 9:30, 288–91, 398–99; and Carlo Volpati, "Paolo Giovio e Genoa," *Giornale storico e letterario della Liguria* 14 (1938): 187.

20. On Federico's desire to carry the war into France after the siege of Parma see A. Luzio, "Isabella d'Este e Leone X," *ASI,*

5th ser., 45 (1910): 259. On the effectiveness of his leadership in defending Pavia see Leonardo Mazzoldi, ed., *Storia di Mantova*, 2:276–77.

21. The "casetta sopra il giardino" was probably above the "giardino di stretta lunga" mentioned in a letter of May 12, 1523, to Benedetto (*IO* 1:97). Matteo Gianoncelli determined that this garden lay on the east side of Como and had belonged to Giovanni da Montorfano. It was not the garden later acquired as the site of the museum. For a reference to a "giardino già del Giovio in Stricta Lunga" see F. Feliciano Ninguarda, *Atti della visita pastorale diocesana* (Como, 1892–94), parte prima (1589–1593): 67.

22. Earlier Giovio had heard that the new pope had been made aware of his debt to the cardinal de' Medici and had naturally assumed he would honor it. *IO* 1:96.

23. Pastor 9:104.

24. *Hadriani vita* (1551), 141–43.

25. G. Oreste, "Girolamo Adorno," *DBI* 1:296–98.

26. ASMo, Cancelleria Ducale Estense, Dispacci da Firenze, n. 13, November 19, 1522. Partially cited by Giulio Bertoni, "Ippolito d'Este, Cardinale di Ferrara," *RSI* 41 (1924): 362–63.

27. Giovio stressed instead that the duke had made his personal peace with Cardinal Giulio before Adrian's arrival in Italy, using the services of his emissary, Antonio Constabile. *Vita Alphonsi* (1550), 46.

28. *IO* 7:95; 9:262. Ariosto was not currently in Ferrara. On Adorno's mission see Oreste, "Girolamo Adorno," *DBI* 1:296–98. For details of his arrival in Venice see Sanudo 33:528, 529. Volpati, probably basing himself on Litta, held that Giovio had preceded Adorno to Venice, but I can find no evidence for this. Carlo Volpati, "Paolo Giovio e Venezia," *Archivio veneto*, 5th ser., 15 (1934): 142. The ambassador, and probably Giovio as well, was housed in the palace of Andrea Corner on the Grand Canal where the Turkish ambassador had been lodged in May, most likely the present-day Ca' Corner Gheltof.

29. Jervis Wegg, *Richard Pace*, 192. For praise of Pace, who later sent Giovio his commentary on the Scottish wars, see *IO* 9:265.

30. Sanudo 33:531.

31. Wegg, *Richard Pace*, 205.

32. *IO* 1:101. In bks. 1 and 2 of the *Histories* Francesco Gonzaga was given credit for his part in the battle of Fornovo, although without exaggeration.

33. *IO* 8:410–11. Giovio later lamented that rats had eaten the notes he took on his interview with Gritti. Biblioteca Communale, Como, MS Sup. 2.2.42, fol. 226.

34. Machiavelli, likewise, taxed the Venetians for the folly of this alliance in the *Prince*, chap. 3, where he observed that to gain "a couple of towns in Lombardy" the Venetians might have made Louis XII master of two-thirds of Italy.

35. *Elogium* of Grimani (*IO* 8:410–12). See also *IO* 9:195–96.

36. For Giovio's friendships with Venetians see Volpati, "Giovio e Venezia." For the sightseeing of Adorno's party see Sanudo 33:549.

37. *IO* 9:283.

38. Sanudo 34:5–7.

39. Cochrane, *Historians*, 168. Sanudo's history was finally edited and published by Rinaldo Fulin, *Archivio veneto* 3 (1873). On Sanudo as historian see Gaetano Cozzi, "Marin Sanudo il Giovane: Dalla cronaca alla storia," *Rivista storica italiana* 80 (1968): 297–314.

40. On these themes see Cochrane, *Historians*, 166–68, and Denis, *Charles VIII et les Italiens*. On Benedetti see Dorothy M. Schullian's introduction to the *Diaria de bello carolino* (New York: Ungar, 1967); and Mario Crespi, "Alessandro Benedetti," *DBI* 8:244–47. In a letter of May 2, 1522, Giovio had requested Equicola to obtain for him the commentary of Jacopo d'Atri, count of Pianella, on the siege of Pavia (*IO* 1:96). Luzio identified Pianella's commentary with the anonymous *Croniche del Marchese di Mantova* preserved in the Biblioteca Trivulziana; see his notes to the letter in *Lettere inedite di Paolo Giovio*.

41. Pietro Bembo, *Lettere*, ed. Ernesto Travi (Bologna: Commissione per i testi di

lingua, 1987–), 2:177 (cited by Castellani, "Contributo alla biografia," 137).

42. Wegg, *Richard Pace*, 207. The portrait is now in the Louvre (see Charles Hope, *Titian*, 66). Perhaps Giovio dreamed of having his own done; while still in Venice he promised one to Equicola (*IO* 1:101). On the *impresa* that Giovio devised for Adorno see *IO* 9:398, and the notes by Maria Luisa Doglio in her edition of Giovio's *Dialogo dell'imprese*, 92–93.

43. *IO* 9:285. Sanudo recorded a similar banquet given by the Mantuan ambassador for Adorno and Pace, to which, with the permission of the senate, twenty-five ladies were invited (Sanudo 33:599, 607). In his collection Giovio had a painting, *La veneciana vestita di verdo* (Volpati, "Giovio e Venezia," 148).

44. *IO* 9:286. See also Volpati, "Giovio e Venezia," 136–37. Sanudo mentioned the arrival of del Vasto on or about December 9 and the visit to the jewels, as well as the visit of Adorno and followers on February 7 to see the jewels (33:538, 564).

45. *Hadriani vita* (1551), 141.

46. Sanudo 33:600.

47. *IO* 4:9–10. Guicciardini took the same viewpoint. *SI* 15.1.

48. *Hadriani vita* (1551), 137 (wrongly numbered 187). On Adrian's penury cf. Negri, March 17, 1523. *Lettere di principi* (1562), 1:83r.

49. Wegg, *Richard Pace*, 207–208; John Julius Norwich, *A History of Venice*, 439, 441. That Venice had been close to agreement with Adorno would appear from Sanudo 34:240, confirmed by Negri, who reported at the end of February that in Rome rapprochement was held a certainty. *Lettere di principi* (1562), 1:82v.

50. Sanudo 34:34.

51. Sanudo 34:39. Giovio is described as "master Paolo Giovio medical doctor and physician of the ambassador," walking as a "corozoso," a dialect term that Prof. Cozzi has suggested to me may be identifiable with "corruccio," or mourning.

52. *Hadriani vita* (1551), 135. Guicciardini also praised him as "persona di grande spirito ed experience benché gio-

vane" who "trattava con molta autorità e con destrezza singolare." *SI* 15.2.

53. *Hadriani vita* (1551), 143; Pastor 9:187.

54. *IO* 1:102. In ancient Rome condemned murderers and traitors were thrown to their deaths from the Tarpeian Rock. For the general expectation regarding Soderini's punishment see Negri to Michiel, June 17, 1523. *Lettere di principi* (1562), 1:86v. For Soderini's perspective see Lowe, *Soderini*, chap. 12.

55. *IO* 1:102–103.

56. See Pastor 9:112–13, and Negri to Michiel, February 28, 1523. *Lettere di principi* (1562), 1:82r.

57. *Hadriani vita* (1551), 144. For the presentation of the bulls to the chapter see ASC, Notarile 201, Volpi, January 17–18, 1523.

58. *Hadriani vita* (1551), 145.

59. Negri to Michiel, March 17, 1523. *Lettere di principi* (1562), 1:83v.

60. The progressive alienation of the Romans can be followed in the letters of the Venetian humanist, Girolamo Negri, secretary to Cardinal Cornaro. His early letters are quite sympathetic to the pope (e.g., April 14, 1522; *Lettere di principi* [1562], 1:75r–76r). On Adrian VI and reform see Robert E. McNally, S.J., "Pope Adrian VI and Church Reform," *Archivum historiae pontificiae* 7 (1969): 253–85.

61. *Hadriani vita* (1551), 118. On Adrian's failure as governor of Spain see Karl Brandi, *The Emperor Charles V*, 94.

62. *Hadriani vita* (1551), 144.

63. See Negri to Michiel, February 28 and March 17, 1523. *Lettere di principi* (1562), 1:82r, 84r.

64. "Però vederemo *et cogitabimus,* disse Papa Adriano." *IO* 1:171.

65. *IO* 1:102. For "washing bricks" cf. Terence, *Phormio* 1.4.8.

66. *Hadriani vita* (1551), 144. The bishop was Girolamo Balbi.

67. Sanudo 34:93–94.

68. May 8, 1523 (*IO* 1:102).

69. Sanudo 34:248–333.

70. *IO* 1:104.

71. O'Malley, *Giles of Viterbo on Church*

and Reform (Leiden: Brill, 1968), 130–31.

72. Sanudo 34:316.

73. Giovio recapitulated his vision of the 1520s in bk. 3 of the life of Pescara. *Vita Piscarii* (1551), 341; *Vita del Pescara* (1931), 322.

74. *SI* 15.2.

75. See Brandi, 205–206. On Gattinara see John M. Headley, *The Emperor and His Chancellor*, and the same author's "Germany, the Empire and *Monarchia* in the Thought and Policy of Gattinara," in Heinrich Lutz, ed., *Das römisch-deutsche Reich im politischen System Karls V* (Munich and Vienna: Oldenbourg, 1982), 15–33.

76. *Hadriani vita* (1551), 146. Girolamo Negri, on the other hand, found the oration "bellissima" (*Lettere di principi* [1562], 1:86v). On the heat see Pastor 9:209.

77. *Pompeii vita* (1551), 175. After studying all the conflicting accounts, including Giovio's, Pastor (9:208) concluded that the pope had returned to the Vatican.

78. *IO* 1:104.

79. *IO* 1:103.

80. Luzio, *Lettere inedite*, 29.

81. Negri to Michiel, September 1, 1523. *Lettere di principi* (1562), 1:87r.

82. *IO* 1:106. For del Nero see Melissa Miriam Bullard, *Filippo Strozzi and the Medici*, 132 n. 46.

83. Federico Gonzaga to Giovanni Battista Malatesta, September 6, 1523. ASM, Archivio Gonzaga, 2965, fol. 52r.

84. Marquis Federico to Benedetto Moraro, September 8, 1523 (ASM, Archivio Gonzaga, 2965, fol. 58v). See Mazzoldi, ed., *Storia di Mantova* 2:339. In his letter describing the ceremony, Federico made no mention of an oration by Giovio, but the previous day he had told his ambassador to assure the cardinal de' Medici that no more welcome emissary could have brought the standard and briefs than "the Reverend Monsignor Paolo Giovio, whom we love most singularly for his rare virtues and for the observant service and faith which he renders to His Most Illustrious Lordship." ASM, Archivio Gonzaga, 2965, fol. 56r.

85. Alessandro Luzio and Rodolfo Renier, "La coltura e le relazioni letterarie di Isabella d'Este Gonzaga," *GS* 36 (1900), 334–35.

86. *Vita del Pescara* (1931), 322–23. See also Luigi Simeoni, *Le signorie* 2:839.

87. On Federico's departure see Mazzoldi, ed., *Storia di Mantova* 2:281, and ASM, Archivio Gonzaga, 2965, 68r-v. For negotiations regarding the stipend and the enlisting of Giovio's services see Federico's letters to the Florentine Otto di Pratica and the priors of September 14, 1523. Ibid., 66v–68r.

88. *Hadriani vita* (1551), 146. Giovio gave his death date as September 13, although most sources place both Adrian's death and Bonnivet's crossing the Ticino on the 14th.

89. *Hadriani vita* (1551), 147. Giovio named the physician as Giovanni Antracino of Macerata, a friend of Colocci and one of the poets of the *Coryciana* (1524). See Gaetano Marini, *Degli archiatri pontefici* 1:322–25. Guicciardini observed that Adrian died "con piacere inestimabile di tutta la corte" (*SI* 15.3).

90. *Hadriani vita* (1551), 145–47. Leopold von Ranke repeated Adrian's dictum in his *History of the Popes*, bk. 1, chap. 3.

91. *Hadriani vita* (1551), 132. For the Latin cf. Virgil *Aeneid* 12.18, "sedato respondit corde Latinus."

92. *Hadriani vita* (1551), 148; *IO* 6:139.

CHAPTER SIX

1. Ridolfi, *Guicciardini*, 180.

2. *Pompeii vita* (1551), 175–77. Guicciardini made a similar observation. *SI* 15.6.

3. *Pompeii vita* (1551), 177. See Judith Hook, "Clement VII, the Colonna and Charles V: A Study of the Political Instability of Italy in the Second and Third Decades of the Sixteenth Century," *European Studies Review* 2 (1972): 291.

4. *Vita Piscarii* (1551), 342. In the preface to the life of Pompeo, Giovio said the cardinal had been his patron for almost twenty years (*IO* 6:142). Since Pompeo died in 1532, the beginning of their relationship would date to ca. 1513.

5. *Lettere di principi* (1562), 1:88r.
6. Pastor 9:246.
7. Castiglione, cited in Cian, *Castiglione*, 114.
8. Pastor 9:247.
9. *IO* 8:407–408.
10. *IO* 1:187. "De loco qui Paradisus dicitur a Sixto edificato" (BAV, Cod. Vat. Lat. 5008, fols. 59v-60r). For this reference I am indebted to the late Prof. Redig de Campos, who was of the opinion that the place could have been under either the Sistine Chapel or the chapel of St. Nicholas. Conclusive evidence has now appeared in a pasquinade that definitely locates Giovio's rooms under the Sistine Chapel. "Questa peste, piú [sic] fera d'Anticristo / sta in Vaticano in una angusta cella / sotto la riverend'alta capella / che fecce il fondator di Ponte Sisto." Marucci, Marzo, and Romano, eds., *Pasquinate romane* 1:384.
11. The bull of Giovio's election to Nocera calls him "familiarem et continuum commensalem" (ASV, Reg. Vat. 1438, 122r). On the papal household see Peter Partner, *Renaissance Rome*, 117–18. As a physician, Giovio would have been numbered among the *camerarii*, the officials ranking just below the domestic prelates and entitled to maintenance for personal servants of their own. See Ferrajoli, *Il ruolo*, 374. A similar roll for Clement VII's court is lacking.
12. Francesco Berni, *Poesie e prose*, ed. Enzio Chiorboli, 100–101. Gaetano Marini discovered at least ten physicians who served Clement VII at various times (*Degli archiatri pontefici* 1:330). In a papal brief of 1527 Giovio was still described as "medicum et familiarem antiquum nostrum." ASV, Min. brev. 1527, xiv, 109r.
13. *Raccolta di novellieri italiani* (Florence, 1834), pt. 2, pp. 2076–77.
14. *IO* 1:111, 109. For favors sought by Castiglione through Giovio see Castiglione to Andrea Piperario, May 8, 1523. *Lettere del Conte Baldessar Castiglione*, ed. Pierantonio Serassi, 1:107.
15. *IO* 1:107. For Giovio's salutations to Castiglione the previous year see *IO* 1:105.
16. *IO* 1:111

17. *IO* 1:108. In the autumn of 1523 Federico was suffering from retention of urine, owed, it was said, to medicine he was taking to cure himself of gonorreah. Mazzoldi, ed., *Storia di Mantova* 3:283, 342 nn. 126, 127.
18. ASMo, Canc. Est., Amb., Roma 30, 31, 34. On Giovio's rapport with Alvarotti see *IO* 2:41, 120, 190, and *Vita Alphonsi* (1550), 47, 54. For Casella see Sanudo 57:553 and *Vita Alphonsi* (l550), 59.
19. *IO* 1:110.
20. *IO* 1:112.
21. For the *commenda* of Sant'Antonio see ASV, Reg. Vat. 1252, fols. 139v–142r, June 13, 1524. See also ASC, Notarile 203, September 1, 1528; and Benedetto Giovio, *Historia patriae* (1982), 258, 267. The researches of Prof. Stefano Della Torre have revealed that in the Trecento the preceptory was originally a priory of the order of the friars hospitalers of St. Anthony of Vienne but had evidently been made into a *commenda* in the Quattrocento, as it was among the benefices possessed by Antonio Trivulzio before becoming bishop of Como. For the Piacenza benefice see C. Poggiali, *Memorie storiche di Piacenza* (Piacenza, 1760), 8:342–43. For this reference I am obliged to Prof. Travi. There are two references in Giovio's correspondence to a pension of 50 *scudi* paid from the endowment of this church, *IO* 1:203 and 246.
22. *IO* 1:108. On the prophecy of Luca Gaurico see Paola Zambelli, "Fine del mondo o inizio della propaganda? Astrologia, filosofia della storia e propaganda politico-religiosa nel dibattito sulla congiunzione del 1524," in *Scienze, credenze occulte, livelli de cultura* (Florence: Istituto Nazionale di Studi sul Rinascimento, 1982), 291–368.
23. Luzio, *Lettere inediti*, 13–14.
24. *IO* 2:205. On the social aspects of the treatise see my article "Renaissance Symposia," 363–74. On Calvo see Francesco Barberi, "Le edizioni romane di Francesco Minizio Calvo, *Miscellanea di scritti di bibliografia ed erudizione in memoria di Luigi Ferrari* (Florence, 1952), 57–98. After finishing the *De romanis piscibus* Giovio had been contemplating a larger work,

De esculentis et poculentis quae veniunt in mensam Romani Pontificis, but after seeing how such works were rewarded he abandoned the idea. *IO* 2:205, 206.

25. Sadoleto to Colocci, 1529 (*Iacobi Sadoleti Epistolae* [Cologne: Birckmann, 1554], 227). On Sadoleto's esteem for Giovio see the analysis by Castellani, "Contributo alla biografia," 145–48. On the academy in this period see Vincenzo De Caprio, "L'area umanistica romana (1513–1527)," *Studi Romani* 29 (1981): 26–46. Negri describes a gathering of the Roman academy at Sadoleto's *vigna* in a letter of June 18, 1525 (*Lettere di principi* [1562], 1:90v). On Sadoleto's *vigne* see David R. Coffin, *The Villa in the Life of Renaissance Rome,* 192.

26. BAV, Ottob. Lat. 2413, lllr–ll6v. For the MS see Kristeller, *Iter* 2:437A. For Vigile and the poem see Saul Levin and T. C. P. Zimmermann, "Fabio Vigile's *Poem of the Pheasant,*" in Paul A. Ramsey, ed., *Rome in the Renaissance* (Binghampton, N.Y.: Center for Medieval and Early Renaissance Studies, 1982), 265–78. The style of the italic calligraphy of the MS suggests composition before 1527. Palladio's *vigna* was on Monte Ciocci, a spur of Monte Mario behind the Vatican, where by 1535 he was able to build a fine villa. See Coffin, *Gardens and Gardening,* 237–38. The villa still stands, although in ruinous condition. Isa Belli Barsali, *Ville di Roma* (Milan: Rusconi, 1983), 382.

27. For Giovio at Giberti's dinner table see Matteo Casella to the duke of Ferrara, January 18, 1527 (ASMo, Canc. Est., Amb., Roma 31, 202-III, 9). Giovio urged Giberti's Calabrian protégé, Antonio Telesio, to publish his "peramoenus" *Liber de coronis* (1525); *IO* 9:234 and Telesio, *De coronis* (Naples, 1762), 168. On Telesio see Antonio Pagano, *Antonio Telesio* (Nicotera: Calabrese, 1935).

Giovio's relations with Berni were more complex (see *IO* 9:246 and 1:152). See also Anne Reynolds, *Renaissance Humanism in Rome: Culture and Politics at the Court of Clement VII* (New York: Garland, forthcoming). Another protégé of Giberti's whose work Giovio admired was the young

Marcantonio Flaminio (see *IO* 9:233 and 2:31). Yet another was the gifted improvisor, Andrea Marone of Brescia (*IO* 9:233 and 8:96–97). For Giovio at Pompeo's court see *IO* 9:229. In Pompeo's circle, Giovio took special pride in the young Roman poet Marcantonio Casanova, whose father was a compatriot from Como (*IO* 9:234–36). On Casanova see also Ubaldini, *Vita di Monsignor Angelo Colocci,* ed. Fanelli, 52–53 and n. 71. Rucellai's "achademia" lasted from 1523 until his death in 1525. In the Ischian dialogue Giovio mentioned, although without enthusiasm, the linguistic experiments in Trissino's *Sophonisba* and in Alessandro Pazzi's *Medea* (*IO* 9:245). In a letter of 1551 Giovio referred to Trissino as "già mio compare" (*IO* 2:191). On the "achademia" see Paolo Farenga, " 'L'Achademia tragica' di Castello e la questione della lingua," in *Quando gli dei si spogliano: Il bagno di Clemente VII a Castel Sant'Angelo e le altre stufe romane del primo Cinquecento* (Roma: Romana Società, 1984), 120–27.

28. Clough, "A Manuscript of Paolo Giovio's *Historiae sui temporis, liber VII,*" 53–83.

29. *IO* 9:257.

30. A Spanish chronicle had already been compiled. On the genesis of Giovio's biography see Costantino Panigada in his edition of *Vita del Pescara* (1931), 488–95. From the mention of the marquis of Pescara as already dead, Panigada concluded that the work was not begun before 1525. However, it is always possible that the phrase could have been an interpolation during revision prior to publication (1549).

31. *IO* 9:257. On Machiavelli's visit see Ridolfi, *Machiavelli,* 319.

32. *Libellus de legatione Basilii magni Principis Moschoviae ad Clementem VII Pont. Max., in qua situs Regionis antiquis incognitus, Religio gentis, mores, et causae legationis fidelissime referuntur* (*IO* 9:73–88). See the excellent introduction by Travi in *IO* 9:67–72. As is clear from the text, the treatise was completed while Gerasimov was still in Rome. In bk. 13 of the *Histories* Giovio said it was written at the request of the pope, but this is not the version given in the

dedication or in the Ischian dialogue (*IO* 9:257). For the interviews with Pietro and Paolino see bk. 3 of the *Histories* (*IO* 3:259).

33. *IO* 2:166.

34. Travi, *IO* 9:72. See Arturo Cronìa, *La conoscenza del mondo slavo in Italia* (Padua: Stediv, 1958), 134–36.

35. *IO* 4:348–49. Pigafetta is generally thought to have been invited to Rome by Clement VII, but Giovio's statement that he came to fulfill a vow would explain the pope's seeming failure to carry through with support. As Mosto points out, Giovio called Pigafetta Girolamo, perhaps confusing him in later years with the writer Fra Girolamo Pigafetta. Andrea da Mosto, "Vita di Antonio Pigafetta," *Raccolta di documenti e studi pubblicati dalla R. Commissione Colombiana* (Rome, 1894), pt. 5, 3:13–47.

36. The article by Francesco Fossati, "Il Museo Giovano e il ritratto di Cristoforo Colombo," *PSSC* 9 (1892): 84–118, has interesting material but is now badly out of date. See the notes on the Columbus portrait by Bruno Fasola in *IO* 10 (forthcoming) and the discussion of Columbus iconography by Samuel Eliot Morison, *Christopher Columbus* (Boston: Little Brown, 1942), 48.

37. Giovio possessed the copy of Verrazzano's report to Francis I on his first voyage, now known as the Cèllere codex, in which the name *Puntum Iovianum* appears. Sometime after the explorer's last voyage, his brother narrated for Giovio and his nephew, Giulio, the story of Verrazzano's murder by cannibals on the coast of Darien. Only in his *elogium* of Cortés, however, did Giovio mention Verrazzano's discoveries and commentary, and in a fashion that suggests he may not have realized just how far north of Darien Verrazzano's celebrated "isthmus" was (it was, in fact, the "Delmarva" peninsula). For whatever reason, Giovio made no effort to immortalize the "Jovium promontorium" in his *Histories*. Lawrence Wroth, *The Voyages of Giovanni da Verrazzano* (New Haven: Yale University Press, 1970), 150–52, 237–39, 250, 255, 259–60.

38. January 17, 1524 (*IO* 1:107).

39. Negri to Michiel, September 1, 1523 (*Lettere di principi* [1562], 1:87r-v). On Giovio and Alcionio see Kenneth Gouwens, "Ciceronianism and Collective Identity: Defining the Boundaries of the Roman Academy, 1525," *Journal of Medieval and Renaissance Studies* 23 (1993): 173–95, and O. Hugo Tucker, "Exile Exiled: Petrus Alcyonius (1487–1527?) in a Travelling-chest," *Journal of the Institute of Romance Studies* 2 (1993): 83–103. For the latter reference I am obliged to Prof. Gouwens. Even Bembo went to great lengths to avoid seeming to rival Giovio. See Carlo Vecce, "Paolo Giovio e Vittoria Colonna," *PSSC* 54 (1990): 88. Girolamo Negri (1494–1557) was secretary to Cardinal Cornaro and a member of the circle of Colocci. See Ubaldini, *Vita di Monsignor Angelo Colocci*, ed. Fanelli, 70 n. 114. For Giovio's praises see *IO* 9:253.

40. *IO* 3:170; 9:172. See Dante Visconti, "Le Lacune delle *Historiae* gioviane," in *Studia ghisleriana*, vol. entitled *Studi letterari*, 285–95. Herrera is mentioned in the life of Pescara (*Vita Piscarii* [1551], bk. 6, 393; *Vita del Pescara* [1931], 416). Giovio had already stored his most valuable belongings before the Colonna raid. *IO* 9:172.

41. *IO* 9:172. It is also interesting that Giovio's friend Pierio Valeriano did not mention the loss in his *De litteratorum infelictate*; nor was the loss of any books noted by Giovio's contemporary Lilio Gregorio Giraldi of Ferrara when he mentioned the redemption of Giovio's histories in his *Poemata* of 1536; *Opera quae extant omnia* (Basel, 1580), 2:915.

42. I am grateful to Prof. Travi for letting me see his transcription of this letter of July 17 [1527], which will be published in *IO* 11.

43. *IO* 9:11; 1:83. Alcionio's praise of Giovio's *Histories* in his *Medices legatus: De exsilio* (1522) suggested that the first decade was complete (bk. 2, fol. fiiir). In the Ischian dialogue Giovio appeared extraordinarily well-versed in the wars of Julius II, which would have been covered in the missing books 8–10 (1498–1512).

44. *IO* 4:1–2; *Il cortegiano*, ed. Vittorio Cian (Florence: Sansoni, 1947), 1.43.

45. *IO* 2:164. See also *IO* 2:232.

46. *IO* 1:261. Charges of ingratitude were, in fact, lodged by later critics.

47. Eduard Fueter, as cited by Emanuella Scarano Lugnani, *Guicciardini e la crisi del Rinascimento* (Bari: Laterza, 1979), 153.

48. *IO* 9:256.

49. *IO* 4:265. The sentence quoted, "Et Hercle, nisi Gibertus . . . sterilitate periissent," was added by Giovio in holograph to the original text of the MS of book 32. See SSC, Archivio Aliati, 28, 6. In the late 1530s Giovio was still receiving Christmas gifts from Giberti (*IO* 1:244). A minor bishopric, as Ariosto's second satire implies, was not much of a plum.

50. November 18, 1523, and March 31, 1524; *Lettere di principi* (1562) 1:88v, 90r. The comprehensive study of Giulio de' Medici as a patron by Prof. Sheryl E. Reiss is eagerly awaited.

51. *IO* 1:204, 9:194.

52. Pastor 9:253.

53. *IO* 1:109.

54. *Vita Piscarii* (1551), bk.3, 343; *Vita del Pescara* (1931), 326.

55. *SI* 15.7.

56. *Vita Piscarii* (1551), bk.3, 346; *Vita del Pescara* (1931), 330.

57. Lannoy noted this at the time. *SI* 16.14.

58. Pieraccini, *La stirpe* 1:315.

59. Ibid. 1:319–20. For the pope's slowness in deciding as an aspect of the Florentine penchant for "enjoying the benefit of time" see Hook, *The Sack of Rome*, 27.

60. Pastor 9:249.

61. *SI* 16.12. Quoted from *The History of Italy*, trans. Sidney Alexander, 363.

62. Hook, *The Sack of Rome*, 40. See also Pastor 9:254.

63. *Vita Piscarii* (1551), 372; *Vita del Pescara* (1931), 377. In his self-justification, written in 1542 after Clement's death, Giberti himself seemed to confirm Giovio's view. Giberti, "Giustificazione," in Giovanni Battista Pighi, *Gian Matteo Giberti*.

64. See T. C. P. Zimmermann, "A Note on Clement VII and the Divorce of Henry VIII," *English Historical Review* 82 (1967): 548–52.

65. In a long relation to Charles V, Sessa described the pope much as Giovio saw him, noting the irresolution but also the aspirations it masked and the avarice. Giovannangelo Di Meglio, *Carlo V e Clemente VII dal carteggio diplomatico*, 27–28.

66. *Pompeii vita* (1551), 178; *Vita Piscarii* (1551), bk. 4, 355; *Vita del Pescara* (1931), 345.

67. Pighi, *Giberti*, vii.

68. *Vita del Pescara* (1931), bk. 5, 377.

69. Ibid., 377–78. Guicciardini asserted that the real purpose of Giberti's mission was to negotiate an agreement with the French king (*SI* 15.11). Giovio did not go this far, and Guicciardini's assertion has been the subject of some dispute. See Pastor 9:267.

70. *Vita del Pescara* (1931), bk. 5, 376. The treaty between Francis I and the pope is given in Sanudo 37:418–19.

71. *SI* 15.12.

72. Pastor 9:271.

73. *Vita del Pescara* (1931), bk. 5, 382.

74. Ibid., 385. On Clement's parsimony see Pastor 9:250. Guicciardini had a similar explanation (*SI* 15.15). In his *Ricordi* he commented, "Nelle guerre chi vuole manco spendere, più spende" (*Ricordi*, ed. Raffaele Spongano, C149, p. 161).

75. *Vita Piscarii* (1551), bk. 6, 391; *Vita del Pescara* (1931), 410. See also Pastor 9:275.

76. Pieri, *Il Rinascimento*, 558–62; and Henry Lemonnier in Ernest Lavisse, ed., *Histoire de France*, vol. 5, pt. 2, p. 36.

77. On the interviews with Francis I (at Marseilles in 1533 and again at Nice in 1538) see *Vita del Pescara* (1931), 435. Sir Charles Oman called Giovio's account of Pavia the most detailed (*The Art of War in the Sixteenth Century*, 186–206). For Pescara's letter to Charles V see M. F. Navarrete, M. Salvá, and P. S. deBaranda, eds., *Colección de documentos inéditos para la historia España* 38 (1861), 408–12. For eyewitness sources Giovio also

had del Vasto and Giambattista Castaldo, who took Francis I prisoner.

78. *Pompeii vita* (1551), 178.

79. "Rimase morto." Pastor 9:275.

80. *Pompeii vita* (1551), 178. See the letter of Cardinal del Monte describing the fighting. *Lettere di principi* (1562), 1:96r-v.

81. *Vita Piscarii* (1551), 409. Dr. Cecil H. Clough has suggested to me the likelihood of strong influence from the ambassador of France Lodovico Canossa on behalf of a French alliance. That Giovio was not in close relations with Canossa is evident from Canossa's letter to Giberti of 1525, "Quanto al Iovio, non saprei molto scrivere di lui, non avendo molta pratica delle condizioni sue: le quali si può pensare che sieno buone" (cited in Castellani, "Contributo alla biografia," 150).

82. *Lettere di principi* (1562), 1:90v.

83. *Vita del Pescara* (1931), 443; *Pompeii vita* (1551), 179. Guicciardini spoke of the pope's "molestia d'animo quasi incredibile" (*SI* 16.7).

84. *Vita del Pescara* (1931), bk. 7, 446–47.

85. *Pompeii vita* (1551), 179. Much turned at this point on the failure of Sforza's ambassador, Tommaso del Maino, to extract the investiture from Charles V. Girolamo Morone cited this in his self-justification, and Giovio mentioned it as a factor (*Piscarii vita* [1551], 414). There were, in fact, many considerations regarding Milan in Charles V's mind. See the account by Gino Franceschini in *Storia di Milano* 8:259–93. Brandi, however, was convinced that Charles had actually executed the charter confirming Francesco Sforza in Milan before the arrival of Castaldo with the letter of Pescara denouncing Morone. Brandi, 229.

86. Cited in Pastor 9:290–91. For Giberti's suspicions see *Vita Piscarii* (1551), 417–18.

87. *Vita Piscarii* (1551), 416.

88. Brandi, 230. Giovio's account is in the third person: "constitit aliquandiu immotus . . . deliberandus" (*Vita Piscarii* [1551], 416). On Castaldo see the entry by Gaspare De Caro, *DBI* 21:562–66.

89. *Vita Piscarii* (1551), 417.

90. Giovio's chronology in this respect is better than Guicciardini's. Guicciardini believed that the visit of Marguerite to Spain might have been the turning point, but we now know Pescara had already acted before the visit. *SI* 16.8.

91. *Vita Piscarii* (1551), 424. On Morone see Carlo Gioda, *Giovanni Morone* (Torino, 1887).

92. *Vita Piscarii* (1551), 424. Guicciardini's judgment was quite similar. *SI* 16.10.

93. *Vita Piscarii* (1551), bk. 5, 419. Guicciardini continually emphasized the same idea.

94. *Vita Piscarii* (1551), 425. Giovio's dating of Pescara's death (November 30) was wrong. See Sanudo 40:420.

95. See T. C. P. Zimmermann, "Francesco Guicciardini and Paolo Giovio," *Annali d'Italianistica* 2 (1984): 39.

96. *Vita Piscarii* (1551), bk. 7, 421.

97. Andrea Navagero, Venetian ambassador in Spain, reported that Gattinara was "a good Italian" (cited Cian, *Castiglione*, 114). On Gattinara's efforts to have Sforza invested with Milan see Headley, *The Emperor and His Chancellor*, 55–56. Headley makes clear the many obstacles to Gattinara's policy, including Lannoy. See also Brandi, 234–35. Giovio's informants on the debate at the court probably included Castiglione's agent at Rome, Andrea Piperario, a writer of papal briefs whom the nuncio kept apprised of events in Spain and through whom he communicated with imperialists such as Schönberg. See Castiglione's letter to Piperario asking him to procure a favor from Giovio (*Lettere*, ed. Serassi, 1:107). A letter of 1525 showed that at this time Giovio was among the clients of Cardinal Salviati, who had been sent as legate to Spain in May 1525, adding the probability that he also obtained information through the dependents of the cardinal. *IO* 1:110. For a draft investiture of Bourbon see *Calendar of Letters, Dispatches, and State Papers . . . Spain* ed. P. de Gayangos, vol. 3, pt. 1 (London, 1873), 563.

98. Cian, *Castiglione*, 109, 112, 126, 129.

99. Pighi, *Giberti*, 23. For an endorsement of the view of Charles V's Italian policy as aggressive, see John Lynch, *Spain under the Hapsburgs*, 2 vols. (New York: Oxford University Press, 1964), 1:68–90.

100. Brandi concluded that the emperor had been proceeding to investiture of Sforza at the very time when Pescara's tidings arrived. Brandi, 226–30.

101. The phrase was Guicciardini's (*SI* 16.16). On Canossa see the article by Mirella Giansante in *DBI* 18:186–92.

102. The conduct of the war by della Rovere exasperated Francesco Guicciardini and moved Giberti to charge that the duke was collaborating with the enemy (Pighi, *Giberti*, 35). In the Ischian dialogue del Vasto commends the duke's prudence in not throwing his much less well-trained troops against the German and Spanish veterans of Bourbon, but Giovio as interlocutor retains his doubts about della Rovere's delays in moving to block Bourbon or relieve Rome (*IO* 9:205, 217). Luigi Guicciardini accounted for della Rovere's conduct by his hatred of the Medici. See Luigi Guicciardini, *The Sack of Rome*, trans. and ed. James H. McGregor, esp. 105.

103. Cited in Jones, *Francesco Vettori*, 186.

104. For Giovio's mission see the dedication of the life of Gonzalo de Córdoba. There has been some suggestion Giovio was sent to see if the duke was really sick. For Giberti's warnings see *Pompeii vita* (1551), 181.

105. *Pompeii vita* (1551), 184.

106. Negri to Michiel, October 24, 1526; *Lettere di principi* (1562), 1:92r.

107. *The History of Italy*, trans. Alexander, 376. The division of Guicciardini's books generally followed the material rather than the year, and the comment on a year is unique. See De Caprio, *La tradizione e il trauma*, 328–29.

108. *IO* 1:113–17. A month later Negri wrote to Venice in a similar vein, "Questa corte homai è diventata un corte da galline" (April 15, 1527); *Lettere di principi* (1571), 2:72v.

109. *Pompeii vita* (1551), 188. See also *IO* 4:18. As part of the effort to block the

truce, Berni had launched his savage pasquinade, "Può fare il ciel però, papa Chimenti" (*Poesie e prose*, ed. Chiorboli, 84). For other similar opinions see Hook, *The Sack of Rome*, 209, citing Sanudo 45:418.

110. Pastor 9:372.

111. *Vita Alfonsi* (1550), 49.

112. Pastor 9:375.

113. Francesco Guicciardini, *Carteggi*, ed. Roberto Palmarocchi and Pier Giorgio Ricci, 13:146–48.

114. Cited in Pastor 9:378.

115. *Pompeii vita* (1551), 190. In March, Clement had offered Ravenna to Venice as pledge for a loan of 25,000 ducats. Sanudo 43:701.

116. *Pompeii vita* (1551), 190. In the Ischian dialogue del Vasto described the amusement of the imperial officers at Ceri's fortifications (*IO* 9:194). On Ceri see Gaspare De Caro, *DBI* 3:309–12.

117. *Pompeii vita* (1551), 191. See the similar account in Sanudo 46:130. Clerics in the papal service usually wore violet.

118. *Pompeii vita* (1551), 192.

119. *Pompeii vita* (1551), 193. The beautiful *nymphaeum* of the Colonna villa at Genazzano can be seen in its ruined state (see Coffin, *The Villa*, 243–45). In book 26 of the *Histories* Giovio noted with satisfaction the death of the Spanish captain who caused the old woman to be strangled and hung up. *IO* 4:88.

120. *Pompeii vita* (1551), 193–94. For a defense of della Rovere's conduct see *IO* 9:205.

121. Hook (*The Sack of Rome*, 209) placed the meeting on June 1.

122. *IO* 4:14. The news of Mohács (August 29–30) reached Rome on the eve of the Colonna raid (September 20).

123. *Pompeii vita* (1551), 192–93.

124. Ibid., 194.

125. The capitulation was signed on June 5; however, the hostages were not actually taken until September.

CHAPTER SEVEN

1. Pastor 9:457. Plague had broken out by June. See Sanudo 45:434.

2. *IO* 9:138. On cardinals finding ass a

delicacy see *IO* 6:180. On the relevance and utility of the pagan tradition of consolation see John McManamon, "Continuity and Change in the Ideals of Humanism: The Evidence from Florentine Funeral Oratory," in Marcel Tetel, Ronald G. Witt, and Rona Goffen, eds., *Life and Death in Fifteenth-Century Florence* (Durham, N.C.: Duke University Press, 1989), 68–87.

3. The text of the letter announcing Giovio's election to the viceroy Lannoy, drafted by Giovio's friend and fellow-academician Blosio Palladio, is reproduced in Marini, *Lettera* (1797), 119–20. The bulls for Giovio's election were executed after the pope's release from captivity, beginning January 1, 1528. ASV, Reg. Vat. 1438, fols. 122r–126r.

4. *IO* 9:167–68. On the outbreak of plague among the pope's household in the castle see the letter of July 13 in Sanudo 45:505.

5. See Giovio's letter of July 17 (1527) requesting a safe-conduct, to be published in *IO* 11 (forthcoming). I am grateful to Prof. Travi for sharing with me his transcript of this letter. In the letter Giovio speaks of de Urbina's "tante offerte" of assistance. In his article, "Vittoria Colonna and Paolo Giovio," *Roma* 11 (1933): 505, Volpati suggested that Giovio had gone to Le Cese, the fief of Fabrizio Colonna near Avezzano, where he revised the *De romanis piscibus*, but Travi's doubts regarding Volpati's source, an inscription in the Como copy of *De piscibus* (see *IO* 9:6–7), have been confirmed by the discovery of Giovio's letter of July 17. For Francesco Formento see *IO* 2:222, 242. The safe-conduct was issued on July 17, stating that the pope was sending Giovio "pro nonnullis nostris et apostolicae sedis negotiis," allowing him and two servants to pass free of customs and requiring papal officials to furnish him escort if necessary. Capparoni, *Paolo Giovio*, 5.

6. *IO* 9:317–18. On Vittoria's relations with Clement VII's counselors see Carlo Dionisotti, "Appunti sul Bembo e su Vittoria Colonna," in *Miscellanea Augusto Campana*, ed. Rino Avesani et al., 1:257–58. On Giovio's relations with Vittoria Colonna see

Carlo Vecce, "Giovio e Colonna," and also Castellani, "Contributo alla biografia," 140–44.

7. *IO* 4:72.

8. There is some doubt as to whether Fregoso died at Ischia, but I see no reason to question Giovio's authority in this. See the note of Vittorio Cian in the 4th ed. of his edition of *Il cortegiano* (Florence: Sansoni, 1947), 515. Taken prisoner in 1522, Fregoso had been obstreperous about his ransom, hence the length of his imprisonment. Some of the papal jewels given as pledges for payment of the pope's ransom were brought for safe storage to Ischia by del Vasto (Suzanne Thérault, *Un cénacle humaniste de la Renaissance autour de Vittoria Colonna châtelaine d'Ischia*, 367–68). I have used the Spanish forms for the d'Avalos family (e.g., Francisco Fernando), rather than the Italian ones (Francesco Ferrando or Ferrante), because of the strongly Spanish allegiance the family retained.

9. *IO* 9:227. On her stoic attitude toward her husband's infidelities see *IO* 9:319. Her father, Fabrizio, was used by Machiavelli as chief interlocutor in *The Art of War*. Federigo da Montefeltro was her maternal grandfather.

10. *IO* 9:167, 299–300. See the chapter on Costanza in Thérault, *Un cénacle humaniste*, 45–59.

11. *IO* 9:297–98.

12. *IO* 9:299.

13. *IO* 9:303–304. See also Thérault, *Un cénacle humaniste*, 301–48; Carlo Volpati, "Paolo Giovio e Napoli," *Nuova rivista storica* 20 (1936): 348–49; and Travi, "La sosta," 111. The French army entered the Regno on February 10, 1528. On Gaurico see Pomponio Gaurico, *De sculptura*, ed. and trans. André Chastel and R. Klein (Geneva: Droz, 1969).

14. Letter of September 7, 1527 (Sanudo 46:54). See also Pastor 9:458. Del Vasto maintained that he had absented himself from the sack (*Pompeii vita* [1551], 197; *IO* 9:174). Like the other officers, he was sometimes in danger of his life from the ragings of the soldiers. See Sanudo 46:317.

15. A letter from Rome dated September 23 mentions del Vasto's absence

(Sanudo 46:181). See his *elogium* by Giovio (*IO* 8:462–63), and the entry by G. De Caro, *DBI* 4:612–16. Giovio describes him as being at that time "iuventae flore et specie corporis, tum virtutis et omnis militaris elegantiae laude [insignis]"; *Vita Piscarii* (1551), 403. On his portraits by Titian, one in armor in Paris (1533) and one in the Prado haranguing his troops (1539–41), see Harold E. Wethey, *The Paintings of Titian* 2:22, 78–80, and pl. 56–58.

16. On Muscettola (1487–1534) see Thérault, *Un cénacle humaniste*, 283, 363–64. There is some confusion between Giovanni Antonio Muscettola and Giovanni Francesco Muscettola, a man of letters whom Thérault concludes could be either the brother or the son of Giovanni Antonio. She even suggests that Giovio's interlocutor might be Giovanni Francesco, but she did not have access to part I of Giovio's Ischian dialogue, which establishes Muscettola's identity beyond all doubt as Giovanni Antonio, as does Giovio's undated letter to Scannapeco (*IO* 1:177–78). On Muscettola see also Vecce, "Giovio e Colonna," 74–75; Hook, *The Sack of Rome*, 104; Pastor 9:457–58, 10:20, 209–10, 228; *IO* 4:95, 203. Clement VII later came to like him and nearly made him a cardinal. For a pasquinade on this proposed elevation and Muscettola's supposed Jewish ancestry see the dispatch of Antonio Romei to Ippolito d'Este, May 12, 1532, ASMo, Canc. Est., disp. Roma 33, 214-V/13.

17. In the dialogue Giovio greets Muscettola as an old friend.

18. Minturno was tutor to the children of the Pignatelli family. See Thérault, *Un cénacle humaniste*, 290–95, 473. A letter of his to Giovio is found in Marquard Gude, *Epistolae*, ed. Pieter Burmann (Utrecht: Halmam and Vandewater, 1697), 129–30. See also *IO* 9:238, and Dionisotti, *Geografia*, 199.

19. *IO* 1:177–78. For the dating of conversations with Sannazaro see Castellani, "Contributo alla biografia," 144–45. On Gravina see *IO* 1:175–76; 8:98–99. In his brief sketch of Gravina, Giovio has an unexplained reference to having gone with him

to "the hostage cardinals" at Naples (Pietro Gravina, *Poemata*, ed. Scipione Capece [Naples: Sulzbach, 1532], appendix). The best guide to Giovio's thought in this period is Travi's "La sosta." For the discussions of Pontano's academy see Mario Santoro, *Fortuna, ragione e prudenza*, chaps. 1 and 2. Pontano's influence can be gauged from the fact that his portrait was one of the first Giovio collected (*IO* 1:92). Giovio's work contains definite echoes of the *De Fortuna* (which was dedicated to his friend and mentor Colocci) as well as of the *De Coelestia*. On Colocci's links to Pontano see Francesco Tateo, *L'umanesimo meridionale* (Bari: Laterza, 1973), 54.

20. *IO* 9:168. The soldiers had begun returning to Rome by September 25 (Pastor 9:459). The hostages had been named in the capitulation of June but not actually taken until now. See Sanudo 46:178, 210, 221. On Vittoria's efforts to have Giberti released see her *Carteggio*, ed. Ermanno Ferrero and Giuseppe Müller, 47.

21. A reference to the presence of a Venetian fleet in the Gulf of Pozzuoli further localized the beginning of the conversations to mid-October (*IO* 9:172; Sanudo 46:264). The third and last conversation of the dialogue is still set during the captivity of the pope, which ended on December 6, 1527, a week after the escape of the hostages. On the period of composition see the masterful introduction to the dialogue by Travi, *IO* 9:149–50, 157–58; see also the reasoning of Ezio Raimondi, "Machiavelli, Giovio e Aristofane," 389–390, and of Carlo Vecce, who has dated the dialogue in the latter half of November, based on del Vasto's presence in Rome on November 12 (Vecce, "Giovio e Colonna," 73). However, Giovio's declaration that del Vasto has arrived "ex Umbris" (*IO* 9:169), not from Rome, suggests the possibility of an earlier date, and the mention of the Venetian fleet seems decisive. The latest verifiable date mentioned in the dialogue appears to be the elevation of Pyrro Gonzaga to the cardinalate, which occurred on January 27, 1528, although news of the intended elevation may have reached Ischia earlier, since Gio-

vio's indirect discourse uses the present and not the perfect passive ("quem . . . cooptari in numerum cardinalium . . . audimus"); *IO* 9:302. See also the *elogium* of Andrea Marone, where the dialogue is described as written "capto pontifice" (*IO* 8:96). Giovio also refers to the dialogue as having been read by Muscettola on Ischia. *IO* 1:177–78.

22. See Vincenzo De Caprio, *La tradizione e il trauma*, pt. 2, and Massimo Miglio, V. De Caprio, D. Arasse, and A. Asor Rosa, eds., *Il sacco di Roma del 1527 e l'immaginario collettivo* (Rome: Istituto Nazionale di Studi Romani, 1986). For reactions of one humanist see Kenneth Gouwens, "Discourses of Vulnerability: Pietro Alcionio's Orations on the Sack of Rome," *RQ* (forthcoming).

23. See Travi, *IO* 9:159–62, and Vecce, "Giovio e Colonna," 68–72. I have attempted to base myself on Giovio's actual thoughts in 1527–28, discounting the revisions of 1530 and 1535. For Giovio's autograph revisions this has been easy, but where whole pages were rewritten by Giovio's amanuensis in 1535 it is difficult to know just how the original thoughts of 1527–28 may have been reworked. The major additions were to part I, especially regarding the Gonzaga family and Francesco Sforza. The MS needs additional study and analysis.

24. On the Quattrocento dialogue see Francesco Tateo, *Tradizione e realtà nell'umanesimo italiano*, pt. 2, or David Marsh, *The Quattrocento Dialogue* (Cambridge: Harvard University Press, 1980). I regret I was unable to consider the models presented in Virginia Cox, *The Renaissance Dialogue: Literary Dialogue in Its Social and Political Contexts, Castiglione to Galileo* (Cambridge: Cambridge University Press, 1992).

25. Travi, "La sosta," 110. The lake is now the port of Ischia, a channel having been cut to the sea by the Bourbon kings.

26. On conflicts between Orange, a favorite of Charles V's, and del Vasto see Setton 3:294. In October 1527, Orange was to be appointed lieutenant of the duke of Ferrara (proposed as imperial captain-gen-

eral) and therefore effective commander (Sanudo 46:220). In January, after the desertion of Alfonso d'Este, Orange succeeded to the supreme command and del Vasto to the command of the infantry (Hook, *The Sack of Rome*, 226). In the dialogue del Vasto condemns political favoritism in military appointments as undermining the development of a capable officer cadre. *IO* 9:211.

27. *IO* 9:172.

28. *IO* 9:169.

29. See Travi, "Dignitatis Italici nominis," in *Lingua e vita*, chap. 5, and Ilardi, "'Italianità' among Some Italian Intellectuals." For an introduction to the literature of the crisis of the sixteenth century see Franco Catalano, "Il problema dell'equilibrio e la crisi della libertà italiana," *Nuove questioni di storia medioevale* (Milan: Marzorati, 1969), 357–98. For English-speaking readers a good summary of the crisis is provided by Lauro Martines, *Power and Imagination: City States in Renaissance Italy* (New York: Knopf, 1979), chap. 14.

30. Pastor 9:457–58.

31. *IO* 9:174; 8:434.

32. *IO* 9:176–82. Giovio's explanation for the influence of the stars is not substantially different from Dante's in *Par.* viii and xiii or Pontano's in *De Fortuna*. Giovio also expresses an early version of the theory of climate which is found developed to the fullest in Bodin's *Methodus*. For Giovio's struggle to renounce astrology see Travi, "La sosta," 113 ff. For a later condemnation of astrology see *IO* 8:81. Giovio's "confession" in the Ischian dialogue recalls, perhaps deliberately, the similar admission by St. Augustine of his early immersion in astrology (*Confessions* 4.3). In the life of Adrian VI, Giovio observed with some sarcasm that perhaps Adrian showed so little excitement at the news of his election to the papacy because his youthful astrological studies had predicted it for him (*Hadriani vita* [1551], 132). On astrology in the Renaissance see E. Garin, *Lo zodiaco della vita* (Bari: Laterza, 1976), in English: *Astrology in the Renaissance* (London: Routledge,

1983); and Paola Zambelli, "Teorie su astrologia, magia e alchemia (1348–1586)," *Rinascimento*, 2d ser., 27 (1987): 95–119.

33. *IO* 9:173. Clement VII's Palm Sunday sermon to the cardinals at Orvieto (April 5, 1528) dwelt on the sack as God's punishment for the sins of the Church (Sanudo 47:235). See also Marjorie Reeves, "Prophecy and the Sack of Rome," in *Prophetic Rome*, 271–78.

34. On the adumbration of these themes in the dialogue see the perceptive remarks of Travi, "La sosta," esp. 109–22. On Pontano's notion, which may have influenced Giovio, that Fortune and the stars order events only when human will and intellect fail see Jerry H. Bentley, *Politics and Culture in Renaissance Naples*, 246–52. On Giovio's concept of Fortune see Yves Giraud, "Esperienza e coscienza della Fortuna nel Giovio," *Atti*, 51–62.

35. Vittoria's transcription of *Il cortegiano* was lamented by Castiglione in the dedicatory letter. Perhaps it was Giovio's reading of it that so alarmed him! *Il cortegiano* is mentioned in the dialogue (*IO* 9:231). For ideas similar to Giovio's see *Il cortegiano* 4.6–9, 21, 33.

36. *IO* 9:178. On Gaurico's prophecy see chap. 6, n. 22, above. On Giovio and Machiavelli see Dionisotti, *Machiavellerie*, 411–44. From his *elogium* of Machiavelli it is clear that by the 1540s Giovio knew the *Florentine Histories* (1532), *The Prince* (1532), the *Discourses* (1531), and *The Art of War* (1521). Especially pertinent to tracing Machiavelli's influence on Giovio's dialogue would be *The Prince*, chaps. 24 and 26, and *The Art of War*, bk. 7. It is easy to suppose that by 1527 Giovio could have seen one of the MSS of *The Prince* in Florence. It seems less probable that by 1527 Giovio knew the *Discourses*, given that the earliest known of the MSS in circulation is 1530. Giovio could easily have seen the MS of the *Florentine Histories* in 1525 when it was presented to the pope. For a study of the manuscripts of Machiavelli see Cecil H. Clough, *Machiavelli Researches* (Naples: Istituto Universitario Orientale di Napoli, 1967). It is also possible that Giovio introduced some of the "Machiavellian" ideas into his dialogue during its revisions in 1531 or 1535. The nature of the manuscript makes it difficult to tell. He could also have gotten some of the ideas regarding mercenaries from Biondo. See Fubini, "Biondo," *DBI* 10:536–59.

37. *IO* 9:183–84. On Giovio's antecedents for the metaphor of decline and rebirth see Angelo Mazzocco, "Decline and Rebirth in Bruni and Biondo," in Paolo Brezzi and Maristella de Panizza Lorch, eds., *Umanesimo a Roma nel Quattrocento* (Rome and New York: Istituto di Studi Romani and Barnard College, 1984), 249–66. Giovio followed Cortesi in accepting Bruni's scheme of decline and rebirth but in linking the revival of culture rather to princely courts. See Ferraù's introduction to Cortesi's *De hominibus doctis*, 25–26.

38. On the connection between military organization and good laws see especially *The Prince*, chap. 12, the *Discourses* 1.21, 3.31, and *The Art of War*, bk. 1. On Machiavelli's concept of *virtù* and military valor see Neal Wood, "Machiavelli's Concept of *Virtù* Reconsidered," *Political Studies* 15 (1967): 159–72.

39. *IO* 9:183–84. In book 1, Giovio is not particularly harsh with Alexander VI, who is depicted as listening to the French merely in order to win more concessions from the Neapolitans. The League of San Marco is not mentioned. Guicciardini may have known even less of it than Giovio, as Dr. Clough has pointed out.

40. E.g., *Florentine Histories* 5.1. Giovio asserts that at the battle of Caravaggio only seven soldiers were killed and two of those through being trampled in the retreat (*IO* 9:189). Cf. also his remarks in *Histories* 2 (*IO* 3:58). See J. R. Hale, "War and Public Opinion in Renaissance Italy," in *Italian Renaissance Studies*, ed. E. F. Jacob (London: Faber, 1960), 94–122.

41. D'Avalos' account of the methods used by Francesco Sforza to select his soldiers (*IO* 9:222) almost sounds like a parody of the criteria attributed by Machiavelli to the Romans in *The Art of War*, bk. 1. The Venetian soldiery conformed to del Vasto's

description of a good mercenary army. See Michael E. Mallett and John R. Hale, *The Military Organization of a Renaissance State: Venice c. 1400 to 1617* (Cambridge: Cambridge University Press, 1984).

42. *IO* 9:220. On the plunder of Italy and especially Lombardy by mercenaries see *The Prince*, chap. 26.

43. *IO* 9:212. One of the arguments advanced by an interlocutor in Platina's *De vera nobilitate* is that wealth enables a virtuous citizen to take exceptional measures in defending the patria. See Tateo, *Tradizione e realtà*, 392.

44. *IO* 9:194. The lengthy account of Clement VII's conclave in the life of Cardinal Colonna may be intended to emphasize that Giulio de' Medici had actively sought a position of leadership for which he was unqualified. Pietro Alcionio was so disgusted with Clement VII he left his service. See Gouwens, "Discourses."

45. *IO* 9:194–96. For Charles V's view see his letter to John III of Portugal, August 2, 1527, cited in John E. Longhurst, ed., *Alfonso de Valdés and the Sack of Rome: Dialogue of Lactancio and an Archdeacon* (Albuquerque: University of New Mexico Press, 1952), 97.

46. *IO* 9:205, 217. For an alternate view of Urbino's strategy see Luigi Guicciardini, *The Sack of Rome.*

47. Blosio Palladio's speech in praise of Leo X argued that God had ordained the Church as the successor to the Roman Empire. See D'Amico, *Renaissance Humanism*, 136. In his work on Muscovy, completed just before the sack, Giovio displayed his belief in the political authority of the papacy by suggesting that Basil III rightly sought the imperial title from the person who crowned the Roman emperor (*IO* 9:75). For the contrasting view of Gattinara and his quasi-messianic concept of the empire, see John M. Headley, "Rhetoric and Reality: Messianic, Humanist, and Civilian Themes in the Imperial Ethos of Gattinara," in *Prophetic Rome*, ed. Reeves, 241–69.

48. *IO* 9:215.

49. *IO* 9:207.

50. Dionisotti, *Machiavellerie*, 413, 420; Raimondi, "Machiavelli, Giovio ed Aristofane," 394–95; Travi, *Lingua e vita*, chap. 10, "L'affermazione del volgare secondo Paolo Giovio," and pp. 150–51. See also Fulvio Vittori, "Pauli Jovii Dialogus I," *PSSC* 40 (1957): 153–93.

51. For the influence of Quintilian on Giovio's theories see my article, "Paolo Giovio and the Evolution of Renaissance Art Criticism," in Cecil H. Clough, ed., *Cultural Aspects of the Italian Renaissance*, 406–24. Giovio seems to have been reluctant to cite Quintilian as an authority, probably because of the hostility of Cortesi et al.

52. On Cortesi's dialogue and Politian's response to it see D'Amico, *Renaissance Humanism*, 128–29. Politian's own *Nutricia* was certainly an antecedent for Giovio's work, but being in verse was not a model. On the limits of Giovio's Ciceronianism see Cataudella in *IO* 6:xvii. For the reference to Giraldi's "periculosissimum librum" see *IO* 9:253. The *De poetis nostrorum temporum* was not published until 1551. See Vittorio Rossi's study, "Per la cronologia e il testo dei dialoghi 'De poetis nostrorum temporum' di Lilio Gregorio Giraldi," *GS* 37 (1901): 246–77.

53. In his reply to Erasmus' *Ciceronianus*, the Roman humanist Giovanni Battista Casali listed Giovio among the "principes assertatores linguae latinae," along with Bembo, Sadoleto, Gravina, etc. (cited in D'Amico, *Renaissance Humanism*, 139). Benedetto Varchi's slur in the *Ercolano* was quite gratuitous, accusing Giovio of not taking the trouble to know Tuscan and of ridiculing Bembo (*L'Ercolano* [Florence, 1580], 206). On the general question of Latin and the vernacular see Dionisotti, *Gli umanisti e il volgare.*

54. *IO* 9:232.

55. *IO* 9:240. The origin of Italian in the barbarian invasions was stressed by Cortesi and later by Romolo Amaseo at Bologna in 1529.

56. *IO* 9:242.

57. *IO* 9:251–52.

58. *IO* 9:241.

59. *IO* 9:262. Giovio's highest praise

was to have equaled the ancients. Cf. *IO* 8:108, 9:245.

60. On anomalies in Giovio's style see Cataudella in *IO* 6:xiv–xx. However, Giovio entered the fray on the Ciceronian side, criticizing the resistance of the grammarian Battista Pio (*IO* 8:123–24), whom Erasmus cited in his *Ciceronianus* (1528) as one who was at least attempting to develop his own style; Erasmus, *Opera omnia* (Amsterdam, 1969–), 1—2 (1971), ed. P. Mesnard, p. 667. Giovio deplored the *Ciceronianus*, accusing Erasmus of unbridled ambition in trying to develop his own unique Latin style (*IO* 8:118). For Giovio's Ciceronianism see also *IO* 8:77–78, 102, 129. His theory of imitation was based on those of Cortesi and Bembo. For the extensive literature on imitation see Scrivano, *Cultura e letteratura*, "Il concetto di imitazione nel Rinascimento," 315–27.

61. *IO* 9:260. On Bembo's position see esp. Giorgio Santangelo, *Il Bembo critico e il principio d'imitazione* (Florence: Sansoni, 1950).

62. *IO* 8:111. See Dionisotti, *Machiavellerie*, 411–44.

63. *IO* 9:248, 255. See above, chap. 3, n. 30.

64. *IO* 9:254–55. For the Platonic *locus* Giovio may have had in mind, my colleagues Alfred Mele and Peter Ahrensdorf have suggested *Phaedrus* 274e. Giovio had a low opinion of the memory theater of Giulio Camillo Delminio.

65. *IO* 9:256.

66. *IO* 9:258. Giovio's contempt for those who did not publish evidently became something of a byword. See Pierio Valeriano, *De litteratorum infelicitate* (Leipzig, 1707), 329–30.

67. *IO* 9:257.

68. On Valla's similar view see Giuseppe Toffanin, *History of Humanism* (New York: Las Americas, 1954), 160. Dionisotti cautions, however, that with the internationalization of Renaissance Latin, it could no longer serve as the basis for cultural nationalism. Cited by Travi, *Lingua e vita*, 74–75.

69. Travi, introduction to the dialogue, *IO* 9:163–64. See also Travi's *Lingua e vita*,

chap. 6, "Le donne ed il volgare." For an introduction to thought on women's equality in Renaissance Italy see Margaret L. King, *Women of the Renaissance* (Chicago: University of Chicago Press, 1991), esp. chap. 3, and Constance Jordan, *Renaissance Feminism* (Ithaca, N.Y.: Cornell University Press, 1990), esp. 250–69. For further particulars on women mentioned in this section of the dialogue see the articles by Carlo Volpati listed in the bibliography.

70. On Giuliano's arguments in Castiglione see King, *Women of the Renaissance*, 187–88, and Dain A. Trafton, "Politics and the Praise of Women," in *Castiglione: The Ideal and the Real in Renaissance Culture*, ed. Robert W. Hanning and David Rosand (New Haven: Yale University Press, 1983), 33.

71. I have accepted the dating for Pompeo's treatise (1523–26) given by Mirella Scala, "Encomi e dediche nelle prime relazioni culturali di Vittoria Colonna," *PSSC* 54 (1990): 105–06, even though Giovio himself implies it was written during Pompeo's later years as viceroy of Naples (*IO* 6:188–89). The *Apologia mulierum* has been edited by Guglielmo Zappacosta, *Studi e ricerche sull'umanesimo italiano* (Bergamo: Minerva Italica, 1972), 159–264. Aside from Pompeo Colonna's *Apologia* other works may have influenced this part of Giovio's dialogue. Trissino's *Ritratti* (Rome, 1524) is a work of a different sort, but Firenzuola's *Epistola in lode delle donne* (1525) was certainly an antecedent, if Giovio knew it. He certainly knew Firenzuola. In the proem to his *Discorsi della bellezza delle donne* (Florence, 1548), Firenzuola mentioned Giovio's presence when Clement VII read parts of his (Firenzuola's) *Discacciamento* and *Ragionamenti*. On Firenzuola see Jacqueline Murray, "Agnolo Firenzuola on Female Sexuality and Women's Equality," *Sixteenth Century Journal* 22 (1991): 199–213. On Trissino and Firenzuola see also Mary Rogers, "The Decorum of Women's Beauty: Trissino, Firenzuola, Luigini and the Representation of Women in Sixteenth-Century Painting," *Renaissance Studies* 2 (1988): 47–88. Gio-

vio's dialogue may in turn have influenced Nifo's *De pulchro et bello* (composed 1529), which in its description of Joanna d'Aragona carried Giovio's evocation of physical beauty to extremes. See Benedetto Croce, "Il *De pulchro* di Agostino Nifo," in *Poeti e scrittori del pieno e del tardo Rinascimento* 3:101–110.

72. *IO* 9:274–77.

73. *IO* 9:277 ff. Giovio's *impresa*, probably done for the marchesa del Vasto during her residence at Milan, emphasized the chastity which she herself observed and enforced on the rest of her household. The device Giovio devised for the duchess of Florence likewise emphasized modesty (*IO* 9:407, 417). See also Thérault, *Un cénacle humaniste*, p. 362.

74. Luigi Cornaro also complained that before the Spanish occupation, social intercourse did not depend on elaborate banquets. Jacob Burckhardt, *Civilization of the Renaissance in Italy*, ed. Hajo Holborn, 283.

75. *IO* 9:313–21. This section of the dialogue is known only in the revised form, the MS having been completely recopied here by the scribe. On Giovio's themes as a reflection of Vittoria's interests see Vecce, "Giovio e Colonna," 75. We do not have an indisputable portrait of Vittoria Colonna. She was painted by Sebastiano del Piombo but there is no certainty that the Barcelona "Vittoria Colonna" is actually she, despite the fact that the lady depicted holds one of Vittoria's sonnets in her hand. See Hirst, *Sebastiano*, 117. Tributes to her became a sort of *genre*, Giovio's being one of the earliest examples to follow that of Cardinal Pompeo. See Thérault, *Un cénacle humaniste*, pt. 3, chaps. 1 and 2; and Scala, "Encomie e dediche."

76. Volpati, "Colonna and Giovio," 501–16. Vecce takes somewhat the same viewpoint.

77. On Giberti as a collector see Negri in *Lettere di principi* (1562) 1:92r. His bath in the Vatican was a model of sophisticated luxury. *Quando gli dei si spogliano*, pl. 31, p. 31.

78. Giovio also relates that she was lashing her pubic parts with thorny lashes. *IO* 9:319.

79. Vittoria Colonna, *Rime*, ed. Alan Bullock (Bari: Laterza, 1982), 205. The sonnet was composed before 1533 (see Tordi's comment in Colonna, supplement to *Carteggio*, ed. Tordi, 20) and may have been composed as early as 1528. For help in construing the Italian I am grateful to Prof. Travi.

80. Dedication to the life of Pescara.

81. Setton 3:295.

82. *Histories*, bk. 25 (*IO* 4:49–54). A more immediate and detailed account is contained in the letter written May 1 describing the event for the pope (*IO* 1:118–23). For a bibliography on the battle see Pastor 10:17. For Giovio's "tragic and grotesque realism" in describing it, see Gianfranco Folena, "L'espressionismo epistolare di Paolo Giovio," 135–36.

83. Cited by Setton (3:297) from Sanudo (47:389).

84. "Di galera, sopra Fonte di Salerno." *IO* 1:118–23.

85. *IO* 4:54. See also *IO* 4:48, 8:117.

86. The envoys were received on June 4. Pastor 10:19–20.

87. Vittoria Colonna, *Carteggio*, 55. Clement VII had gotten wind of a possible change of allegiance on the part of Doria and was urging caution on all parties (*IO* 4:80). In chap. 31 of the *De romanis piscibus* Giovio mentioned being taught to bone a murena by Sanga which they had caught at Civitavecchia (*IO* 9:47). For Sanga and Giovio's Roman friendships see Castellani, "Contributo alla biografia," chap. 4.

88. *IO* 4:61. It may seem surprising in view of the disparagement of the concept of Fortune in the dialogue to see it used for events of 1528, but book 26 was written in 1551, and toward the latter part of his life, as Giraud has shown, Giovio tended to use the concept of Fortune more. Giraud, *Atti*, 51–62.

89. Cited in Lavisse, ed., *Histoire de France* 5, pt. 2, p. 58.

90. *IO* 4:61.

91. Giovio placed their arrival the day

before the French retreat, which he dated as August 28 (*IO* 4:66). Using other authorities, Thérault (*Un cénacle humaniste*, p. 378) dated their arrival the 31st. Simeoni accepted Giovio's date for the retreat, as do I. Simeoni, *Le signorie* 2:861.

92. *Histories*, bk. 26 (*IO* 4:70); *Pompeii vita* (1551), 194–95, 197. On the magnificent exequies for Lautrec at Rome see *IO* 4:71.

93. *IO* 4:61.

94. *IO* 4:72.

95. *IO* 4:81–83. Genoa rose against the French on September 13, 1528.

96. Autobiographical fragment.

CHAPTER EIGHT

1. See André Chastel, *The Sack of Rome*, 186–87; and Sanudo 48:226. Giovio mentioned the white beard as impressing the emperor at Bologna (*IO* 4:116). A canon of the Fifth Lateran Council forbade clerics beards, but the pope grew it in protest at his captivity.

2. Cited in Hirst, *Sebastiano*, 112. The sense of anomie is a typical response to such a catastrophe.

3. *IO* 1:123–24. The bulls relating to his election are dated January 1, 1528 (ASV, Reg. Vat. 1438, 122r–126r). The election was approved in consistory on the 13th and provision made for Giovio's receiving income during the vacancy (Acta Misc. 18, fol. 180; Wilhelm Van Gulik and Conrad Eubel, *Hierarchia catholica*, ed. Ludwig Schmitz-Kallenberg 3:230). Nocera, disliking the Spaniards, had declared for the French in 1528. After Lautrec's death it was reduced to obedience by Fabrizio Maramaldo, without a sack, the historian of Nocera believed, but Giovio's remark would suggest otherwise. Gennaro Orlando, *Nocera dei Pagani*, 3 vols. (Naples, 1884–87), 3:17–19.

4. See Travi, "Paolo Giovio nel suo tempo," *Atti*, 313–30. For Giovio's motto see the *Dialogo dell'imprese* (*IO* 9:419). Pierio Valeriano's pessimistic *De litteratorum infelicitate* reflected the mood of humanists after the sack. We look forward to the stud-

ies of Kenneth Gouwens on their reactions. On Guicciardini's bitter pragmatism after 1527 and the imperative for the individual to save himself see Roberto Lopez, *The Three Ages of the Italian Renaissance*, 60.

5. *IO* 4:37. This episode is narrated by Giovio with the revolt of 1527, but the pope's grave illness occurred in 1529. Book 25 was not written until the end of his life, and Giovio probably compressed the events.

6. On the burning of Careggi in 1527 see Stephens, *Fall of the Florentine Republic*, 251.

7. See Berni's three sonnets of 1529 on the pope's illness (nos. 24, 33, 34), in *Poesie e prose*, ed. Chiorboli, 100–101.

8. *IO* 4:41. The episode is included with the events of the winter of 1527–28, but Giovio was on Ischia at that time. The allusion to renewed health suggests that the pope's exclamation was actually made to Giovio in the winter or spring of 1529. By Easter 1529, Clement had been well enough to give the benediction *urbi et orbi*. On the pope's shame at losing the principate of Florence cf. Machiavelli, *The Prince*, chap. 24. For the duke of Sessa's comments on Clement's nepotism see Di Meglio, *Carlo V e Clemente VII*, 26–28.

9. On Gattinara's Italian policy see Headley, *The Emperor and His Chancellor*, chap. 6.

10. Sanudo 51:294–96, 399, 433. See George L. Gorse, "Triumphal Entries into Genoa in the Sixteenth Century," in *All the World's a Stage: Art and Pageantry in the Renaissance and Baroque* 1:193–96.

11. *IO* 4:105.

12. Alfred Morel-Fatio, *Historiographie de Charles-Quint*, 358.

13. Sanudo 51:476; *IO* 4:107.

14. *Cronaca del soggiorno di Carlo V in Italia* [by Luigi Gonzaga?], ed. Gennaro Romano, 96.

15. On the papal entry and the triumphal arch erected by Bandinelli see Annamaria Petrioli Tofani, "Contributo allo studio degli apparati e delle feste Medicee," *Firenze e la Toscana dei Medici nell'Europa del '500* (Florence: Olschki, 1983), 2:646–

49. For summaries of the entries of pope and emperor and the coronation ceremonies, with bibliographies, see Bonner Mitchell, *The Majesty of the State: Triumphal Progresses of Foreign Sovereigns in Renaissance Italy (1494–1600)*, 133–49.

16. *IO* 4:113–15. The remark about Giovio's Veronese eye is Chabod's (*Scritti sul Rinascimento*, 261). There is a considerable literature on the imperial coronation at Bologna. See the bibliography in Bonner Mitchell, *Italian Civic Pageantry in the High Renaissance*, 19–25.

17. For less flattering descriptions see Wethey, *Titian* 2:36, and Sanudo 51:371.

18. *Pompeii vita* (1551), 200 (wrongly numbered 220).

19. *IO* 4:116. For the facade of his friend Tommaso Cambi's house in Naples Giovio wrote the program for a series of scenes glorifying Charles V, one of which features the investiture of Francesco Sforza, with the inscription "Singularis clementia cum insigni liberalitate." See the text as published by Kliemann in *Atti*, 221–23; for more on Cambi, see n. 72, below.

20. *IO* 4:116, 117.

21. *IO* 4:118. See also *IO* 9:386, and Claudia Rousseau, "The Yoke Impresa of Leo X," *Mitteilungen des Kunsthistorischen Institutes in Florenz* 33 (1989): 113–26.

22. *IO* 4:118. See also *IO* 4:25–26. For a discussion of Giovio and Florentine republicanism see Dionisotti, *Machiavellerie*, 411–44.

23. To Clement VII, April 7, 1530. Pietro Bembo, *Opere* 5:13–14.

24. ASMo, Canc. Est., Roma 33, December 9 and 25, 1529.

25. *Consalvi vita* (1551), 247–48; *Vita di Consalvo* (1931), 157. On Diego Hurtado de Mendoza, count of Mélito and viceroy of Valencia, see Helen Nader, *The Mendoza Family in the Spanish Renaissance* (New Brunswick, N.J.: Rutgers University Press, 1979), 125. For de Leyva see *IO* 4:113.

26. Giuseppe Coniglio, *I Gonzaga* (Milan: Dall'Oglio, 1967), 273.

27. Gaetano Giordani, *Della venuta e dimora in Bologna del Sommo Pontefice Clemente VII per la coronazione di Carlo V . . . cronaca* (Bologna: Alla Volpe, 1842), 77–78; Vittorio Cian, *Un decennio nella vita di M. Pietro Bembo*, 148–49. For Giovio's praise of Veronica Gambara see *IO* 9:287.

28. See Travi, *Lingua e vita*, 5–16. The translation is from Cecil Grayson, *A Renaissance Controversy, Latin or Italian* (Oxford: Clarendon Press, 1960), 7. On Amaseo see the entry by Rino Avesani, *DBI* 2:660–66. His lectures were printed in R. Amaseo, *Orationum volumen* (Bologna: Rubrio, 1564), 101–46. See also Vecce, "Giovio e Colonna," 71.

29. See Travi in *IO* 9:149 ff.

30. *IO* 2:179–80. The reputation of Francophilia may also have been owing to Giovio's letter to the pope of 1528 describing the battle of Capo d'Orso, which was given the title *Li veri particulari della felice vittoria del illustre signor Conte Philippino Doria contra l'armata cesarea etc* (1528).

31. The charter, dated the day of the coronation, was published by Primo Luigi Tatti, *Annali sacri della città di Como*, appendix to the third decade (Milan, 1735), 173–79.

32. *IO* 4:116–17. Amaseo's speech was reprinted in his *Orationum volumen*, 74–100. See also Giordani, *Cronaca*, 61–62. A good recent description of the coronation is given by Anthony M. Cummings, *The Politicized Muse* (Princeton: Princeton University Press, 1992), chap. 11.

33. In the life of Alfonso, Giovio made clear how crucial the duke's personal diplomacy had been in winning the emperor over. *Vita Alphonsi* (1550), 52.

34. Travi has termed Bologna the end of the dream of Italian independence ("La sosta," 121).

35. Coniglio, *I Gonzaga*, 274. For festivities see Bonner Mitchell, *Italian Civic Pageantry*, 68–70.

36. According to Vasari's life of Piero della Francesca, Giulio Romano had given Giovio the portrait copies of Quattrocento worthies made by Raphael's pupils before the frescoes of Piero della Francesca were destroyed during preparation of the Vatican stanze. For the festivities see the *Cronaca*

del soggiorno di Carlo V. For the palazzo del Te see Egon Verheyen, *Il Palazzo del Te* (Baltimore: Johns Hopkins University Press, 1977); and Frederick Hartt, *Giulio Romano* (New Haven: Yale University Press, 1958). Hartt (pp. 127, 139) has speculated that Giovio might have done the program for the sala di Psiche, on which Giulio and his assistants were working as early as 1528, and that the *putto pisciatore* on the ceiling and the theme of the purgative role of water may have been related to Giovio's attempt to cure the duke of "ostinata retentione di urina."

37. Giambattista Giovio, "Elogio," 86, citing an *ottava rima* of Giovio's nephew and companion, Giulio Giovio. Giovio, alas, did not make the roll of literary greats in canto 46 of the soon-to-be-published revised edition (1532) of *Orlando*.

38. Autobiographical fragment (*IO* 1:125). The ceremony took place on April 8, 1532.

39. Autobiographical fragment.

40. *Elogium* of Ippolito (*IO* 8:446).

41. On Ippolito's birth see John Stephens, "Giovanbattista Cibo's Confession," in Sergio Bertelli and Gloria Ramakus, eds., *Essays Presented to Myron P. Gilmore*, 2 vols. (Florence: La Nuova Italia, 1978), 1:255–56; *IO* 8:445; Pieraccini, *La stirpe* 1:345 ff.

42. *IO* 1:131–32. On Giulia Gonzaga see Mario Oliva, *Giulia Gonzaga Colonna*, and *IO* 9:302.

43. March 13, 1531. Cited by A. Bertolotti, "Ancora della famiglia Morone," *Archivio storico lombardo* 3 (1876): 301.

44. Cian, "Gioviana," 302–303. For assistance in translation I am indebted to my colleague Dr. Dirk French. For Ippolito's hunts see also Coffin, *The Villa*, 131. The apparent allusion to the rhetorician and historian Marcus Cornelius Fronto as Giovio's guide to horseflesh is not clear, except as a pun. Giovio at least fared better than Celso Mellini, who was drowned on one of Leo X's hunts. See Ubaldini, *Colocci*, ed. Fanelli, 31.

45. "Voglio pur dire che un de questi giorni si trovò attaccato a pasquino un de questi animalacci dishonesti che con l'ale sparte vanno svolazzando tutta la notte ne dolci nidi de le madonne di costa et di Roma. et se depingono su muri de le taverne con piedi et ale, et vi era di sotto questo distico: etc." (ASMo, Canc. est., disp. di Roma, 33, 214-V/13, Antonio Romei, May 12, 1532). Drawings of this type are mentioned as found on the walls of inns in *Il cortegiano* 2.93.

46. Asked by Marforio what he would give Giovio, were he a god, Pasquino replies, "Impetrarem ut bona fide historias conscriberet." *Pasquillorum tomi duo* ("Eleutheropoli" ["Free City" and a possible pun on Luther but actually Basel], 1544), 300. In 1535, on the vigil of Epiphany, appeared: "In Jovium: Supra dorsum meum fabricaverunt peccatores" (ibid., 330 [actually 430]). Another (perhaps aimed at Giovio's nephew) ran: "Gianonico Jovio: Peccata nostra ipse pertulit in corpore suo" (ibid., 408 [actually 508]). For the significance of these and other pasquinades about Giovio see Cian, "Gioviana," 335–55. Another lengthy pasquinade provided me by Prof. Kenneth Gouwens called him "diffuttuta episcopa" (BAV, Cod. Vat. Lat. 5225, vol. IV, fol. 903v). For other pasquinades attacking Giovio, see Marucci, Marzo, and Romano, eds., *Pasquinate romane* 1: 384–85, no. 390; or BAV, Cod. Urb. Lat. 1619, fol. 83: "Venalem livor Jovium, appellatque loquacem etc." See also sonnet 29 in Niccolò Franco's scurrilous *La priapea* ("Peking," 1784"). On pasquinades in general see the bibliography in Marucci, Marzo, and Romano, and in Massimo Firpo, "Pasquinate romane del Cinquecento," *RSI* 96 (1984): 612–21.

47. *IO* 8:442.

48. See Litta, "Giovio."

49. "Qui giace Paolo Giovio ermaphrodito / Che ora fece da moglie, or da marito." See ahead, chap. 9, n. 105. "Il Lasca" contributed a couple of pasquinades of the same tenor, one of which resembled the purported pasquinade of Aretino. The second touched all bases: "Qui giace il Giovio pescator maturo / istorico mendace, adulatore / prelato indegno e grande af-

frontatore; / viator, non temer, passa sicuro" (Antonfrancesco Grazzini detto il Lasca, *Le rime burlesche*, ed. Carlo Verzone [Florence: Sansoni, 1882], 636). Verzone also found in Cod. Mgl. 271 an unattributed pasquinade, "Qui giace il Giovio: a sì gran nome corra / Tutto lo stuol di Soddoma e Gomorra."

50. Biblioteca Communale, Como, MS sup. 2/2/42. For sentimental friendship see Giovio's letter to Raimondi of September 17, 1536, or his letter to Vasari of September 2, 1547. *IO* 1:187–88; 2:108.

51. *IO* 8:445–46. Varchi's description of Ippolito at this same time confirms Giovio's portrait. Benedetto Varchi, *Storia fiorentina* 4:345–46. For Ippolito's poetry see E. Weaver, "Inediti vaticani di Ippolito de' Medici," *Filologia e critica* 9 (1984): 122–35.

52. Wolfgang Kallab, *Vasaristudien* (Vienna and Leipzig: Grasser, 1908), pt. 1, 48–49; Vasari, *Der literarische Nachlass Giorgio Vasaris*, ed. Karl Frey, 2.

53. *Nachlass Vasaris*, ed. Frey, 2.

54. Ubaldini, *Vita di Monsignor Angelo Colocci*, ed. Fanelli, 76 ff.; Gnoli, *La Roma di Leone X*, 151.

55. Michele Maylender, *Storia delle accademie d'Italia*, 5 vols. (Bologna, 1926–30), 4:325. On Blosio's villa and gardens see above, chap. 6, n. 26.

56. *IO* 1:138.

57. Giovio is not listed as a member in any of the principal contemporary sources for the Vignaiuoli that I have examined, including the letter from Berni to Giovanfrancesco Bini of April 12, 1534, in Dionigi Atanagi, ed., *Delle lettere facete et piacevoli* 1:30–31, and the undated letter to Uberto Strozzi of Marco Sabino prefaced to Mario Equicola's *Institutioni al comporre in ogni sorte di rima della lingua volgare* (Milan, 1541).

58. December 16, 1531 (Atanagi, ed., *Lettere facete et piacevoli* [1601], 1:252–53). Vergerio was in Venice on November 4, 1531, and is not known to have been in Rome until he appeared as a papal secretary in mid-July 1532; Anne Jacobson Schutte, *Pier Paolo Vergerio* (Geneva: Droz, 1977),

46. However, Prof. Schutte has told me she sees no reason why this letter cannot be taken as evidence of an earlier arrival in Rome. On Fondoli see Ubaldini, *Vita di Monsignor Angelo Colocci*, ed. Fanelli, appendix 10, p. 126. Although in frequent conflict with the irascible Mai, Muscettola was serving during this period as imperial agent in Rome. See Pastor 10:210. For Gianfrancesco Bini, a papal secretary and later clerk of the Sacred College, see *IO* 1:236, and the entry by G. Ballistreri, *DBI* 10:510–13. For Marco da Lodi, a familiar of Ippolito's, see *IO* 2:81. For Balami, a papal physician, see *IO* 1:200, 209, 263, 336; 2:81; and Paola Zambelli, *DBI* 5:307–308.

59. ASM, Canc. est., disp. Roma, 33, 214-IV/54, Ant. Romei to card. d'Este, November 28, 1531.

60. *IO* 4:187; but see also *IO* 1:128. For Giovio's estimate of Orange see *IO* 1:130.

61. *IO* 2:219.

62. *IO* 1:128.

63. *IO* 1:130.

64. Vecce, "Giovio e Colonna," 82–93. At Bologna, Giovio also had Bembo correct his copy of the *Faunus*. On the likelihood of Bembo and Colonna having met before see Vecce, ibid., and Dionisotti, "Appunti," in Avesani et al., eds., *Miscellanea Augusto Campana* 1:260–61.

65. June 24, 1530. *Carteggio*, 62–63.

66. Dionisotti, "Appunti," 264–65.

67. July 15, 1530 (*IO* 1:125–26). For the sequence of the correspondence see Vecce, "Giovio e Colonna," 86–93.

68. *IO* 1:126. For Bembo's thanks see his letter of September 15, 1530. *Opere* 5:275.

69. Dionisotti, "Appunti," 271–72; Vecce, "Giovio e Colonna," 90–93.

70. I was able to examine the charter in 1963 thanks to the chancellor, Msgr. Vincenzo Striano. The identity of at least one of Giovio's vicars is known, Luca Sicardo. Archivio di Stato, Florence (hereafter, ASF), Notarile 178 (Giovanni Piero Carmignani, 1551–54), 53r-v, entry of October 2, 1551.

71. Pastor 12:536 n. 4, citing the index

of briefs of Paul III for 1539. The inability of bishops to administer their sees because of exemptions and special privileges was a major complaint to the reform commission of 1535. See Hubert Jedin, *A History of the Council of Trent*, trans. Ernest Graf, 1:441–42.

72. *IO* 1:213. Cambi appears frequently in Giovio's correspondence. A Florentine knight and banker, Cambi was established in Naples because of a homicide committed in Florence. He died in 1549. See Tordi's note in Colonna, supplement to *Carteggio*, 83.

73. *IO* 1:133. See also Colonna, *Carteggio*, 74; Alessandro Luzio, "Vittoria Colonna," *Rivista storica mantovana* 1 (1884): 20.

74. *Pompeii vita* (1551), 202–203. See Giuseppe Coniglio, *I vicerè spagnoli di Napoli* (Naples: Fiorentino, 1967), 35–38.

75. "Vita Petri Gravinae a P. Iovio ad Iohannem Franciscum Campaneum," appendix to Pietro Gravina, *Poemata*, ed. Scipione Capece (Naples: Sulzbach, 1532). See Vecce, "Giovio e Colonna," 88–89. On Gravina see Benedetto Croce, "Un umanista gaudente: Pietro Gravina," in *Uomini e cose della vecchia Italia*, 3d ed., 2 vols. (Bari: Laterza, 1956), 1:13–26. Giovio's letter to Scannapeco is found in *IO* 1:174–79, his *elogium* of Gravina in *IO* 8:98–99. For a discussion of Giovio's theory of biography see my essay, "Paolo Giovio and the Rhetoric of Individuality," in Thomas F. Mayer and Daniel R. Woolf, eds., *The Rhetorics of Life-writing in Early Modern Europe*.

76. *IO* 1:131, 134; ML, MA 1346, 112. The *referendario* was the local channel for petitions to the ducal government.

77. March 1, 1531 (*IO* 1:132). On the building of the Giovio palazzo see Stefano Della Torre and Rosanna Pavoni, "La casa," in Pavoni, ed., *Collezioni Giovio: Le immagini e la storia*, 38–44; Matteo Gianoncelli and Stefano Della Torre, *Microanalisi di una città*, 404–405.

78. *IO* 1:133. On the withdrawal of the Spanish garrison see Benedetto Giovio, *His-*

toria patriae (1982), 173–74. On the War of Musso see Mario Fara, "La signoria di Gian Giacomo Medici sul Lario," in *Larius*, vol. 2, pt. 2, pp. 443–53.

79. The letter was written at the beginning of February 1532 (*PSSC* 8 [1891]: 243–46). "A dextra post atrium habebis cubiculum, zeteculam, museum, et diaetam, loca ex ordine succedentia." The precise meaning of these terms is difficult to reconstruct. "Cubiculum" would be a bedroom. A "diaeta," as used by Pliny the Younger would be a summer living room or garden room. See Coffin, *Gardens and Gardening*, 188. "Zetecula," according to my colleague Prof. Dirk French, is probably a diminuitive of "diaeta." An inscription on the museum, seen on the painting of it at Como, read, NON COENACVLA PICTA NON DIAETAE RIDENTEM FACIVNT DOMVM SED HORTVS. In view of Giovio's later use of the term, Benedetto's use here of "musaeum" is most interesting. See ahead, chap. 9, n. 129.

80. The Lucini house was eventually added, but the family had to wait until Count Giambattista Giovio acquired it in 1775.

81. To Giulio Giovio, April 28, 1532 (*IO* 1:135). A remark in a letter to Cardinal Farnese, July 24, 1543, suggests that Giovio may have acquired the Fonte Pliniana through the generosity of the Farnese. *IO* 1:317.

82. Letter of July 1527, to be published in *IO* 11.

83. Pastor 9:328.

84. *Commentario de le cose de' Turchi* in Francesco Sansovino, ed., *Dell' historia universale dell'origine et imperio de Turchi* 2:86v.

85. Ibid., 87r. At Bologna, Giovio had compiled an account taken "from many of the most accurate descriptions" of the siege, which was printed "at the order of the pope under the name of the nuncio" (the same Vincenzo Pimpinella whose speech had bored him in 1523); to Giovan Iacopo Calandra, February 8, 1530 (*IO* 1:124). Giovio said he was enclosing a copy of the

printed tract. No copies are known to exist, but SSC has a relation to pope Clement VII dated "ex Moravia 16 Nov. 1529" and entitled "La espugnatione di Vienna et la fuga dil Gran Turco con li particulari di tutto il successo." The text begins, "Essendo io venuto in Moravia con la Maiestà del Re [Ferdinand] etc." (SSC, Archivio Aliati, 28, 5, 162v–168v). The use of the first person singular has created some confusion and led to the assumption that Giovio was in Austria in 1529, but the letter to Calandra explains that the account was written as though from the legate, Vincenzo Pimpinella, archbishop of Rossano. The catalogue of the Chigi collection, BAV, records a copy in MS Chigi 2204, "Del Gran Turco la obsidia sopra Vienna d'Austria per lettere del Reverendo Archivescovo de Rosano alla Santità de N. S. et al Reverend. et Ill. Card. de Monte legato de l'alma Roma," December 6, 1529.

86. Letter of February 20, 1531 (cited in Pastor 10:189).

87. "qual . . . indirizzo a V. S.ia accio ch'ella leggendolo in poco tempo sappia quel che in lunghissimo forse non saprebbe senza il libro" (Antonio Romei to Ippolito d'Este, August 7, 1532; ASMo, Canc. Est. Disp. Roma 33, 214-V/20, 1r). A copy of Blado's edition with a 1532 colophon apparently exists in Michigan. See Robert G. Marshall, ed., *Short Title Catalog of Books Printed in Italy and of Books in Italian Printed Abroad, 1501–1600, Held in Selected North American Libraries*, 3 vols. (Boston: Hall, 1970), 2:51. The earliest copy I personally have seen is that printed by Blado in Rome in 1535. A reference to the siege of Vienna as having occurred "last year" suggests Giovio composed the work in 1530, as does the optimism it expresses for concord between Francis I and Charles V following Francis' marriage to Charles' sister, Eleanor of Portugal (July 7, 1530).

88. Chabod, *Scritti*, 264. Without further study it is impossible to suggest Giovio's sources. Stefano Taleazzi's treatise may have been one, and, if Giovio happened to find a copy, Biondo's little treatise written for Alfonso of Aragon, *De expeditione in Turchos*, may have been helpful for the crusade against Murad II (Flavio Biondo, *Scritti inediti e rari*, ed. Bartolomeo Nogara [Vatican City: Tipografia Vaticana, 1927], 28–58). On Taleazzi see Setton 2:525–26 and 3:154. Giovio may have known Andrea Cambini's *Commentario della origine de' Turchi et imperio della casa ottomana* (Florence, 1529?). On Cambini see the entry by Mirella Giansante, *DBI* 17:132–34, who puts the first edition in 1529. For a brief survey of Italian writings on Eastern history which might have been available to Giovio see Cochrane, *Historians*, 324–37. On Giovio's sources for oriental history see V. J. Parry, "Renaissance Historical Literature in Relation to the Near and Middle East (with Special Reference to Paolo Giovio)," in *Historians of the Middle East*, ed. Bernard Lewis and P. M. Holt (London: Oxford University Press, 1962), 277–89.

89. Jiminez de Quesada, *El antijovio*, 622. In his old age Giovio bemoaned that he was even accused of sitting Turkish-style on cushions. *IO* 2:191.

90. *Commentario*, 87r.

91. *Commentario*, 90v.

92. *IO* 1:135. For accounts of preparations see Pastor 10:196ff. and Setton 3:358ff.

93. Sanudo 56: 817–18. Ippolito's demands for support were, as usual, excessive. Giovio related to the Ferrarese agent that he had asked for 8,000 ducats a month—4,000 for his suite and 4,000 to maintain a guard of 200 horsemen. Letter of June 26, 1532 (ASMo, Canc. est., Ambs., Roma 34, 220-II/41, p. 3).

94. July 24, 1532 (Guicciardini, *Carteggi*, ed. Palmarocchi and Ricci, 15:180). Ippolito de' Medici had left Bologna on July 20; Giovio arrived on the 22nd (ibid., 15:179–80).

95. July 21, 1532 (Guicciardini, *Carteggi*, 15:179);. Dionisotti, *Machiavellerie*, 248.

96. They left on July 24. Sanudo 56:770.

97.

Venisti, bone Paulle, Paulle amate
Quantum ullus potis est amari amicus;
Qui mecum Ticini otio beato
Soles condere candidos solebas,
Argutis salibus facetiisque.
Venisti. O fine fine me beatum!

D'Arco, *Nicolai Archii Comitis numerorum libri IV*, 71–72. One clause suggested that Giovio also had with him the Ischian dialogue: "Illustres lego feminas virosque"; the clause "Proelium lego Parthicum inchoatum" suggests Giovio had written parts of books 28 and 30 antecedent to the 1532 crusade. For the prior reunion with Giberti in Verona see *IO* 1:135.

98. Sanudo 56:817–18.

99. *IO* 4:211; Sanudo 56:868, 869, 922.

100. *IO* 1:135.

101. *IO* 4:216. For the siege see Setton 3:365.

102. *IO* 4:228. Here Giovio calculated the fighting host as 90,000 foot and 30,000 horse. In his autobiographical sketch he said the "monstra mirabile" took place on September 27, 1532.

103. *IO* 4:210.

104. *IO* 4:210.

105. *IO* 4:218.

106. *IO* 4:219–20.

107. *IO* 4:213–14.

108. *IO* 4:230–32.

109. In his account of the background of the crusade Giovio said nothing about the demand of the Catholics at Regensburg for a council. On the issue of the council see Jedin 1:276–80. On Francis and Suleiman see Setton 3:360–63. In 1532 we find Giovio already establishing contact with John Zápolya, tapping every source for his eyewitness history. See the letter of Zápolya to Giovio dated December 10, 1533, in Santo Monti, ed., "Gioviana: Documenti gioviani inediti," *PSSC* 16 (1904): 42.

110. Autobiographical sketch. For October 20, 1532, Sanudo reported, "Fo gran freddo" (57:111).

111. *IO* 4:210–11, 234. Among Giovio's papers there is a schematic diagram showing the order of march from Vienna to Udine through Neustadt, Bruck-an-der-Mur, and Villach. Autograph MS, "Viaggio da Vienna in Italia per la dritta qual facessemo nel ritorno dalla guerra," BNR, MS A 153.9.

112. Sanudo 57:87–92.

113. *IO* 4:233. On the rebel column see Sanudo 57:88 ff. It has been mistakenly assumed that Ippolito was arrested in San Vito al Tagliamento, but Giovio's identification of St. Veit with ancient Verunum in Norcia leaves no doubt. Mario Oliva's reasoning is correct in questioning San Vito al Tagliamento (*Giulia Gonzaga*, 144 n. 6).

114. Pastor 10:214.

115. *IO* 4:234; Sanudo 57:105, 108, 111–12, 173. See also Alessandro Luzio, *Un prognostico satirico di Pietro Aretino*, xii; Lynne Lawner, *Lives of the Courtesans*, 45.

116. Giovio said that he sat for the portrait in Venice (*IO* 8:445). On the scimitar see *IO* 4:211. See also Hope, *Titian*, 76 and 107 n. 3. The portrait is now in the Pitti.

117. For a description of one such evening see Sanudo 57:332–33. See also Bonner Mitchell, *Italian Civic Pageantry*, 70–72.

118. Sanudo 57:302.

119. Verheyen, *Il Palazzo del Te*, 15 (see the letter of March 10, 1531, reproduced as doc. 47 on p. 142).

120. Francesco Maria's opinion was that Rangoni and the count of St. Pol were equally at fault. *IO* 4:94.

121. May 6, 1531 (*Histories*, bk. 31, *IO* 4:254).

122. *Vita Alphonsi* (1550), 54.

123. *IO* 4:254. On the correctness of Giovio's judgment, as confirmed by other contemporary sources, see Pastor 10:228.

124. Book 31 may have been composed as early as 1533 and no later than 1538, during all of which time Giovio remained an admirer of Charles V. See my "Nota storico-critica," *IO* 5:244.

125. *Vita Alphonsi* (1550), 53. See also Giovio's remarks to Cardinal Farnese in 1545. *IO* 2:24.

126. Treaty of June 9, 1531 (Pastor 10:212).

127. Giovio does, however, note that the pope used the council as a rebuttal to those who disapproved of his meeting with Francis, implying that the coming colloquy with Francis was a step in winning French support for a council (*IO* 4:254). The most detailed study of Clement's policies toward the situation in Germany is Gerhard Müller, *Die römische Kurie und die Reformation 1523–1534* (Gütersloh: Mohn, 1969). For the divorce see *IO* 4:246, and Zimmermann, "A Note on Clement VII and the Divorce of Henry VIII," 548–52.

128. ". . . de libertate, de vita et de reliquis fortunis tum primum bene sperare inciperent" (*IO* 4:248). For the text of the league and the negotiations leading to it see Sanudo 57:464–578, 600–609. Giovio included the Florentines in the pact *scilicet* because of the pope, although they were not formally members; he omitted Mantua, probably because it was not a contributing member, as Federico had objected to de Leyva's captaincy. On the understanding that the league included Florence because of the pope see Sanudo 57:577–78.

129. The tract was entitled *Legatio David Aethiopiae Regis, ad sanctissimum D. N. Clementem Papam VII una cum obedientia eidem sanctissimo D. N. praestita. Eiusdem David Aethiopiae regis legatio ad Emanuelem Portugalliae regem. De regno Aethiopiae ac populo, deque moribus eiusque populi nonnulla* (Bologna, February 1533). An Italian translation appeared the following month. On the legend of Prester John see Francis M. Rogers, *The Quest for Eastern Christians* (Minneapolis: University of Minnesota Press, 1962), and by the same author, *Travels of the Infanta Dom Pedro of Portugal* (Cambridge: Harvard University Press, 1961).

130. Summarized from Salvatore Tedeschi, "Paolo Giovio e la conoscenza dell'Etiopia nel Rinascimento," in *Atti* (1985), 93–116. The letters were republished by Damião de Gois (with a few corrections which he says were necessitated by a misunderstanding of the Arabic by the original Portuguese translator) in his *Fides, religio, moresque Aethiopium* (Louvain:

Rescius, 1540), Diiiv., Eiiir., Fiiiv.–Giiir. De Gois also failed to translate Alvares' treatise, which he claimed to possess. Giovio possessed a portrait of David III, the iconography of which may have gone back to the Portuguese painter on the mission, Lazaro d'Andrade, but the fact that d'Andrade remained in Ethiopia created uncertainties regarding the attribution.

131. Sanudo 57:589.

132. *IO* 4:248–49. On the Genoese welcome see Gorse, "Triumphal Entries," 197–200.

133. On the trip see Pastor 10:224, and Giovio's autobiographical sketch. On the consecration see Ferrajoli, *Il ruolo*, 40; Biagio Baroni, *Diaria*, BAV, Cod. Vat. Lat. 12422, 264v–265r. Priestly orders were not generally taken by careerists until appointed bishop. Paul III had been a cardinal twenty years before taking them.

134. Giovio and Guicciardini are in essential agreement on this tactic of Clement's. *IO* 4:248; *SI* 20.7.

135. September 22, 1533. Chastel, *Sack*, 201.

136. *IO* 4:254; Pastor 10:232 ff. The fleet had relieved the city from a Turkish siege aimed at recapture.

137. Autobiographical fragment.

138. *IO* 4:254.

139. *Histories*, bk. 31 (*IO* 4:255).

140. *IO* 4:255.

141. Even in his autobiographical sketch Giovio stressed the link between Modena and Reggio and the rapprochement with Francis. In regard to the outcome he was correct. Pastor (10:234) cited a draft memorandum in Francis' hand of an agreement specifying that Urbino and Milan would go to the duke of Orléans. See also the account of the meeting in Knecht, 229–31.

142. For Giovio's account of the interview see *Vita Piscarii* (1551), 405. His account of the captured king is particularly fine, as when Francis' simple speech moves the victors to tears (ibid., 403–404). Cosimo I's minister, Lelio Torelli, wrote of the passage: "Questo è certo, che 'l Re di Francia morto, qui'vi per lui riuscita doppiamente, prima per l'ordinario come si vive

doppo morte, ne' scritti de' scrittori illustri, poi particularmente il Re Francesco che per le bocche del volgo in quella giornata viene biasmato e vilipeso, et quivi non solamente è salvato da infamia ma honorato per coraggioso et valoroso et prudente et vincitor della sua fortuna." Biblioteca Nazionale, Florence (hereafter, BNF), Carte Strozziane, I ser., CCCLIII, pp. 19–20.

143. *IO* 4:256. In his autobiographical sketch Giovio said the pension was 1,000 francs on the priory of "Fiscanone." In a letter of 1546 he specified "Fiscanone di Rovano [Rouen]," *IO* 2:60. This benefice was one of those conceded to the king of France by Leo X and Adrian VI.

144. Alfred von Reumont, *La gioventù di Caterina de' Medici*, trans. S. Bianciardi (Florence: Le Monnier, 1858), 137.

145. Autobiographical fragment; *IO* 1:142.

146. ASM, Archivio Gonzaga 882, Fabrizio Peregrini to the duke, Roma, November 18, 1533.

147. *IO* 1:136.

148. Ibid. At this time Aleandro was wrongly believed to favor a council. Jedin 1:277.

149. To Molza, March 3, 1534 (*IO* 1:137). "Palemone" must be a reference to Boccaccio's *Teseida*, for which in translation I have used the Chaucerian spelling. The confections of San Biagio were a slice of *pan giallo* kept from Christmas and served on February 3, the feast of San Biagio, protector of the throat. Giovio would have just eaten them the previous month. For *pan giallo* see ahead, chap. 9, n. 76. On the *Polyanthea* and the *Margarita* see *IO* 9:254.

150. Benedetto's *Historia patriae* runs to 1532 and speaks of Clement VII as still pope. See the preface by Gianoncelli to the Como 1982 edition. Copies of Giovio's *Histories* had been sent to Como in 1532. See *IO* 1:135.

151. Autobiographical fragment.

152. Caterina Santoro, *Gli Sforza*, 389. For a fuller analysis see Chabod, *Epoca*, pt. 3. At Bologna in 1532 Sforza made earnest appeals to have the contribution to the emperor reduced (Sanudo 57:383). On hatred of the Spanish soldiery see Pastor 9:303.

153. To Ippolito de' Medici. *IO* 1:136.

154. Letter cited to Ippolito; autobiographical sketch; Pastor 10:322.

155. *IO* 4:266–67. Grana was now bishop of Segni. On his skill in funeral orations see Giovio's remarks in the Ischian dialogue, *IO* 9:249. For the speech see John M. McManamon, "The Ideal Renaissance Pope," *Archivum historiae pontificiae* 14 (1976): 15.

156. *IO* 4:256. It is possible that these passages condemning Clement's diplomacy at Marseilles were inserted in the *Histories* after the resumption of hostilities between Francis and Charles. Nonetheless, in his contemporary letter to Ippolito, Giovio suggested that the pope do something to counteract the suspicions of the Italians that he had raised the possibility of war. *IO* 1:136.

157. *IO* 4:265. Guicciardini's well-known evaluations are found in *SI*, bks. 16.12 and 20.7. Varchi's judgment was even harsher. See Umberto Pirotti, *Benedetto Varchi* (Florence: Olschki, 1971), 165–66.

158. *Pompeii vita* (1551), 182; *IO* 4:266. A Venetian ambassador observed in 1526 that Clement VII's "entire pleasure was to discuss hydraulics with his engineers." Coffin, *The Villa*, 250–53.

159. *IO* 1:261.

CHAPTER NINE

1. *IO* 1:147.

2. ". . . quanto ancora per li advisi che [la S. V.] mi da delle cose del mondo, sopra le quali con la solita sua prudentia ne discorre, tutto quello che al juditio mio ne si puo dire." ASF, Mediceo del Principato 184, fol. 42v., Cosimo to Giovio, September 28, 1542.

3. E.g., Musso to Cervini, *CT* 11:406 n. l; or the legates to Cardinal Farnese, "se può dire col Iovio, che sia cima d'huomo" (ibid., 10:124); or Serristori to Cosimo I, *Nuntiaturberichte aus Deutschland*, ed. Preussisches Historisches Institut in Rom, pt. I, vol. 10 (Berlin, 1907), 55, or Cervini to Dandino, ibid., vol. 11 (Berlin, 1910), 409.

4. *IO* 1:147; Sforza to Giovio, March

30, 1535, published by Carlo Volpati, "Paolo Giovio e l'ultimo duca di Milano," *Archivio storico lombardo*, 8th ser., no. 3 (1951–52): 198. On the popularity of Giovio's letters see Ferrero's introduction to his correspondence (*IO* 1:69–71). Many of Giovio's letters are known only through contemporary copies, as, for example, most of his letters to Rodolfo Pio. See Cecil H. Clough, "The Pio di Savoia Archives," in Berta Maracchi Biagiarelli and D. E. Rhodes, eds., *Studi offerti a Roberto Ridolfi* (Florence: Olschki, 1973), 213 n. 24.

5. *Dialogo dell'imprese* (*IO* 9:374). See also *Commentario de le cose dei Turchi*, ed. Sansovino, 2:72r-v. For an introduction to the debate between Tuscan, Florentine, and the *lingua cortegiana* see Bruno Migliorini, *Storia della lingua italiana* (Florence: Sansoni, 1960), chap. 8, or in the English translation, *The Italian Language*, by T. Gwynor Griffith (London: Faber, 1974).

6. For Giovio's language I have followed the analyses by Ferrero in *IO* 2:261–63; by Folena, "L'espressionismo"; the unpublished *tesi di laurea* of Antonella Ghielmetti, "La lingua di Paolo Giovio nell'epistolario," UCM, 1988; and Travi's fundamental study, *Lingua e vita*. On the old *gergo* see Franca Ageno, "A proposito del 'Nuovo modo de intendere la lingua zerga'" in *GS* 135 (1958): 370–91. An example of peculiarly Giovian jargon would be the adjective "gibertalis," meaning with Gibertian discipline. An example of ironic lexical coinage would be "pasticciere [pasticher]?" for secretary. An example of ironic metaphor would be the figure "in groppa [on the crupper]," as in the expression "io mi avveggo che la spiritualità va in groppa alla temporalità [I see that spirituality goes on the crupper after worldliness]." For a very critical assessment of the gap between theory and practice in Giovio's language see the review of *IO* 1 and 2 by Maria Corti, *GS* 136 (1959): 653–58.

7. *IO* 1:301. See the list of Cardinal Cervini's *burlevole cifre* given by the editors of *CT* 10:888–89.

8. Folena, "L'espressionismo," 127.

9. On the autobiographical component of the letters see Rota, "Paolo Giovio,"

927. On Giovio's letters see especially Guido Giuseppe Ferrero, "Politica e vita morale del '500 nelle lettere di Paolo Giovio," *Memorie della R. Accademia delle Scienze di Torino*, 2d ser., vol. 70, pt. 2 (1942): 57–102. See also the reviews of Ferrero's article by Carlo Dionisotti, *GS* 118 (1941): 156–60, and of *IO* 1 and 2 by Gennaro Sasso, *GS* 133 (1956): 606–14, and 136 (1959): 647–52.

10. *IO* 1:332. On the freedom of personal correspondence see the excellent summary of Renaissance epistolography by John M. Najemy, *Between Friends: Discourse of Power and Desire in the Machiavelli-Vettori Letters of 1513–1515* (Princeton: Princeton University Press, 1993), chap. 1, and G. Fragnito, "Per lo studio dell'epistolografia volgare del Cinquecento: Le Lettere di Ludovico Beccadelli," Bibliothèque d' Humanisme et Renaissance 43 (1981): 62–87.

11. My translation is a free one but, I think, faithful to the intent of Fedeli's almost untranslatable Italian. "Monsignor Jovio mi scrive, alcuna volta, et è bene intertenersi con tutti perché da gli avvisi di molti non è che alcuna volta non se ne cavi servitio, e se ben l'ha licentioso et del satirico nel scriver, et sii sempre a un modo, pur si può dar mente alla intentione del suggieto, et non alla struttura delle parole"; cited by F. Stefani, "Paolo Giovio," *Archivio Veneto* 1 (1871): 370–76. Angelo Massarelli commented apropos of one of Giovio's letters, "Il Card. S. Croce hebbe una lettera del Iovio burlevole, ma non senza qualche consideratione" (*CT* 1:287).

12. ". . . et apresso lettere di Mons. Giovio, a quali havendo sentite leggere di S. Campana, oltr' al parergli che le sieno piacevoli, le giudica anchora appassionate.." Riccio to Grifoni, May 4, 1543; ASF, Mediceo del principato 360, 229r.

13. "mi andai schermente." Autobiographical fragment.

14. February 16, 1535 (*IO* 1:146).

15. *Elogium* of Ippolito (*IO* 8:446). Giovio's version has recently been confirmed by discovery of Cibo's confession. See John Stephens, "Giovanbattista Cibo's Confession," in Bertelli and Ramakus, eds.,

Essays Presented to Myron P. Gilmore, 2 vols. (Florence: La Nuova Italia, 1978), 1:255–69. For Varchi's account see his *Storia fiorentina* 5:137 (bk. 14).

16. *Histories*, bk. 34 (*IO* 4:341); Varchi, *Storia fiorentina*, bk. 14, *Opere*, 5:127–28.

17. August 20, 1535 (*IO* 1:161).

18. *IO* 8:447; 4:341. In a letter to Sforza of October 14, 1535, Giovio still showed some uncertainty (*IO* 1:166). Pieraccini concluded that the cardinal had been carried off by pernicious malaria. Pieraccini, *La stirpe* 1:358 ff.

19. *IO* 8:447; 1:161.

20. February 12, 1535 (*IO* 1:142). On Montmorency see ahead, Conclusion, n. 13.

21. On the project *De imperiis et gentibus cogniti orbis* see Travi in *IO* 9:67–72. On the proposal for a philosophical treatise see SSC, Archivio Aliati, 28, 5, fols. 370v–371r.

22. *IO* 1:142. On the metaphor "inzaffranato [saffroned—yellowed—a reference to the yellow badge of heretics or Jews]," see Folena, "L'espressionismo," 144.

23. July 17, 1524; *Epistolae*, ed. P. Burmann (Utrecht: Halmam and Vandewater, 1697), 142. In 1524 Tagliacarne, of Sarzana, was tutor to the French princes, whom he accompanied to Spain, 1526–1530. Giovio paid him a bland compliment in the Ischian dialogue (*IO* 9:258) and asked to be remembered to him in a couple of letters to Pio (*IO* 1:143, 190).

24. February 16, 1535 (*IO* 1:146). On January 17, 1536, Negri reported Giovio as being among those attending Paul III at dinner. *Lettere di principi* (1581) 3:38r.

25. February 16, 1535 (*IO* 1:144–47). On Paul III see also *Histories*, bk. 42 (*IO* 5:124).

26. On Giovio and the crusade see my article, "The Publication of Paolo Giovio's *Histories*: Charles V and the Revision of Book XXXIV," *La Bibliofilia* 74 (1972): 49–90. On the entry into Naples of "Carolus Africanus" see Bonner Mitchell, *Italian Civic Pageantry*, 101–104. For Giovio's portrait of Barbarossa see L. Klinger and J. Raby, "Barbarossa and Sinan: A Portrait of Two Ottoman Corsairs from the

Collection of Paolo Giovio," *Ateneo veneto* 9 (1989): 47–59.

27. December 8, 1535 (*Lettere di principi* [1581], 3:38r). On the visit to Nocera see Giovio's letter to Carpi, December 28, 1535. *IO* 1:170.

28. To a cardinal, perhaps del Monte or du Bellay, but not, as supposed by the editor, Pio, who was not yet a cardinal (Naples, December 12, 1535; *IO* 1:169). It thus appears that Giovio had already written the preliminary parts of book 34 and perhaps had even begun to sketch in the action at Tunis. Certainly the optimism of book 34 and its opening paean to Charles V and Paul III suggest near-contemporary composition.

29. *IO* 1:169.

30. To Carpi, December 28, 1535 (*IO* 1:170–71). Giovio cannot mean Sepúlveda, who was appointed *cronista* of Castille, succeeding Bernardo Gentile, in 1536. Morel-Fatio supposed Giovio meant Guevara, who had held the post since 1526, conflating news of a coming new appointment with Guevara's tenure. Since 1509 there had customarily been two *cronistas* of Castille (Morel-Fatio, *Charles-Quint*, 109–10). See also Augustin Redondo, *Antonio de Guevara* (Geneva: Droz, 1976), 102, 303–11.

31. *IO* 1:172, 170.

32. Vecce, "Giovio e Colonna," 71, 89; Travi, *IO* 9:160–62.

33. *IO* 4:346. See Hayward Keniston, *Francisco de los Cobos* (Pittsburgh: University of Pittsburgh Press, 1958), 174.

34. Del Vasto to Giovio, July 24, 1535 (*Lettere di principi* [1570], 1:129v); *IO* 1:171; "Chatalogo degli spoglie affricane portato da Jovio a Roma per ornamento della sua bottega che mi ricordo" SSC, Archivio Aliati, 25, 5, 322r and v.

35. *IO* 1:180–82, and letter to Benedetto Giovio, February 6, 1536, UCM, Fondo Negri da Oleggio. *IO* 11 (forthcoming).

36. *IO* 1:172.

37. *IO* 1:183 and letter to Benedetto, February 6, 1536. Marzocco was the lion-symbol of the Florentine Republic.

38. To Vincenzo Fedeli, January 31,

1544 (*IO* 1:331). Lorenzo delle Teste was presumably Sforza's physician. He does not appear in Juliana Hill Cotton's *A Medical Register of the Italian Renaissance* (Oxford: Privately printed, 1976), but I have not searched Cotton's papers, in deposit at the Wellcome Library, London.

39. Letters of December 18, 1543, March 9 and 30, 1535 (private collection). On Sforza see Paola Oldrini, "Francesco II Sforza," in Giorgio Chittolini, ed., *Gli Sforza, la chiesa lombarda, e la corte di Roma* (Naples: Liguori, 1989).

40. *IO* 1:155, 163.

41. *IO* 1:173.

42. *Histories*, bk. 43 (*IO* 5:133). There are several disapproving allusions in the letters to such an agreement, e.g., *IO* 1:225, 331, 347. On the negotiations at Naples and Giovio's perspicacity see Chabod, "Epoca di Carlo V," in *Storia di Milano* 9:60–70.

43. Letter cited to Benedetto Giovio. See also *IO* 1:187.

44. On the entry see Chastel, *Sack*, 210ff., and Mitchell, *Italian Civic Pageantry*, 125–29. See also Mitchell's "The SPQR in Two Roman Festivals of the Early and Mid-Cinquecento," *Sixteenth Century Journal* 9 (1978): 95–102.

45. *IO* 1:184. On Manetti see Léon Dorez, *La cour du Pape Paul III* 1:130–31, 264.

46. In his *Consolatoria* of 1527, Guicciardini spoke of "el cammino della monarchia di Italia a che si vedeva andare Cesare." *Opere*, ed. Emanuella Lugnani Scarano, 3 vols. (Turin: UTET, 1970–81), 1:499. See also Pastor 11:233.

47. May 3, 1536 (*IO* 1:184).

48. May 12, 1536 (*IO* 1:185–86).

49. See Hallman, *Italian Cardinals*, 46–63.

50. To Pio, December 10, 1536 (*IO* 1:189). In his autobiographical fragment Giovio said he left Rome on September 8. Letter no. 66 in *IO* is dated Rome, September 17, but the editor transcribed it from Domenichi's edition, which may have mistaken 7 for 17.

51. Alessandro was asking for information as well as for papers belonging to Al-

fonsina de' Medici, wife of Piero di Lorenzo, that Giovio had inventoried when they were consigned to his care at her death in 1520. August 14, 1535; ASF, Mediceo del principato, 181, fol. 235.

52. To Pio, December 10, 1536 (*IO* 1:189). Giovio said he was to leave Genoa on November 9; the emperor departed on the 16th for Spain.

53. *IO* 1:201.

54. Travi in *IO* 9:162; see also *IO* 1:171.

55. Preface to vol. II (*IO* 4:2).

56. December 10, 1536 (*IO* 1:189).

57. *IO* 1:204. See my "Nota storico-critica," *IO* 5:244.

58. Aretino's pension, awarded in 1536, was for 200 *scudi*. Luzio, *Pietro Aretino*, 54.

59. *IO* 1:191. See also *IO* 2:123.

60. On the Turkish alliance of 1536 see De Lamar Jensen, "The Ottoman Turks in Sixteenth-Century French Diplomacy," *Sixteenth Century Journal* 16 (1985): 455–56.

61. *IO* 1:193.

62. On Giovio and Pole's mission see Mayer, "Reginald Pole," *Sixteenth Century Journal* 16 (1985): 431–50. In his letter to Agostino Landi, written from San Fiorano (north of Piacenza) on March 10, 1537, Giovio said he had met the prelates at "Ogliera," a locale of uncertain whereabouts, and had then gone on to Piacenza (*IO* 1:194). Prof. Mayer, who has reconstructed Pole's itinerary from contemporary letters, tells me Pole may have left Rome on February 16, 1537, and that he and Giberti were in Bologna by the 27th. They departed for Modena on the 28th, arrived in Piacenza on March 3, and left there on the 5th with a safe-conduct from del Vasto, who would thus have been able to alert Giovio to their presence. Leaving Asti on the 9th, the prelates reached Chieri the same day. My hypothesis is that Giovio left Milan on the 4th or 5th and, going by way of Pavia, intercepted Giberti and Pole at Voghera, near Tortona, which would fit the time frame of their journey and also allow him time to have traveled back through Piacenza to San Fiorano by the 10th. Thanks to the courtesy of Dott. Vanni Tesei of the Biblioteca "A. Saffi" of Forlì, I have been able to examine a reproduction of Giovio's holograph letter,

which allows for a reading of "Oghera" as readily as Ferrero's "Ogliera."

63. On Giberti's esteem for Giovio see Adriano Prosperi, *Tra evangelismo e controriforma: Gian Matteo Giberti* (Rome: Edizioni di Storia e Letteratura, 1969), 59.

64. *IO* 1:191–93. On the still unpaid pension see the letter to Pio, *IO* 1:190.

65. May 4, 1537 (*IO* 1:197).

66. Federico Chabod, *Per la storia religiosa dello stato di Milano durante il dominio di Carlo V* (Bologna: Zanichelli, 1938), 29, 176.

67. March 21 and September 6, 1537; *Annali della Fabbrica del Duomo di Milano*, vol. 3 (Milan, 1880): 263–64, 265–66. For this reference I am much obliged to Prof. Stefano Della Torre. Among the names is senator Gualterio Corbetta, to whom there is a letter of Giovio's dated April 10, 1537, *IO* 1:195–96.

68. ". . . non obstante aliquo lapsu temporis." ASC, Notarile, Cart. 345, D. Volpi, March 28, 1563.

69. ASC, Notarile 206, Volpi, November 9, 1537. See also Litta, "Giovio." Nothing is known of Feliciano's age or the identity of his mother. He was adopted without right of inheriting Giampietro's goods, although with the right of inheriting goods to be assigned him by codicil to Paolo's will. As he was not mentioned in Paolo's last will, he presumably did not survive.

70. May 4, 1537 (*IO* 1:196).

71. "Io gli lo arccomando, et la prego a far' che non si doglia, per che non conseguendo quello che iustamente desidera, si doleria più di Vostra Signoria et di me che del debitor' principale" (ASF, Mediceo del Principato, 5024, no. 1, del Vasto to Cosimo I, April 29, 1537). Giovio also induced the viceroy of Naples, Pedro Alvarez de Toledo to write. Ibid., undated.

72. *IO* 1:199–200. Details of the campaigns are found in books 37 and 38 of the *Histories.*

73. *IO* 1:200. For a summary of events leading to the Venetian-papal alliance agreed to in principle in September 1537, see Setton 3:422–34.

74. To Cosimo de' Medici, Milan, December 11, 1537 (*IO* 1:201). Doria's letter

to Cosimo is dated from Milan, December 10, 1537 (ASF, Mediceo del principato 2834). I am grateful to Prof. George Gorse for sharing with me this reference.

75. Vasari is the authority for the painting having been done for Giovio (life of Bronzino in "Accademici del Disegno," in Bettarini and Barocchi, eds., *Le vite* 6:232). The portrait has been dated 1533 by Craig Smyth, but some scholars date it as late as 1540. I am grateful to Prof. George Gorse, for letting me see a draft of his article on the portrait. According to Vasari, Bronzino painted Doria after being recalled from Pesaro by Pontormo for assistance with Poggio a Caiano. Giovio was in Florence briefly in early May 1534, en route from Como to Rome. He was there again briefly in 1536 before being invited by Alessandro de' Medici to Pisa and Genoa. He visited in September 1538 as guest of Cosimo de' Medici while en route to Rome, and returned in June 1539 at the time of Cosimo's wedding festivities. Any of these visits could have been the occasion Vasari described. It is unlike Giovio to have paid for the portrait himself, and perhaps Alessandro or Cosimo did so. Vasari mentioned a friendship between Giovio and Bronzino, which is substantiated by passages in Giovio's letters. See *IO* 2:156; 2:78.

76. December 3, 1537 (*IO* 1:200). Giovio was still in Milan as of the 11th and was back by the 30th (*IO* 1:202, 211). *Pan giallo*, a Como tradition, was a bread made with yellow corn meal from America and hence a rich Christmas treat. It is customarily called "pan de méj [millet]" but is actually made with corn and rye. See Franco Soldaini, ed., *Comaschi a tavola* (Como: Edizioni della Famiglia Comasca, 1987), 244.

77. *IO* 1:200.

78. *IO* 1:198.

79. December 30, 1537 (not 1538 as indicated by the editor), *IO* 1:211. This letter was dated by Giovio according to the Milanese custom of beginning the new year with Christmas. It is one of the very few errors in Ferrero's splendid edition of the letters.

80. *IO* 4:407. For miseries caused by the

taxes, the reluctance of Caracciolo and del Vasto to impose more taxes, and Giovio's importance as a source in this, see Chabod, "Epoca," 90–95, 282, 323, 330, 341, 359.

81. *IO* 4:371.

82. January 28, 1538 (*IO* 1:204).

83. Ibid.

84. *IO* 1:205.

85. *IO* 1:205–206.

86. See also William S. Maltby, *Alba*, 39. The Florentine agent at Rome, Angelo Niccolini, had a report from Nice of sun, oppressive heat, bad water, and indifferent wine. ASF, Mediceo del principato 3261, fol. 46r.

87. *Histories*, bk. 35 (*IO* 4:364). See Knecht, 285. Charles had mocked Francis' timidity by boasting of the perfect order of his retreat. The interview at Nice was also a source of information on the battle of Pavia. *Vita Piscarii* (1551), 405; *Vita del Pescara* (1931), 435.

88. To Montmorency. *IO* 1:208.

89. *IO* 4:409.

90. SSC, Archivio Aliati, 28, 5, fols. 309r–321r. See Dante Visconti, "Nota su alcuni MSS giovini," *Clio* 1 (1965): 111. In a letter of 1539 Giovio referred to "quello discorso io portai a Sua Cesarea Maestà in Villa Franca [Villefranche]" (*IO* 1:224). Another copy was sent to Montmorency with an accompanying letter of August 18, 1538, mentioning that the emperor had already seen and approved it (*IO* 1:208). The treatise was printed in some later editions of Domenichi's translation of the *Histories*, beginning with the edition of G. M. Bonelli (Venice, 1560), with the title "Consiglio di Mons. Giovio intorno al modo di far l'impresa contra infideli." See Ferrero's note in *IO* 1:208, where he cites internal evidence confirming composition in 1538. I have used the text from the *Sopplimento di Girolamo Ruscelli nell'istorie di Monsignor Paolo Giovio* (Venice: Salicato, 1572), 89–100. There are, however, differences between the MS and printed text which merit study. Giovio's *Discorso* undoubtedly incorporates materials from Stefano Taleazzi's treatises written for Julius II and Leo X. Some of its arguments may even go back to Pius II's famous letter

to Muhammad the Conqueror (ca. 1460). On Taleazzi see Setton 2:525–26 and 3:154. On Leo X's project for a crusade see G. L. Moncallero, "La politica di Leone X e di Francesco I nella progettata crociata contro i Turchi e nella lotta per la successione imperiale," *Rinascimento*, 1st ser., 8 (1957): 61–101.

91. The grant was confirmed by Paul III in June 1538 (ASV, Reg. Lat. 1688, 67v–68v). In a letter dated September 8, 1552, Giovio asked the ducal chancery at Florence to draft a letter to the cardinal of Trent requesting by him to secure resumption of payments by the bishop of Pamplona of the 300 ducat pension awarded by Charles V and courteously paid for fourteen years, i.e., since 1538 (*IO* 2:239). See also SSC, Archivio Aliati, 28, 7, fol. 16r., where a financial transaction of Giovio's dated February 7, 1548, records the pension "Dal S.or Don Petro Pacheco che lui cì debbe su'l vescovato di Pampalogna."

92. Sepúlveda, *De rebus gestis Caroli V*, bk. 30, chap. 33, in Sepúlveda, *Opera* (Madrid, 1780), 2:534–35. See the comments on Sepúlveda and this episode by Morel-Fatio (*Charles-Quint*, 108–109), who does not attempt to unravel the circumstances but accepts the general accuracy of Sepúlveda's account.

93. Giovio himself admitted that he was looking for a "lame mule" at Naples in 1535 and that he was disappointed by Charles V at Genoa in 1536. It is unlikely that the episode described by Sepúlveda took place at Bologna, either in 1530 or in 1532, since Giovio was then the client of Ippolito de' Medici, not Alessandro. Nor could Alessandro have been Giovio's advocate at Naples, as he did not arrive there until January 1536, long after Giovio had left. If Alessandro sought a pension for Giovio, it would have had to have been at Genoa in the autumn of 1536. Sepúlveda's story thus seems to have been a composite of events.

94. Nice and the subsequent meeting of Charles and Francis at Aigues Mortes were widely perceived in Germany as the prelude to an alliance against the Turks. On these grounds, Cornelius de Schryver wrote an epic poem to celebrate the meeting. Corne-

lius Scribonius Grapheus, *Pacis inter Carolum V Imp. Caes. Aug. & Franciscum I Gallorum Regem* (Antwerp: Coccius, 1540).

95. E. Parma Armani, "Il palazzo del principe Andrea Doria a Fasolo in Genova," *L'Arte*, 3d ser., 10 (1970): 12–64.

96. *IO* 1:206. Giovio dated his note to Farnese "Da piaza Doria, in casa di messer Dominico, 29 Iunii."

97. *IO* 1:206–207.

98. Brandi on the other hand (p. 389) believes that these talks, although friendly, convinced Charles that peace with Francis was hopeless.

99. *IO* 4:411–13. On the embassy see Angiolo Salomoni, ed., *Memorie storico-diplomatiche degli ambasciatori . . . che la città di Milano inviò a diversi suoi principi. . .* (Milan: Tipografia Pulini al Bocchetto, 1806), chap. 21, 85–90.

100. *IO* 4:414, 420. See Chabod, "Epoca," 322. On del Vasto's governorship see Gaspare De Caro's entry in the *DBI* 4:611–16.

101. *IO* 4:403–404, 420–26. For Giovio's sources see the *elogium* of Capello, *IO* 8:458–60 and 1:233.

102. *IO* 4:425.

103. Chabod, *Scritti*, 263.

104. See Setton 3:445–46. Despite Venetian impatience, Gonzaga had insisted on awaiting Doria and his galleys before commencing any action. Another complicating factor may have been the negotiations preceding the battle in which Barbarossa apparently offered to come over to the imperial side in return for Tunis. Brandi, 415–16.

105. Francesco married Isabella della Selva. Giambattista Giovio, "Elogio," 43; Litta, "Giovio."

106. Aretino's letter was dated June 23, Giovio's response August 15, 1538 (*IO* 1:207). See the annotated edition of Aretino's letter in G. G. Ferrero, ed., *Scritti scelti di Aretino e di Doni* (Turin: UTET, 1962), 163–65. Even before Giovio penned his response Aretino had sent another letter dated August 11 along with a copy of the second Marcolini edition of book I of the letters, in which the letter praising Giovio

appears. On this edition see Ferrero, ibid., 163. One of Nicolò Franco's verse attacks on Aretino begins, "Aretin mio, il Jovio m'avisa / che dal Marchese avrai provisione" *Rime di Nicolò Franco contro Pietro Aretino* (Lanciano, 1916), 19.

There is no real authority for attributing to Aretino and Giovio the unflattering pair of epitaphs they are said to have exchanged. Giovio's supposed epitaph for Aretino goes: "Qui giace l'Aretin, poeta tosco / Che disse mal d'ognun fuor che di Cristo / Scusandosi con dir: non lo conosco." Aretino's runs: "Qui giace Paolo Giovio ermaphrodito / Che ora fece da moglie, or da marito" (Cian, "Gioviana," 354–55). Cian's rejection of the tradition was reinforced by Carlo Bertani, *Pietro Aretino* (Sondrio: Quadrio, 1901), 181–82. The linkage of the "satyr" medal sometimes called a portrait of Giovio to either Giovio or to a Giovio-Aretino "quarrel" is quite without foundation. See Raymond B. Waddington, "Before Arcimboldo: Composite Portraits on Italian Medals," *The Medal* 14 (1989): 12–23. In his *Prognostico satirico* of 1534, Aretino styled Giovio "parasito apostolico" and "dio del vituperio della sede apostolico" (Luzio, *Un prognostico satirico*, 5).

107. *De chorographia Larii lacus*. See Travi in *IO* 9:333–50. The sense of "spiritual beatitude" that successive generations of artists and writers have found in contemplating the beauty of Lake Como has been recounted by Prof. Gianfranco Miglio in his magisterial "Introduzione al mito del Lario," *Larius* 1:xix–cxxxi.

108. See Visconti in *Larius* 1:67–70. On Sfondrato's mission to Savoy see bk. 34 of the *Histories* (*IO* 4:339). For Giovio's praises of him see *IO* 1:271–72.

109. Although the imperial charter is dated October 23, 1537, Sfondrato would certainly have known in advance of the grant and may have requested the information before the formal confirmation, at a time normally more propitious for lake travel than late October.

110. *IO* 9:335–37. For Como's Roman past see Giorgio Luraschi, *Comum oppidum* (Como: Noseda, 1974), and "L'età antica

di Como," in *Atti dei convegni celebrativi del centenario 1878–1978* (Como: Società Storica Comense, 1979), 87–105. See also the volume *Novum comum 2050* (Como: Società Archaeologica Comense, 1993).

111. Giovio may have been correct. Ruins of a Roman villa's foundations have been found in the harbor of Lenno. See *Larius*, ed. Miglio, 1:12. Pliny's letter describing his villas on the lake is *Ep.* 9.7. For the supposed villa at Bellagio there is, unfortunately, no archaeological evidence.

112. See the notes of Mario Fara in *Larius*, vol. 2, pt. 2:347–53 ("Il castello di Musso") and 443–53 ("La signoria di Gian Giacomo Medici sul Lario"). Giovio had recently interceded with the marquis del Vasto to secure better treatment for Gian Giacomo and his brother when they were arrested under suspicion of disloyalty to the emperor. See Giovio's letters of January 30 and February 22, 1537, to their brother Gian Angelo de' Medici, the future Pius IV. *IO* 1:191–92.

113. Leonardo's drawings and comments on the Fiumelatte are in the Codex Atlanticus.

114. See Pliny the Elder, *Nat. hist.* 2.103; Pliny the Younger, *Ep.* 4.30. The spring is the site of a splendid but unfortunately deteriorating villa built by Count Giovanni Anguissola who retired there as governor of Como after the murder of Pier Luigi Farnese.

115. *IO* 9:348–49; see also 9:144.

116. *De chorographia Larii Lacus* (Venice: Ziletti, 1559). See Travi in *IO* 9:324–32. Giovio's own copy, made by his amanuensis Luigi Raimondi and illustrated with a topographical drawing of the lake, is dated 1537, as is the copy in the Biblioteca Ambrosiana, which was probably the copy sent to Boldoni. Boldoni's letter to Sfondrato is dated much later, January 27, 1539.

117. *IO* 1:92. In 1549 Giovio claimed to have been collecting portraits for more than thirty years (*IO* 2:132; see also *IO* 8:479). On the stanza "Mercurio e Palladio" see Linda Klinger, "Paolo Giovio e le collezioni rinascimentali di ritratti," *IO* 10 (forthcoming). It was probably in the palace

of the Cancelleria, but no such stanza can be located today.

118. *IO* 1:94.

119. On antecedents for Giovio's collection see Linda S. Klinger, "The Portrait Collection of Paolo Giovio" (Ph.D. diss., Princeton University, 1991). Also valuable are Rosanna Pavoni, ed., *Collezioni Giovio*; Eugène Müntz, *Le musée de portraits de Paul Jove*; and Paul Ortwin Rave, "Paolo Giovio und die Bildnisvitenbücher des Humanismus," *Jahrbuch der Berliner Museen* 1 (1959): 119–54.

120. *IO* 1:141; Müntz, *Paul Jove*, 5.

121. *IO* 8:35.

122. February 12, 1535; *IO* 1:141.

123. Matteo Gianoncelli, *L'antico museo di Paolo Giovio in Borgovico*, 6. In the appraisal of 1537 the property is listed simply as "a house called 'the Tower' with garden" and as belonging to "Benedetto et fratello de Zobio," suggesting that construction was not yet under way; but in his autobiographical fragment Giovio says that in 1537 he alternated between Como and Milan "edificando il museo." For general discussions of the museum and its location, see also Stefano Della Torre, "Il museo" in Pavoni, ed., *Collezioni Giovio*, 14–17, and his "Le vedute del museo gioviano," *Quaderni Erbesi* 7 (1985): 39–48, and "Note per l'iconografia di Plinio il Vecchio," in *Plinio, i suoi luoghi, il suo tempo* (Como: New Press, 1984). Although Della Torre's work supersedes all earlier studies, there is useful material in Zygmunt Wazbinski, "Musaeum Paolo Giovio w Como," *Acta Universitatis Nicolai Copernici* 99 (1979): 115–44, and in Paul Ortwin Rave, "Das Museo Giovio zu Como," *Miscellanea Bibliothecae Hertzianae* (Munich: Schroll, 1961), 275–84, who speculates that the architect may have been Domenico Giuntalodi. Additional land was purchased on April 8, 1538; ASC, Notarile 206, Volpi.

124. For the statement in the will see Giorgio Bordoli, ed., "Il testamento di Paolo Giovio," *PSSC* 50 (1983): 113. For the phrase "the teeth of the tax gatherer," see the letter of February 12, 1535, in which Giovio praised the prince who can

rule "senza poner dente contra a chi ha da vivere" (*IO* 1:141). In 1538 d'Avalos became sole governor of Milan.

125. Mention of the plane tree occurs in Pliny the Younger, *Ep.* 3.1. Benedetto thought a mosaic pavement in the convent of the Umiliati in Borgo Vico had been part of Caninius Rufus' villa (*Opere scelte* [Como, 1887], 231). See Weiss, *The Renaissance Discovery of Classical Antiquity*, 117. The site of the villa has now been identified with virtual certainty by Prof. Giorgio Luraschi as being on the opposite side of Como. "La villa romana di Via Zezio in Como," *Como*, no. 3 (Autumn 1976).

126. Letter without date but probably ca. 1544–45. *PSSC* 8 (1891): 186.

127. *IO* 8:35.

128. Bruno Migliorini, *Parole d'autore* (*onomaturgia*) (Florence: Sansoni, 1977), 73. The other to use the term *museum* was Alberto Lollio. See also Julius von Schlosser Magnino, *La letteratura artistica* (Florence: Nuova Italia, 1967), 195–97; Gigliola Fragnito, "Il museo di Antonio Giganti da Fossombrone," *Scienze credenze occulte livelli di cultura*, Convegno Internazionale di Studi, Florence, 1980 (Florence: Olschki, 1982); and Paula Findlen, "The Museum: Its Classical Etymology and Renaissance Genealogy," *Journal of the History of Collections* 1 (1989): 59–78. I am grateful to Prof. Gouwens for the last reference.

129. February 1, 1532; *PSSC* 8 (1891): 244. On the refurbishing of the palazzo see above, chap. 8, n. 79. Benedetto employed the traditional custom of Quattrocento Latin whereby the diphthong became a long "e"; hence the spelling *museum*. Interestingly, Benedetto did not use the word *museum* in editing the Cesarini Vitruvius (Como, 1521), a detail suggesting that he and Giovio came upon the concept later. Pliny the Elder used the word to describe artificial grottoes, which, he said, the Greeks called *musaea*, "homes of the muses" (*Nat. hist.*, 36.42); cited in Coffin, *Gardens and Gardening*, 30.

130. *IO* 9:338. On the classical prece-

dents see Rosanna Pavoni, "Il Museo," and "Il collezionismo," in Pavoni, ed., *Collezioni Giovio*, 14–17, 19–25.

131. *PSSC* 8 (1891): 201.

132. *IO* 1:207. *In solidum* is probably a pun on "solid" and the Roman gold coin a *solidus*. In a letter of 1551 Giovio said he could now live frugally, being free of "il rabbioso capriccio d'edificare." *IO* 2:206.

133. Bordoli, "Il testamento," 112–13. It was necessary to show that the museum had not been built with ecclesiastical income.

134. *IO* 1:202.

135. There are several references to this letter, which exempted only the Premonstratensian canons from extending him hospitality (*IO* 1:189, 190, 304). By now Giovio had a respectable episcopal household. His nephew Giulio, Benedetto's son to whom he had renounced the *commenda* of Sant'Antonio, seems to have joined him as a more or less constant companion, perhaps as his chaplain. (For a chaplain see *IO* 1:132.) Luigi Raimondi, scion of an old Como family and a relative of Benedetto's wife Maria, was serving at this time as secretary and amanuensis. He has been identified as the transcriber of one of the MSS of the *Larius* in 1537 (Visconti, "Nota," 101). On Raimondi see Giambattista Giovio, *Gli uomini della comasca diocesi antichi e moderni nelle arti e nelle lettere illustri* (Modena: Società Tipografica, 1784), 203–204. On Giulio Giovio see Ernesto Travi, "Profilo di Giulio Giovio," in *Umanesimo e Rinascimento a Firenze e Venezia: Miscellanea in onore di V. Branca*, 5 vols. (Florence: Olschki, 1983), 3:749–70.

136. *IO* 1:201.

137. It seems that his quest for the pension was successful, although payment continued to be erratic. After Forlì's death in 1552 Giovio arranged to collect some arrears from the bishop's estate. *IO* 2:246.

138. To Pio, September 27, 1538 (*IO* 1:209–10). I have rendered "quello adopratore delle forficette," a seeming piece of medical jargon, as "bungler."

CHAPTER TEN

1. Autobiographical fragment.

2. Babbi to Cosimo, January 7, 1546; ASF, Mediceo del principato 3590, fol. 34r.

3. Fabrini to Riccio, September 3, 1549; ASF, Miscellanea Medicea 22, ins. 20, fol. 271r.

4. "... non mi occorse trombetta migliore che quella del Jovio." Niccolini to Grifoni, February 24, 1539 (ASF, Mediceo del principato 3261, fol. 265r). For further details see Zimmermann, "Paolo Giovio and Cosimo I de' Medici" (Ph.D. diss., Harvard University, 1964).

5. Brandi agrees with Giovio that it was after Nice and Villefranche that Charles V realized Francis I would never give up. Brandi, 389–90.

6. *IO* 1:214. On this mode of executing criminals see Samuel Y. Edgerton, Jr., *Pictures and Punishment During the Florentine Renaissance* (Ithaca, N.Y.: Cornell University Press, 1985), 233.

7. Autobiographical fragment. For the festivities see Andrew C. Minor and Bonner Mitchell, *A Renaissance Entertainment* (Columbia: University of Missouri Press, 1968), and *IO* 9:389–90.

8. *IO* 1:219.

9. Bks. 36 and 37 were completed no later than October 1540. In a letter to Farnese (October 1540), Giovio said he had finished through the battle of Castelnuovo (Hercegnovi), which occurred on August 7, 1539. *IO* 1:261.

10. The work is dedicated to the cardinal, not proof positive but most likely the sign of a commission. The colophon carries the date November 1539. In a letter of December 27, 1539, Giovio urged the cardinal to see that the printers were diligent in correcting any spelling errors in the MS, which was prepared by "a bizarre German," hence probably in Como (*IO* 1:263). Ferrero gives the date of the letter as 1540, but as it was written from Mantua, Giovio must have used the Mantuan style of dating the new year with Christmas.

11. *Vita Sfortiae* (Florence: Torrentino,

1551), 114. On humanist biography see Cochrane, *Historians*, 52–53. On Giovio and gunpowder see J. R. Hale, *Renaissance War Studies*, 400–401.

12. *IO* 1:219. In SSC, Archivio Aliati 28, 5, fols. 396–411, there is an "Informatione sull'impresa di Castel Nuovo data per messer Martino d'Avila." See Visconti, "Nota," 112.

13. *Histories*, bk. 37 (*IO* 4:432).

14. *IO* 1:221.

15. *IO* 1:216–22.

16. *IO* 1:223–27. The letter was published by Ferrero from a copy in the Biblioteca Ambrosiana. It is undated and without addressee, but internal evidence makes it certain it was sent to Raynce. Ferrero suggests December 1539, on the basis of d'Avila's arrival in Rome on November 20.

17. See also *IO* 1:214–15.

18. In his letter to Raynce, Giovio predicted that, were Charles V to give up Milan, peace would come, in which the sultan would join, seeing that the Christian states were in concord with each other through "maintaining equal the balance of states and powers" ("stando anche loro in pace fra sé per mantenere eguale la bilancia de li Stati e delle potenzie"), *IO* 1:227. Giovio here expanded the concept from the Italian states to Europe as a whole. Fueter agreed with Giovio on the centrality of Milan to the European balance of power. Eduard Fueter, *Geschichte des europäischen Staatensystems von 1492–1559* (Munich: Oldenbourg, 1919; rpt., Osnabrück: Zeller, 1972), 284 ff. (latter source).

19. *IO* 1:229.

20. *IO* 1:225, 231, 237.

21. To Raynce, January 3, 1540 (*IO* 1:228). On fears of a second League of Cambrai see also his letter to Federico Gonzaga of January 1540. *IO* 1:229.

22. *IO* 1:228. There were even some suspicions that d'Annebault may have secretly encouraged Venice in the proposed treaty with the Turk, as the embassy did nothing to weaken Francis I's friendship with Suleiman. See Knecht, 294–95, and J. Ursu, *La politique orientale de François I*

(Paris: Champion, 1908), 110–15. Details of the embassy's welcome are from book 39 of the *Histories* (*IO* 5:2–3). Aretino described the warmth of the Venetian welcome in a letter of December 25, 1539, to Charles V that also mentioned "il celeberrimo Iovio, assiduo testimonio de gli atti del fatal capitano" (*Il secondo libro delle lettere* [Bari: Laterza, 1916], 193; ibid. [Milan: Mondadori, 1960], 610–13). On Venetian attitudes toward the Turks see Dionisotti, "La guerra d'Oriente nella letteratura veneziana del Cinquecento," *Geografia*, 163–82.

23. *IO* 1:233; cf. Terence, *Eunuchus* 1.105. The slave, however, says he leaks only fabrications and lies, not truth, which he holds. Perhaps for this reason in the *Histories* Giovio dropped this metaphor in favor of a storm-tossed and leaky ship (*IO* 5:5). On the desire to see Orléans in Milan see Giovio's letter to Maffei, January 24, 1540 (*IO* 1:233). For Francesco Foscari's complaint of leaks from the debates of the Pregadi in 1523 see Sanudo 17:262.

24. *IO* 1:240. Among those Giovio mentioned or later asked to be remembered to were "il cavalere Capello" (Bernardo Capello? see *IO* 1:294), Marco Contarini, a "messer prete Eliodoro" who had given him some seeds for the garden of the museum, and "signor Valerio" (Zuan Francesco Valier?), *IO* 1:242; also Daniele Barbaro and Marco Foscari (*IO* 2:4), Giorgio Zorzi (*IO* 2:199), Ottavio Raverta, bishop of Terracina (*IO* 2:149), and Giovanni Vendramin (*IO* 1:332). In 1543 Giovio entertained the patriarch, Girolamo Quirini, at the museum (*IO* 1:317). See also Volpati, "Giovio e Venezia." In 1551 Giovio asked to be remembered to Paul de Labarthe, sieur de Termes, who had formed part of d'Annebault's suite. *IO* 2:193.

25. *IO* 1:235.

26. February 25, 1540 (*IO* 1:240). The letter is addressed to Donato Rollio, who is almost certainly, as Ferrero suggests, Donato Rullo, the friend of Flaminio and of Gualteruzzi and later a victim of the Inquisition.

27.
Giovio, se ben havete il corpo infermo
Tanto che non può gir senza sostegno
Non è pero, ch'l vostro kiaro* ingegno
Non sia, come fu mai, vivace e fermo.

Con esso usate poi sì fatto schermo
Contra 'l tempo, e la morte, che il lor regno
Per voi s'atterra; e fate illustre, e degno
Ogni vil loco tenebroso, et hermo.

La bella historia vostra a morte fura
I nomi, i luoghi, e l'opre et lji* dà vita
Da le insidie del tempo alta e sicura.

Questa anchor fia sì vaga, e sì gradita
Ch'ogni alma eletta harà per gran ventura
D'esser dal mondo in quelle charte udita.

* (Trissino was still clinging to his orthographic reforms.) Monti, ed., "Gioviana," *PSSC* 20 (1912–13): 203.

28. See Luzio, *Pietro Aretino*, 51.

29. *IO* 1:227. For Aretino's thanks see *Lettere di M. Pietro Aretino*, 6 vols. (Paris, 1609), 2:117r–18r.

30. January 24, 1540 (*IO* 1:232). Giovio was also trying to lure "il Salviati" to Milan to execute a dozen portraits from medals. *IO* 1:238–39.

31. February 6, 1540 (*IO* 1:236–37).

32. Knecht, 294.

33. *IO* 1:237, 241–42.

34. Giovio missed the conclusion of the treaty (October 2) by less than a month. See Setton 3:448.

35. June 8, 1540 (*IO* 1:241–42).

36. Cf. Thucydides 1.70.

37. *IO* 5:5. On the conspiracy of the Cavazza see P. Labalme in David Rosand, ed., *Titian: His World and His Legacy* (New York: Columbia University Press, 1982), 125–26. On the grain question see Gabriele Lombardini, *Pane e denaro a Bassano tra il 1500 e il 1700* (Vicenza: Neri Possa, 1963), 41, a reference for which I am grateful to Dr. Clough.

38. *IO* 5:8–10.

39. *IO* 5:11. During this summer of 1540, it should be noted, Giovio helped his banker Tommaso Cambi design a fresco honoring Charles V for the facade of his

house in Naples, using *invenzioni* and mottos that reflected his earlier admiration. See Kliemann's edition of the letter to Cambi in *Atti*, 221–23.

40. On July 16 Giovio told Cardinal Farnese that the d'Avalos had left Como for Milan the day before yesterday, having been there twenty-two days, which would give an arrival of June 22 and a departure of July 14 (*IO* 1:248). Writing to the marquis of Savoy on June 17, 1540, Don Lope de Soria advised, "Los Señores Marques y Marquesa partieron ayer para yr a Coma a holgar y buscar el fresco no enbarzante que al Señor Marques era venida un poco de gota en un pie dize que sanara con bevar frio. Va con ellos el señor don Antonio de Aragon hermano de la Señora marquessa y el obp.o Jovio los aguarda con muchas conselas y pinturas" (Archivo General de Simancas, Estado 1187, no. 29). The time discrepancy is puzzling. Perhaps the court sojourned in the Brianza en route. However, Giovio is explicit, for in a letter to Giulio Landi on July 13 he said the d'Avalos had been there twenty-two days. *IO* 1:246.

41. June 24, 1540 (*IO* 1:243). At some point Giovio also had Vittoria's *impresa* painted in the museum (*IO* 9:406), but his lack of mention of it here in 1540 confirms my inclination to believe it was composed later. On Carlo Gualteruzzi of Fano, a lawyer, novelist, agent of Bembo, and friend of Vittoria Colonna, see Ornella Moroni, *Carlo Gualteruzzi e i corrispondenti*. On his being one of the *spirituali* see Mayer, "Reginald Pole," 444.

42. July 2, 1540 (*IO* 1:244–45). Interestingly, Giovio's letter began with an acknowledgment that "in questo acerbo caso la crudezza del dolore avanza ogni grandezza d'animo." On the legitimacy of grief to the humanists see McClure, *Sorrow and Consolation*, 4.

43. Indirectly through Carpi and the secretaries Bernardino Maffei and Raynce, and in a letter to the cardinal himself (*IO* 1:231, 233, 243). After having been substituted by Monluc in 1540, Raynce had taken service with Cardinal Farnese.

44. July 16, 1540 (*IO* 1:248). For exemptions from the tithe see *IO* 1:222 and 263.

45. From Rome, October 13, 1540 (*IO* 1:253). See also *IO* 1:246.

46. September 17, 1536 (*IO* 1:188).

47. Gianoncelli, *L'antico museo*, 68.

48. *IO* 1:146, 162, 183, 231.

49. Giovio's offer to write the life of Paul III was made in a letter to Cardinal Farnese datable October 1540 (*IO* 1:261). In the letter Giovio claimed that his proposal had met with the approval of Cervini and Maffei. Evidence of Paul III's enjoyment of Giovio's letters at this period comes from a letter of February 1540, in which Raynce sent on to Cardinal Farnese at Ghent copies of letters from Giovio describing his museum and offering opinions on events, "in which His Holiness has taken the greatest pleasure" (*Acta nuntiaturae gallicae*, vol. 1, *Correspondance des nonces en France Carpi et Ferrerio 1535–40*, ed. J. Lestocquoy (Rome: Gregorian University, 1961): 529. If not Paul III, Giovio had at least convinced del Vasto's secretary, Gutierrez, of his loyalty to Cardinal Farnese. See Gutierrez's letter to the cardinal of August 17, 1543: "Ma sopra tutto lo [Giovio] amo et osservo per esser tanto et tanto servitor di V. S. Ill.ma et una tromba di sua grandezza et summa cortesia" (Archivio di Stato, Parma, Racc. MSS., 115, p. 21). On the expectation of loyalty to a patron see Diana Robin, *Filelfo in Milan* (Princeton: Princeton University Press, 1991), 13–17.

50. January 24, 1540 (*IO* 1:231). On Carafa's objections to Bembo see Gigliola Fragnito, *In villa e in museo: Saggi sul Rinascimento perduto*, 30, and Dionisotti, *Geografia*, 187. For Giovio's "messer Cato" I have used the Chaucerian "Daun [dominus] Cato."

51. *IO* 1:247–48.

52. Pastor 11:135–36.

53. For a typical Giovian sarcasm about Theatines see *IO* 1:218. On the reluctance in general of the literary careerists in the curia to sacrifice their careers for political or religious motives see Dionisotti, "La lette-

ratura italiana nell'eta del Concilio di Trento," *Georgrafia*, 185–86.

54. Pastor 12:535.

55. To Farnese, July 16, 1540 (*IO* 1:248). The colloquy of Hagenau lasted from June 12 to July 28.

56. For Giovio's sense of traditional piety see *IO* 1:298.

57. *IO* 1:251–52. In 1541 the diet of Regensburg did vote money and troops to defend Buda, which Ferdinand had taken in May 1541, against a Turkish counterattack.

58. Dante Visconti, "La famiglia Gallio," *PSSC* 40 (1957–1959): 202.

59. *IO* 1:246, 252, 254.

60. Archivio di Stato, Parma, Racc. MSS., 114, ins. 2, fol. 17; cf. *IO* 1:232.

61. *IO* 1:254.

62. Jedin 1:439.

63. Cited in Pastor 11:209.

64. Jedin 1:441–42. The bishops' memorial is printed in *CT* 4:481–85, but the list of signatories has been lost from the original document. Giovio's own difficulties with exempt orders in his diocese have been noted. In these same months he was mounting a campaign to secure a monopoly over the export of wine from his see, exploiting his new friendship with Eleanor of Toledo to obtain the consent of her father the viceroy. *IO* 1:262–63.

65. Cardinal Farnese to the nuncio to Venice, October 14, 1540. Archivio di Stato, Parma, Racc. MSS., 114, ins. 2, fol. 19. This is a final draft of the letter on which Farnese had written the close "come fratello" but then did not sign, which raises questions as to what was finally sent. This is the only mention we have of this pension, probably a grace of Giovio's patron, Giberti.

66. *IO* 2:175. The bull of conferral is dated December 16, 1540 (ASV, Reg. Vat. 1546, fols. 45v–47r. According to Litta the benefice was renounced to Giovio's nephew, Alessandro, the next year. A former Benedictine abbey, San Giuliano had been made into a secular commenda in the fifteenth century. See Matteo Gianoncelli, *Como e suo convalle* (Como: New Press, 1975), 53. For Giovio's possession see

ASC, Notarile 207, Volpi, January 15, 1541 (bulls registered with chapter, along with a letter of del Vasto dated December 28, 1540).

67. March 10, 1543 (*IO* 1:307). For the commenda of the archpresbytery of St. Stephen at Menaggio, conferred February 16, 1542, see ASV, Reg. Vat. 1581, fols. 169r–170r.

68. *IO* 1:265–66. Ascanio Colonna had refused to submit to the salt tax of 1540.

69. The party took place on February 20. Pastor 11:353.

70. *IO* 1:256–58.

71. Contarini's letter was dated June 9; del Vasto's report June 28. Pastor 11:462, 468; Jedin 1:446.

72. *Histories*, bk. 40 (*IO* 5:65–66). Bonner Mitchell, *Italian Civic Pageantry*, 66–67.

73. September 17, 1541 (*IO* 1:269–71). Giovio's recourse here to fate is reminiscent of his explanation for why Clement VII should have trusted the old enemies of his house (*IO* 9:194). See Giraud, "Fortuna nel Giovio," *Atti*, 51–62.

74. In his glossary Ferrero comments on the phrase "cima d'arrosto" but not on the adjective "freddo," which would seem to indicate a cooling of Giovio's admiration (*IO* 2:279). "Cima d'huomo" does not necessarily imply moral approbation. Cf. Cervini and colleagues to Cardinal Farnese, Trent, June 20, 1545, when speaking of Charles V: "Se può dire col Iovio, che sia *cima d'huomo* et quel che non gli riesce per una via, cerchi per l'altra et che ami piu sè, che quasivoglia." *CT* 10:124.

75. *IO* 1:270. The fall of Buda is narrated in bk. 39, the arrival of Suleiman in bk. 40.

76. *IO* 1:271–72.

77. *IO* 8:230. Giovio's *elogia* of Leonardo, Raphael, and Michelangelo were all composed between 1525 and 1532 and most likely in 1527–28. For the dating of the three lives see my arguments in "Giovio and Renaissance Art Criticism," 422–23 n. 50.

78. Karl Frey, "Zur Baugeschichte des St. Peter," *Jahrbuch der Königlich Preussischen Kunstsammlungen*, Beiheft 33

(1912): 9 n. 2. The college, composed of sixty members of various nations, was created by Clement VII by the bull *Admonet nos* of December 12, 1523. Pecchiai, *Roma nel Cinquecento*, 174. For Giovio as a member of the executive board which carried on the daily work see Pastor 12:655.

79. *IO* 1:229.

80. Michelangelo to Bartolomeo Ferrantini, December 1546 or January 1547. *Il carteggio*, ed. Paola Barocchi, Renzo Ristori et al. (Florence: Sansoni, 1965—), 4:251–52.

81. November 8, 1541 (SSC, Archivio Aliati, 28, 5, 84r; UCM, Fondo Negri da Oleggio).

82. *IO* 1:273–75. On Charles' letter see Brandi, 456. On the campaign see also Maltby, *Alba*, 46–47. Giovio's unpublished "Discorso sopra l'impresa di Algeri" (SSC, Archivio Aliati, 28, 5, 222r–224r) suggests that he saw the emperor's letter, since he incorporated Charles' own justification for the expedition.

83. June 2, 1542 (*IO* 1:280). The book is one of the two Giovio promised to bring the duke of Florence in a letter of February 9, 1543. *IO* 1:306.

84. *IO* 1:278–79.

85. On the motto *VIRTVTI FORTVNA COMES* see Giovio, *Dialogo dell'imprese*, ed. Doglio, 40–41.

86. Setton 3:462.

87. To Stefano Colonna. *IO* 1:279.

88. *IO* 1:287, 290; see also *IO* 1:282. I accept Ferrero's dating for this letter of 1542 but would place it not in June but in late July, after war was a certainty. Knecht (303–304, 362) places Francis I's declaration of war on July 12 after he had heard from Constantinople. Jedin (1:456) and Setton (3:462) place it on July 10, before he had heard from Constantinople. In either event, Giovio was correct that the Turk was closely involved in French plans.

89. *IO* 1:293.

90. September 20 and December 18, 1542 (*IO* 1:295, 297). Copies of letters of Vitelli and the physician Bartolomeo Carabeto to Giovio on the desultory progress of the Hungarian campaign can be found in

ASF, Mediceo del Principato, 358, fols. 308r–310r and 315r–316r.

91. *Histories*, bk. 42 (*IO* 5:118).

92. *IO* 1:291. Contarini was posthumously condemned for heresy by Paul IV. See Molza's moving Latin verses of 1542, "The dying poet to his friends," and Benedetto Accolti's verse appealing to the Muses on Molza's behalf, in Alessandro Perosa and John Sparrow, eds., *Renaissance Latin Verse* (Chapel Hill: University of North Carolina Press, 1979), 265–67, 277. After much suffering Molza returned in the spring of 1543 to his native Modena, where he died in 1544.

93. *IO* 1:293, 298–99. For Benedetto's letters see *PSSC* 8 (1891): 240, 243, 247. Both brothers speak of their common "brother." The only known brother was Giampietro. However, Benedetto's letter reads "M. Antonio orbati simus," creating a puzzle yet to be solved.

94. *IO* 1:304.

95. *IO* 1:305.

96. *IO* 1:306–308. On San Gallo's plan for Cervini's villa see Stanley Morrison, "Marcello Cervini, Pope Marcellus II, Bibliography's Patron Saint," *Italia medioevale et humanistica* 5 (1962): 301–19. Cervini was a member of Tolomei's Vitruvian academy, which probably explained Giovio's desire to see the villa. For his impressions of it see *IO* 1:307. As Girolamo Muzio later charged in one of his invectives, Giovio seldom stayed in an inn or paid for a meal, preferring to lodge with friends and acquaintances en route; *Archeografo Triestino*, new ser., 7, pts. 1–2 (August 1880): 13–14. See Giovio's amusing letter to the secretary of the marquis del Vasto, Francesco Guttierez, without date but ca. 1542–43, explaining how he could travel from Rome to Milan almost without paying for lodging or meals. *IO* 1:299–301.

97. *IO* 1:308, 311–12. On *De imperiis* see also *IO* 1:142, and Travi in *IO* 9:67. Alberti was active at Bologna 1538–41 but did not officially become the inquisitor of the city until 1551. See Abele Redigonda, "Leandro Alberti," *DBI* 1:699–702.

98. *IO* 1:309, 311.

99. "Il bel duca Ottavio chiavò in Pavia quattro volte la prima notte la sua Madama" (*IO* 1:312).

100. *IO* 1:314. In fact, Charles had 3,000 Spanish foot, 4,000 Italian, and 500 light horse. As his secret letter to Philip shows, he had not finally made up his mind, even after investing Philip with Milan (Brandi, 493–95). The return of the fortresses to Cosimo was finally approved at Pavia on June 12. Giorgio Spini, *Cosimo I de' Medici e la indipendenza del principato mediceo*, 214.

101. *IO* 1:317. In his letter describing Giovio's museum Doni spoke of the great heat that summer, as did Giovio (*IO* 8:34).

102. *IO* 5:137.

103. *IO* 1:317.

104. *Histories*, bk. 43. For a detailed account see Setton 3:470 ff.

105. *IO* 5:134. In a letter to Cardinal Farnese of September 23, 1544, Giovio mentioned having completed the storming of Strigonia, etc., which formed the latter part of book 43. *IO* 1:349.

106. Brandi, 496; Jedin 1:481.

107. See Pastor 12:176–77; Brandi, 497–98. Charles certainly did not dismiss the pope's proposal out of hand. Brandi cites don Diego Hurtado de Mendoza, Charles' ambassador to Venice, as warning him that "Milan is the gateway to Italy."

108. Giovio's support of Paul III's peace efforts and his disgust at the devastation of northern Italy found a poetic echo in the sonnet, "Ecco che già tre volte, Italia mia," which his friend Veronica Gambara composed after Busseto. Veronica Gambara, *Rime e lettere*, ed. Felice Rizzardi (Brescia: Giammaria Rizzardi, 1759), 9. For Giovio's approval of Paul III's neutrality see *IO* 1:340.

109. *IO* 1:319.

110. *IO* 1:317–18. By "mal della verula," Ferrero suggests, Giovio probably meant syphilis, contracted from her husband. Ironically, sometime during these Lombard visits Giovio composed an *impresa* for the marchioness celebrating her as the apotheosis of chastity. *IO* 9:407; see also *IO* 5:65.

111. July 22, 1543 (*IO* 1:315–16).

112. *IO* 1:322. Although Giovio wrote Cardinal Farnese, nothing came of the matter. On del Vasto's problems in Milan see Chabod, "Epoca," 95–96, and Gaspare de Caro's entry in the *DBI* 4:611–16.

113. *IO* 1:317–18.

114. *IO* 1:311. In March Giovio had described the museum as nine-tenths complete (*IO* 1:306). For the *stanza d'onore* see Gianoncelli, *L'antico museo*, 66.

115. To Maffei, August 16, 1543 (*IO* 1:319–20). The house, which he bought from Giacomo da Corte, was just to the north of the enlarged family palace. See Gianoncelli and Della Torre, *Microanalisi*, 402–404, and Della Torre, "La casa" in Pavoni, ed., *Collezioni Giovio*, 38. The intervening houses were acquired by the Giovio family after Paolo's death.

116. On Doni see Paul F. Grendler, *Critics of the Italian World*, 49 ff. Doni's description is best read in Anton Francesco Doni, *Disegno: Fac simile della edizione del 1549 di Venezia, con una appendice di altri scritti del Doni riguardanti le arti figurative*, ed. Mario Pepi (Milan: Electa, 1970), 98–100. The earlier edition by A. Luzio, "Il Museo gioviano descritto da A. F. Doni," *Archivio storico lombardo*, 2d ser., 16 (1901): 143–50, was reproduced by G. G. Ferrero in his *Scritti scelti di Aretino e di Doni* (Turin: UTET, 1962), 402–408. The description for Jacopo Tintoretto was apparently intended for Ludovico Domenichi. See Klinger, "The Portrait Collection," 69.

117. PAVLVS IOVIVS EPISCOPVS NVCERINVS OB ERVDITI INGENII FOECVNDITATEM MAX. REGVM ATQVE PONTIFICVM GRATIAM LIBERALITATEMQVE PROMERITVS, CVM IN PATRIA COMO SIBI VIVENS SVORVM TEMPORVM HISTORIAM CONDERET MVSEVM CVM PERENNI FONTE AMOENISQVE PORTICIBVS AD LARIVM PVBLICAE HILARITATI DEDICAVIT. MDXLIII (Gianoncelli, *L'antico museo*, 57). On the opening of gardens in Rome and Naples to public enjoyment, and on Pontano's suggestion in his

dialogue "On Splendor" that the splendid man used gardens and villas to entertain *cives peregrinosque*, see Coffin, *Gardens and Gardening*, 246, 250–51.

118. *PSSC* 8 (1891): 200–202.

119. The "Musaei Ioviani Descriptio" (*IO* 8:35–38) begins as though it had been composed with publication in mind, but the central part reads as though adapted from a response to Ottavio Farnese, to whom the *Elogia* were dedicated. All the descriptions should be read in conjunction with the later paintings of the museum, on which see Stefano Della Torre, "Le vedute del museo gioviano."

120. Pliny the Younger, *Ep.* 9.7. English translations of Giovio's description are based on Florence Alden Gragg, trans., *An Italian Portrait Gallery*, 22–27.

121. The painter is unknown. The Hippocrene spring was actually on Helicon, but Doni apparently followed a Renaissance tradition of assigning it equally to Parnassus. See Coffin, *Gardens and Gardening*, 78–79.

122. Among the mottoes were: *Saluti consulere*; *dignitatem tueri*; *censum respicere*; *lite carere*; *libertate frui*; *immortalitati studere*. Gianoncelli, *L'antico museo*, 60.

123. *IO* 1:222. The "Tivano" blows southward down the lake from about 3:00 A.M. to midday, the "Breva" northward in early evening. From the descriptions by Benedetto and Doni, we know that this room was frescoed with representations of Apollo and the muses with their appropriate instruments and the insignia attributed to them by the poets of antiquity. Benedetto had edited Vitruvius, and, if not a member, Giovio was certainly in close contact with Claudio Tolomei and members of his Vitruvian academy—whence, probably, his desire to see Cervini's villa on Monte Amiata. The museum as the product of Giovio's deliberate reconstruction of classical values has been stressed by Wazbinski, especially its Plinian archaeology, its use as a pantheon, and its dedication to the Muses. See Klinger, "The Portrait Collection," 75.

124. Klinger, ibid., 71–76. By 1543 only a small portion of the portraits had ac-

tually been installed. See Pavoni, "Il museo" and "Il collezionismo," in Pavoni, ed., *Collezioni Giovio*, 14–17, 19–26, and *IO* 10 (forthcoming).

125. *IO* 1:317, 318, 320, 322, 323, 326, 328.

126. October 9 and 25, 1543 (*IO* 1:325–27). Giovio's portrait of Suleiman was probably a copy of Titian's, done in 1539 for Guidobaldo della Rovere. See J. M. Rogers and R. M. Ward, *Süleyman the Magnificent* (London: British Museum, 1988), 46–51.

127. *IO* 1:328–30. Cardinal Farnese left Rome on November 28 for France and met Charles V in January at Kreuznach.

128. The siege had been raised when the attackers learned of the landing of the relief force by Andrea Doria at Villefranche. Setton 3:471.

129. September 23, 1544 (*IO* 1:349).

130. *IO* 5:169. Francis I also concluded that Barbarossa and Doria had their own game to play. One is reminded of Stilicho and Alaric. See Knecht, 365–66, and Setton 3:471.

131. Achille Neri, "Una lettera inedita di Girolamo Muzio," *GS* 4 (1884): 229–40. On Delminio see the article by Giorgio Stabile in the *DBI* 17:218–30 and the study by Lina Bolzoni, *Il teatro della memoria: Studi su Giulio Camillo* (Padua: Antenore, 1984).

132. *IO* 1:331–32. On the fatal enema see also *IO* 1:313, 347. On the letter to Fedeli see F. Stefani, "Paolo Giovio," *Archivio Veneto* 1 (1871): 370–76.

133. *IO* 1:332. Paul III had silenced the cardinal of Burgos in consistory by declaring that Charles V's alliance with England was worse than Francis I's with the Turk. Pastor 12:186.

134. *IO* 1:333.

135. Cited in Pastor 12:670. Brandi (p. 508) saw the mission as primarily nepotistic; Pastor accepted it as sincere (12:187–89); Jedin (1:493) was closest to Giovio in acknowledging nepotism but sensing that the Church's best interest lay in conciliation.

136. *IO* 1:333. Note Giovio's feeling that Clement's undue severity lost England.

137. *IO* 1:337–38. Assuming it was books 39 and 40 that Giovio mentioned to Cardinal Farnese as already seen (letter of October 28, 1543, *IO* 1:327), by these two and a half new books he must have meant 41, 42, and part of 43.

138. Gianoncelli, *L'antico museo*, 63.

139. *IO* 1:341. On the implicit comparison of del Vasto and de' Medici see *IO* 1:331.

140. Maltby, *Alba*, 55–56.

141. *IO* 5:190–91. See the extended discussion by Oman, *The Art of War*, 229–43. Oman believed Giovio to have been in error with regard to certain particulars, although otherwise detailed and valuable. Oman himself was in error, however, on the date of the battle, which he placed on April 11 instead of the 14th, and he tended to give too much credence to the French sources.

142. *IO* 5:191.

143. *IO* 1:340–41.

144. *IO* 5:203–209. Giovio's willingness to credit Francis with some restraint in dissuading the fleet from attacking Spain after Nice may have been owing to conversations with the papal nuncio to France in this period, Girolamo Dandino, who returned to Rome in 1544 and with whom Giovio corresponded often, beginning in 1545. See the entry on Dandino by Anna Foa, *DBI* 32:413–23.

145. *IO* 1:340. It was to Henry's influence that Giovio correctly attributed the surprise departure from Rome on May 22 of Charles V's ambassador to the pope, Don Juan de Vega. See Pastor 12:192.

146. *IO* 1:340. Pastor (12:194) cites the passage as a good example of Giovio's insight. On Ippolito's departure at the end of June see *IO* 1:342. On the gem see *IO* 1:335–36. On the unearthing of Maria's tomb during the renewed work on St. Peter's see Pastor 12:638.

147. *IO* 1:333, 340.

148. *IO* 1:341

149. June 28, 1544 (*IO* 1:342).

150. "Io non vorrei però che le troppe grandezze vi insuperbissero, et che voi vi scordaste di noi altri come havete fatto fin qui con perpetuo silentio sapendo massime quanto le vostre lettere si leggano volentieri; et quanto da nre. parte sieno desiderate. Però Mons. mio se volete purgar la contumacia scrivete una lettera lunga: piena di discorsi sopra questi ultimi avvisi del essersi già approssimati doi esserciti a tre leghe" (Maffei to Giovio, September 6, 1544; Archivio di Stato, Parma, Racc. MSS., cart. 114, ins. 2, fol. 44). In a letter of the 12th from Perugia the cardinal also spoke of a letter he had written from Assisi asking for Giovio's considered opinion (ibid., fol. 51). On this correspondence see the remarks of Ferrero in *IO* 1:30–34.

151. *IO* 1:343–45. After receiving Giovio's letter of the 11th, the cardinal himself wrote, "Se la prima vostra lettera fu tanto grata quanto vi scrissi, per l'altra mia pensate che è stata la di xi in risposta della mia d'Ascisi pieni di quelle cose che si aspettano dalla vostra bussola" (Cardinal Farnese to Giovio, September 15, 1544; Archivio di Stato, Parma, Racc. MSS., cart. 114, ins. 2, fol. 53). The correspondence contains numerous allusions to dispatches being forwarded to Giovio. He was certainly well-informed. He knew, for example, that there had been a preliminary French-imperial colloquy in August, which he thought had taken place at Bar-le-duc (it had actually taken place at Saint-Amand). See Charles Paillard, *L'invasion allemande en 1544* (Paris: Champion, 1884), 368–69. Giovio's account of the forged letters authorizing the surrender of Saint-Dizier, although unsubstantiated, accords with other contemporary versions. *IO* 5:219; Paillard, ibid., 245.

152. See Brandi, 521.

153. September 18, 1544 (*IO* 1:346–47).

154. To Farnese, September 23, 1544 (*IO* 1:348–49).

155. To Giovanni della Casa, September 27, 1544. Moroni, *Gualteruzzi*, 150.

156. *IO* 1:351.

157. October 28, 1544 (*IO* 1:354); see also letter of October 14 to an unknown correspondent (1:353). In a letter of November 8, 1541, Giovio called Tournon

"mecenati optimo." SSC, Archivio Aliati, 28, 5, fol. 84r.

158. *IO* 1:352; Giovanni Bianchetti to Giovanni della Casa, November 1, 1544, in L. Campana, "Msgr. Giovanni della Casa e i suoi tempi," *Studi storici* 18 (1909): 354, doc. 12. For the possible basis of this report see Giovio's remark about Madame d'Etampes in his letter to Farnese of September 18, 1544. *IO* 1:349.

159. *IO* 1:353.

160. Cf. *IO* 1:302.

161. In his letter of September 23, 1544, to the cardinal, Giovio offered to become a friar not if peace came but if Luca Gaurico's predictions came true that Charles V would break a leg. *IO* 1:349; see also *IO* 2:59.

162. Carlo Gualteruzzi, letter of September 27, 1544. Moroni, *Gualteruzzi*, 150.

163. Campana, "Giovanni della Casa," 354–55, doc. 12. See also *CT* 10:194.

164. *IO* 5:220.

165. *IO* 5:222.

CHAPTER ELEVEN

1. *IO* 1:338.

2. *IO* 1:319.

3. *IO* 2:138.

4. See Partner, *Renaissance Rome*, 140–41.

5. *IO* 2:19. A figure in the neighborhood of 800 to 1,000 gold *scudi* seems reasonable for Giovio's introit. For purposes of comparison, the salary of 300 *scudi* accorded Piero Vettori when he was called to teach at Pisa was considered extremely handsome (Angelo Maria Bandini, *Memorie per servire alla vita del Senator Pier Vettori* [Livorno, 1756], 15–16). In 1527, twelve years before he had been made a cardinal, Bembo's "tiny fortune," the income of at least twenty-eight separate benefices (twenty-six of them given him by Leo X) is calculated by Hallman to have been in the neighborhood of 1,593 ducats a year (Hallman, *Italian Cardinals*, 38–39). As an example of Giovio's "rich style," see the description of his episcopal baldacchino made

in 1547 and its cost, 81 ducats, in Como, Biblioteca Communale, MS Sup. 2/2/42, fol. 52. Other inventories of clothing, furnishings, and portraits are found on fols. 222, 223, 243, 245, 246, 253v, some of which were published by Monti, "Giovi-ana." By the end of his life Giovio had 3,000 *scudi* invested in the Monte of Florence. ASF, Riscontro della deposieria, Deposieria generale 770, fol. 89v; 773, fol. 48v. For these references I am obliged to Dr. Corti. See also Mediceo del principato 477, fol. 742r.

6. *IO* 1:87.

7. For advice on the cardinal's confessor see *IO* 2:16; for a brazen solicitation see 2:82.

8. *IO* 2:8.

9. E.g., *IO* 2:153.

10. *IO* 2:6. Philippe de Commynes, *La historia famosa di Monsignor di Argenton* (Venice: Tramezzino, 1544).

11. January 24, 1540 (*IO* 1:234). Dionigi Atanagi of Cagli was secretary to Giovanni Guidiccione, bishop of Fossombrone. See the entry by Claudio Mutini in the *DBI* 4:503–506. On the academies see Abd-el-Kader Salza, *Luca Contile*, 17–22, and Luigi Sbaragli, *Claudio Tolomei* (Siena: Accademia per le Arte e per le Lettere, 1939), 49–53. See also the description of the Virtù by Caro in a letter to Varchi of March 10, 1538 (Annibale Caro, *Lettere familiari*, ed. Aulo Greco, 3 vols. [Florence: Le Monnier, 1957], 1:68–70 and n. 5), which reproduces a description of the Virtuosi in a letter of Luca Contile of July 18, 1541. Giovio's critical judgment in regard to the "poesia nuova" has been sustained by Dionisotti, *Geografia*, 141.

12. *IO* 2:36. Another poet is specified as "Caesareus," whom neither Ferrero nor I can identify. In a letter of August 1, 1550, to an unknown recipient Giovio declared himself to have been the patron of six poets: "Raineri, Phaerno, Cocciano, Vacca, Possevini, and Vitali" (UCM, Fondo Negri da Oleggio). Another, perhaps late, protégé was the Neapolitan poet Giovanni Battista Agrippa, as evidenced by an unpublished letter of Agrippa to Giovio, March 13, 1550

(see Christie's sale catalogue *Early Printed Books*, item 310). There is a deeply felt tribute by Mirteo to Giovio in Jan Gruter, ed., *Delitiae CC Italorum Poetarum*, 2 vols. (Frankfurt, 1608), 2:99: ". . . O Iovi, Iovi, habes me; habes puto, et scis / Quidnam dicere nunc volo, medullis / Quod me cogit ab intimis libellos / Omnes negligere, et omnium tabellas; / Non tuas modo cum tuis, sed omnes, / Sed meipsum proque, quod magis dolendum est." For this reference I am indebted to the late John Sparrow, Esq. See also *IO* 2:42. Marcantonio Casanova was the son of a Como citizen resident at Rome and a protégé of Giovio's. *IO* 9:234–36.

13. *IO* 1:299; to Marcello Pollonio, December 16, 1543, UCM, Fondo Negri da Oleggio, and *IO* 11 (forthcoming).

14. *IO* 9:406. See *Dialogo dell'imprese*, ed. Doglio, 111. Giovio does not mention the *impresa* in 1540 (see chap. 10 above, n. 40), which leads me to believe that it was composed now and painted in Vittoria's stanza at the museum in 1549–50. On Giovio's reaction to the flight of Ochino (1542) see *IO* 2:26. I cannot agree with Vecce that the absence of letters suggests a break owing to Giovio's role in the publication (1536) of Vittoria's unsuccessful "Pistola." Vecce, "Giovio e Colonna," 89.

15. On Gualteruzzi see Moroni, *Gualteruzzi*; on Giovio's frequent dinners with Raynce see *IO* 1:294. For Angleria see *CT* 10:691 n. 1.

16. See esp. *IO* 2:36, 40, 43. On Dandino see Anna Foa in *DBI* 32:413–23. On Bernardi, the cardinal's former tutor and frequently Giovio's traveling companion, see Paola Zambelli in *DBI* 9:148–51. Angelo Perozzi da Camerino is mentioned by Giovio in letters (e.g., *IO* 2:36, 40, 43). He contributed verses on Uguccione della Fagiola to the *Elogia*. On Giovio and Romolo Amaseo see the article by R. Avesani in *DBI* 2:663.

17. *IO* 2:9–10, 12–13.

18. *IO* 2:22–24. Ferrero dated the letter, which lacks the name of the recipient, as September 1545, with which I agree, but I doubt it was written to Cardinal Farnese. Giovio had no way of knowing that Juan de Vega, the emperor's ambassador in Rome, drew up at this time a memo suggesting how, with papal help, the empire could be made hereditary in the Hapsburg family. Brandi, 533.

19. *IO* 2:59. The dictum is from Terence, *Andria* 1.68.

20. *IO* 2:22.

21. *IO* 2:22–24.

22. *IO* 2:24. In his essay "Chierici e laici nella letteratura italiana nel primo '500," Dionisotti suggested that 1527 signaled to humanists the failure of belligerent politics on the part of the Church (*Geographia*, 70–71). While he had his own analysis for the failure of 1527, Giovio in his later years certainly came to accept the principle and practice of neutrality for the Church. For a denunciation of papal nepotism see the *elogium* of Cesare Borgia, *IO* 8:376–78.

23. *IO* 2:12–13.

24. *IO* 2:14.

25. Jedin 1:517.

26. *IO* 2:14.

27. Setton 3:481.

28. *IO* 2:29–30; diary of Angelo Massarelli, October 14, 1545; *CT* 1:287. On the truce negotiations and the legates' response see Setton 3:481, 490.

29. Jedin 1:538.

30. *IO* 2:118–20.

31. Fossati, introduction to the *Historia patriae* (1982), xxii–xxiii. I am indebted to Dr. Sibilia for verifying the dates of Benedetto's *rogiti*.

32. *IO* 8:126.

33. Renzo Meregazzi in *IO* 8:10–14.

34. *IO* 8:39.

35. *IO* 8:235. Giovio's first use of the term *elogia* was in 1542 (*IO* 1:292). For chronology of composition and the origins of the term *elogium* see Meregazzi in *IO* 8:1–14.

36. On the lives as *exempla* see *IO* 8:39.

37. Gregorovius, *History of the City of Rome in the Middle Ages*, bk. 14, chap. 4. Since there are so many diverse editions, it seems preferable to cite by book and chapter rather than volume and page.

38. Burckhardt, *Civilization of the Renaissance* (1954), 179.

39. *IO* 2:68.

40. Quintilian, *Institutio Oratoria* 3.7.10–25. Among ancient biographies, Giovio specifically mentioned Suetonius' *De vita Caesarum* but not the obvious prototype for the *elogia* of men of letters, the *De viris illustribus*, lives of literary figures, of which the *De grammaticis et rhetoribus* survives along with a few lives of Roman writers. Giovio did, however, mention lives of grammarians by Pliny, which may have been a confusion of the moment *IO* 1:174). Giovio's recommendation to Vasari that he entitle the *Lives of the Artists* to be *Vite degli eccellenti artefici* would seem to reflect his familiarity with Nepos' lives, although they were attributed to Probus (1st ed., Venice, 1471) until proven by Parrasio to be by Nepos. Giovio was also familiar with Diogenes Laertius' lives of the philosophers, translated by Ambrogio Traversari by 1433 and first printed in Venice in 1475. *IO* 1:174.

41. For a full discussion of antecedents see Rave, "Paolo Giovio und die Bildnisvitenbücher des Humanismus," 119–54.

42. See also Cicero, *Brutus* 42. There are, in fact, many errors in the *Elogia* which were probably owing to lack of verification through hasty composition, something Giovio avoided in the *Histories*. For example, in the *elogium* of Decio, Giovio said the jurist was recruited to Pavia from Pisa, when he had actually been recruited from Padua. However, he had previously taught at Pisa for many years. On Giovio's haste and lack of scrupulous documentation see Italo Gallo, "Piceni e Picentini: Paolo Giovio e la patria di Pomponio Leto," *Rassegna storica salernitana*, new ser., 3 (June 1986): 44; and Charles Schmitt, "Thomas Linacre and Italy," *The Aristotelian Tradition and Renaissance Universities* (London: Variorum, 1984), 41 n. 1, for a legend about Linacre originating in the *Elogia*.

43. *IO* 8:109–10 (trans. Gragg, *An Italian Portrait Gallery*, 123). Although a leading proponent of ecclesiastical reform, Giles of Viterbo possessed three episcopacies at his death in 1532. Hallman, *Italian Cardinals*, 24.

44. See his defense of his life of Gravina against the attack of Girolamo Scannapeco. *IO* 1:174–79.

45. Klinger, "The Portrait Collection," introduction and chap. 4. See also Francis Haskell, *History and Its Images* (New Haven: Yale University Press, 1993), 44–70.

46. Cecil H. Clough, "Italian Renaissance Portraiture and Printed Portrait Books," in *The Italian Book, 1465–1800: Studies Presented to Dennis E. Rhodes*, ed. Denis V. Reidy (London: British Library, 1993), 183–223.

47. See my article, "Paolo Giovio and the Rhetoric of Individuality." In a letter to Daniele Barbaro of December 5, 1544, Giovio insisted on the necessity of both image and text (ASF, Mediceo del principato 1170a, fasc. 2, ins. 6, fol. 16v). I am obliged to Prof. David Wright for this reference. For Giovio on physiognomy see *IO* 2:190.

48. *IO* 8:39. The lives of Leonardo, Michelangelo, and Raphael are all that exist of the lives of makers of art. No *elogia* of the "facetissimorum etiam hominum" have survived.

49. For Varro's *Imagines* see Pliny the Elder, *Nat. hist.* 35.2, and Rave, "Bildnisvitenbücher, 121.

50. *IO* 2:7–8.

51. *IO* 2:29. On Pigge see *IO* 4:120.

52. Meregazzi, *IO* 8:17.

53. *IO* 2:30.

54. *IO* 2:31.

55. March 19, 1546 (*IO* 2:33).

56. *IO* 2:37–38, 47–48.

57. September 18, 1546 (*IO* 2:48).

58. *IO* 2:48.

59. See Giovio's letter of January 16, 1545, to Dandino, legate to France, in which he spoke of "tante rase e longole *de iustificatione gratiae inhaerentis vel imputatae*." *IO* 2:59.

60. To Pietro Bertano, bishop of Fano, an imperialist, January 11, 1547. *IO* 2:64.

61. The characterization of Cervini is from Hudon, *Cervini*.

62. December 27, 1546 (*IO* 2:61–63).

63. January 11, 1547 (*IO* 2:64).

64. Pastor 12:291–92.

65. *IO* 2:43.

66. September 6, 1543 (*IO* 2:43).

67. August 15, 1546 (*IO* 2:38). This metaphor leaves for the papal states only the parts between the belly and the legs.

68. Ibid.

69. August 15, 1546 (*IO* 2:37).

70. August 15, 1546 (*IO* 2:39). On Giovio's analyses of the war and their importance see Brandi, 551, 554.

71. September 10, 1546 (*IO* 2:44). Cf. Livy 2.12.10, and Virgil *Aeneid* 6.851. I am grateful to Dr. Kliemann for suggesting Livy and to my colleague Gary Fagan for helping find the passage.

72. *IO* 2:66, 48, 45.

73. December 14, 1546 (*IO* 2:58).

74. *IO* 2:56–57. Giovio's term for the children was *gemelli*. Alessandro, future duke of Parma, was born in 1545.

75. *IO* 2:62–63.

76. December 14, 1546 (*IO* 2:58).

77. The commission Giovio obtained for Vasari in 1543 was the allegory of justice now in Naples (Capodimonte); *IO* 1:303. On Giovio's efforts to obtain the fresco commission for Vasari see *IO* 2:3.

78. See the edition of the *invenzioni* by Kliemann in *Atti*, 221–23.

79. I have followed principally: Julian Kliemann, "Il pensiero di Giovio nelle sue 'invenzioni,'" in *Atti*, 205–207; Clare Robertson, "*Il Gran Cardinale*": *Alessandro Farnese, Patron of the Arts* (New Haven: Yale University Press, 1992), 53–68, 210–15, and her "Paolo Giovio and the *Invenzioni* for the Sala dei Cento Giorni," in *Atti*, 225–37; Ernst Steinmann, "Freskenzyklen der Spätenrenaissance in Rom. I. Die Sala Farnese in der Cancelleria," *Monatshefte für Kunstwissenschaft* 3 (1910): 45–58.

80. At this point I am following a brilliant new reading of the frescoes by Dr. Julian Kliemann, shared with me at "I Tatti," and now published in his *Gesta dipinte: La grande decorazione nelle dimore italiane dal Quattrocento al Seicento* (Milan: Silvana, 1993), 37–51.

81. On the rhetoric of the ideal pope see John McManamon, "The Ideal Renaissance Pope," *Archivum historiae pontificiae* 14 (1976): 9–70.

82. On "ius destributiva" and Bembo see *IO* 2:65.

83. August 15, 1546 (*IO* 2:38–39).

84. August 25, 1546 (*IO* 2:40).

85. *IO* 2:38–39.

86. In December 1546 there was a prospect of Vittoria Farnese's marrying the young marquis of Pescara. See *IO* 2:56. She was ultimately married to Guidobaldo della Rovere, duke of Urbino, on June 29, 1547. When told the frescoes had been done in a hundred days, Michelangelo was said to have commented, "And it is evident."

87. December 18, 1546 (*IO* 2:61).

88. Vasari, "Descrizione dell'opere di Giorgio Vasari," in *Le vite*, ed. Bettarini and Barocchi, 6:388.

89. Ibid., 6:389. Cf. *IO* 8:39. For a dating of the lives of Michelangelo, Raphael, and Leonardo, composed probably around 1528 and certainly before 1532, see my article, "Giovio and Renaissance Art Criticism," 422–23 n. 50.

90. For the most recent assessments of the long scholarly controversy see Robertson, "*Il Gran Cardinale*," 68, and Charles Davis, "L'origine delle *Vite*," in *Giorgio Vasari*, Catalogue of the Exhibition, Arezzo, 1981 (Florence: Edam, 1981), 213–14. Vasari says simply "in questo tempo," placing the narration of the conversation right after his account of the Cancelleria frescoes. Immediately after their completion, however, he left for Tuscany, some time before the cardinal returned to Rome. I cannot agree with Boase, who moves the episode forward to the first six months of 1543 on the grounds that Molza, who died in February 1544, is mentioned as being one of the group who gathered at the cardinal's dinner table (T. S. R. Boase, *Giorgio Vasari* [Princeton: Princeton University Press, 1979], 44–46). For one thing, it seems to me more likely that Vasari, writing twenty years later, would forget that Molza was no longer there in 1546 sooner than he would forget the year of so important an event. We know that Molza, a "protector" of Vasari at the court of Ippolito de' Medici, was bedridden at least by 1542, the year before Vasari returned to Rome. To argue

against Boase's theory there is also the fact that Giovio was only in Rome the first month and a half of 1543, and that Cardinal Farnese himself was away for part of that period. It seems entirely likely that the conversation as reported by Vasari would have arisen during 1546 when Giovio was intensely absorbed in the writing of the *Elogia*. Finally, and perhaps most decisively, one can ask why, in the preface to the first edition of the *Elogia* (1546), Giovio would have mentioned his intention of composing the *elogia* of artists if, as Boase suggests, he had known about Vasari's project since 1543? Giovio's renunciation of his own plans for a series of *elogia* of artists was integral to Vasari's account. The conversation reported by Vasari must have taken place late enough in 1546 that the *Elogia* were already in press. Whether through diffidence or whatever, Vasari had clearly not mentioned his project to any of his "protectors" at Rome. Davis points out that the preface to the first edition of the *Lives* suggests that by 1546 Vasari had in hand much more than notes, but this is also implied in the story itself by Giovio's reaction to what Vasari brought him.

91. November 27, 1546 (*IO* 2:55). See also *IO* 2:91, 108.

92. December 10, 1547 (*IO* 2:116).

93. January 29, 1548 (*IO* 2:118). The title recalls Cornelius Nepos' *De excellentibus ducibus*.

94. For assessments of Vasari's debts to Roman humanism and to Giovio see Herbert Siebenhuener, "Studi topografici per le *Vite* del Vasari," *Studi Vasariani*, Atti del convegno internazionale per il IV centenario della prima edizione delle *Vite*, 1950 (Florence: Istituto Nazionale di Studi sul Rinascimento, 1952), 109–10; Anna Maria Brizio, "La prima e la seconda edizione delle *Vite*," *Studi Vasariani*, 83–85; Zygmunt Wazbinski, "L'idée de l'histoire dans la première et la seconde édition des *Vies* de Vasari," *Il Vasari storiografo e artista: Atti del congresso internazionale nel IV centenario della morte* (Florence: Istituto Nazionale di Studi sul Rinascimento, 1976), 6; Julian Kliemann, "Su alcuni con-

cetti umanistici del pensiero e del mondo figurativo vasariani" in Gian Carlo Garfagnini, ed., *Giorgio Vasari tra decorazione ambientale e storiografia artistica* (Florence: Olschki, 1985), 80–82. For the impact of Giovio's *Elogia* on Vasari see my article, "Giovio and the Rhetoric of Individuality." On Giovio's use of *ekphrasis*, Vasari's primary mode of criticism, see my "Giovio and Renaissance Art Criticism." In his life of Pisanello, Vasari cited Giovio on the technique of bas relief.

95. Vasari's impatient expression, "quella cicala del Iovio," occurred in a letter to Aretino, October 6, 1541 (Vasari, *Nachlass Vasaris*, ed. Frey, 110). Giovio's affection for Vasari is evident in expressions such as "Amatame, perch'io vi adoro" (*IO* 2:61) or "baciandovi dolcemente la fronte sotto al leggiadro vostro ciuffo riccio" (*IO* 2:108).

96. December 14, 1546 (*IO* 2:59).

97. December 27, 1546 (*IO* 2:62). The first five books, Giovio said, dealt with the wars of Charles VIII, from 1494 to 1498. Of these, book V (1498) is lost. Giovio's language now becomes ambiguous: "Gli altri libri saranno fenestrati, con protesto che sono scritti. E sono XXXIIII profumati, quali si mostrano ogni dì." At first reading it seems that these thirty-four books covered the remaining forty-six years, 1499–1544. However, the original book XXX, one of the few later books for which the original MS survives, corresponds to the published book 42 and covers events of 1542–43. Hence, Giovio must have meant "e sono [in tutto] XXXIIII profumati." My "Nota storico-critica," *IO* 5:245, must be revised in this regard.

98. *IO* 9:89. On the composition see Travi's discussion, *IO* 9:67. Since the "description" of England concluded with Henry VIII's marriage to Catharine Parr, Giovio must have completed it after 1543 but before Henry's death on January 28, 1547.

99. See Mayer, "Reginald Pole." The phrase "bloody and cruel tryant" is from *IO* 2:69.

100. *IO* 2:34–35. In the *elogium* of del Vasto, Giovio in fact asserted that the mar-

quis died of sorrow (*IO* 8:463). The "infe-licissima marchesa's" letter is printed in Giovio, *Lettere volgari*, ed. Domenichi, fol. 19r-v. On the sentiments expressed by Giovio see McClure, *Sorrow and Consolation*, esp. p. 14. For del Vasto's letter to the pope see BNF, Carte Strozziane, I ser., 353, p. 5.

101. To Dandino, January 1547 (*IO* 2:67).

102. May 4, 1547 (*IO* 2:83).

103. *IO* 2:69.

104. Giovio, *Lettere volgare*, 31v.

105. *IO* 2:105–107. Giovio's letter was published anonymously in Germany in 1547, along with an anonymous *Dialogus de bello germanico*, dated July 1546, between Ariovistus and Caesar (*Epistola Pauli Iovii Historici, ad Iohannem Fridericum Saxonum, & Philippum Chattorum principes*). The Società Storica Comense possesses a copy of the rare volume.

106. *IO* 2:104.

107. Jedin 2:440–42, and Hudon, *Cervini*, 86–88.

108. *IO* 2:76. For Cervini's reply see *CT* 11:153.

109. *IO* 2:80.

110. *IO* 2:76.

111. *IO* 2:101–102.

112. *IO* 2:103, 108.

113. *IO* 2:112, 116. To describe the pope Giovio uses the phrase "in suo sprezzato dolore."

114. *IO* 2:92, 100. For Gonzaga's letter to Giovio praising the museum see Giovio's *Lettere volgari* (1560), 33v–34r (misnumbered as 41–42).

115. *IO* 2:89.

116. *IO* 2:112–13.

117. *IO* 2:97. On the truce see Setton 3:485. Giovio's phrase "the Turkish dog" is taken from a letter of December 17, 1545 (*IO* 2:30). Luther, who died on February 18, 1546, had thought the 1545 truce a disaster for Germany.

118. *IO* 2:98.

119. *IO* 2:115.

120. ASV, Fondo Pio 57, fol. 39r, Dandino to Raynce, March 31, 1547.

121. To Farnese, September 5 and 10, 1547 (*IO* 2:109–10). On Alessandro see

Giambattista Giovio, *Gli uomini della comasca diocesi antichi e moderni nelle arti e nelle lettere illustri* (Modena, Società Tipografica, 1784), 109–10.

122. *IO* 2:117. A subsequent letter of November 26, 1551, to the chancellor of Milan thanks him for transferring the office from Cesare to Francesco Giovio. *IO* 2:210.

123. *IO* 2:118.

124. *IO* 2:119. The letter is without date but from the context was clearly written before the pope's response in consistory on the first of February. Giovio lends no support to Jedin's hypothesis that Paul III was being led by his scheming family.

125. July 13, 1548 (*IO* 2:124–25).

126. To Ippolito d'Este, January 1548 (*IO* 2:119).

127. For details see my article, "Ferrante Gonzaga ed il vescovado di Como," *PSSC* 41 (1960–67): 108–109.

128. *De vita Leonis Decimi . . . libri IIII: His ordine temporum accesserunt Hadriani Sexti Pont. Max. et Pompeii Columnae Cardinalis vitae* (Florence: Torrentino, 1548). The life of Adrian VI was first published in 1546 as an appendix to the *Elogia*. See Michele Cataudella in *IO* 6:ix–xx. Aida Consorti's biography, *Il cardinale Pompeo Colonna*, 2d ed. (Rome: Consorti, 1909), was largely based on Giovio's.

129. Preface to *Illustrium virorum vitae* (Florence: Torrentino, 1549), 3. See also *IO* 2:138–39.

130. See Giovio's remarks to Tommaso Cambi, advising against the adulation of Charles V ("Invenzione per la faciata della casa in Napoli di Tomaso Cambio, 1540," ed. Stefano Della Torre, *Atti*, 221–23). For Giovio's theories on biography see his letter to Girolamo Scannapeco, *IO* 1:174–79; Vecce, "Giovio and Colonna," 88–89; Zimmermann, "Giovio and the Rhetoric of Individuality." On humanist biography see Cochrane, *Historians*, 52–58; Riccardo Fubini, "Papato e storiografia nel Quattrocento: Storia, biografia e propaganda in un recente studio," *Studi medievali* 18 (1977); and Michele Cataudella in *Atti*, 63–70.

131. For Giovio's remarks see *IO* 1:261.

For Guicciardini's use of Giovio, see my article "Guicciardini and Giovio." For Burckhardt see the epigraph to chap. 3 above. On the Leonine Golden Age see above, chap. 3, n. 20.

132. To Guicciardini, May 12, 1536, and dedication to Alessandro (*IO* 1:185; 6:3). See also Cataudella in *IO* 6:ix–x. Giovio said that Ippolito assigned him the pension on the see of Forlì when the work was almost complete. The bishop began to pay him, but by May 1536 Giovio claimed he was owed 250 *scudi*, which would seem to indicate completion late in 1533. The dedication to Alessandro says the life was complete by the death of Clement VII. The life of Leo as published has four books, a sign to Cataudella of further revision before publication, as is the compliment to Paul III near the end (*IO* 6:x). For an earlier version see *IO* see 9:257.

133. Cosimo to Giovio, January 21, 1546 (ASF, Mediceo del principato 6, fol. 461). Giovio to Cosimo, February 18, 1546 (*IO* 2:31–32). See also Cataudella, *IO* 6:x.

134. Letter to Cosimo, ibid. For Giuliano's motto see *IO* 9:387 and Doglio's notes in her edition of the *Dialogo dell'imprese*, 65.

135. June 9, 1548 (*CT* 11:428).

136. For Giovio's impatience see Bracci to Riccio, May 22, 1546 (ASF, Mediceo del principato 1172, ins. 2, doc. 50; partially quoted by Cian, "Gioviana," 337). For the courtiers' dissatisfaction with Doni's press, which had a run of about twenty editions, see Riccio to Bracci, May 28 1546; ASF, Mediceo del principato 1172, ins. 3, doc. 19.

137. On Torrentino's coming to Florence see Leandro Perini, "La stampa in Italia nel '500: Firenze e la Toscana," *Esperienze Letterarie* 15 (1990): 30–35.

138. Stanley Morrison, "Marcello Cervini," *Italia medioevale et humanistica* 5 (1962): 311. For praise by Alciato see *IO* 3:2.

139. Judith Bryce, *Cosimo Bartoli* (Geneva: Droz, 1983), 167–68.

140. *IO* 2:143. On Torelli and his place in Cosimo's administration see *Carteggio*

universale di Cosimo I de' Medici: Inventario, ed. Anna Bellinazzi and Claudio Lamioni (Florence: La Nuova Italia, 1982), xxiv. It is clear the duke read the lives (ASF, Mediceo del principato 1170a, fol. 547r, Pagni to Riccio, May 5, 1548). I owe this reference to Prof. Wright.

141. Giovio to Torelli, May 12 and 26, 1548 (*IO* 2:120–21); Buonanni to Torelli, November 17, 1548 (ASF, Mediceo del principato 3267, fol. 349r.); Torelli to Buonanni, November 25, 1548 (BNF, Carte Strozziane, I ser., CCCLIII, pp. 19–20).

142. *IO* 2:67, 74.

143. First dedication and *IO* 9:257. See Panigada's commentary to the life of Gonzalo de Córdoba, *Le vite del Gran Capitano e del Marchese di Pescara* (1931), 488.

144. *IO* 2:116. The dedication is dated September 13, 1547.

145. For Giovio's sources see Panigada (1931), 488–95.

146. "Diffusissime" (*IO* 9:257).

147. See Prescott's judgment cited by Panigada (1931), 492.

148. July 3, 1548 (*IO* 2:124). A reference to the death of Francis I in book 6 indicates the revisions of 1548.

149. In his letter to Girolamo Scannapeco, written probably in 1534 or 1535, Giovio mentioned the life in a manner implying that it was either finished or in process of composition. *IO* 1:179.

150. For comparisons of Giovio with subsequent historians see Panigada (1931), 495–504.

151. *IO* 2:120, 126.

152. September 14, 1548 (*IO* 2:127, 254–55). See Grendler, *Critics*, 56. Doni's *Medaglie* was printed in Venice by Giolito in 1550.

153. Cosimo to Giovio, January 21, 1546 (ASF, Mediceo del principato 6, fol. 461r); Giovio to Cosimo, February 18, 1546 (*IO* 2:32).

154. *IO* 2:124; Giambattista Busini to Benedetto Varchi, November 23, 1548 (*Lettere a Benedetto Varchi*, ed. G. Milanesi [Florence: Le Monnier, 1860], 10). The

hint of a dedication was contained in a letter to Torelli of May 26, 1548, *IO* 2:121.

155. *IO* 1:319.

156. "Or questo sì che non vi potemo mancare; e così lo effettuaremo" (August 17, 1549, *IO* 2:137). In Italian, the demonstrative, "questo," also signifies "the latter." See also *IO* 2:174–75.

157. Buonanni to Cosimo, September 18, 1548 (ASF, Mediceo del principato 3267, fol. 243v). On della Croce see Dorez, *La cour du Pape Paul III* 1:36.

158. September 22, 1548 (ASF, ibid., 252v).

159. To Cardinal Gaddi, October 7, 1548 (*IO* 2:129).

160. Pastor 12:443.

161. *IO* 2:134. Sardi's replies are interesting for Giovian historiography. Modena, Biblioteca Estense, MS α.G.1.18.

162. *IO* 2:135–36 (without date). Assigned by Buschbell to March 1548, but reassigned by Ferrero to 1549.

163. August 17, 1549 (*IO* 2:137–38). Giovio termed his ultimatum a "polizza perentoriale."

164. Zimmermann, "Ferrante Gonzaga." For Giovio's suspicions see *IO* 2:174.

165. *IO* 2:124, 174–75.

166. *IO* 2:139–40.

167. *IO* 2:139, 178–79. For possessions left in Rome see Monti, ed., "Gioviana," *PSSC* 16 (1904): 62.

CHAPTER TWELVE

1. *IO* 2:140–41.

2. *IO* 2:140.

3. He arrived on September 12 (*IO* 2:141, 143). On Riccio see Gigliola Fragnito, "Un pratese alla corte di Cosimo I: Riflessioni e materiali per un profilo di Pierfrancesco Riccio," *Archivio storico pratese* 62 (1986): 5–57.

4. Pagni to Riccio, September 14, 1549 (ASF, Mediceo del principato 1175, ins. 6, fol. 40).

5. Guidi to Riccio, September 16, 1549 (ibid., fol 21).

6. *IO* 2:141–42. On Giovio's relations with the cardinal see Renzo Ristori and P. Zimmermann, "Una lettera inedita di Paolo Giovio al Cardinale Benedetto Accolti," *ASI* 122 (1964): 505–507.

7. Conti to Riccio, September 29, 1549 (ASF, Mediceo del principato 1175, ins. 6, fol. 23).

8. Torelli to Riccio, June 20, 1549 (ASF, Mediceo del principato 1175, ins. 3, fol. 33r).

9. For "vecchio tenere antico servitore" see *IO* 2:123.

10. *IO* 2:18–19.

11. *IO* 8:285. Giovio must have enjoyed contesting Machiavelli's opinion of King Robert; see *Florentine Histories*, bk. 3, chap. 5. Pius II agreed with Giovio on the nature of Florentine democracy; see bk. 2 of his *Commentaries.*

12. Torelli to Riccio, June 20, 1549 (ASF, Mediceo del principato 1175, ins. 3, fol. 33).

13. *IO* 2:144.

14. Cosimo to Giovio, January 24, 1549 (ASF, Mediceo del principato, 190, fol. 56v); Cosimo to Giovio, October 2, 1549 (ibid., 192, fol. 13).

15. October 2, 1549 (*IO* 2:143). See also Cosimo to Giovio, October 2, 1549 (ASF, Mediceo del principato, 192, fol. 13). In the absence of the MS from which the *Histories* were printed, the extent to which Cosimo and Torelli may have acted as censors is impossible to determine, but the events narrated in the present chapter make it seem doubtful that they did to any extent.

16. *IO* 2:143, 147; ASF, Mediceo del principato, 192, fol. 13r-v; ibid. 638, fol. 257. On the seven arrases see Candace Adelson, "Florentine and Flemish Tapestries in Giovio's Collection," in *Atti*, 239–81.

17. *IO* 1:191, 192. On Giangiacomo see Mario Fara, "Gian Giacomo Medici detto il Medeghino," *PSSC* 40 (1957–1959): 9–151.

18. October 9, 1549 (*IO* 2:148). The Villa Gualtera, now Simonetta, suffered in the bombardments of World War II, and the gardens are ruined. On Giovio and Gonzaga's plans see Ludwig H. Heyden-

reich and Wolfgang Lotz, *Architecture in Italy, 1400 to 1600*, trans. Mary Hottinger (Harmondsworth: Penguin, 1974), 292.

19. *IO* 2:147–48.

20. *IO* 2:149.

21. Monti, "Gioviana," *PSSC* 20 (1912–13): 210. See also *IO* 2:151.

22. *IO* 2:150. This visit seems to have been the occasion on which Giovio was sought out by Francesco Ciceri of Lugano on behalf of a friend whom Giovio had supposedly wronged. See his letter to Gianantonio Volpi, della Croce's vicar, dated December 16, 1549. Francesco Ciceri *Epistolarum libri XII et orationes quatuor*, ed. Pompeo Casati, 2 vols. (Milan, 1782), 1:219–20.

23. *IO* 2:150, 153–55.

24. *IO* 2:151.

25. *IO* 2:158. The election took place on February 8. There is an account of the conclave in Setton 3:505–25, but see Thomas F. Mayer, "Un parlamento di *lavanderas*: Il conclave di Giulio III," *Annali dell'istituto storico italo-germanico* (forthcoming).

26. [April] 1550 (*IO* 2:162).

27. *IO* 2:162.

28. August 1, 1550 (UCM, Fondo Negri da Oleggio).

29. This was the order established with Torelli in June of 1549. Giovio to Riccio, November 18, 1549 (*IO* 2:150), and Torelli to Giovio, April 21, 1550, acknowledging the last two books and the letter of Alciatus (ML, MA 3308). The inventory of Torrentino's possessions at his death included "two chests, said of Giovio." Perhaps these contained the manuscripts from which printing was done (G. J. Hoogewerff, "Laurentius Torrentinus," *Het Boek* 15 (1926): 380). Giovio himself mentioned the transcription of "un magno libro" of volume two to give to the duke. *IO* 2:218.

30. November 18, 1549 (*IO* 2:150).

31. Francesco Vinta to Giovio, January 14, 1550 (ML, MA 3308). Vinta, Cosimo's ambassador to Milan, was forwarding to Giovio the quires that came in his packets from Florence.

32. *IO* 2:156. Torelli to Giovio, February 15 and April 21, 1550 (ML, MA 3308).

33. March 15, 1550 (*IO* 2:159).

34. Sauli's response, dated October 17, 1550, made some corrections which, however, Giovio chose not to incorporate. Private collection.

35. De Luna to Giovio, August 18, 1550. Private collection.

36. *IO* 2:167. Torrentino's *editio princeps* was by any standard a fine piece of typography, with generous margins and spacing.

37. Torelli to Giovio, June 23, 1550 (ML, MA 3308).

38. To Torelli, July 2, 1550 (*IO* 2:164). The tomb Giovio cites can still be seen in the cathedral of Parma with the inscription, *IO MARTINVS MAIAVACCA IV DOCTOR ET EQVES NOLENS DISCRETIONI HEREDVM STARE VIVENS POSVIT MDXX*.

39. For Marco Foscari see *IO* 1:233; 2:4; 5:5.

40. July 2, 1550 (*IO* 2:164). On fenestrations see also *IO* 2:62.

41. August 16, 1550 (*IO* 2:171). The colophon to the *editio princeps* says printing was completed August 2.

42. August 10, 1550 (UCM, Fondo Negri da Oleggio.

43. [June] 1550 (*IO* 2:168). Ferrero dates the letter July–August but subsequent discovery of Torelli's reply makes a redating necessary.

44. "stracchetto" (*IO* 2:172).

45. Pagni to Riccio, September 12, 1550. "Sua Ecc.a ha inteso con grande piacere l'arrivo di Mons.r Jovio, et mi ha comandato le scriva che se li faccino carezze et le dica che qua venga a suo piacere quando sara posato" (ASF, Mediceo del principato 1176, ins. 6, fol. 1). Sauli, Giovio's host in Bologna, was bishop of Bari.

46. *IO* 2:169, 176–77. Torrentino had sent a copy to the emperor in thanks for the imperial privilege. Torrentino to d'Arras, August 17, 1550 (Royal Palace, Madrid, Cartas Italianas, MS 2259). For this reference I am obliged to the late Edward Sanchez.

47. February 27, 1550 (*IO* 2:158).
48. August 30, 1550 (*Lettere volgari*, fol. 69r).
49. February 27, 1550 (*IO* 2:158); September 19, 1550 (*IO* 2:174).
50. Torelli to Riccio, June 20, 1549 (ASF, Mediceo del principato 1175, ins. 3, fol. 33). See also *IO* 2:175.
51. From Alciato's response, dated October 7, we know that Giovio's letter was dated August 30, 1549. On his early relations with the Giovio brothers see Castellani, "Contributo alla biografia," 152–54.
52. Torelli to Giovio, April 21, 1550, acknowledging the last two books and the letter of Alciatus (ML, MA 3308).
53. The original of Alciato's letter has never surfaced. See Vittorio Cian, "Lettere inedite di Andrea Alciato a Pietro Bembo—l'Alciato e Paolo Giovio," *Archivio storico lombardo* 17 (1890): 828–44; Roberto Abbondanza, "A proposito dell'epistolario dell'Alciato," *Annali di storia del diritto* 1 (1957): 500.
54. In happier times Giovio had called della Croce "la dolcezza della camera del Papa, re della modestia, tiranno della fede . . . ma non già teatino" (*IO* 1:156). Although Tatti tried to make della Croce into a native of Como, he was, in fact, a Milanese patrician. Primo Luigi Tatti, *Annali sacri di Como* (Milan, 1734), 608, 612, 619.
55. See Cosimo I to Granvelle, April 31, 1546 (ASF, Mediceo del principato 7, 91r).
56. *Histories*, bk. 30 (*IO* 4:230–31). The MS is lost, so it is impossible to tell if Giovio made alterations in his original version, but the speech as it presently stands does not seem overly rhetorical.
57. September 20, 1550 (*Lettere volgari*, 70r).
58. September 19, 1550 (*IO* 2:174–75).
59. *IO* 2:174.
60. *Lettere volgari*, 69v. See *Delle lettere del Commendatore Annibal Caro scritte a nome del Cardinale Alessandro Farnese*, ed. Angelo Comino, 3 vols. (Padua, 1765), 1:328–30.
61. October 4, 1550 (*IO* 2:178–79).
62. August 1, 1550 (UCM, Fondo Negri da Oleggio).

63. October 25, 1550 (*IO* 2:181). Giovio had just written Carpi on October 17 (SSC, Fondo Aliati 28, 5, 202v, and UCM, Fondo Negri da Oleggio) requesting some favor from him and Farnese, so he must have gotten the anonymous letter between the 17th and 25th. The courier he names as Alfonso—his "Portughese"? Our knowledge of the anonymous letter comes from Cosimo's letter to Serristori (see following note). In the Vatican Library, along with a letter of Alciato's nephew, Cian found a poetic attack on Giovio, "In Paulum Jovium," which began, "Est ausus impudenter impurus senex / Quem nostis optime, Jovi cognomine / Farnesiorum, claram et inclytam domum / onorare probis impiis audax scelus/etc." BAV, Cod. Barb. Lat. 2097, fols. 27v–28v.
64. BNF, Carte Strozziane, I ser., CXXXVIII, fol. 110r-v, a *Seicento* copy without date published by Cian, "Lettere inedite," 835–36. The first sentence is preserved in Mediceo del principato 16, fol. 165v., where it forms part of a letter written by the duke from Pisa on December 29, 1550, and may, accordingly, be so dated.
65. October 4, 1550 (*Lettere volgari*, 70v–71r). Ippolito had made his formal entry into Tivoli on September 9, 1550. The incident is found in bk. 2, *Histories; IO* 3:46.
66. October 15, 1550 (*IO* 2:179).
67. *IO* 2:169, 197–98. Giovio may not have known at this point that the cardinal d'Este and d'Urfé did not get on.
68. *IO* 2:169–71. Giovio had met Arras at Rome. *IO* 1:294.
69. Brandi, 588; Morel-Fatio, *Charles-Quint*, 65.
70. *IO* 2:170.
71. Arras to Giovio, undated (*Revista de Archivos, Bibliotecas y Museos*, Tercera Epoca, año 9 [1905], July–December: 140). See my article, "Charles V and the Revision of Book 34," *La Bibliofilia* 74 (1972): 49–90.
72. Zimmermann, "Revision," 87. On d'Avila's commentary see Morel-Fatio, *Charles-Quint*, 114, and Georg Voigt, "Die Geschichtschreibung über den Zug Karls V

gegen Tunis," *Abhandlungen der Philolo-gisch-Historischen Classe der Königlich Säch-sischen Gesellschaft der Wissenschaften* 6 (1874): 194.

73. *IO* 2:58–59, 180.

74. Zimmermann, "Revision," 87.

75. Ibid., 88. This letter was published by Spini from the *Minute*, showing minute variations in style as dictated (Cosimo I de' Medici, *Lettere*, ed. Giorgio Spini [Florence: Vallecchi, 1940], 116–18). On Giovio's visit see *IO* 2:186.

76. Zimmermann, "Revision," 88.

77. See chap. 9, n. 92.

78. November 26, 1550 (*IO* 2:183–84). Giovio left Pisa on November 24 (Agnolo da Bibbiena to Riccio, November 24, 1550; ASF, Mediceo del principato 1176, ins. 6, fol. 43). The adage Giovio alludes to, *veritas filia temporis* (Truth is the daughter of time), originated with Aulus Gellius and was included by Erasmus in his *Adagies*.

79. *IO* 2:184–85.

80. Transcribed by Kliemann in *Atti*, 221–23.

81. *IO* 2:169.

82. *Elogia* (*IO* 8:34) trans. Gragg, *An Italian Portrait Gallery*, 20 (slightly emended to render more satisfactorily the sense of the difficult phrase *non procul ab invidia*).

83. The phrase is Raleigh's, from the preface to the *History of the World*.

84. *IO* 1:86.

85. *IO* 2:192–93, 196; Cochrane, *Historians*, 369; Dionisotti, *Machiavellerie*, 428. Varchi was tutor to Piero Strozzi's children.

86. *IO* 2:196. See Dionisotti, *Machiavellerie*, 434.

87. *IO* 5:444–48. For conversations with Guicciardini over the assassination of Alessandro see *IO* 4:450.

88. *IO* 4:469–70. On the belief that Cosimo did not expect boot greasing see *IO* 2:164, 219. On Cosimo's dislike of flattery see Filippo Cabrina, *Cosmi Medices Magni Ducis Hetruriae vita* (BNF, Magliabecchiana XXV, 49, 8v), and Eric Cochrane, *Florence in the Forgotten Centuries*, 82.

89. January 30, 1551 (1550 old style); Giovio, *Lettere volgari*, 71v–72r. On Co-simo as a patron see Cochrane, *Florence*, 72–73, and Dionisotti, *Machiavellerie*, 432, who cautions that Cosimo did not extend the same liberty of expression to other historians.

90. *IO* 2:194, 196, 199.

91. *IO* 2:191.

92. For Giovio's epitaph for Soderini see Giambattista Busini, *Lettere sugli avvenimenti dell'assedio di Firenze dirette a Benedetto Varchi*, ed. Giovanni Rosini (Milan: Silvestri, 1847), 5.

93. *IO* 2:189–91. See also *IO* 2:192, 194, and the letter of Francesco d'Este of March 10, 1551, in *Lettere volgari*, 73r-v. The dedication to Ippolito bears the date May 7, 1550. For the cardinal's acknowledgment of the dedication and life see his letter of July 24, 1550 (SCC, Archivio Aliati 28, 5, fol. 194r-v).

94. For example, Giovio had Alfonso seizing Reggio during the papal vacancy of 1521–22, when, in fact, he repossessed it during the vacancy of 1523. Burckhardt commented on the incomprehensibility of Alfonso's nature to his contemporaries. *Civilization of the Renaissance* (1954), 167.

95. *Vita Alphonsi* (1550), 13.

96. January 30, 1551 (*Lettere volgari*, 72v). Berni's poem begins, "Ser Cecco non può star senza la corte, / Nè la corte può star senza ser Cecco: / E ser Cecco ha bisogno della corte, / E la corte ha bisogno di ser Cecco." "Ser Cecco" was Francesco Benci, an official of the Camera Apostolica. See Berni, *Poesie e prose*, ed Chiorboli, 74–75.

97. *IO* 2:194.

98. "La spesa del iovio va ogni giorno multiplicando." Tommaso de' Medici to Riccio, Pisa, October 4, 1550 (ASF, Mediceo del principato 1176, ins. 7, fol. 10). Domenico Mellini, the Florentine academician and confidant of the duke in his later years, recalled that Cosimo had held "open house" in Florence for Giovio "with a noble and rich table for him and all his household." Domenico Mellini, *Ricordi intorno ai costumi, azioni e governo del serenissimo Gran Duca Cosimo I* (Florence, 1820), 6.

99. May 20, 1551 (*IO* 2:197). On Giulio Giovio see Ernesto Travi, "Profilo di Giulio Giovio," in *Umanesimo e Rinascimento a Firenze e Venezia: Miscellanea in onore di V. Branca*, 5 vols. (Florence: Olschki, 1983), 3:749–70. Paolo Giovio the Young, now archpriest of Menaggio, eventually became bishop of Nocera and figured in the later sessions at Trent. On "messer Marco nostro" see *IO* 2:218. Visconti identified "Marco nostro" as Marco Gallio, the older brother of Tolomeo Gallio, the future cardinal ("La famiglia Gallio," *PSSC* 40 [1957–1959]: 202). In 1548 Marco is mentioned as putting the MSS of the *Histories* together in Rome (UCM, Fondo Negri da Oleggio, Giovio to his nephews, February 26, 1548). Tolomeo had also been Giovio's secretary for a while but had wished in 1549 to stay on in Rome and so had passed to the service of Antonio Trivulzio (Carlo Castelli, "Tolomeo Gallio," *PSSC* 50 [1983]: 17–18). Castelli speculates that Tolomeo then entered the service of Cardinal Gaddi in order to avoid traveling abroad with Trivulzio, named nuncio to France in 1550. His hypothesis is confirmed by the fact that Tolomeo was a witness to Giovio's disposition of the vicarship of Nocera in a document executed in Florence on October 2, 1551 (ASF, Notarile 178, Giovan Piero Carmignani, fol. 53r-v).

100. See also Mellini, *Ricordi*, 6. Giovio described an unexpected parturition that occurred while he was attending the duchess in her antechamber. *IO* 2:195.

101. Cabrina, *Cosmi Medices vita*, 8v.

102. November 12, 1551 (*IO* 2:209–10). The letter was quoted by Vasari in the life of Pisanello. See George Francis Hill, *A Corpus of Italian Medals of the Renaissance before Cellini*, 2 vols. (London: British Museum, 1930), 1:7, 13.

103. The obverse was reproduced as a frontispiece for volume one of the 1557 edition of Domenichi's translation of the *Histories*. For the medal see above, chap. 2, n. 35.

104. Cosimo to Giovio, August 10, 1551 (ASF, Mediceo del principato 194, fol. 105v, and *IO* 2:200–201). See also

Claudia Rousseau, "The Pageant of the Muses at the Medici Wedding of 1539 and the Description of the Salone dei Cinquecento" in *"All the World's a Stage: Art and Pageantry in the Renaissance and Baroque*, ed. Barbara Wisch and Susan Munshower, 2 vols. (University Park: Papers in Art History from the Pennsylvania State University, 1990), 2:453.

105. Grendler, *Critics*, 45. On the Florentine Academy see Armand L. De Gaetano, *Giambattista Gelli and the Florentine Academy*, 100–36. I have searched its *capitoli* and membership rolls and have not found any indication that Giovio became a member. BNF, Magliabecchiana IX, 42, 91.

106. *La vita di Alfonso da Este*, trans. Gelli (Florence: Torrentino, 1553), 4. On Bartoli see Judith Bryce, *Cosimo Bartoli* (Geneva: Droz, 1983). For Vettori see *IO* 2:212.

107. Giovio to Galeazzo Florimonte, [December] 1551 (SSC, Archivio Aliati, 28, 5). I presume that "Arlenio" or, as sometimes seen, "Arlemio," is an Italianization for "Haarlem."

108. *IO* 2:186–87, 192, 199, 215. Varchi's numerous transcriptions of materials in Giovio's possession can be found in the BNF, Carte Strozziane, I ser., CCCLIII.

109. Michele Lupo-Gentile, *Studi sulla storiografia fiorentina alla corte di Cosimo I de' Medici*.

110. For relations with Segni see *IO* 2:221. Marchese Roberto Ridolfi kindly lent me the photostat in his possession of a letter dated Florence, September 19, 1549, from Segni to Vettori also mentioning relations with Giovio. "Stamattina essendo ito a visitare il vescovo Jovio, alle sei parole mi domando di voi, et mi pregò vi facessi intendere che e desiderava parlarvi" (British Library, Add MSS 10280, no. 95). For relations with Nerli see Lupo-Gentile, *Storiografia*, 50, and Giuseppe Sanesi, "Alcune osservazioni e notizie intorno a tre storici minori del Cinquecento," *ASI*, 5th ser., 23 (1899), 268. Of the Florentine historians still in exile, Giovio had known Busini in Rome (*Lettere del Busini*, 2) and Nardi in Venice (*IO* 1:235).

111. *IO* 2:137. On Domenichi see Angela Piscini, *DBI* 40:595–600. His translations, executed during Giovio's lifetime, are a necessary adjunct to Giovio's Latin as they provide a key to his often obscure use of ancient names for sixteenth-century peoples and places.

112. *IO* 2:78. Salviati, whom Giovio also knew, had returned to Rome in 1550.

113. *IO* 9:386. See Dionisotti, *Machiavellerie*, 417; *Dialogo dell'imprese*, ed. Doglio, 63 n. 76.

114. *Lettere volgari*, 75r. For Gaddi as a patron see Dorez, *La cour du Pape Paul III* 1:108.

115. Farnese to Cosimo, July 6, 1551 (ASF, Mediceo del principato 3720). Farnese arrived sometime between the 6th and 22nd, the dates of his last letter to Cosimo from Casteldurante (modern Urbania) and his first from Florence. On his lodgings see Riguccio Galluzzi, *Istoria del granducato di Toscana*, 5 vols. (Florence: Del Vivo, 1781), bk. 1, chap. 7, 1:82–83.

116. *IO* 2:195.

117. June 23, 1551 (*IO* 2:198).

118. For excessive heat in June see *IO* 2:199 and the dedication of the *Dialogo dell'imprese*.

119. *IO* 2:204; 9:373. It was not published until after Giovio's death (Rome: Antonio Barre, 1555).

120. Mariagrazia Penco in *IO* 9:353–71.

121. Alessandro D'Alessandro, "Prime ricerche su Ludovico Domenichi," *Le corti farnesiane di Parma e Piacenza*, ed. Amedeo Quondam, 2 vols. (Rome: Bulzoni, 1978), 1:179, 190; Frances Yates, *The Art of Memory* (Chicago: University of Chicago Press, 1966), 135.

122. De Gaetano, *Gelli*, 164; Bryce, *Bartoli*, 214.

123. D'Alessandro, "Ludovico Domenichi," 194.

124. *IO* 2:229.

125. D'Alessandro, "Ludovico Domenichi," 194; *IO* 2:229.

126. *Dialogo dell'imprese*, ed. Doglio, 9–29; Mauda Bregoli-Russo, "*Il dialogo delle imprese* di Paolo Giovio e il *Ragionamento* di Lodovico Domenichi,"

Critica letteraria 40 (1983): 445–51, and the same author's *L'impresa come ritratto del Rinascimento* (Naples: Loffredo, 1990).

127. Giovio's historical derivation largely skipped the use of devices in the Quattrocento, of which he was well aware from his collection of medallions, probably because he was thinking of the knightly and courtly tradition. See Kristen Lippincott, "The Genesis and Significance of the Fifteenth-Century Italian *Impresa*," in Sydney Anglo, ed., *Chivalry*, 63.

128. *IO* 2:209.

129. *IO* 2:208, 210.

130. *IO* 2:202.

131. To Castaldo, September 16, 1551 (*IO* 2:202–203).

132. October 3, 1551 (*IO* 2:204–205).

133. *IO* 2:210.

134. *IO* 2:215.

135. Like Giovio, Porzio may have been a student of Pomponazzi's, although it is more probable that he had been the pupil of Nifo. See F. Fiorentino, "Della vita e delle opere di Simone Porzio," in *Studi e ritratti della Rinascenza* (Bari: Laterza, 1911), 83–153.

136. On Gelli's translation see De Gaetano, *Gelli*, 56–65.

137. May 20, 1551 (*IO* 2:196).

138. Camillo Porzio, dedication to *La congiura de' baroni*, in Porzio, *Opere*, ed. C. Monzani (Florence: Le Monnier, 1855), 3. See Ernesto Pontieri, "Camillo Porzio storico," *Archivio storico per le provincie Napolitane* 37 (1957): 121–79. It may be that Giovio's "regrets" originated in his conversations with Sannazaro in 1527–28. *IO* 1:177.

139. *IO* 2:196, 197, 215. A "Nicolao dalla Magona" whom Giovio also mentions may be the professor of medicine, Niccolò Boldoni. Francesco Robortello had already left for Padua. For professors at Pisa see Charles B. Schmitt, "The Studio Pisano in the European Cultural Context of the Sixteenth Century," *Firenze e la Toscana dei Medici nell'Europa del '500*, 3 vols. (Florence: Olschki, 1983), 1:19–36.

140. *IO* 2:109, 110, 182, 194.

141. Medici to Giovio, April 17 and 23, 1551 (*Lettere volgari*, 74r–75r); Giovio to

Carpi, December 26, 1551 (*IO* 2:214). The official act is dated August 21, 1551 (Van Gulik and Eubel, *Hierarchia catholica* 3:230). Giovio then requested relief from the bulk of the fees involved (November 7, 1551, *IO* 2:208). Giovio also thanked Florimonte and Romolo Amaseo, the pope's Latin secretaries. To Florimonte, s.d. but a companion letter to letter #387 in Ferrero, *IO* 2:212 (SSC, Archivio Aliati, 28, 5). Giovio also continued to seek exemption from the the tithe for Nocera. *IO* 2:165, 234.

142. *IO* 2:214–15.

143. December 26, 1551 (*IO* 2:213–14). On this letter as an exemplar of uncompromising Renaissance culture standing its ground in the face of Reform and Counter-Reform see Dionisotti's review of Ferrero's "Politica e vita morale nelle lettere di Paolo Giovio," *GS* 118 (1941): 159–60.

144. January 30, 1552 (*IO* 2:218).

145. *IO* 2:217. On Gaddi's "mortal dissenteria" see Giovio's letter to Conversini of October 3, 1551, cited in n. 148, below.

146. The news reached Rome on January 14; see Setton 4:576 ff. On the gift of the horse in 1547 see *IO* 2:80.

147. *Histories*, bk. 39; *IO* 2:218.

148. *IO* 2:202–203; Giovio to Giovanni Conversini, bishop of Iesi, October 3, 1551 (*Delle lettere miscellanee del Sig. Bonifazio Vannozzi*, 2 vols. [Rome, 1608], 2:306). It is clear that Giovio never thought much of Ferdinand's chances of securing Hungary and regarded Zápolya as the real king. See the epitome of book 23 of the *Histories*.

149. Castaldo to Giovio, July 29, 1552 (BNF, Carte Strozziane, I ser., CCCII, fols. 219r–221v). See the account in Setton 4:565–80. Giovio later learned the assassination had been by the hand of Sforza Pallavicino (letter to Giovanni Conversini, September 7, 1552; *Lettere del Vannozzi* 2:308). See also the entry on Castaldo by Gaspare De Caro, who also finds Castaldo politically naïve (*DBI* 21:562–66). His 1548 portrait by Titian, now in Dortmund, shows his weariness.

150. D'Alessandro, "Ludovico Domenichi," 184–86. See also Galluzzi, *Istoria* 1:93; Grendler, *Critics*, 131–32. For im-

portant new evidence of Cosimo's attitude see Fragnito, "Pierfrancesco Riccio." The book that chiefly attracted the zeal of the inquisitors was the *Beneficio di Cristo* (Venice, 1543), a work infused with the Protestant doctrines of predestination and justification by faith. Many of Giovio's friends had a hand in spreading it, including Flaminio, Carnesecchi, Bartoli, and Riccio. Gelli had written a very popular dialogue between a cooper and his own soul entitled *I capricci del bottaio*, published by Doni in 1548 without the author's consent, in which there is not only criticism of the clergy—certainly nothing new for Florence—but a call for a vernacular Bible. Prof. Mayer tells me that Torelli also had investigated heretical ideas.

151. Domenichi worked, however, from the Latin translation of 1549. D'Alessandro, "Ludovico Domenichi," 183; Galluzzi, *Istoria* 1:93.

152. Grendler, *Critics*, 133.

153. D'Alessandro, "Ludovico Domenichi," 182–83; Galluzzi, *Istoria* 1:93.

154. D'Alessandro, "Ludovico Domenichi," 188. See also F. Bonaini, "Dell'imprigionamento per opinioni religiose di Renata d'Este e di Lodovico Domenichi," *Giornale storico degli archivi toscani* 3 (1859): 268–81. A recent study of Renée is that of Charmarie Jenkins Blaisdell, "Renée de France between Reform and Counter-Reform," *Archiv für Reformationsgeschichte* 63 (1972): 196–226.

155. D'Alessandro, "Ludovico Domenichi," 188–89.

156. According to Giambattista Giovio, just before leaving Como for Florence, Giovio had interceded on behalf of five canons of the cathedral charged with heresy by Michele Ghislieri. A letter, unfortunately now lost, written by Giovio to Carpi on August 15, 1550, supposedly resulted in suppression of the charges. Giovio, "Elogio," 51.

157. Among Giovio's friends and acquaints who dabbled at one time or other in reformed ideas were, besides Flaminio, Carnesecchi, and the Florentines mentioned in n. 150 above, Calvo, Ziegler,

Calcagnini, Bernardi, Rullo, Gualteruzzi, Contarini, Pole, Fascitello, and Vittoria Colonna. On Giovio's contacts with the *spirituali* see Mayer, "Reginald Pole."

158. November 7, 1551 (*IO* 2:208).

159. January 30, 1552 (*IO* 2:217–18).

160. January 18, 1552 (*IO* 2:217).

161. *IO* 2:217–18.

162. February 29, 1552 (*IO* 2:219–20). Giovio's will mentioned the recent donation of leatherwork to the museum by the duke of Alba and Cardinal Mendoza (*PSSC* 50 [1983]: 113). There is also a very cordial letter dated May 30, 1550, from Mendoza urging Giovio's return to Rome. Private collection; see also *IO* 8:150.

163. Preface to the life of Adrian VI. *IO* 6:107.

164. Preface to bk. 7 of the *Elogia* of heroes. *IO* 8:479.

165. *IO* 2:220–21.

166. *IO* 2:218–25. The *facultas testandi* was dated April 4, 1552.

167. *IO* 2:220.

168. *IO* 2:222.

169. *IO* 2:225, 228.

170. *IO* 2:224–25.

171. To Giulio Giovio, May 14, 1552 (UCM, Fondo Negri da Oleggio).

172. *IO* 2:225–26.

173. *IO* 2:221. On the use of Giovio's account of the siege by the Florentine historians see Lupo-Gentile, *Storiografia*, and Felice Scolari, "L'assedio di Firenze (1529–30): Francesco Ferrucci e il nostro storico Paolo Giovio," *PSSC* 27 (1930): 13–39.

174. *IO* 2:219.

175. *IO* 2:226.

176. *IO* 2:221.

177. *IO* 2:219.

178. It should be noted that if Leo X and Clement VII gave individual Florentines lucrative offices, they also milked the city for money to further their foreign policies. See Bullard, *Filippo Strozzi*.

179. *Histories*, bk. 27 (*IO* 4:97–103). See Dionisotti, *Machiavellerie*, 433–34.

180. Cf. Guicciardini, *Ricordi*, ed. Spongano, C3, pp. 6–7.

181. Cochrane, *Florence*, chap. l; Dioni-

sotti, *Machiavellerie*; Stephens, *Fall of the Florentine Republic*.

182. *IO* 2:228, 229.

183. *IO* 2:235–37.

184. *IO* 2:230.

185. *IO* 2:231, 235, 236. By July 4 Giovio had received some of what he needed, but not, he said, the dates of Francis I's crossing into Italy and his meeting with Henry VIII (*IO* 2:237). Presumably Giovio meant the meeting of Francis I and Henry VIII at the field of cloth of gold on June 1520, which appears in the epitome of bk. 20. However, the epitome of 20 should have been already printed. The date had been given erroneously in the *Descriptio Britanniae*. Mayer, "Reginald Pole," 440.

186. *IO* 2:239.

187. *IO* 2:220, 231.

188. *IO* 2:217. Letter of July 16, 1552 (UCM, Fondo Negri da Oleggio).

189. To Giulio, May 14, 1552 (UCM, Negri da Oleggio).

190. Bordoli, "Il testamento," 87–116.

191. *IO* 2:241.

192. *IO* 2:242.

193. *IO* 2:243.

194. See my article, "A Sixteenth-Century List of the Intronati," *Bullettino senese di storia patria* 72 (1965): 91–95. The list was Giovio's, copied by Varchi.

195. To Conversini, September 7, 1552 (*Lettere del Vannozzi*, 2:308).

196. *IO* 2:245.

197. *IO* 2:244.

198. *IO* 2:246.

199. *IO* 2:247. On Savonarola see Roberto Ridolfi, *Vita di Girolamo Savonarola*, 2 vols. (Rome: Belardetti, 1952), 1:13; on Guicciardini see Varchi, *Storia fiorentina* 3:195.

200. Contile was now secretary to the cardinal of Trent. *IO* 2:246–47.

201. [November–December 1552] *IO* 2:232. Despite the fact that the *Histories* are spoken of as completed, Ferrero accepted the date of this letter, transcribed from Domenichi's edition of the *Lettere volgari*, as May 23, 1552. In my opinion it must at least follow the letter to Contile of November 12 and is probably a letter of December.

See also the similar judgment of Dionisotti, *Machiavellerie*, 411. On the expression "ho alla coda una frotta di quegli anta che tutta notte canta," see Folena, "L'espressionismo," 157. Annibale Raimondi, a mathematician and astronomer of note, was a relative of Giovio's sister-in-law, Maria Raimondi.

202. *IO* 2:232–33. For the incident see *IO* 4:459.

203. E.g., *IO* 2:59, 151.

204. In a brief note to the duke Giovio's great-nephew described the death as having taken place "all' 8 hore della presente notte" (December 12, 1552; ASF, Mediceo del principato 412, fol. 391r). Since the night was divided into eight equal "hours" beginning at sundown, this was probably shortly after 2 P.M., sundown coming in Florence about 4:30 in mid-December and sunrise about 7:30. The source for the nature of Giovio's final illness was a letter from Nerli to Segni, December 15, 1552: "hebbe breve male di dolori cholici et di fiancho." Cited by Sanesi, "Alcune osservazioni," 267.

205. Cosimo to Riccio, December 12, 1552 (ASF, Mediceo del principato 638, fol. 395).

206. Mellini, *Ricordi*, 6. "La morte di questo huomo raro è doluta a tutta questa città, et alle recquie e stato gran concorso di populi" (Riccio to Cosimo, December 13, 1552; ASF, Mediceo del principato 412, fols. 416r–417r). Judging by the *copialettere* the duke came from Poggio to Florence on December 12, but it was not the custom for rulers to attend the funerals of commoners.

207. "La sepultura si farà fatto da detto arciprete secondo il volere di V. Ecc.a, ma si aspetterà al dargli principio la dichiaratione sua per respetto del luogo, che nella chiesa di S.o Lorenzo non ne sono altre sepulture, se non della sua casa Ill.ma secondo il volere dell'avo Cosimo, et fino a' questo tempo s'è observato" (Riccio to Cosimo, December 13, 1552; ASF, Mediceo del principato, 412, fol. 416v).

208. "Secondo il testamento di detto Mons.re il corpo suo ha da restare in quel luogo dove è mancato lo spirito et allogato in sepultura di pietra d'un pezzo con epithaphio ordinato da lui, quale non se possuto vedere, perche le casse et confini sono stati inventariati et sigillati dal com.rio di S. Sta" (Riccio to Cosimo, December 13, 1552; ASF, Mediceo del principato 412, fol. 416r). The MS of the old bk. X (17–18) contains such an epitaph: "Paulus Iovius ab urbe in patriam post 37 annum revectus, editis historiis et re familiari aucta hoc sibi vivens sepulchrum posuit, cum aetatis reliquum litteris genio et Christiana pietate negocio vacuus imponeret." Other epitaphs composed by friends can be found in Giovio's commonplace book (Biblioteca Communale, Como, MS Sup. 2/2/42, fols. 9 [by Gabriele Faerno], 94, 107, and 181 [by Antonfrancesco Raineri]). See Monti, "Gioviana," *PSSC* 20 (1912–13): 209–10. In designing his own tomb and epitaph (which was not used) Giovio seemingly forgot his snide comment in the *elogium* of Sabellico that the tomb and epitaph he had prepared for himself while living would have been even more fitting had they been erected by the affection of another. *IO* 8:78.

209. For details on the provisional tomb see my article, "La presunta data di nascita di P.G.," *PSSC* 52 (1986–87): 189–92.

210. A receipt from the sculptor for partial payment of 50 gold *scudi* dated May 27, 1555, is reproduced by Giambattista Giovio, "Elogio," 107. According to the receipt the monument was to be constructed "come apare nel disegnio del sopra deto Mons.r Jovio." See Christie's auction catalogue, *Early Printed Books, Manuscripts and Autograph Letters* (November 17, 1976), 94. Cirri states that the statue was completed in 1560 and placed on the original sepulcher, which to judge from Riccio's letter to Cosimo (cited above, n. 206) must have been somewhere in the left aisle. The completed monument bears the following inscription: PAVLO IOVIO NOVOCOMENSI EPISCOPO NVCERINO HISTORIARVM SVI TEMPORIS SCRIPTORI SEPVLCRVM QVOD SIBI DE-

CREVERAT POSTERI EIVS INTEGRA FIDE POSVERVNT INDVLGENTIA MAXIMORVM OPTIMORVMQVE COSMI, ET FRANCISCI ETRVRIAE DVCVM. ANNO MDLXXIV.

211. Gianoncelli, *L'antico museo*, 47–50.

CONCLUSION

1. Clough, "A Manuscript of Paolo Giovio's *Historiae sui temporis, liber VII*," 56.

2. Klinger, "The Portrait Collection," 202.

3. Giambattista Busini, *Lettere a Benedetto Varchi sopra l'assedio di Firenze*, ed. G. Milanesi (Florence: Le Monnier, 1860), 244.

4. "Delle historie del Jovio mi pare, che si ragioni come di cosa scritta per buffoneria: et per dire il vero la historia del Guicciardini gli ha dato una gran bastonata" (Giannotti to Varchi, March 3, 1563). Donato Giannotti, *Opere politiche e letterarie*, ed. F. L. Polidori, 2 vols. (Florence: Le Monnier, 1850), 2:425; Filippo Nerli, *Commentari de' fatti civili occorsi dentro la città di Firenze dall'anno 1215 al 1537* (Augsburg, 1728), 182.

5. Benedetto Varchi, *Errori di Paolo Giovio nella storia*, ed. Vincenzo Follini (Badìa di Fiesole, 1821). See also Umberto Pirotti, *Benedetto Varchi* (Florence: Olschki, 1971), 170–71; Cochrane, *Historians*, 375; and Dionisotti, *Machiavellerie*, 428.

6. Federico di Scipione Alberti, *Le difese de Fiorentini contra le false calunnie del Giovio* (Lyons: Giovanne Martino, 1566).

7. *IO* 8:34.

8. On a number of occasions Giovio spoke of his intentions of publishing in his lifetime as a pledge of his impartiality and good faith, given that participants and witnesses would still be living (e.g., *IO* 3:5; 2:182; 9:256).

9. Girolamo Cardano, "Neronis encomium," *Opera omnia*, 10 vols. (Lyons: Huguetan and Ranaud, 1663), 1:216. Giovio's account of Pavia occurred in the life of Pescara, bk. 5. Torelli agreed that it dis-

played Francis I as "coraggioso et valoroso et prudente et vincitor della sua fortuna" (November 25, 1548; BNF, Carte Strozziane, I ser., CCCLIII, pp. 19–20). For Giovio's admiration of de Leyva see, for example, *Histories*, bk. 26, *IO* 4:93.

10. *Lettere volgari*, 15v, 101r. For letters produced from archives see Franca Bevilacqua Caldari, "Un brano delle *Historie* del Giovio in una lettera inedita del Cardinale Jean du Bellay," *Studi romani* 19 (1971): 431–52. On the defenders of Giovio see Cochrane, *Historians*, 375–76, and his, "Paolo Giovio e la storiografia del Rinascimento," *Atti*, 19–30. For Paleario's praise of Giovio as "father of history," see Aonio Paleario, *Opuscula doctissima* (Bremen: Villeriani, 1619), 177, 419. In the preface to his history, Porzio called Giovio "padre delle moderne istorie." Camillo Porzio, *La congiura dei baroni*, ed. E. Pontieri, 2d ed. (Naples: E.S.I., 1964). On Atanagi's defense see Eckhard Kessler, ed., *Theoretiker humanistischer Geschichtsschreibung* (Munich: Fink, 1971), 49–53.

11. Jean Bodin, *Method for the Easy Comprehension of History*, trans. Beatrice Reynolds (New York: Columbia University Press, 1945), bk. 1, p. 62.

12. Pierre Bayle, "Paul Jove," *Dictionaire historique et critique* (Rotterdam, 1695–1697), vol 2, pt. 1: 179–82. On Bodin's preferences see Anthony Grafton, *Defenders of the Text*, 28–29.

13. *IO* 1:142, and Caldari, "Un brano delle *Historiae* del Giovio." In bk. 41 Giovio hinted that Montmorency's efforts to achieve a rapprochement with Charles V had been "parum synceris" in presenting to the king only details favorable to rapprochement, and that Francis I had shown his magnanimity by not following the example of Louis XI with the count of Saint-Pol or Suleiman with Pasha Abrahim (*IO* 5:85–86). Giovio himself felt that his laments about Montmorency's conduct at the time were well known and sufficient to document his integrity (e.g., *IO* 2:233). His view of Montmorency was quite consistent with his attitude toward the negotiations of

1539–40 and his disbelief, even anger, that Francis I would allow himself to be duped by Charles V. On Giovio's sympathy with the aims of Montmorency's policy of reconciliation see *IO* 1:208.

Yet it is worthy of further investigation that in the *Histories* Giovio did not give Montmorency more credit than he did for the invitation to Charles V to cross through France in 1539–40 and for his attempts to arrange peace. See the defense of Giovio by Girolamo Ruscelli in his "Sopplimento nell'istorie di Monsignor Giovio" appended to the vernacular edition of the *Histories* by Bonelli (Venice, 1560). Prof. Samuel Kinser, a leading authority on de Thou, tells me he believes that Giovio probably offended de Thou's elevated sense of the good historian's impartiality.

14. Citations from Bayle.

15. Girolamo Tiraboschi, *Storia della letteratura italiana*, 2d ed., 8 vols. in 16 (Milan, 1822–26), 1:452 (the principal article on Giovio occurs in 12:1306–21); William Roscoe, *The Life and Pontificate of Leo X*, rev. ed., 2 vols. (London: Chatto and Windus, 1876), 1:265; 2:379–81.

16. Cited from Luigi Rovelli, *Paolo Giovio*, 35.

17. *Encyclopedia Brittanica*, 11th ed. (Cambridge: Cambridge University Press, 1911), 15:527.

18. Croce, "La grande aneddotica storica di Paolo Giovio," *Poeti e scrittori*, 2:27–55. See Croce's letter to Gianfranco Miglio, cited by Sergio Lazzarini, "Miglio e la storiografia locale," in *Multiformità ed unità della politica: Atti del convegno tenuto in occasione del 70° compleanno di Gianfranco Miglio* (Milan: Giuffrè, 1992), 177; Eduard Fueter, *Geschichte der neueren Historiographie* (Munich, 1911), 51–55. Fueter had a low opinion of humanist history in general. When Giovio boasted of his "golden pen" in the service of his patrons, he probably meant not that he would exaggerate or flatter but that he would employ the highest literary style to write of their deeds. Cf. his letter to Cardinal Rodolfo Pio in which he spoke of his "venerazione di

quella dorata penna con la quale [Bembo] scrive l'eterne istorie." *IO* 1:232.

19. Ridolfi, *Guicciardini*, 422; Felice Scolari, "Pregi e difetti di Paolo Giovio storico e uomo," *PSSC* 27 (1930): 60.

20. Leopold von Ranke, *Zur Kritik neurer Geschichts-schreiber* (Leipzig, 1884), 70–78.

21. Pastor 8:238–41; 7:187.

22. Edoardo Alvisi, *La battaglia di Gavinana* (Bologna: Zanichelli, 1881), 2–3.

23. Chabod, *Scritti*, 243–67. Gino Franceschini used Giovio extensively as well for his chapters in vol. 8 of the *Storia di Milano*, 17 vols. (Milan: Fondazione Treccani degli Alfieri, 1953–66).

24. Lupo-Gentile, *Storiografia*.

25. Dionisotti, *Machiavellerie*, 434.

26. Reynolds, "Latin Historiography," *Studies in the Renaissance* 2 (1955): 56–57.

27. Caldari, "Un brano delle *Historiae* del Giovio"; Zimmermann, "Charles V and the Revision of Book 34," *La Bibliofilia* 74 (1972): 49–90.

28. Emanuella Scarano Lugnani, *Guicciardini e la crisi del Rinascimento* (Bari: Laterza, 1979), 155.

29. Cochrane, *Historians*, 366–76, and his "Paolo Giovio e la storiografia del Rinascimento," *Atti*, 19–30.

30. Traiano Boccalini, *Ragguagli di Parnasso*, ed. G. Rua (Bari: Laterza, 1910), centuria seconda, ragguaglio 94.

31. Letter to Tommaso Cambi, *Atti*, 222; letter to Scannapeco, *IO* 1:174–79. For condemnation of flattery by historians see the *elogia* of Campano, Sabellico, and Polydore Vergil.

32. For Giovio's belief in *fides historiae* see, e.g., *IO* 8:462. For his condemnation of "timid omissions" see his critique of Raffaele Maffei, *IO* 8:131.

33. *IO* 1:174.

34. *IO* 9:255. For Giovio's dependence on the precepts of Lucian see Reynolds, "Latin Historiography," 57, and *IO* 1:174. On "prudence" in Renaissance historical thought see Santoro, *Fortuna, ragione e prudenza*, and Albert Russell Ascoli, "Machiavelli's Gift of Counsel," in Ascoli and

Victoria Kahn, eds., *Machiavelli and the Discourse of Literature* (Ithaca, N.Y.: Cornell University Press, 1993), 230–37. The notion of reading as an act of judgment is stressed by Kahn in *Rhetoric, Prudence, and Skepticism in the Renaissance* (Ithaca, N.Y.: Cornell University Press, 1985).

35. *IO* 9:256; 2:104. A phrase in the preface to Giovio's *Histories* suggests he may have been aware of introducing new methodology into the humanist tradition: "Sperabam enim hunc laborem meum, quadam ingenii liberalitate sponte susceptum, multo utiliorem atque iocundiorem posteris futurum quam si *earum artium praecepta* [scribendae historiae] novis commentariis locupletare contendissem [italics mine]." On Lucian and an overview of the tension between "style" and "substance" in Renaissance historiography see Beatrice Reynolds, "Shifting Currents in Historical Criticism."

36. Dionisotti, *Machiavellerie*, 418.

37. *IO* 3:6; see also *IO* 1:312 and 2:226. The influence of Polybius on Giovio was suggested by Reynolds, and more recently by Mayer, "Reginald Pole," 438–39, who has been able to show that Giovio's account of Henry VIII might have been modeled on Polybius' story of Philip V's corruption by bad advice, as well as to suggest other connections, including Domenichi's interest in Polybius. It is unlikely that Giovio knew Polybius' maxims for writing history as they were formally laid down in bk. 12.25–28, since only the first five books were readily available in Perotti's Latin translation (Rome, 1473, and subsequent reprintings, including the popular Aldine editions of 1518, 1520, and 1521). However, the maxims also appear scattered throughout the first five books (e.g., on eyewitness testimony see 4.2.; on causation, 3.31–32, 36; on criticism of sources, 1.14–15, 2.56, 3.26, etc.). For Polybius' statements on the importance of universal history see esp. 1.4 and 3.32, both of which were accessible in the Perotti translation, e.g., the Aldine edition of 1521 (bk. 1), 75v. Bodin, who noted Giovio's similarity to Polybius in

writing universal history, scornfully disallowed the comparison in every other respect; *Methodus*, bk. 4.

38. Polybius 3.31–32; Thucydides 1.21–22.

39. The fullest expression of Renaissance historical theory was Pontano's dialogue, "Actius," in Giovanni Pontano, *Dialoghi*, ed. Carmelito Previtera, 127–239. For an astute analysis of Pontano's conservatism as a theoretician of history and his dependence on Roman models see Girolamo Cotroneo, *Trattatisti dell'ars historica*, chap. 3, "La 'poetica soluta' di Giovanni Pontano," 87–120. Giovio was tutored in Pontanian standards by Sannazaro (Actius Syncerus), for whom Pontano's dialogue was named (*IO* 1:177). On Campano's influence see F. De Bernardo, *Un vescovo umanista alla corte pontificia: G. A. Campano (1429–1477)* (Rome: Università Gregoriana, 1975) with the review of R. Fubini, *RSI* 88 (1976): 745–55.

40. Pontano, "Actius," 219–22. For the effects of the humanist preoccupation with classical military history on military affairs and, ultimately, on Machiavelli, see Cecil H. Clough, "Niccolò Machiavelli's Political Assumptions and Objectives," *Bulletin of the John Rylands Library* 53, no. 1 (1970): 71–75.

41. Pontano, "Actius," 209; *IO* 5:81.

42. In the *De hominibus doctis*, Cortesi advocated strict imitation of the style of Cicero (see the edition by Giacomo Ferraù). On Valla and the origins of historicism see Donald R. Kelley, *Foundations of Modern Historical Scholarship* (New York: Columbia University Press, 1970), chap. 2. On Facio's polemic against Valla see Linda Gardiner Janik, "Lorenzo Valla: The Primacy of Rhetoric and the De-Moralization of History," *History and Theory* 12 (1973): 389–404 (for Facio's insistence on *dignitas* see esp. 397–98).

43. Facio condemned the inclusion of anything the historian as moralist could not approve of (Janik, ibid., 399). While Platina certainly did not espouse this view, Campano's life of Braccio and Manetti's influen-

tial life of Nicholas V omitted almost all negatives. On dilemmas of the Lombard historians see esp. Ianziti, *Humanistic Historiography*. Pontano was franker in regard to King Ferrante than the generality of humanist historians dared to be, but he published after the dynasty had fallen; see Bentley, *Politics and Culture*, 239–41, who argues that Pontano's practice of history was more complex and sophisticated than the *Actius* would suggest.

44. On Giovio's conversion see *IO* 9:256. For Vergerio on methodical doubt see *De ingenuis moribus*, trans. Garin, 89.

45. For Giovio on history and war see *IO* 2:104. On Giovio's belief in the greater importance of the factual side of history over the literary, see, for example, *IO* 9:256. For an example of "dignity" constraining historical style see Fubini, "Biondo," *DBI* 10:545. Alcionio's praises of a portion of Giovio's *Histories* (presumably the first decade), dating from 1522, reflected perfectly the Ciceronian expectations of the Roman academy. Pietro Alcionio, *Medices legatus de exsilio* in *Analecta de calamitate litteratorum* (Leipzig, 1707), 149–50.

46. See Giovio's obeisances to the "brevity of history" (bk. 39, *IO* 5:11; bk. 40, *IO* 5:81). Guicciardini also cited "the laws of history" regarding brevity in *SI* 4.12. For criticism of Pontano for not always maintaining *dignitas* see *IO* 8:77.

47. Burckhardt believed that the use of a dead language deprived all humanist history of contemporaneity (*Civilization of the Renaissance* [1954], 178). For Montaigne's feeling that the literary nature of humanist history circumscribed its substance and his consequent admiration of Guicciardini for his grasp of process, see Felix Gilbert, "The Renaissance Interest in History," in Charles S. Singleton, ed., *Art, Science, and History in the Renaissance* (Baltimore: Johns Hopkins University Press, 1967), 378. The best critique of Giovio's Latin is Alciato's in *IO* 3:3. John Addington Symonds found it "fluent and sonorous rather than pointed or grave" (*Encyclopedia Brittanica*, 11th ed., 15:527). Croce found it "molto bello" (letter to Gianfranco Miglio, May 6, 1952, cited by Lazzarini, *Multiformità*, 177).

48. On Guicciardini and the humanist historiographical tradition see the essays by F. Gaeta, N. Rubinstein, and E. Cochrane in Istituto Nazionale di Studi sul Rinascimento, *Francesco Guicciardini nel V centenario della nascita* (Florence: Olschki, 1984). See also Donald J. Wilcox, "Guicciardini and the Humanist Historians," *Annali d'Italianistica* 2 (1984): 19–33.

49. For the view of method as the dividing line see Franco Gaeta, "Osservazioni sul percorso storiografico di Francesco Guicciardini," in *Guicciardini nel V centenario*, 156–57. When Camillo Porzio styled Giovio "father of modern histories," he may well have had in mind not only his contemporary focus but his innovations in method. Porzio, *Opere*, ed. C. Monzani (Florence: Le Monnier, 1855), 3.

50. Mark Phillips, *Francesco Guicciardini: The Historian's Craft* (Toronto: University of Toronto Press, 1977).

51. Dionisotti, *Machiavellerie*, 412. The most extensive discussion of Giovio's political limitations is Gennaro Sasso's reviews of *IO* 1 and 2 in *GS* 133 (1956): 606–14, and 136 (1959): 647–52.

52. On the tradition of character sketches see the illuminating remarks of Peter E. Bondanella, *Machiavelli and the Art of Renaissance History* (Detroit: Wayne State University Press, 1973), chap. 1.

53. Examples would be his accounts of the debates in the council of King Charles VIII and his officers before the battles of Fornovo in bk. 2, or among the defenders of Alba Regia (Székesfehérvár) in bk. 43.

54. On Giovio's importance to military history see Chabod, *Scritti*, 257–59, and Pieri, *Il Rinascimento*, 518, and his review of Panigada's edition of the lives, *La nuova Italia* 16 (1932): 434–36.

55. On Biondo's discouragement with mastering the interminable wars of contemporary history see Fubini, "Biondo," *DBI* 10:545, and Donald R. Kelley, "Humanism and History," in Rabil, Jr., ed., *Renaissance Humanism* 3:243.

56. *SI* 16.7–11. See Zimmermann, "Guicciardini and Giovio."

57. *SI* 18.14.

58. It is particularly significant that Guicciardini followed Giovio's structure in the life of Leo X, even though it was not strictly chronological.

59. Giovio's reliance on human agency has been stressed by Reynolds, "Latin Historiography," 56, and Cochrane, *Historians*, 373. On Livy's stress on morals over causes and its influence on Pontano and the humanists see Cotroneo, *Trattatisti*, chap. 3. The phrase "a tragic vision of greatness humbled and liberty lost," is J. R. Hale's, from his insightful introduction to Guicciardini, *History of Italy and History of Florence*, trans. Cecil Grayson (New York: Twayne, 1964), xlvi.

60. Quintilian, *Institutio oratoria* 10.1.31, trans. H. E. Butler, (Cambridge and London: Loeb Classics, 1922). Sallust makes a similar observation in the exordium to his *Bellum Catilinae*, whose ideas on glory, ambition, honor, averice, and the deterioration of human society undoubtedly influenced Giovio.

61. *IO* 3:5 and 2:169.

62. *Vita Piscarii* (1551), 272. By and large, Giovio's patrons seem to have agreed with him, but while some sought him out, others certainly needed prodding. On "true glory" cf. Castigione, *Il cortegiano* 1.43. On Charles V's desire for "solidam gloriam quae proprium est virtutis praemium" see Sepúlveda's *De rebus gestis Caroli V*, bk. 30, chap. 30, and *Opera* (1780), 2:532. (For the phrase "solida gloria" see Cicero, *Tusc.* 3.2). On humanists and the *Pro Archia* see Hanna H. Gray, "Renaissance Humanism: The Pursuit of Eloquence," in P. O. Kristeller and P. P. Wiener, eds., *Renaissance Essays* (New York: Harper and Row, 1968), 205, as reprinted from the *Journal of the History of Ideas* 24 (1963).

63. Dedication of the *Elogia* of heroes to Cosimo I de' Medici. *IO* 8:235.

64. To Suleiman the Magnificent (*IO* 2:245). On the social utility of a thirst for glory see Hans Baron on Petrarch's deliber-

ate misreading of *Tusc.* 4.19 in "Petrarch: His Inner Struggles and the Humanistic Discovery of Man's Nature," in J. G. Rowe and W. H. Stockdale, eds., *Florilegium Historiale: Essays Presented to Wallace K. Ferguson* (Toronto: University of Toronto Press, 1971), 30. See also Fubini on Biondo's view that the stimulus of glory and the love of virtue were protectors of the social bond and the preconditions for the salvation of souls (Fubini, "Biondo," *DBI* 10:557). For Valla's grouping of monastic asceticism and Christian pessimism with Stoicism and Cynicism see Fubini, *Umanesimo e secolarizzazione*, 177. For Machiavelli's view of the utility of a love of glory and his critique of Christianity for discouraging it, see Russell Price, "The Theme of *Gloria* in Machiavelli," *RQ* 30 (1977): 588–632, esp. 590. For a full discussion of the topos of *amor laudis* see Alberto Tenenti, *Il senso della morte e l'amore della vita nel Rinascimento*.

65. *De arte rhetorica* 11.2. See Donald Kelley, *Renaissance Humanism* (Boston: Twayne, 1991), 97.

66. See, for example, Giovio's expression of this idea to d'Alviano (*IO* 1:83) or to Granvelle (quoting Cicero), 2:170.

67. *IO* 8:236.

68. *Vita Piscarii* (1551), bk. 3, 330; *Vita del Pescara* (1931), 320. In the *Elogia* Giovio sketched Bourbon as an example of ill-fame, along with such figures as Ezzelino da Romano, Cesare Borgia, and Sultan Selim the Grim. On Machiavelli's distinctions between *vera gloria* and *falsa gloria* see Price, "The Theme of *Gloria*," esp. 590, 610–18.

69. *Vitae duodecim Vicecomitum* in *Illustrium virorum vitae* (Florence, 1551), 91. Giovio's irony here has frequently been overlooked. See the stimulating analysis of possible irony in Machiavelli's use of *virtù* by Victoria Kahn, "*Virtù* and the Example of Agathocles in Machiavelli's Prince," in Ascoli and Kahn, eds., *Machiavelli and the Discourse of Literature*, esp. 206.

70. Burckhardt pointed to chivalry as one of the factors that gave the revival of

antiquity a distinctively Italian character (*Civilization of the Renaissance* [1954], 130). The legacy of chivalry to Renaissance courtliness and behavior has recently been explored in a far-ranging study by Aldo Scaglione, *Knights at Court* (Berkeley: University of California Press, 1991). A lucid and comprehensive overview of Renaissance moral philosophy and its sources has recently been given by Paul O. Kristeller, "Humanism and Moral Philosophy," in Rabil, ed., *Renaissance Humanism* 3:271–309. See also the discussion of the cardinal virtues in Platina by Tateo, *Tradizione e realtà*, chap. 8, "La disputà della nobiltà," 395–96.

71. *IO* 8:45. Riccardo Fubini has suggested that Giovio's apparent preference for Bruni's version, despite the appearance of better ones, demonstrates once again his attachment to the culture of the Quattrocento.

72. On the distinction between Trecento and Quattrocento Florentine humanism in this regard see Ronald G. Witt, *Hercules at the Crossroads* (Durham, N.C.: Duke University Press, 1983), chap. 13. On Bruni and Aristotle see Fubini, *Umanesimo e secolarizzazione*, 172–73. On Pontano's influence on Giovio see chap. 7 above, n. 19. On his philosophy see Carol Kidwell, *Pontano: Poet and Prime Minister* (London: Duckworth, 1991).

73. SSC, Archivio Aliati, 28.5, fols. 370v–371r.

74. For the emphasis on individual experience see John M. Headley, "Tommaso Campanella and the End of the Renaissance," *Journal of Medieval and Renaissance Studies* 20 (1990): 157–74.

75. In his old age Giovio asked Pier Vettori to see if the Laurentian Library contained Politian's translations of Epictetus. *IO* 2:212. On Renaissance Stoicism see William J. Bouwsma, "The Two Faces of Humanism: Stoicism and Augustinianism in Renaissance Thought," in Heiko Oberman and Thomas A. Brady, Jr., eds., *Itinerarium Italicum* (Leiden: Brill, 1975), 3–60.

76. On skepticism see Kristeller, "Humanism and Moral Philosophy," 280. On

Cicero's *Academica* in the Renaissance see Charles B. Schmitt, *Cicero Skepticus* (The Hague: Nijhoff, 1972).

77. For "rebirth of good letters" see the *elogium* of Petrarch (*IO* 8:42–43). On rhetorical aspects of the *Elogia* see my article, "Giovio and the Rhetoric of Individuality."

78. *IO* 8:376.

79. *Histories*, bk. 27 (*IO* 4:116).

80. *IO* 5:69; 8:487.

81. *IO* 8:385.

82. For example, Giovio reported that, at Pavia, Francis I refused to surrender to the duke of Bourbon. *Vita del Pescara* (1931), 430.

83. *Vita Piscarii* (1551), bk. 1, 278. For the Aristotelian scheme see the *Nicomachean Ethics* 2.6.

84. *Histories*, bk. 15 (*IO* 3:340).

85. On the humanist polemics see Fubini, *Umanesimo e secolarizzazione*, chap. 4, pp. 137–81.

86. *Nicomachean Ethics* 4.3.

87. *Histories*, bk. 26 (*IO* 4:61); *Vita Piscarii* (1551), bk.2, 311; *Vita del Pescara* (1931), 269.

88. *Histories*, bk. 43 (*IO* 5:148).

89. *Vita Piscarii* (1551), 405. In some MSS of Poggio's oration at Constance on the vices of the clergy, *humanitas* alternates with *humilitas*. Fubini, *Umanesimo e secolarizzazione*, 303–38.

90. *Nicomachean Ethics* 4.3.

91. *IO* 9:196; *Il cortegiano* 4.36. See also Pontano, *De magnanimitate*, which sprang from talks at Rome with Giovio's friend Colocci (Kidwell, *Pontano*, 288). On Pompeo's *civilis humanitas* see *IO* 6:187.

92. "Quippe qui non adumbratam sed veram et vividam, non Fortunae adminiculis quaesitam sed a fonte ipso propriae virtutis profluentem gloriam sectaretur" (*IO* 4:116). Cf. Cicero: "Est enim gloria solida quaedam res et expressa, non adumbrata" (*Tusc.* 3.1).

93. *IO* 9:194–96; 8:410–12; 9:277.

94. *IO* 5:83.

95. See Yves Giraud, "Esperienza e coscienza della Fortuna nel Giovio," in *Atti*, 51–62.

96. *Vita Piscarii* (1551), bk. 6, 405;

Vita del Pescara (1931), 436. The cult of *virtù* in Giovio's Rome is illustrated by the academy founded by his friend Claudio Tolomei, the Accademia della Virtù, with its presiding officer the Re della Virtù. Machiavelli's use of the term *virtù* has been the subject of considerable discussion and debate, but whether he intended by it "masculine energy," the antithesis of passivity and the antidote to Fortuna, or functional excellence, he used the term, like Giovio, according to the Latin root sense. On *virtù* as "masculine energy," see Sebastian de Grazia, *Machiavelli in Hell* (Princeton: Princeton University Press, 1989), 212, 243, or Hanna Fenichel Pitkin, *Fortune Is a Woman: Gender and Politics in the Thought of Niccolò Machiavelli* (Berkeley: University of California Press, 1984); for *virtù* as functional excellence, or *areté*, see Mark Hulliung, *Citizen Machiavelli* (Princeton: Princeton University Press, 1993), 136, and Kahn, "*Virtù* and the Example of Agathocles," 195–217. In his note, "On Machiavelli's Idea of *Virtù*," *Renaissance News* 4 (1951): 53–55, Felix Gilbert called attention to the use of *virtù* in contemporary medical terminology as that which gave vitality to a human being, a particularly appropriate usage for Giovio and close to his actual sense of the term.

97. For Giovio's ideas on imitation see the discussion of the Ischian dialogue in chap. 7 above. The phrase "imitation as the last refuge of the mediocre" occurs in Albert Russell Ascoli's discussion of chap. 6 of *The Prince* in his essay "Machiavelli's Gift of Counsel," 238–39. For a bibliography of interpretations of Machiavelli with regard to humanist notions of imitation see Kahn, "*Virtù* and the Example of Agathocles," 196–97.

98. The condemnation of those who do not use their gifts occurs in the Ischian dialogue, which also contains Giovio's most extensive discussion of talent and training in all spheres of life (*IO* 9:258). In the *De litteratorum infelicitate*, Pierio Valeriano has Colocci observe, "In illis vero, qui nihil scripsere, neque scripturi fuerant, qui uti facete, qui mos est hominis, Jovius noster

dicere solebat, semina intra renes praemortua secum extulerunt, parum jacturae fecimus, quamvis jucunda alioquin eorum consuetudine privati doleamus" (Leipzig, 1707), 329–30. For conflict between career officers and noble superiors see *Histories*, bk. 44, *IO* 5:181. For debates on the nature of nobility see Tateo, *Tradizione e realtà*, chap. 8, 355–422; Claudio Donati, *L'idea di nobiltà in Italia, secoli XIV–XVIII*; Albert Rabil, Jr., ed., *Knowledge, Goodness, and Power: The Debate over Nobility Among Quattrocento Humanists* (Binghampton, N.Y: Mediaeval and Renaissance Texts and Studies, 1991).

99. See chap. 7, above.

100. See Clough, "Chivalry and Magnificence in the Golden Age of the Renaissance," in *Chivalry in the Renaissance*, ed. Sydney Anglo, 25–47; A. D. Fraser Jenkins, "Cosimo de' Medici's Patronage of Architecture and the Theory of Magnificence," *WJ* 33 (1970): 162–70; Tateo, *Tradizione e realtà*, 391, 411; Machiavelli, *The Prince*, chap. 21. In the Cancelleria fresco scheme, Paul III's "building St. Peter's" personifies magnificence.

101. *IO* 1:90; see also 4:246, 368. In Giovio's analysis of Clement VII, the pope's parsimony was clearly a failing of both magnificence and magnanimity.

102. For Giberti's dislike of bad manners see Giovanni della Casa, *Il Galateo*, ed. Dino Provenzal (Milan: Rizzoli, 1950), 17–19.

103. See Burckhardt, *Civilization of the Renaissance* (1954), 277.

104. Tenenti, *Il senso della morte*, 41.

105. Lucien Febvre's conclusions are to the point here; see *The Problem of Unbelief in the Sixteenth Century: The Religion of Rabelais*, trans. Beatrice Gottlieb (Cambridge: Harvard University Press, 1982).

106. *Il cortegiano* 4.32.

107. *IO* 1:298.

108. *Vita Piscarii* (1551), 270; *Vita del Pescara* (1931), 199.

109. "Unde mox eius philosophiae beneficio inanes, nihilque profuturas sollicitudines animo detraxerim, et me ipsum angore et metu magna ex parte liberarim" (*IO*

9:138). Cf. *Tusc.* 2.4.11: "nam efficit hoc philosophia: medetur animis, inanes sollicitudines detrahit, cupiditatibus liberat, pellit timores." On Landino and philosophy as medicine of the soul see Arthur Field, *The Origins of the Platonic Academy of Florence* (Princeton: Princeton University Press, 1988), 242–46. On Petrarch and the *Tusculan Disputations* see Hans Baron, *From Petrarch to Leonardo Bruni* (Chicago: University of Chicago Press, 1968), 55, 83.

110. *IO* 9:253. The equation of Stoics and ascetics may be another echo of Valla. See Fubini, *Umanesimo e secolarizzazione*, 177.

111. *IO* 6:160.

112. The concept of "papal humanism" was suggested by D'Amico in *Renaissance Humanism in Papal Rome*. Giovio's friend Mario Maffei represented for D'Amico this type of humanist.

113. Eric Cochrane said much the same: "For Giovio, Catholic Christianity was simply one of the essential components of the culture into which he happily had been born—like Latin poetry and Brianza wine" (*Historians*, 372). On the easy coexistence of Cicero and Christ see Lopez, *The Three Ages*, 21, or Tenenti, *Il senso della morte*, 25. On Giovio's religion see Msgr. Pietro Gini's fundamental study, with which I am in substantial agreement, "Paolo Giovio e la vita religiosa del Cinquecento," *Atti*, 31–50.

114. *IO* 8:75, trans. Gragg, *An Italian Portrait Gallery*, 76. True to his humanist predelictions, the word Giovio used for friars was not *fratres* but *cucullati sacertdoti*.

115. *IO* 9:253.

116. *IO* 1:268.

117. "Ne ciò mi maraviglio io di lui, sapendo come egli parla, et che à chi gli allega la scrittura, egli suol rispondere la Bibia al Giovio, An?" (November 11, 1550; Girolamo Muzio, *Lettere Catholiche* [Venice: Valvassori, 1571], 99–102). While in the service of the duke of Ferrara, Muzio had sung the praises of the courtesan Tullia of Aragon. See Lynne Lawner, *Lives of the Courtesans*, 46.

118. The cardinals inquisitors included in 1550 cardinals Sfondrato, Morone, and Pole. Pastor 13:210.

119. See Tenenti, *Il senso della morte*, 25. Even Valla ridiculed the idea of "virtue as its own reward." See Jill Kraye, "Moral Philosophy," in Charles B. Schmitt, ed., *The Cambridge History of Renaissance Philosophy* (Cambridge: Cambridge University Press, 1988), 363.

120. Burckhardt, *Civilization of the Renaissance* (1954), 340, 370.

121. *IO* 9:419. Cf. also Giovio's 1549 assertion, "Dio *qui est omni fato prudentior*" (*IO* 2:150). There are many comments of Giovio's rebuking the idea of *raison d'état* or the deliberate use of cruelty, e.g., *Vita Piscarii* (1551), bk. 7, 416–17; *Vita del Pescara* (1931), 457; the *elogium* of Sultan Selim (*IO* 8:404), or of Louis XII (8:385). For Giovio's views on Fortune see Giraud in *Atti*, 51–62; for his views on astrology see *IO* 9:176–82, and Travi, "La sosta," 109–18.

122. On Pontano's failure to address the contradictions between human freedom and historical determinism see Cotroneo, *Trattisti*, chap. 3.

123. Fubini, "Biondo," *DBI* 10:536–59. For the way in which religious leadership was combined with a secular monarchy by the papacy see Paolo Prodi, *The Papal Prince*, trans. Susan Haskins (Cambridge: Cambridge University Press, 1987).

124. E.g., *IO* 2:224–25.

125. *IO* 8:237. In the iconography of the Cancelleria frescoes, the pope is represented in Giovio's scheme as the true successor to the universal monarchs Alexander and Caesar. Kliemann in *Atti*, 207.

126. *IO* 8:145, trans. Gragg, *An Italian Portrait Gallery*, 167. Giovio actually returned to an idea of Valla's, expressed in the preface to the *Elegantiae*, that the Roman empire was coterminous with Latin. See Donald R. Kelley, *Foundations of Modern Historical Scholarship*, 36.

127. Cited by Giraud in *Atti*, 53.

128. On the invasions' undermining civic virtue see Lopez, *The Three Ages*, 42.

129. On Giovio and the yearning for *il quieto vivere* see Travi, "Paolo Giovio nel suo tempo," in *Atti*, 313–30, and Rota, "Paolo Giovio." For an important recent development of the theme of withdrawal see Gigliola Fragnito, *In villa e in museo*. On de Sanctis and withdrawal see Lopez, *The Three Ages*, 74.

130. See Klinger, "The Portrait Collection," esp. 9–12.

131. I am grateful to Drs. Clough and Gouwens for suggested wordings here. The work of Anthony Grafton and Lisa Jardine, *From Humanism to the Humanities* (Cambridge: Harvard University Press, 1986), clarifies some of the mythical and therefore vulnerable aspects of humanist educational theory. The transformation and legacy of humanism has been analyzed by Grafton in *Defenders of the Text*. On collecting in the later sixteenth century see Fragnito, *In villa*; Clifford M. Brown, *Our Accustomed Discourse on the Antique: Cesare Gonzaga and Gerolamo Garimberto: Two Renaissance Collectors of Greco-Roman Art* (New York: Garland, 1993); and Paula Findlen, *Possessing Nature* (Berkeley: University of California Press, 1994).

132. Gregorovius, *History of Rome*, bk. 14, chap. 4, vol. 8, pt. l, p. 345.

133. See epigraph to the preface in the present volume.

134. Burckhardt accused Giovio of excusing the perjury of Giangaleazzo Visconti by the example of Caesar, when he was in reality condemning it. *Civilization of the Renaissance* (1954), 320.

135. Ibid., 179.

136. For Bembo's comment on Giovio's "graceful and learned style" see his letter to Clement VII, April 7, 1530, *Opere* 5:13–14.

137. Garin's phrase ("l'inafferrabile, l'indeterminato e indeterminabile, ciò che sfugge alla presa dell'uomo") is cited by Umberto Bosco in his essay, "Il senso del limite," in *Saggi sul Rinascimento italiano* (Florence: Le Monnier, 1970), 19.

138. *IO* 2:102. See also his comment to Cosimo I de' Medici, "E spero satisfare con la penna alla mira del scapello della secunda bussula, perché pochi ne sono nella prima." *IO* 2:32.

139. *IO* 2:137.

140. *IO* 8:36–37.

141. *IO* 1:176. The phrase "Il nostro Monsignor Giovio, quale de niuna cosa fà maggior' professione" occurs in a letter of the marquis del Vasto to Cosimo I, April 29, 1537 (ASF, Mediceo del principato 5024, no. 1).

Select Bibliography

WORKS BY GIOVIO

Pauli Iovii opera. Rome: Società Storica Comense and Istituto Poligrafico dello
Stato, 1956—.
  1. *Epistularum, pars prior.* Edited by Giuseppe Guido Ferrero. 1956.
  2. *Epistularum, pars altera.* Edited by G. G. Ferrero. 1958.
  3. *Historiarum sui temporis, tomus primus.* Edited by Dante Visconti.
    1957.
  4. *Historiarum sui temporis, tomi secundi, pars prior.* Edited by D. Vis-
    conti. 1964.
  5. *Historiarum sui temporis, tomi secundi, pars altera.* Edited by D. Vis-
    conti and T. C. Price Zimmermann. 1985
  6. *Vitarum, pars prior* (Leo X, Adrian VI, Pompeo Colonna). Edited by
    Michele Cataudella. 1987.
  7. *Vitarum, pars altera* (Visconti dukes of Milan, Muzio Attendolo Sforza,
    Gonzalo de Córdoba, Francisco Fernando d'Avalos, Alfonso d'Este).
    Edited by M. Cataudella. Forthcoming.
  8. *Elogia.* Edited by Renzo Meregazzi. 1972.
  9. *Dialogi et descriptiones* (*De piscibus,* 11–64; *Moschovia,* 73–88; *Descrip-
    tio Britanniae,* 89–128; *De optima victus ratione,* 137–46; *Dialogus de
    viris et foeminis aetate nostra florentibus,* 167–321; *Larius,* 330–50; *Di-
    alogo dell'imprese,* 373–443). Edited by Ernesto Travi and Mariagrazia
    Penco. 1984.
  10. *Iconographia.* Edited by Stefano Della Torre, Pierluigi De Vecchi,
    Bruno Fasola, Linda Klinger, Rosanna Pavoni, Clare Robertson, and
    Robert Simon. Forthcoming.
  11. *Opera minora.* Edited by E. Travi. Forthcoming.

INDIVIDUAL GIOVIAN WORKS, EDITIONS, MANUSCRIPTS, ETC.

Autobiographical sketch. BNR, MSS Autografi, A. 153.1. A single sheet can-
  celed with diagonal ink lines.
Commentario de le cose de' Turchi. In Francesco Sansovino, ed., *Dell' historia
  universale dell'origine et imperio de Turchi,* vol. 2, fols. 70v–90v. 2 vols.
  Venice: Sansovino, 1560.
Dialogo dell'imprese militari e amorose. Edited by Maria Luisa Doglio. Rome:
  Bulzoni, 1978.
Larius. See 9 above, and under Miglio, Gianfranco and Pietro Gini, eds.
Lettere volgari di Mons. Paolo Giovio. Edited by Lodovico Domenichi. Venice:
  Sessa, 1560.
Illustrium virorum vitae. Florence: Torrentino, 1551. *De vita et rebus gestis XII
  Vicecomitum Mediolani Principum; De vita et rebus gestis Magni Sfortiae;
  De vita et rebus gestis Consalvi Ferdinandi Cordubae cognomento Magni; De
  vita et rebus gestis Ferdinandi Davali cognomento Piscarii.*
De vita et rebus gestis Alphonsi Atestini Ferrariae Principis. Florence: Torrentino,
  1550.

De vita Leonis Decimi Pont. Max. libri quatuor: His ordine temporum accesserunt Hadriani Sexti Pont. Max. et Pompeii Columnae Cardinalis vitae. Florence: Torrentino, 1551.

Le vite del Gran Capitano e del Marchese di Pescara. Translated by Ludovico Domenichi. Edited by Costantino Panigada. Bari: Laterza and Figli, 1931.

WORKS BY OTHER AUTHORS

Alcionio, Pietro. *Medices legatus de exsilio* (Venice: Aldus, 1522). Also in *Analecta de calamitate litteratorum.* Leipzig, 1707.

Anglo, Sydney, ed. *Chivalry in the Renaissance.* Woodbridge, Suffolk, U.K.: Boydell, 1990.

Arsilli, Francesco. *De poetis urbanis, ad Paulum Iovium libellus.* In Blosio Palladio, ed., *Coryciana.* Rome: Arrighi, 1524.

Atanagi, Dionigi, ed. *Delle lettere facete et piacevoli.* Vol. 1. Venice: Salicato, 1601.

Atti del convegno Paolo Giovio: Il Rinascimento e la memoria. Como: Società Storica Comense, 1985.

Bembo, Pietro. *Opere.* Edited by Anton Federigo Seghezzi. 11 vols. Milan: Classici Italiani, 1808–1810.

Bentley, Jerry H. *Politics and Culture in Renaissance Naples.* Princeton: Princeton University Press, 1987.

Berni, Francesco. *Poesie e prose.* Edited by Enzio Chiorboli. Geneva and Florence: Olschki, 1934.

Bordoli, Giorgio, ed. "Il testamento di Paolo Giovio." *PSSC* 50 (1983): 87–116.

Brandi, Karl. *The Emperor Charles V.* Translated by C. V. Wedgwood. London: Jonathan Cape, 1960.

Bullard, Melissa Miriam. *Filippo Strozzi and the Medici.* Cambridge: Cambridge University Press, 1980.

Burckhardt, Jacob. *The Civilization of the Renaissance in Italy.* Edited by Hajo Holborn. New York: Modern Library, 1954.

Caldari, Franca Bevilacqua. "Un brano delle *Historiae* del Giovio in una lettera inedita del Cardinale Jean du Bellay." *Studi romani* 19 (1971): 431–52.

Capparoni, Pietro. *Paolo Giovio Archiatra di Papa Clemente VII.* Grottaferrata: "S. Nilo," 1913.

Castiglione, Baldassar. *Lettere.* Edited by Pierantonio Serassi. 2 vols. Padua: Comino, 1769–71.

Castellani, Silvia. "Contributo alla biografia di Paolo Giovio." Unpublished *tesi di laurea*, University of Florence, 1992.

Chabod, Federico. "Epoca di Carlo V." *Storia di Milano*, q.v., vol. 9, pt. 1.

———. *Scritti sul Rinascimento.* Turin: Einaudi, 1967.

Chastel, André. *The Sack of Rome.* Translated by Beth Archer. Princeton: Princeton University Press, 1983.

Christie's Sale Catalogue. *Early Printed Books, Manuscripts, and Autograph Letters.* London, November 17, 1976.

Cian, Vittorio. *Un decennio nella vita di M. Pietro Bembo.* Turin, 1885.

———. "Gioviana: Paolo Giovio poeta fra poeti e di alcune rime sconosciute del secolo XVI." *GS* 17 (1891): 277–357.

———. *Un illustre nunzio pontificio del Rinascimento: Baldassar Castiglione.* "Studi e Testi," 156. Vatican City: BAV, 1951.

———. "Lettere inedite di Andrea Alciato a Pietro Bembo—l'Alciato e Paolo Giovio." *Archivio storico lombardo* 17 (1890): 811–65.

Clough, Cecil H. "A Manuscript of Paolo Giovio's *Historiae sui temporis, liber VII*: More Light on the Career of Ludovico degli Arrighi." *PSSC* 53 (1988–89): 53–83. Also published in *The Book Collector* 38 (1989): 27–59.

Cochrane, Eric. *Florence in the Forgotten Centuries.* Chicago: University of Chicago Press, 1973.

———. *Historians and Historiography in the Italian Renaissance.* Chicago: University of Chicago Press, 1981.

Coffin, David R. *Gardens and Gardening in Papal Rome.* Princeton: Princeton University Press, 1991.

———. *The Villa in the Life of Renaissance Rome.* Princeton: Princeton University Press, 1979.

Colonna, Vittoria. *Carteggio.* Edited by Ermanno Ferrero and Giuseppe Müller. 2d ed., with a supplement ed. by Domenico Tordi. Turin: Loescher, 1892.

Collezioni Giovio. See Pavoni, Rosanna.

Concilium Tridentinum: Diariorum, actorum, epistolarum, tractatuum nova collectio. Edited by the Görres-Gesellschaft. Freiburg-im-Breisgau: Herder, 1901—.

Cortesi, Paolo. *De hominibus doctis.* Edited by Giacomo Ferraù. Palermo: Il Vespro, 1979.

Cotroneo, Girolamo. *Trattatisti dell'ars historica.* Naples: Giannini, 1971.

Croce, Benedetto. *Poeti e scrittori del pieno e del tardo Rinascimento.* 3 vols. Bari: Laterza and Figli, 1945–52.

Cronaca del soggiorno di Carlo V in Italia. [By Luigi Gonzaga?] Edited by Gennaro Romano. Milan: Hoepli, 1892.

D'Amico, John F. *Renaissance Humanism in Papal Rome.* Baltimore: Johns Hopkins University Press, 1983.

D'Arco, Niccolò. *Nicolai Archii Comitis numerorum libri IV.* Verona, 1762.

De Caprio, Vincenzo. *La tradizione e il trauma: Idee del Rinascimento romano.* Manziana: Vecchiarelli, 1991.

De Gaetano, Armand L. *Giambattista Gelli and the Florentine Academy.* Florence: Olschki, 1976.

Della Torre, Stefano. "Le vedute del museo gioviano." *Quaderni erbesi* 7 (1985): 39–48.

Denis, Anne. *Charles VIII et les Italiens: Histoire et mythe.* Geneva: Droz, 1979.

Di Meglio, Giovannangelo. *Carlo V e Clemente VII dal carteggio diplomatico.* Milan: Martello, 1970.

Dionisotti, Carlo. "Appunti sul Bembo e su Vittoria Colonna." In Rino Avesani et al., eds., *Miscellanea Augusto Campana.* 2 vols. Padua: Antenore, 1981.

———. *Geografia e storia della letteratura italiana.* Turin: Einaudi, 1967.

———. *Gli umanisti ed il volgare fra Quattrocento e Cinquecento.* Florence: Le Monnier, 1968.

———. *Machiavellerie.* Turin: Einaudi, 1980.

Dizionario biografico degli Italiani. Rome: Istituto dell'Enciclopedia Italiana, 1960—.

Donati, Claudio. *L'idea di nobiltà in Italia, secoli XIV–XVIII.* Bari: Laterza and Figli, 1988.

Dorez, Léon. *La cour du Pape Paul III.* 2 vols. Paris: Librairie Leroux, 1932.

Erasmus, Desiderius. *Opus epistolarum*. Edited by P. S. Allen. 12 vols. Oxford: Clarendon Press, 1906–1958.

Ferrajoli, Alessandro. *Il Ruolo della Corte di Leone X*. Edited by Vincenzo de Caprio. Rome: Bulzoni, 1984.

Folena, Gianfranco. "L'espressionismo epistolare di Paolo Giovio." *Atti dei convegni Lincei* 71, Convegno sul tema: L'espressivismo linguistico nella letteratura italiana. Rome: Accademia Nazionale dei Lincei, 1985.

Fragnito, Gigliola. *In museo e in villa: Saggi sul Rinascimento perduto*. Venice: Arsenale, 1988.

———. "Un pratese alla corte di Cosimo I: Riflessioni e materiali per un profilo di Pierfrancesco Riccio." *Archivio storico pratese* 62 (1986): 5–57.

Fubini, Riccardo. *Umanesimo e secolarizzazione*. Rome: Bulzoni, 1990.

Gianoncelli, Matteo. *L'antico museo di Paolo Giovio in Borgovico*. Como: New Press, 1977.

Gianoncelli, Matteo and Stefano Della Torre. *Microanalisi di una città*. Como: New Press, 1984.

Gilbert, Felix. *Machiavelli and Guicciardini*. Princeton: Princeton University Press, 1965.

Giovio, Benedetto. *Historiae patriae libri duo*. Como: New Press, 1982.

———. "Lettere." Edited by Santo Monti. *PSSC* 8 (1891): 91–259.

Giovio, Giambattista. "Elogio di Msgr. Paolo Giovio." In Andrea Rubbi, ed., *Elogi italiani* (8:5–124). 12 vols. Venice: Marcuzzi, 1782–83.

Gnoli, Domenico. *La Roma di Leone X*. Milan: Hoepli, 1938.

Gorse, George L. "Triumphal Entries into Genoa in the Sixteenth Century." In *All the World's a Stage: Art and Pageantry in the Renaissance and Baroque*, ed. Barbara Wisch and Susan Munshower, 1:188–256. 2 vols. University Park: Papers in Art History from the Pennsylvania State University, 1990.

Grafton, Anthony. *Defenders of the Text: The Traditions of Scholarship in an Age of Science, 1450–1800*. Cambridge: Harvard University Press, 1991.

Gragg, Florence Alden, trans. *An Italian Portrait Gallery: Being Brief Biographies of Scholars . . . by Paolo Giovio*. Boston: Chapman and Grimes, 1935.

Grendler, Paul F. *Critics of the Italian World*. Madison: University of Wisconsin Press, 1969.

Gregorovius, Ferdinand. *History of the City of Rome in the Middle Ages*. Translated by Annie Hamilton from the 4th German edition. 2d ed., rev. 8 vols. in 13. London: George Bell, 1900–1902.

Guicciardini, Francesco. *Carteggi di Francesco Guicciardini*. Edited by Roberto Palmarocchi and Pier Giorgio Ricci. 17 vols. Rome: Istituto Storico Italiano per l'Età Moderna e Contemporanea, 1938–1972.

———. *The History of Italy*. Translated by Sidney Alexander. New York: Macmillan, 1969.

———. *Ricordi*. Edited by Raffaele Spongano. Florence: Sansoni, 1951.

Guicciardini, Luigi. *The Sack of Rome*. Edited and translated by James H. McGregor. New York: Italica Press, 1993.

Hale, John R. *Renaissance War Studies*. London: Hambledon, 1983.

Hallman, Barbara McClung. *Italian Cardinals, Reform, and the Church as Property, 1492–1563*. Berkeley: University of California Press, 1985.

Headley, John M. *The Emperor and His Chancellor: A Study of the Imperial Chancellery under Gattinara*. Cambridge: Cambridge University Press, 1983.

Hirst, Michael. *Sebastiano del Piombo*. Oxford: Oxford University Press, 1981.

Hook, Judith. *The Sack of Rome*. London: Macmillan, 1972.

Hope, Charles. *Titian*. New York: Harper and Row, 1980.

Hudon, William V. *Marcello Cervini and Ecclesiastical Government in Tridentine Italy*. DeKalb: Northern Illinois University Press, 1992.

Ianziti, Gary. *Humanist Historiography under the Sforzas: Politics and Propaganda in Fifteenth-Century Milan*. Oxford: Clarendon Press, 1988.

Ilardi, Vincent. "'Italianità' among Some Italian Intellectuals in the Early Sixteenth Century," *Traditio* 12 (1956): 339–67. Reprinted in Ilardi, *Studies in Italian Renaissance Diplomatic History*. London: Variorum Reprints, 1986.

Jedin, Hubert. *A History of the Council of Trent*. Translated by Ernest Graf. 2 vols. London: Thomas Nelson, 1957–1961.

Jiminez de Quesada, Gonzalo. *El antijovio*. Edited by Rafael Torres Quintero. Bogotá: Instituto Caro y Cuervo, 1952.

Jones, Rosemary Devonshire . *Francesco Vettori*. London: Athlone, 1972.

Klinger, Linda S. "The Portrait Collection of Paolo Giovio." Ph.D. diss., Princeton University, 1991.

Knecht, R. J. *Francis I*. Cambridge: Cambridge University Press, 1982.

Kristeller, Paul O. *Iter italicum*. 6 vols. Leiden: E. J. Brill, 1963–92.

Lavisse, Ernest, ed. *Histoire de France*. 9 vols. Paris: Hachette, 1901–1911. Esp. vol. 5 (1904), pt. l, "Les guerres d'Italie," and pt. 2, "La lutte contre la maison d'Autriche," by Henry Lemonnier.

Lawner, Lynne. *Lives of the Courtesans*. New York: Rizzoli, 1987.

Lettere facete et piacevoli. See Atanagi.

Lettere di principi. 3 vols. Venice: Ziletti, 1562–81. Vol. 1: edited by Girolamo Ruscelli (1562); vol. 2: edited by Giordano Ziletti (1571); vol. 3: edited by Giordano Ziletti (1581).

Litta, Pompeo, ed. *Famiglie celebri d'Italia*. 185 parts. Milan and Turin: Giusti and subsequent publishers, 1819–1899.

Lopez, Roberto. *The Three Ages of the Italian Renaissance*. Charlottesville: University Press of Virginia, 1970.

Lowe, K. J. P. *Church and Politics in Renaissance Italy: The Life and Career of Cardinal Francesco Soderini, 1453–1524*. Cambridge: Cambridge University Press, 1993.

Lupo-Gentile, Michele. *Studi sulla storiografia fiorentina alla corte di Cosimo I de' Medici*. Pisa: Scuola Normale Superiore, 1905. Reprinted from *Annali della Scuola Normale Superiore di Pisa* 19 (1905): 1–163.

Luzio, Alessandro. "Isabella d'Este e Leone X." *ASI*, 5th ser., 40 (1907): 18–97; 44 (1909): 72–128; 45 (1910): 245–302.

———. *Lettere inedite di Paolo Giovio tratte dall'Archivio Gonzaga*. Mantua: Segna, 1885.

———. *Pietro Aretino nei sui primi anni a Venezia e la corte dei Gonzaga*. Turin: Loescher, 1888.

———. *Un prognostico satirico di Pietro Aretino*. Bergamo: Arti Grafiche, 1900.

Luzio, Alessandro and Rodolfo Renier. "La coltura e le relazioni letterarie di Isabella d'Este Gonzaga." Nine installments. *GS* 33–42 (1899–1903). Citations are from 36 (1900): 325–49.

McClure, George W. *Sorrow and Consolation in Italian Humanism*. Princeton: Princeton University Press, 1991.

McNanamon, John M. "The Ideal Renaissance Pope: Funeral Oratory from the Papal Court." *Archivum historiae pontificiae* 14 (1976): 9–70.

Maltby, William S. *Alba*. Berkeley: University of California Press, 1983.

Marini, Gaetano. *Degli archiatri pontefici*. 2 vols. Rome, 1784.

―――. *Lettera . . . nella quale s'illustra il ruolo de' professori dell'Archiginnasio Romano per l'anno MDXIV*. Rome, 1797.

Marucci, Valerio, Antonio Marzo, and Angelo Romano, eds. *Pasquinate romane del Cinquecento*. 2 vols. Rome: Salerno, 1983.

Mayer, Thomas F. "Reginald Pole in Paolo Giovio's *Descriptio*: A Strategy for Reconversion." *Sixteenth Century Journal* 16 (1985): 431–50.

Mazzoldi, Leonardo, ed. *Storia di Mantova*. 3 vols. Mantua: Istituto Carlo D'Arco, 1961–1963.

Miglio, Gianfranco and Pietro Gini, eds. *Larius*. Milan and Como: Società Storica Comense, 1959―.

Mitchell, Bonner. *Italian Civic Pageantry in the High Renaissance*. Florence: Olschki, 1979.

―――. *The Majesty of the State: Triumphal Progresses of Foreign Sovereigns in Renaissance Italy (1494–1600)*. Florence: Olschki, 1986.

―――. *Rome in the High Renaissance*. Norman: University of Oklahoma Press, 1973.

Monti, Santo, ed. "Gioviana: Documenti gioviani inediti." *PSSC* 16 (1904): 1–62; 20 (1912–13): 203–15.

Morel-Fatio, Alfred. *Historiographie de Charles-Quint*. Paris: Champion, 1913.

Moroni, Ornella. *Carlo Gualteruzzi e i corrispondenti*. "Studi e Testi," 307. Vatican City: BAV, 1984.

Müntz, Eugène. *Le musée de portraits de Paul Jove*. Paris: Librairie Klincksieck, 1900. Reprinted from *Mémoires de l'Académie des Inscriptions et Belles-lettres* 36, pt. 2 (1900): 247–343.

Noseda, Magda and Cesare Sibilia. "Fondi archivistici gioviani" (pamphlet). Como: Società Storica Comense, 1983.

Norwich, John Julius. *A History of Venice*. New York: Knopf, 1982.

Oliva, Mario. *Giulia Gonzaga Colonna*. Milan: Mursia, 1985.

Oman, Sir Charles. *The Art of War in the Sixteenth Century*. New York: Dutton, 1937.

Partner, Peter. *The Pope's Men*. Oxford: Clarendon Press, 1990.

―――. *Renaissance Rome, 1500–1559*. Berkeley: University of California Press, 1976.

Pastor, Ludwig von. *The History of the Popes from the Close of the Middle Ages*. Translated by F. I. Antrobus et al. 40 vols. London: Routledge and Kegan Paul, 1891–1953.

Pavoni, Rosanna, ed. *Collezioni Giovio: Le immagini e la storia*. Catalogue of the Exhibition, "Paolo Giovio." Como: Musei Civici, 1983.

Pecchiai, Pio. *Roma nel Cinquecento*. Bologna: Cappelli, 1948.

Pieraccini, Gaetano. *La stirpe de' Medici di Cafaggiolo*. 2d. ed. 3 vols. in 4. Florence: Valecchi, 1947.

Pieri, Piero. *Il Rinascimento e la crisi militare italiana*. Turin: Einaudi, 1952.

Pighi, Giovanni Battista. *Gian Matteo Giberti*. Verona: Melchior, 1900; rpt., Verona: Valdonega, 1955.

Pillinini, Giovanni. *Il sistema degli stati italiani, 1454–1494*. Venice: Libreria Universitaria, 1970.

Pontano, Giovanni. *Dialoghi*. Edited by Carmelito Previtera. Florence: Sansoni, 1943.

————. *Quando gli dei si spogliano: Il bagno di Clemente VII a castel Sant'Angelo e le altre stufe romane del primo Cinquecento.* Rome: Romana Società, 1984

Rabil, Albert, Jr. *Renaissance Humanism: Foundations, Forms, and Legacy.* 3 vols. Philadelphia: University of Pennsylvania Press, 1988.

Raimondi, Ezio. "Machiavelli, Giovio ed Aristofane." In Sergio Antonelli, ed., *Saggi di letteratura italiana in onore di Gaetano Trombatore.* Milan: Istituto Editoriale Cisalpino–La Goliardica, 1973.

Rave, Paul Ortwin. "Paolo Giovio und die Bildnisvitenbücher des Humanismus." *Jahrbuch der Berliner Museen* 1 (1959): 119–54.

Reeves, Marjorie, ed. *Prophetic Rome in the High Renaissance.* Oxford: Clarendon Press, 1992.

Reynolds, Beatrice R. "Latin Historiography: A Survey: 1400–1600." *Studies in the Renaissance* 2 (1955): 7–66.

————. "Shifting Currents in Historical Criticism." *Journal of the History of Ideas.* Reprinted in P. O. Kristeller and P. P. Wiener, eds., *Renaissance Essays,* 115–36. New York: Harper and Row, 1968.

Ridolfi, Roberto. *Vita di Francesco Guicciardini.* Rome: Belardetti 1960.

————. *Vita di Niccolò Machiavelli.* Rome: Belardetti 1954.

Rota, Ettore. "Paolo Giovio." In *Letteratura italiana: I minori* 2:927–48. Milan: Marzorati, 1961.

Rovelli, Luigi. *Paolo Giovio.* Como: Cavalleri, 1928.

Sadoleto, Jacopo. *Opera.* 4 vols. Verona, 1737.

Salza, Abd-el-Kader. *Luca Contile.* Florence: Carnesecchi, 1903.

Sanesi, Giuseppe. "Alcune osservazioni e notizie intorno a tre storici minori del Cinquecento." *ASI,* 5th ser., 23 (1899): 260–88.

Santoro, Caterina. *Gli Sforza.* Milan: dall'Oglio, 1968.

Santoro, Mario. *Fortuna, ragione e prudenza nella civiltà letteraria del Cinquecento.* Naples: Liguori, 1967.

Sanudo, Marin. *I diarii.* Edited by Rinaldo Fulin et al. 58 vols. Venice: Visentini 1879–1903.

Scala, Mirella. "Encomi e dediche nelle prime relazioni culturali di Vittoria Colonna." *PSSC* 54 (1990): 95–112.

Scolari, Felice. "L'assedio di Firenze (1529–30): Francesco Ferrucci e il nostro storico Paolo Giovio." *PSSC* 27 (1930): 13–39.

Scrivano, Riccardo. *Cultura e letteratura nel Cinquecento.* Rome: Edizioni dell'Ateneo, 1966.

Sepúlveda, Juan Ginès. *Opera.* 4 vols. Madrid, 1780.

Setton, Kenneth M. *The Papacy and the Levant.* 4 vols. Philadelphia: American Philosophical Society, 1976–1984.

Simeoni, Luigi. *Le signorie.* 2 vols. "Storia politica d'Italia." Milan: Vallardi, 1950.

Spini, Giorgio. *Cosimo I de' Medici e la indipendenza del principato medioceo.* Florence: Vallecchi, 1980.

Stephens, John N. *The Fall of the Florentine Republic, 1512–1530.* Oxford: Clarendon Press, 1983.

————. "Giovanbattista Cibo's Confession." In Sergio Bertelli and Gloria Ramakus, eds., *Essays Presented to Myron P. Gilmore* 1:255–69. 2 vols. Florence: La Nuova Italia, 1978.

Stinger, Charles L. *The Renaissance in Rome.* Bloomington: Indiana University Press, 1985.

Storia di Mantova. See Mazzoldi.

Storia di Milano. 17 vols. Milan: Fondazione Treccani degli Alfieri, 1953–1966.

Tateo, Francesco. *Tradizione e realtà nell'umanesimo italiano.* Bari: Dedalo Libri, 1967.

Tenenti, Alberto. *Il senso della morte e l'amore della vita nel Rinascimento.* Turin: Einaudi 1957.

Thérault, Suzanne. *Un cénacle humaniste de la Renaissance autour de Vittoria Colonna châtelaine d'Ischia.* Florence: Sansoni, 1968.

Travi, Ernesto. "Giovio, gli Orti Oricellari, e Machiavelli." *Testo* 5 (1983): 52–61.

———. *Lingua e vita nel primo Cinquecento.* Milan: Edizioni di Teoria e Storia Letteraria, 1984.

———. "Paolo Giovio a Pavia accanto a Marcantonio della Torre e Leonardo." *Communitas,* Annali del Centro Studi Storici Val Menaggio, 1979–82: 121–25.

———. "La sosta a Napoli di Paolo Giovio." *Quaderni* 4 (1987): 109–29. Reprinted in Travi, *Uomini e forme in Lombardia,* 57–72. Rome: Bulzoni, 1993.

Ubaldini, Federico. *Vita di Monsignor Angelo Colocci.* Edited by Vittorio Fanelli. "Studi e Testi," 256. Vatican City: BAV, 1969.

Valeriano, Pierio. *De litteratorum infelicitate libri duo.* Venice: Sarzina, 1620; Leipzig: Gleditsch, 1707.

Van Gulik, Wilhelm and Conrad Eubel. *Hierarchia catholica.* Edited by Ludwig Schmitz-Kallenberg. Vol. 3. Münster: Regensberg Bücherei, 1923.

Varchi, Benedetto. *Storia fiorentina.* 5 vols. Milan: Classici Italiani, 1803–1804.

Vasari, Giorgio. *Der literarische Nachlass Giorgio Vasaris.* Edited by Karl Frey. Munich: Müller, 1923.

———. *Le vite.* Edited by Rosana Bettarini and Paola Barocchi. Florence: Sansoni, 1966—.

Vecce, Carlo. "Paolo Giovio e Vittoria Colonna." *PSSC* 54 (1990): 67–93.

Vergerio, Pier Paolo. *De ingenuis moribus.* Edited and translated by Eugenio Garin. In Garin, ed., *L'educazione umanistica in Italia,* 49–106. Bari: Laterza and Figli, 1949.

Vettori, Francesco. *Sommario della storia d'Italia.* In Vettori, *Scritti storici e politici.* Edited by Enrico Niccolini. Bari: Laterza and Figli, 1972.

Visconti, Dante. "Le lacune delle *Historiae* gioviane." In *Studia ghisleriana,* 2d ser., vol. 3, *Studi letterari,* 285–95. Pavia: Tipografia del Libro, 1967.

———. "Nota su alcuni MSS gioviani." *Clio* 1 (1965): 98–114.

Volpati, Carlo. "Paolo Giovio e Genoa." *Giornale storico e letterario della Liguria* 14 (1938): 92–99, 182–89.

———. "Paolo Giovio e Napoli." *Nuova rivista storica* 20 (1936): 347–62.

———. "Paolo Giovio e l'ultimo duca di Milano," *Archivio storico lombardo,* 8th ser., no. 3 (1951–52): 195–201.

———. "Paolo Giovio e Venezia." *Archivio veneto,* 5th ser., 15 (1934): 132–56.

———. "Vittoria Colonna e Paolo Giovio." *Roma* 11 (1933): 501–16.

Wegg, Jervis. *Richard Pace.* London: Methuen, 1932.

Weiss, Roberto. *The Renaissance Discovery of Classical Antiquity.* Oxford: Basil Blackwell, 1969.

Wethey, Harold E. *The Paintings of Titian.* 2 vols. London: Phaidon, 1969–1971.

Zimmermann, T. C. Price. "Ferrante Gonzaga ed il vescovado di Como." *PSSC* 41 (1960–1967): 103–13.

―――. "Francesco Guicciardini and Paolo Giovio." *Annali d'Italianistica* 2 (1984): 34–52.

―――. "Nota storico-critica." In *IO* 5:239–48.

―――. "A Note on Clement VII and the Divorce of Henry VIII." *English Historical Review* 82 (1967): 548–52.

―――. "Paolo Giovio and the Evolution of Renaissance Art Criticism." In Cecil H. Clough, ed., *Cultural Aspects of the Italian Renaissance: Essays in Honour of Paul Oskar Kristeller.* Manchester: Manchester University Press, 1976, 406–24.

―――. "Paolo Giovio and the Rhetoric of Individuality." In Thomas F. Mayer and Daniel R. Woolf, eds., *The Rhetorics of Life-writing in Early Modern Europe: Forms of Biography from Cassandra Fedele to Louis XIV.* Ann Arbor: University of Michigan Press, 1995.

―――. "Renaissance Symposia." In Sergio Bertelli and Gloria Ramakus, eds., *Essays Presented to Myron P. Gilmore.* 2 vols. Florence: La Nuova Italia, 1978, vol. 1, 363–74.

Index

About the Author

T. C. PRICE ZIMMERMANN is Charles A. Dana Professor of History at Davidson College.